History of the

UNIVERSITY OF ALABAMA

VOLUME I · 1818-1902

VOLUME I · 1818-1902

History of the

UNIVERSITY OF

ALABAMA

by JAMES B. SELLERS

PROFESSOR OF HISTORY IN THE
UNIVERSITY OF ALABAMA

1953

UNIVERSITY OF ALABAMA PRESS

UNIVERSITY, ALABAMA

COPYRIGHT 1953 BY
UNIVERSITY OF ALABAMA PRESS

PRINTED AND BOUND BY THE
BIRMINGHAM PRINTING COMPANY
BIRMINGHAM, ALABAMA

TO

MY MOTHER AND MY WIFE'S MOTHER

MARTHA ELLEN SELLERS

AND

MARY JANE AUTREY

Preface

THE WRITING of the history of the University presents many problems to the student of history imbued with the conventional concepts as to values, proportions and objectives. The basic difficulty lies in the fact that the possible readers are so many different groups. In the history of a state university many groups are entitled to consideration. The taxpayers, the alumni, the faculty, and students of social history all have enduring interests in the University. The antiquarian and the human interest journalists often crowd out the conventional historian.

Any reader will understand the difficulty a writer associated with one school and one phase of a university would have in presenting the problems and progress of all schools. The modernization of the University consists of the development of the various departments, not of the University as an entity. Without the help of my colleagues this part would have been most inadequate. The deans of the several schools of the University have been very sympathetic with this study and have placed much valuable data at my disposal.

To the University Research Committee I am very thankful for making grants-in-aid which have enabled me to do the vast amount of research necessary in writing the book. I am indeed grateful to President John M. Gallalee for his sympathetic consideration in granting me some time off from teaching to complete this study. To Mrs. W. K. E. James I wish to express my sincere appreciation for her unceasing interest and coöperation in making this study possible, and for permission to use the picture of her father, Robison Brown, facing page 485. I also wish to express my sincere appreciation to my colleagues, Dean A. B.

Moore and Professor Frank L. Owsley, for reading the manuscript and making many helpful suggestions.

I am indeed grateful to Mrs. D. F. Mulvihill for the assistance she gave me in preparing this volume. To Mrs. R. S. Van de Woestyne I am very much indebted for her sympathetic aid and critical advice in the preparation of the manuscript. I wish to express my appreciation to Mrs. Max Howard for the assistance she gave me in writing this volume. Among others to whom I am indebted for their assistance are: Mrs. Cade Verner, of the Alabama Collection, who placed much valuable source material at my disposal; and Mrs. M. B. Owen and her assistants, especially Miss Frances Hails, of the Alabama Department of Archives and History. I owe a debt of gratitude to Professor James B. McMillan for his many constructive suggestions and to my wife, Carrie Autrey Sellers, who has assisted me in the whole undertaking.

J. B. S.

Tuscaloosa
January, 1953

Contents

PART I: THE OLD UNIVERSITY

INTRODUCTION:	A NEW UNIVERSITY IS BORN	3
I	THE FOUNDATIONS	7
II	BUILDING THE UNIVERSITY	28
III	THE FIRST FACULTY 1831-1837	43
IV	THE FACULTY 1837-1860	67
V	THE LIBRARY	98
VI	THE STUDENTS	115
VII	CURRICULUM AND CLASSROOM	145
VIII	STUDENT ORGANIZATIONS	175
IX	PROBLEMS OF DISCIPLINE: FACULTY VERSUS STUDENTS	197
X	PROBLEMS OF DISCIPLINE: REBELLIOUS YOUTH	226
XI	THE MILITARY YEARS 1860-1865	258
XII	THE DESTRUCTION OF THE UNIVERSITY	281

PART II: REBUILDING THE UNIVERSITY

XIII	REOPENING THE UNIVERSITY 1865-1871	291
XIV	THE PRESIDENTS 1871-1901	314

XV	BUSINESS MANAGEMENT AND CAMPUS DEVELOPMENT *1871-1901*	343
XVI	THE SCHOOLS AND THEIR TEACHERS	372
XVII	THE LIBRARY	404
XVIII	SCHOLASTIC STANDARDS	416
XIX	FACULTY PROBLEMS	435
XX	STUDENT LIFE	454
XXI	MILITARY DISCIPLINE	486
XXII	EXTRA-CURRICULAR ACTIVITIES	514
XXIII	COMMENCEMENTS AND HONORS	536
XXIV	SECULAR AND SECTARIAN OPPOSITION	552
	BIBLIOGRAPHY	573
	ENROLLMENT OF STUDENTS AND GRADUATES *1831-1902*	581
	NOTES	583
	INDEX	631

Illustrations

	Facing Page
VIEW OF THE ORIGINAL CAMPUS	36
PRESIDENT'S MANSION	37
GORGAS HOME	52
OBSERVATORY	53
ROUND HOUSE	53
ALVA WOODS	292
BASIL MANLY	292
LANDON CABELL GARLAND	292
WILLIAM RUSSELL SMITH	293
NATHANIEL THOMAS LUPTON	293
CARLOS GREENE SMITH	293
JOSIAH GORGAS	293
THE CAMPUS IN 1852	308
THE CAMPUS IN 1888	309
WOODS HALL	340
CLARK HALL	341
MANLY HALL	356
GARLAND HALL	357

BARNARD HALL	436
TUOMEY HALL	437
BURWELL BOYKIN LEWIS	452
HENRY DELAMAR CLAYTON	452
RICHARD CHANNING JONES	452
JAMES KNOX POWERS	452
WILLIAM STOKES WYMAN	453
THOMAS CHALMERS MCCORVEY	453
JULIA STRUDWICK TUTWILER	484
AMELIA GAYLE GORGAS	484
THE COEDS OF 1899	485
DRESS UNIFORM, 1890	485
A CADET COMPANY	500
OFFICIAL SEALS	501

Part One

THE OLD UNIVERSITY
1818-1865

INTRODUCTION

A New University Is Born

APRIL 12, 1831, was an important day in Tuscaloosa. In the Episcopal Church, leading citizens of the town and state had gathered for ceremonies which they were well aware had upon them the mark of history in the making. There were United States congressmen in the assembly, members of the state legislature, city officials, judges, lawyers and doctors, the makers and moulders of a still young state. There were Tuscaloosa townspeople who had dropped their daily tasks to be present for the big event. There were strangers who had traveled long distances over difficult roads, scholarly newcomers about to build careers for themselves in a new environment, young sons of pioneer planters who regarded the day as peculiarly their own. As the church filled, they waited expectantly.

Then the church organ pealed out the opening hymn. The choir sang. The Reverend A. A. Miller, rector, delivered an "appropriate" prayer. The Honorable Samuel B. Moore, governor of Alabama, rose to speak. The anticipated moment had come. In an address "neat, brief, sensible, and to the point,"[1] the state's chief executive performed the ceremony for which the day had been planned. When in closing he turned to the bespectacled Vermonter at his side and delivered into his hands the keys to the University of Alabama, the audience nodded with satisfaction. Their University, the "Seminary of Learning" provided for by Congressional grant even before Alabama attained statehood, was a reality at last.

Appraising eyes fastened upon the stranger who was being invested with the rights and privileges of the presidency of that University. They saw a youngish man in his late thirties. He was "of medium height, compactly built, of robust health, with a round face, fairly handsome." His florid complexion hinted at abundant energy. And his "well-shaped head, high and somewhat bald" seemed to be an appropriate domicile for the brain he was reputed to possess.[2] He was not a man one would warm to; but a sound scholar if one could credit the glowing reports of "honors well and recently acquired, thick upon him," which had heralded his coming. A man who could command respect. That was evident in his bearing. A disciplinarian probably—to be such was all to the good. Young men needed a strong hand.

Deliberately, almost with hesitation, the Reverend Alva Woods began his inaugural address. Reporters of the event wrote afterwards that he spoke with "ease and grace" and "without ostentation or rhetorical flourishes" as he discoursed on "the importance of learning and knowledge to the safety, liberty, prosperity, and moral and religious improvement of man."[3] "The justness of his views of popular instruction," commented the Huntsville *Southern Advocate,* "and the diffusion of the lights of science, commanded universal assent." Particularly "fortunate for the destiny of the institution," that newspaper thought, was the remark which President Woods saw fit to make in deprecation of "an inroad upon the funds of the University." An "expression of almost universal approbation" had, the writer observed, "pervaded the audience" at that point.[4]

Did the University trustees in the audience share wholeheartedly that general approbation? It was a particularly important occasion for them, the culmination of nine years of hard and often heartbreaking work. With little or no compensation, they had performed the functions of real estate operators, financiers, planners, architects, builders, educational experts, business administrators. They understood well the import of the reference to legislative effort to grant relief to University debtors, but they must also have been uneasily conscious that plans for necessary compromise were already shaping in their own board. Did they feel, when their new appointee singled them out for special exhortation, that he had too quickly constituted himself their mentor? When he reminded them— as if they needed reminding—"of the importance of husbanding the resources of the institution, and regarding them as sacred to the cause of learning and the diffusion of knowledge,"[5] did they have some faint uncomfortable inkling that this stern and uncompromising moralist might in the years just ahead be a difficult fellow to man-

INTRODUCTION

age, a focus for controversy and for conflict within the University walls?

If the trustees had misgivings, they must have lost them as they left the inaugural services and, traveling a little distance along the Huntsville Road, looked proudly at the fine new institution their labors had built. There it stood, surrounded by eighty acres of its own land. South of the road, fruit trees marked the site for the experimental farm. North of the road the necessary plant for an institution of learning was a reality of brick and stone and wood. There was the Rotunda with its dome and its colonnade, one of the finest buildings in the whole South. There was the Lyceum in which classes would be held. There were the quarters for the students, Washington and Jefferson halls, the faculty homes, and Steward's Hall, where as many as one hundred students could be served their meals.

The community, and indeed the whole state, was proud of the new University buildings. They had been minutely described and warmly praised in a long article the previous October in the Huntsville *Advocate:*

the choice of so agreeable and healthy a situation—the taste and elegant plan of the buildings, their strength, convenience, and durability, with the great economy of money which has been displayed throughout, does honor to the minds of those connected with their erection, and indicates a cheering and well-founded hope, that under the fostering care of a wise and beneficient government, this institution brought forward under such happy auspices, will go on to prosper,—be the pride and honor of this young and happy commonwealth,—and continue the home of literature—of science and of the arts.[6]

The University was ready now for the students, ready for the youth who would make it a living reality. And six days after the inauguration of President Woods, the students came. There were fifty-two of them on the opening day, nearly one hundred before the first session ended. They came by stage and by carriage, by ox cart and on foot. They brought with them both the earnestness and the unruliness of sons of pioneer stock. They moved into the dormitories and into the classrooms. An early dream had become an actuality.

No shadow of impending calamity fell across the April days of

1831 which saw this dream's fulfillment. But the University whose birth then was celebrated with such rejoicing was destined to die in flames in another April, only thirty-four years in the future, the victim of raid by Croxton's Army in the very last days of the war. The foundations of the University of Alabama as we know it today rest on the ashes of that raid.

The very fact that the pioneer University ended so soon makes it possible to study and appraise it as a unit, to examine the formative period of the institution, to understand the practical problems of its building, to know what manner of men guided its beginnings and what manner of students put the impress of their young vigor upon it, and to find in these beginnings the roots of the traditions which have made the University what it is today. Such is the purpose of this study.

CHAPTER I

The Foundations

THE STORY begins in 1818, on April 20, almost thirteen years to the day before Professors Saltonstall and Tutwiler welcomed to the campus the first students of the University of Alabama. On that day, the Congress of the United States, passing an Act Respecting the Sale of Public Lands in the Alabama Territory, stipulated that "there shall be reserved from sale, in the Alabama territory, an entire township, which shall be located by the Secretary of the Treasury for the support of a Seminary of Learning within the said territory."[1] A year later, on March 2, 1819, in the Act for the Admission of Alabama to the Union,[2] a second township was added to the grant.

The Convention of the Territory of Alabama which met in Huntsville on July 5 of that year had thus before it, for acceptance or rejection, proposals to set aside for the support of an institution of higher education some sections, or 46,080 acres of land. The convention lost no time in accepting the proposition in an ordinance "irrevocable without the consent of the United States" and in instructing the General Assembly of the new state so to administer the land grant as to build up funds for the seminary:

The General Assembly shall take like measures (as were to be taken in reference to the 16th Sections) for the improvement of such lands as may have been, or may hereafter be granted by the United States to this State for the support of a Seminary of Learning and the moneys which may be raised from such lands by rent, lease, or sale, or from any other quarter for the purpose aforesaid, shall be, and remain, a fund for the exclusive support of a State University for the promotion of the arts, literature, and sciences; and it shall be the duty of the General Assembly, as early as may be, to provide effectual means for the improvement and permanent security of the lands and endowments of such institutions.[3]

The General Assembly went at its task promptly. At its first session, held in Huntsville, in October, it authorized Governor William W. Bibb to appoint commissioners to lease the University land and to begin at once to look for a University site, "having due regard to the advantages of health, to the nature and situation of the surrounding country, and to the general convenience of the State."[4] When he made his inaugural address,[5] the governor, like his lawmakers, warmly praised Congress for the encouragement given to education.

Finding a place to put the new institution proved unexpectedly difficult. Although two tentative sites were earmarked in 1822, final choice was not to be made until the closing days of 1827. Administration of University land also turned out to be no simple matter; it was to continue as a vexing problem until well into the thirties.

The legislature appears, however, to have been in no mood to make haste slowly. At Cahawba, in 1820, it declared "That a Seminary of Learning be and the same is hereby established, to be denominated 'The University of the State of Alabama,' "[6] and the following year the embryonic university was duly provided with a board of trustees, among whose duties, it is interesting to note, was the selection of a site "for a female institution; which institution shall be considered as a branch of the University of the State of Alabama, and shall be governed by the same laws, so far as the same may be applicable."[7]

For nearly a decade this board of trustees was the University. The 1821 General Assembly, in An Act Supplementary to an Act to Establish a State University, outlined its organization and its duties so completely that, with a few revisions the following year, no further legislative redefinition was needed until 1843. The reorganization effected in that year was further amplified and amended in 1848 and again in 1858.

The original charter of the board called for twelve trustees, who, with the governor of the state as ex officio president, should constitute "a body politic and corporate, in deed and in law, by the name of the Trustees of the University of Alabama."[8] Joint ballot of both houses was to be used in the election of two trustees from each judicial circuit, and these men were to remain in office for three years.[9] A board of twelve men scattered throughout the state may have proved unable to convene itself quickly for the transaction of business, for in 1822 the number was increased to eighteen by the addition of six new members who lived "within fifty miles of the University." Their term of office was set to coincide with that of the original appointees, so that on expiration of the first board's term, the legislature might again proceed to elect eighteen replacements.[10]

The board thus constituted carried out the preliminary planning for the institution. Not until 1843 was the board composition altered. At that time room on the board for the judges of the State Supreme Court was made by cutting down the number of representatives from the judicial districts. The circuit in which the University was located was still to have its two representatives, but other circuits were to have one each. A plan of insuring continuity by rotating the terms of the trustees was introduced at the same time. When elections had been conducted by the general assembly, the board was instructed to classify the trustees elected into three groups having two, four, and six-year terms respectively. Maturity of the University and increasing problems of its administration may have dictated at this time the new provision that no one under thirty years of age was eligible for election to the board.[11]

Once more in the period under consideration the board was enlarged, this time in 1858, when two additional trustees from the judicial circuit in which the University was located were provided for. The legislature restricted representation from Tuscaloosa County, however, providing that no more than two trustees from the third circuit were to be residents of that county. And it further stipulated that the increase in the number of trustees should not change the number required for a quorum.[12]

Careful provisions regarding the meetings of the board were included in all the laws relating to the trustees. The board was required under the 1821 law to hold at least one meeting at Commencement and to report annually to the legislature the financial situation of the University. The governor was nominally the chairman of these meetings, but it was recognized that his duties might prevent his carrying out this responsibility. If he was unable to attend, the trustees were authorized to elect a president pro tempore to preside at the meeting.[13]

For other meetings needed for the transaction of University business, authority was first given to the president and four trustees. A year later the law was liberalized somewhat. Two trustees with the president or three trustees without the president were empowered to issue a call, provided that they gave reasonable notice, stated the purpose of the meeting, and did not introduce into the sessions thus called any new business without approval of at least seven members present.[14]

The legislature kept for itself the prerogative of filling vacancies on the board. But in both the 1822 and the 1843 legislation, authority to choose temporary replacements during recess of the General Assembly was specifically given to the trustees themselves. There was brisk business in elections and in temporary appointments. The turnover on the board during the years from 1821 to 1865 was very great. Some 138 men served as University trustees in that period, with the term of their service averaging five and one-third years. Twenty-nine had served four-year terms; three had remained on the board only a single year. The trustee having the longest service record was Francis Bugbee, who, appointed in 1836, remained on the board for twenty-three years.[15]

Trustee absences, particularly after the University was a going concern, were frowned upon in the reorganization act of 1843, which provided that two consecuitve absences from regular meetings was tantamount to resignation.[16] But certain practical considerations led to provisions both in 1848 and in 1858 that absences of the Supreme Court judges and of the additional members elected in the latter year should not be taken into account in determining a quorum.

On the first board, elected on December 19, 1821, the twelve men, serving under the chairmanship of Governor Israel Pickens, were George W. Owen and John Murphy, from the first circuit; Henry Hitchcock and George Phillips, from the second; Jack Shackelford and Hume R. Field, from the third; Nicholas Davis and John McKinley, from the fourth; Thomas Fearn and Henry Minor, from the fifth; and Clement C. Billingslea and Robert W. Carter, from the sixth.[17]

They solemnly lifted their right hands in assent to the prescribed oath of office: "I do solemnly swear (or affirm) that I will faithfully discharge the duties assigned me as trustee, to the best of my skill and ability, without partiality or affection. So help me God."[18]

Nothing had been said about compensation for the discharge of duties. That was to come the following year, when the legislature voted to allow three dollars a day for time actually spent on University meetings and three dollars extra for every twenty-five miles traveled in going to and from meetings. Members of the legislature serving as trustees were excepted from these pay provisions while they were attending legislative ssesions and presumably could fit in trustee meetings without additional expense. Allowances were to be paid out of the University fund. When the University was organized and professors appointed, these allowances were to stop.[19] It is interesting to note that when the time for discontinuing the payments came, the trustees conveniently forgot this stipulation. The law enacted in 1833 continued the system of honoraria, dropping any reference to a terminal date.[20]

If the General Assembly in 1821 had been forgetful about pay for its new public servants, however, it had managed to remember a formidable list of things it expected the University board to do. The board members were empowered to receive lands, tenements, hereditaments, personal property, and sums of money for the purpose of promoting the interests of the University. They were the custodians of the University's land and other assets. They were responsible for planning and building and administering an institution which should reflect credit to the state. They were authorized to elect by majority vote of the whole board necessary officers for the University, to fix their salaries, and to remove them from office if they proved incompetent. They were responsible for prescribing courses of study and for the enactment of University rules. And when the University should at last be functioning, they were to confer on approved students diplomas or certificates signed by them and sealed with the common seal of the trustees of the University.[21] They had a big job before them. Perhaps it is not surprising that four of the original twelve trustees resigned before the end of the term for which they had been elected. In December, 1823, the places of Owen, Hitchcock, McKinley, and Minor were filled by the appointment of George Buchanan, Bolling Hall, Arthur F. Hopkins, and David Moore. Samuel W. Oliver was brought on the board at the same time to replace Robert W. Carter, who had died in October.[22]

From the beginning, the board of trustees did a great deal of its work through special and standing committees. Most of the early committees were concerned with the disposition and handling of University lands. In 1822 the first of these was the committee to prescribe oaths of office for agents of seminary land. Some others were as follows: committee to draft ordinance authorizing sale of land, 1822; committee to inquire into the expediency of suspending sale of lands in Conecuh and Monroe counties, 1822; committee to draft memorial to the legislature on locating a site, 1822; and committee on renting lands, 1824. Later, committees were concerned with buying land for the University site; for contracting to erect buildings; for nominating professors and tutors; and for having a clock made for the University. On November 18, 1830, the following standing committees were appointed: propositions and grievances, accounts and claims, University land, library, University regulations, and annual report. Many other committees of varied natures followed these, such as a committee to install the president in 1831; to fill temporarily vacant professorships in 1837; to draft plans for professors' houses in 1843; and to protect University property from depredation in 1853. Perhaps the most important was the executive committee, which began functioning in 1837. It consisted of four trustees appointed annually and the president of the board. The duty of the committee was to carry out the measures and ordinances of the board and to report their proceedings to the next annual meeting. This committee has continued to play an important part in the operations of the University. After their appointment the usual procedure of committees was to make investigations and then at a later date report to the board. The recommendations of the committees were either accepted, modified, or rejected.

It is questionable whether such extensive authority over the University should have been left to the discretion of men few of whom were educators themselves. The very complexity and magnitude of their task made it almost inevitable that mistakes would be made in judgment and in administration. Yet their courage and their devotion contributed largely to the success of the new Univer-

THE OLD UNIVERSITY 13

sity. They worked faithfully, for the most part, and they worked hard.

The endowment of the new University was land—two townships, 46,080 acres of it. The first and foremost duty of the trustees was to handle that land so that funds for building and maintaining a college should be soundly obtained and soundly invested. They began that task in an atmosphere of controversy touched off by two governors.

The law which established the University had also set the minimum price for the lease of improved college land at two dollars an acre, ordered the land surveyed, and warned trespassers that they would be fined triple damages.[23] To Governor Thomas Bibb, the leasing process seemed cumbersome and slow. "Our object should be so to dispose of the land as to ensure the greatest annual income at the least expense," he told the General Assembly in 1821. Public auction for cash was the course that he recommended. That would quickly establish a fund which, properly invested in a state bank, would provide sound income for the institution.[24] Six days later, the incoming Governor Israel Pickens disagreed with Bibb. On the basis of "daily observation, connected with the present condition of our circulation medium," he said, outright cash sales would be most unwise. Twice as much money, in his opinion, would accrue to the University if land sold could be paid for on an installment basis.[25]

Governor Pickens' plan was accepted. The General Assembly fixed a price of seventeen dollars an acre for the land, one-fourth of the purchase price to be paid at the time of the sale, the remainder in four annual installments. Then they vested in the newly constituted board of trustees the right to sell the land and to receive the money paid. The trustees were required to make annual financial reports to the legislature, and they were forbidden to reduce, in any way, the capital stock arising from land sales.

Careful provisions were made against defaulters. Persons who failed to pay installments promptly forfeited the land and the money paid on it. Three months after forfeiture, the trustees were instructed to dispossess the defaulter unless he had meanwhile given adequate bond and security to cover unpaid installments.[26]

When the trustees held their first meeting in April, 1822, they proceeded at once with plans to carry out the orders of the legislature. They appointed bonded agents in three districts—John Hunter for Cahaba, Thomas Owen for Tuscaloosa, Quin Morton for Big Springs (Franklin County)—and arranged to pay them $250, $120, and $120 respectively, plus five dollars for each day they were actually at work. Each agent was responsible to the trustees of the district. He was instructed to examine the land and to report to the president of the board one month before the next board meeting whether he believed it to be worth seventeen dollars an acre. Apparently the agents were authorized to sell land if opportunity arose, for the trustees issued careful instructions on sales procedures. Each purchaser was to be given a certificate of sale, signed by the superintendents and the agent, giving the exact location of the land—"number of the range, township, section, quarter or part of a quarter section and fractional section, and the number of the lot"—and the terms of payment agreed upon. Money received from sales was to be exchanged for United States notes and specie. And, of course, complete reports were to be regularly submitted to the trustees.[27]

Before any land was sold under this plan, however, the legislature performed the first of its many changes of policy which was to cause both confusion and financial loss as University land gradually was converted to University capital. Leaving the minimum price set at seventeen dollars per acre, the legislators eased the burden on purchasers by spreading payments over eight years instead of four. Then they re-adopted the leasing principles which only a year earlier they had ruled out, adopted them in peculiarly unwieldy form by permitting sale to be transformed into lease at the will of the purchaser:

at the expiration of the term of credit, or within three months thereafter, herein before prescribed upon the sales of said lands, the purchaser, his heirs or assigns, shall have the right, upon the payment of all interest then due upon said purchase, and upon surrendering up the certificate of purchase, to convert said purchase into a lease for ninety-nine years, renewable forever, upon condition that the lessee, his heirs, executors, administrators or assigns, shall pay to the said Trustees interest at six per cent per annum, upon the amount of the original purchase money due at the time of converting said sale into a lease.[28]

To operate a plan of this kind successfully would have required greater clerical and business skill than most of the University's appointed agents possessed. And those agents were not all conscientious and competent even by the standards of the day. In the many transactions which converted sales to leases, considerable sums were lost because purchasers, turned lessees, failed to pay either the original purchase price or interest upon it. Within a year the trustees were asking for more stringent legislation to help them collect money owed to the University.[29] And within ten years the confusion had developed to such a point that special investigations were needed to bring order into the records of land transactions.

The General Assembly turned a critical eye also upon the price it had set for University land. Sales were slow in 1822 and 1823. Was the minimum price of seventeen dollars too high? This time the trustees held out against the lawmakers. They reported to the legislature in 1824:

In regard to the minimum price of the University lands the Board are unanimously of opinion that any reduction at this time would be inexpedient . . . . It is admitted that portions of the land may not soon be saleable at seventeen dollars per acre, yet the Board consider that the delay in the sale of these portions will be of less importance than the sacrifice which would attend a general reduction.[30]

Having carried their point, however, the board began almost at once to give consideration in their own meetings to the very points advanced in the legislature's proposals. It was true that much of the unsold land would not sell for a long time at the present asking price. It was true that there would be advantage in turning the less valuable land into immediate cash. It would help to save on the expenses of leasing those lands and protecting them against trespassers. By classifying the land according to quality of soil and advantage of location, a scale of prices could be worked out which might step up sales and bring to the University active and accumulating capital.[31]

The General Assembly received such proposals from the trustees in January, 1826, and promptly accepted them. Three persons in each judicial circuit, chosen by joint vote of both houses of the General Assembly, were directed to divide the land into three graded classifications. For top quality land the seventeen-dollar minimum price was retained; in the other two classes minimums of twelve and eight dollars were set.[32]

Times were good in the 1820's. University land sales moved ahead without too much difficulty for several years. There was a minor complication when the trustees found that approximately 904 acres in Madison County, part of the original grant, had been sold by the federal government. A memorial to Congress sent in December, 1827, was acted upon in 1829, and the missing acres were restored by the substitution of equivalent new land.[33]

Selection of the University site in 1827 freed for the market land which had been held for possible sites. This included a considerable tract in Tuscaloosa, where the original grant comprised the section of the present city which lies south to the A.G.S. Railroad and west to Queen City Avenue. In at least one instance the trustees showed lack of foresight in dealing with this land. They leased a considerable part of the eastern section of their holdings on 99-year lease and some years later sold their reversionary interest to a land company, thereby losing the benefits which would have come to the University with the great appreciation in value of the land.

As the 1830's opened, the economic background for land operations changed. Cotton prices were declining, and the prices asked for University land remained fixed. The federal government reduced prices on its Alabama lands to $3.50 an acre. Some of the University holdings had deteriorated in actual value because of the destruction of forests and exhaustion of soil. Large new tracts of fertile lands purchased from Indian tribes were about to be placed on the market.[34]

Not only were new sales difficult in this situation, but also payments on sales made in the 1820's were alarmingly slow. People who had bought land in the years between 1823 and 1825, when prices were high and when the flat rate of seventeen dollars an acre was charged, were in real trouble. Most of them had paid one-fourth of the purchase price at the time of sale and, finding themselves hard pressed to keep up the installment payments, petitioned the lgislature for relief.

The General Assembly was sympathetic. Several times it acted to relieve individuals of debt burdens on terms which seem, in retrospect, to have been most unfair to the University. Edmund Prince, of Franklin County, was one of the recipients of legislative generosity. In 1830 the lawmakers decreed

That the trustees of the University of this State be, and they are hereby required to cancel and deliver up to Edmund Prince, of the County of Franklin, any bond, promissory note or other writing, which he may have executed to them in consideration of the rent of one hundred and fifty acres of the University lands, lying in the County of Franklin . . . .[35]

The year which saw the opening of the doors of the new University also saw violent controversy over legislation to provide general relief to land purchasers. One bill, which would have allowed buyers to relinquish the debt due for the part retained, passed the Senate with a large majority before it was finally stopped by narrow margin in the House. The *Southern Advocate,* flying to the defense of the University, expressed indignation in no uncertain terms:

A bill of a most disastrous character to the interest of the University has passed the Senate and is now in progress through the other branch of the General Assembly, and we fear it will become a law . . . . The legislature are only Trustees of the bounty of General Government— and the terms of the Trust are, that it shall be managed for the sole benefit of the cause of education. How can they then exercise absolute control over the land, even to the giving of them away for a mere song?[36]

The trustees of the University, however, could not avoid facing the realities of the situation. If they stood firm and exacted forfeitures while most of the principal was still owed, they could probably realize only four to five dollars an acre. The only practical course appeared to be a more liberal policy which would give debtors a longer time in which to pay their debts. Their first move in this direction touched off a fight both within the board and in the public press.

In April, 1831, the same month that the University opened, a majority of the board supported an ordinance which declared that "in order to secure the University, the debt and interest due from purchasers . . . who are represented to be unable to pay those heavy payments now due for their land," such purchasers should be allowed "a further credit of five years, in equal installments, each installment to be paid on the 1st. of January, in every year." Safeguards against abuse of this time extension were added to the ordinance:

Provided, however, that the first installment shall be paid on or before the first day of January, 1832; and also provided, that each individual herein named, shall well and truly execute a deed or deeds of trust, in favor of the University of Alabama, upon personal and real estate to the full value of fifteen hundred dollars, to secure what is now due upon each quarter section held by the same.[37]

Trustees S. W. Mardis and William Acklin, Jr., brought in a minority report. The board, they argued, had no power to grant such relief. It had, by its action, rescinded contracts, put the University in a position to lose the interest on a large part of its debts for five years. The legislature had clearly intended to give to the board no such discretion regarding the handling of University land. It was extremely doubftul, they said, that the action would save a single bad or doubtful claim. And they protested that among the men benefited by the ordinance were several of known wealth, fully able to pay their debts. If any relief to debtors was necessary, surely it should be given to all alike, not merely to a few singled out for special favor by the board.[38]

The press sided with Mardis and Acklin. Newspapers in Mobile and Huntsville, as well as in Tuscaloosa, took up the cry, condemning the trustees' action as both unwise and illegal. "Eighteen thousand dollars have been thus disposed of!" shouted the Tuscaloosa *Inquirer:*

. . . certain enumerated persons, who jointly owe a debt of more than sixty thousand dollars, are permitted to pay the debts they respectively owe, in five annual installments without interest . . . . The legislature was certainly competent to pass laws providing for the sale, &c., of these lands. It has said the lands shall be sold for a given sum, and that the debts due therefor shall bear interest. The Board of Trustees nullify the act of the Legislature, and say the debts shall not bear interest.[39]

With "astonishment and indignation" the *Southern Advocate* declared that the board had exhibited "an exertion of power unprecedented in our history, and ruinous to the fair prospects of our State University." If the trustees could do this, what could keep them from deciding to give the land away outright? Clearly the trustees' ordinance was "contrary to law . . . null and void, and consequently not obligatory on their successors."[40]

The Mobile *Commercial Register* also condemned the ordinance as "obnoxious" and a "nullity." Any arrangements made under it would almost certainly be rendered void. The University

THE OLD UNIVERSITY 19

funds, the *Register* said, were a sacred deposit which the present generation held in trust for their successors; no considerations should induce them to violate that trust.[41]

The storm did not quickly subside. Five months later the editor of the *Southern Advocate* was still eyeing with suspicion a board of trustees that showed such indifference to the real interests of the University:

The greatest danger it has to apprehend is from its Trustees. These may be, and perhaps some of them are now, men in political bustle—in whose care the concerns of education will meet with but little regard, if these prove to be, or should be supposed to be, opposed to the interest or wishes of that portion of the public which is represented by them. We hope, however, for the best, and that feelings of patriotism will be found sufficiently powerful to foster this rising institution, until it is made, what it ought to be, an honour to our State and a source of pride to our citizens.[42]

In spite of such admonitions, the trustees continued their liberal policy toward University debtors. In 1833 they extended to twelve months the time limit for conversions from purchase to lease, with the provision that purchasers wishing to become lessees must have paid one-half of the principal of the purchase money and all the interest due on the last half. They also tightened up forfeiture proceedings, instructing their agents to enter upon and hold all forfeited lands and to prosecute if necessary to obtain possession.[43]

The limelight of public scrutiny which fell upon the board, once the University was open, may have made its deliberations more difficult. In January of 1832 the trustees formally resolved that outsiders would be admitted to board meetings thenceforth only on invitation.[44] To make this rule effective they decided to hire a doorkeeper, and four days later put James A. Bates in that position with a stipend of six dollars for his services.[45] In the August sessions of 1833 and 1834 Thomas L. Baskins and Benjamin Oppett were official doorkeepers. Baskins got two dollars a day for his services; Oppett, three dollars.[46]

In 1833 the trustees decided that the time had come for a checkup on University lands. They appointed a committee, which soon found itself in a tangle that carelessness and incompetence had been weaving for ten years. Reporting to the board in January, 1834, the committee expressed "astonishment that the vast concerns of the Institution, involving transactions upwards of a million dollars, have been suffered, by the accumulation of undigested reports and other papers, to commence and continue in the most perplexing confusion."[47]

It had been almost impossible to find out exactly what land had been sold and what remained unsold and to determine accurately the debts still owed to the University. The committee had found, for example, records of fifteen payments, made between 1823 and 1827, which did not show to what account they had been paid. In order to straighten out the record, they had had to examine all the records of all the agents who had handled land transactions since the organization of the board.[48]

They had, however, managed to bring order out of confusion. Going back to original land patents, they had prepared a tract book in which the size and location of every parcel of land was carefully described. They had noted that, although their researches showed variations of from five acres to full sections in the quantities which various tracts were computed to contain as compared with the original grants, the overall difference amounted to but a fraction of an acre. The committee had carefully entered in the tract book an account of all reported sales, including names of buyers, date of sale, rate per acre, and the aggregate amount. They had relied on reports of land agents for this record, and they warned those agents that they would be held responsible for any discrepancies.

Then, to avoid repetition of such confusion in the future, the committee recommended drastic tightening up of land-sale procedures:

That no bond or other property be put into the hands of agents or other persons, without entry being made at once, describing it in every particular; That no cash be credited to an individual, without a clear indication of the account to which it was paid; That the agent be required to keep a complete tract book; And that these books be considered the property of the Board and subject to the inspection of the members.[49]

Findings of the committee were supported the following year when a joint committee of the legislature, investigating the financial condition of the University, had occasion to examine again the University records. Those records, this committee said, had been so kept as to "place the affairs of that interesting and important institution in a most perplexed and confused situation."[50]

The difficulties which the trustees encountered in their handling of University lands did not all stem from public criticism or the inadequacies of some of their agents. Sometimes the law itself seemed to block their effort to make the lands yield maximum profit to their institution. When, in 1833, John J. Winston defaulted on his bond, the trustees, believing that the amount of Winston's debt was greater than the value of the land which he might be required to forfeit, brought suit against him. If the University had been a private corporation, it could have waived the right of forfeiture and sued for the purchase money. But, ruled the Supreme Court, the University was adjudged a public corporation. The statutes clearly stated that land should be forfeited if the purchaser failed to make stipulated payments. The University, therefore, "must be content to receive the land in satisfaction of its demands against the defendant, whether it be more or less valuable." The Alabama Supreme Court in the case of *Trustees of the University of Alabama v. Winston* set an important precedent for other courts dealing with state institutions. In several states, however, the concept of a state university as a public corporation was not fully adopted for a number of years.[51]

Once more, in 1834, the University sustained a heavy blow through action of the General Assembly. A commission was appointed to appraise the lands which, having been sold for seventeen dollars or more an acre, had been declared forfeited because of debt. Holders of certificates were then given the right to repurchase the land at its new markdown value.[52] Many people took advantage of this act, and the University fund suffered an immense loss in principal.

The trustees' investigating committee of 1833 reported that 42,540 acres of the original grant had been sold for $377,681, or approximately $8.87 per acre on an average.[53] In 1836 Benjamin F. Porter, agent and attorney for the University, reporting after "two years of incessant and arduous investigation," estimated that only 562 acres remained unsold and noted that, although the proceeds from the sale of 45,305 acres were $382,715.57, losses to the University fund from "forfeitures, relief laws, resales, deducted interest, relinquishments, leases, . . ." could be estimated as $144,239.18.[54]

In 1859 the trustees reported to the General Assembly that University lands had brought in an aggregate sum of $441,451.93.[55] Had the original price of seventeen dollars an acre been received, the total would have been almost twice as large.

As the University lands turned into money, the work of the trustees became more and more complicated. It is interesting to note that, although the board found it advisable to protect its privacy by employing a doorkeeper in 1832, no treasurer to protect its financial affairs was appointed until 1848. In that year Henry A. Snow assumed the responsibilities of a new job. He was required to give bond of $10,000 and was given complete charge of handling University funds. He received an annual salary of $100.[56]

The legislature in 1822 gave explicit instructions for the management of University money. From the first payments on lands sold, a "sum not exceeding $500,000" was to be set apart as a building fund. Interest on subsequent payments was to be invested in the stock of the United States and "applied exclusively to sinking the amount of money hereby appropriated to the erection of buildings." When the amount so invested should equal and offset money spent for buildings, the capital stock should never be diminished.[57]

Monies received from University land sales were, according to a law passed in 1823, to be turned over by the trustees to the state treasurer for safe custody.[58]

When the Bank of the State of Alabama was established in 1823, University funds to the amount of $100,000 became part of the capital of the institution. The Governor and the president and directors of the bank were authorized to issue to the University trustees stock or certificates of debt, bearing six per cent interest.[59]

The limitation of the University's investment in the capital stock of the bank was to be a matter of controversy for years to come. As early as 1826 the trustees of the University earnestly asked that they be allowed to increase the amount of their bank investment, so that "the interest on the stock already obtained should also be invested, that it may not lie wholly unproductive in the Treasury."[60] It was years before such increase was allowed, and even then no increase in interest was provided. It may be said, with some justice, that the University made a forced loan to the bank. It never was permitted to become a stockholder or to share in the bank's profits.

Dealings with the bank and other financial matters became so entangled by 1834 that the General Assembly appointed a joint committee to straighten them out. The committee was instructed to determine on what authority the board of trustees had borrowed $60,000 from the state bank and spent it, to look into the bookkeeping discrepancies in the university records, and "to make any other and further inquiries they might think proper."[61]

Findings of this committee in the area of procedures and records did little more than echo those of the committee which had made a similar investigation for the trustees themselves the previous year. A scrutiny of the management of the University funds, however, greatly chargined the committee. University disbursements, the investigators found, had exceeded appropriations made by the legislature and the entire income fund of the institution to the amount of $26,890.91. By what authority had the trustees allowed such expenditures? By what authority had they borrowed money from the bank? There was nothing in the law to give them these rights. They had, in effect, diminished the capital stock of the University, and this was direct violation of law.[62]

The trustees were severely censured for carelessness. The General Assembly's committee sternly recommended to them

The propriety of inquiring into the University, and to ascertain whether it is in a flourishing or a declining condition, and if they ascertain that the Institution is not in so flourishing a condition as the munificent endowment—the large expenditures which have been made, and the generous and liberal salaries of the Professors and the President would induce the State to expect, that they take such steps without delay, as will probably produce the desired result, and make full report thereof, to the Legislature at their next session.[63]

"Shameful negligence and mismanagement," declared the Mobile *Commercial Register,* had been brought to light in this investigation. The trustees had been guilty of "an entire disregard of the requisitions of law, and a recklessness and prodigality in the use of the funds." Perhaps they had been guilty also of "a more censurable dereliction of duty." The new board had better take prompt steps to correct such abuses or "the university would dwindle and die."[64]

In 1833 the long-awaited permission to increase the University's investment in the state bank to $300,000 was granted.[65] By 1837 the question of University indebtedness to the bank came before the legislature again, and a ten-year struggle for just relief to the University had opened. In that year the trustees reported to the General Assembly that their bank debt, contracted for the construction of buildings, amounted, with interest, to $85,318.01. To pay this debt would mean using all funds available in the treasury and dipping into capital stock to the amount of $45,609. The total remaining, with estimated dues and unsold land, would then be $259,503.[66]

Asking the General Assembly for relief, the trustees carefully pointed out the justice of their grievances. The terms upon which the bank used University funds were, they said, unduly favorable to the bank. The bank had also had the use of large University deposits for which no benefit had come to the University. Much of the profit which the state had derived had come from the University fund. They made a special point of the fact that the General Assembly, in its legislation for the relief of purchasers of University land, had deprived the University of funds greatly exceeding the amount of the bank debt.[67]

As the legislature turned a deaf ear to these pleas, the University continued to pay the interest on its debt. Five years passed. Governor Benjamin Fitzpatrick brought the question up again in December, 1842, saying,

The University fund pays annually a considerable sum in the way of interest, on a debt due the bank. I recommend to the Legislature to adopt some measure which will ultimately result in extinguishing the debt, and relieve that fund from the yearly drain to which it is now subjected.[68]

Not only did the legislature remain indifferent, but it failed to act upon a similar recommendation from the governor in the following year. Even the proposal from the trustees in 1845 that a compromise be effected, by offsetting the bank debt with the money which the state owed the University on "losses occurring through the state's mismanagement," failed to stir the lawmakers into action.

Governor J. L. Martin broke the deadlock in 1847. He did so in a message, delivered on December 6, in which he appealed to the pride of the legislators, expressed his confidence in the University's future, and then admonished his hearers to recognize the moral responsibility they had in relation to that institution:

THE OLD UNIVERSITY   25

Between the University and the bank of the State, there is an unsettled account. The bank has a claim against it, on account of money borrowed, at an early day, for the erection of buildings, while the University presents an equitable claim against the State, on various grounds, for a much larger amount. There can be no doubt but that the relation of the State to the University is strictly fiduciary. The obligations she has assumed with regard to it are engrafted on the constitution, and make part of the fundamental law, by which you came into existence as a State. You assumed the care of the University fund, as a grant of the General Government, in the capacity of a trustee, under the most solemn of all sanctions, pledging the "faith and credit" of the State for its custody and productiveness.

He closed with a recommendation that "the necessary investigation" be made and a settlement be reached "on principles of justice and liberality consonant with the enlightened spirit of the age, and becoming the dignity and honor of the State of Alabama."[69]

The next General Assembly heard the report of the committee charged with the investigation and negotiation recommended by Governor Martin. The committee found that the bank debt of the University now totalled $100,000. The loss which the University had sustained because of relief laws was estimated at $255,745.73. The large debt hanging over the University was holding back many very valuable and necessary improvements and causing great embarrassment in the management of its affairs. The committee recommended liquidation of the mutual indebtedness between the University and the state, and the legislature moved at last to settle a long controversy.

All notes held by the state against the trustees were to be cancelled. All claims which the trustees had against the state were to be dropped, and the trustees were to file a written relinquishment of such claim with the secretary of state. The University fund, fixed at $300,000 by the senate, was reduced to $250,000 through House action, and the faith and credit of the state were pledged for the fund's permanent security and the punctual payment of interest on it at the rate of six per cent.[70]

The trustees probably felt at the time that the reduction in the University fund was not quite in accordance with the compromise they had agreed to accept. They took no action, however, for more than a decade. Then, in 1859 they presented a claim for the $50,000 which, they said, had been wrongfully withheld from the University fund since 1848. They petitioned for a restoration of the fund to the agreed $300,000, and for interest from February, 1848, on the missing $50,000.

Once again gubernatorial support helped to secure legislative action. Governor A. B. Moore said that he was convinced that the University did indeed need money:

It appears that all the surplus means have been expended in the erection of a new dormitory, and two houses for the Professors: that extensive repairs are necessary to other buildings, and that the philosophical apparatus is incomplete and imperfect . . . these repairs cannot be made, nor the deficiencies in the apparatus supplied, without some provision for that purpose.

He called the attention of the legislature to the fact that the trustees were not asking for an appropriation from the state treasury, and he said that, in his opinion, "the able argument" made in behalf of the restoration of the fifty thousand dollars could hardly be "answered or resisted." "I ask your calm deliberation," he said in closing, "and if you conclude that this sum is unjustly withheld, it should be restored."[71]

Whether the legislature was moved by the governor's appeal to fairness or by the assurance from the trustees that the additional funds were needed and would be spent for a fine new military department, it did take the desired action. The endowment fund was restored to $300,000, and the state treasurer was instructed to calculate six per cent interest on $50,000 from February 21, 1848, to February 21, 1860, and to pay this amount to the University treasurer or authorized agent.[72] The following year the interest rate on the fund was changed to eight per cent.[73]

How the University managed to keep itself afloat with the handicaps placed upon it by a none-too-generous legislature is an interesting question which is hard to answer because of the inadequacies in the records of its receipts and disbursements from 1831 to 1865. One or two reports through these years give some light on the matter. The annual report of the board of trustees which covers the period between November 26, 1832, to September 3, 1833, shows interest on $215,977.36 of state stock in the amount of $12,958.54 and student

THE OLD UNIVERSITY

fees totaling $2400. The income total that year was thus $15,358.54. Disbursements for salaries of faculty and officers in the same year amounted to $16,740.[74] In 1842 the trustees reported

We have in our University six Professors, and two Tutors, all men of superior minds, and qualifications, with all the facilities of their different departments, and toward the expense of securing the services of all these, the students pay some three thousand dollars, while the University contributes the sum of at least $15,000 annually; so that all the high and ennobling advantages of education, at an expense of $18,000 a year, are offered to the youth of our state, at a charge upon them of only $3,000.[75]

Income on the University fund could never have exceeded $18,000, or six per cent on the allowed $300,000. Probably it never reached that amount because it was offset by interest on loans for buildings. From 1848 to 1860 the state paid to the University a pittance of $15,000 annually on an investment of more than $400,000.

CHAPTER II

Building the University

NO SHADOW of impending financial problems and quarrels with the legislature clouded the trustees' meeting on December 4, 1825. There was a balance of $67,343.49 in the treasury. The time had come for action. They could really begin the building of the University. "The situation of our finances," they said, "and the superior claims of the growing youth and prosperity of our State unite in pressing the expediency of commencing this great work."[1]

Deciding upon a location for the University was the necessary first step. And here some progress had already been made. Three years earlier, at the April 5, 1822, meeting of the board, the president had expressly called attention to the instructions given in the act just passed by the General Assembly, and had said, "Gentlemen . . . . you are notified to examine, and to report to the Legislature, at their next session, such place, or places, having due regard to health, and the fertility of the sourrounding country, as shall appear to be most suitable for the location of the University."[2] The board was ready with recommendations when the legislature met, but these recommendations were somewhat general. The trustees could not be wholly specific because none of them knew all the suggested sites.

Much would depend upon whether the General Assembly wished to put the University in the northern part of the state or in the central section. If a northern site was considered "expedient," the trustees suggested Athens, or some place near it in Limestone County, to be "most suitable." If a central site was desired, they would make the following suggestions: "some point within Township 17 and Range 18 in Autauga County; Wilson's Hill in Shelby County; the place called Gage's in Perry County; and some place near the town of Tuscaloosa."[3]

While the legislature considered these suggestions, the superintendents of sales at Big Spring and Cahawba were authorized in 1822 to negotiate for the purchase of two tracts of land, not larger than 160 acres in size, at prices not to exceed seventeen dollars an acre. One of these tracts was to be in Limestone County near Athens; the other near Coosada in Autauga County. The purchase was to take effect, however, only if and when the University chose one of these tracts as its location.

Nothing more had happened by 1825. And nothing came of the trustees' urgent request for action that year. Governor Murphy appears to have made the next move. In his message to the legislature on November 20, 1827, he suggested that an early decision on the University site might be reached if commissioners from each judicial district were appointed to inspect the proposed sites and report their findings to the General Assembly.[4]

The University board was growing impatient by this time. In December they told the General Assembly so, urging not only that the money was ready and the needs of youth great but also that justice to the pioneers who had built the state demanded that a place soon be provided for the education of their sons.

If any portion of our citizens can have superior claims upon the representative branch of our State, the hardy, industrious and enterprising pioneer who has contributed his mite to the improvement, aggrandizement and political importance of our State, presents himself to our consideration in the most favorable attitude, and claims at least, the gratitude and attention of his country; so far as to have his children educated in the land of their fathers. . . . Our sons should be educated in our own state. Persons thus educated, give both a moral and political impress to the great outline of our Municipal character, and even extend a happy influence upon the private and more limited sphere of human action.[5]

The legislators may have been moved by this eloquence, or they may have felt that their task of site selection became compassable when the trustees narrowed down the area of choice by a recommendation that, in order to minimize sectional jealousy, the University be placed as near the center of the state as "health and convenience will permit." On December 29, the legislators began action in earnest and, in joint evening session of both houses, chose a site for the University. Thirteen locations were on the list when they started voting, and it took nineteen ballots for a decision. The lands considered were the following: the University lands near Gage's; Greensborough, in Greene County; Lagrange, in Franklin County; Athens, in Limestone County; Montevallo, in Shelby County; Honeycomb Springs, in Jackson County; Somerville, in Morgan County; Moulton, in Lawrence County; Davis, in Autauga County; Greenville, in Butler County; Tuskaloosa; Elyton; and Village Springs. Five contenders lasted until the final ballot, when the vote stood as follows: Tuskaloosa, 47; Montevallo, 18; Lagrange, 10; Athens, 5; and Bellfont, 1. The speaker then declared Tuskaloosa to be the duly selected site for the location of the University of Alabama, and the trustees were given authority to select, within fifteen miles of that town, the exact place for the buildings.[6]

Messrs. Phillips, Shackleford, Benson, Morton, and Oliva were appointed a committee to receive proposals. On March 22, 1828, they presented to the board three possible sites: Marr's field, Childress' place, and Taber's place. The trustees voted. Seven favored Marr's field, the other locations receiving two votes each. The site for the University had been selected at last.[7]

To round out their tract, the board was authorized to purchase fifty acres of land owned by James Paul adjacent to the University site. They paid $1,250 for this land, saying that they did so "to prevent immoral persons from settling on same," and also because they had a practical eye on "the superior quality of the clay for making bricks for the buildings and the quantity of wood thereon which could be spared therefrom for burning them."[8]

Two days after the vote on the sites, the trustees had before them the first estimates on "two blocks of dormitories, one block of professors' houses, a chemical laboratory, and lecture rooms," presented by Captain William Nichols, architect, and the building committee, Hume Field, Jack Shackleford, George Phillips, and Quin Morton. This indicates that work on building plans had been going along simultaneously with work on site selection. It is generally accepted that the buildings of the University were patterned somewhat after those of the University of Virginia. Although there is no documentary proof of the fact, it seems reasonable to suppose that the architect or the building committee had prior to March, 1828, made a trip to the University of Virginia to study its plan. Most of the early plans of the first buildings, as well as the buildings themselves, vanished in flame in 1865. There are, however, documents relating to work on the buildings, to contracts, to settlements of complaints, and to the work performed by the state architect, who, it is noted, prepared in advance a complete layout of the campus.[9] One can only guess, though with considerable sureness, that the buildings referred to in the trustees' minutes of March 24, 1828, included Washington and Jefferson halls; a building called the Lyceum, which stood about where Woods now stands; and the first group of professors' houses, which, with the Lyceum, formed the north side of the University square. Although the first general plan was lost, some old records show the relation of the buildings to this general plan. Houses and dormitories bear the letters E through K. The letter L indicates the Rotunda, center of the group; M, the Lyceum. N and O refer to two "hotels," one, the present Gorgas Home, the other, probably never completed.

The estimated cost of the first group of buildings was $56,000, a sum which would not build one such edifice today. The trustees agreed to make available a building fund of $50,000; $10,000 for the first year of the building program, $30,000 for the second year, and the balance for the third year.[10] It is interesting to note how accurately the building schedule was kept. The University was built and ready for students in the three-year time limit set.

After determining the University site, agreeing upon an architectural plan, and setting aside funds for construction, the trustees could and did proceed at once to let the contracts for the actual building. Copies of these contracts are in the records at Montgomery, and estimates of the costs of some of the buildings are included in the "Journal of the Board of Trustees."[11]

Workmen building the University in the years between 1828 and 1831 found close at hand much of the material they needed. Constantine Perkins gave sandstone, quarried near the Warrior River; brick were burned and made on the spot; lumber from the University's own timber tract was cut and shaped by hand. Separate contracts were entered into for all such services. Much of the labor was, of course, performed by slaves, but the stonemasons, trained artisans of Scotch descent, built their pride of craft into the strength and beauty of the buildings they helped to erect.

What did the University look like when, in the winter of 1830-31, it stood almost ready to receive its first students? In October, 1830, the *Southern Advocate,* proudly describing the new institution for the benefit of all interested citizens, published a detailed article which is the fullest record left of the plan and appearance of the early University. The writer spoke first of the location. The eighty or more acres of land lay across the high road from Tuscaloosa to Huntsville. The southern division was enclosed; it was occupied partly by fruit trees, since it was intended for an experimental farm. North of the road, where the land was higher, stood the University buildings, also well enclosed.

Then he turned to the buildings themselves, describing each with minutest care. There was the Laboratory, or Lyceum, the principal building for instruction, standing at the center of the northern side of the University square. It was two stories high with a portico with six Ionic columns, approached by a handsome flight of steps. It was forty-five feet wide and seventy-five feet deep. Inside there were six apartments: a theater for chemistry lectures and two smaller rooms on the first floor; three "splendid" rooms, one of them measuring forty-five feet by thirty feet, on the second floor. Each apartment had its own fireplace; the large second-floor room had two. Two "handsome" staircases were placed one on either side of the lobby.

Just west of the Laboratory were the two faculty buildings, each of which was forty-five feet by thirty-five feet, with a space of forty-five feet between them. Each could accommodate four families. Between them and "immediately resting on them," was a one-story recitation room. The buildings for the professors were three stories high and so arranged that each family had six large, airy rooms, with kitchen and outbuildings.

Facing each other, on the west and east sides of the square, were Washington and Jefferson halls, the two dormitories. Each could accommodate easily forty-eight students, four in each of the twelve apartments, which included a sitting room with fireplace and two bedrooms. The twin buildings, ninety-eight feet by thirty-six feet, included cellars used for storing fuel.

Provision for feeding the students who would come to live in Washington and Jefferson halls was made in the hotel (later to be called the Gorgas Home), which stood behind Washington but which was placed about eighty yards back from the line of the square "rendering it more retired and agreeable for its purpose of a boarding house." The hotel was a handsome two-story building. In its brick-paved dining hall, fifty-six by twenty-two feet, as many as one hundred students could eat in comfort. The other rooms behind the great hall could be used as "places of deposit for desserts, culinary utensils, and for other conveniences." The kitchen was well placed and well constructed.

When the *Advocate* writer described the Rotunda, standing in the center of the University square, he became more enthusiastic, saying that "it not only adorned the institution, but it also added honor to its architecture, and to the artizans employed in its construction." It was, in his opinion, "one of the finest in the southern states." Circular, as its name suggested, the Rotunda was three stories high and was surmounted by a dome. There was also a spire in front. A fine colonnade of twenty-four pillars surrounded it. Inside, on the first floor, was the hall which would be used for commencements. Upstairs was the room set aside for the University library.

An excellent start, the writer noted, had been made also on landscaping the University grounds. Advantage of spaciousness of the forty-acre site had been taken, and walks had been well laid out. Trees and flowers and shrubbery had been planted "at proper distances." Such planning "adorned the University," the writer remarked, adding that "flower gardens and walks with shady trees are truly delightful in this climate."

Having carefully described the University as it looked in the autumn of 1830, the *Advocate* writer then gave his readers a brief preview of the future. Two more buildings for the faculty and another hotel would be built, he said, on the east side of the Laboratory. Four or more new dormitories, "of uniform appearance with those already erected," would be placed to the south of Washington and Jefferson on both sides of the square. Eventually, when the University added a Medical School, the south side of the square, next to the high road, which was now open would be completed with buildings corresponding in plan to those on the north side. "Thus a uniform plan would be constantly attended to, and every new building as it was erected would fit into its place according to the original plan of the architect."

Full completion of such "fine" plans would take time, the writer warned. He did not expect that the University would be finished in his day. Concluding his article, he warmly praised "the simplicity, the justness, and the science of the plans" and paid "unhesitating" tribute of "admiration for the efforts of taste and genius which had executed them."[12]

The *Advocate* writer was a good prophet. The elaborate plans for the University building were destined to remain incomplete in his day and, indeed, forever. But the years between 1830 and 1865 saw at least four distinctive new buildings added to the University plant. Two of them were dormitories: Franklin Hall, built in 1833; and Madison Hall, which also had meeting and study space, built in 1854. One, the President's Mansion, the pride of the men who built it in 1841, is still in use today. The fourth, which was to be romantically saved from the flames of 1865 through the intercession of a brave lady, was the Observatory, built in 1844 and added to in 1858.

Franklin Hall appears first in the trustees' records of 1832, though it was still unnamed at that time. The board, noting that an expected increase in enrollment would necessitate the construction of a new dormitory, authorized the comptroller of public accounts to pay Captain William Nichols $300 for his services as superintendent of buildings and for the plan and estimates of a new dormitory.[13] A year later the board turned its attention to "the new Dormitory now building," appropriated $6000 for building costs, and authorized the borrowing of this money from the state bank or any of its branches.[14]

In a period when building costs were low, the President's Mansion was constructed in 1841 for $18,000. Apparently the trustees spared no expense to make it the dignified and elegant home their University presidents deserved; their satisfaction with their accomplishment is reflected in their comments on the building as it neared completion. It was built, they said, of stuccoed brick and sandstone which came from property near by. This "very spacious structure, built in the Greek style of architecture," is two stories high and contains "twelve large apartments." Its six Ionic columns reach to the roof, and it has an overhanging iron balcony on the second floor, and a double winding stairway leading to the elevated entrance. A great hall runs through the center of the building and is flanked on each side by large rooms. The windows of the rooms are deeply recessed."[15]

Professor F. A. P. Barnard was the prime mover and planner in the undertaking which gave the University its Observatory. As early as 1838 he was urging the need for such facilities for his students in astronomy. The board of trustees passed on his communication to the legislature that year, but nothing happened.[16] Professor Barnard, however, went right ahead with his plans, and in 1840 he was rewarded by an appropriation of $2000.[17] Under his watchful eye, the building began to take shape. By 1844 it was ready for use, a structure fifty-four feet long and twenty-two feet wide. By 1858 an addition was necessary. Professor Barnard worked hard to secure the best possible equipment for the Observatory. Its five-foot telescope, with object glass four inches in the clear, was especially constructed for the University by Simms of London, and there were other fine pieces of astronomical and physical apparatus. At that time the Observatory was considered one of the best equipped in the country.[18]

When, in July, 1853, the trustees began planning for the building which, in honor of James Madison, was to be known as Madison Hall, student life had developed so that attention must be given to needs other than those of shelter, food, and recitation. The board authorized its president and James Guild to procure suitable plans for a new building, similar in appearance and in position to Franklin Hall, to be placed east of the Rotunda. It was to have dormitory space and study rooms, but it was also to have "a sufficient number of public rooms for the working of the establishment," including two for the meetings of the Erosophic and Philomathic societies. The sum of $10,000 was appropriated for this building.[19]

No doubt the trustees, if they were like board members in any other time, enjoyed watching building after building rise on their University campus, visible evidence of the flourishing state of their institution, lasting monuments to the men guiding that institution's affairs. They could not, however, give all their time to these large and gratifying matters. As soon as the University began to operate, details of maintenance occupied more and more of their time. Records of their meetings are sprinkled with references to window blinds and lightning rods and "privvys" as well as to further plans and policies.

The April 1831, which saw the first students on campus found the trustees deep in discussion of a report from the building committee on improvements needed for the "security of the University buildings, and the accommodation of the Faculty and Students." Among the items which the committee considered immediate needs were window blinds for the professors' houses, recitation rooms and laboratories; grates for burning coal in the University buildings; barns, stables, and carriage houses; a well with a pump; shelves and cases; fencing materials; one hundred cherry trees "to protect the houses," and "2 privvys for Students." The estimated cost for these improvements was $6000, the committee said. The trustees appropriated this amount and authorized the employment of a superintendent to carry out the plans.[20]

Trustees' meetings in January, 1832, dealt with seats for the Rotunda, housing for the University bell, and a dispute over a freight bill involving a member of the faculty. William Morrison, apparently under contract to make the Rotunda seats, was voted an additional $160 for his work, the sum to be payable on completion of the job.[21] According to plans previously submitted by the building committee, the sum of $500 was appropriated to build a cupola on the Laboratory for the bell.[22] And "Doctor Wallis" was directed to pay Captain J. Cleveland the balance due on the freight bill for transporting chemical equipment from Mobile to Tuscaloosa.[23]

P. P. Ashe was given $308.75 in December, 1832, to pay for furniture in the "hotel" and for repairs on this building and its garden.[24] A few days later, the professor of chemistry was given permission to buy a stove to warm the recitation room "by means of heated air;" he was authorized to spend $100 for this purpose.[25] The winter of 1832-33 must have been a cold one!

Lightning rods were featured in the trustees' minutes in August, 1834. The board authorized the placing of such protection on University buildings and the employment of a mechanic to decide where they should be placed and to install them.[26] Lightning rods were

VIEW OF THE ORIGINAL CAMPUS

CENTER: the Rotunda. LEFT: Franklin and Washington halls. RIGHT: Jefferson and Madison halls. BACKGROUND: the Lyceum and faculty homes. The steward's hall (Gorgas Home), Observa- tory, and Mansion are not shown in this view. The Mound, traditional site of student exercises, was the original foundation of Washington Hall. A classroom connects two of the homes.

PRESIDENT'S MANSION

Built in 1841 of sandstone quarried nearby and brick burned on the building site, the President's Mansion was one of the four buildings spared when the University campus was raided by Union troops in 1865. The Gorgas Home, the Observatory, and the Round House were the other buildings saved. The Mansion has served exclusively as a home for the presidents.

THE OLD UNIVERSITY 37

discussed again eight years later, when the trustees again authorized this equipment.[27]

No money was involved in a matter which occupied the attention of the board in the summer of 1835. A certain Colonel William D. Stone apparently had offered the University an air gun. By formal resolution, the president of the University was authorized "and required" to accept the gift.[28]

Trespassers and marauders were recognized as a problem that year. In November the University stewards were directed to enclose the campus, repair the fences, and prosecute people who persisted in "tearing or breaking" the fences.[29] Apparently this action was not enough, for, within two years, the trustees again noted the condition of University property and this time gave the building committee permission to hire a man to take care of the "grounds, etc., fences, enclosures, vineyards, etc., and to ornament the grounds with suitable shade trees, to repair the said fences, and enclosures and to prune and otherwise improve the vineyards and preserve the groves of the University."[30] Then they voted $2000 for repairs. It is interesting to note, however, that they did not specify in detail, as they had done in 1831, just what the money should be used for.[31]

Board actions taken in December of 1840 included an ordinance requiring each student to furnish for his room, "a lock or such other fastening as he may see fit,"[32] possibly to absolve the University from the responsibility of doing so; a resolution to permit President Manly to enclose the grounds between the President's Mansion and "Mrs. Banks," south of the Huntsville Road, subject to restrictions previously agreed upon;[33] and a resolution authorizing the executive committee to spend "not more than fifty dollars" to buy a screw press.[34]

It is a little hard to determine what was involved in the business which the trustees transacted at their meeting on December 19, 1843, when they appropriated $325 to pay R. T. Brumby for the erection of a dining hall attached to his home, since an essential part of the arrangement was that Brumby was to deed to the University a piece of land next to his home "supposed to contain about seven acres."[35] The record of the following year shows no such vagueness in an appropriation of money for an equatorial telescope "to complete the observatory." A maximum limit of $2500 was placed on the purchase, but great care should be taken, said the trustees, that the best possible instrument at that price be found. Payment of $500 in advance and the balance on delivery was also carefully specified.[36]

Minor emergencies were a regular concern of the governing board in the early days of the University. Once in a while a major catastrophe confronted them, as when, in April, 1848, a defective flue started a fire which destroyed the homes of Professors Dockery and Garland.[37]

The trustees early became employers, hiring agents who were entrusted with the sales of University land. Before the University was ready for students, the trustees had become also, as was quite natural, slaveowners and contractors for slave labor, with all the complications which that relationship implied in a state in which the slave population was increasing faster than in any other state of the Union.

Their first recorded purchase of a slave was in 1828. At that time, Ben, who was brought to work under the direction of the architect, planted trees and preserved fences on the University site.[38] Ben was sold after the buildings had been completed, along with a horse which also had apparently been needed in the construction tasks.[39] The steward was instructed at that time to hire slaves as University servants,[40] and, during the next few years, the system of hiring rather than outright ownership seems to have been in force. Not until 1838 does another authorization for the purchase of a slave appear in the trustees' records.[41] A second slave was bought four years later,[42] and purchases became more frequent from that time on. A bill of sale dated January 7, 1845, shows that among the slaves purchased that year by the trustees was a "Negro man named Moses, aged about twenty-eight . . . sound and healthy and a slave for life." The trustees paid $700 for Moses.[43] Eight years later they paid almost twice as much, $1300, for Isac,[44] whether because he was worth that much more or because of rising prices for slaves is not certain. Later in the same period Professor George Benagh was sent to Virginia with authority to spend as much as $7000 to buy slaves.[45]

It is probable that the trustees preferred to hire slaves from owners in Tuscaloosa because the University had no facilities for housing them and, in any case, had to keep them and board them in

Tuscaloosa. An account of 1831 shows that board for twelve weeks for Ben cost ten dollars. (The same bill included a fifteen dollar item for feeding the horse for the same period.)[46] Costs had risen by 1839, for in that year Benjamin Whitfield boarded three slaves and charged ten dollars a month for each of them.[47] The University steward, who boarded two University slaves in 1842, received no money, but he was allowed to use the services of his boarders during meals and during vacations.[48] Appropriations in 1848 included $144 for boarding Moses, Arthur, and Sam.[49] The period covered by this amount is not stated, but a receipt issued by Alex Baird in 1850 indicates that he was boarding University slaves for as little as three dollars a month.[50]

The University had to clothe its slaves in addition to feeding and housing them. Cottonade coats and pants, flannel coats, summer vests, summer hats, winter coats, shoes, and slippers are items which appear in the old records. Sometimes the clothing was made by local seamstresses: Mrs. J. C. Buchannan was hired in 1839 to make five shirts, two round jackets, and three pairs of pantaloons.[51] Sometimes the clothing was purchased; two pairs of satinet pants and a satinet vest were bought, also in 1839, from merchants in Tuscaloosa for "servant boy Sam."[52] In 1860 a warrant on the treasurer for the payment of insurance on slaves and clothing items totalled $201.22.[53]

Hired slaves were used around the University for many tasks, both skilled and unskilled. They were hired from Tuscaloosa slave owners, and in at least one case from members of the University family, for "carpenters James, William, and an apprentice, Edward," who began to work for the University in the years between 1837 and 1840, belonged to Professor H. S. Pratt. After Pratt died, his widow continued the arrangement for many years. Hired slaves were employed for "coloring" the buildings, carrying water to the Rotunda during commencement, plastering, blacksmith work, cutting and hauling wood, brickmaking and bricklaying and "toting." Usually they were hired by the week or month, but occasionally the term of employment was as long as a year. The rate of hire varied according to the task and to the ability of the worker. Common laborers received about ten dollars a month; painters and plasterers, commanded from a dollar to a dollar and a quarter a day; blacksmiths, around a dollar and a half. Carpenters were at the top of the list. A good one brought his owner two dollars every day he was hired. Carpenter William, one of the carpenters most frequently hired by the University, may have demanded even more, for, in addition to general work, he was skillful enough to be trusted with building desks and bookcases.[54]

The University was responsible for boarding both its own slaves and the hired ones. Sometimes it was responsible also for their clothing. When Ned was hired for the year of 1841, for $110, it was with the express stipulation that the University should be at no expense for clothing him;[55] but when Paul was hired, in 1858, for $150, the University undertook, not only to clothe him, but also to pay taxes on him, to meet any doctor's bills Paul incurred, and to expect no rebate on account of Paul's loss of time through illness unless he actually died. In that case Paul's owner was to collect the amount due only to the date of his death.[56]

The same problems which confronted other slaveowners had to be dealt with by the University. There were slaves whose health required attention and expense. Isac, whose bill of sale in 1853 noted that he was "about twenty-five years of age . . . sound and in good health, both of mind and body," appears not to have been so robust in 1857, when Dr. Reuben Searcy rendered a bill for medicines and for thirty-three visits within three months to "Man Isac" as well as charges for liniment for Moses and for "opening rising on foot" of the latter slave.[57] Also, from time to time, slaves turned out to be unruly. Sam appears to be one of these. Although the trustees tried to have him sold in 1848, he was still around in 1851, and in that year he so severely injured Tom, a slave hired from Alex Glascock, that Tom could not work for a month.[58] In one instance the University unknowingly served as a refuge for "runaways." In 1852 Professor Scherb reported that he had found some Negroes sleeping in Room 18, Franklin Hall. They had been there for some time, "keeping large fires all night, and snoring at a great note." Upon being questioned, they said they belonged to Mr. Baird, and, in all probability, they were returned to him.[59]

For the most part, however, the University slaves seem to have been capable servants, and in time, some of them became almost traditions of the institution they served. Moses, one of these, was suspected of being unduly fond of drinking. He was admonished

THE OLD UNIVERSITY

and was told that he would be sold if he continued this practice. This threat evidently had the desired effect, for mention of Moses is found in later years.[60] His solemnity, according to a story in the Mobile *Tribune* in 1859, earned him the name of "Preach." It must have been a seriousness mixed with wit, however, for the story goes on to tell of one occasion when teasing students called out to him:

"I say, Preach, what are you going to do when the devil gets you?"

The answer came back, patly and promptly:

"Wait on the students."[61]

In 1850 servant Sam, in addition to his regular duties, was allowed to fit up a cellar under the South end of the Washington building as a barber shop for the students.[62]

Two maintenance supervisors, a proctor and a steward, were quite early placed on the University staff, and the trustees spent a fair amount of time overseeing the supervisors. Appointment of the proctor was authorized in December, 1837,[63] but another year passed before the job was actually filled. The proctor seems to have been the personnel man and, to some extent, the purchasing agent. Under faculty supervision, he was to manage the improvements on buildings and grounds and to hire and direct University servants. One of his chief duties was to provide fuel for the students, but he was carefully instructed not to deliver fuel to students unless the student had deposited with the treasurer enough money to pay for it or was willing and able to pay on delivery. The students, by the way, were to be charged the current rate for this fuel plus a ten per cent service charge. For these services the proctor was to be paid not more than $35 a month. When they established this position, however, the trustees set aside an appropriation of $1500 to carry it out.[64]

If the proctor was carefully supervised, the steward was even more so. The trustees gave him so much attention, particularly during the years 1844 and 1845, that one feels justified in reading between the lines of the record some indication of friction between this employee and the faculty.

In December, 1844, the trustees noted that the steward might be permitted to clear and enclose "the small portion of land in the rear of his buildings" if by so doing he did not injure the appearance or usefulness of the University buildings.[65] A year later the trustees put the steward under $2,000 bond and made him responsible for collecting student bills for room and board. Every student was to be required to obtain from the steward a receipt in full for such payments.[66] That was passed on Christmas Day. The following day the trustees approached other problems more directly related to the steward's original job. They told him that he must not use University coal or fuel to heat the dining room or any other part of Steward's Hall; furthermore, they curtailed permission formerly given him to use the slaves he boarded during vacations. They specified in great detail the work these slaves should be doing during holidays: receiving coal, cleaning, whitewashing, and so on, and all "to the satisfaction of the faculty." The trustees expressly stated that the holiday chores which the steward asked the servants to do must not be allowed to interfere with these duties.[67]

Making a University rise out of the new earth of a new state, equipping this University with the best available furnishings and educational tools, staffing it with the maintenance staff who would keep it smoothly running—these were tasks which required thought and energy and conscientious work from the trustees. These tasks, however, were not wholly foreign to the trustees, who were on somewhat familiar ground. But building a façulty for the new institution of learning was different. Few, if any, of the men on the board had experience as educators. Yet they tackled the most difficult of their tasks with vigor and perhaps with some of the cocksureness which amateurs in the field of education often show. They combed the country for their candidates and wrangled over each appointment before they made it. And gradually they brought together an able and distinguished group of men who, even though causing the board more headaches than did the legislature, set a high standard of education for the young University. The story of the first faculty is another chapter.

CHAPTER III

The First Faculty
1831-1837

FOUR MEN made up the faculty of the University of Alabama when on April 12, 1831, the institution inaugurated its first president and made ready to receive its first students. Less than seven years later they were all gone from the campus, after experiences which could not have made altogether pleasant memories. Yet they helped to shape the raw materials of the University and put upon it the stamp of their personalities.

Two of them had come from the East and the North—President Alva Woods from Vermont and Professor Gurdon Saltonstall from New York state. Two had been born in the old South—Professor Henry Tutwiler in Virginia and Professor John Fielding Wallis in Maryland. All were mature men, with honorable experience behind them, except for Tutwiler who, at twenty-four years of age, was "a delicate stripling of a youth."

Nearly sixty years later, William R. Smith, a student in the first University class, wrote his *Reminiscences*[1] of these men as persons and as teachers, in thumb-nail sketches which let us see them as the boys they taught saw them more than a century ago. Of the Reverend Alva Woods, Smith wrote

As he appeared to the writer, now nearly sixty years ago, he was of medium height, compactly built, of robust health, with round face, fairly handsome; a well shaped head, high and somewhat bald, and florid complexion. He wore glasses habitually. About him there was a deliberation of manner that might well be called hesitation; as if, indeed, he was constantly meditating upon every movement of mind and body.

Dr. Woods, Smith said, "was graciously received by the professors and students, for he was heralded by a fair fame." But he added a paragraph of observation which goes far to explain why the first president failed to hold throughout his term of office the support of those same professors and students:

His feet fell very lightly as he walked, and his restless eye indicated that his ear was in suspense. There was an air of vigilance about him that threw one on his guard against a watchfulness that appeared almost offensive. With such a characteristic it is quite impossible that he should have inspired the boys with any feeling akin to affection; on the contrary, he was an object of awe.[2]

Those nimble feet were to stand the president in good stead when, as sometimes happened, the students forgot their awe in anger!

Smith had less to say about Professors Saltonstall and Wallis, but what he did say is pithy. Of Saltonstall:

I remember this professor chiefly as an elegant and engaging person, of lofty stature and benignant countenance. He was of easy manners and uncomplaining disposition; too good-natured even to rebuke a rebellious pupil for an unmitigated breach of discipline.[3]

Of Wallis:

He was of retiring and solitary habits, of dejected, melancholic appearance. He was a widower, and demeaned himself as one who had lost his heart's treasure, and had but few of those livelier solicitudes which engage the more joyous.[4]

The explanation of Saltonstall's early relinquishment of a post requiring disciplinary skills distasteful to him, and the explanation of Wallis's difficulties with his associates are more than hinted in those brief notations.

Only one of the four early faculty members seems to have stirred in young Smith's heart any real affection. Professor Tutwiler stands out from the pages of the *Reminiscences* as a warm, sensitive, and friendly human being.

Professor Tutwiler was altogether the most noted and marked of the first corps of professors. He was . . . in appearance as timid and modest as a woman—so gentle in his demeanor and so graceful and apt in his mode of imparting instruction that every boy fell absolutely in love with him. . . .

. . . Professor Tutwiler was seldom seen in or out of the school-room without having a small volume in his left hand. He had a diamond edition of the ancient classics, and carried about with him either Virgil, Horace, the Anabasis, Iliad, Cicero, Terence, or Eurispides. These were his quiet companions, from which he seemed to be inseparable. He was never without a pencil; and would stop in his walks, under the shade of an oak, and enrich the margin of his book with some useful hint or scholarly annotation.

This gentle scholar apparently loved boys as well as books. His former student remembered with admiration the wide scope of the young man's knowledge:

. . . he was a whole Faculty within himself . . . as much at home in the chemical laboratory as he was in his own room with the classics . . . familiar with all the sciences, and always at work . . . handy with the telescope. . . .

And he remembered the patient, personal relationship the teacher established with boys not many years his juniors:

He took charge of the classes in Latin and Greek, and was recognized as the professor of ancient and modern languages; but he also took charge of students in the primary departments; for in the beginning of the exercises of the University no systematic collegiate classes could be readily formed. On this account he had to do, in some way, with every boy—the least and the most advanced—and so at once became the friend, companion, and instructor of all. . . .

The associations which Tutwiler built in that way were, Smith noted, lasting friendships:

It may be asserted as a fact that the feeling entertained for him by the earlier students . . . amounted to real affection, which suffered no diminution by the lapse of time. And this was reciprocal; for Professor Tutwiler watched the career, with exceeding anxiety, of all his pupils in after years, noting with pride the development of any excellence, and rejoicing in their success.[5]

In the University family of 1831, Tutwiler had only one real rival for the affections of the students—the president's wife. Even after nearly sixty years, Smith described her in lyrical terms:

But besides the intellectual halo surrounding Dr. Woods, there was one more celestial—his charming wife. . . . Her beauty was without a flaw; and her graceful and gracious manners carried her straightway to the hearts of the students. It was quite impossible to spend an evening in her presence without softening toward the man on whom she lavished the boundless wealth of her loveliness.[6]

With Ann Eliza Wallis, who came to Alabama with her widowed

father, Mrs. Woods probably gave the University family its only touch of femininity in those early years. Ann Eliza, by the way, may be considered the University's first coed, though, of course, she was never actually enrolled. After she graduated from the Alabama Female Academy, her father arranged to have his colleagues tutor her in the same courses which they were currently giving at the University.[7]

Gathering together this first faculty had been no easy task for the trustees. As early as January 2, 1829, they had made a start, under the authority given them by the General Assembly, to find a teaching staff for the University whose buildings were beginning to rise in Marr's Field. Messrs. Fearn, Lewis, and Elliott were appointed to study the needs of the University and to start writing letters to possible candidates for teaching positions.[8]

It took the committee only three days to decide upon their recommendations regarding the academic needs of the University, the number of professors required, and the subjects essential for the first curriculum. On January 5, they reported

. . . it will be proper to commence the courses of instruction in this Institution with four Professors, one of whom shall be appointed to preside over the Faculty—that it will be proper in the selection of such Professors to have particular regard to their qualifications for teaching the following Branches of Literature and Science, viz:

1. Antient Languages, including the higher grade of Latin and Greek languages; Antient and Modern History, Geography, Antient and Modern, with the use of the Globes, to be assisted by a Tutor.
2. Mathematicks and Natural Philosophy, including the higher branches of Numerical Arithmetick, Algebra, Trigonometry, Plane and Spherical Geometry, Mensuration, Navigation, Conic Sections, Fluxions or Differentials, Mechanicks, Statics, Hydrostatics, Hydrantics, Pneumatics, Acoustics, Optics, and Astronomy, to be assisted by a Mathematical Tutor.
3. Natural History, including Botany, Zoology, Mineralogy, Chemistry and Geology, with the Application of Chemistry to the Arts and Agriculture.
4. Moral Philosophy, including Mental Science, generally, Belles-letters, Logick, Rhetorick, and Political Economy.[9]

The report was accepted. The president of the board was added to the committee on procurement of faculty.[10] And the four men started the task of combing the country for teachers able to teach the

THE OLD UNIVERSITY   47

somewhat formidable array of subjects they had agreed to offer.

Meeting the following December, the trustees learned that their committee was ready with applications. The importance of the step they were about to take was well recognized. Not only did they appoint as a special committee Messrs. Phillips, Hubbard, Benson, Oliver, Field, Rhodes, and Crawford to "arrange" the applications[11] but they also attempted to stiffen the appointment procedures. A motion, which would have set faculty terms at three years with reappointment permitted and which would also have required a majority vote of the whole board for such appointments, was lost by a vote of 8 to 4.[12]

The meeting on December 19, called for the purpose of electing the faculty, got off to a good start. It was easily agreed that the chair of moral philosophy should be filled first. Dr. Philip Lindsley, the only one nominated for this post, was unanimously elected.

To some of the trustees that seemed like a good day's work. They moved to postpone action on other appointment, but the motion was lost. Dr. Gurdon Saltonstall, graduate of Union College in New York state, and Dr. Patterson of the University of Virginia were nominated for the professorship in mathematics. Saltonstall was elected by a vote of ten to two.

Again an attempt to put off the rest of the appointments for another day was lost, and the trustees buckled down to the election of teachers for the departments of natural history and ancient languages and to the appointment of a steward.

John Fielding Wallis won the position of professor of natural history by a vote of 7 to 5 over Dr. Elisha Mitchell. The Reverend William Hooper had two opponents in the contest for the chair of ancient languages; he got eight votes, however, whereas Rev. Nathaniel Harris and Mr. Benjamin B. Hopkins got two each. Choice of a steward took two ballots. On the first, Mr. P. P. Ashe got six votes; Mr. William Colgin, four; Mr. William Cannon, one; and Mr. Dennis Dent, one. The two low men were withdrawn and Ashe won on the next ballot eight to four.

Still on the list of appointments was an adjunct professor of chemistry. A motion to proceed with that election was, however, lost. The trustees stopped work for the day, having selected, they believed, four excellent teachers and a competent steward.[13]

They met three times in the following week before they settled upon the postponed appointment of an adjunct professor of chemistry. As Dr. William A. King was the only nominee on December 21, that matter was tabled [14] as was also the nomination of John I. Wyche the next day.[15] Apparently there was some disagreement as to whether the University really needed to make this appointment so early, for on December 23, a motion was made and lost to postpone the election indefinitely. A second motion represented a compromise stand; it provided that even if the adjunct professor of chemistry were appointed then his salary should not begin until the University was actually in operation. This settled, the trustees were willing to act. They made Dr. King adjunct professor of chemistry.[16]

Early in the new year they took one further step. Dr. Lindsley became, by unanimous and unopposed vote, the president-elect of the University of Alabama.[17]

Six months later the board found itself almost back where it had started. The appointments of Saltonstall and Wallis had apparently held. But the president-elect and the professor of ancient languages had both declined appointment, and the adjunct professor of chemistry had died. Work on the University buildings was going ahead rapidly. If a faculty were to be ready as soon as the University plant, the trustees would have to move fast.

The move they made was to authorize appointment of an agent:

to collect and lay before the Board at their next meeting all the information he can procure as to the qualifications of persons who may be willing to accept [the positions] of Professor of Languages &c and President of the Faculty of the University of Alabama.

This agent was given permission to "visit any part of the United States," and he was to be adequately paid for his services.[18]

James G. Birney, trustee from the fifth district, was given this important job, paid $500 in advance, and sent off on his scouting mission.[19] By November, 1830, he was back again with his report. The trustees paid him an additional $400 for a job well done,[20] and then proceeded, on November 25, to act on his recommendations, adding to his well-documented information on the candidates some other material on new candidates of their own.

Their desire to have Dr. Lindsley connected with the University must have been strong. He was again nominated in spite of his refusal to accept the appointment made the year before, and the new candidate, the Reverend Alva Woods, narrowly won his election in a six to five vote. Three ballots were necessary to make Henry Tutwiler professor of ancient languages. The first gave three votes each to him, to Mr. Woolsey, and to Mr. Mustrat, and one vote each to two other contenders, Mr. Cunningham and Mr. Harris. The second ballot was also inconclusive; the third gave Tutwiler his appointment by a vote of eight to three. Dr. Woods was then unanimously named president. The job was done.[21]

The trustees were justifiably proud of their work as faculty builders. They said so when they met on January 15:

The Board passed ample surety in the distinguished literary and scientific [achievements] of these gentlemen, that all will be done which zealous devotion and well cultivated talents of the highest order can effect, to place the University of Alabama on that lofty eminence, which they fondly hope it is destined to occupy among the literary institutions of our country.[22]

It did look like an excellent faculty. At its head was a man who had already demonstrated at Transylvania College, Lexington, Kentucky, his ability to fill the job of college president. The Reverend Alva Woods, born in Shoreham, Vermont, August 13, 1794, the son of a Baptist clergyman, had a brilliant record of scholarly attainments to show for his thirty-seven years. He had gone to school at Phillips Academy in Andover, Massachusetts; graduated from Harvard in 1817 and from the Andover Theological Seminary four years later, having taken a year out of his theological studies to serve as assistant principal of his preparatory school. He had been a professor at the Columbian University in the District of Columbia from 1821 to 1823; and at Brown University, Providence, Rhode Island, from 1824 until his appointment, in 1828, as president of Transylvania. He had traveled as well as taught; the year 1824 saw him attending lectures in London and at the universities at Oxford, Cambridge, Edinburgh, and Glasgow, and visiting "the principal institutions of literature, science, and art in Paris, Lyons, Genoa, Leghorn, Florence, Rome, Naples, Milan, and Geneva."[23] Certainly he was a man of parts, who could lead the new institution with distinction.

Gurdon Saltonstall, the tall, good-natured mathematics professor, may have been well-known to the trustees as a competent physician in the town of Tuscaloosa. His roots, however, like Dr. Woods', were in the North. He went to college at Union College in Schenectady and then studied medicine at the College of Physicians and Surgeons of Columbia University in 1814 and 1815, receiving, according to Union College records, the degree of M.D. He may also have served for a time as private in Captain Samuel Swartout's company, second artillery regiment, New York, in the late months of 1814.[24] The trustees probably were as impressed as William R. Smith with this "elegant and engaging person."

John Fielding Wallis, melancholy though he may have been, brought to his new job school experience which must have looked very good indeed to the trustees. Born on the Eastern Shore of Maryland, educated at Princeton, Wallis had moved, as a young man, to Georgia, where he established at Cherokee Corner, Oglethorpe County, a successful boarding school.[25] He was already on the job, the only one of the four appointees actually at work for the University in January, 1831. As early as June, 1830, he began urging the trustees to let him go abroad to buy chemical apparatus for the University. Reluctant at first to entrust to anyone but the president the responsibility for spending the $20,000 appropriated for the purpose of "purchasing a Library and Chemical and Philosophical apparatus,"[26] the board finally gave him the permission he wanted, authorized him to spend half the appropriation, and gave him leave of absence until July 1, 1831.[27] Such energy and enterprise must have made a favorable impression.

Young Tutwiler was, of course, the least experienced of the staff, but the trustees, reading the warm letters of recommendation which came from many of the boy's associates at the University of Virginia, must have recognized a man of exceptional promise in this appointee. Tutwiler was one of the first graduates of the University of Virginia and one of the first men to whom that University gave the degree of Master of Arts, an honor seldom bestowed in those days. He had had a few years of teaching experience between his graduation in 1829 and his coming to the University of Alabama in 1831.

Oddly enough, the trustees had more difficulty in getting the new faculty on the grounds for the opening of the University on April 18, 1831, than they had in finding them in the first place. Just who were there to greet the first students is hard to determine accurately. Wallis certainly was not; he was off hunting "chemical and philosophical apparatus" and would not start his classroom duties until July. William R. Smith remembered that Saltonstall and Tutwiler were the only two teachers on hand to conduct examinations and decide "upon the fitness of the applicants."[28] Owen supports Smith in this statement, saying in his study of "The Genesis of the University of Alabama,"

The examinations for admittance were conducted by Professors Henry Tutwiler and Gurdon Saltonstall. The ceremonies were very simple, on account of the fact that the president was detained, winding up some business at Transylvania University, and the other professors not having yet taken their chairs. It consisted in merely handing in the name and age, and setting a little while on the examination benches.[29]

But two questions arise if one accepts these statements. The first has to do with Professor Saltonstall. Four days before the University opened he had been given a leave of absence until July 20 and had been put on the payroll as of July 15.[30] If under these circumstances he actually came out to the campus to lend a hand with the enrollments, it is indeed evidence of the uncomplaining good nature which Smith attributes to him. If he was a physician in Tuscaloosa, as some reports say, he may, however, have found it possible to leave his practice for the day to help Tutwiler.

The second question is more puzzling. Where was the president? Certainly he had been in Tuscaloosa on April 12. The successful inauguration ceremonies at the Episcopal Church that day had pleased all the trustees and particularly the committee appointed to make arrangements for the president's installation: Messrs. Jesse Garth, Quin Morton, George Starr, and William Acklin.[31] From the newspaper accounts it is evident that the Reverend Alva Woods was not only there but that he delivered the first of the speeches which were to win him fame in the years ahead.[32] Had he made the long journey from Lexington, Kentucky, and then, without waiting for the University to open, traveled all that long distance back again? The records of the board of trustees shed no light on this question. We do know that both Woods and Tutwiler were put on the University payroll as of February 1, 1831, "the time at which they respectively commenced preparation for their removal to this University to take upon themselves the duties assigned to them."[33] Smith suggests that the arrangement in President Woods' case may have provided explicitly for overlapping jobs:

It seems to have been understood at the time of his acceptance of the position as president of our University, that he would be allowed to remain at Lexington until the completion of the unexpired term of his office. Thus it happened that he was not present when the University of Alabama opened for the reception of pupils. It was not until several weeks after the organization of the classes that Dr. Woods made his appearance in Tuscaloosa.[34]

One other individual, not quite a member of the faculty, had added himself to the staff before the University opened. He was Mr. William McMillan, who considered it obvious that the institution must have a museum and who set himself to collecting specimens of birds, animals, and other natural history exhibits. At first his idea got very little encouragement from the trustees. In fact, it was flatly turned down in January and July of 1830.[35] It was referred to a committee when the board met in December.[36] By January, 1831, however, persistence was rewarded. The board voted to employ Mr. McMillan as librarian and collector of natural history specimens,[37] but they hedged the appointment with reservations. The president could dismiss him "at any time he deemed proper," and his payment would be only for the length of time he had been employed. With this safeguard the trustees were willing to let him go on working and even to give him $50 for work he had already done in collecting specimens.[38] On the whole, they were rather pleased with their action. It was a triumph of so new a university to have a natural history museum complete with curator:

Impressed with a belief in its great utility, and importance, the Board have taken measures to form a museum for the University—and for that purpose have employed Mr. McMillan, a naturalist, to collect and prepare specimens of natural history—the same individual has also undertaken to collect such antiquities of this State as may come within his knowledge, in this way not only the Natural History of our own country may be collected in a few years, but by a system of exchanges with foreign institutions, many valuable specimens may be obtained from them, this undertaking has already been commissioned and a considerable number of specimens prepared, which are now at the institution.[39]

GORGAS HOME

Originally called the "hotel" or "steward's hall," and for some years known as Pratt House, this is the only survivor of the original buildings constructed in 1828-1830. Before 1847 it housed the college dining room and kitchen and the steward's living quarters. For a time the student infirmary was in two of the second-floor rooms. The Gorgas family have lived here since 1879, and it was made a historic shrine in 1943.

OBSERVATORY

ROUND HOUSE

THE OLD UNIVERSITY 53

Between the inauguration of the president and the opening of the University, the trustees took account of stock. It was obvious that four faculty members, even with a librarian-curator thrown in, would not be able to carry the work of the University. A teacher of modern languages and a teacher of elocution and English literature were needed to round out the staff. They could serve also as tutors in other departments if that seemed desirable to the president. The board authorized the faculty to look around for such men and to report at the next board meeting "the name or names of individuals, . . . together with such testimonials as may be in their possession, as to their qualifications."[40]

The Reverend Henry Hilliard was the only one nominated on the following December for the post of professor of English literature. He was appointed with the understanding that he should, if needed teach mathematics or ancient languages.[41] Sauveur Francios Bonfils, a native of France and a graduate of the University of Pisa in 1815, won his election to the chair of modern languages over two other candidates, Mr. D. Norris and Mr. Beauchini. His appointment was to begin on January 20.[42] The board then asked the president if he needed yet more teachers, and at his suggestion chose Calvin Jones to be tutor in ancient languages.[43]

Except for changes made necessary by resignations and dismissals, the faculty organization remained relatively stable for the next six years. William W. Hudson, a graduate of Yale College, came to replace Professor Saltonstall in January, 1833.[44] Professor Richard T. Brumby succeeded Wallis in 1834.[45] Two young graduates of the University, James F. Bailey and John M. Smith, were given brief appointments in a preparatory department experiment in 1836.[46] And John L. Gay had an even briefer appointment to round out the stormy year of 1837. Some courses apparently were dropped; Professors Hilliard and Bonfils were not replaced when they resigned. But no new items were added to the curriculum in that period.

On the eve of the opening of the University, the trustees had also adopted for its government careful rules that included the duties which they expected their faculty to perform. They had said,[47]

The faculty during the Session shall devote themselves to the instruction and discipline of the University.

They shall reside on the College premises and occupy such rooms as may be designated at a meeting of the Faculty. . . .

The President shall preside at Commencements, examinations and exhibitions, and in case of absence, sickness or death of the President, the senior Professor present shall have all the powers of the President in the government of the University during such disability or until the next meeting of the Board of Trustees. . . .

[The President] shall officiate in the usual devotional exercises, morning and evening, and in his absence the duty shall devolve on the other college officers. . . .

The Faculty shall hold frequent meetings to deliberate on the concerns of the college, to secure the most perfect uniformity of discipline, and to inflict necessary punishments . . . the Faculty shall distribute among themselves the various classes and exercises; and each member of the Faculty shall hear the recitations, which may be thus assigned to him.

For a brief time the president was also required to attend all meetings of the board of trustees. This requirement was repealed January 2, 1832;[48] whether to relieve President Woods of an added responsibility or to relieve the trustees of his presence is not stated.

In 1832 the trustees became more specific about the non-academic duties of the teaching staff. They ruled that

. . . as often as once in two months the Faculty shall address circular letters to parents or guardians, giving them information of all absences from college exercises, together with any remark which may be thought necessary upon the general conduct and scholarship of the Students.
. . . each member of the Faculty shall have under his special care a certain number of the Students' rooms, which he shall visit every night.
. . . each member of the Faculty shall as often as once in two months report to the Faculty all damages done in the rooms under his care.[49]

Faculty responsibilities thus covered a wide area—from teaching to discipline. As no great difficulty was involved in arranging the schedules, the discharge of teaching responsibilities was possible. But one wonders at the versatility of those early professors who, in a day of specialization, were able to teach not only their own subjects but also anything else necessary. Some early faculty minutes record the assignments of the early faculty at a time when the University had been in operation approximately nine months.[50]

Mr. Jones had the entire instruction of the sub-freshman class and instructed the freshmen in ancient languages. Mr. Hilliard

THE OLD UNIVERSITY

heard one exercise a day with the freshmen and one with the sophomores. To the first group he taught geography, English grammar, and history; to the second, elements of rhetoric and elocution. Both classes had a daily assignment in reading, orthography, or composition. Mr. Hilliard was assigned also the freshman class in mathematics.

Mr. Bonfils was scheduled for one lesson a day in French with the sophomores and one with the juniors. If anyone wanted to study Spanish or Italian, Professor Bonfils was to make arrangements for other classes.

Mr. Wallis was assigned one daily sophomore class in natural history, followed by one in botany or "some similar subject." He was to teach chemistry, geology, and mineralogy to seniors and in some cases to juniors. Until Mr. Jones arrived, Wallis was to carry his sub-freshman work as well as his own schedule.

Professor Saltonstall's job was to teach each day one sophomore class in pure mathematics and one junior-senior class in natural philosophy, accompanying his instruction with frequent "experimental lectures."

Professor Tutwiler was to have the three upper classes in Latin and Greek; the seniors were to be "favored with Lectures," and all students were to be called on for frequent written translations.

President Woods, in addition to filling in for Mr. Hilliard until that gentleman arrived on campus, was to instruct juniors in logic, rhetoric, and moral philosophy and give to the seniors courses in intellectual philosophy, evidences of Christianity, and elements of criticism. He was to accompany his courses with lectures and to require frequent exercises in composition and speaking. All this, of course, was in addition to his administrative duties.

It was not the teaching load that caused the faculty trial and tribulation in the next few years. Even when Hilliard and Jones resigned in the fall of 1833 and their respective department positions were abolished, the faculty minutes note cheerfully that, even with this curtailment of staff, duties were so distributed that no professor had more than three or less than two regular classes each day.[51]

Discipline was another matter. Caught between a student body young and mettlesome as young colts, and a president who had learned discipline in the shadow of the New England Puritans, the faculty found themselves in constant turmoil. They never did learn to handle either the students or the president, and their efforts to do so have elements of both comedy and tragedy.

Before the University opened, the Huntsville *Advocate* had examined the prospects of good discipline in the new school and found them bright. The University of Alabama, said the editor, would certainly not be another example of the "laxative discipline which abounds in the southern seminaries." The fact that it was not tax supported would be an advantage. In states where universities depended on tax monies, the enforcement of strict discipline might cause parents to exert political pressures to withdraw funds. Not so at the independent University of Alabama.

Our professors will therefore naturally feel themselves under no dread of the kind above mentioned; and they will be the more able to enforce the rules of the University with firmness and integrity. And should any number of the students happen to combine against them and leave the institution, the only evil that would result from this would be fewer numbers. And what would the deserters do? They must either go to some instituiton at hand where their education would not be so justly dealt with or they would be under the necessity of going to the north, where discipline is very rigidly enforced, and where they would come in contact with the industrious and studious habits of the northern youth. . . . The discipline necessary in the University will no doubt be taken into consideration soon by those most competent to legislate upon the subject; and with the example and experience of New England before them, we have no doubt they will form a code of rules calculated to do justice to the education of the students, and also, with an eye to the honor and future fame of the institution—Amicus Veritates.[52]

It may have been exactly this "example and experience of New England" which caused the trouble, for the early rules of the University of Alabama were modelled closely on those of the University of Transylvania, from which President Woods came. And those rules were, in their turn, based upon the current regulations at Harvard. The young sons of pioneers were thus expected to live up to approximately the same standards of gentlemanly conduct that had obtained at Harvard in the 1820's. There were variations in the wording of the three sets of regulations, and the system of fines in force at Harvard—fines ranging from fifty cents for disrespect to authorities to twenty dollars for forming a combine to do an unlaw-

THE OLD UNIVERSITY 57

ful act—were not adopted either at Transylvania or at Alabama. But in substance the three systems bear a striking similarity and perhaps bear witness to a certain inflexibility and lack of adaptability on the part of the man who carried them from one institution to another— the Reverend Alva Woods.[53]

The difficulty which President Woods encountered in putting the impress of Harvard on the University of Alabama had many causes, some of which related to the president's own personality. Basic, however, was the nature of the material with which he tried to work. Clark, in his *History of Education in Alabama,* sums up the reasons for the "lawlessness and insubordination" which characterized the seven years of Dr. Woods' presidency by putting the blame, not upon any "neglect of duty" on the part of the faculty, nor "want of executive ability" on the part of the president, but squarely on the shoulders of the students of that day.

> The students were largely influenced in their conduct and manners by their environment. The civilization of the State was, at the time, the civilization of a frontier people. The State had not yet been redeemed from the wilderness. A large part of the eastern and north-eastern region was still in possession of the Creek and Cherokee tribes of Indians. A large part of the white people had not yet learned to submit patiently to the wholesome restraints of the law. It is not strange that the sons of the pioneers were restless under the wise restrictions of college government.[54]

Dr. Woods took a far less tolerant view. He ruled the students with an iron hand. And he was as hard on their parents as he was on the sons. If there was unruliness on the campus, he sternly censured the homes from which the unruly students came. Toward the end of his regime, he summed up his ideas of discipline in a baccalaureate address:

> Why is the parent so often called to weep over his son's waywardness and disregard of parental counsels? Because that son was never taught that obedience to parents is the first duty of childhood.
> Why are instructors of youth sometimes vexed with turbulent, unmanageable pupils, who show no regard for law or order!—Generally, it is because those youth were never taught in the nursery the first lessons of submission to lawful authority. Perhaps they were sent abroad because they were found unmanageable at home. The period during which they might have been made docile and tractable, is passed away. . . .
> Why is our country sometimes disgraced with riotous mobs, tramp-

ling on all civil authority and placing property and even life itself at the mercy of unbridled passions? Those rioters were never trained up in childhood in the way they should go. They were never taught subordination and self-government. . . . .

Our *literary* institutions are more republican in their nature, more practical in their character, and better suited to the wants of the people at large, than are similar institutions in the old world. The severity of the ancient discipline, has been replaced by the milder system of moral suasion. But is there no danger that the education which we give, should lose in accuracy and profoundness what it may gain in diffusion; and that our gentler system of discipline may fail to supply all the necessary motives to powerful action? In the zealous efforts made by some to promote infant education, is there no danger that the mind may be forced to a premature growth, which shall stint its future progress and forever incapacitate it for reaching the higher eminence of intellectual excellence? . . . .[55]

There is little evidence that Dr. Woods, his faculty, and his students resorted often to "the milder system of moral suasion" in their dealings with each other. Their relations seem to have swung between periods of armed truce and periods of open warfare. The president fulfilled the prediction of "Amicus Veritates" in at least one respect: no fear of reprisal from politically powerful parents kept him from expelling unruly students. And there were many. "Only one student expelled this week. Nothing more of importance to communicate," Charles W. Tait wrote his grandfather in June of 1832.[56] One or more expulsions a week must have made serious inroads in a student body of less than one hundred boys.

For the faculty as well as the students, the atmosphere from the first was tense and strained. The easygoing Dr. Saltonstall was the first to give under the strain. In the spring of 1832 nine trustees wrote to him, asserting that his inadequacy as a teacher of mathematics was driving students away and asked for his resignation. Dr. Saltonstall apparently made no move until the trustees met in December. Then in a letter he presented his side of the case. If students were dissatisfied with the mathematics work, he said, it was because they had been admitted to the University with completely inadequate preparation in the subject. He asked that the trustees conduct an official investigation to see whether he was a good teacher or not. After all, he pointed out, the letter which had asked him to resign was unofficial; it did not come from the board as a board.[57]

THE OLD UNIVERSITY   59

The board had, only a few days earlier, set up a special committee, including Messrs. Davis Hubbard, John B. Hogan, Joab Lawler, George Starr, and George Phillips, to ascertain "how far the faculty of the University generally have performed the high trusts committed to their hands,"[58] but neither this committee nor any other group gave to the mathematics professor the hearing he wanted. On December 27, the board acted on his case; they requested his resignation, removed him from office, and declared his position vacant, all in one resolution.[59] It is small wonder that Dr. Saltonstall resigned after that. The trustees quickly filled the vacant post by the appointment of William W. Hudson.[60] The appointment was for the calendar year of 1833 only; but Hudson continued as professor of mathematics for four years.

Professors Hilliard and Jones went next. The reasons for their resignations are vague. Professor Hilliard had only the year before won promotion to professorial rank; so his teaching must have been satisfactory. Perhaps the question of retrenchment entered into the matter. The posts of professor of English literature and tutor of ancient languages were not filled again for some years; the duties performed by Hilliard and Jones—"with the exception of the Constitution of the United States"—were distributed among the other professors.

By the spring of 1834 campus warfare was out in the open, with President Woods in the thick of the fight. "The students have been assailing Dr. Woods' study again," wrote Sarah Haynsworth Gayle, on March 5. "Were I in his place I would positively make myself an object of fear to them if I could not be one of love and reverence. The University will go down to the ground. What can be the reason?"[61]

The same season, young Clement Clay, writing to his father, described a near riot, involving most of the faculty and students. The nimble president is shown in anything but a dignified light in this account:

Matters have been growing worse every day, till on Saturday night there was an open and audacious rebellion. About ten students, at 9 o'clock, collected on the blowing of a horn, and commenced dressing themselves in white. Mr. Hudson ran into the room in which they were, and succeeded in detecting two or three—left them and returned to his room—a bottle was thrown after him, but did not strike him—the assailant unknown—they after this dispersion met again with their horn and tin pan in the Campus, with pistols and clubs—commenced firing—shouting, etc. Mr. Tutwiler went out to them, and they left him and came in pursuit of Dr. Woods—met him coming to the dormitory and began to throw brickbats at him—he ran and as he turned the corner of the house a pistol was fired in the direction towards him—he availed himself of an open window and jumped in it. They fortunately, on his turning the corner, ran around the opposite side of the house, and not seeing him, went into the cellars, and then into the woods, to find him. He then came to all rooms and marked all out—went in his own room without a light. The insurgents by this time had added ten more to their number and returned. Unable to find him they rocked his window and finally started up stairs to take him out if he should be in it. . . . (But Woods hid in another room and they then went down and paraded on the Campus). Dr. Wallace came out, and they told him if he approached it was at his peril, cocking their pistols at the same time . . . . Dr. Woods in the meantime, escaped over home without their knowledge. They broke in the chapel—rung the bell—stoned Mr. Hudson's windows, and about 1 o'clock stillness was procured by their own drowsiness. Mr. Tutwiler, alone, among the faculty commanded some respect from them. . . .[62]

"I would not," the young Clay adds wisely, "risk my life in Dr. Woods situation for his salary!" The episode he described took place in February. In April he wrote his father again, saying that some of the students involved in the affray had been expelled. Two of them came back, however, and attacked the president with cowhide whips, dealing out lashes strong enough to "lift a two-thousand pound percheron off his feet." Dr. Woods, by this time in excellent running trim, escaped up the stairs, gathered a posse of students and gave chase to the intruders.[63] A couple of months later the trustees formally ordained that no expelled student would be allowed to set foot on campus.[64]

With campus discipline in such a shocking state, it is not surprising that President Woods should ask the board of trustees to make an investigation into the causes of the situation. On August 13, Major Hubbard, chairman of the board, addressed a questionnaire to the three men whom Woods considered responsible for some of the disturbances: Professors Wallis, Tutwiler, and Hudson. They were asked what they thought was the cause of the dissension. They were asked whether they had advised students to leave the University. They were asked whether they had discussed faculty affairs with students. Each one, in his answer, protested his innocence of any breach of professional ethics.[65]

Action so rapidly followed the questionnaire that it seems unlikely the trustees bothered to weigh the answers they received to it. They picked out Professor Wallis as their candidate for chief culprit. They wrote him sternly:

. . . the board are of the opinion, that your views of discipline and college government are such as they ought not to approve, and that if they are permitted to avail, the insubordination already existing to an injurious extent cannot be subdued, but will be extended until it affects the entire body of students.

The board have thought proper thus to communicate its impressions, from which you will be able to determine whether or not you will agrue [sic] your situation in the University—or leave the Board to take such other steps as they may think proper.[66]

They asked for an "immediate answer" and they got it. Their communication and Professor Wallis's reply are both dated August 14. It was a great "mistake," Wallis said, to blame him or his colleagues, Tutwiler and Hudson, for the sad state of discipline in the University:

It is abundantly known to the students, & we believe to yourself, that from *us* the students expect least of indulgence.

Then, in a burst of indignation, the harried professor blurted out his own opinion of the trouble:

If it be asked whence came everything, for the last two months in the form of public reproof, rebuke or admonition, it must be answered from the minority. . . . That a majority should rule we have always been willing, but we cannot conceive that your honorable Board would wish us to make a sacrifice of moral principle, to secure presidential favor . . . . If the writer be in fault he is prepared to take the consequences, if not, he confides in the magnimimity [sic] of the Board to secure his reputation from the influence of intrigue and envy.[67]

Professor Wallis then offered his resignation.

The trustees, confident that they had found the troublemaker and eliminated him, breathed a sigh of relief, which is clearly heard in the memorandum which they formally issued the following day. They did not feel, they said, that it was the place of a board of trustees to interfere with the "strictly personal dessentions" which were unavoidable in any faculty. It was quite a different matter, they argued,

when the officers manifest disregard for the interest and prosperity of an institution, or when dissentions among them become highly accremonious attended with public crimination and recrimination, evincing a disposition on the part of either portion to effect the popular standing, and reputation and thereby usefulness of any member of the faculty—reckless of the injury thus necessarily resulting to the institution over which they preside.

In such a case it became "the imperious duty of the trustees . . . to adopt the most summary method of removing the evil."[68]

Wallis "summarily" disposed of, the trustees appointed Richard T. Brumby to take his place and looked for a cessation of their troubles. Yet the troubles went on. In the summer of 1835 the whole student body and most of the faculty became embroiled in a town-gown feud, involving a Mr. James H. Dearing, who had the misfortune to live near the road the students took to town and who thus had his life made miserable by mischievous and sometimes malicious invasions of his property and privacy. The echoes of that battle sounded in the public press, and special letters had to be sent to explain it to worried parents and guardians.[69]

When Steward's Hall became a constant battleground, with biscuits flying and heads getting cracked and general disorder rampant, it was necessary to rule that at least one faculty member should eat in that hall and try to keep some semblance of order. At first the rule merely offered free meals to the faculty members on duty. Perhaps that inducement was not enough, for a few months later a regular rotation of assignment was arranged, beginning with the president and giving each teacher his turn in the order in which his name appeared in the *Catalogue*.[70]

Professor Bonfils resigned in 1836. Nothing is known of the circumstances surrounding the resignation. He had always held a somewhat favored position among the faculty. The professorship he wanted had been his within a year of his original appointment.[71] Even earlier, he had been given permission to hear all his recitations after breakfast, although most of the staff had a class before breakfast, following morning prayers. A special room had been given him as a study. And when he was ill in 1833 President Woods and Professor Wallis cheerfully took over his classes.[72] Perhaps the time came when even these small perquisites could not make up for the discomfort of the general turmoil.

Life was becoming intolerable for Professor Tutwiler also. His relationship with President Woods had always been strained. William Smith, looking back to his student days, thought that jealousy was part of the trouble:

> It was unfortunate for Dr. Woods to be brought into personal contact with Professor Tutwiler, of whom, before the arrival of the president, the students had grown passionately fond and, who, until the president's advent, had been looked upon as the head of the college.[73]

At odds with his chief from the start, Tutwiler had isolated himself from his colleagues when, in 1835, he had refused to join with the rest of the faculty in signing the whitewash letter to parents about the trouble with Mr. Dearing.[74] Letters written to the young classics professor by his friend and classmate, Gessner Harrison, of Virginia, reflect his unhappiness. The letters Tutwiler wrote, pouring out his troubles to his friend and, no doubt, giving his interpretation of the situation, have unfortunately been lost.

The explosive situation blew up in 1836. Strangely enough a circus furnished the final spark. In spite of the fact that circuses were definitely out of bounds for University students, some eighty or ninety, according to Oran Roberts, who was one of the culprits, managed to see the circus of the spring of 1836.[75] Six of the culprits were suspended on April 20 and were told not to come back to college until February 1, 1837. An uproar followed. The students petitioned for reinstatement of their fellows. In a communication signed by the Honorable B. F. Porter, the Honorable H. W. Collier, and others, the citizens of Tuscaloosa also petitioned. The faculty rejected both pleas. Such a reinstatement, they said,

> would produce a very injurious effect upon the discipline of the University, by opening the *certainty* of punishment in cases of detected and acknowledged transgressions;

and they reminded the citizens of Tuscaloosa that they had a stake in the "prosperity of the University" and should therefore support the "maintenance of good order and wholesome discipline" on which that prosperity depended.[76]

The suspended students, unable because of travel difficulties to get out of town at once, helped to keep things stirred up for a week or more. Their classmates left on the campus were indignant at the unfairness of punishing six when ninety were guilty. Someone suggested that a confession signed by all the circus-goers would be good strategy; the faculty could hardly suspend ninety out of a student body of approximately one hundred. Forty advocates of fair play signed.[77] The faculty promptly suspended them until August.[78] Ten of the group were given permission to stay with relatives in Tuscaloosa during the period of their suspension, and they helped keep things lively. One student incurred, by his improper conduct in church, an additional sentence of six months.[79] With more than one-third of the student body away, college activity was reduced to a minimum. Between May 9 and August 1 of that year only three entries were made in the "Faculty Minutes."

Even more rigid discipline seemed to be necessary. In the spring of 1836 new and more stringent laws were passed. But the students who were left on the campus protested so vehemently that these rules were withdrawn until the start of the new school year. Particularly obnoxious was the provision that students should be marked daily in each class and that a record of their merits and demerits be published monthly. This method encouraged favoritism, said the students, for those called on frequently for recitation got the good marks; the others got only demerits.[80]

By the spring of 1837 rebellion was at its height. When a student petition for the rescinding of the new rules was refused by the faculty, the students countered with rioting and gun fire. Immediately the faculty voted to suspend all students who had missed classes during the riots unless they agreed to sign a pledge of good conduct, give up their firearms, and promise not to interfere again with the administration. The students refused.[81] Many left the campus. The ones left were completely defiant. The faculty were defeated.

Tutwiler was the first to resign that year. But by the end of the school term, it was apparent that the rout was complete. Some 101 students are listed in the University *Catalogue* for 1837, but only one senior, Joseph Dunnam Jenkins, qualified for a degree. Between July and December President Woods and Professor Brumby went

THE OLD UNIVERSITY   65

through the motions of hearing daily recitations with the juniors and sophomores. Mr. Smith, the preparatory teacher, heard the freshman class in geometry. A new professor, John L. Gay, was brought in to teach ancient languages from September to December.[82] And on December 6, the resignation of Woods, Gay, and Smith became effective. Of all the men who had served on the faculty since April, 1831, only Professor Brumby was at his post when the year ended.

The board of trustees were back where they started. Patiently they began to build again. A committee appointed in July had helped tide the University over the crisis period by temporary appointments. Its chief assignment, however, was to "correspond with distinguished literary men" to find again candidates capable of giving to the University a good administration and a good teaching staff competent to cover these subjects: English literature, mathematics, natural philosophy and civil engineering; chemistry, mineralogy, and geology; ancient languages and modern languages.[83] When December came the trustees were ready with new appointments that would carry their University into its second phase and lay a foundation of permanence for the next quarter-century.

What happened to the men who came to start the young University in that spring of 1831?

After delivering the last of his famous addresses, a valedictory on December 6, which some praised for its "beautiful style" and "the force, vigor and purity" of its language,[84] and which some criticized as "lengthy, erudite, cold and formal"[85] the Reverend Alva Woods, first president of the University of Alabama, went back to Providence, Rhode Island. He seems never to have held again a position comparable to the one at the University. Years later, in 1876, he wrote to a Dr. Hitchcock, telling him of his service as chaplain and Bible teacher in the Rhode Island state prison, of his work as trustee of Brown University and of the Newton (Massachusetts) Theological Institution, where he had helped these schools establish lectureships and scholarships.[86] He died in Providence, in 1887.

Little is known of Saltonstall after his unfortunate experience at the University. It is known, however, that his colleague, Wallis, went back to his school at Cherokee Corner as its president.[87]

Professor Tutwiler must have held his faith in boys throughout all his unhappy years at the University. After he left the University, he taught six years in LaGrange College in north Alabama and five years in Howard College at Marion, Alabama. At Greene Springs, Alabama, in 1847, he founded a school for boys. Twice, in later years, the University of Alabama sought to bring him back as its president; twice he refused the appointment.

On December 6, 1837, relegating thoughts of the men who had served the University as its first faculty the trustees, the students, and the townspeople of Tuscaloosa got ready to inaugurate another president, hailed by the *Independent Monitor* as "a gift from heaven." He was the Reverend Basil Manly, who was to serve the University as a competent administrator for the next eighteen years.

CHAPTER IV

The Faculty
1837-1860

BASIL MANLY, second president of the University of Alabama, had fewer academic laurels than his predecessor. His foremost interest was the church. Already, at thirty-nine, he had a record of twenty-one years of gospel preaching, first, as a "licensed preacher" when he was still in his teens, and, later, as pastor of several churches in South Carolina. Born near Pittsborough, North Carolina, on January 29, 1798, he had been graduated with first honors in 1821 from the South Carolina College. Before coming to his new post, he had been a leader in the movements which established Furman University at Greenville, South Carolina, and the Baptist Theological Seminary at Louisville, Kentucky.

Years later, Dr. Boyce, delivering Dr. Manly's funeral discourse, made this curiously oblique reference to his scholarly attainments:

It required some scholarship in others to perceive the depth of the investigation he had made of the subjects he had studied, or to recognize the wide range to which he had extended his researches.

The second president of the University apparently wore his learning without ostentation. But he possessed in abundance qualities even more important in the position to which he was called in December, 1837. He had administrative skill, warmth of personality, kindness of heart, and the saving grace of a sense of humor. Dr. Boyce continued his praise:

He was upright and honest, faithful and laborious. He was a man of rare practical wisdom, entering heartily into sympathy with the young men intrusted to his guidance and counsel. His methods of governing were firm and positive, but always kind and fatherly. In him, as executive officer of the Faculty, judgment was always tempered with mercy. . . . With these mental acquirements was united a spirit of playfulness and humor which gave a charm to his conversation. No one could better appreciate true wit or genuine humor. No one enjoyed an innocent pleasantry more than he. To the outside world this only made him more companionable and fitted him better for his work. It never led to levity. It never tempted him to give pain to others.[1]

To aid Dr. Manly in rebuilding a faculty broken by strife were three new professors: Frederick Augustus Porter Barnard, professor of mathematics, natural philosophy, and astronomy; Professor Samuel M. Stafford, professor of ancient languages; and Professor Horace Southworth Pratt, professor of English literature. A single survivor from the old faculty welcomed them: Professor Richard T. Brumby, professor of chemistry, mineralogy, and geology.[2] Professor Pratt was to serve the University only three years; he died in 1840. The other three in this "second faculty" group were to bring to the young institution sound and sustained leadership and to build the foundations for its increasing reputation as an institution of learning both at home and abroad.

With his appointment to the University faculty, Professor Brumby, who had succeeded Wallis in 1834, found himself professionally. He had worked hard for his education in his home state of South Carolina, where he was one of a large family in somewhat poor circumstances. He was graduated from South Carolina College, having done his preparatory school work at the classical school of the Reverend John Marshall at Statesville, North Carolina, and at a third school in Lincolnton, North Carolina. After his admission to the bar in 1825, he practiced law two years. Then he spent a year in the West, went home to Lincolnton, moved to Montgomery, and finally arrived in Tuscaloosa, where he tried his hand at newspaper work as editor of the *Expositor*, which advanced the cause of nullification.[3]

Considering this rolling stone for the position left vacant by Wallis, the trustees had some misgivings about his qualifications for the job. They made him temporary instructor first, encouraging him by awarding him the degree of Master of Arts.[4] In August, 1835, the temporary appointment was made permanent;[5] Brumby became professor of chemistry, mineralogy, and geology. Before he finished his University service, he had added physiology, conchology, and agricultural chemistry to the curriculum. He had definitely

THE OLD UNIVERSITY

decided upon his vocation. "He loved the pursuits of science," said one who knew him, "and for many years had consecrated all his time and talents to it [science] with singular devotion. . . . He was always to be found in the laboratory. There he toiled with laborious, persevering industry."[6]

Samuel M. Stafford, like young Tutwiler, whom he replaced, seems to have had the instincts of a teacher. For years before coming to Alabama, he had been the master of a flourishing boys' boarding school at Winnborough, South Carolina. It is said that the trustees chose him for the chair of ancient languages in 1837 not only because of his high reputation as a classical scholar but also because the pupils he prepared for South Carolina College made such excellent college records. Although he was a native of North Carolina, his alma mater was South Carolina. Clark writes of Stafford and of his nineteen years in the service of the University of Alabama:

By his accurate scholarship, his many private virtues, his official fidelity and ability, he gained the unqualified admiration of all who were ever associated with him.[7]

One of his students, George Little, adds a note of sadness to the record of Stafford's life:

His health failed. . . and he had to give up his work. His wife, who had been Miss Maria Brooks, then bought the old Presbyterian Female Institute and for several years conducted it under the name of the Stafford School. This was the building that was finally bought by the city and used as a public school and still retains its old name of Stafford School. This school was established about 1840 by ten Presbyterians who gave one thousand dollars each for the building.[8]

Probably the most brilliant of the teachers who worked with President Manly was Frederick A. P. Barnard, the versatile young man who stepped into the professorship of mathematics and natural philosophy in 1838. He was born in Sheffield, Massachusetts, on May 5, 1809, and was thus still in his twenties when he first came to Alabama. He had gone to school in his own village at Saratoga Academy and at an academy in Stockbridge, not far from his home. After graduation from Yale in 1828, he had taught in the American Institution for the Deaf and Dumb at Hartford, tutored in mathematics at Yale, and had been a member of the faculty of the New York Institution for the Deaf and Dumb. Choice of his teaching assignments may have been determined by his own handicap of deafness, which was beginning while he was at Hartford but which he never completely lost.[9]

Into the classrooms of the University of Alabama the young man brought vigor and originality. He introduced the course in organic chemistry, the first to be given in any southern university and probably the first given as a distinct listing anywhere in the United States. He had little patience with textbooks, preferring to make his chemistry courses purely demonstrative. Consequently, he needed assistants in his experiments. As the University budget provided nothing for this purpose, Barnard sometimes had to pay his assistant out of his own salary. For eight months the son of Professor Olmsted of Yale worked with him. Sometimes he employed Sam, a skilled slave.[10]

William R. Smith, who knew Barnard and admired him tremendously, felt that the young chemistry professor had had "a hard tussle with his inclinations" before he settled down to the service of science. "When science got the better of him," Smith wrote, "it was a great triumph to the brickbat world." The pen picture which Smith gives of the "admirable Frederick" touches upon the many talents and the many enthusiasms which made Barnard, in the minds of a generation of young students, "a marvel of intellectual brilliancy and practical versatility."[11]

He could take a hand at any game, and play it well. He was conceded the *best* at whatever he attempted to do; he could turn the best sonnet, write the best love story, take the best daguerreotype picture, charm the most women, catch the most trout, and calculate the most undoubted almanac. . . .

He was, when Smith knew him, "young, dashing, and handsome . . . a trifle eccentric in manner and habit, with a mind ever on science and literature, and a heart and eye bent on the enjoyment of the legitimate pleasures of the hour." Those legitimate pleasures included excursions into such hobbies as photography and literature. "When the surprising Daguerron art was making its earliest appearance in this country," Smith writes, "he became so keenly excited . . . that he united with Dr. Harrington, and set up in the city of Tuscaloosa a gallery for taking pictures, and to this he devoted all the time he could spare from the University duties."

An accomplished chemist, he went into this business with sleeves rolled up and manipulated the camera with such skill as to produce really fine specimens of the art, so that the faces of the belles and beaus of Tuskaloosa were speedily duplicated to the infinite gratification of the young and the old.

"The interest he took in such things as these," Smith adds, "was absolutely absorbing; and this he made no effort to conceal."

With the same ebullient enthusiasm, he threw himself into literary experiments.

When Judge Meek established the *Southron* he found in Barnard an earnest coadjutor. Barnard, at that period of his life, was full of literary enthusiasms—gushing over with fancies exuberant—as much so as if he had just passed into a fledgling junior. He had a good knowledge of the art of poetry, especially as to the construction of the different sorts of versification. He could turn a sonnet after the manner of Petrarch, and could discourse learnedly on the differences of the Italian and the English models. . . .

His literary efforts ranged from the didactic to the ludicrous:

Professor Barnard was a very industrious and prolific writer. Besides contributing many articles to newspapers, he wrote for the magazines, especially for the *American Journal of Education*. From science and literature, he would expand into the most graceful humor, as the occasion might justify. At other times he was grave and didactic.[12]

Sometimes, Smith says, the professor's "acute perception of the lucicrous" and "quick appreciation of the absurd" led him to the "perpetration of mock-heroic poems, bordering on the satirical."

Beneath these enthusiasms and these brilliant displays of talents Dr. Barnard had a deep seriousness. While he was on the University faculty, he took orders in the Episcopal Church. Just before he left Alabama in 1854 he was ordained a deacon in that church and preached his first sermon, on "Justification of Faith," in Christ Church in Tuscaloosa.[13]

Professor Barnard's personality must have been truly magnetic to so blind his students and the citizens of Tuscaloosa. An entirely different picture of this brilliant, though unique, man is given in correspondence concerning him which has recently been made public. Despite the fact that he was an ordained deacon in the Episcopal Church, he was fond of strong drink.

As early as 1841 he was the recipient of a letter written by his colleagues, President Manly and Professors Brumby and Stafford, concerning his behavior:

With sincere respect and affection for you, we feel constrained by a sense of duty to implore upon the delicate task of importunation and warning. The occasion which calls for such a step was furnished by the events of Saturday evening last taken in connection with other similar instances of excess and exposure, transpiring at intervals. In other occasions we have borne, in silence, what our high regard for you made us deeply deplore. But this late unfortunate occurance was attended by such circumstances of exposure and notoriety as deeply convince us that if friendship can accomplish anything for your severity and happiness it must be *now*.

It ought not to be concealed from you, that, in addition to all the Moral aspects of the case, which are sufficiently serious, your situation in the University cannot be maintained, (whatever our feelings in regard to you) without an immediate and thorough concern on your part, removing even the liability to the reoccurrance of such deplorable scenes.

We implore you, by the concord subsisting among us,—by our mutual toils, responsibilities, hopes, and fates, by all that is respectable and dear in your own eyes, forbear; for God's sake, forbear! You can have no safety but in entire and perpetual abstinence from every thing that can intoxicate. This is our deliberate judgment, as the result of anxious and friendly observation.

May you receive this, as it is meant, in love; and may your life be useful, honorable, and happy.[14]

Perhaps upon receipt of this strong, straightforward letter, Professor Barnard decided to mend his ways as advised, for the next known communication concerning his behavior was six years later, when in 1847 President Manly notes that

Barnard was drunk during Thursday and Thursday night—was seen by Richardson during the day and by Dr. Burkett and other Trustees during the night. This taken in connection with his recent inattention to business and loss of literary pride satisfies me that *he will not do*.[15]

A year later when Professor Barnard conversed with Professor Dockery, it was Dockery's decided opinion that, judging from Barnard's breath and from his "well-known" manner he was very drunk. At that time he was no longer "young, dashing and handsome" as he was decribed earlier, for he was becoming fat and bloated and was often not well. At last, in 1854, sixteen years after he had made his first appearance on the campus of the Uni-

THE OLD UNIVERSITY

versity, he left. His departure was noted by President Manly in the following manner:

One great incumbus thrown off—Barnard is gone. . . . He has genius and extensive acquirements, but his physical and moral defects disqualify him from being a useful or reliable officer.[16]

The University of Mississippi called him to its department of mathematics and natural philosophy in 1854 and soon thereafter made him its president. Barnard's description of the transfer to Oxford is a reminder that the deep South was still frontier even in the 1850's, and it is also a reminder of the friendly good nature of one of the greatest professors the University of Alabama ever had.

There were many difficulties attending our removal to Oxford. We had to drive there, of course; and on the very evening before we were to start, a valuable horse that I had had for several years took suddenly ill and died. My books and furniture had to be sent by a very roundabout way, first down the river four hundred miles to Mobile, thence by sea two hundred miles to New Orleans, thence up the Mississippi five hundred miles to Memphis, and then sixty miles by wagon to Oxford. We made our trip without accident; but at the places where we stopped it was not encouraging to me to hear the professor whose place I was to fill constantly mentioned as a man whose loss to the University was simply irreparable. I entered on my new position with a feeling of sincere discouragement, but, as time passed, I began to have reason to think that my success consoled the authorities of the University for the loss of my predecessor.[17]

Barnard stayed at the University of Mississippi until 1861. Four years later he was chosen president of Columbia University in New York, where he remained until his death in 1889. Barnard College, established that year, was named for him, an appropriate honor, since his interest in the education of young women had begun back in his University of Alabama days when he used to reserve seats in his lecture rooms for the young ladies of the Tuscaloosa Female Institute.[18]

Ten years after Barnard's death, an Alabama alumnus toasting his memory at an alumni banquet, bore witness to the place he held in the affection and trust of the students more than a half-century before. Warfield C. Richardson, class of 1843, spoke of the spies and informers set to watch the students of his day and of the eagerness with which the average faculty member listened to the tattletales. Then he added,

There was one striking exception, however—one who refused to lend himself to these odious methods—one who would not dog the steps or pry into the conduct of any man. I refer to him who was familiarly known as "Old Fap." Say what you will of Dr. Barnard and bitter things have been said of him truly. Say what you will of Dr. Barnard and bitter things have been said of him falsely. Say he was fickle, say he was vain, say he was frivolous, say that he was unorthodox, say he loved the Union, when other men were disunionists, say what you will—I only know that he was a gentleman through and through, bone and muscle, body and soul. With some, he is embalmed today in the bitter spices of hate and malice, but he is canonized in the hearts of the friendless boys who knew him best.[19]

President Manly and his faculty, starting their job of rebuilding the University teaching force were given an entirely new set of "Laws" to guide them. First published in 1838, these regulations tersely indicate the magnitude and complexity of their responsibility.

They were, in the first place, expected to possess a versatility which would dismay the most competent professor of the twentieth century. Here is the job description the trustees handed its new faculty in 1838:

The President shall give instruction in Moral and Mental Philosophy. The Professor of English Literature shall give instruction in Rhetoric, Belles Lettres, Logic, and Modern History, and have the superintendence of Composition and Declamation. The Professor of Mathematics shall give instruction in Pure Mathematics and Civil Engineering, Natural Philosophy and Astronomy. The Professor of Chemistry, in Chemistry, Mineralogy, and Geology, and shall illustrate the connection of these sciences with Agriculture and the Arts. The Professor of Ancient Languages shall teach Latin and Greek Languages, Ancient History and Geography. The Professor of Modern Languages shall teach the French, Spanish, and Italian Languages. The Tutors shall give instruction in such branches, and assume such duties, as may be assigned by the Faculty.[20]

Let no one think, however, that the teachers were allowed to specialize even according to these broad definitions. The assumption seems to have been that a well-educated man could, in an emergency, teach anything that needed to be taught. In 1845, for example, when the chair of English literature was vacant, the chemistry professor taught classes in rhetoric and English analysis and inspected the

English compositions of the junior and sophomore classes; the new geology professor taught logic and elocution, superintended the ordinary declamation of all classes, and inspected the English compositions of freshmen and seniors; and the president himself was assigned the task of inspecting and superintending the compensation and delivery of the public speeches made by members of the two upper classes.[21]

Effort was made, however, to keep a reasonable balance in the loads assigned to the teachers:

In case of inequality in the amount of labor performed among the Professors and Tutors, the Faculty may make a more equal distribution; and each officer shall attend to the duties and exercises which may thus be assigned to him. The Board of Trustees shall have the power at all times to modify the duties required of the different officers and to impose additional duties.[22]

New rules clarified the procedures for appointments and for resignations and established a system of rank by seniority:[23]

A member of the Faculty intending to resign, must give six months' notice to the President of the Board.

Whenever a vacancy shall occur in the offices of instruction in the University, or any officer be incapable of performing his duties for any reason, the Faculty shall have the power to fill such vacancy or to make provision until the next meeting of the Board of Trustees.

The Professors shall take rank according to seniority of appointment.

When any person shall have been elected to, and have accepted, the office of a Tutor in the University, he shall continue in office for a term not less than two years, unless he shall be permitted by the Executive Committee, or the Board of Trustees, to resign sooner.

The disciplinary authority of the faculty was also clarified:

Each officer shall have authority to govern and control any student, provided he does not exercise this authority contrary to the laws of the Board, or Faculty, or the views and wishes of the President of the University.[24]

And finally, the general relationship between the board and the faculty was defined and procedures set for the conduct of faculty business:

The Faculty are charged with the immediate government and direction of the University, and have authority to make all bye-laws [sic], orders,

and regulations, necessary for carrying into effect their powers and duties, not inconsistent with the laws of the Board of Trustees. . . .
The Faculty shall have weekly meetings for reviewing the state of the college, and considering such cases as may be brought before them. One of their number annually, shall be appointed as their secretary, who shall keep a fair and full record of their proceedings, in a well bound book; which book shall be at all times subject to the inspection of the Board of Trustees. No act of the Faculty which is not recorded in the Faculty-Book shall be considered valid. The decision of the Faculty shall be by majority of voices, that of the President being always one to give effect to the decision of the majority; and in case of an equal number of votes on each side, the presiding officer shall have the casting vote. The Faculty may hold special meetings by their own adjournment.[25]

With minor changes the laws of 1839 remained in effect through 1865. After the upheavals which had all but wrecked the University in 1837, the new faculty led by President Manly brought a stability to University affairs which made it possible to develop the curriculum and to strengthen the educational program. This is not to say that there were no shifts and changes and even explosions in the faculty of the next two decades. Tracing the course of the major departments during the period shows both the growing continuity and the occasional difficulties.

The department of English literature suffered most from changes in its staff. When Professor Horace Southworth Pratt took the chair in 1837, it had been vacant since the resignation of Professor Hilliard in 1833. In 1840 it was vacant again; Professor Pratt had died. Stephen Olin was offered the post, but he refused. So for the next year the work in English was distributed among the other faculty members.[26] The Reverend Edward D. Sims, a graduate of the University of North Carolina, occupied the chair from 1841 to 1845. When he died, the University made an unsuccessful attempt to call the Reverend A. A. Lipscomb of New York,[27] and then settled upon Frederick W. Thomas, who enjoyed what was probably the shortest tenure of any professor the University ever had.

When Thomas arrived on the campus, he discovered that the president of the board had heard "certain representations unfavorable to him," and that he was not to begin his teaching until the board of trustees had investigated these charges. President Manly had received a letter from William Robinson, father of a student at the University, to the effect that the conduct of Professor Thomas on board a boat from Montgomery to Mobile was such that if he remained a member of the faculty, student Robinson would be removed. The unfavorable conduct reported was that Thomas had been drunk all the way to Mobile and that he had taken into his stateroom a Negro slave girl, who, it seems, was retrieved by the owner.

On being confronted with this information, Professor Thomas replied that he had taken a little opium and brandy in compliance with the orders of a physician to correct a physical disorder. The opium and brandy were either taken in large amounts or were extremely potent, for, by his own admission, he was in a wild, unconscious state from the time he left Montgomery till three or four days after he arrived at Mobile.

Neither the president of the University nor the governor had the power to displace him, this task being peculiar to the trustees. Thus Professor Thomas was given permission to teach until a meeting of the board could be convoked.[28] Less than two weeks later he was, by faculty action, excused from visitation of rooms.[29] By March the faculty, now thoroughly convinced that Mr. Thomas was not a fit man for their staff, were holding special meetings on his case. First, they relieved him of the freshman elocution class.[30] Two days later they issued an indignant resolution that they "could no longer be associated with such a man."

It having appeared that Prof. Thomas had been guilty of conduct unbecoming his station, and had returned to the University this morning in a condition to unfit him for the discharge of duty it having appeared also, that his classes are not profitably spending their time, and the Faculty being satisfied that he is incompetent to give instruction in the studies belonging to his department. His latest public exposure, moreover, having occurred so soon after his having forced himself upon the University, without any satisfactory clearing up of the grave imputations made as to his conduct before his arrival; the Faculty unanimously, [resolved] that they could no longer be associated with such a man, and that they would, one and all, put their names to a paper asking him to withdraw forthwith from the premises.[31]

Professor Thomas did not wait for the seven o'clock morning deadline, which the faculty set for reply to this ultimatum. He told them flatly that same evening that he had no intention of resigning.

Whereupon, his colleagues summarily relieved him of all his classes, redistributed his work among Professors Barnard, Dockery, and Brumby, and dispatched a notice to the governor telling him what they had done and asked for supporting action.[32]

That was enough for Thomas. He resigned. He said in his letter to the trustees,

Since entering upon the discharge of the duties of the professorship, to which you did me the honor to elect me, I have found the station less agreeable than I had anticipated. I am desirous, therefore, of resigning my chair in the University, and desire that my resignation may be accepted, to take effect at the end of the first quarter after my assumption of its duties. With respect, I am, Gentlemen, Your ob't Serv't, F. W. Thomas.[33]

Mr. Thomas's successor, a man who was to serve the University faculty in varied capacities and was to succeed President Manly in the presidency, was appointed by the trustees in the summer of 1847.[34] Landon Cabell Garland, born in Nelson County, Virginia, March 21, 1810, was graduated from Hampden-Sidney College at the age of nineteen. For seven years he served as professor of natural sciences at Washington College (now Washington and Lee), before accepting a call to Randolph-Macon College, in Ashland, where he served for ten years. During part of that time he had, because of the illness of Stephen Olin, assumed the duties of the presidency of Randolph-Macon. Then came his call to the University of Alabama.

A man of such position and substance could not effect a change quickly. The chair of English literature at the University of Alabama remained vacant for another six months until Dr. Garland could make "definite and lasting arrangements" for the long journey and for the shipment of books and household goods by way of Norfolk and Mobile. When, early in December, 1847, the Garland family was ready to start for its new home, it required something of a caravan to make the journey. For the Garlands had six children to bring along—"William Henry, Lucinda Rose, Maurice Hamner, Louise and Landonia, twins, and Jennie"—and they also had three wagonloads of Negro slaves. The journey was further delayed when one of the nurses became ill with pneumonia, at McMinnville, Tennessee. There the caravan remained for ten days, until she was out

THE OLD UNIVERSITY 79

of danger and could be moved to the home of a physician, where she stayed during convalescence.

Dr. Garland's kindness to his slaves is traditional. One of his biographers writes,

Dr. Garland was very fond of his slaves. When he and his wife were married, a special gift bestowed upon them by their parents was the choice of slaves for their servants. In the course of years, however, the number of slaves increased from three to sixty. Nevertheless, "Old Master's" black women folks wanted to stay with him and refused to be sold to owners of their husbands, as Dr. Garland had prospered. His policy . . . had always been to keep families as nearly intact as possible; consequently, he bought the women's husbands.[35]

As a professor at the University of Alabama in 1848 had little use for three wagonloads of slaves, Dr. Garland hired them out to citizens of Tuscaloosa, but continued to worry about their welfare even after they were freed.[36]

In the Alabama classroom Garland quickly established his genius for teaching and for handling boys with firmness and understanding. Comments which students made about him as they looked back upon classroom experiences in later years throw light upon the secret of his success:

A good recitation would light up his features with a peculiar smile of approbation; a poor recitation wounded him, yet never brought forth a sarcastic rebuke. His look of disappointment was the most touching reproof to a lazy student. . . .
No earnest student could spend an hour in his recitation in those days without feeling himself stronger and better, not so much from the lesson learned as from the inspiring influence that emanated from the living master.[37]
. . . he seemed to gain obedience and respect through the love and affection the boys and young men felt for him. [Many times he] helped to lighten the consequences of their misdoings, and it was this gentleness and tolerance and understanding of young men, untinged by any hint of weakness, that endeared him so greatly.[38]

Years later Dr. Garland himself, installing his successor at Vanderbilt University, put into words his own theory of college discipline:

You may lay anything upon young men if done with sympathy. There is but one way in the world to manage young men and that is to treat them as highminded and honorable young men. Take them as men utterly incapable of anything but the truth. . . . You cannot govern a young man except by sympathy and confidence.[39]

Except for one year, 1854-1855, when he left the campus to become president of the North-East and South-West Railroad, then building a line from Meridian, Mississippi, to Wills Valley, Alabama, the University enjoyed the services of this wise and human educator for nineteen years: as professor of English literature, of mathematics, and as president. When the University was burned in 1865, Garland had been its president for ten years, and he remained president of the destroyed institution nominally until June, 1866. Then he went to the University of Mississippi as professor of physics and astronomy. In 1875 Vanderbilt University, in Nashville, Tennessee, called him to become its president. He retired from this post in 1893. He died two years later on the Vanderbilt campus.

In 1849, the Reverend John Wood Pratt came to the University as professor of English literature, a post which he held for five years before becoming professor of logic, rhetoric, and oratory. After Pratt left the University, in 1865, he became president of Centre College in Danville, Kentucky.[40]

The chair of modern languages, like that of English literature, had been vacant for some years. It had been discontinued when Professor Bonfils resigned in 1836, and it was not restored until 1841.[41] There is evidence, however, that even before formal re-establishment of the post the trustees had been casting about for likely candidates, for, in New England Henry Wadsworth Longfellow wrote to his father on August 2, 1839,

By the way, I had yesterday the offer of a professorship in the University of Alabama at Tuscaloosa. I declined and recommended S———. Good climate and two thousand dollars a year.[42]

James C. Dockery became professor of modern language in 1842 and served eight years. Then Charles F. Henry, tutor, filled in until 1852. Emmanuel Vilalis Scherb, a graduate of Harvard University, who held the post for a single year, 1852-53, was apparently one of the unfortunate individuals who was cordially disliked. The students evidenced their dislike by insubordination and pranks. The faculty and trustees let their antipathy creep into the record when Scherb left: the treasurer was authorized to pay him $300 due as

THE OLD UNIVERSITY 81

salary for the remainder of the college year and the additional sum of $50, "claimed by, and properly withheld by the Treasurer," if Professor Scherb agreed that that payment would settle in full his account with the University.[43]

More fortunate was the appointment of Scherb's successor, Andre DeLoffre, of France and Selma, Alabama. He held the job, first as instructor and later as professor, until the University closed in 1865.[44] Some of his students remembered him with a touch of amusement in their admiration. George Little says,

Dr. Manly asked him how he pronounced his name. He replied: "You must not pronounce it De Loafer." . . . He was a Huguenot and attended the Presbyterian Church. . . . De Loffre was a very fine teacher of French and induced to teach Spanish although he knew very little about that language. He had the custom of requiring the students to recite an irregular verb every day. One day I rattled off the verb so fast that he could not keep up with me. After the class he asked Charlie Manly: "Do you think Mr. Little means to insoolt me" Manly replied, "No, that's the way he recites all of his lessons."[45]

In the chemistry department the history between 1837 and 1865 is one of expansion and change rather than shift of personnel. The work was reorganized in 1846 so that Professor Brumby might concentrate on chemistry and natural history and a new man might be brought in to cover the work in mineralogy and geology and to develop agricultural chemistry. It is interesting to note that Professor Barnard, already moving toward an interest in chemistry, was one of the promoters of this plan. He told the trustees that he considered work in agricultural chemistry so important both to the University and to the state that he would willingly continue sharing the English literature classes with his colleagues if that would make possible the establishment of the new chair.[46]

For the first incumbent of the new position the trustees picked a rather remarkable Irishman, one Michael Tuomey, born in Cork on St. Michael's Day, 1805. Tuomey's career had included schoolteaching, at the age of seventeen, in Yorkshire, England; farming in Pennsylvania; a private school head-mastership in Maryland; tutoring in the home of John Dennis in the same state; studying at Rensselaer Institute, Troy, New York; railroad construction engineering in North Carolina; teaching mathematics and natural science in a girls' school in Virginia; and establishing a seminary in Petersburg, Virginia. His interest in geology probably developed in his Virginia days. He gathered a large collection of materials in geology, paleontology, and minerals, and soon found himself called to South Carolina to become state geologist. While he was working at that position, Alabama called him to become not only a professor at the University but also its first state geologist.[47]

Tuomey's contract with the University explicitly provided for this dual function. Advised by the trustees, he was to spend a maximum of four months each year exploring the state.[48] During the summer of 1847, he was given an advance from the contingent fund, so that he could hire a wagon and an attendant for his explorations.[49] That his field trips were fruitful is evidenced by the fact that his geological reports are still consulted and still found accurate and useful.[50]

Professor Brumby resigned in 1848 and turned over his work in chemistry to the eager Dr. Barnard. Once more good F.A.P. showed his instinct for the kind and gracious act:

Certain friendly resolutions were presented by Professor Barnard in regard to Prof. Brumby on occasion of his leaving us. These were adopted, ordered to be signed by the President and secretary and sent to Prof. Brumby.[51]

So Brumby went off to become professor of chemistry at South Carolina College, and Barnard carried on in his place until 1854. In that year both Barnard and Tuomey left the University, and for the next two years examination of the records of both faculty and students shows no evidence that any work in chemistry was given. Tuomey was back again, but briefly, in 1856 and 1857, and with him came an even more versatile Irishman, John William Mallet, who headed the chemistry department until 1860.[52]

Professor Mallet was only twenty-four years old when he came to the University, but he already held a degree from the University of Dublin and his doctorate from the University of Göttingen. He had had exceptional educational advantages ever since his birth, October 12, 1832, at Drumondra House, the county seat of his grandparents. His English father, a distinguished civil engineer and Fellow of the Royal Society, had provided the best of private teachers for his eldest son; surrounded him with a fine library, in which the

THE OLD UNIVERSITY 83

boy early learned the fascination of chemical studies by Black, Lavoisier, Fourcroy, Vauquelin, Davy, Henry, and Thompson; and while he was still in his teens had taken him into a kind of partnership in his own work. It was to get information for his father that the young Mallet made a visit to America in 1853. He had no intention of remaining this side of the Atlantic. But he visited an old Göttingen classmate at Amherst College and soon found himself in the Amherst classroom, where he taught a little French and German at first and then took over the work in analytical chemistry. When Professor Tuomey needed an assistant on the staff of the Alabama Geological Survey in 1855, he selected Mallet. Even after Mallet had become a part of the University faculty, first as assistant and later as full professor of chemistry, he continued to act as analytical chemist for the survey and, after Tuomey's death, edited for publication the second survey *Report*.[53]

After leaving the University of Alabama in 1860, he joined the staff of the newly established medical college in Mobile. Although in 1861 he joined the Confederate Army, serving under General Josiah Gorgas, he never relinquished his British citizenship.[54] The brief visit to the United States, which began in 1853, ended only with his death in 1912.

Scientists remember and honor Mallet for distinguished research and discovery. It is probable, however, that the students of his day remembered the young teacher best for his brushes with the young ladies of Mrs. Stafford's School. Once a week the girls in their long calico skirts, high-heeled, high-topped boots, and sunbonnets, filed decorously through the woods and into Professor Mallet's classroom. The temptation was too much for the boys. Some of them put on long skirts and sunbonnets, too, and came to class with the young ladies. When the class was over, it was discovered that someone had locked the doors and no one could get out.[55]

Even without pranks like this to plague him, Professor Mallet may have felt that the young ladies and Mrs. Stafford were a little more than he cared to cope with. Crenshaw Hall wrote his mother in 1858 that he thought Mr. Mallet had purposely given the girls at Mrs. Stafford's a rigid examination in order to discourage the idea of continuing chemistry instruction there:

. . . the other day after we had stood our examination, Mrs. Stafford requested Prof. Mallet to try the knowledge of her students, she said she wished to see how the young ladies compared with the students of the University so she walked into the examination room with great dignity to hear the examination. The end of it was that everyone failed. I suppose he gave them a pretty hard examination, as he did not wish to stick his name to anyone's diploma who did not have a good knowledge of his department. Of course it would be to his discredit so to have done. I expect that Mrs. Stafford feels quite sick after that extraordinary catastrophe. The boys have made the girls feel so. I don't think Mallet will be bothered any more by Mrs. Stafford to give her scholars lectures, and maybe that was one of the reasons why he made them all fail, as he had to lecture without getting pay for it.[56]

Caleb Huse, first commandant of the University's military college, took over the work in chemistry after Mallet's resignation in 1860.

The department of ancient languages in this period functioned smoothly. Professor Stafford held the chair from 1837 to 1856 and was then succeeded by William Stokes Wyman, who had been a tutor of ancient languages in the department since 1852.[57] Wyman continued in the post until 1865 and then came back again when classes were resumed in 1871. Work in Greek was directed from 1856 to 1860 by Archibald John Battle, who, like Wyman, had served an apprenticeship as tutor before he became professor. He resigned in 1860 to visit Europe.[58]

No such continuity marked the course of the mathematics department, but it did draw into its teaching staff, at least temporarily, two of the ablest of the teachers. Professor Barnard taught in the department from 1837 to 1849; Professor Garland filled the same chair from 1849 to 1854. Among the tutors and professors who came and went during these years, three stand out. One was Arnoldus V. Brumby, tutor from 1837 to 1840, a brother of Richard T. Brumby. He was a West Point graduate and had served against the Seminole Indians in 1836. His wife was the daughter of John Fielding Wallis, one of the first professors of the University.

George Benagh, a graduate of Randolph-Macon College, is the second. He worked as a tutor under Garland from 1850 to 1852 and then was raised to professor. After Garland was made president,

THE OLD UNIVERSITY

Benagh became the professor in charge of all the work in mathematics, natural philosophy, and astronomy. His career had a sad ending. In 1863 while he was swimming in the Warrior River, he was drowned.

The third is Robert K. Hargrove, professor of mathematics from 1855 to 1857. Apparently he combined theology with his mathematical studies, for he went from the University into a career in the Methodist Church. He served as pastor of several churches, was president of the Centenary Institute at Summerfield, Alabama, became president of the Tennessee Female College at Franklin, Tennessee, and in 1882 was ordained a bishop of his church.[59]

A brief glance at one other department rounds out this summary of faculty shifts and changes in the years between 1837 and 1865. Traditionally the president of the University was also professor of moral and mental philosophy and political economy; a post which changed automatically with the administration. Dr. Manly occupied the chair faithfully until 1855. Dr. Garland was head of the department when the University was reduced to ashes.

By present standards the faculty of the University of Alabama in the ante-bellum days was somewhat short on scholarly degrees. The presidents could all claim the title of "Doctor"; Woods and Manly wrote D.D. after their names; and Garland was a Doctor of Laws. But the only Ph.D. degree was the one John W. Mallet earned at the University of Göttingen. Most of the other professors and the tutors held the degree of Master of Arts, a degree easy to obtain in those days. Many colleges gave it with practically no post-graduate requirements. And when the University of Alabama hired a young teacher without his master's degree, it was a simple matter to remedy that lack. Among those to whom the University gave masters' degrees were the following men: Henry W. Hilliard and Richard T. Brumby, 1834; Henry Tutwiler, 1837; Arnoldus V. Brumby, 1838; James C. Dockery, 1842; and Benjamin F. Porter, 1843.

But if formal tags of scholarship were lacking, the substance was undoubtedly there. Of the small number of science teachers, at least four made lasting and significant records: Barnard, Brumby, Tuomey, and Mallet.

The indefatigable F. A. P. Barnard left his mark not only on literature and photography but also on the map of the United

States. In 1846 he was appointed by the governor as Alabama's representative on a joint commission to fix the disputed boundary between Alabama and Florida. He was not at all disturbed when the representative from Florida failed to appear. He performed the task himself:

The real boundary was the thirty-first degree of north latitude, but the difficulty arose from two different lines having been marked. His first proceeding was to observe for latitude. For this purpose, he was obliged to depend on a reflecting circle and an artificial horizon. He soon satisfied himself that the one marked by small mounds corresponded with this degree of latitude, and that the other was a mere "random" line, and crooked. Both parties concurred in fixing the line in conformity with the report of Dr. Barnard.[60]

Professor Brumby was a scientific pioneer not only in the University but also in the whole American South. Says one commentator,

Professor Brumby's labors in the University of Alabama were of the most valuable character and reflected the highest honor upon him. There is no doubt that he gave the first impetus to the cause of science in that part of the country, and imparted to it a dignity and importance which it had not previously enjoyed.[61]

Another biographer speaks especially of his reasearch with goldplating:

Brumby's work with goldplating was significant because of the fact that within a decade after Faraday's researches in 1834, he carried out this goldplating without any instructions whatever.[62]

In 1838 he published the first systematic report of the mineral resources of Alabama. And when, in 1846, Sir Charles Lyell, exploring for the Geographical Society of England, visited Alabama, he paid special tribute to the work which Brumby had done:

It would have been impossible for me, during my short visit, to form more than a conjectural opinion respecting the structure of this coal field, still less to determine its geographical area, had not these subjects been studied with great care and scientific ability by Mr. Brumby.[63]

Michael Tuomey and his assistant and successor, John Mallet, built on Brumby's foundations in the Alabama Geological Survey for which they both worked so brilliantly. Mallet analyzed many rare minerals while he was at the University. He is credited with

THE OLD UNIVERSITY

the first exact atomic weight determination ever made in America. His studies and experiments to find the atomic weight of lithium were published in the *American Journal of Science* in 1856. He noted then his points of disagreement with the findings of scientists abroad and stated for himself results which in later years have been proved valid.[64] He continued his researches in atomic weights throughout his life. Two of his important later papers have to do with the atomic weights of aluminum and gold.[65] While he was in the Confederate Army, he added other achievements in yet another branch of applied science. As superintendent of Ordinance Laboratories under General Gorgas, he was both a trouble-shooter and a production manager; and he found time to be an inventor as well. He invented a shell with polygonal cavities—though what the virtue of such a shell was is not clearly stated.[66]

In the years when the University was being built up by the reputation of the faculty, the institution gradually but surely took its place as a member of the national and international community of higher education. Occasional entries in faculty minutes record requests for co-operation and offers of assistance from other universities and institutions. A few have little to do with scholarship, as, for example, the request in 1853 from the state insane asylum that the trustees set a day some time in Commencement Week for laying the cornerstone for the original asylum building. The trustees, probably with entire solemnity, decided that the afternoon of Commencement Day would be most appropriate.[67]

The director of the Observatory in Washington, D. C., wrote in 1846, offering a copy of the "Observations" for 1845 and inviting comment and criticism of the Observatory's program.[68] Three years later the Smithsonian Institution asked that the University of Alabama keep a meteorological journal, a request which was no doubt welcome to Professors Garland, Tuomey, and Barnard, to whom it was referred.[69] Another request for meteorological records came in 1853, when an extended series of these observations was being projected by the British and American governments under "Lt. Maury" (presumably Matthew F. Maury).[70]

It was in this period that the University took its first step into pressure politics on a national level. When the president of Harvard University wrote asking that the faculty at Alabama join with faculties of other colleges and universities to protest to Congress against the duties on books and philosophical apparatus, the faculty readily agreed that import duties should be waived when books and equipment were to be used in institutions of higher learning. They not only agreed to coöperate with the Harvard effort but they also asked the board of trustees to do so.[71]

Such indications of recognized scholarship and reputation seem all the more notable when one realizes the heavy burdens these men carried in addition to classroom and laboratory work. Chapel and faculty meetings were compulsory; the former came every day, and in times of stress faculty meetings seem to have come even oftener. Only occasionally and by special dispensation was a teacher relieved of attendance at these meetings. Professor Benagh was excused from attending prayers and marking absentees there when he was appointed secretary to the faculty, but provision was made that the tutors of modern and ancient languages continue to take the record.

Disciplinary problems were most time consuming of all. Though the University faculty held together reasonably well after the upheavals of 1837, disciplinary crises continued to recur. The continuous battle between the students and their mentors was not actually brought under control until the University became, in 1860, more of a military post than a school.

Compensation for these exacting and comprehensive jobs was low by modern standards, but the faculty at the early University enjoyed certain perquisites which helped to make up for low salaries.

They enjoyed, first, a measure of academic freedom insured by law. The legislature in 1821 had provided

That no person shall be excluded from any liberty, liberties, community, office, or situation in said University, on account of his religious persuasions, provided, he demain himself in a sober and peaceable and orderly manner, and conform to the rules. . . .[72]

Tax exemption was a second valuable gift of the General Assembly. Laws enacted in 1822 contained this provision:

That the estate, both real and personal, of the said Corporation shall be free and forever exempt from taxes, and the persons of all officers, servants and students belonging to the said University, shall, during their continuance there, be exempt from taxes, serving on juries, working on roads, and ordinary military duty.[73]

The plum which probably mattered most, however, was housing. When the decision was made to build the University on Marr's field, it was obvious to the trustees that they could not expect to attract a teaching staff to an institution so far from Tuscaloosa unless they made provisions for faculty housing as well as for student dormitories. The original architectural plans called for four blocks of faculty housing, but only two of these were actually built. Together these units were supposed to house eight families. Even in the early days, when the faculty was very small, this provision was inadequate, and much time in trustees' meetings had to be given to fitting faculty members into the available space. When Professors Bonfils and Hilliard were added to the staff in 1832, the board appointed a special committee to find room for them in the University buildings.[74] Two weeks later the committee made the suggestion that Professor Bonfils could have the house formerly occupied by Mr. Saltonstall, who had resigned. What they did about Mr. Hilliard is not on record.[75]

When the faculty was reorganized in 1837, the trustees definitely recorded a policy of providing for faculty members a dwelling house and "grounds attached thereto," with preference in University buildings being given to professors with families.[76] But in board meetings they continued to discuss housing and its related problems.

In 1838 Professor Pratt was given permission to use for his family the building formerly occupied by the preparatory school if he repaired the house at his own expense. At the same time President Manly and Professors Brumby, Stafford, and Pratt were told that they might use jointly a parcel of land just east of the laboratory lot provided they did not involve the University in any expense for fencing.[77]

An appropriation of $100 for a "good and substantial walled well" near the faculty dwellings (if one could be built for that price) was made in 1840.[78]

By 1844 the trustees began to wrestle with the problem of adding to the housing available for faculty. They appointed a committee of two to draft plans and get cost estimates for another faculty house.[79] Year by year, however, they tended to solve the problem in makeshift fashion by turning over for residential use parts of buildings planned for other purposes. Two rooms in the upper part of

Steward's Hall were ordered fixed for the use of Professor Barnard in late 1844; Professor Sims was to be transferred to the house formerly occupied by Barnard, but he died before the arrangement could be made.[80] Discontinuance of Steward's Hall as a boardinghouse in 1847 made more room available for faculty use. When the board authorized its remodeling for professors' housing, it reserved the right to reconvert to a boardinghouse whenever the need for such facilities should again be felt, and it reserved for general University use the basement dining room. Having completed this action, the board, at the same meeting, took formal cognizance of the fact that the promotion of two professors had underlined the importance of additional campus housing. "Whereas a residence off of said premises will be inconvenient for the professors and render their services less effective," the resolution read, "now, therefore, to promote the best interests of the University and to do equal justice to all professors. . . ." When the resolution had passed, Professor Tuomey had been assigned to Steward's Hall; Professor Garland was to move into Professor Barnard's former house; and Professor Barnard was to have a rent allowance of $250 a year until a new building could be erected.[81]

This resort to a rent allowance appears to have been fairly common. In 1844 Professor Sims was granted $200 to pay rent on the house he occupied that year.[82] In 1848 Professors Garland and Dockery were given rent allowances of $26.50 and $33.25 respectively for the period from the end of April to mid-July, and a sum of $150 each was allotted to Professors Garland, Dockery, and Barnard for rent for the ensuing year. They were to use only such part of this money as was "necessary."[83] Five years later the trustees were, probably of necessity, more generous: they granted $200 to Professor Pratt and the same amount to Professor Garland for their rent allowance.[84]

President Woods, during his whole term, and President Manly, during a part of his, took potluck with the rest of the faculty in the matter of housing. But, from 1838 when the first appropriation of $5,000 was made for the purpose[85] until its completion three years later, the President's Mansion drew admiring attention from the community as well as the University family. By 1841 the building had taken the original appropriation and a second appropriation of

$10,000, made in 1839;[86] yet costs were still mounting. The results, however, were beginning to justify the expenditures, according to public opinion expressed in the *Alabama Journal* at Montgomery:

> The plan of the building presents a specimen of the finest architectural proportions and beauty, perhaps, in the State and though, from the high prices of work and materials at the time, the contracts were given out, the building will cost much more than the Trustees contemplated; yet it cannot, perhaps, be considered as on a scale of magnificence beyond the wealth and dignity of the State.[87]

This President's Mansion and Steward's Hall, now known as the Gorgas Home, are the only two buildings standing today which were officially used for faculty housing in the early University.

An effort to provide for the University family in death as well as in life was made in 1839, when the death of a student named Samuel James made the trustees aware that, in a day of difficult transportation and inadequate embalming processes, a University burying ground was almost essential. The board buried James on the campus, designated the ground surrounding his grave as a college cemetery, and appropriated $100 to fence it in.[88] James' body was later disinterred. According to Dr. Manly's diary, another student, William J. Crawford, who died of typhus fever July 6, 1844, was buried in the same grave dug first for James. Dr. Manly also recorded the burial of two slaves in the college cemetery. Jack, a University-owned slave who, Dr. Manly said, was an African, a Methodist, honest, and faithful, was buried there May 5, 1843. The other slave, Boysey, a seven-year-old boy, belonged to Dr. Manly; his death, on November 22, 1844, was attributed to whooping cough. Later, however, this plot became, in effect, a private burying ground for the family of Professor Horace S. Pratt.

Professor Pratt died in 1840 at his brother's home in Cobb County, Georgia, and was presumably buried there. But his family continued to live in Tuscaloosa, and as members of the family died, they were buried in the University burying ground. In 1854 Mrs. Pratt asked the board of trustees to give her title to that portion of the cemetery in which her relatives were buried. The board said it was glad to do so—the cemetery fence needed repairs and the University could not afford to fix it. They gave Mrs. Pratt ownership of a plot forty-two by twenty-eight feet, on condition that the title revert to the University if the plot should be abandoned as a cemetery and the bodies interred there removed.[89] Four tombstones, all undoubtedly those of members of the Pratt family, are still enclosed in this area. They mark the graves of Mrs. Isabella Drysdale Pratt, Professor Pratt's widow, who died in 1864; Horace Southworth Pratt, apparently a son, who died in 1853; Jane Horatio Pratt and Mary A. Drysdale, about whom no dates are recorded.

Even with the gratuities which went with appointment to the faculty of the early University, salary was important. And around the question of how much to pay and to whom to pay it, discussion and even controversy centered in the meetings of the trustees and of the faculty themselves.

When the trustees were casting about for the first faculty, they took their first definite action in 1829 to establish a salary scale:

That the Salary of the Professors first to be appointed in the University of Alabama shall be $1500, per Annum, together with such fees for Tuition as may be required by the Board of Trustees, which they retain to themselves the power to fix at a moderate rate, provided, however, that the compensation of each Professor shall not be less than $2000 annually.[90]

This generous provision, the Board told the legislature that year, was necessary to attract the best men to the faculty:

The Board, believing that the great end and purposes of the institution would be greatly advanced by the selection of persons of superior literary acquirements and attainments in Science, determined to assign to each professorship such a salary per annum as would provide suitable compensation therefor, and at the same time accord under the circumstances with a prudent economy.[91]

"Suitable compensation" for the adjunct professor of chemistry was thought to be $1000; and that for a tutor, $800.[92] By November and December of the year before the University opened, the trustees were ready to fill in some of the details about faculty compensation. The president, they ruled, might receive $3000 if he carried the work of a professor as well as of administrator.[93] The following April they recorded arrangements made with the men chosen as the first faculty: President Woods and Professor Tutwiler were put on the payroll as of February 1, 1831, the time when they started to make preparations for moving to Tuscaloosa.[94] Professor Wallis, who had been out buying scientific apparatus for some months, started to draw his salary on July 1, 1830.[95]

Efforts were made to hold the salaries to the agreed scale. When in 1831 Mr. Bonfils and Mr. Hilliard came to teach modern languages and English literature, they were rated on the level of the "adjunct professor of Chemistry" and were given $1000.[96] But a year later when they were given rank of professor, it was with the stipulation that the promotion should "never be considered as furnishing any claim to an increase in salary."[97] Professor Hudson, who came at the beginning of 1833, got $1500, but it was noted by him and by the trustees, that the man he replaced, Mr. Saltonstall, had been getting $2000.[98] Professor Brumby, who came in 1834, started at $1200,[99] but he was raised from instructor to professor the following year and then was given the same $2000 salary as his predecessor, Mr. Wallis.[100]

Irregular appointments for assistants and for special services show less consistency. The persistent Mr. McMillan, who early worked himself into a position of collector of specimens of natural history, with a yearly stipend of $200 and retroactive compensation of $50,[101] was given a raise of $200 in 1831, provided that he would make over to the University title to all specimens he had collected or should collect in the future.[102] Professor Brumby's assistants, Washington D. Miller and Richard Furman, apparently had to take out some of their compensation in board bills. Miller had his board bill of $97.50 paid in August, 1835, as "partial compensation" for his work, and when he left his job in December, 1836, payment of $114 was to compensate him for his services from the date of his appointment to December 31, 1836.[103] Furman, who replaced Miller, had his salary set as equivalent to his board and tuition. He was, however, given a slight cash salary the next year when he was appointed bell ringer at $80 a year.[104]

The stipulation that tutoring fees could supplement salary was, in the case of the favored Professor Bonfils, extended to include tutoring of persons off the campus, "provided that this shall be done in such manner as the faculty may direct not interfering with his duties in the University."[105] Perhaps the outside work did interfere. In 1832 the trustees voted him an extra $500 in lieu of the privilege of outside teaching and made it retroactive to the first of that calendar year.[106] And a year later they brought his salary up to the full $2000 which put him on a par with other professors.[107] By 1835 the language professor had regained his privilege of teaching in the community. The trustees said that he might visit "any literary institution in the town of Tuscaloosa to hear recitations in the French language or for other purposes," and they again cautioned that this must not "interfere with the discharge of his official duties at other times."[108]

The $2000 salary, which had quickly become established by practice, was recognized in 1837 when the trustees ruled on procedures relating to a brand-new faculty. The president, they said, should get $3000 and the use of a house and grounds; professors should get salaries of $2000 and also get housing when "convenient."[109] This scale was followed rather consistently for the next five years. By 1842, however, pressure of financial burden and failure to get relief from the legislature was forcing the trustees to consider means of cutting down University expenses in every possible way.

Money had never been easy, of course. As far back as the summer of 1834 the trustees had been writing words of caution on the state of the budget similar to those written, before and since, by many boards to many faculties:

Gentlemen: the situation you occupy will enable you by the exercise of vigilance and caution greatly to aid the trustees in curtailing and preventing the expenditures of this university—while therefore we would by no means have you, in any instance, descend below the most dignified course in the management of concerns of the institution, we trust you will take upon yourselves the additional duty of assisting us in avoiding every expense not strictly for the promotion of the true interest of the University.

You are aware that the appropriations of this Board must in many instances, be in accordance with your advice—the present deranged state of the University funds, which we hope to be able to obviate, makes this request necessary, which under other circumstances might seem improper —doubting not of our entire and cheerful concurrence. . . . [110]

The funds were more "deranged," if possible, ten years later, and the means of "obviating" the derangement had not been found. The trustees took a small step in the direction of salary cuts in late 1841, when they set $1500, rather than $2000, as the salary for the newly re-established professorship in modern language.[111] A year later the axe fell. The president's salary was cut to $2500; professors' salaries, to $1700; and tutors,' to $800. The tutors were to take their cut at once; others were to have theirs as of July 1, 1843.[112]

The board sought to temper the bad news with a vote of confidence in the high attainments of the faculty. With notices of salary reductions each member of the teaching staff received a copy of this comforting statement:

Resolved, unanimously, by the President and Trustees of the University of Alabama, that while economy & a just regard to the interest of the University have induced them to diminish the salaries of its several officers, that they have every confidence in the learning, ability & high qualifications of the President and Faculty of the University, individually and collectively.[113]

Protest from the faculty was slow in coming, but when it came the following October, it challenged the legal right of the trustees to revise salaries downward. They asked that salaries be restored and the matter referred for settlement "amicably" by the state Supreme Court. The faculty were, they said in their communication to the trustees, gratified at the expression of confidence in their work made by the trustees. They were quite willing to make necessary sacrifices for the cause of education. But they felt "constrained" to protest that one party to a contract may not justly alter the terms of that contract without the consent of the other party. Teachers who accepted posts at the University of Alabama endured hardships and inconveniences because they had confidence in the permanence of their new positions. If salaries could be changed at the whim of the trustees, there would be "distrust and uneasiness, unfriendly to the confident and zealous discharge of their duties while they remain and sufficient to render welcome any proposition of advantageous settlement elsewhere." Said the professors,

We are not disposed to overrate the value of our services to the University and we are as incapable of making a threat as the Trustees are incapable of *being affected by it*. But, with all modesty, we would suggest, that a vacancy in our stations, under all the uncertainties involved in the late action of the Board of Trustees, would not present such attractions as to command the services of men possessing sufficient character and force, to be valued and desired where they are. Such only, we are persuaded, you would wish to succeed us, what ever may be thought of ourselves.[114]

The trustees were unmoved at this veiled threat of mass resignation. They merely sent another polite resolution of "undiminished confidence in the learning, industry, ability & good conduct of the Presiden [sic] and professors of the University," and reiterated their stand:

That the reduction of salaries at the last meeting of this Board was made under an imperious sense of duty as well for the Welfare of the parties concerned as in obedience to public opinion & that stern necessity forbids this Board from increasing said salaries.[115]

Perhaps the suggestion of the faculty that the board had exceeded its legal right in making the reductions may have bothered some trustees. They tried to make good that right by going on record that they could reduce salaries whenever they thought it expedient to do so.[116]

Evidently this assertion of authority went unchallenged by all of the faculty except George S. Walden, a tutor from 1841 to 1844. In response to his petition the Supreme Court in 1849 handed down its decision in favor of Walden:

Having enacted and published an ordinance stipulating that the salary of tutors in the university should be $1,000 per year, and that all tutors should serve for a period of two years unless sooner permitted to resign, the board decided to reduce the compensation of a tutor employed under this ordinance for his second year of service from $1,000 to $800 without his consent. He sued on his contract, and in the Supreme Court of Alabama affirmed a judgment for $200 in his favor.[117]

By the time this judgment had been given, however, the faculty had settled down to the new salary scale. Even the bell-ringer took his cut. Henry Brooks, who held that important position in 1843, was given twelve dollars a month for his services.[118]

Appointments in the fifties show further efforts in economy. In 1853 tutors in ancient and modern languages were paid salaries of $800 each.[119] Professor Scherb, who, for a brief period, held the chair of modern languages at that time, had been offered $900, with the explanation that the trustees would have given him more if they had not had to appoint a tutor of ancient languages that year.[120]

A jolt which drove the trustees to reconsider salaries was the resignation in 1854 of three outstanding professors: Garland, Barnard, and Tuomey. An investigation showed that inadequate salary

THE OLD UNIVERSITY

was at least one reason for these resignations. The trustees were forced to recognize that the cost of living had been increasing while University salaries had remained static and that, moreover, salaries in other vocations were becoming increasingly attractive. They granted some slight relief, raising professors from $1700 to $2000, and tutors from $800 to $1000, but leaving the president with his salary still fixed at $2500.[121]

Even after this action, the trustees continued to find ways of cutting corners for economy's sake. When Professors Barnard and Tuomey resigned, the chair of chemistry and natural history was combined with that of mineralogy, geology and agricultural chemistry, and one $2000 appointment was made to cover the whole field. The professorships of modern language and ancient language in 1855 were to be filled at $1500 and $1200 respectively.[122] As a result of depreciated Confederate currency, the board of trustees raised the salaries of the faculty members during the Civil War in order to help them meet the increased costs of living. In 1863 President Garland's salary was $12,524.85. The salaries of the other teachers ranged from $4000 to $6000. Colonel J. T. Murfee, commandant of cadets, was paid $6,678.06.[123]

It is perhaps remarkable that, with a salary scale which in a period of more than thirty years changed very little with the changing needs of the time, the University was yet able to attract and hold the kind of teachers whose achievements we have briefly considered in this chapter.

CHAPTER V

The Library

A LIBRARY for the University was to the Alabama trustees at least as important as a faculty. Looking over the architects' first plans for the buildings in 1828, they noted with pride that these plans included "a principal building for public lectures, Commencements, Library &c."[1] And they forthwith instructed the president of the board to "open correspondence with the principal booksellers in the United States as preparatory to the purchase of a library for the University."[2]

Two years passed before these plans began to take any formal shape. Then in January, 1830, the trustees took the next step, the setting aside of money. They appropriated $20,000 for the purchase of a library and of chemical and philosophical apparatus.[3] By summer they had definitely earmarked $10,000 of this sum for the use of Professor Wallis in his acquirement of chemical and philosophical apparatus.[4] Another six months passed before they set the library fund at $6,000.[5]

In the summer of 1830 the trustees received also a gentle nudge toward action from Mr. D. Woodruff, bookseller of Tuscaloosa, who had heard that the trustees were thinking of buying books in Europe. He urged that they patronize home enterprise instead, saying that as he had "one of the best book houses in the Union," he felt sure that he could fill their needs.[6]

A special library committee was appointed that December to "inquire into the best practicable mode of obtaining a library for the University."[7] Within a month the committee submitted a careful report and a draft of ordinances to govern the selection of a library.[8]

Preliminary listing of books needed and negotiations to get bids became the responsibility of the president of the University. It is pleasant to note that the enterprising Mr. Woodruff was not forgotten:

Sec. 1. Be it ordained by the Trustees of the University of Alabama that it shall be the duty of the President of the University of Alabama as soon as may be—to make out a list of all such Books as in his opinion may be necessary to form a library for the commencement of instructions in this university, calculated for the use of one hundred students, and forward one of such lists to Mr. David Woodruff of Tuscaloosa, one to Mr. Lowar and Hogan of Philadelphia, one to Mr. Cog Carrill of New-York and to such other book-sellers of Philadelphia, Newyork or Boston as he may think proper, and request them at what price or for what sum they will undertake to furnish the Books contained in the said list, and deliver them safely at the University.

The president was authorized to accept the best bid, and the steps by which the payments for the books were to be made were carefully outlined:

Sec. 2. And be it further ordained, that it shall be the duty of the President aforesaid as soon as answers may be received from the persons to whom lists shall have been furnished to accept . . . the proposal of such person or persons as in his opinion will be most conducive to the interest of the university and to close a contract with such person or persons for the purchase of said Library and shall require such Bookseller to cause the books to be shipped immediately, directed to the Trustees of the university of Alabama, and delivered safely at the university, and to forward his or their bill for payment.

Sec. 3. And be it further ordained that it shall be the duty of the President of the University, as soon as he may have closed a contract with any person or persons for the purchase of a Library as aforesaid, to inform the President of the Board of Trustees of such contract, and of the sum, which he may have agreed to pay for such Library, and it shall be the duty of the President of the Board of Trustees as soon as he may be informed that the books for said Library have been safely delivered at the University to issue his Warrant upon the Comptroller of public accounts for the amount which shall have been agreed upon between the President of the University and such Bookseller or Booksellers or to cause payment to be made in any other manner that may have been agreed upon.

Sec. 4. And be it further ordained that for the purpose of carrying this ordinance into effect, the sum of six thousand dollars of the University fund be and the same is hereby appropriated and placed subject to the Warrant or draft of the President of the Board.

While President Woods was concluding his affairs at Transylvania, this ordinance was presented. It is improbable, therefore, that the students who came to the campus in April, 1831, found many books assembled to help them in their studies. By December, however, Dr. Woods was able to present to the trustees a report on the books he had purchased. It would be interesting to know what these books were that formed the nucleus of the University library. Unfortunately, Dr. Woods' report was merely received and referred to the committee on accounts, and no record of the books covered was made in the minutes.[9] The board did, however, authorize the transfer to the library fund of $1500, which had previously been given to Professor Wallis for the purchase of a collection of minerals from Mr. Nuttall.[10]

The regulations governing the library included in the ordinances of the University when it opened in 1831 were changed very little in the years before 1865. The rules included in the laws of 1839 are typical of the entire period:[11]

1. There shall be a librarian annually appointed by the Board of Trustees whose duty shall be to take charge of all the books and other matters belonging to the Library and; in all things pertaining to his office, not expressly provided for in these laws, he shall be subject to the direction and control of the Faculty.

2. The Librarian shall keep the Library neat and clean—shall register all books, whether donations or purchased—shall record all books lent and returned, charge and collect all fines incurred for violations of the Library Laws, and shall call in all books, without exception, in the week preceding Vacation and Commencement. If any book or article shall be presented to the Library, the Librarian shall record the name and residence of the donor.

3. The Library shall be opened not less than once a week, during session time; the books shall be delivered out, and returned in such order and manner as the Librarian may direct.

4. The use of the Library shall be tendered, free of expense, to the Trustees of the University, to all such persons as have made a donation to the Library of the value of one hundred dollars, to the officers of instruction, resident graduates, and the students, but no graduates shall be considered resident and as such entitled to the use of the Library unless they actually reside within the College walls.

5. The officers of Instruction are entitled to the use of the Library at any hour. They shall, however, keep a book, in which the names of

the works taken by them from the Library shall be regularly recorded; and they shall subject themselves to a fine of one dollar, for any neglect of this rule, to be paid the Librarian. No other persons, entitled to the use of the Library, shall take a book therefrom, except in the presence of the Librarian, or one of the Faculty who shall take a note of the same, before the book is delivered.

6. No student, at any time, shall have, in his possession more than three volumes, which may be kept two weeks; except such as are preparing for a public exhibition who may be allowed a greater number, on application to the President. . . . If books are not returned within the specified time, the drawer shall pay, for every week's detention beyond the limitation, 10 cents, for a 12mo, or book of smaller size; 20 cents, for an 8vo; 30 cents, for a quarto; and forty cents for a folio. If any book, taken from the Library, be lost or damaged, the delinquent shall have the privilege of immediately replacing the volume or sett—otherwise he shall pay the value of the volume or sett, if defaced; double the value, if much injured; and three-fold, if lost; and the amount shall be applied to the use of the Library.

7. Students are forbidden to take down or displace any book, and are particularly required to observe order and decorum, while receiving books from the Librarian, under penalty of a fine not exceeding fifty cents, and such other punishment as the case may require.

8. Books, valuable for their plates, their rarity, their antiquity, or of which the character fits them for consultation rather than reading, may be withheld from circulation by the Librarian.—No book taken from the Library can be used by a Student, as a text book.

9. If any Student shall lend a book of the Library, to any person, not a fellow-student, or shall permit it to be carried out of the immediate vicinity of the University, he shall be reprimanded by the Librarian: and if the offence be repeated, all access to the Library shall be denied him. No person, entitled to the use of the Library, shall be allowed to carry a book out of the immediate vicinity of the city of Tuskaloosa; except officers of instruction, employed abroad in scientific investigations.

10. The Librarian shall keep a book, properly ruled, in which any person entitled to the use of the library, and any Literary Visitor may write the title, author and publisher, size and price of such book or books, as they may think ought to be in the Library; and each person so recommending a book, shall add his signature to the recommendation. The Librarian shall lay the said book before the Trustees, at their annual meeting.

11. If fines, inflicted under these laws, remain unpaid, the delinquent's

privilege of the Library shall be suspended, until payment is made. No Student's diploma shall be signed by the Faculty, until he produces evidence that he is not a defaulter at the Library.

12. The care of enforcing these laws, when not enforced by the Librarian, devolves on the Faculty, even in the case of members of their own body, or of the Board of Trustees.

13. The Librarian shall receive, as a compensation for his services, an annual salary of one hundred dollars.

Such rules indicate the degree to which the board of trustees determined library policy. Moreover they made the appointment of the librarian. Always they held the purse strings with a firm hand. One notable exception they made to library rules was in 1837; they accorded to the retiring President Woods the privilege of using the library whenever he wished to do so[12]—a privilege of doubtful practical value, it may be said, since Dr. Woods was to live out the rest of his life in Providence, Rhode Island.

The trustees were always quite willing to leave to the faculty the details of enforcement of rules and the day by day administration of the library. And the faculty found many items of library business coming into the agendas of their meetings. At least twice, in 1832 and 1833, they had occasion to remind the librarian of the rule against lending books containing valuable plates and, especially, books which contained translations of textbook materials which students might use as an easy aid to learning.[13] They very early intensified the rules on renewals by providing that students might not renew books which had been applied for by other students.[14] A vote in 1836 that the library was to be opened only by the librarian and books were to be taken out only through him suggests that some laxity in library procedures may have developed by that time.[15]

Enforcement of the rules on fines and tardiness in returning books and periodicals also occupied its share of faculty time. Two entries in the minutes of 1852 are typical. One reads: "Ormand, who had heretofore been reported as a defaulter to the Library (having taken out *The Pioneer* and never returned it) has never complied with the law by replacing it. The Faculty therefore inflict a fine of $3.00, that amt. being taken to be three times the value of the book lost."[16] The second orders fines of fifty cents each for sev-

THE OLD UNIVERSITY
103

eral other student defaulters "unless some law of the library is thereby contravened."[17] Students were not the only offenders. Several entries instruct the librarian to call upon all officers to return reviews belonging to the library, and it was expressly stated that officers might keep reviews only one week, subject to renewal unless some other person had asked for them.[18]

A somewhat major matter of library administration was under discussion by the faculty in 1843. It had become apparent that there was need for a better arrangement of books and also for a sharpening of the rules for keeping order in the use of the library. President Manly suggested that the librarian, A. W. Richardson, be asked to undertake the first of these tasks, and that, inasmuch as the job was a big one, he should receive $50 from the library fund in addition to his regular salary.[19] This was at least the second time that the books in the library had been systematically rearranged. Oran Roberts, one-time student librarian, remembered a similar housecleaning in 1834-35:

It was that year that the books in the Library in the Rotunda were rearranged, according to subjects treated, so as to make it easy to find any book, that might be applied for, upon the subject of which it treated being mentioned. Marion Baldwin and some other students performed the work.[20]

By 1843 the library had apparently grown so much that its rearrangement could not be left to volunteers among the students.

The new rules which the faculty adopted at that time also indicate new problems developing in a growing library. These rules, supplementing the library laws already in force, may be summarized as follows:

1. The library was to be open at noon on two successive days each week, Wednesday and Thursday. The first day was for making application for books; the second, for receiving them.
2. The librarian was to enforce strictly all the trustees' laws in reference to the use of the library.
3. The librarian was to ascertain what books were missing, which, according to the printed catalogues and manuscript lists, should have been in the library, and to ascertain if the books could be traced.
4. Each member of the staff was to hand in a list of all the books he had in his possession and to keep the list on file.

5. At the end of the year, a committee of two from the faculty was to examine the library and report to the faculty.
6. The librarian was to see to the binding of such pamphlets, reviews, etc., as the faculty might decree.
7. The librarian, being responsible for the library, must refuse to give to anyone except a member of the faculty the key, which must be returned to the librarian as soon as the immediate use for which it was obtained was over.[21]

Once more in this period, in 1852, new regulations for the use of the library were issued, providing for additional library hours and also for somewhat more formal procedures for the issuance of books:

1. The Librarian shall keep the Library open on Mondays and Thursdays for one hour during the noon recess and Saturday afternoon from 2 to 4 o'clock.
2. The Librarian shall record all periodicals received into the Library or given out.
3. No talking shall be had in the Library, except the Librarian and that in such a manner as not to disturb the others.
4. Any person desiring a book, shall write down the title and the Library number of the book upon a slip of paper and hand it to the Librarian and the Librarian shall take the book from the shelves. No student shall take a book from the shelves upon any pretence.[22]

The regulations regarding library conversations and the circulation rules reflect difficulties which were inherent in the very nature of the building which housed the library. Oran Roberts, looking back upon his college experiences, well remembered the inadequacies of the Rotunda as a library, especially because of the strange acoustics of the place:

In the session of 1835-6, which was my Senior year, I was elected Librarian by the Trustees of the University, as I supposed upon the recommendation of the Faculty. It was then usual for a member of the Senior class to be the Librarian of the University. It was my duty to select and give out the books that were applied for by the professors and students, and keep an account of it so as to secure their return. The books had been classified by subjects, so that there was no difficulty to select the books, that were applied for. The library was in the Rotunda, situated in the center of the square made by the other buildings. Applications were made for books by the student one day before the time for delivery, which was early every Saturday morning. It was my business also to attend visitors who sought to go into the library. The library was in the

THE OLD UNIVERSITY   105

second story of the building, which was circular, both at the sides where the book-shelves were placed and also the dome, which had no pillars to support it, and the room was about eighty feet in diameter.

A striking characteristic of that room was the immense reverberation of sound, produced by ordinary conversation, or by walking on the floor. The least harshness in the voice of a person speaking reverberated with such a confusion and increase in the volume of the sound, that he could not be heard at the distance of three feet of another person. If a person would stamp his foot upon the floor the sound produced was like thunder in loudness, and its reverberations would continue with lessening loudness, and finally die away after half a minute or longer. I found but few persons who could speak in that room so as to be distinctly heard. To be heard very distinctly one had to speak deliberately and announce the word spoken with precision and without the least harshness in the sound of the voice. There were many more females than males, who could speak so as to be heard well. I very soon learned to speak as to be heard distinctly all over the room. I have thought since then that a building so constructed would be well adapted to training the voice in elocution, and that Demosthenes found the cave, to which he resorted in which to speak, to answer the same purpose, though another reason for doing so is given.[23]

In this big, echoing room, books were easily lost, stolen, and damaged, as were other items housed in the Rotunda. In 1845 damage to natural history specimens stored on the floor of the library caused concern to the faculty. They decided that they should be taken off the floor and put away, either in the cases already built under the bookshelves on the west wall or in boxes specially made for them under the direction of the president. While they were making these rearrangements, the faculty also asked their secretary to see what could be done, in the way of curtains, to improve the lighting of a large picture in the library room.[24]

At a faculty meeting in 1849 the librarian told the professors that someone had entered the library room and displaced books. Professors Manly and Tuomey were instructed to look into ways of "shutting out ingressions hereafter by means of windows." So serious was the situation that the two men were authorized to go ahead with the construction of any means to protect the Library without first reporting to the full faculty.[25] Another step made to safeguard books was the provision in 1852 of wire doors for the library cases. Incidentally, the resolution authorizing the purchase of these doors also provided for the purchase of "a dozen spit-boxes for the library room provided the contingent fund is able to bear the expense."[26]

Care of periodicals was a constant source of worry. In 1837 the librarian was ordered to collect all the unbound numbers of standard reviews then in the library and to obtain estimates on the cost of binding them in uniformity with the works to which they belonged.[27] Binding of pamphlets and periodicals and rebinding of valuable books in bad repair was also ordered in a faculty meeting in 1844.

Sometimes the authorization of the binding of periodicals only created new problems. Early in 1849 the faculty learned, to its distress, that Mr. Cammer, who had had the order for binding some forty-seven volumes, had done a good job on only thirty volumes. The other seventeen contained odd volumes bound together. Only half the agreed-upon price was paid to Mr. Cammer on the incomplete sets, and Mr. Gould and Mr. Richardson were instructed to try to collect the missing numbers and to prepare for binding in complete sets all the valuable periodicals up to the close of 1848.[29] Apparently Mr. Cammer lost business through his carelessness, for, when Messrs. Gould and Richardson had assembled the materials, the faculty did not further patronize Mr. Cammer. Professor Barnard, who was going to take a trip to Mobile or New Orleans, was urged to take with him such reviews and pamphlets as were ready for binding and also unbound books whose constant use made their binding necessary for their preservation. He was requested to see that the work of binding was properly done and to bring the books back with him when he returned.[30]

Working with the faculty on all these problems, these University librarians must have amply earned their stipend of approximately $100 a year. Sometimes the trustees appointed the librarian; sometimes the faculty appointed him. For part of the period students worked in this capacity, earning money to offset college expenses. Oran Roberts felt that the work brought more than financial reward to such students.

Being Librarian gave me an extensive knowledge of books, and the subjects treated of in them, and enabled me to employ my leisure time in a general course of reading and also to prepare myself for the discussion of the subjects debated upon in the society.[31]

The first librarian was William McMillan, the persistent collector of natural history specimens, who, in January, 1831, was given the position in addition to his other responsibilities.[32] He seems to have been somewhat dissatisfied with his employment at the University. At any rate he did not remain long. His letter of resignation in January, 1832, was referred to the committee on propositions and grievances.[33]

At that point the trustees delegated to the faculty the appointment of the librarian. They were authorized to select a student librarian and pay him $110 a year.[34]

James Carlisle, assistant to Professor Wallis, was the first faculty appointee. He was paid the full $110 for his services in 1832,[35] and he was, in consideration of this extra work and also "in consequence of his health," excused from one of his recitations each day.[36]

No reason is given why the trustees at the end of this year withdrew from the faculty the authority to appoint a librarian.[37] From 1833 to 1837 the board itself at its regular meetings proceeded to make these appointments. Arrangements regarding compensation varied from year to year. John G. Davenport, named in 1833,[38] was allowed $88.61 for his services to October 21, 1833.[39] His successor, Thomas M. Peters, got "the usual compensation of $110."[40] But Marion Baldwin had $40 for tuition deducted from his salary in 1835,[41] and so did Oran M. Roberts the following year.[42] Richard Furman, student librarian from July 1 to October 20, 1836, got $51.25 for his services,[43] but when Joseph Dunnam Jenkins served that December, his compensation for his library work cancelled his board bill at Steward's Hall.[44]

The use of students as librarians was discontinued in the reorganization which took place in 1837. Samuel H. Rives, librarian at the time of this action, was allowed to continue his work until February 1, 1838,[45] but, thereafter a member of the faculty was to be assigned to this position.[46] Arnoldus V. Brumby was the first appointee under this new plan. He added $150 to his tutor's stipend by his library work.[47] He was succeeded in 1839 by Sterling S. Sherman, who served as librarian until January, 1842.[48] In 1841 the trustees once again intrusted to the faculty the responsibility for library appointments,[49] and in 1842 the faculty selected Richard T. Brumby.[50]

In the following year, however, Mr. Brumby lost his appointment in a contested election, which is difficult to understand in view of the small stipend and large drudgery involved in the position being fought over. Professor Brumby and Tutor John Gorman Barr were the nominees. President Manly, Professor Stafford, and Tutor James Somerville voted for Brumby; Professors Barnard, Sims, and Dockery voted for Barr. The president declared it a tie and postponed further action.[51] Barnard entered a protest when the faculty met again. He said that tutors had no right to vote and that the president had no right to create a tie by voting with the faculty and then to decide the matter by casting another vote. Professors Sims and Dockery felt that Barr really had won the election. But President Manly, who was opposed to Barr, insisted that, regardless of the vote, no candidate could be elected without his approval. Professor Barnard thought that elections should not be subject to the use of the presidential veto. Professor Brumby had apparently withdrawn from the contest by this time, but Austin Williams Richardson, a student, was a new candidate. No tutors voted this time. Professors Barnard, Sims, and Dockery were loyal to their candidate Barr; Professors Brumby and Stafford voted with the president for Richardson. Another tie followed. And, in spite of Barnard's objections, President Manly again used his vote to break the tie to declare Richardson elected.[52] The disgruntled trio entered a formal protest in the "Faculty Minutes." A month later President Manly also used the "Faculty Minutes" to record a lengthy defense of his action as thoroughly consistent with the laws of the trustees.[53] Late in 1844 tutors were formally given the right to vote in faculty meetings[54] but the point of the presidential vote was apparently discarded.

Richardson was succeeded in 1845 by another man with the same surname, Wilson Gaines Richardson, a tutor in ancient languages. He served until 1849.[55] About that time curtailment of college expenses led the trustees to rule that the duties of the librarian would, hereafter, be apportioned among the faculty and other officers without extra compensation.[56] Robert Simonton Gould, a tutor in mathematics, offered to do the work with the understanding that he should be allowed free use of the Library after his retirement from the University.[57] Tutor Wilson G. Richardson took the position for three months beginning in November, 1849,[58] and then Professor Stafford filled in for the remainder of that school year.[59] Archibald John Battle, tutor in Latin and Greek, was librarian in 1850 and 1851. William Stokes Wyman, a resident graduate, supplied briefly, beginning October 4, 1851, with the understanding that he would be released from all college charges while he was performing the duties of librarian.[60] He left in January, however, and Professor Tuomey who served for the rest of that term,[61] was succeeded in April by Charles Francis Henry, tutor in the French and the Spanish languages.

This rapid turnover was not to be ignored by the trustees. In July, 1852, they reversed their previous action and gave permission to the faculty to appoint a librarian from among the students and to pay him the same salary paid to the bellman.[62] John W. Bishop, a junior, was selected.[63]

During 1854 and 1865 three other men were librarians: Josias Duckett Rhodes, a student, (1854 to 1856); Professor William S. Wyman (1856-1857); and Professor Andre DeLoffre (1857-1865).

These rapid changes at the librarian's desk could not have contributed much to the smooth running of the library.

During all these years, however, the library continued to grow and develop. After the original grant for books had been expended, an annual grant of $400 was provided for the purchase of books selected by the faculty.[64] This appropriation was in effect, however, only from 1836 to 1842; then the trustees cut it in half.[65] The grants were divided among the departments, each professor being free to buy with his allowance the books he preferred. In 1843 the faculty gave Professor Dockery permission to spend his library money when he went to New Orleans for a visit.[66]

Even when the grant had been reduced to $200 a year, money was occasionally left in the library fund. In 1843 Professors Barnard, Stafford, and Sims were appointed as a committee to decide what should be done with one such surplus. They drew up a list of books, which was approved by the faculty and subject to the advice of the librarian, and they asked that O. Rich, a bookseller in London, be consulted about the prices of the most necessary books on their list.[67]

Like all faculties, the men who made up the faculty of the early University of Alabama complanied frequently that the library was inadequate. Professor Brumby said to the trustees in 1841,

The Sciences which I teach are rapidly advancing; & hence, while my colleagues are supplied with all necessary books, I am constantly behind the scientific world, because I cannot have access to the costly works filled with plates, which are published annually. And I ask you to examine the catalogue of the University Library with special reference to my department. You will find it to contain a comparatively meager list of antiquated, though valuable volumes.[68]

The trustees seem not to have been moved by this plea. But in 1845 they did make a special appropriation of $400 for the increase and improvement of the library.[69] Encouraged by this generosity, the faculty met in February, 1846, "for the purpose of considering a list of prices of books received from Wiley and Putnam, New York, and of taking steps toward the preparation of an order for the increase of the library." At the same meeting "the president made an exhibit of the state of the library fund, and such a selection was agreed upon to fall within the means available." The matter was then referred to a committee consisting of Professors Stafford and Barnard, who were authorized to revise the list and to make "such alterations and substitutes as might seem desirable." And they were ordered "to report on Friday."[70]

Similarly, the journals and periodicals in the library failed to satisfy the professors. In the first days of the library there had been a special fund for the purchase of periodicals, but after 1839 the regular library fund and the annual appropriations for book acquisitions were expected to cover periodicals as well as books.[71] In 1846 Professors Brumby and Barnard together petitioned the trustees for an appropriation of $100 to increase the volumes of journals in the library. Such action, they said, was necessary if the University was to "sustain an honorable character among the colleges of the country."[72] The trustees, who only the year before had made a special library appropriation, rejected the request.[73]

It is interesting to note that among the periodicals which the University had regularly in its library during this period were the following: *Quarterly Review,* published by the American Protestant Association;[74] *Boston Quarterly Register,* published by the Education Society;[75] *Southern Educational Journal,* by Franklin H. Brooks;[76] *New Englander,* published in New Haven; and *DeBow's Commercial Review,* published in New Orleans.[77]

THE OLD UNIVERSITY 111

Even when there was money for books and periodicals, it was not easy in those days to get library materials safely from publisher or bookseller to the library shelves. In 1840 several years after he had left the University, Professor Tutwiler wrote to President Manly about an experience which was probably all too typical. He had, Tutwiler said, ordered some books from New York while he was still on the faculty. These books were to be sent in care of Prince and Garrett in Mobile and then to him in Tuscaloosa. The books reached Mobile safely, but all one summer they lay in the warehouse of Prince and Garrett until a friend saw the bundle and sent it on a boat to Tuscaloosa. The books were addressed to Professor Tutwiler, who, everyone knew, had left the University. Therefore, the captain or someone else aboard, thinking that nothing could be gained by delivering the books to him there, as a friendly gesture landed the books at Erie. That was the last anyone heard of the package. Meanwhile, the bookseller had billed Tutwiler for the books and Tutwiler had paid the bill. Later he asked that President Manly arrange to have him reimbursed in the amount of $10.21 for the lost package.[78]

The library fund was used for direct library purchases: $15 to Professor Stafford for a five-volume set of *The Life of Washington* in 1842;[79] $45.75 to Professor Sims for books imported in 1843.[80] It was also used for a miscellaneous assortment of expenditures which would seem very much out of place in a modern library record. President Woods reported a bill of $12.75 for freight and charges from New York to Tuscaloosa on two boxes containing donations of books from the British government.[81] President Manly advanced twenty cents to pay a Negro drayman to bring a box of books from the steamer *Fashion*—he was reimbursed by Professor Tuomey.[82] The *Fashion* had earlier been paid fifty cents for freight and $2.25 for other charges on a box of books, perhaps the same box for which the twenty cent drayage fee was paid.[83] In 1846 a record book for the library cost $3.50.[84] In 1856 a blank book costing $2.00 was bought by Professor Wyman from Hogan and Foster and charged to the library fund.[85] Professor Barnard was reimbursed by President Manly for forty cents which he had paid to have two boxes of books brought from Tuscaloosa.[86] A freight bill of $5.75 for two boxes of books brought up the river by Kinney was ordered paid in

October, 1847.[87] These items are undoubtedly typical of others of the period.

The library grew by gifts as well as by purchases. In 1836 President Woods was authorized to acknowledge in a suitable manner the receipt of the "rare and valuable" collection of books presented to the University of Alabama by the British Government and to express "our deep sense of the magnanimity and delicate liberality manifested in that donation."[88] Again in 1839, the British government was the donor when it presented ten books to the University.[89] A "Business Directory of the Western Valley" came from Gordon and Curry of Mobile in 1845,[90] and in that same year the publisher of Arnold's *Lectures on Modern History* gave a copy of that book to the library.[91] The donation of Donne's *Blackstone* was accepted by the faculty in 1842.[92]

Henry Gapett and/or Henry Gasset of Boston interested himself or themselves in providing the University library with materials on Freemasonry. Henry Gapett is the name recorded as donor in 1843 of three volumes on Masonry, one volume on anti-Masonic conventions, and two volumes on anti-Masonic pamphlets, given on condition "that the books be placed conspicuously on the shelves of the library."[93] A copy of the *Letters of John Quincy Adams on Free Masonry,* which came to the library some five years later, was recorded as the gift of "Henry Gasset of Boston."[94]

Other gifts recorded in the faculty minutes of the 1840's include the following: scientific reports published and presented by the state of Massachusetts;[95] a French and a Greek dictionary from Dr. Hullum of Tuscaloosa;[96] two volumes of *Dana's Zo-ophytes of the Exploring Expedition,* presented to the state of Alabama by the "general government" and turned over to Judge Collier for deposit in the University library;[97] and a number of books by Dr. Martyn Payne of New York, presented by the author.[98]

Perhaps the most unusual offer of all was one made by a certain "Ebenezer Henderson, LLD of Greenbank House, St. Helens, near Liverpool, England." He made the first attempt at buying an honorary degree in the history of the University. The matter first came up in a faculty meeting in October, 1852 when a letter from Mr. Henderson was read. It contained an offer of "copies of his various works upon astronomy—optics—geometry and mechanical philoso-

THE OLD UNIVERSITY 113

phy—and also an orrey [orrery] made by Jas. Ferguson F.R.S. and once in the possession of D. Franklin [sic]; also intimation that he would like to have conferred upon him the honorary degree of LLD and tendering certificates." The faculty voted "that the thanks of the Faculty be returned for his presents, and the certificates offered be invited."[99] During the next summer the matter was again considered. Apparently the old faculty had much to say about the conferring of honorary degrees, for they "resolved to pass over for the present the subject of conferring the honorary L.L.D. upon Mr. Henderson of England—until the books which he has presented to the library shall have arrived."[100] No record of an honorary degree for Ebenezer Henderson appears in any University publication. Perhaps the donor changed his mind. Perhaps he was unwilling to send the books without firm promise of the degree in advance. Or perhaps the books, if indeed they did come, were thought by the faculty inadequate to warrant the bestowal of the degree.

Books bought and books given were listed in at least two printed catalogues during the period before 1865. The first was undertaken in 1837, when Richard Furman, librarian pro tem, was "authorized and required" to make a catalogue of the books "arranged under their proper heads" in the library and to arrange for the printing of 500 copies.[101] The following year Mr. Furman was paid $50 for making out the catalogue and supervising its printing.[102]

The second was compiled in 1847-48 by Wilson Gaines Richardson, and 225 copies of it were ordered to be sold unbound, at seventy-five cents a copy.[103] Two bills paid in connection with this catalogue are on record: one, for binding 210 copies at twenty-five cents each; the other, for printing the catalogue at $1.75 a page for 257 pages, a total of $449.75. In the first place, librarian Richardson himself had apparently paid the printing and binding bills, for the two bills are made in his favor, and the money was directed to be paid to him.[104]

Richardson had used as model for this catalogue that of the Signet Library of Edinburgh. The names of authors and titles were recorded alphabetically. "An alphabetical index was added as an exponent of the subjects treated, as far as these could be gleaned from the title pages."[105]

When this catalogue was published midway in the period between the University's founding and the Civil War, the number of books in the library was 4,231, not counting pamphlets and other unbound material. A collection of this size would be considered inadequate for a University library today, but it served the educational needs of a simpler time and helped to stimulate the thinking of generations of eager University students.

CHAPTER VI

The Students

THE OPENING of Alabama's own "institution of learning" meant that ambitious fathers need no longer send their sons far from home to be educated as cultured gentlemen. That they did not fully avail themselves of this opportunity was a matter of concern to both University and state leaders. In 1850 Governor Collier addressed to the citizens of the state a plea for more active support of the University:

The smallness of the number of students in our University may to some extent be attributed to the fact that about one third of the young men of this State, who receive a collegiate education, are sent to the colleges of other states. This is greatly to be regretted, as its tendency is not only to disparage our own literary institutions, but to estrange the youths sent abroad from the associations of home, and repress their solicitude for the prosperity of their own State, to say nothing of the loss we sustain by the abstraction of a large sum of money, that should be expended in our midst. . . . We would appeal to the patriotism and self-respect of the people, and ask them, if it is not our duty to give a preference to our own schools and colleges.[1]

High on the list of the competitors for Alabama students was the University of Virginia, at Charlottesville, founded in 1819. For years newspapers in Alabama carried the advertisements of this university side by side with those of the University of Alabama, and it was, perhaps, to be expected that a generation of fathers not too far from the memories of the Old Dominion often wanted to send their boys back home to school.

Alabama attracted to its University few students from other states to offset this trend. Usually there were two or three Mississippi boys enrolled in the student body, but students from other states were few and infrequent. For example, in 1837, when the enrollment was 101, four students came from Mississippi, two from North

Carolina, and one from South Carolina. In 1845 one student came from North Carolina. In 1857 a student from Texas and one from Georgia were the only out-of-state enrollments in a college of 144.

Builders of the University had planned for an initial enrollment of about 100 students. They had provided dormitory space in Washington and Jefferson halls for 96 boys. They had instructed their library committee to obtain books for a student body of approximately 100. But they had not intended to stop at this limit. The building of Franklin Hall in 1832-33 and of Madison Hall in 1853-54 increased the student dormitory facilities, but the enrollment figures do not show a proportionate increase. The median enrollment for the period is 101; the average, 96. In the period before 1860 the highest enrollment recorded was 158 in 1836; the lowest, 38 in 1838. It should be noted here that the high enrollment in a year of University turmoil probably represents a cumulative total of a rapidly changing student enrollment. Only one man was graduated in the fatal year of 1837, and only 8 in the next year. In the thirty years prior to 1860, students graduated from the University numbered only 370. The largest graduating class on record was the class of 1859 with 26 members. The average for the period was 12.[2]

On April 15, 1831, the trustees, who three days earlier had inaugurated the first president of their University, passed a resolution that the University should be opened for students on Monday, April 18, and that notices to that effect should be placed in the newspapers.[3] The next day they set up the regulations which should govern admissions. Students under fourteen years of age were not to be admitted. Each applicant was to be examined by the faculty to be sure that he had an acquaintance with English grammar, a knowledge of arithmetic and geography, an ability to commence the reading of the higher Greek and Latin authors, and testimonials of good character.[4]

When Professors Tutwiler and Saltonstall, on the appointed opening day, greeted the fifty-two young men who were to be the University's first students, even these admission requirements proved too stiff to apply. These enrolled in the following order: Silas L. Gunn, Marion Banks, John Colgin, John G. Davenport, William W. King, Robert B. McMullen, Alexander B. Meek, John L. Tindall, Jr., James A. Johnson, William C. Ashe, Leroy P. Allen, Burwell Boykin, John D. Bracey, Jacob H. Baker, Charles W. Caldwell, Thomas L. Carson, John W. Caldwell, James L. Childress, William A. Cochran, John Thomas Crabb, John T. Fortson, John H. Gindrat, James M. Williams, George W. Gaines, William C. Henry, Charles L. Williams, James D. Webb, John J. Hill, Numa Hubert, William B. Inge, Samuel W. Inge, John W. Lewis, Daniel P. Marr, John G. Maull, James W. McQueen, Joseph R. N. Owen, Algernon S. Pinkston, Alexis D. Pope, Green M. Wood, Whitmill W. Rives, Joseph S. Reese, Sardine G. Stone, Boling Smith, William R. Smith, Adison J. Saffold, George D. Shortridge, William C. Sorsby, Thomas Sorsby, James Meriwether, Benjamin A. Mosely, Stephen W. Harris, and Nathaniel Moore.

During the years before 1865 the Black Belt was the great feeder for the University. Greene county furnished 135 students, of whom 40 graduated. Montgomery county came next with 140 students, of whom only 23 graduated. Dallas county furnished 131 students, 20 of whom received their diplomas. Jefferson county, which today is a great reservoir for student material, furnished only 27 students for the 34 years prior to 1865.

When it came to towns, Tuscaloosa, because of its proximity, led with 404 matriculates, of whom 87 graduated. Montgomery came next with 125, of whom 20 graduated. Eutaw furnished 60, of whom 18 graduated. Selma was represented by 50 matriculates, 9 of whom graduated. Fifty-nine entered from Marion and 15 graduated. Only 13 students entered from Elyton which was to become Birmingham afterwards. Of this number 3 graduated. Cahaba, the old capital of the state, had 19 students registered, of whom not a single one received a sheepskin. Fosters, only a small community in Tuscaloosa county, was represented by 26 students, of whom 8 graduated.

Tutwiler and Saltonstall gladly took advantage of the permission given them by the trustees to relax the rules for the first year if they "deemed it desirable" to do so.[5] Young William R. Smith, who remembered that opening day as a time for "merely handing in the name and age, and setting a little while on the examination benches," made this observation also about the admission processes:

. . . it is believed that no applicant was rejected on the ground of deficiency in learning—all were admitted; and as a consequence of this it may be said that for the first year of the college the institution assumed rather the cast of an "old field school" than of a university, for there were many boys not sufficiently advanced to enter regularly even the freshman class.[6]

Before the year was over, Professor Saltonstall, at least, was probably regretting that he had not interpreted somewhat more rigidly the requirement of "a knowledge of mathematics." To the complaints which so soon began to be heard about his teaching, he could only offer the defense that the preparation of the students in his subject was shockingly poor.

Most of the splendor of the University's opening had gone into the inauguration of the president. Whatever color and life there was in the opening day itself must have been created by the youth and energy of the boys starting on a pioneer adventure of University life. They and the others who came straggling along to swell the ranks of the first University enrollment to 95 found that reaching the University was no small matter in itself. The state of Alabama was only a dozen years old. Tuscaloosa was a new town, practically on the frontier. There were no railroads. Some of the students came by stagecoach; some, bringing personal slaves with them, drove up in stately family carriages; some came by oxcart; and others, no doubt, came on foot over dusty roads. Sons of the richer planters had pockets well lined with money for tuition and college expenses. Less fortunate boys brought hams and other farm produce to offset their college bills.

The sole senior in the first college group, John A. Nooe, was not there on opening day. He came some weeks later with President Woods, from Transylvania College, in Kentucky, and he was the first alumnus of the University. After graduation in 1832, Mr. Nooe lived in Memphis, Tennessee, where he was a respected and able lawyer.

Of the first comers, the examining professors gave junior rank to the following: A. B. Meek, Marion Banks, George D. Shortridge, William W. King, John G. Davenport, and R. B. McMullen. Frank Bouchelle joined this class a few days later. Twelve were assigned to the sophomore class. The others were a miscellaneous group, most of them probably not even able to qualify as freshmen. The University could not afford to be too particular about its academic standards then—or for many years to come.

THE OLD UNIVERSITY 119

Enrollment continued to be a simple process all through the early years. A prospective student simply came to Tuscaloosa and presented himself for examination to some member of the faculty. If he passed that examination, he paid his tuition and started going to classes. The faculty met on the first day of each college session to examine new students and assign them to their classes, but that did not mean that new students, coming along any time during the term, were not welcome. Oran Roberts, who entered the University in 1833, has left a record of his enrollment experiences, a record probably typical for many students in his day. He wrote,

On the 13th day of February, 1833, my brother and I called upon the President, Alva Woods, and told him of our business. He, after talking with us about my preparation, and where I lived, appointed a time and place for me to meet the Faculty to be examined for admission. It was the same afternoon in Prof. Tutwiler's residence. The Faculty was then composed of President Alva Woods, Prof. Tutwiler, Prof. Hudson, Prof. Bonfils, Prof. Wallace, and Prof. Hilliard.

I stood a good examination in Latin and Greek, and Arithmetic, but was deficient in every other requirement. The consultation about me was then and there had in my presence. My proficiency in Latin and Greek strongly inclined them in my favor, when Professor Hilliard volunteered to give me private lessons in Geography, and in some other studies, which resulted in my being accepted as a student in the Freshman Class, which was then more than three months advanced with their studies. . . .

Upon being told that I would be admitted (I well understood that I was on probation) I was directed to pay my tuition ($40) to some one, to whom I do not recollect, as there was no red-tape then, as everything was managed by the professors. That being done I was directed to a room on the second floor of the Washington Dormitory. . . . At that time there were four in each set of three rooms all four using the front room where the fire place was, and two of them occupying each one of the connected bed-rooms. . . .[7]

Also characteristic of other adolescent University boys were young Roberts' feelings the next day when his brother "came by the University in the hack on his way home" to say good-bye to the fledgling student:

I went off to myself north of the buildings and had a good cry. I had never been five days separated from my relatives before, and felt alone in a new world.[8]

With the resilience of youth, Roberts found that the period of homesickness soon passed as he "found company in books." Perhaps his "faithful Negro (Prince)", who came along with him and was later hired out in the town to help pay college expenses,[9] helped the boy over the first lonely days.

Oran Roberts' memory about the amount of his tuition may not have been wholly accurate. At the time of the opening of the University, the trustees had ruled "that in order to extend the advantages of education as widely as possible, the charges for tuition, room rent, use of library and use of public rooms shall be only thirty dollars, for the collegiate year."[10] In December, 1837, leaving the tuition fee at $30, the trustees provided that each student must, in addition, make a deposit of $15 to pay for repairs, servant hire, fuel, and other contingencies. Unexpended amounts were to be refunded at the end of each session, but students who overdrew their deposit were to make up the difference at that time.[11] This contingent deposit was reduced to $10 in 1842.[12] A year later it was upped again to $12, and at the same time tuition was raised to $40.[13] Provision for advance payment of fees semiannually was made in 1837;[14] this provision was repeated in the regulations of 1842.[15] In 1848 was instituted a more elaborate installment plan whereby students paid $18 at the beginning of each of the first two terms and $16 at the beginning of the third term. Twelve dollars of this amount was for the contingent fund.[16] Except in cases of prolonged illness or death no refunds were allowed. Students who lived off campus got a slight reduction on contingent fund deposits in 1843; they were not required to pay the amount that related to fuel.[17]

Special arrangements were made for students who wanted to take the same course a second time for "greater proficiency." After August, 1847, they could do so without paying tuition fees.[18] An ordinance passed in 1845 required law students to pay $25 semiannually, and it was noted that they were not to be given any reduction on this fee if they were late in entering.[19]

Concern for the student unable to pay even these modest fees was early voiced by the board of trustees, and provision for scholarships was made at the very beginning of the University. Concern for the self-respect of the recipients of these scholarships seems to have been less marked. They are consistently referred to as "charity students."

The board of trustees as early as 1830 sent to the legislature a

THE OLD UNIVERSITY 121

resolution which would have allowed free tuition to a number of students from each county of the state. The number from each county was to be determined in proportion to the white population.[20] There is no record that the resolution in this form was given legislative approval, but in 1831 the trustees acted as though limited approval, at least, had been forthcoming. They ruled that tuition fees, in whole or in part, might be remitted at the discretion of the board to "assist poor and promising youths," and they invited the judge and commissioners of each county to propose for free admission one young man of promising talents from that county.[21] Governor John Gayle spoke well of this arrangement in his 1833 message to the General Assembly. He said that every county in the state should take advantage of it.[22] In 1842 the trustees were apparently being overwhelmed for requests for these scholarships; they ruled that it was "inexpedient" to admit on this basis more than one student from each county.[23]

Special scholarships for theological students were set up in 1853. Upon presentation of certificates from any ecclesiastical body or church or from a well-accredited minister of the gospel, candidates for the Christian ministry were to have all fees waived. This privilege was open to students of all denominations. But the faculty was authorized, at the same time, to withhold the exemption if the deportment of the student did not measure up to his designation.[24]

Whether the early students came as paying or charity members of the University, the life they lived on the campus followed the same pattern. It was a life governed by the ringing of bells, a life restricted (or such was the faculty intention) by the campus fences and by a multitude of rules. Rebellious and unruly sons of pioneers kicked over the traces with healthy frequency, but they also spent time and earnest energy in getting the education for which they came.

The students assigned to Washington and Jefferson halls had to provide most of the comforts which go to make a dormitory room. Only the fireplace grates and the window shades were furnished. The students provided their own furniture and their own bedding. The results were far from luxurious. A letter from Crenshaw Hall to his father in 1858 must have had many duplicates among the son-to-father letters of the period:

I want to get out of it as soon as I can.. It seems like I am destined to be unfortunate here, for I have twice been sick, the two worst times I could have been . . . . We have . . . no mosquitoes to disturb our peaceful slumbers, but rats we have an amount of. They play at a great rate.[25]

The University proctor was responsible for keeping the bare rooms reasonably warm and sufficiently lighted, but the students paid for the luxuries of fuel and light in their contingent fees. Early regulations defined the proctor's duties in considerable detail:

The Proctor shall provide, at the most convenient seasons, and on the best terms, suitable supplies of coal or fire-wood, and candles or lamp-oil, and shall deliver to the students at their rooms, what they may want of these articles, from time to time, provided the amount thereof shall not exceed the amount deposited by each student with the Treasurer for that purpose. He shall keep particular accounts with each student. He shall charge all articles furnished them at what they cost, with an additional sum to compensate for unavoidable waste or loss. If the amount deposited be not sufficient to allow each student necessary supplies, the Proctor may demand more; if that amount be more than sufficient, the excess shall be refunded.[26]

By 1850 these laws had been revised and simplified:

The Proctor or other officer acting in his place, shall also provide, at most convenient season, and on best terms, suitable supplies of coal.[27]

Actual building of the fires, as well as the cleaning of the rooms, was, of course, the job of the University servants. They also swept the private rooms, made the beds, brushed the students' shoes "on Wednesday and Saturdays afternoons," and performed other menial tasks.[28]

Assignment of rooms was made by lot. On the second day of each session, one hour before evening prayers, the drawing for rooms took place under faculty supervision. Before a student could draw, he had to produce evidence that he had paid his fees and got his uniform.[29] If students enrolled the previous session wished to keep the room they had lived in then, they were not required to take part in the drawing.[30] Four students might draw together for a suite of rooms. When the building of Franklin Hall afforded more dormitory space, two students instead of four were permitted to occupy an "apartment."[31]

THE OLD UNIVERSITY 123

Students drew for their rooms in the same order in which their names were listed in the *Catalogue*—regular seniors first, then "irregular" seniors, regular juniors, "irregular" juniors, and so on down to the irregular students taking freshman work. The selection for those last was apt to be somewhat limited. The system must have worked with reasonable success, however, for it was in use as late as 1857. Bolling Hall, a senior that year, wrote to his mother:

When I came here my old-room-mates desired me to take in Crenshaw [his brother] to room with us so that we are very well fixed in that respect. We also in drawing for rooms were lucky enough to get first choice and have (we think) the best room in college. Our room is in the Franklin Building.[32]

All students except those who lived with their families or relatives in Tuscaloosa were required to live in the University dormitories. And they were required to spend in the bare and Spartan quarters provided for them most of the twenty-four hours of every day. The authorities of the University liked to know that the students under their charge were safe from any mischief.

Early rules stated that unless students were in class they must be in their rooms from nine in the morning until one in the afternoon, from two until evening prayers and from seven until bedtime.

During these hours every student will be expected and required to be in his own room quietly pursuing his studies, and every known violation of this regulation will subject the offender to censure, according to the nature of the case, provided, however, students may be allowed to play on musical instruments between the hours of 9 & 10 in the evening.[33]

In 1838 a slight change was made in the hours, but no relaxation in their stringency, when the study hours were decreed to be "from the first bell in the morning until the bell that denotes the close of the recitation hour; from 9 o'clock A.M. until 12M; and from 2 o'clock P.M. until evening prayers; and from 7 o'clock until 9 o'clock at night."[34] In the 1850 laws the evening prayer hour was defined as five o'clock, but no other change was made.[35] In both sets of regulations appears this stern admonition:

During study hours, the students shall be in their rooms quietly attending to business, except when required to go to recitation, or to attend an officer. Business in the city, or any thing short of an absolute necessity, cannot be accepted as an excuse for absence during these hours. It is a misdemeanor to be absent from one's own tenement or entry, without permission, after 9 o'clock at night.[36]

Even the students who lived with their families off the campus came under this ruling to a great extent. In 1842 the faculty rescinded its permissions for these students to go home and study after their day's recitations:

In regard to certain members of the senior class, residing in town, who have offered an excuse for absence from their rooms during the study hour of the day, that not having recitations following those hours, they preferred studying at home, it was resolved that hereafter they shall be required to be in their rooms in study hours as usual.[37]

Rules like these were made to be broken. The struggle of the faculty to enforce them is one of the stormiest chapters in the history of the University of Alabama before 1860. Under the earliest regulations the faculty were made to serve as policemen on patrol duty in the dormitories. Said the board of trustees on April 16, 1831.

And be it further ordained that the officers of the College may visit the rooms of Students at any hour of the day or night whenever they have reason to suspect a violation of the laws, and in all cases of improper noise or disturbance it shall be their duty to visit the rooms. Should any student refuse to admit an officer to his room it shall be punished as a misdemeanor.[38]

Perhaps, in the minds of the trustees, the faculty did not sufficiently avail themselves of this permission to visit student rooms. The "may" was changed to "shall" before the college was a year old. The new regulation read,

And be it further ordained that each member of the Faculty shall have under his special care a certain number of Students rooms, which he shall visit every night in the week and also every day in the week with the exception of the day time of Saturday and Sunday—Should any officer be necessarily prevented from attending to this duty, he shall procure some other member of the Faculty to visit the rooms in his place—and should any Student not be found in place, and not give within a sufficient time a satisfactory reason of his absence he shall be reported to the Faculty, and by them to the parent or guardian—and should such absences continue to occur during the hours of study, it shall be the duty of the Faculty after having tried admonition in vain to dismiss such Student from the institution.[39]

So the faculty dutifully divided up among themselves the dormitories that had to be patrolled. The president took the south entry of Jefferson Hall, and Mr. Hilliard took the north entry. Mr. Jones and Mr. Wallis covered Washington Hall's two entries. Mr. Tutwiler and Mr. Saltonstall were made responsible for the student rooms in their own houses.[40]

The dual problem of making the students obey the rules and making the faculty enforce them continued all through this period. In the disturbed year of 1836, the faculty, meeting on March 1, solemnly admonished each other about their laxity in the visitation of rooms and as solemnly promised to mend their ways.

Whereas it is reported that the Faculty are negligent, or at least irregular in visiting the students rooms, & as it is important for the Faculty to know certainly whether there be any neglect, & the extent of it, therefore, Resolved, That the members of the Faculty pledge themselves to one another that they will invariably execute the law in relation to the visiting of rooms especially at night and that they will faithfully report, at their weekly meeting, every instance in which they have neglected this duty.[41]

The laws of 1838 returned to the faculty the privilege of deciding the number of visitations necessary to maintain law and order.[42] By this time, however, the professors seem to have entered into the spirit of the injunction and proceeded with the visitations at an even brisker rate than before. In 1842 they were visiting rooms five times a week at irregular hours.[43] In 1843 regular visitations were set at three and four times a week. In 1845 there was another reduction. Each visiting officer was to "make three and four visits a week, on alternate weeks." It was further provided at this time that each faculty member assigned to such duty

shall report the times of his visits, and any failures on his part. Also that the visiting officers shall take measure to detect and suppress all noises in study hours, or at any improper times and that in case of any serious disturbance, all shall unite in putting it down.[44]

The occasions when such united effort was needed to put down serious disturbances were rather frequent. They culminated in the famous Doby Rebellion, in which were involved not only the recalcitrant students and the united faculty but also the press and the public for miles around.

While the professors went about their police duties, they were expected to be on the lookout for unseemly disorder and especially for any damage to University property. There were very specific rules about the student rooms and their care. For instance, the type and location of the essential coal box was determined by faculty edict:

That a box of a certain pattern be placed in each room for the purpose of holding coal, and that the deposit of each student be one dollar and that these boxes be paid for out of the deposit money. That no student shall be permitted to have coal upon the floor of his room.[45]

The very starkness of the rooms should have limited the amount of damage done, but students then were as resourceful as present-day students. The original general ruling of the trustees that "students shall always be liable to be assessed for damages done to rooms or to any University property"[46] was quickly proved inadequate. In January, 1832, the trustees spelled out the responsibility for protecting University property and ruled,

that each member of the Faculty shall, as often as once in two months, report to the Faculty all the damages done in the rooms under his care, and the Faculty shall cause the necessary repairs to be made, and the amount to be charged to the authors when known, otherwise to the occupants of the rooms.[47]

In 1833 when these damages ran up to an amount equalling the $2.00 per student which had been deposited with the librarian, the whole amount was turned over to the treasurer. Three years later the faculty discovered to its consternation that enterprising students had cut a new door through the brick partition between two rooms. They ordered the occupants of the rooms to have the wall repaired within four weeks or pay $2.00 to the treasurer.[48]

Rules about damages were clarified and simplified in 1838. The new laws provided that damage to student rooms was to be made good by the occupants; damage to the entry, by the occupants of the entry; and damages to the public rooms, by assessment of the whole student body unless the actual culprit was known. Once a year the proctor was to see that repairs were made and assessments collected. A student refusing to pay his share of such assessment was kept out of class until he did.[49] The laws of 1850 left these provisions unchanged, but added damage to gates, fences, and other University property to the list of items for which the students might be held responsible.[50]

Watchfulness over the health of the boys bending over their books in the bare dormitories was not a part of the monitoring duties of the faculty. Nowhere was provision made for infirmary care for students who became ill. They simply stayed in their rooms, taking care of themselves as best they could or being cared for by their roommates. Letters home often voiced the homesick complaints of boys whose chills, sore throats, headaches, and pains in the joints were not getting the solicitude they had received back home. Bolling and Crenshaw Hall both had their turn on the sick list. When Bolling had roseola in the winter of 1857, he managed to keep on going to classes, a fact which must have subjected all his schoolmates to the danger of contagion. He did, however, tell his father that he was so very sick that he found it hard to keep up with his studying.[51] Crenshaw was even sicker the following fall; he was confined to his room with high fever and chills. His brother took care of him and finally called a doctor, who prescribed calomel, rhubarb, and clover powders all at the same time. It was hard, nurse Bolling said, to get proper food for Crenshaw while he was ill. But Mr. Fowler, who ran a boardinghouse, kindly agreed to bring meals to his room. Bolling said that several other students were also ill with sore throats and chills. Some of them thought that the trouble had been caused by the dust stirred up by the stagecoach in which they returned to school.[52]

Although dormitory facilities for the students were reasonably adequate, boarding arrangements were less satisfactory. The faculty struggled with that problem all through the period under discussion. The University owned and operated the steward's hall (now the Gorgas Home),[53] and until 1847 many of the students ate their meals there. Those who did not wish to avail themselves of this arrangement had to get faculty approval to eat in boardinghouses in town. Such approval had to be obtained also if they wanted to change boarding places.[54] Members of the faculty sometimes boarded students to eke out their meager salaries. Professor Bonfils was one of these. In 1833 the trustees told him that he had their permission to "board any number of Students of his class not exceeding six in number on such terms as he can agree upon."[55] Three years later a group of "responsible" persons were permitted to lease University-owned land near the campus with the understanding that they would take student boarders in the homes they built there.[56]

Apparently the University officials failed to anticipate the disorder which might result when students, penned in their study and classrooms most of the day, came over to the steward's hall for food and a brief respite from discipline. They made no rules about conduct in the dining hall in their original ordinances. They early discovered their oversight and in 1834 enjoined the steward to "report promptly to the Faculty every instance of improper conduct in the dining hall."[57] Such reports must have been frequent and futile. Oran Roberts gave a vivid picture of the old dining hall and the battles of biscuits which made life miserable for the waiters and for Judge Brown, the steward. He wrote,

The old gentleman was occasionally very much annoyed by the boys at their meals. If the biscuits were too hard, one of them might be seen flying toward a negro-waiter, which would be succeeded by a whole volley of them from all parts of the hall, until every waiter had fled through the back-door. Whereupon the old gentleman would appear at the back-door, usually bare-headed, and say 'Boys, O Boys, don't don't.' Every boy at the table would have his head down eating with all his might. Of course nobody did it, to all appearances then. They were too busy.[58]

The laws of 1839 attempted to deal with this situation. Faculty monitoring of the dining hall was added to faculty monitoring of rooms.

The Students must be careful to abstain from all rude, boisterous, violent, and indecorous behaviour in the Hall, and about the premises of the Steward, and must behave towards the Steward and each other with the decorum observed in well-bred society. They must take their seats in such order and manner as may be prescribed by the Faculty, two of whom in rotation may always take their meals with the students, without being charged for board; and if any student by his ungentlemanly or improper conduct, should become objectionable to the Steward, on complaint being made, the Faculty may, at their discretion, require the offender to seek accommodations elsewhere, and may inflict such further censure or punishment, as the case may seem to require.[59]

Words, even stern ones, failed to solve the problem. The steward's hall continued to be a focus for student disorders which ranged from mischievous explosions of youthful high spirits to episodes of

THE OLD UNIVERSITY   129

violence. In 1847 the trustees decided to discontinue the student dining room.[60] Boarding problems were even more difficult after that. Crenshaw Hall, arriving on campus in the fall of 1857 with the sore throat and chills brought on by the dust of the journey, thought he might have to go back home because he was unable to "speak for" a boarding place before all available dining rooms were filled. Mr. Fowler, who brought meals to his sick-room also reserved a place for him in his dining room, although he already had twice as many boarders as he had intended to take. Crenshaw had to pay $15 a month for his board although it was "nothing extra in the eating line," but it was better than nothing.[61]

Eleven students petitioned the faculty in 1853 for permission to build a cabin in the woods near the University and to use it as a boardinghouse. The permission was given "with the express understanding that the Faculty can and will abolish [the dining room] immediately in case of any disorder and that it cannot be used for any purpose except an eating house."[62] As a further safeguard the faculty chose one of its members to select the site and three others to draw up plans for the cabin.[63]

Off-campus boardinghouses had their part in building up student tradition of the years passed. George Little remembered and wrote of several operating in the fifties:

Old Benjamin Whitfield, who was a great Baptist, boarded about forty of the students. One morning breakfast was late and the boys started to raise the windows to get in the dining room. Mrs. Whitfield appeared with her broom and drove them away. Mr. Baird, a stonecutter, who had a famous strawberry patch, also kept boarders. David Johnston had a boarding house out at the Baker place. He charged only ten dollars a month for meals and most of the poorer students ate with him.[64]

The $10 to $15 a month rate for student board seems to have been typical. During the period when the steward's hall was in operation, charges for eating there kept within this range except at the very beginning, when the trustees set them at $80 for the school year, and during the years 1837 to 1839, when they briefly raised them to $18 a month. In 1834 the rate was $10 a month; in 1839, $15; in 1842, $10; and in 1843, $12.[65] The original intent of the trustees had been that all students except those living at home would board with the steward,[66] but this provision was changed even before the University opened.[67] Board bills were payable half-yearly in advance, but the steward was required to refund unused amounts if a student moved away from the hall.[68]

With tuition never more than $40 during this period, with the contingent fees ranging around $10 to $15, with laundry taken care of by persons in the neighborhood at $1.50 a month, and with board bills running under $15 a month for most students a young man with $200 in his pocket could, in those days, cover the essentials of his college life.

That college life was a routine governed by bells—bells which rang for recitations, for rising and retiring, for mealtime and study time. Their imperious demands gave a sense of rush and hurry to the University day which one student described as follows in a letter home:

> I have not much time to spare for writing this letter, but I must take time to let you know how I am getting on. Hard times still press on us and we hardly have time to turn around or sit down to studying good before the bell rings the signal for us all to rush to the recitation room. Whilst I was writing the first 4 lines, or rather just as I finished them, the bell rang the signal for us to rush to the Rotunda to boom forth like the great Demosthenes.[69]

Ringing the bells was at first the responsibility of the college servants, but in 1837 Richard Furman, a student, was appointed bell-ringer at a salary of $16 a month. He took up his quarters in a room on the second floor of the Laboratory, where the bell-rope hanging through the ceiling was convenient to his hand. He was required to report to the faculty any student attempt to keep him from ringing the bell at the stated hours. He was under faculty direction and supervision.[70]

At sunrise or even earlier the rising bell rang, followed soon by the bell for morning prayers. Morning recitations were signalled by bells at nine, eleven, and twelve; afternoon classes, by bells at two, four, and five; the evening study period, by bells at seven and nine-thirty. That was the typical schedule, but the faculty spent considerable time in their meetings tinkering with it and adjusting it to seasonal needs or to their own whims. During the short days of fall and winter, they sometimes allowed the bell-ringer to be a little late with the morning bells and a little early with those in the after-

THE OLD UNIVERSITY
131

noon. In the spring bells rang somewhat later, giving extra time for recreation. When the evening study bell was changed from seven o'clock to seven-thirty in May, 1849, however, the faculty took careful note that "the half hour thus subtracted from study at night is intended to be compensated for by study in the morning."[71] In May, 1853, the faculty ordered "that the morning bell for prayers be rung ten minutes later than the usual time; that is 10 minutes after sun-rise, for the present."[72] This must have seemed late to those who, the previous spring, had heard the prayer-bell faithfully sounded at five-thirty.[73]

The bell-ringer was only human. He slipped occasionally. In 1848 he was reprimanded for laxity when his superiors of the faculty scolded him for irregularity in ringing the morning bell and for omitting entirely the bell at nine o'clock at night.[74]

Morning prayers were the first order of business of the University day. They consisted of "reading the Scriptures and prayer by the officiating officer, to which may be added psalmody, at the discretion of the President."[75] They were held before the first class and, of course, before breakfast. Sleepy teachers and sleepy students alike were required to attend "punctually" and to file in and out of the services "in a respectful manner."[76] At first chapel was held in the East Room over the Laboratory; later it was moved to the Rotunda.[77] Students took their places in the same order as they were listed in the *Catalogue*.

From chapel the students, still breakfastless, went to the first recitation of the day. This arrangement brought protests from both faculty and students. In 1832 Professor Bonfils was granted his request to have all his classes after breakfast,[78] but a group of students who petitioned the faculty twenty years later for omission of before-breakfast recitations on Mondays did not fare as well. The faculty twice postponed action on this matter and then decided that it was "inexpedient at present to grant the petition."[79] Students who lived in town were allowed to miss chapel if they had no before-breakfast classes.[80] Off-campus students with early classes were out of luck, especially in the later years; they often had to scurry out to campus for their first class, rush home for breakfast, and scurry back again for a second class only an hour later.[81]

The campus day got into full swing after breakfast. The University laws required that there be three recitations or lectures daily for each class or student. The second morning class came just before noon. An afternoon class was scheduled just before evening prayers.[82] The rest of the day and all of the evening was given to carefully restricted study hours when students were expected to be in their rooms.

Evening prayers closed the day in the early years. In 1846, however, the faculty were authorized to use their discretion about the advisability of continuing them.[83] By 1850 the practice had apparently disappeared, for there is no mention of evening prayers in the laws enacted that year.

Sundays, like other days, began with morning prayers. From time to time the faculty tried to provide other religious services befitting the day. In 1832 a regular Sunday afternoon service was instituted, but it was sparsely attended.[84] Students were required to attend two prayer services on Sundays as well as on week days; they did not flock in large numbers to this third voluntary service. Some members of the faculty suggested combining evening prayers with the preaching service. President Woods, however, vetoed that idea. And a year later a committee was appointed to try once more to make arrangements for preaching on Sunday afternoon in the chapel, so that the students might be given "religious as well as literary privileges."[85]

By 1839 the faculty had been "authorized to institute regular Christian worship on the Sabbath-day, in the Rotunda," and they were also authorized to make attendance compulsory. Said the University laws on this service, "when it shall be so instituted, every student shall attend the same, and report himself with becoming solemnity."[86] Apparently the faculty, interpreting this ruling as permissive rather than mandatory, sometimes provided the services and sometimes did not. Bolling Hall wrote his mother in 1857 about one of the spasmodic efforts to set up special Sunday services:

The faculty now have a law that there shall be preaching in the chapel every Sunday; which I suppose they will keep up until Pratt gets tired of it, when they will be very apt to repeal.[87]

With or without the preaching, Sunday on the University campus was observed with all the strictness of the times. The laws about it were clear and stern:

THE OLD UNIVERSITY 133

The students shall refrain from their usual exercises and diversions on the Sabbath, and whatever is unbecoming the retirement and sacredness of the day; and they shall not play on any musical instrument, on that day, except for the purpose of sacred psalmody.[88]

On Sunday or any other day any levity or disorder at a religious service was subject to prompt and severe punishment, which might even lead to dismissal if the president saw fit to inflict that penalty:

The faculty may adopt any mode most convenient to them for ascertaining tardiness or absence from prayers, or other religious exercises. Any want of reverence at such, may be punished according to the nature and aggravation of the offense; and if any student shall persevere in habitual inattention or delinquency, he may be dismissed by the President, without public censure; unless the case should appear to require formal dealings.[89]

The students who obeyed the bells in the earliest days of the University did so in a uniform prescribed by the faculty and consisting of

A frock coat of dark blue colth, single-breasted, with standing collar, ornamented on each side with a gilt star, a single row of gilt buttons in front, and six buttons on the back. A black stock and a black hat with narrow brim. . . .[90]

Authorization for this uniform had been given by the trustees when the University first opened. They had suggested that the faculty, in choosing it, have "due regard to economy and to the seasons of the year."[91] Since Professors Tutwiler, Hilliard, and Hudson were commissioned in 1833 to select the uniform,[92] the one decided upon was probably their recommendation. Students were required to get their uniforms before they could draw for rooms,[93] and they were required to wear them on campus or within five miles of campus.[94]

The students did not submit willingly to this regulation which made them carry the student label when they went in to town. By 1842 disregard of the uniform rules had become so general that the faculty attempted to set penalties which would stop it. A first offense brought ten demerits; a second, an additional ten demerits and an "admonition."[95] Those offending for a third time risked suspension unless they could produce as good an alibi as did one senior that year. When the faculty summoned him to show cause why he should not be suspended, he pled that someone had taken his hat from his room and that he had no other. That seemed reasonable to the faculty; they let him off with a warning not to do it again.[96] They were more inclined to be lenient in this case because the weather that July was sweltering and it seemed cruel to force students to take examinations in full uniform. They not only excused the single culprit but decreed that students need not appear in uniform for examinations.[97]

By the following year the faculty were willing to give up trying to make students wear uniforms off campus, but they postponed action until they could talk the matter over with the resident trustee.[98] The decision of the trustees to abolish the uniform requirement was made on December 8, 1843.[99] Permission was still given the faculty to prescribe a uniform again if they felt it expedient to do so, and the same provision was written into the laws of 1850.[100] It is interesting to note that the students, having fought against the uniform successfully, turned about-face in the years that followed and in 1847 petitioned for its re-adoption. Their petition was turned down on grounds of economy and expediency.[101] Uniforms did not again appear on the University of Alabama campus until they appeared as marks of military training in the 1860's.

Academic gowns were required as student dress for public occasions in the early years of the University, but after a year of heated faculty debate they, too, were dispensed with in 1843.[102]

The lighter side of college life was limited both by the circumstances of the times and by the rigorous discipline which the faculty tried to impose. Even the delivery of letters, which loom so large in importance on any college campus, was a problem. The University proctor was the official postman. He was charged with the responsibility of getting campus mail to the post office and also of getting the postmaster to make arrangements for the delivery of incoming mail. Although travel was difficult and resources for recreation were few, the students did manage to inject into the University regime a good deal of amusement, which ranged from harmless and healthy play to rowdiness and even worse.

Hazing had its place in student life then as it always has. Oran Roberts remembered a particularly effective bit of initiation given to him when he entered college. It featured ghostly moans and sheeted figures. But the freshman seems to have had the better of his initiators:

THE OLD UNIVERSITY 135

As usual then, as it is in some schools still, every youth that enters must have his metal tried. I was peculiarly a fit person for this trial, being a raw-boy from an obscure mountain region, although I was not then aware of any such custom. Another thing that pointed me out for the trial was, that I had entered school the last of the class. A month or two after I had entered, I was engaged to a late hour in the night in hard study over my lessons, being alone in my sleeping-room, when becoming tired I blew out the light and went to bed. Before going to sleep the door to my room was opened, and by the dim light furnished by the windows and door I discovered two tall objects, covered with white sheets, passing into the room, mumbling out some sort of utterances, calling on me. As quick as thought, for I really never knew what I thought, I bounded out of bed, rushed at the front figure, caught hold of him, and, with all my might, wrenched him around me, and threw him on the floor, and at once made a grab at the other figure as he retreated, and got from him the bosom of his ruffle shirt, and by that time a voice called out: 'Roberts, Oh, Roberts, Are you going to kill a body, you have thrown me down with my head against the corner of your trunk.' They were Alexander B. Meek and John Tindall. I said not a word but sullenly got back into bed, as may be supposed very mad.[103]

Physical exercise was certainly considered unessential by the planners of the University. They took a dim view of what they called "sport" and made their definition of that term very broad when they handed out demerits. Two students were criticized in the faculty minutes of May 10, 1852, for engaging in "sport during study hours."[104] They had been playing Mumble the Peg, which may have been a fad at the time, for five other students were before the faculty for the same crime the next day.[105] Later two students met faculty disapproval for the "sport" of racing a rabbit on the campus.[106] George Little puzzled his head to account for two demerits handed out to him. He asked Dr. Manly about them. "Sport on the campus," was the reply. "You were playing during study hours in front of Franklin Hall." Little then remembered that he had indeed swung one day on the limb of a cedar tree.[107]

The hour between supper and evening study and sometimes Saturday afternoon hours were less cramped. Students had some semblance of freedom then. Oran Roberts remembered the evening walks with his friends:

It was customary then for the students, after an early supper, to take a walk upon the campus and out on the road South of it, when often they would engage in running, jumping, and wrestling to test their physical powers.[108]

George Little said that when he was in college the favorite sport was town ball. This game was much like baseball, but it was played with a soft rubber ball and the runner was out if hit by the ball while running between bases. Hunting, fishing, and swimming in the Warrior River near the University shoals on Saturday afternoons were also among Little's memories. On Friday evenings, he recalled, boys went calling on the girls. Suppers in student rooms, with food supplied by Negroes, who brought peanuts, candy, tobacco, and sometimes cooked 'possum, may have been either licit or clandestine forms of student recreation.[109]

Occasionally members of the faculty unbent a little to join in the student fun or to help make it. When George Little was a freshman, he was startled one day by having Professor Tuomey invite him to go riding with him in his two-horse barouche. He accepted with alacrity, however; and so began a lifelong friendship.[110] Bolling Hall, out walking with a friend, met Dr. Garland, starting off for a hunting trip with his gun and two pointers. Garland sent Bolling back for his other gun, and the two went hunting together. Garland got two or three pheasants that trip; Bolling, one.[111]

Dr. Garland seems to have been more willing than most of his colleagues to fraternize with the students. Probably it was at Dr. Garland's suggestion that Rose Garland gave in May, 1858, a party to which all juniors and seniors were invited. Strawberries and ice cream were in abundance, and even the fact that the disgruntled freshmen and sophomores tried to break up the party did not keep those present from having a wonderful time.[112] Garland figured also in Crenshaw Hall's story of the parties and picnics arranged that same spring for students who stayed in school during the spring vacation. The festivities culminated with a concert in the Rotunda, at which Dr. Garland was in high spirits. Bolling Hall's letter to his mother sounds almost as though he did not quite approve of the undignified behavior of the learned man. He wrote,

I suppose it was very good (the concert), but I couldn't exactly appreciate it. Dr. Garland, I suppose, appreciated it highly as he amused the boys greatly by his antic motions. It is said that good music always runs him half crazy and judging from that I suppose we must have had good music the other night.[113]

The faculty made a valiant effort to keep the students from

seeking amusement in the town of Tuscaloosa. In 1833 they solemnly passed the following resolution:

Whereas it is commonly reported that some students of this institution are in the habit of resorting to town, particularly at night, to the great detriment not only of their own character but of the reputation of this University, & of the honor of the whole state, therefore,

Resolved, unanimously, that no student be excused to go to town at night during session terms except by the faculty, & then only for the most weighty and urgent reasons; & that application be made to the whole Faculty for such permissions, with the reasons of them be kept by the Secretary.[114]

It was a losing battle, however, and by 1836 the faculty were ready to make at least a strategic retreat. They "respectfully suggested to the Trustees to consider the propriety of revising the regulations concerning the intercourse of students with the town of Tuscaloosa."[115] When the new laws were issued in 1838, no prohibition against going to town was included. Of course, the students were required to be in their rooms during study hours and after nine o'clock in the evening unless they had special permission. Though their time for visits to town was limited, there was no longer a ban against such visits.[116]

They went on various missions and expeditions and errands, some praiseworthy and some of such character as to build up the traditional town-gown feud to major proportions. Oran Roberts was much impressed with the cultural opportunities offered to a mountain boy in the city of Tuscaloosa. He wrote of visits to the legislature, the courts, and the churches. He said,

It fastened on me the lasting impression, that the University of the state ought to be located at the Capitol of the state, in order to give its students, coming from all parts of the country, the greatest advantages obtainable in attending such an institution. And I fortunately lived to be able to actively participate in producing that result in the state of my adoption.[117]

The state of Roberts' "adoption" was Texas. He moved there in 1841, was elected governor in 1878, and probably had a part in deciding that the University of Texas, organized in 1883, should be located in the capital city of the state.

Crenshaw Hall wrote of the frequent concerts "down town,"

though he seemed rather bored with the whole idea of musical entertainment:

There is a concert down town tonight of some description, but they come so often and I never attend them that I hardly notice.[118]

Other students may have been more eager to take advantage of this particular kind of entertainment. Dancing may have interested even more students.

Here again faculty ideas and student determination conflicted. Dancing, at least at public parties, was nominally forbidden. When the University opened, the trustees had ruled that any student attending such a party should be solemnly admonished and if he did not mend his ways be suspended or dismissed from the University.[119] Yet, within two years, if the memory of Oran Roberts is to be trusted, students were going to a dancing school in a downtown hotel and also attending the public dancing parties which the instructor gave every week or two. The boys liked these parties because there they met ladies from the nearby Methodist school. Opportunities to meet girls were not very plentiful.[120]

For years the students went on dancing and the faculty went on "admonishing" them, but with appreciable leniency. In 1846 fifteen students were permitted to go to a dancing school in Tuscaloosa two nights a week, with the stipulation that they return to their rooms by eight o'clock. Two other students were given similar permission to take lessons on a "musical instrument."[121] The following year ten students got an even better concession; they could stay out for their dancing school until half past eight.[122] The rules were somewhat more severe by 1849. Students going to dancing school that year could go only on Friday evening and were required to be in their rooms studying by eight o'clock.[123]

Dancing parties at the University were another matter. Permission to hold them was never forthcoming. In 1846 managers of a student party at Steward's Hall asked consent to allow dancing at the party. The faculty side-stepped by replying that they did not undertake to regulate such matters.[124] In 1854 when students asked permission to use the Rotunda for a commencement dance, the request was refused.[125] Yet somehow, in spite of obstacles, the students managed to get in a considerable amount of dancing. George Little remembered that at this time it was "the favorite amusement of the students," though he added that the only dances he ever went to were the "stag dances in the dormitory." He noted also that

The students were entertained a great deal in the homes in Tuscaloosa and there was a regular ball room in the hotel on the Roseneau corner.[126]

Students were present at one party to which they were probably not invited. On Saturday night, July 3, 1847, James S. Banks, Thomas Gray, Tom Herndon, and H. S. King attended a party given by Negroes at the house of S. H. Ross. They caused no damage, and after frolicking about a short time they departed.[127]

Regulations concerning the school year, the time of Commencement, the length of vacations, and the disposition of holidays were subject to frequent change during the period. As originally outlined in the ordinances, the college year was to "embrace but one Session beginning and ending with the civil year, but there shall be a regular vacation extending from the fourth Wednesday of July to the first Wednesday of October."[128] At first there was a short Christmas holiday, but both faculty and trustees thought that it was unnecessary luxury. The faculty resolved in the summer of 1834 that, in their opinion, it should be abolished:

Whereas it is found that the Christmass holidays, usually granted for recreation, exert a very unfavorable influence on the regular, studious, and moral habits of the students,

Therefore, Resolved, That, in the opinion of the Faculty, it would be desirable to dispense with the Christmass holidays, and instead of them, to add one week to the end of our present vacation, which is shorter than is usual in Colleges.[129]

Almost simultaneously the trustees decreed that the faculty should not be authorized to extend the Christmas vacation to a period longer than two days, exclusive of Sunday.[130]

The question of Christmas vacation was adjusted the next year when Commencement was shifted from its original mid-summer position to December. A vacation after Commencement Day, the Wednesday preceding December 25th, seemed appropriate. The change was made at the recommendation of the faculty, who told the trustees that they believed that "the prosperity of the University would be promoted by having the public exercises of commencement or graduation day, take place during the Session of the Legislature." They added the thought that this would tend to awaken in our public men, a greater interest in the welfare of the State institution; and also to encite the Students to higher Literary efforts to meet public expectation.[131]

With Commencement as the pivot, several vacation plans were tried. First, two more or less equal vacations were decided upon: One to start on Commencement Day and extend to the first Monday in February; the other to start on July 1 and continue to the first Monday in August.[132] Apparently that did not work well, for the next year the Christmas vacation was shortened to two weeks, and the summer vacation extended from July 15 to September 15.[153] In 1837 the trustees ruled that the college year should begin and end with the Wednesday after the second Monday in December.[134]

Three vacations were provided in 1840. The first was the three-week period right after Commencement; the second, three more weeks following the first Monday in April; the third, the long vacation from the last of July to the first of September. That made it possible to divide the college year into two terms, the first running from Commencement to the end of July—approximately six months of class work; the second, beginning the first of September and including the three and one-half months remaining before Commencement.[135]

The next year, however, the trustees again favored the biannual vacation system. The first vacation comprised three weeks in April; the second, from the end of July to the first of October. The first college session then ran from December to the end of July, and the second, from the first of October to Commencement.[136]

Not until the Alabama legislature moved from Tuscaloosa to Montgomery, the new state capital, did some kind of stability begin to appear in the college year of the University. In December, 1846, the trustees moved Commencement back to the traditional summer time; they need no longer think of the publicity value of the occasion for the legislators. The second Monday in August was first designated,[137] but the following year[138] it was changed to mid-July. The spring vacation, which was lengthened to a whole month in 1846, was, in 1847, curtailed once more. The faculty were authorized to grant a vacation in the spring if they thought best, but they were limited to one week for this holiday.

Vacations, especially short ones, presented serious problems for the students, for travel was difficult and the schedules of stagecoaches inconvenient and inadequate. The planning of the Christmas holiday trip which Bolling Hall and his brother made in 1857 to their home near Montgomery is typical of the planning necessary for many boys if they wanted to spend holidays at home. At first, Bolling did not think he could make it at all:

The College exercises would terminate on Wednesday the 23d day of December. If this is so I do not see that we can go home then; for I should dislike to spend so much money only to stay home two or three days.[139]

That was in October. By December, with Christmas coming closer, anticipation became almost a reality. The boys found that they could leave on Tuesday evening, December 22 and arrive home by Thursday. The details which Bolling gave to his mother in a letter at this time present a vivid picture of travel difficulties the students encountered.

The stage leaves here on Tuesday evening, and will arrive at Randolph the next morning, fifty-seven miles from here. You spoke of sending the carriage. I think that if father wishes us to come home, that he had better let us go as far as Randolph by stage, and there meet the carriage, for you see by so doing we would travel all night the first night, and on Wednesday morning we would be fifty-seven miles on our way home, instead of being here. . . . In this way we could easily get home Thursday and the carriage would only stay out two nights. . . . Crenshaw and myself, though anxious to see you all, are willing to forego this pleasure if father thinks it will cost too much for such a short time. . . . One of the greatest reasons for wanting the carriage to meet me at Randolph is that I do not believe it would be possible to drive it in safety over the road between here and there where the mud is nearly always up to hubs of the wheels even when traveling up hill.[140]

The trip by stage must have proved satisfactory. When the boys came back from their spring vacation the following April, they were allowed to take this conveyance all the way. They had, Crenshaw reported, arrived in Tuscaloosa at six in the morning, having spent the first night at the home of the Walkers and then driving all the second night except for a two-hour rest at Randolph.[141]

The faculty showed surprising helpfulness with problems such as those which confronted the two Halls. They were even willing at times to adjust examinations to meet stage schedules. "Those students who are dependent on the Pickens stage for conveyance to their homes" they ruled, just before the spring vacation of 1848, "may be examined and discharged by Wednesday night."[142] Spring examinations in 1851 were set so that those who had to go to their homes by boat would be through in time to take the evening boat on Thursday, though the rest of the students were not dismissed until the next morning.[143] Travel by boat, incidentally, was rather common, though it was always complicated and roundabout. In 1858 about ten students went home to Montgomery together in this way. They had to take the boat at Tuscaloosa, go down the Warrior and Tombigbee rivers to Mobile Bay, and then up the Alabama River to Montgomery.[144] Fortunately, they were bound for a summer vacation; they could not otherwise have made the trip in time.

The single holidays which dot the present school calendar were not observed by the early University of Alabama. The exception to this rule was the Fourth of July, and that was an exception only because the students fought a running battle with their elders who had earlier made the following decree:

the only celebration of the 4th of July proper to be had at this literary Institution is a literary celebration . . . under our authority no permission will hereafter be granted for any other.[145]

The reason for this decision was, the faculty noted, "'recent observation." The Independence Day celebration of 1833 had apparently started in a sufficiently decorous manner but had ended with such student rowdiness as to make the professors cringe. Sara Haynesworth Gayle, who lived in Tuscaloosa at the time, wrote about it in her diary:

The 4th of July has gone by in the stillest dullest way imaginable—no demonstration of public sentiment more than the ceremonies of the college. Young Meek delivered an address said to be admirable, suitable to the day, and Burwell Boykin, one on Temperance, very good also. A dinner followed where some of the students signalized themselves by their drunken extravagances. They are much mistaken as to the proper mode of securing to themselves fame. At present they limit themselves to the shaving of horses tails, and tying balls dipped in brimstone, and set on fire, to those of the professors' harmless dogs and philosophic geese.[146]

The professors had the welfare of their "harmless dogs and philosophic geese" firmly in their minds when, two years later, the

THE OLD UNIVERSITY
143

students asked permission to have another Fourth of July dinner. The faculty refused, and quoted their action of the summer of 1833. They also reminded the students that they could not "without permission entertain company or make any public entertainment;"[147] to do so would break the college rules.

A combined meeting of the two literary societies, with reading of the Declaration of Independence by a member of Philomathic and an oration by a member of Erosophic, was the feature of the "Sixty-Fifth Anniversary of American Independence" celebrated on July 3, 1841.[148] So full of decorum were subsequent celebrations—some relaxation of classes in 1843 and 1845,[149] and a truly literary celebration in 1858, with orations by Professor Benagh and John McLaughlin[150]—that it is almost a relief to read of the escapade of July 4, 1849, when some of the students celebrated by going swimming, and, in doing so, shocked the ladies of the town. As the faculty got the story,

> several young men, said to be students, whilst bathing in the river opposite the University, had exposed themselves in a position where they could be observed by some ladies who were upon the bank.[151]

The faculty deferred consideration of this "outrage" for a time; but when investigation showed no evidence of "intentional impropriety," they finally forgot all about it.

Extra holidays were usually special and unpredictable events. In 1844 classes were dismissed for a day because of the death of William J. Crawford of the sophomore class.[152] The inauguration of a governor in 1845 rated a half-holiday so that students could go to the ceremony.[153] News of the death of Lafayette in 1834 was the occasion for a service in one of the churches, at which Judge Goldthwaite of the state Supreme Court delivered the eulogy. Students were encouraged to attend these ceremonies.[154] On February 24, 1853, forenoon classes were omitted for the annual Concert of Prayer for Colleges in Tuscaloosa.[155] But Thanksgiving Day came and went with little notice except that afternoon classes were customarily omitted.[156]

Washington's Birthday received little recognition except in 1842, when committees from the two literary societies waited upon the faculty with a request for permission to miss classes on that day and attend a celebration in town, where Washington's *Farewell Address* was to be read and an oration given. The faculty granted the permission but not without indulging in a pompous little gesture of disapproval of celebrations in the city. They said,

The Faculty are not desirous to recognize celebrations in the city, unless of such a nature as to claim general participation. Yet on such a day and as the students have but rarely solicited the remission of exercises, the Faculty yield to their request so far as to suspend business in college, from nine until two o'clock on Tuesday, the 22nd inst.[157]

The faculty and the trustees were never quite successful in forcing the young students of the new University of Alabama into the mold of decorum and studiousness they considered appropriate. Yet the tradition of lawlessness which grew up concerning the early days of the institution is only one part of the truth. The typical student of those days lived plainly, enjoyed simple pleasures, worked hard, and, in the classrooms and societies of the campus got the rudiments of an education which was a credit to the day—or to any day.

CHAPTER VII

Curriculum and Classroom

SHAPING a course of study to meet the needs of the youth of Alabama was the knottiest problem the builders of the University had to face. Basic to the problem was the inadequacy of secondary education in the state at the time. Many boys came to the University with a smattering of schooling. Others came from homes where they had been carefully tutored. Some were as mature as today's college students; some were youngsters just entering their teens. The University could not afford to turn away students whom it needed for its very existence. It could not afford to set its standards so low that its reputation among other institutions of learning suffered.

The dilemma was a real one. Professor Saltonstall soon found the same students he blithely admitted with perfunctory examination in April of 1831 so ill prepared as to be unteachable; they brought to an end the brief teaching career of a promising professor. President Manly, less than a decade later, stated the problem in his first report to the trustees. He said,

> Having been compelled, among the applicants examined, to reject the larger portion as being utterly unprepared to take the classes to which they aspired, the Faculty are led to conclude that there can not, in all probability, be a large increase in our numbers for some years to come. Low as the University has placed its requirements for admission, the schools in the country seem to be unprepared to meet them. Before the University can have numbers, the schools must be elevated.
>
> A question will arise: Shall the University come down to the schools or must the schools be brought up to the University? We are persuaded that your enlightened body cannot hesitate a moment for the answer. Nor can you be at a loss to predict what is to be the effect on the schools, of insisting on some definite standard of admission to the University. The Faculty are well satisfied that the principles on which they have been permitted to commence their administration are the only principles

on which success, if practicable at all, can be secured, and all they can reasonably ask is that the board will patiently await the result of an experiment on these principles.[1]

President Manly's effort to raise admission standards may be reflected in the enrollment figures of his administration. And the sharp drop from 101 in 1837 to 38 in 1838 may have been due as much to the selective policies of the new president as to the upheaval the University had just gone through. Not until 1844 did the enrollment climb above the 100 mark. Yet the problem of inadequate preparation continued to plague President Manly through the whole term of his office.

The University catalogues of the 1840's stressed in polite and positive terms the need for well-prepared students:

It will have been perceived that the arrangements of this University presuppose in the student some degree of intellectual maturity, some adequate power of self government, some decidedly formed feeling of social and moral responsibility. Until the mind and character of a young man be thus formed, he is too young, whatever be his years, to enter a public Institution, with advantage to himself, safety to the Institution, or honor to his friends.[2]

These were fine, forceful words worthy, even today, of a place in any college catalogue. But they may not have been definite enough to register with the parents of prospective students the exact meaning the faculty intended them to convey. By 1850 the catalogue statement was much more explicit:

The Faculty would state that applicants are found, almost universally deficient in elementary branches; in arithmetic, the grammars, and very frequently, also, in geography. It will not be inappropriate to urge upon parents and teachers, the importance of a thorough and faithful preparation, according to the foregoing statement of requisitions.[3]

About this same time President Manly wrote to James Tait's father a letter which indicates the extent to which some of the students were found "deficient." He wrote,

My dear Sir:
James was not able to enter college free from conditions. He was found deficient on the following studies; and was conditioned accordingly;— viz—Decimal Fractions and cube root, in Arithmetic; Ancient and Modern Geography; Aeneid of Virgil, 3rd to 6th books inclusive; and 4 ora-

tions of Cicero against Catiline.—He has fulfilled Modern Geography. The others remain to be fulfilled.—
Had there been a good school in Tuskaloosa, I would have thought it better to put him there for a year; but then there was none. We concluded to try him, in college. No doubt he suffers disadvantages from his defective preparation; yet, with energy and perseverance, he may work his way through; and attain a respectable grade.—[4]

Just before President Manly resigned he made one more attempt to raise the entrance standards. It was decided that after October, 1854, no student would be admitted to any class in the University "to whom it would be necessary to assign a single condition in any subject essential to the college course."[5] Enrollment dropped from 121 in 1853-54 to 112 in 1854-55. That fact could have been the reason why the rule was dropped after a single year.

The admission requirements which the trustees had adopted when the University opened were elaborated but not essentially changed in 1837. The requirement of "an acquaintance with English Grammar, Arithmetic, and Geography," remained unchanged—and unclarified; so did the requirement that the candidate for admission present "testimonials of good character." But the "ability to commence the reading of the higher Greek and Latin authors" was now spelled out in considerable detail. It meant exactly this:

. . . an ability to translate four books at least of Caesar's Gallic War, Sallust's Catilene and Jugurtha, and Eclogues Georgics and four Aeneids of Virgil, and two books at least of Xenophon's Anabasis or Cyropoedia.[6]

It is interesting to see this definiteness in the field of the classics juxtaposed to the vagueness of other requirements. There was apparently no difference in opinion among the faculty or the trustees of the early University of Alabama regarding the foundation stone of liberal education. Work in modern languages and English literature might be put into the curriculum one year and dropped the next. Sciences seemed to develop according to the enthusiasms of the men who taught them rather than along any carefully worked-out plan. But the classics were clearly the backbone of the course. Governor Collier, addressing the citizens of Alabama on the state of their University in 1850, ran no risk of contradiction from citizens, from the faculty of the University, or even from the students of that day when he said,

Classical education lies at the foundation of intellectual eminence. Some have become scholars and chaste writers and speakers, without an acquaintance with the ancient classics, but they are so few as to constitute rather exceptions to a general rule. Not only our own but other polite modern languages are to so great an extent derived from the Greek or the Latin, that few can justly pretend to be critical scholars who are not acquainted with the two latter.[7]

Typical of the curriculum in the first decade of the University is that of 1837. The faculty noted in their minutes in February not only the subjects studied but also the arrangement of the class schedule. Freshmen, sophomores, and juniors presented themselves, hungry and sleepy, at six o'clock in the morning for their first classes. The seniors were allowed to breakfast before they came to their first class at nine o'clock. The freshman schedule called for mathematics at six, ancient languages at eleven, and "Mr. Smith" (which apparently meant grammar and modern geography) at four in the afternoon. The sophomores recited in ancient languages every morning at six and in mathematics every afternoon at four, but their middle-of-the-day classes varied. They had modern languages at noon on Monday and Friday, chemistry at noon on Wednesday, and moral philosophy at eleven on Tuesday and Thursday. Juniors had modern language at six on Monday, Wednesday, and Friday mornings, and moral philosophy at the same early hour on Tuesday, Thursday, and Saturday. Their ancient language classes came daily at four in the afternoon, and their mathematics classes daily at noon. Seniors started the day with modern language at nine. Chemistry came at eleven for them, and their day ended with moral philosophy at four in the afternoon.[8]

The faculty did not believe in overloading the student schedule. As the standard load consisted of three classes a day no student was allowed to take more "unless for very weighty and special reasons the Faculty shall so determine."[9] The rule against having more than one recitation a day in any one department was dictated by expediency. There were apparently not enough courses on a given level so that a student doubling up in this way would not be taking simultaneously courses designed to follow each other.[10] At the time of the sample schedule outlined above, each student was required to take one modern language—it was one of the periods when a modern language faculty member was available. He might choose this himself or leave the choice to the faculty.[11] Another curious requirement of that same year was the ban placed by the trustees on making the Constitution of the United States any "part or portion of the course of studies prescribed."[12]

After the change in administration the new laws of the University in 1839 set forth a new curriculum statement. It covered much the same ground as the earlier ones, but was somewhat more explicit in regard to the courses offered and subjects covered.

The Freshman class shall pursue the study of the Latin and Greek Languages, and of Algebra and Geometry.

The Sophomore Class shall pursue the study of the Latin and Greek Languages; Trigonometry, Plane and Spherical; Surveying, Mensuration; Navigation; Analytical Geometry; and differential and integral Calculus; and Logic.

The Junior Class shall continue the study of the Learned Languages, and shall also study Natural Philosophy, Rhetoric, Chemistry, and Ancient and Modern History.

The Senior Class shall study Moral and Intellectual Philosophy, Astronomy, and its applications, Principles of Taste and Criticism, Civil Engineering, Evidences of Christianity, Vegetable and Animal Physiology, Mineralogy, and Geology, and shall continue the study of the Learned Languages.[13]

Arrival on the campus of a new president and a battery of versatile and enthusiastic professors is undoubtedly reflected in this statement. Barnard, Stafford, and Manly were full of new ideas, and Brumby, also, was ready to branch out in new directions. From the curriculum modern languages were missing; the post vacated by Professor Bonfils had not been filled. English literature, too, was missing. Professor Pratt, who was to teach it, had died.

By 1850 French had come back for the sophomores and juniors. Other courses, also, had been added: for freshmen, Greek literature and elocution; for juniors, calculus and botany; for sophomores, history; and for the seniors, an impressive array, including optics, agricultural chemistry, zoology, political economy, conchology, meteorology, Spanish, and a continuation of the classics.[14]

Professor Barnard's free-ranging enthusiasms, together with the arrival in 1846 of the brilliant Irishman, Michael Tuomey, account for some of the innovations. They, with Professor Mallet, who came a few years later, gave to the early curriculum of the University of Alabama a somewhat unusual degree of emphasis on the sciences.

Apparently some of the classes listed in the curriculula of the early days failed to materialize. Although civil engineering was listed as a senior course in the laws of 1839, the board of trustees asked in 1843 that civil engineering instruction be added. It should be given, they said, in such a manner as to be most conducive to the interests of the University.[15]

On the other hand, there were courses of semi-official status which did not appear in the catalogue listings. At least three gentlemen—Mr. N. Foster, in 1842; Mr. McHelm, in 1845; and Mr. W. J. L. Millar, in 1851—were given permission to teach penmanship to University students provided these classes did not interfere with University hours and study.[16] For the third of these penmen, President Manly wrote a truly handsome testimonial:

The Subscriber hereby states that Mr. W. J. L. Millar has superintended the exercises, *in writing,* of a voluntary class, formed in the University of Alabama;—that the improvement of all, who have taken the requisite pains, has been satisfactory to themselves, and gratifying to those who have witnessed it; and that the deportment & social position of Mr. Millar, so far as they have come to the Knowledge of the Subscriber have been such as to give weight to his instructions, & to render him agreeable to respectable persons in Tuskaloosa.

Two members of my own family, a daughter & Son, have received private lessons from Mr. Millar;—their improvement, in the space of a fortnight, has been marked & decided; and they now, obviously, need nothing more than frequent & steady practice, on the principles they have received from him, to fix, in each appropriately, the attainment of an elegant handwriting.[17]

Toward the end of his administration President Manly, still struggling with the problem of maintaining and improving educational standards in a college whose students too often lacked the foundations for the kind of higher education he wanted them to have, felt that some progress was being made. In his report to the trustees in 1851, he noted the improvement in study habits that he had observed:

It is apparent that more study has been accomplished this year than heretofore in a similar period. The classes occupy higher grades, especially in some departments of study, than ever before. In mathematics they are severally as high as it is proposed to take them. And the Faculty are convinced that this advance has not been made at the expense of accuracy and thoroughness. Dispositions and habits more student-like

THE OLD UNIVERSITY   151

have certainly been engendered. Among the means which have contributed to these pleasing results the chief is the examination of every student on every subject partly by writing as well as orally. The effects of this change have been so elevating and salutary that the Faculty desire to improve and extend the system.[18]

His satisfaction with progress was not so great, however, as to keep him from searching for yet better educational plans. In the summer of 1852 he was commissioned by the trustees to visit the leading universities and colleges in the country and report to the board his findings about the methods of study being used there. In the American educational scene at the time, according to Clark's *History of Education in Alabama,* two systems were being vigorously debated. The first, on which the curriculum of the University of Alabama had hitherto been largely based, was the "time-honored curriculum requiring four years for the attainment of the degree of bachelor of arts, with a division of the students into classes, called, respectively, senior, junior, sophomore, and freshman." The second was "the eclectic system, first introduced by Mr. Jefferson into the University of Virginia, which abolished the class system and permitted all students, under certain necessary restrictions, to pursue the studies of their choice."[19]

President Manly must have been impressed with the experiments going on in Virginia. Or perhaps the trustees of the University of Alabama were independently impressed, as such boards have often been before and since, with the argument that students should be allowed to take "useful" courses and omit those which would be of no practical value in later life. In July of 1854, the trustees took action to "require" the faculty to convert to the "Virginia system":

The President of the Board and the Trustees now present are unanimously in favor of modifying the present system of instruction in the University of Alabama, and respectfully request the Faculty of the University to report to an adjourned meeting of the Board, on Monday, the 25th of September next, the plans and details for the initiation and continuance of a system conforming, as near as our circumstances will allow, to the arrangements of the University of Virginia.[20]

The order was signed by Messrs John A. Winston, Wm. H. Forney, John N. Malone, Ed. Baptist, and H. W. Collier.

Professors Barnard, Pratt, and Benagh were appointed to draw up the requested report. It was really the work of the redoubtable

Barnard, and it was a blistering defense of the old college curriculum. When the report was ready, Professor Pratt concurred with Barnard in signing it, but Benagh, who was afraid of offending his father-in-law, the governor, dissented. Barnard objected to the idea that "the University should give instruction to all who chose to demand it, and that it should give them whatever instruction they chose to demand, so that the students should study what they chose, all that they chose, and nothing but what they chose." To him the theory was arrant nonsense. It was "emphatically not the system of the University of Virginia." If it were adopted, the college curriculum would be "practically abolished, and educational chaos would be brought into existence, and a small army of instructors would be required to meet a varied and capricious demand for the instruction of an indefinite number of classes."[21] How much of this sentiment he put into his report which, according to Fulton brought him "prominently forward as a progressive student of the whole subject of education" is not clear. But he probably did not mince words in the two hundred pages he laid before the trustees.

But the board was not to be turned aside from its purpose of emulating the University of Virginia. They adopted, to take effect with the college year of 1854-55, some changes which they felt would move the University toward the "Virginia system." It was in that year that Professor Barnard resigned from the faculty to go to the University of Mississippi. Was there, perhaps, a connection between these two events?

Up to the time of the adoption of the new system the University of Alabama had had rigid rules regarding the admission of "special" students as all students were expected to take the full prescribed course. Some exceptions, however, had been made for those who, because of "indigence, advanced age, or infirm health," seemed to deserve special concessions. But all such students were required to give "special assurance . . . of the moral character and habits of the applicant.[22]

But with the new plan students might choose under certain limitations as many or as few courses as they liked from the offerings of the University. The concessions now were made for the students

THE OLD UNIVERSITY 153

who wished to take everything the University offered; they might enter at fourteen years of age instead of fifteen. The regulations governing the election of courses as they were first formulated were these:

Each Student under the age of twenty-one years, desiring to select a particular or special course of study, shall be required to produce from his parent or guardian, if he has one, a written declaration of his special object in coming to the University; and the Faculty shall then prescribe him for the course of study which will accomplish his object in the shortest time, and in the best manner—consistent with other regulations of the University.

A Student shall not enter on any study he may select until he has passed such an examination as will satisfy the Faculty that, by proper application, he may prosecute it successfully. . . .

The officers, severally, in each department, shall examine all applicants for admission, according to the course of study for which each may apply; and shall report their qualification, to the Faculty, who must decide on the position and course of exercises which each must take, according to the fitness exhibited for the successful prosecution of the course of study he may select.

No Student shall be admitted into the University until he is, at least, fifteen years of age; but one who intends to pursue all the studies taught in the University, may begin the course at fourteen years of age.[23]

Accordingly, these rules were slightly modified in the *Catalogue* of 1857-1858. These changes evidence the fact that the students may have changed their minds frequently about their electives and may also have worked out for themselves too many tractable schedules. The new rules read,

Students who desire to pursue a select course of study may be allowed to do so, provided:
1st. That their choice be made at the beginning of the collegiate year;
2nd, That they take up studies sufficient to occupy their time;
3rd, That they shall have made all the acquisitions necessary to a successful study of the branches they wish to prosecute.
4th, That they present the written consent of their parents or guardians to such a course.[24]

The actual course offerings, however, did not change greatly with the change in system. The listings in 1855-1856 are typical:[25]

CURRICULUM AND CLASSROOM

COURSE OF INSTRUCTION

FIRST YEAR

Term I
Harkness' Second Latin Book
Lessons on Reasoning (Whately)
Algebra (Bourbon) through quadratics
Latin Exercises

Term II
Xenophon's Anasbasis
Satires and Epistles of Horace
Algebra (completed)
Geometry (Legendre) 5 books
Elocution
Latin Exercises

Term III
Herodotus
Odes and Epodes of Horace
Mythology (Eschenburg's Manual of Classical Literature)
Geometry (completed)
Latin Exercises.

SECOND YEAR

Term I
Isocrates and Demosthenes (Graeca Majora)
Horace's Art of Poetry
Plane Trigonometry Legendre)
Surveying (Legendre)
Mensuration (Legendre)
Fasquelle's French Course, Exercises and Regular Verbs
Rhetoric, Day
Latin Exercises

Term II
Homer's Iliad, begun
Juvenal
Grecian and Roman Antiquities (Eschengurg's Manual)
Analytical Geometry Loomis
Rhetoric, Day
Fasquelle, continued Calculus, Differential (Loomis)
Latin Exercises

Term III
Homer's Iliad, continued
Cicero de Senectute
Calculus, Integral (Loomis)
Fasquelle's exercise and gram. Synopsis finished.
Latin exercises

Arnold's Latin Prose Composition, throughout the year.
Loomis' Logarithmic Tables, for reference, throughout the year.

THIRD YEAR

Term I
Cicero de Amicitia
Greek
Chemistry, including Electricity and Magnetism (Lectures)
Statics (Smith De Fiva's Classic Fr. Reader)
History of English Literature (Spaulding)
Latin Composition

Term II
Cicero de Amicitia, continued
Greek
Inorganic Chemistry finished
Dynamics, Hydrostatics & Hydrodynamics (Smith)
Translations into French (Rasselas)
Latin Composition

Term III
Tacitus de Moribus Germaniae
Greek
Organic Chemistry (Lecturers)
Zoology (Agassiz and Gould)
Acoustics (Lectures)
Human Physiology (Lectures)
Optics (Jackson)
Rasselas continued for and exercises for conversation

Arnold's Latin Prose Composition, throughout the year.

THE OLD UNIVERSITY

FOURTH YEAR

Term I	Term II	Term III
Mental Science (Wayland)	Political Economy (Wayland)	Greek and Latin
Moral Science (Wayland)	Greek and Latin	Agricultural Chemistry (Lectures)
Greek and Latin	Botany (Lectures)	Meterology (Lectures)
Spherical Trigonometry	Conchology and Palaeontology (Lectures)	Civil Engineering Lectures
Astronomy	Geology (Lectures)	Spanish Reader Valasquez
Mineralogy (Dana and Lec.)	Astronomy, completed	
Spanish, Velasquez and T. Simonne's method	Velasquez, &c., continued	

Arnold's Latin Prose Composition, throughout the years.

* * *

Clark says that the so-called Virginia system was tried for three years, starting in 1854, and that then, since there was no "marked improvement in the morals or scholarship of the students" it was abandoned.[26] Study of the catalogues, however, does not wholly support this statement. A modified course selection system seems to have been in effect until 1859 and 1860, when a still more radical departure from the old curriculum and system was made.

Adopted for the election of courses were new rules which limited the full autonomy of student choice. The conditions under which students selected courses were as follows:

1st. That the previous attainments of a Student do warrant his entering upon the studies selected, of which the Head of a Department shall be the sole judge, as far as his own Department may be concerned.

2nd. That each Student shall enter three, at least, of the Departments, unless good cause be shown for the relaxation of this requirement.

3rd. That, if from any cause whatever, it be found upon experiment a Student has undertaken more than he can successfully accomplish, the Faculty may at their discretion require him to discontinue one or more studies for the time.[27]

All students were required to meet certain requirements in English grammar, geography, and arithmetic, no matter what their electives.

The novel feature of the plan was the elimination of the four classes. Students were no longer classified as freshmen, sophomores, juniors, and seniors. Instead they worked in "departments." The course of instruction was divided into eight of these departments: ethics, logic, Latin, Greek, modern languages, pure mathematics, natural philosophy, and chemistry. The work of each department was then divided into three "classes." Thus in Class I of the ethics department, mental and moral philosophy were studied. In Class II of the same department, the time was devoted to political economy. Ethics Class III was given to the study of constitutional law. Chemistry Class I was an "Experimental Course on Heat; Electricity"; Class II worked in mineralogy and geology; and Class III in applied chemistry. The work of Class II in any department could not be undertaken before Class I had been mastered, nor could the work of Class III be taken before Class I and Class II. The program for each class was designed to cover a year's time.

After one year of this plan, President Garland said that he thought that it had resulted in lowered scholarship. It had had, however, some excellent by-products:

In honourable bearing and in polite intercourse with their instructors, the conduct of the students has been more commendable than it formerly was.[28]

Lest this be construed as meaning that the general conduct of the students had improved, the president added,

In morals I perceive no change for the better or worse. They have always had it in their power to indulge in vice, if they were so disposed to do; and the greater liberty of the system to which they are now subjected does not seem to have increased the tendency to indulgence.[29]

A single year, with the eight departments of instruction functioning as separate entities, was perhaps too small a sample to allow fair judgment of the possibilities of the plan. But the drastic move which turned the University into a military academy swung the academic life of the students into a more regimented pattern once more. The experiment of 1859-1860 remained just an experiment.

The trustees, as well as the legislators, from whom they had their authority, were ambitious for their University. They saw it developing professional schools as well as a worthy undergraduate department. They saw it including, in some fashion never quite clear, provision for the higher education of women. In the early

THE OLD UNIVERSITY 157

years of the University, these plans and dreams were sporadic, but there were several attempts to increase the scope of the curriculum.

The first of these was dictated by necessity. The inadequacy of preparation for college afforded by the schools of the time made it seem almost imperative that the University itself establish a preparatory department so that students arriving on campus poorly equipped with educational tools would not continue to set a low scholastic standard for the whole school. During the last two years of President Woods' administration a preparatory department functioned as a recognized part of the University.

On December 18, 1834, the faculty made the first plans for this department. They agreed that the interests of the University and of the community would be promoted by the appointment of a preparatory teacher. James Bailey, who had just been graduated from the University, seemed to have the "approved character and scholarship" needed for the position. The faculty agreed to appoint him, subject to the approval of the trustees. Professors Bonfils and Hudson were requested to draw up any regulations they thought necessary for the proposed preparatory department.[30]

Within a month the regulations were ready and approved. The teacher of the preparatory school was, under these rules, to devote six hours a day—four in the morning and two in the afternoon—to teaching those students, and only those, who might be placed under his care by the faculty. He was to report to the faculty at least once a month about the state of the school, the number of classes, and the progress and proficiency of the students. Classes were to be held in the recitation room between the professors' houses. No student under twelve years was to be admitted without special permission from the faculty. Students who did not live on campus, and who, therefore, did not have to pay for fuel, service, or rooms, were to pay $30 for the college year for tuition.[31]

Mr. Bailey started with seven students, culled from the regular freshman class. He was to eliminate their deficiency in their preparation in Latin. For another six, his assignment was preparatory work in Greek.[32] In April of the same year there were nine regular preparatory students.[33]

By August the faculty were apparently so well pleased with the progress of the preparatory school that they directed that for the new college session a notice of the preparatory school be included in the announcement in the Tuscaloosa papers. To the school was added a new faculty member, John M. Smith, also of the class of 1834. The faculty willingly assured parents that they could "safely rely on the services of this gentleman." He would "exercise a constant and parental care over his pupils." To make it possible for non-residents of Tuscaloosa to avail themselves of this new service, Professor Bonfils had agreed to take some preparatory students into his family and "to give special attention to their moral and intellectual development." Judge Brown had also agreed to take some as boarders.[34]

It was, perhaps, optimistic to assign two teachers to the preparatory department of a college whose regular faculty numbered only three times that number. By 1837 the faculty recognized that Mr. Smith was not needed full time in the preparatory department. Consequently he was given the assignment of hearing freshman recitations in English grammar and modern geography—with the use of globes. His colleagues were sure that he could discharge this assignment "without interfering with his more appropriate responsibilities of fitting students for the freshman class." That same year, those appropriate duties put emphasis on "receiving and teaching" all the thirteen-year-olds "provided they can be prepared for the Freshman class in twelve months—and of this the Faculty shall judge."[35] The age limit for admission had, it seems, been placed at thirteen years, but there were still exceptions. Luther M. Clements, well in advance of his thirteenth birthday, was admitted "for special reasons" that year.[36]

The turmoil of 1837 took its toll of the preparatory department as it did of the senior college. When it ended, Mr. Smith was teaching freshman geometry as well as grammar and geography[37] and, in fact, was helping to hold the University together long enough for the transition between presidents Woods and Manly to be effected. Both Bailey and Smith received for their services as preparatory school teachers salaries of $1,000 a year.[38]

When the preparatory school was formally abandoned in December, 1837,[39] no further direct effort was made by the University to train its own candidates for college admission. And the problem of college preparation was still troubling educators of Alabama when Governor Collier, in 1850, made his long and earnest appeal for un-

THE OLD UNIVERSITY 159

derstanding by the citizens of the state of their institution of learning. He made a special point of the need for better teachers and better teaching in Alabama's secondary schools:

If the people of this State are sufficiently impressed with the importance of education, why is it that the large fund we have devoted to common school instruction effects so little good. . . .
If education were appreciated, attention would be paid to the selection of teachers, not only competent to teach what they profess, but to elevate the standard. The complaint that a great majority of the teachers of our preparatory schools are incompetent to prepare their students for admission to the University would be rarely heard.[40]

The University made one attempt, on paper at least, to solve one phase of this problem. If it could not successfully be its own preparatory school, it could perhaps train teachers for other schools. When in 1843 the board of trustees asked the faculty's opinion of a Normal department, the faculty reported to the board their full approval of the idea.[41] To this end plans were formulated when the board met that December. The stated purpose of the Normal school was to educate teachers for the primary and preparatory schools of Alabama. Students who entered the Normal course were to file written declarations that it was their *"bona fide* intention" to become teachers in Alabama schools. Each county was to have the privilege of sending one student tuition-free. Others might enroll for $30 a year. The course was to be regulated by the faculty. The students for Normal courses were to be kept separate from the regular student body; they were neither to live in the dormitories nor to board at the Steward's Hall.[42]

The Normal department was duly listed and described in the University *Catalogue* for 1844. Students were to follow, the prospectus stated, "substantially" the same course as that of the college, "adapted to the varying conditions and wants of individuals, together with particular instruction in the art and business of a teacher." They were encouraged to enroll for the full three-year course, but might enroll for a shorter period if they wished to do so. They might not enroll for less than one college session. The admission requirements were certainly not too exacting:

An applicant must be competently informed in the common branches of reading, writing, spelling, and elementary arithmetic he must have attained, at least, seventeen years of age, must be of good moral character, and must file his declaration in writing with the secretary of the Faculty, that he intends to teach in this state.[43]

There is no record that the Normal department drew any students that year. By 1845 all mention of it had dropped from the *Catalogue*.

The trustees were also, at this time, exploring the possibilities of adding professional schools to their University. In 1843 they had appointed a committee to study the advisability of establishing a medical school, but this committee had brought in an adverse report.[44] While the normal department was struggling to come to reality, however, the trustees had other matters to consider. They were busily and happily planning a law school. Like the normal department, this new enterprise was in due time set up by formal vote of the board and given status by a colorful description in the University *Catalogue*. Like the Normal department, it remained, apparently, neither more nor less than this ordinance and this prospectus. The students who might have given it life failed to materialize. Yet the plans as the the trustees saw them are not without interest.

The Law School, said the trustees when they met in December, 1845, should be quite distinct from the undergraduate college. University students were not to attend law lectures, and these lectures were to be given outside University premises. Law students were not eligible for dormitory or dining hall; they might, however, be given library privileges if they "subscribed" to a declaration formulated by the faculty. The Law School faculty was to consist of a single professor of law. He was to confer with the judges of the state supreme Court in planning his lectures and instruction and in choosing his textbooks. He was to sit with the faculty of the University only when matters relating to his own work were under discussion. His salary was to be whatever his students paid as fees; the funds of the University were not to be used at all in connection with the new department. It is interesting to note that in matters of discipline the University faculty were to retain their authority over law students as well as over others; they might dismiss a law student as quickly as any other student if they felt it necessary to do so.[45]

The appointment of the Honorable Benjamin F. Porter, who

THE OLD UNIVERSITY 161

must have accepted the position of professor of law at the University, was announced in the *Catalogue* for 1846. The curriculum and requirements for law-school applicants were set forth as follows:

The course of study shall embrace instruction in the most important elementary works, and be completed in two years. Illustrations and explanations, orally, will accompany every examination; and Moot Courts be frequently held, in which the investigation of principles of law, and the Practice and Pleadings of Courts, will exercise the minds of the students.

The students of Law will be entitled, under suitable regulations, to the use of the University Library; and such as will have attained the age of twenty-one years, who sustain a good moral character, and who have completed a regular course of study and passed the proper examinations, shall receive, with the sanction of the Board and Faculty, the degree of Bachelor of Law.

Such as do not complete the course, may receive, under like sanction, a Certificate, such as may be deserved.

Tickets shall be issued semi-annually, and the charge shall be, twenty-five dollars half yearly in advance. Entrance at other times than the beginning of a half-year, shall produce no abatement of the tuition fee.[46]

If a few inquisitive students had been willing to try this novel and attractive plan, the University Law School might have dated its beginning in 1846 instead of in 1872.

Three failures in their attempts to establish new schools in the University must have lessened the zeal of the trustees. In fact they turned a somewhat chilly shoulder in 1851 to Peter Hamilton of Mobile, who suggested that the University should arrange to have members of the faculty give courses of lectures during the winter or spring months in his city of Mobile. The president was instructed to reply to Mr. Hamilton in a "suitable" manner, but there is no record of what his reply actually was.[47] Nevertheless, to Mr. Peter Hamilton belongs the credit for having first introduced into University deliberations the idea of extension work.

The "female institution" which the University founders regarded as an important branch of their new college, and for which they directed that three sites should be selected,[48] did not reach even the blueprint and catalogue stage until much later. It may be that the trustees shared with Governor Collier the opinion that, on the whole, girls were doing better than boys in taking advantage of educational opportunities in the Alabama of that day. Governor Collier put it this way:

The remark is very common, as well at the North as at the South, that the education of females is quite in advance of the education of males. It is not, of course, meant that the standard in favor of the former is disproportionately high, but rather that a larger proportion of the former than the latter avail themselves of the higher standard. This state of things is to be attributed to the fact that the mind of the female is much more ductile than that of the male. . . .[49]

Whatever the reason, Professor Wallis's informal arrangements for the teaching of his daughter and Professor Mallet's adventures with the young ladies of Mrs. Stafford's School were the only experiments in coeducation fostered even unofficially in the University of Alabama prior to 1860.

In what ways and by what teaching methods the classics-centered curriculum of the early University was put into action to shape raw youngsters into educated men is not an easy question to answer.

Some of the textbooks used are indicated in the listing of the courses. And it is known that the problem of getting these books was often a source of vexation of both faculty and students. An effort was made in the early years to patronize home industry by placing textbook orders with a bookstore in Tuscaloosa. In 1849 after the faculty noted that "serious disappointment" had been "suffered" because of late deliveries on needed books they decided in the future to order books from New York. John Wily had the first chance to show that he could do better than the local dealer.[50] But after one year the order was transferred to Robert B. Collins, also of New York.[51] He may have given satisfaction, for there are no more entries on this matter in the faculty minutes.

Students bought their books and, therefore, were critical when professors decided to change texts from year to year. Lucien Owen wrote home in 1857:

I have paid out $7.50 for books and probably will have to buy two or 3 more. I have borrowed books heretofore. The books of the junior class are all different from what they were last year. Some are compelled to purchase new ones.
P.S. Please send my Comstocks Philosophy down by Jim. I will need it.[52]

THE OLD UNIVERSITY 163

It is evident also that in the scientific courses much stress was placed on "specimens" and "collections," used both as exhibits and as classroom materials. The early appointment of Mr. McMillan was based wholly on his offering of such materials. Professor Brumby, too, was an indefatigable collector. A letter by him in the *Flag of the Union* for January 27, 1841, invited "public spirited and intelligent men" to help him in gathering his new collection "in Geology, Mineralogy, Conchology, and Paleontology, consisting exclusively of the rocks, minerals, shells, and fossils of the State." He suggested that such a collection would be "an honorable and enduring memorial of the intelligence and enterprise of the people of Alabama," but he did not forget to add that it would be useful in the classroom as well:

Such a cabinet would enable the proper officer of this institution to teach the general principles of the science with increased benefit to his classes; and, what is of great importance, to complete his annual instructions with a brief course of lectures on the local geology of Alabama, illustrated by rocks and fossils from every important place.[53]

Demonstration experiments by the professors probably had a part in the science classrooms, and there is one reference to experiments carried out by the students themselves. Professor Tuomey, in one year, asked for an annual appropriaiton of $60 to cover the cost of breakage and chemicals for class experiments in agricultural chemistry.[54]

In general, however, the minds of the faculty seemed to focus more naturally on questions of student deportment than on theories of education. There was an early rule that each professor keep daily notes of the progress and relative merit of each student. He was to record everything that related to mental improvement and general conduct, and he was to report on his notes at each weekly faculty meeting.[55]

Random excerpts from the faculty ledger from 1843 to 1860 indicate that the professors worried constantly and often helplessly over non-academic aspects of classroom conduct. Here are a few of the ways in which the students enlivened the class hours: talking in recitation, prompting, throwing paper balls, disturbing declamation, playing tricks on another student, sleeping in recitation room, reading, using texts, cracking and eating pindars, eating peas, having a stick in recitation room, screaming in the entry while going to recitation, scribbling and passing notes, boxing, reading newspapers, handing bottles around and talking, knocking on bench, drawing pictures on blackboard, lying down on bench, cutting bench with knife, whistling, spitting on the floor, going to fire during recitation, laughing, disturbing class with a wasp, shooting chalk, pretending to fall from seat, whispering and gesturing in imitation of student, and taking the professor's hat out of the recitation room on a rainy morning. If this deportment appears more like high-school conduct than it does like University behavior, it should be remembered that many of the boys in the University of Alabama classrooms were of high school age.

The students, like the faculty and like students of any day and school, considered classroom routine unimportant in comparison with the picturesque incidents and the hardships they suffered in the learning process. Reminiscences and letters add much to the color of the picture of classroom life but very little to its outlines.

William Richardson remembered how students of his day outwitted a methodical professor who called students to recite in the order in which their names came in the little box of cards he kept on his desk. By sprinting from chapel to class, an enterprising student could arrive before the teacher, find his card in the pile, and place it where he wanted it. If he knew the first part of the lesson, he put his card on top of the pile. If he knew the middle part best, the card slipped into the stack about halfway down. If he was strong only on the end of the assignment, the card went to the bottom of the heap. If he knew nothing about the lesson, he pocketed his card for the day. The professor, Richardson said, gradually came to realize that the runners were getting high marks, but he was quite satisfied with the explanation that "a brisk run in the early morning always stimulated the fluids and was provocative of lively cerebration." In fact, he found this explanation "so eminently obvious and satisfactory that Prex at once begged *all* the boys to run."[56]

Roberts remembered that an ingenious device for getting around his assignments in English composition turned out to be an important part of his education:

During my Sophomore year we recited to Dr. Woods in Moral Philosophy, Rhetoric, or some other such studies and had to write an original

THE OLD UNIVERSITY 165

composition every two or three weeks upon subjects selected by ourselves, or rather by each one for himself. I wrote a few times upon some general subjects, that I thought I could give some ideas in regard to them. Very soon my fund of subjects were exhausted. I had no general information outside of my class-books, had never had access to a library before coming to the University from which I was enabled to read up on literary or other subjects. In other words I did not know what to write. My perplexity was great, still something must be done. I do not recollect where or how we got the idea, but so it was, that Coleman and I got a book apiece out of the library, (I think they were Johnson's Essays,) selected subjects from them, read the essays over carefully, so as to get the ideas, or facts contained in them, and reproduced them in our own language and style; thereby illustrating, that "necessity is the mother of invention." I then commenced regularly to get books upon history and biography out of the library and from that time on pursued a general course of reading, which gave me a capacity for original composition, by drawing from stores of information, that I had thus acquired.[57]

Richardson and Roberts may have seen their college days through the mists of memory. But there was nothing but direct and vivid experience in the letters which the two Hall boys wrote home, telling of their worries about their marks, their difficulties with professors who, then as now, appeared unfeeling and lacking in mercy. Crenshaw wrote both his mother and his father in the autumn of 1857 about his discouragement and his anxieties. Professor Pratt, who seems to have been a personal friend of the family, was the villian of the first letter:

This evening was the first chance I have had to find out what he conditioned me on. He said Logic, English and Geography. I then asked him why he conditioned me in Grammar and Geography as I thought I did very well in them. Well, he said, I did do very well but as I was applying for the Junior year, I had to stand a very close examination on them. He said if I had been applying for the Fresh. class it would have been a different thing, as he would have had me in his department and learned me all these things. I know Jack [Professor Pratt] did me injustice though he may not have done it from any dislike but merely to show his smartness and how strict he was in his department, but I would prefer his practicing on somebody else. He is the most deceitful looking man in the Faculty. I think I did very well in the other departments and was conditioned in nothing. I believe if I had known every word in the Grammar by heart, Jack would have conditioned me. . . . Well, I say so far that it has been very hard on me as I have not time to sleep half enough if I make a respectable stand. It occupies all of our time to get our lessons and then we can not get them perfectly for they are too long. I have some consolation however in the reflection that I am no worse off than the majority of my class, as they have to study day and night also. There is no student in college, Seniors and all, but who says we are entirely too hardly pushed and that we cannot stand it. Everything is raised too much.[58]

The second letter, also, complains of overwork as well as a certain indifference and lack of helpfulness on the part of his brother:

I do not have a fair chance in Mathematics Department as the most of my class do as there is none of my own class rooming with me. We do not study Mechanics from the text book as Bolling did last year, but take lectures from Prof. Benagh. He often gives Propositions that it takes us until twelve o'clock to work and write off in our notebooks. Now, when there is anything I do not understand, I have to hunt up someone to ask. Perhaps I forget some of the lectures. Bolling has no time to explain to me. He is as busy as I am. As the Standard of Seniorship is also raised, I am afraid by the time I become Senior that the Standard will be so high and the studies increased so much that I will not get along.[59]

Brother Bolling meanwhile was writing of his first introduction to logic and his complete boredom with it:

I am not doing well in my studies this term, Pratt's department disheartens me more than any other, for I find that fifteen or twenty pages of Wilson's logic is more than I can master. This is the most uninteresting subject that I have ever attempted to study. So far as I have been yet it has been altogether definitions. There are few in the class who do much better than I do. In Garland's department, although we have twice as many pages to get over, still as I can see some sense in it, I have done heretofore much better.[60]

Letters like these close the gap of a century. They might be the letters of any college boys to any parents.

Dread of the daily assignment and the daily recitation paled in comparison with the greater dread of the public examinations. They took place once a year and were in the nature of a Roman holiday. The faculty not only put the students through their paces without mercy but also demonstrated to the general public the scope and quality of the education being given at the University of Alabama.

When the University was less than a year old, the first of these public examinations was advertised in the local newspaper, with a description of the nature of the performance to which the ladies and gentlemen of the town were "respectfully invited:"

On Monday last, commenced the examination of the several Classes. This Examination is still in progress; In most cases, the American and English modes of College Examination are continued.—The oral method, usually practiced in the United States is most interesting to spectators generally. But the written examination, carried on at the same time, enables the Faculty, with more accuracy, to ascertain, graduate, and record the exact attainments of each student. In this latter examination, a list of written questions on any part of the work read, or a portion of Laitn, or of Greek is presented to each Student, who is required immediately without intercourse with anyone to write answers and translations.

Ladies and Gentlemen, generally, are respectfully invited to attend. The Examination begins each morning at 10 o'clock; and each afternoon at half past two. The following is the order:
    Monday morning—The Vergil Classes
    Monday Evening—Logic and Moral Philosophy
    Tuesday Morning—Arithmetic
    Tuesday Evening—Xenophon's Anabasis, Euripedes
    Wednesday Morning—Algebra
    Wednesday Evening—Ancient Geography and Anabasis
    Thursday Morning—Horace and Tacitus
    Thursday Evening—Geometry
    Friday Evening, at 2 o'clock—The speaking of original compositions; and an address before the Erosophic Society by Judge Shortridge[61]

Senior examinations were an especially grueling ordeal. They covered the whole college course. Those for the underclassmen covered only the school year just ending. The trustees made a point of being present in the audience when these examinations were in progress. It gave them a feeling that their University was a credit to them and to the state.

In 1833 the senior examinaitons started on Tuesday, July 9, at eight o'clock in the morning, with tests in natural philosophy and ancient languages. Wednesday morning was given to modern languages; Thursday morning, to chemistry and other natural sciences; and Friday morning, to moral and mental philosophy.[62] Examinations for the other classes were scheduled later at the close of the same term: the freshmen, on Monday; the sophomores, on Tuesday and Wednesday, the juniors, on Thursday and Friday. The complete schedule was as follows:[63]

Freshmen	Monday	8 a.m.	Jones (Ancient Languages)
		10:30 a.m.	Hilliard (English Literature)
		3 p.m.	Hudson (Mathematics)
Sophomores:	Tuesday	8 a.m.	Hilliard (English Literature)
		3 p.m.	Hudson (Mathematics)
	Wednesday	8 a.m.	Tutwiler (Ancient Languages)
		3 p.m.	Wallis (Chemistry and Natural History)
Juniors	Thursday	8 a.m.	Hudson (Mathematics)
		12 noon	Hilliard (English Literature)
		3 p.m.	Bonfils (Modern Languages)
	Friday	8 a.m.	Tutwiler (Ancient Languages)
		3 p.m.	Woods (Mental and Moral Philosophy)

Writing some years later, Oran Roberts remembered his own final examination in mathematics:

At the public examination at the close of that session, I received tacitly encouragement from Professor Hudson again, by his giving me the most difficult problem to solve before the audience. I understood the reason of it afterwards. He was not willing to give it to one who depends upon his memory in solving problems, as many of the students did, and he knew that I did not, and was willing to risk my judgment.[64]

Examinations on the important subjects of English grammar and geography were not included in the public performances which marked the close of the school term. But they were not forgotten. They had a place of their own, near the close of the year and before the finals, and every student was expected to pass them if he wished to graduate. The *Catalogue* of 1855-56 describes these examinations which were known as "The English Examination."

There will be an English Examination near the close of the College year, and previous to the Annual Examinations, which shall embrace the subjects of English Grammar and Modern Geography; and students of every grade shall be held due to this examination, who had not passed a satisfactory examination on these subjects at the period of their admission.

A student must sustain examinations on these subjects satisfactorily; in order to receive a diploma, or a certificate of proficiency in any department.

The examination of applicants for admission, in Modern Geography, will be conducted by means of a blackboard. The knowledge of the applicant, will be tested, by his ability to fill up the blanks in an outline map, drawn upon the board. Examinations in English Grammar, will be conducted entirely in writing. A thorough knowledge of the rules of Syntax is not all that will be required. The applicant will be required to correct certain sentences which shall be furnished to him, containing errors in orthography, syntax and punctuation, and he will then be expected to parse the sentence as corrected, and to give the rules for the corrections he may make.[65]

From time to time the trustees considered making tangible awards to students who excelled in scholarship. In 1843 the board decided to give prizes of "suitable" books to the best students, not to exceed three, in each class. They told the faculty to choose the books, pay for them out of the contingent fund, and inscribe them with a statement of the reason for their award. The average cost per book was set at $2.00.[66] The awards were never made. The faculty, after investgating the contingent fund the following June, voted,

in the present exhausted [state] of the Treasury, it is impossible to comply with the requisitions of the Ordinance of the Board of Trustees requiring the presentation of premiums to the most meritorious scholars.[67]

Ten years later when the matter came up again, the trustees made more elaborate plans. They voted $500 to be used as prizes,[68] and they had announcement of these prizes and details about them published in the *Catalogue* of 1853-54. The final examination premiums, for which seniors would compete on their whole college record, were to be silver and bronze medals "of a large and costly design, the dies for which are now sinking in New York." The description of these medals was intended to stimulate the desire for scholarship in every student's breast:

The medal has been selected for the distinction because of its beauty and value as a work of art, and because of the constant public testimony which it will bear, to the eminent success of the owner whilst at the University. Each medal, in additions to its appropriate design, will also bear the name of the successful student, and the grades obtained by him in each of his studies.[69]

Medals for about one-third of the senior class were to be provided.

The medals for which sophomores competed on the basis of two years of work were to have their names inscribed on "golden crosses or stars, to be worn upon the coat." About one-fourth of the class was expected to receive these medals.

No student with an average grade below 85 per cent would be

eligible for these prizes, but a student with an average less than 85 per cent might be given a special prize if he had 95 per cent in one of his subjects. There were to be special premiums for juniors in declamation and for seniors in composition.

No mention of these prizes appears in the *Catalogues* of subsequent years. Money was too scarce in the 1850's to permit much generosity on the part of the trustees, even to stimulate scholarship. From 1857 through 1860, however, the catalogues list honors and appointments made during the year. The listing includes the award of a declamation prize medal, the names of students chosen to make orations at Commencement, and the names of students with meritorious records in scholarship and deportment. In the year 1858-59 nine seniors, one junior, eight sophomores, and one freshmen made the merit list. In 1860 only nine altogether were thus honored.

In the first days of the University, requirements for the bachelor's degree were as simple as requirements for entrance. The original ordinances simply stated that

no Student shall be considered as a candidate for the first degree, unless he has honorably sustained all his examinations, and has performed every exercise which has been assigned him, nor untill he produces evidence, that all his College dues have been paid.[70]

Provision was made at the same time for advanced and honorary degrees: it was to be possible for "Bachelors of three years' standing and of good moral character" to be admitted to the "Second degree, upon seasonable application to the President, and with the assent of the Trustees." Persons who "had received a degree from other regular College or university" were to be admitted to the same rank in the University of Alabama, "with the approbation of the Faculty and Trustees." Honorary degrees were to be conferred "on account of distinguished merit."[71]

John Nooe was the first to attain the A.B. degree, in 1832, and he was followed the next year by seven students. They were as follows: Marion Banks, Francis C. D. Bouchelle, John G. Davenport, William W. King, Robert B. McMullen, Alexander B. Meek and George D. Shortridge.[72]

Nooe added another first in 1835 when he became the holder of the University's first master's degree. The citation shows the bestowal of the degree to have been simple and without the customary requirements which hedge about the master's degree in modern times:

John A. Nooe, having received three years since the degree of Bachelor of Arts, as a regular graduate of this Institution, and having since pursued, as it is believed a general course of Literary improvement, is now entitled according to College usage, to receive the second degree, or the degree of Master of Arts, and that it be recommended to the Trustees to authorize the conferring of said degree.[73]

Three of the 1833 graduates, Davenport, King, and Meek, were similarly honored in 1836.

So many students came to the old University unprepared to carry college work and so many left after a term or two that it seemed advisable, without cheapening the actual degree, to give some recognition to students who did not complete the course. In 1833 provision was made for certificates of limited graduation. These read,

We certify that A.B. has completed, in a satisfactory manner, the studies of the department of.............that while accomplishing this partial education, his obedience to the laws, his respect for his Teachers, & his general conduct, have been deemed worthy of approbation, & that he is recommended, wherever he may go, to the friends of learning and morality.[74]

Slightly less effusive was the certificate devised for those who had attended the University for one session and had behaved themselves well:

I certify that A.B. has been for the space of...months a member of this Institution: that during this short period his general conduct has been commendable; & that he is now honorably dismissed with the best wishes for his future welfare.—
          President
In addition to the above, we certify that A.B. has attended the following studies under our instruction: ...., ..., ..., that he has made for the time good proficiency in the same; & that his deportment so far as we know, has been good.[75]

Certificates of this kind were given in the presence of the faculty, not in the formal graduation ceremonies.[76]

Requirements for graduation as formulated in the laws of 1839 were more definite, though hardly more exacting from the point of view of scholarship.

Candidates for the first degree (that of Bachelor of Arts) must have been at least one year in the University and must have sustained their examinations well, all through their College course they must produce testimony that they are not delinquents at the Library; and they are liable to be examined, at their final examination, on all the College studies. If there be any deficiency in these particulars, the Faculty may withhold the degree. Before receiving his diploma, each graduate must pay a proportionate part of the cost of diplomas.

Candidates for the second Degree (Master of Arts) besides having taken the first degree, must have studied some art, science, or profession, after leaving College, and must exhibit evidence of being qualified to add something to the general weal, the sum of human happiness; they must also leave their names with the President of the University, at least two months before Commencement; they must perform such exercises as may be assigned them; and must pay the price of their diplomas. . . .

The degree of Master of Arts will not be ordinarily conferred until the third year after graduation. A resident graduate, who shall remain one year in the University, and pursue a course of study under the direction and to the satisfaction of the Faculty, and shall sustain a fair character, and perform at Commencement such exercises as may be assigned to him, may receive the second degree in one year after receiving the first.[77]

Milford F. Woodruff of the class of 1848 took advantage of the provisions in the last paragraph of these regulations. At least he tried to. After graduation he asked permission to work, as resident graduate, for his master's degree. Professors Brumby and Garland were appointed to plan a course for him, and it was agreed that if he performed his work in a satisfactory manner he would be recommended for a M.A. in 1849.[78] His course included these texts: Vattel's *Laws of Nations,* Smythe's *Lectures on History,* Hallman's *Middle Ages;* Kent's *Commentaries on American Law,* Introduction to Robertson's *Charles V,* Agassiz and Gould's *Principles of Zoology,* and Mr. Somerville's "connexion of the Physical Sciences."[79] When June, 1849 came, however, Mr. Woodruff was in Nashville, Tennessee. As he could not fulfill that part of the requirements which called for performing at Commencement "such exercises as may be assigned to him," the faculty voted to withhold his degree.[80] He finally received it in 1851.[81]

The introduction of the semi-Virginia plan made other changes necessary in the requirements for degrees in 1855-56:

Upon a student's completing, and standing an approved examination

THE OLD UNIVERSITY 173

upon all the studies in any department, he shall receive the degree of GRADUATE in that department, and a certificate bearing the seal of the University, shall be delivered to him at Commnecement in the usual mode.

Candidates for the degree of Bachelor of Arts, must spend at least one year in the University, and must sustain examinations upon all the studies taught in it.

The Faculty may nominate candidates for honorary degrees; but these shall not be conferred except by unanimous vote of the Board of Trustees.[82]

The following year the requirements were more specific:

Candidates for the Degree of Bachelor of Arts must spend at least one year in the University, and must sustain examination in all the studies of the course. They must present certificates from the Librarian that they are not delinquents at the Library, and from the Proctor, that they are not indebteded for repairs and damages.

The fee for the Bachelor's Degree including the Diploma, is $2.00—which must be paid as early as the Saturday before Commencement Day. The Degree of Master of Arts is conferred on every Bachelor of Arts of three years standing, who has, in the meantime, sustained a good moral character and has studied some art, science or profession. Application must be made to the President at least two months before Commencement. The fee including the Diploma is $2.00.

The stipulation that "The University will not be responsible for *the safekeeping of any Diploma* after the Degree has been conferred," closes this 1857-58 statement.[83]

Once again, when the curriculum was drastically changed in 1859, degree requirements were also changed. Students who completed the studies in all three classes of any one department were to receive in public a Diploma of Graduation from that department and were to be regarded as alumni of the University. Students who completed with a grade of not less than 50 per cent the studies of Classes I and II in all eight departments were to be given the degree of Bachelor of Arts and Sciences. Students who completed the work of all three classes in all eight departments with a grade of 75 per cent or better were entitled to the degree of Master of Arts and Sciences. The degree of Master of Arts, bestowed almost automatically three years after the bachelor's degree, was discontinued. Fees for degrees and diplomas remained at $2.00.[84]

The young University started off almost at once to give honorary degrees to deserving and distinguished friends. First on the list was the Reverend Albert A. Muller, of Nashville. He was designated Doctor of Divinity in 1833. The 1834 honors went to seven men. The Reverend Stephen Olin, then president of Wesleyan University, Middleton, Connecticut, received a D.D. and the Honorable Abner S. Lipscomb of Texas, an LL.D. Three ministers, the Reverend D. P. Bestor, the Reverend C. G. McPherson, and the Reverend A. H. Sample, were made honorary Masters of Art. And the same degree was bestowed on two members of the University faculty, Professors Henry W. Hilliard and Richard T. Brumby, to give them added prestige and dignity in their classrooms. In 1837 an LL.D. went to the Honorable William Crawford of Mobile; an honorary M.A. to Henry Thompson of Texas; and an M.A. to Henry Tutwiler, the young professor of ancient languages.

In 1846 the board of trustees conferred on Daniel Pratt of Autauga county, gin maker and leading industralist of the state, the most unusual degree, Master in the Mechanic and useful Arts.[85]

By the time the University closed in 1865, the trustees had granted eighty-four honorary degrees. Eight of these had been LL.D.'s; twenty, D.D.'s; and fifty-six, M.A.'s. In proportion to earned degrees numbering only a few hundred this list seems long, but it undoubtedly gratified the University officials to honor its friends with these tokens of esteem and to add to the prestige of the University by adding their names to its roster.

Plenty of good, solid work went on in the early classrooms of the University of Alabama. The men who shaped and reshaped its curriculum were honest and earnest teachers. If sometimes they were lacking in understanding of youth, they were strong in their conviction of the importance of education. Governor Collier was not whistling in the wind when he urged the citizens of Alabama to "appreciate and patronize" their own University instead of "discouraging and depressing" its leaders by sending their sons to distant schools whose standards were by no means better:

We speak advisedly when we bear witness to the morality, learning and faithfulness of the faculty of the University of Alabama. They are altogether competent to impart education quite as extensive and thorough as can be obtained within the time usually allotted to a collegiate course, either in the North or South.[85]

CHAPTER VIII

Student Organizations

PROVISION for extracurricular student activities, social or serious, was not in the minds of the University planners. They envisioned a student world limited by the college fences and the walls of classroom and dormitory. They scheduled minutely every waking hour of each student's day. But they reckoned without the students. Gregarious, high-spirited, and young, the boys, who were also the builders of University life and tradition, managed with remarkable speed to equip their college with an array of organizations to meet the perennial need of the student for self-expression and group activity. Before the University closed in 1865 the list of these organizations, which had begun with the literary societies typical of campuses of the day, had expanded to include the beginnings of the newer fraternities. The faculty alternately encouraged and frowned upon these groups but was powerless to keep them from forming.

The University had been in operation less than a year when the first student organization came into being. In fact, the Erosophic Society was so well established by December, 1831, that its members were asking the board of trustees to assign a room for their meetings.[1] By December of the following year two societies instead of one were making the same request. The trustees acquiesced and assigned a room for the use of the Erosophic and Philomathic societies.[2]

It is generally agreed that the Erosophic Society was founded first. William R. Smith said so, and, as one of the first students, he should know. But the two groups came into being so nearly simultaneously that the matter of seniority is not important. William C. Davis, Jr., who, in 1932, wrote the centennial history of the Philomathic Society, gives one view of the impulses which brought both groups into being:

Prominent in the minds of the first students of the University were a great love for knowledge and a high appreciation of the value of discourse and debate. It was, therefore, only natural that, when the University had been in existence only a few months, a literary society was organized which has existed continuously for a century and has had among its members many of the most famous men the state has produced. In keeping with the ideals upon which the society was founded, it was given the name Philomathic, meaning "love of knowledge."[3]

Even to the definition of the name, this paragraph could equally apply to the rival group, the Erosophic Society. And if Mr. Davis, looking through the mists of a century, may have somewhat overlooked other reasons for the formation of a student club in his emphasis upon the "love for knowledge and the high appreciation of the values of discourse and debate," no one would deny that earnest idealism was a cornerstone of these typical student organizations.

Although Mr. Davis is unable to set an exact date for the organization of the Philomathic Society, he concludes, on the basis of a letter then in the possession of Miss Mary Gorgas that it must have been not later than the spring of 1832. That letter, an invitation to Governor John Gayle to become an honorary member, is an expression of the high aims of the society's youthful founders:

Sir: The members of the Philomathic Society, having united themselves for the promotion of piety and virtue, and wishing to acquire an extensive acquaintance of historical and other literary subjects, the discussion of which may afford interest and utility to those seeking knowledge; and being aware that such ends are promptly assisted by the bright example of those persons who are really friends to literature and virtue, have appointed us, the undersigned, to solicit of you the privilege of enrolling your name among the honorary members of said society.[4]

Another clue to the dates of the founding of these two first societies lies in the accounts of anniversary celebrations, though there is not complete consistency in the dates chosen for these events. The Erosophic Society apparently celebrated its first birthday in May, 1832, and, according to the newspaper account, it must have been an impressive event:

The anniversary of this Collegiate Society was celebrated on Saturday last. The procession, composed of members of the two literary societies, with the Faculty of the University, the Governor, and other honorary members of the Erosophic Society, made a very handsome display.

The Rev. Mr. Hilliard delivered the anniversary address. It occupied about three quarters of an hour in delivery. We were much pleased with its sentiments, with the style in which they were expressed, and with the elegant historical and literary illustrations. . . .

We were happy to learn that it is to be printed in pamphlet form, by order of the Society.[5]

The Philomathic Society chose December 7, 1839, as the date for the celebration of its seventh anniversary. Professor F. A. P. Barnard delivered the address on that occasion.[6] On the basis of these two records, one might conclude that the Erosophic group started the same spring the college opened and that Philomathic was at least a year younger. But this evidence is by no means conclusive. Throughout the years "anniversary" celebrations had a variety of dates. John Foster spoke to the Philomathic Society in 1844 on "The Literary Spirit of the Present Day." That celebration was reported in the newspapers of February, 1844.[7] Gradually, also, the society celebrations came to be synchronized with commencement events and so to lose their significance as birthdays.

Actual incorporation of the societies did not come until both had been in existence more than ten years. The Erosophic Society was incorporated by legislative act on February 10, 1843; the Philomathic Society, on January 25, 1845. The wording of both acts of incorporation is similar:

That the............Society of the University of Alabama be, and hereby is, established and declared a body corporate and politic, and by that name shall have power to receive and hold personal property by gift, purchase, or devise; also to sue and be sued, plead and be impleaded, to have and to use a common seal, and to pass all laws for the internal government of said Society, not inconsistent with the constitution and laws of this State, nor with the by-laws and regulations of the Trustees and Faculty of the University of Alabama. . . . all property belonging to said Society, shall forever be, and remain free from taxation.[8]

Saturday was the meeting day for these societies. In 1833 the faculty ruled that meetings should be held in the daytime, but apparently this did not meet with the approval of the organization leaders, for in 1834 the faculty, "for reasons offered," gave their permission for evening meetings of both groups.[10] W. S. Wyman, who was a student from 1848 to 1851 and who later became president of the University, remembered Saturday morning meetings:

The University held only one class on Saturday and it came before breakfast. The two literary societies, the Philomathic and the Erosophic, met at 10:00 a.m. Every student belonged to one of these societies. The meetings were well attended and the interest taken was very great. Fines were imposed for absence and no student could receive his "Society Diploma" unless all his dues were paid to date. Each society held a public celebration during commencement, and at this time it was customary to present each member of the graduating class with a diploma written in bad Latin and printed on good parchment. The diplomas were adorned with huge seals and long streamers of red and white ribbon. These diplomas were prized nearly as highly as the Bachelor's Diploma.[11]

At the beginning of 1854 the two societies, needing new scope for their activities, asked that all Saturday morning recitations be abolished. The faculty decided that "it was inexpedient to grant the request," adding that if the "secret clubs" beginning to spring up on the campus were abolished they might be more inclined to allow society meetings on Saturday evenings.[12]

Much serious work went into the literary societies. It is probable that members worked with more zest in preparation for the society debates than they did on formal course assignments. In the autumn of 1857 Bolling Hall wrote to his father of his resolution to make the most of the opportunities the Erosophic Society offered him:

I have determined hereafter to debate every Saturday. I am on the debate next Saturday and from that day I intend paying more attention to the Erosophic than I have ever done before. I will have a much better chance to do this than I had last year as all the best debaters are gone and shall find myself more on an equality with the members than before. I always before hated to get up and speak when I knew that the members were desirious of hearing some other person and also when I knew that I might make a failure.[13]

Oran Roberts was probably one of many youngsters who found the training received in these societies of great value in after-college years. He wrote that his election as president of Erosophic at the close of his junior year had made it necessary for him to familiarize himself with the rules of Jefferson's *Manual*. He wrote also of the experience he got in the debates themselves:

During that session Bowden and I, by previous agreement, selected different sides upon the subjects debated, prepared ourselves in advance, and closed nearly every debate after those members of the Society, who had been selected as they stood upon the roll, had completed their speeches. Many years afterwards he and I met in the Courts of Texas, and being employed on different sides of important suits, spoke against each other again.[14]

Society life was not, however, all seriousness. At least some of the members had moments when they felt that love of learning should take second place to good fun. Bolling Hall wrote entertainingly to his father of one episode in which a picnic almost disrupted the Erosophic Society:

There was a picnic given by some of the citizens . . . to which a majority of the members were invited. That majority to save their fines came into the Hall at the ringing of the bells and endeavored to put off the meeting until next Saturday. Some of the members said that it was against the Constitution to put off the business of the Society for any purpose, much less a picnic. When the vote was put, the majority, of course, voted to adjourn. Some of the opposite side then got up and made a motion to adjourn forever, and thus, of course, to break up the Society. Those who made this motion, it was well known, had no real desire to break up the Society, but they said that their motion was as much in order as the other. The others said that the president had no right to put this question to the vote although they knew it would not be carried. From this they proceeded to personalities and got to a pretty high pitch before they quit, but at last they stopped and the picnicers were let off. But the best of it was that they were kept even longer by the "quarrelling debate" than if they had permitted the business to have gone on in regular order.[15]

The controversies of the day were reflected in the debates of the societies and in the records, which show that in at least one instance stirred-up feelings resulted in more than words. The Philomathic Society as early as 1837 found itself embarrassed because James G. Birney, abolitionist, was saying publicly that he considered himself one of its members. Birney had been made an honorary member of Philomathic, perhaps in recognition of his services as scout for the faculty of the early University. But life was moving fast and he was no longer *persona grata*. The anti-abolition current was running very swiftly. The Philomathic Society took formal action to purge itself and asked that all the newspapers of the state publish the fact that Birney had been expelled from honorary membership in 1836, because of "his espousal and endeavors to propagate opinions which militate and are at direct variance with the rights of the South, the peace of society, and the perpetuity of our government."[16]

The Erosophic and Philomathic societies undoubtedly filled a need in the hearts of the University students. They proudly wore the emblem of their group—that of the Erosophic was a large block "E" on a building with a Latin inscription.[17] As dues were never very high, the payment could usually be made from the students' allowances.[18] And they found in their own club rooms at least one place on the campus which the faculty did not rule. Davis described the hall assigned to Philomathic; it must have been matched by that of Erosophic:

[The Philomathic Society] had a special hall for its meetings, which was well kept and decorated with beautiful pictures. The Society also owned its own library which at one time contained as many as 2500 books. On various occasions Legislatures of the state in making appropriations to the University specified that so much should go to the literary societies.[19]

The two literary societies were the ranking student organizations of the period, providing between them club membership for every student and proceeding with a minimum of faculty regulation and interference. But they were not the only organizations to be formed on that early campus.

The Othomisian Debating Society, formed in 1846 according to the established pattern, was short-lived. Saturday afternoon, the meeting time planned to avoid conflict with the other societies, was not satisfactory to the members, and a petition to meet in the evening was not honored by the faculty.[20]

Much more apprehension was felt by the faculty when the first secret societies, forerunners of the modern fraternity, began to appear on the campus. A "secret and exclusive" society, the Eutrapelian, was granted permission to organize in 1845. But the permission also carried a warning. It was given "with the understanding that they do not stand upon the same footing with the other societies, but will be liable to be dissolved, should the Faculty find any cause to be dissatisfied with them."[22]

Reluctant permissions for other groups followed in the next five years. In 1847 Delta Kappa Epsilon was chartered, perhaps the first of the national fraternities.

The President gave notice that he had been informed of the institution in the University of a branch or chapter of the Delta Kappa Epsilon [which had] purposes of mutual improvement.[23]

Kuklos Adelphon was set up the next year by William B. Augustus, who was given formal permission to form a secret society by that name.[24] In the spring of 1855 internal dissensions resulted because members of the minority faction disclosed secrets. The dissolution of this circle and of other circles resulted in the majority faction's acceptance of a charter from Phi Gamma Delta at the University of Alabama. A group of five students in 1849 had sought and had obtained permission to form another secret society "for their improvement." The faculty were particularly frank about their apprehension in this case, saying,

Leave was granted to the parties mentioned to form their society (which is without a name as yet) but the faculty express their apprehension that these societies may operate injuriously, or be abused; and in that case they will take the necessary measures for suppressing them altogether. This society, in particular, is required to give notice to the faculty of any change that may be made in their constitution.[25]

Alpha Delta Phi was added to the list in 1850.[26]

When George Little was in college, from 1851 to 1855, three of these fraternities were flourishing, but the nameless "secret society" of 1849 had disappeared. He remembered that Phi Gamma Delta was founded during his college years and that S.A.E. came to the campus the year after his graduation. He remembered D.K.E. as the strongest and Alpha Delta Phi as the most select:

There were four Greek letter fraternities at the University in my day of which D.K.E. was the strongest. The Alpha Delta Phi was very small and very select. The Phi Gamma Delta was started while I was there. The Kuklos Adelphon was the other fraternity but the year after I graduated the S.A.E. was founded. . . . One year the D.K.E. bragged that they had all the officers in the literary society. This aroused the antagonism of the other students and the next year they did not elect a single man.[27]

A most unusual state of affairs must have existed in 1851, for President Manly was told that difficulties had sprung up between two of the societies. The same informer also told him that either Delta Kappa Epsilon or Alpha Delta Phi had a rule that each member of the group must supply himself with a pistol. The rule must have been enforced by the group, for student William A. Cochran, a member of one of the fraternities, was the recipient of a message from Manly concerning his possession of a revolver.[28]

For some years the faculty and trustees seem to have cherished the hope that these new disturbing groups which they distrusted would vanish if they did not pay too much attention to them. Colonel Bugbee, one of the trustees, put this hope into words when he wrote in 1852 that he believed these secret societies were "ephemeral in their character." He said,

These societies unless they can build up a library, or do something to bind them together, cannot exist long.[29]

In an effort to rid the University of these secret societies, the faculty made an appeal to them in November, 1852, to disband. As was to be expected, this appeal met little response.[30] The faculty must have tired momentarily of the battle, for during the same month they granted the fraternities permsision to use rooms in the old Capitol building which had just been given to the University. They stipulated that the president was to select the rooms and that if the fraternities requested and received any of the Capitol's old furniture they must give a proper receipt for it.[31]

The fight between the authorities and the students concerning the secret societies continued, for in 1854 an application was presented by J. N. Arrington, J. G. Foster, and Robert Perrin for permission to form another fraternity. As the faculty still felt that these secret societies were flourishing at the expense of the literary societies, the petition was refused.[32]

By 1856 the hope of seeing the fraternities dissolved without action by the authorities had vanished. The faculty made an attempt to put them out of business through requiring each student to sign a pledge that he would not participate in the activities of such societies:

We and each of us do further solemnly promise that we will not directly or indirectly unite ourselves to any secret organization hitherto existing among the students or that may hereafter be introduced or be attempted to be introduced among them, nor ever attend any meeting connected with any such association, with the exception of the Erosophic and Philomathic Societies.[33]

THE OLD UNIVERSITY

In connection with this ban, it is interesting to note that Delta Kappa Epsilon celebrated its one-hundredth anniversay at the University of Alabama on November 21, 1947.

Distrust of secret societies made difficult the introduction to the University of Alabama of one Greek letter organization not popularly regarded as a fraternity. As early as 1849 Professor Barnard was trying to bring to the campus a chapter of Phi Beta Kappa. The faculty authorized him in July of that year to take the preliminary steps toward this end.[34] Nearly eighteen months later the faculty learned that a letter had come from the Connecticut Alpha of Phi Beta Kappa reporting that it had approved a resolution authorizing the installation of a chapter in the University of Alabama. It was now in order, the letter stated, for the University to apply to other chapters for their concurrence.[35]

Two considerations made the faculty reluctant to take the action suggested. The fact that the letter came from the North was enough to taint it with suspicion. Moreover, they were being greatly disturbed with "the multiplication of societies," and they felt "objections" on principle to secret societies. They let the letter from Yale rest. A member of the board of trustees was the man who prodded them into action three months later. Mr. Bugbee wrote the faculty of his own desire to have the establishment of a Phi Beta Kappa chapter seriously considered. He assured them that it would be strictly a college society over which they would have complete control. Although the faculty received this letter on March 3, 1851, they did not actually take up the matter until March 10.

It was then that they learned to their amazement and consternation that the University already had a Phi Beta Kappa chapter. Professor Barnard was not a man to be put off when he wanted something. He had received a charter for the new society from New Haven in the fall of 1850 and had promptly used it. Alabama Alpha of Phi Beta Kappa had been organized for some time.[36] More than a year passed before they recovered from the shock sufficiently to do anything about the outlaw organization on their doorstep.

Then in the summer of 1852 the two sides of the controversy moved almost simultaneously to close the gap between them and to regularize the Phi Beta Kappa chapter. Probably the initiative was with the faculty, for there were faculty discussions that July which included the interesting idea that the establishment of a Phi Beta Kappa chapter might be "the occasion to merge, if possible, the secret societies" and therefore the means of "securing our object deemed so very desirable by the Faculty, viz., the voluntary abandonment of these societies." The discussions culminated in a letter to the trustees, asking their help in dealing with the "self-constituted tribunal" which was assuming prerogatives belonging to the faculty and, in general, becoming something of an embarrassment and a nuisance.

We find ourselves needing a defence of our personal and official acts in a community, with which we have no connection, and from which, as a secret society, we can obtain no open authentic reports—a self-constituted tribunal near us assuming to scan and review our proceedings as a Faculty, and to redistribute collegiate honors and rewards on principles of their own:—which began its career by assuming and appropriating to itself a prerogative, which, we are taught by the highest authority, belonged exclusively to the Faculty of the University of Alabama—and which has exercised that prerogative as to the elction of members in some cases which have publicly transpired, in a manner directly opposite to what we understand of the declared objectives of the Society, and not in accordance with the judgment and award of the Faculty in regard to collegiate standing and honors. . . . With our present views we cannot sanction an organization so perverted and irregular—effected not only without our authority but in direct hostility to us; and which has been used, to some extent, to disaffect our own alumni to us.[37]

Members of the "perverted and irregular" organization sat, no doubt, in the faculty meetings at which this communication was decided upon. It is an evidence of their wisdom and sense of strategy that the letter had no sooner been dispatched than the faculty were in receipt of a communication from Phi Beta Kappa which was calculated to soothe their ruffled feelings and pave the way for an amicable solution. The message, presented by "Messrs Ormond, Shortridge, and Whitfield, a committee to present the resolutions to the President of the University," began with acknowledgement of the weakness which lack of faculty official support gave the organization:

Whereas this Society was organized without the sanction or consent of the Faculty of the University as contemplated by the parent society, from which cause the countenance and support of the Faculty have been withheld from it, and without which it will probably languish and fail in the accomplishment of its purpose,

Now therefore to concentrate and harmonize all these influences so essential to our prosperity, and to enable this society to fulfill its appropriate functions by holding out additional inducements for the attainment of high scholarship and elevated moral character, and to prevent even the appearance of this society being placed in antagonism to, instead of being an adjunct and aid to the University . . . .

Then the message suggested the basis on which both sides could unite "in a friendly re-organization of this society." All elections made by the society were to be officially confirmed. And, thereafter, the society was to have the same relation to the University of Alabama as its parent society had with Yale College.[38]

It took only two days for the threatening storm clouds to disappear. On July 15, the faculty voted full agreement with the organization plan suggested:

The Faculty shall give their full consent to a reorganization of the Society, by which all elections that have hitherto been made shall be confirmed, *as of this day*—and the society shall hold the same general relation to the University that the parent society holds to Yale College.

One or two important provisos were attached to the resolution:

Further, to avoid future misunderstanding, the Faculty declare the above assent to be taken as yielded only in case such original papers have been received as will authorize such organization according to the rules and usages of the parent society. And further, this assent to the resolution of the Society is not to be taken as either authorizing or requiring that the present constitution and laws shall or may be altered to correspond with those of the parent Society—but the Faculty prefer and expect that the Society will continue their constitution and laws as they at present exist and that whatever changes shall be thought best, be accomplished in the usual way.[39]

Student membership in organizations not directly a part of the college was always discouraged, and often it was expressly forbidden. One group wanted to join the Odd Fellows in 1845, but they were forbidden to do so because the meetings would be held in town.[40] Request for permission to form a military company for exercise in their spare time was denied, but another group was granted a similar request in 1846.[41] That same year students who wanted to join the Volunteer Military Company of Tuscaloosa were told that such membership was against the University laws.[42]

When a chapter of the Sons of Temperance was organized on the campus in October, 1848, however, the faculty welcomed it with open arms,[43] hoping it would help solve one of the most troublesome problems of college life. The Sons wanted to hold their meetings in the library. The faculty opposed this idea, but gave them a choice of a room in one of the dormitories or a room near those of the literary societies.[44] They could even take down the partition if they did so without damaging the building.[45] They could have the seats previously used in the recitation rooms of Washington Dormitory.[46] They could, in short, have every facility that a welcoming faculty could arrange to give them.

All the organizations on the campus gradually came to consider the commencement season as the crown and climax of their year. As the student societies grew in number and in strength, the graduation ceremonies, simple at first, became longer, more elaborate, more varied, until they were indeed the complete expression of the serious side of the life lived on the campus. Commencement was the coming to fruition of the labors of the faculty in classrooms, of the long study hours in dormitory rooms, of the debating practice of the literary clubs, and of the whole intellectual effort of the University year. Some lighter touches were added as the years went by, but they served only to emphasize the variety and the solidity of the intellecual feast.

The central focus of the program was always the senior orations. Work on these declamations began early in the year; after evening prayers the seniors practiced selected or original discourses approved by the president.[47] This program included juniors by 1836.[48] And before the period ended commencement orations had been supplemented by two other occasions when seniors gave original addresses before the faculty and students.[49] Emphasis on public speaking was strong, and appreciation of the art of oratory must also have been general, else the public would never have thronged as they did on hot summer days to sit on hard benches to listen to the youthful graduates hold forth on historical lore and philosophical abstractions.

It may be said that the commencement oratory began before commencements did. Although there were no students ready to graduate in December, 1831, orations were given on the Friday of

THE OLD UNIVERSITY 187

examination week. And the young orators set a difficult pace for their successors to follow. The following subjects were approved.[50]

Moral Culture   *Marion Banks, Tuscaloosa*

The Connection of Education with Liberty and Happiness
Burwell Boykin, Sparta
Mutual Influence of Literature and Religion
John G. Davenport, Butler
The Love of Character   *William W. King, Montevallo*

Causes of National Prosperity and Decline
Robert B. McMullen, Tuscaloosa
The Character of Lafayette   *Alexander B. Meek, Tuscaloosa*

The Present State of Europe   *George D. Shortridge, Tuscaloosa*

The American Indians   *William R. Smith, Tuscaloosa*

The Liberty of the Press   *Thomas A. Walker, Montevallo*

The Prospect and Claims of our Country
John A. Nooe, Franklin County

Senior orators in December, 1833, held the pace well. They appeared at the exhibition following their final examinations with the following discourses:[51]

James F. Bailey	The Style and Moral Tendency of Addison's Periodical Writings
Clement C. Clay	The Unhappy Fate of Poland
Isham H. Kelly	The Character and Writings of B. Franklin
James H. Mastin	Europe in the Middle Ages
William Parham	Europe after the Revival of Literature
Thomas M. Peters	Character and Writings of Henry Brougham
John B. Read	The Influence of Imagination on Character
John M. Smith	Popular Education, The Foundation of Popular Liberty.

All of these students made another appearance in July of the following year. With three others they made up the graduating class, and each graduate was listed on the program for an oration:[52]

James F. Bailey	The Writings and Eloquence of the late **Robert Hall**, of England
Clement C. Clay	The True Sources of National Greatness
Isham H. Kelly	The Moral Character of George Washington
James H. Mastin	The Importance of History

William Parham	A Eulogy on La-fayette
Thomas M. Peters	Language as a Vehicle of Thought
John B. Read	The Influence of Christianity on Individuals and Nations
John M. Smith	The Advantages of Education to Individuals and to the Community
William A. Cochrane	The Comparative Influence of Poverty and Wealth on the Attainment of Eminence (excused from speaking)
Walter H. Crenshaw	The Discovery of America, and its Moral Influence on the World
Charles W. Tait	The Ruins of Pompeii and Herculaneum (Excused from speaking)

Again, in 1835, it was practical to use the entire senior class of eight on the commencement platform. Their subjects, too, are impressive and wide-ranging:[53]

Marion Baldwin	The Inauguration
George Gaines	Neglected Genius
William B. Inge	The Reign of Bonaparte
George Meriwether	The Connection and Relative Value of Physical, Moral, and Intellectual Education (Excused)
John E. Moore	College Life
Reuben Mundy	The Character of the Pilgrims Who First Settled New England
William E. Powe	The Connection Between Education and Liberty, and Between Ignorance and Slavery
Eggleston D. Townes	Pernicious Effects of the Union of Church and State

Oran Roberts graduated the next year, and he, too, gave a picture of a simple ceremony, serious and full of youthful eloquence.

At the Commencement in December 1836, there were twelve in the Senior Class who graduated. There were no grades publishd, and no honors conferred. The only approach to it was in the selection by the Faculty of five or six of the Class to deliver speeches at the Commencement. I recollect that Bowdon delivered the valedictory, and that Pickens and I delivered speeches. I have no recollection as to the others, but from my knowledge of the numbers of the Class I should judge that Miller and Johnson and Elijah Wallace also delivered speeches.[54]

Probably the most colorful part of the early commencements was the awarding of the coveted diplomas. They were written in Latin, as

THE OLD UNIVERSITY

became a University founded upon the classics, and they had attached to them with ribbon the old seal of the University of Alabama. The trustees had made provision for that seal at its first meeting in April, 1822, when it heard in the report of the committee on rules for land agents and forthwith approved the following recommendation:

That it is inexpedient, at this time, for the Board of Trustees to act upon the powers delegated to them by law, further than, that they should pass an ordinance, authorizing the President of the Board to procure a seal for themselves, and successors, with engravings of such appropriate emblems as he shall approve.[55]

The seal adopted was strongly classical in feeling and design. Some years later, the report of the committee on seal describes it as follows:

In the foreground is the figure of Minerva. Her head is surrounded with a halo. In her left hand is an olive branch. Her right hand holding a pair of compasses, rests upon a globe. Lying at her feet on the left side, are a scroll and a book.
    The Parthenon is seen to the left, in the distance. Upon the upper part of the rim is the inscription, "Universitat Alabam. Sigill."[56]

Professor Robert E. Jones, recently of the department of classical languages of the University, thinks that this mark of the classics on the emblem of the University, as well as its architecture and its curriculum, is particularly worthy of note.[57] He describes the old seal thus:

The old seal of the University of Alabama represents a standing female figure with her right hand resting on a globe and in her left hand holding a branch, while rays emanate from her head and at her feet are several objects too small to be identified except for an open scroll. Around the seal are the words UNIVERSITAT. ALABAM. SIGIL. (UNIVERSITATIS ALABAMIENSIS SIGILLUM). The radiance emanating from the head indicates that the figure is that of a divine being, and the olive branch (which it could well be) in the left hand suggests Athena, who as goddess of wisdom would be especially appropriate for a university. The subject of the sculptures of the west pediment of the Parthenon was the contest of Athena and Poseidon for Attica, when Athena caused an olive tree to spring from the soil.[58]

Whether the early recipients of the University diplomas studied as closely as Professor Jones the emblem of their University is, of course open to question.

Just when the simple commencements began to be elaborated by the addition of related events, both social and organizational, is not easy to determine. One is perhaps safe in inferring that as soon as there were organized alumni the elaboration began. And the Society of Alumni was organized as soon as there were enough graduates to make a respectable meeting. It held its first anniversary in December, 1836, with A. B. Meek as orator. There were thirty-six regular alumni by that time, and "many more" who had graduated in several departments. They had a typical "old grad's" meeting, as the orator rang the changes on the virtues and the future of the University.[59]

In 1839 the Society of Alumni met at the Erosophic Hall and then proceeded to the Rotunda to hear an address by Walter H. Crenshaw.[60] Ten years later they had assumed more of the traditional responsibilities of an alumni association. They met not only to renew old associations but also with the definite purpose of helping the University. They decided to prepare in praise of the school an address which should "vindicate" it from "the unfounded aspersions and unjust prejudices that have been arrayed against it." They would, they said, see that this vindication had wide circulation.[61]

By the 1850's their commencement time meetings of the alumni had become a fixed and important part of the festivities. Judge Stansel of Pickens County, who delivered the address in 1857, stirred up considerable controversy by the nature of his speech. The *Independent,* published in Gainesville, apprised its readers of the local reactions to the speech:

It appears to have been well received in a literary point of view; but there was considerable dissent from it on account of the "ologies" it teaches. The *Monitor* was of the opinion it warred against Christianity; the *Observer* explained and defended.[62]

Probably the Society of Alumni was on safer ground the next year when the Reverend R. P. McMullen from Tennessee spoke on "Truth" and made the single point that "Truth is the only Liberty."[63]

The Erosophic and Philomathic societies also had moved into the commencement orbit by 1842. In that year the faculty politely

THE OLD UNIVERSITY   191

suggested that instead of holding two celebrations just before commencement the two organizations should hold a joint celebration and alternate in choosing a speaker.[64] Two of these orations give some idea of the lofty tone which the two societies required in their annual meeting. In 1857 Colonel Burwell Boykin, of Mobile, was invited to speak, but he died before he could fill the engagement, and Colonel J. G. Barr of Gainesville read for him the speech he had prepared on "The Contributions of Science to the Use of Man."[65] The Honorable E. C. Bullock, the speaker the following year, chose a shorter subject—"Civilization." This topic, apparently, meant simply the mores of the South, for one newspaper praised the oration in these words:

As the most perfect type of true civilization, he well exhibited our own Sunny South as the incomparable model. Those who heard the address will long remember that the present phantasies "spiritualities" and fearful agrariansim and "isms" generally of our New England neighbors received little mercy from his comparison of these with the high toned chivalry and civilization of the South.[66]

Other innovations and modifications were creeping into the commencement schedule during the thirties and especially the forties. A small note of social emphasis crept in as early as 1837, with the trustees' appropriation of $150 for the "collation on Commencement Day."[67] And the idea of a baccalaureate sermon was first broached in 1835, when the faculty were instructed to have a religious discourse in the Rotunda on the Sunday before commencement.[68] The first commencement sermon, however, was not delivered until 1839, when President Manly was the preacher.[69] Five years later the trustees, instructing President Manly to place in the archives copies of the commencement sermons, told him to be sure to include the "able, eloquent, and chaste commencement sermon delivered on Sunday 12 (22') of Decr. instant. in the Methodist Church" and the "very appropriate classical, eloquent, and chaste addresses," which he himself had made.[70]

In addition to these new features for commencement, the forties saw further elegance added to the student oration program itself. The trustees ruled in 1846 that at least one senior was to deliver his oration in some modern language other than English.[71] Charles M. Burford was the student chosen in 1849 to present this demonstration of the skill with which languages were taught in the University. He spoke on "La Vie Conjugale." A patient audience sweltered through his eloquence and that of sixteen other young scholars. This varying of the program did not lighten the main business of commencement. In the newspaper account of that 1849 celebration the mere list of the orations is overwhelming:[72]

Salutory Oration, in Latin   *Peter F. Hunley*
"Possunt, quia posse vindentur"   *Manly L. Hester*
"National Prosperity as Effected by Education"   *John M. Owen*
"Foreign Immigration"   *Walter Cook*
"Character of Nathan Hale"   *James H. Fitts*
"Self-Development"   *Thomas B. Slade*
"The Beauties of Virtue"   *Lucian V. B. Martin*
"Our Country's Prospects"   *John H. Lee*
"La Vie Conjugale"   (French oration)   *Charles M. Burford*
"Military Virtues"   *Alburto Martin*
"Our Country—Her Themes for Romance"   *Phillips Fitzpatrick*
"The Influence of Mathematical Science, with An Application"
　　　　　　　　　　　　　　　　　　　　　　　　Charles E. Bridges
"Banks—Their Necessity and Value"   *Edward L. Jones*
"The Statesman"   *John Moore*
"National Faith"   *Andrew J. Jenkins*
"Intellectual Conditions and Prospects of Alabama"   *Samuel M. Meek*
Valedictory Address   *Charles M. Burford*

It seems probable that there were some nodding heads in the audience by the time diplomas were awarded to these boys and to James D. Webb of Greensboro. Ten M.A's were also given that day—six "earned" and four honorary.

With the coming of the fifties, commencements really began to boom. In 1850 a new organization, the Alabama Historical Society, had made its appearance on the campus and had claimed the usual right to a part in the graduation program. With the dates already pre-empted by the other societies, the Historical Society meeting helped to lengthen the period which had to be alloted for commencement. By 1852 it took five days to get all the meetings, assemblies, orations, and social gatherings arranged so that they did not overlap.

The suggestion in 1850 that an Alabama Historical Society be formed came from Mr. Alexander Bowie of the board of trustees. Invitations were extended to "individual gentlemen of distinction or literary taste throughout the state,"[73] and when the first meeting was called, some sixty of these notables were present to enroll. They elected Chancellor Bowie as president; Colonel Pickett, first vice-president; General E. D. King, second vice-president; Honorable W. Moody, treasurer, and Joshua H. Foster, secretary.[74] Dues were set at $5.00, and membership was declared open to any "gentleman" who so notified the secretary and who paid his dues. The purpose of the society was simply stated; it was "to collect, preserve, and publish the floating fragments of our State history."[75]

The collecting of the "floating fragments" no doubt went on the year around, but the yearly meetings in commencement week were a favorite time for the presentation of treasures. In that week, in 1852, for instance, the historical society received contributions both tangible and intangible—but all historical—from Professor Tuomey, Judge Bowie, and Mr. A. S. Nicoloson. The *Jacksonville Republican* quoted the story from the Tuscaloosa *Monitor:*

Professor Tuomey presented some sea shells with an account of their natural history, &c. and also a strand of beads made of shells, taken from a human skeleton found in one of the Indian Mounds in Tuskaloosa County. A letter was also read from Judge Bowie, relative to a Spanish dollar, having the date 1519, found in a mound in this [Benton] County, which the Judge supposed indicated a point in "DeSoto's route." Mr. A. S. Nicoloson delivered the annual address, which the *Monitor* says was an able vindication of Southern Slavery.[76]

The schedule for that year's commencement is carefully recorded in the faculty minutes and is probably typical of the commencements of the decade. The week started on Sunday with the commencement sermon. Monday morning was set aside for the oration before the Alabama Historical Society, with the same organization holding its business meeting that afternoon. Tuesday belonged to the Erosophic and Philomathic societies. On Wednesday morning the junior exhibitions were held, and Wednesday afternoon the Society of Alumni had its annual oration. The commencement ceremonies and the bestowal of degrees came on Thursday morning.[77]

For the actual flavor of the celebrations, however, for the color and life and variety which, by that time, had come to cluster around that all-important week, one turns to the contemporary newspaper accounts. One appeared in the *Advertiser and State Gazette*:

The valedictory addresses were delivered to the graduating members of the two literary Societies, by W.H.C. Price, of Macon County, on the part of the Erosophic Society; and R.K. Hargrove, of Pickens, for the Philomathic Society. The addresses of these two young men were highly creditable, and may be regarded as undoubted indications, not only of the high order of education furnished by the University,—but of the happy conduction and the very beautiful efforts of the Societies themselves. In these speeches, elegance of style, force of thought, logical reasoning and the powers of declamation were all combined.[78]

The second, published by the *Independent* of Gainesville, was apparently based on material originally appearing in the *Monitor* in Tuscaloosa in July, 1856:

We learn from the *Monitor* that on Saturday afternoon, the 12th, the dull and vacant streets of old Tuskaloosa began to give some indications of the coming crowd of visitors that usually congregates there on occasions of Commencement. Familiar faces that had not been seen for a twelvemonth, and others who were familiar some years ago, were seen on the sidewalks, and old classmates that had not met for years, warmly greeted each other, and talked of "maters and things in general" that had transpired since they met.

Rev. Mr. Nevius, (Episcopal) of Tuskaloosa, preached the Commencement Sermon. Bishop Elliot, of Georgia, had been appointed to preach the sermon, but did not appear.

On Monday, contrary to the usual order of things, there was no "speech making," as had been expected. The orator of the Alumni, who would have been entitled to the day, had not arrived. On that morning, however, the Trustees held their first meeting of the year. There were present Messrs. Baptist, Blanchard, Bugbee, Forney, Ormond, Stansel, and Tait, together with President Garland.

Tuesday morning was the time appointed for the oration before the Literary Societies of the College. Hon. William L. Yancey had consented to deliver this oration, says the *Monitor,* and his high reputation as an orator drew forth a large and intelligent audience. The subject selected by the orator was the distinctive characteristics of the Northern and Southern people of the Union, and it was treated in a manner befitting the reputation of the speaker.

On Wednesday morning, the Junior Class delivered original addresses. At night, Mr. W. C. Richardson delivered a poem before the Phi Beta Kappa Society, which was highly spoken of.

THE OLD UNIVERSITY 195

On Thursday, the last day of the Exercises, the Rotunda was early filled to overflowing by strangers and citizens, to hear the addresses of the Graduating Class. The young gentlemen all acquainted themselves with honor, and without intending to make any distinctions, we must be allowed to give expression to the unqualified pleasure with which we listened to the address of Mr. Garrett, in defense of the claims of the University. It was well worded and well spoken.

The Graduating Class consisted of N. L. DeVotie, of Montgomery, who delivered the Valedictories and French Speech; H. M. Somerville, of Tuskaloosa, Latin Salutatory; J. J. Garrett, of Greene, Select English Oration; J. D. Rhodes, of Perry, Philosophical Oration; J. W. Young, of Wilcox; R. C. Yancey, of Montgomery; E. P. Morrisett, Monroe; A. C. Hargrove, Tuskaloosa; P. C. Lee, Dallas; N. E. Cockerel, Sumter; J. W. Kerr, Tuskaloosa; W. Foster, Tuskaloosa; J. B. Rudolph, of Lowndes, Graduate in Ethics, Mod. Language, Chemistry, Geology, &c.[79]

The third, from the same newspaper four years later, deals with the literary society celebration which was still rivaling the actual commencement ceremoney for interest and brilliance:

Upon Tuesday morning the annual address before the literary societies of the University of Alabama was delivered by that distinguished orator, the Rev. P. P. Neely, of Marion. It was indeed a most splendid oration, marked by the glowing beauties of language and the power of thought. . . . The large audience listened in breathless silence, broken only by frequent and loud applause. It is to be hoped that he will furnish the societies with this address for publication. . . . This [the exhibition of the class in oratory] is always a very interesting part of the Commencement season, and attracted a large crowd, amongst whom shone, as bright as stars, many of the lovely daughters of Alabama. All of the speeches, both as regards composition and declamation, were very creditable, and several were of a high order of excellence.[80]

One wonders if the students of those days were overwhelmed by this week-long flood of oratory, if commencemnet looked to them as it looked to the gentlemen of the press, if they felt about their own graduations as students of today feel, and if there were anything to offset the long tedious flow of words. A few student eye accounts are preserved in old letters and reminiscences. George Little writes with the authentic flavor of matter-of-factness and pleasure in the social aspects of the close of University life:

The subject of my graduating essay was Mental Symmetry. My eyes were much inflamed after final examinations and Dr. Manly excused me from reading it. Dr. W. W. Lord, of Vicksburg, read an original poem at commencement and the graduating address was delivered by a lawyer named Moss, who I think was from Columbus, Miss. Osborne Parker delivered the valedictory and was married that night by Dr. Manly to Miss Laura Owen. . . William Parker delivered the salutatory in Latin. W. G. Gamble delivered a Spanish oration and Charles Manly one in French. There were twenty-two graduates in my class out of sixty-six who had entered. Commencement in those days was in the middle of July and the dust and heat were terrible, but in spite of this hundreds of carriages would drive out and the auditorium would be packed. The night before the graduating exercises Dr. Manly gave us a watermelon supper on the back porch of his home. On commencement day the faculty all wore gowns and Dr. Manly delivered his farewell remarks in Latin, saying to each graduate: *"Accipe hoc diploma"*. The final event of commencement week was the University ball in the United States court room at the old Washington Hotel.[81]

For the space of commencement week, trustees, faculty, parents, and townspeople could indulge in untarnished pride. The University of their dreams, where all students were diligent and orderly, where the loftiest ideas had currency, and where nobility was a mark upon every brow was real for that week. They would go away with exalted hopes, but a few short weeks later, the college year would begin again, with students behaving like undisciplined children more often than like scholars and gentlemen. The tug of war between students and their natural enemies, the faculty, would begin again. The town-and-gown feud would break out in some new spot. Commencement came but once a year. But the problems of discipline were a steady headache to University leaders almost every hour during the rest of the college year.

CHAPTER IX

Problems of Discipline: Faculty versus Students

SCHOLARLY PRESTIGE built by the University on its days of commencement and public examinations was all too evanescent in the public mind. The chief popular reputation the school gained during the pre-war days was that of a trouble spot where unruly and destructive boys, brandishing dirks and pistols, rode roughshod over their mentors, outraged the townfolk, and made University life a continuous, disgraceful brawl. Although legislatures investigated, newspapers deplored, and alumni sought to explain and soften, the story of student misdemeanors would never really down. Lack of discipline was a handicap as the University struggled to get the support, both moral and financial, which it sorely needed.

The reputation was never wholly deserved. Yet the problem of student discipline was paramount in the life of the early University. On that rock the first president had been shipwrecked, and his successors avoided the same fate only with herculean effort. Much time in faculty meetings had to be given to the disciplinary problems which each day brought forth. And the teachers found their policing duties at least as arduous as their work in the classroom and far more time consuming.

In so far as rules could bring about order and good conduct, the faculty and administration cannot be charged with laxity. Probably that fact, in itself, was one cause of the trouble, for the laws which governed student life were so rigid as to be an invitation to rebellion for frontier youth, many of them still in the undisciplined, restless early years of adolescence. In general the authorities attempted to accomplish two things; to force the stamp of studious regimentation upon boys unused to routine and to curb the expression of high spirits displayed in boisterous, destructive, and mischievous ways.

The many "Thou shalt's" governing the routine of college life made spirited lads restive and an even greater number of "Thou shalt not's" prohibitions on the most harmless amusements as well as on serious offences. To both demands the students reacted as wiser disciplinarians might have expected them to react.

The attempt of Dr. Alva Woods to transplant to the campus of the University of Alabama the standards of student conduct obtaining at Harvard had been proved by 1837 to be a miserable failure.[1] But after Dr. Woods and his first faculty had left the campus in undignified rout, new rules were framed and adopted which were just as strict and just as ill adapted to the students.

Sitting restlessly in chapel at the beginning of each college session, the students listened to the reading of the rules:

The Faculty and Students shall all punctually attend morning and evening prayers. . . .

The Students shall refrain from their usual exercises and diversions on the Sabbath. . . .

The order of entering and departing from the Chapel, or of being seated therein shall be prescribed by the Faculty. . . .

During study hours the Students shall be in their rooms quietly attending to business. . . .

It is a misdemeanor to be absent from one's own tenement or entry without permission after nine o'clock at night. . . .

No student shall attend on any public amusement, or show, or exhibition without permission from the Faculty, or President. . . .

Playing at games of Hazard, betting, keeping dogs or liquors, visiting a tavern, or any such place, for the purpose of entertainment or amusement, keeping company with persons of publicly bad character, and every immorality of every description, are strictly forbidden. . . .

Cleanliness, both in and around the buildings is particularly enjoined. Water and any kind of dirt or rubbish must not be thrown from any of the college windows. . . .

No shouting, dancing, nor any boisterous noise can be permitted in the passages, or rooms of the College, at any times. To collect in groups during study hours is a particular misdemeanor. . . .[2]

As the reading of the list droned on perhaps the boys on the hard benches found their imaginations caught less by the admonition that they govern themselves by the "high and generous motives which would influence gentlemen" than they were by the interesting suggestions for mischief presented by the detailed catalogue.

When the reading was over, each student received a printed copy of the laws, which also served as his certificate of admission. On each copy was printed this form:

........................is admitted into the........Class of this University on Probation, on the ....day of A.D. 183...

President[3]

Poring over this document, the student learned—if he, indeed, did pore over it—that the University of Alabama graded infractions of rules according to heinousness. There were simple "misdemeanors" and there were "high offenses." He discovered that if he transgressed he might be admonished, removed, suspended, degraded to a lower class, refused promotion or a degree. He might, indeed, be expelled, but that could occur only by action of the trustees.

"Misdemeanors" were somewhat generally described. They were simply "all offenses against the laws of the University, or the principles of good order, not characterized as high offenses." They could move into the category of "high offenses" if they were "repeated or persisted in, or attended with circumstances of atrocity."[4]

"High offenses" made more interesting reading. They included specificly and in detail everything from "flagrant immorality against the laws of God and man" to bonfires and fireworks:

. . . any flagrant immorality against the laws of God and man, gross disrespect to any officer of the University; riotous and noisy behaviour to the disturbance of the University or of the inhabitants of Tuscaloosa; disobedience to the sentence of the Faculty; obstructing the officers in the discharge of their duties; being in any way concerned, however remotely, in a duel; keeping of wines, liquors, gun-powder, or any deadly weapon; maliciously defacing any property of the University; combinations to conceal or perpetrate mischief, or to resist the laws; indecency or obscenity in language, dress, or behaviour; habitual extravagance, after due admonition; attendance on public sports or theatrical exhibitions; playing at any game for money or other things of value; associating with persons under sentence of suspension or expulsion, or with persons of known vice or dissoluteness, or any other prohibited person; being concerned in any bon-fire, fire-works or unauthorized illuminations; intoxication; and any offense against the laws of the land which would subject the offender to disgraceful punishment.[5]

The list was indeed formidable, but as the University administrators may have had some awareness of the ingenuity with which boys can invent new mischief, they added a blanket clause to cover such contingency. It gave to the faculty "in case of offences not enumerated or for which no specific penalty is provided" the right to "adjudge the offence and inflict such punishment, not inconsistent with the laws, as may seem to them just and requisite."[6]

The students were required to know these laws. Ignorance was never accepted as an excuse. But the faculty had an even greater burden. They were required to enforce them. Both the laws established by President Woods and the laws adopted in 1839 were explicit as to this responsibility. The early laws specified that it is

confidently expected that the students will be influenced to conduct any literary exertion by higher motives than the fear of punishment, but when such motives fail, it will be the duty of the Faculty, with paternal solicitude, to endeavor, by conversation, admonition and warning to save the delinquent so long as it can be done without injury to the institution; when these means are inaffectual [sic], they will proceed to give official notice to parents or guardians, and when the case may require it, to inflict one or more of these punishments: public admonition, suspension, private or public dismission, or if the case calls for expulsion, to bring it before the Board of Trustees for their consideration.[7]

The laws of 1839 invested the faculty with "discretional parental authority" and directed them

constantly to treat the Students with mildness and moderation; and in case of offenses, to endeavor with paternal solicitude, by conversation, admonition, and warning, to save the delinquent so long as it may be done without injury to the institution; and, except in cases which manifest deliberate wickedness, to avoid inflicting the higher censures, until the discipline of advisory measures shall have been tried in vain.[8]

"Discretional parental authority" was a heavy burden for faculty shoulders. And the burden was made even heavier than it needed to be by the passage of the "exculpation rule" as part of the laws of 1839. This rule, intended to facilitate the detection of culprits through an honor system, had the effect—which wiser heads would have anticipated—of turning minor incidents into full-fledged rebellions in which the students were arrayed against their natural enemies, the faculty. The provisions of the rule were stated thus:

In ordinary cases, or for mere College misdemeanors, no student shall be called on to give information against another; but when several are known to contain among them the guilty person or persons, that the innocent may not equally suffer with the guilty, they are all liable to be severally called up, and each to be put upon his own exculpation; unless the magnanimity of the guilty shall relieve the Faculty from the necessity of this expedient, by an ingenuous confession of his or their own fault. If any Student, when thus permitted to declare his innocence, shall decline to exculpate himself, he shall be considered as taking the guilt of the offense upon himself, and encountering all the consequences. If a student shall deny that he is guilty, that shall be taken as *prima facie* proof of his innocence; but if it shall afterwards appear, from satisfactory competent evidence, that he really was guilty, he shall be considered unworthy to remain in the University. Should the author or authors of any misdemeanor, by concealment of his or their own guilt, permit an innocent fellow-student to suffer punishment for any offence of which he, or they, and not the other, was guilty; for such dishonorable conduct he shall be immediately dismissed, and the case reported to the Board of Trustees.[9]

The faculty had occasion to try out this all-inclusive law in the spring of 1840, when two "disgraceful outrages" marred the peace of the campus. The first was vandalism in the chapel room of the Rotunda, where students tore a Bible to pieces and displayed "placards of an inflammatory character." The second was breaking and entering a tutor's room, with theft of private papers and articles of value. The faculty moved first to determine the culprits in the second episode. All the residents of the entry in which the unfortunate tutor lived were summoned. They were put on their honor to answer this question:

Were you concerned, either mediately or immediately, in breaking open the room of Tutor Whiting, or were you present, aiding or abetting or looking on?

Solemnly, one by one, Tutor Whiting's neighbors answered in the negative. The plan was a failure. Students had no intention of getting caught in that trap.

The faculty appealed for help to the president. Holding a special faculty meeting, they suspended from classes the suspected students living in Tutor Whiting's entry. When they called the whole student body in for exculpation proceedings, again the answer from each boy was an innocent "No." Then the president indefinitely suspended the students from the entry where the incident happened. The remaining students expressed disapprobation in rioting on the campus.

Orthodox detective methods had meanwhile discovered the real culprit, who, because he had lied as well as "outraged" Tutor Whiting's privacy, was reported to the trustees for expulsion. Things had got to such a pass, however, that the faculty thought it expedient to declare a vacation and to send all students home for several weeks, sending with them a letter explaining to parents and guardians the whole unhappy event. Before students came back to school they were required to sign a statement, once more clearing themselves from responsibility in recent distubrances, and promising coöperation in the future in making the exculpation law work. The mutilated Bible figured in this statement, the first article of which read,

I do not know of any student now in the University who was engaged directly or indirectly in destroying the Bible and otherwise desecrating the place of worship. . . . I do not know any person now out of the University who was so engaged. . . .[10]

A second attempt to make the law work in 1842 was hardly more successful. It was another two-pronged incident. Some students had shot firearms and used "low and exceedingly blasphemous language" on the college grounds, and these or other students the following night had gathered outside the Alabama Athenaeum, a seminary for young ladies, and "insulted and alarmed the inmates with boisterous shouts, profane language, and the discharge of firearms."

When at prayers the next morning (April 2, 1842), the president notified the students that they would be exonerated, several students who had been in the Athenaeum disturbance voluntarily confessed. The faculty then confined their interrogation to the campus incident. Twenty-seven students said they were innocent; two admitted some degree of guilt. But forty-eight refused to answer. These were sent home to think it over. Some did. When they asked for permission to come back and vindicate themselves, the permission was granted. But it is not clear whether the actual culprits were ever really found.[11]

Three years later an even less serious incident had the result of plunging the campus into riot because the hated exculpation law was invoked. Boys who lived in Washington Hall so far forgot the conduct becoming gentlemen that they shouted from their windows at ladies walking through the college grounds and even flashed light in their faces with mirrors. Called up for reprimand, the boys who lived in the rooms from which the light might have been thrown refused to confess or deny the charge and were "forthwith suspended for contumacy." Their fellow students—also—forthwith—rioted, and, in their turn, refused to defend themselves and were suspended. The faculty must have been encouraged the next day when a number of students, of their own volition, came forward to confess that they had had some part in the disorders. But, instead of leaving well enough alone, the faculty pressed their advantage by requiring the culprits to sign a humiliating document which read,

We, whose names are hereunto subscribed, do hereby declare our cordial disapprobation of the acts of Wednesday, the 19th instant, which, though thoughtlessly done, we perceive with regret, were in violation of the decorum and the respect due to ladies; and we promise that while we are students of this University we will not engage in any act which we have reason to suppose will be interpreted as an insult to a lady.

We also hereby express out disapprobation of the disorders of Monday night, and, so far as we participated in disorder or a breach of the laws on either occasion, we ask forgiveness of the Faculty.

This extreme measure was grating to the feelings. Eleven students signed in silence. A few refused to sign and were suspended. And the same sentence was meted out to the others who, though they signed, did so with "offensive words" which described their feelings about faculty tyranny.[12]

The same disposition on the part of the faculty to invite trouble by excessive emphasis of breaches of discipline and the same readiness of students to retaliate appears in an incident of 1847, which involved the riding of horses without permission and throwing of a stone at Professor Brumby. The crimes occurred at the end of the school term, December 21, 1847. Professor Brumby had been a target for "missiles" when he started over to Washington Hall to find out who had taken the horses from a faculty member's stable. It would have been the better part of wisdom to have let the holiday bring a measure of forgetfulness, but the faculty were made of sterner stuff. On January 1, they held a special pre-term meeting and decided to put on probation all students except those known to be innocent. They were probably surprised and shocked when some "unknown persons" took all door-knobs from the public rooms in the Lyceum and the Rotunda to prevent all regular exercises from being held. Only three students complied with the order that time, but others must have taken advantage of an overnight extension of time to change their minds and avoid suspension, for classes which could certainly not have been held with so large a part of the student body absent did continue. Two culprits were finally exposed. Robert E. Herndon confessed and was refused an "honorable dismission" on January 17, and on February 7, William Saffold admitted that he had thrown the stone at Professor Brumby. Apparently he made honorable amends, for he was reinstated in the school.[13]

What the professors lacked in finesse they made up for in diligence. Patiently, to each meeting of the faculty, each teacher brought his report of student misdeeds. Often there was little time for other business after these had been duly considered. Special faculty meetings were often called at which students guilty of serious misdemeanors were given an opportunity to explain and apologize. When, as the years went on, a system of demerits was introduced, the faculty carefully compiled these lists and read them in the chapel the morning following their regular faculty meeting. One hundred demerits warranted dismissal from the University. Parents were apprised of their sons' shortcomings and earnestly asked to help in the enforcement of the necessary discipline which would make the youngsters into gentlemen and scholars. When matters seemed to get serious, boys were sent home for a short period of suspension or forever.

Some of the disciplinary action had to be taken when student antagonism toward the faculty expressed itself in overt acts. Thomas M. Mathews was suspended in February, 1833, for "insurbordination and contempt of lawful authority" toward Professor Bonfils. The period of this student's dismissal would have kept him away from the campus for ten months unless he should satisfy the authorities that he felt "properly" about his misdeeds and was ready to apologize.[14] Richard Croom got into similar trouble, with similar penalties on May 8, 1835. He had not only shown disrespect to a

THE OLD UNIVERSITY 205

professor but he had been noisy around the buildings, inattentive to his studies, and had not mended his ways when admonished.[15] John Inge in 1842 avoided suspension by making "a humble, penitent apology"[16] for calling Mr. Foster a nickname in "a loud and insulting tone." Other counts were against him, however, and he was soon involved in a general disturbance which resulted in dismissal.[17] Jeremiah E. Sanders, reported for insolence in Mr. Walden's classroom, also had his apology accepted[18] but, like Inge, he did not mend his ways after this warning. Only a few days later he was in trouble for "improper conduct in Steward's Hall" and for "grossly indecorous and insulting conduct" toward the steward, Mr. Caruthers. That time he was sent home.[19]

Sometimes students complicated these cases of lack of respect toward the constituted authorities by showing youthful spirit and dignity. One such incident started when Professor Walden, seeing Francis M. Robinson "being mean to a small boy," remarked that such conduct was "not very manly." Robinson's insolent reply resulted in the calling of a special faculty meeting at which Robinson refused to offer either apology or defense. He was withdrawn from the University until such time as he was ready to apologize and to acknowledge the right of any officer to control him. The boy made a gesture toward complying the following week, but the "tone and tenor" of his letter was "such as to meet the unanimous disapprobation of the members" of the faculty. They held another special meeting to consider Robinson's second attempt at apology and to edit his note, returning it to him with "such erasures and interlineations marked as would render the communication acceptable." They also reminded him that a satisfactory apology had to be accompanied by a disclaimer, made in private to the president, of any responsibility for firing a bullet or buckshot into Mr. Walden's room the previous week. Apparently Robinson had been goaded into taking retaliatory measures as his relatively minor offense had assumed the proportions of a major crime. There the record stops; there is no further reference to Robinson in the minutes.[20]

Another rebel was Robert Tait, who was summoned to appear before the faculty on March 31, 1843, but he failed to do so. As the term was just ending then, it was April 25, before the faculty could consider the case. By that time they had apparently forgotten what it was that had made Robert's summons necessary in the first place. His original misdeed had been eclipsed by the crime of ignoring a faculty summons. Tait's first attempt at a letter of explanation was regarded as "breathing a rebellious spirit" and his second was just as unsatisfactory. The tenor of these notes may be reflected in the faculty comment that the boy was particularly "culpable" because of "his assumption that a student has the right to judge of the propriety of obeying a summons of the Faculty . . . according to his view of the reasons which induced the Faculty to make the summons." They told the culprit that he would now have to make an "unequivocal expression of regret" not only for his first disobedience but also for his "rebellious" letters. Tait at that point wrote the apology required. After talking with him the President, satisfied that his penitence was genuine, reinstated[21] him.

When the president took initial action without allowing the faculty to become involved in disciplinary action, matters sometimes went more easily. Oliver T. Prince, who shouted at a professor one March day in 1848, was severely and promptly admonished by the President. So ended that case.[22]

Once in a while a student wrote, not in apology, but in aggressive insult. No record was made in the faculty minutes of the contents of one such letter, written to Professor Pratt in 1852 by William James Gilmore, but they agreed that Professor Pratt had every reason to consider it "improper." Gilmore worsened his case in a second letter "pretending to be a retraction." The faculty said "that the language of this paper, as well as its appearance, take from it the merit of even a retraction, and that it is wholly deficient as an apology." Gilmore was dismissed, but he was later reinstated after a satisfactory apology to the president and to Professor Pratt.[23]

In this accumulation of stories of apologies exacted by teachers for "insults" from students, at least one incident records a reversal of circumstances. In 1849 in a class of Professor Dockery's, students applauded the recitation of one of the class members. Professor Dockery told the students that this practice was against University rules and that students who thus far forgot themselves were deficient in good breeding and gentlemanly deportment. The hot young blood of the old South regarded this as an insult not to be tolerated even from a professor. The next day they asserted their

THE OLD UNIVERSITY

independence by applauding again. When Professor Dockery told those who did not care to behave themselves to leave the class, all but four went out. And they did not come back until Professor Dockery was willing to assure them that he had intended no insult.[24]

Student differences with the faculty were by no means confined to words. More than one teacher found himself in actual physical danger when the ire of the students or their spirit of mischief got into play. Frequently President Woods was a target for student violence.[25] Similarly President Manly was not immune to attack. On February 1, 1841 Richard Legrand Capers was expelled for an assault on the president and on the steward.[26] Manly described the incident in the following leter:

University of Ala.
June 14, 1841

My Dear Brother,

... We have had no difficulty in the college this year. In the latter part of the month of January a low and dissolute fellow, by the name of Capers, on being excluded for his vices and contempt of the laws, attempted to insult me and the Steward by pulling our noses. Mine was fortunately so short that the fellow could not get hold of it fairly, and therefore no harm was done.

The circumstances, as you ask for them, were briefly this. A fellow by the name of Capers, poor and destitute, and unhappily dissolute and low, applied for admission into college in January, 1840—and on account of his being an orphan, poor and friendless, was admitted by very great and unusual indulgence. When I found him failing to pay punctually his college dues, I proposed to him to abate all college charges, according to a provision of our board in favor of the destitute. This he declined; and said his brother would bountifully supply him. When I found him drinking, visiting houses of ill fame, and in his intoxication committing various outrages, the faculty was induced to give him a further trial on his promise of amendment. At last, things getting no better, he was sent for and warned that his standing was very precarious, and that the first offense would discharge him. Not long after, it was ascertained that he was a defaulter to the steward—had not paid his board. Before the steward reported him to me formally, I took pains to go to the fellow, and call him aside, and tell him that I had called not as an officer, but a friend, to admonish him that this difficulty was hanging over him, that he ought to take pains to remove it at once, that if the steward should report him, the faculty had no alternative but must dismiss him forthwith, according to the laws, all which he very well knew. Still he let the matter run on 10 days longer, and the steward (who had before banished him from his table for his ill-manners) reported him to the faculty. I was directed by the faculty to send for him, and if he pleaded want of means, I was to allow him time to write to his brother and receive an answer, before enforcing the regulation. When he came, he said he had the money in hand, and could pay at any time. I then told him that he must pay, and hand me the evidence of payment, within 24 hours from that time. This was Monday morning. I waited until Tuesday noon; when, hearing nothing from him I sent him a written order to the effect that his privileges in his class are suspended. It seems that, after receiving this order, he went and paid the steward, and offered him some insolence at the same time. But he came not to me, nor communicated with me in any manner; but finding that his name was not called by the officers in the list of his class, he took himself off to town and remained away (supposed in a house of ill fame) until the following Thursday night. Then he came to me, and wished I should recall the order for his exclusion from his class; still, however, offering no evidence that he had paid and no apology for having delayed to pay beyond the time I had ordered, or for his leaving college for several days, I told him I should not recall the order, that he had trifled with me as a man, by giving no heed to my private friendly counsels, and that he had showed contempt for the laws and authority of the University; which I was determined no student should do. He thought it very hard, and asked me if I would allow him to bring his case before the faculty. To this I assented readily, told him to write his appeal, and I would present it on the following evening. He still offered no apology or explanation of his conduct. The faculty accordingly sent him an order, to this effect that they saw no reason to deviate from the decision heretofore announced to him, and that he must leave the premises forthwith. This letter was sent him by the secretary on Saturday. Nothing more was heard directly from him, until after prayer on Monday afternoon following: while I was standing in the chapel door talking to some students who had business with me, I saw him approaching. My first thought was not to recognize him at all, as his being on the premises was a violation of the laws. But I soon concluded that I would at least see what he had to say. When those to whom I was talking were gone, he approached me impressively and asked if there was no chance for his restoration. I told him I thought not. He said he should like to know the reason. I replied that my conversation with him had not been vague nor ambiguous, that he knew, himself, how he had trifled with the laws and shown contempt for authority; and that the very fact of his presence there, without permission, at that time, was a further instance how little he regarded the laws of the Board, or the order of the Faculty.

On this, he attempted to pull my nose; failing to get hold he slapped me in the face—all in a twinkling. So little did I expect such a thing, that I scarcely was conscious of what was passing. My first consciousness found me advanced toward him a step or two, with my fist drawn back, but as he stood at a respectful distance (cussing and raging, however) it immediately struck me what would be said if I should advance on him and brat him. I stood, therefore, silent, in that attitude for a minute or more; and finding him not disposed to renew the assault, I simply remarked to him, that "the time had been, when as not restrained by christian principles, I would make him smart for that," and then turned and walked home. The fellow then went down to the steward's house and attempted the same indignity on the steward. There was no person nearer to me when he attempted to strike me than the college buildings, about 100 yards distant. At the steward's house the students who were at table prevented a collision between him and the steward; and while the latter went upstairs to get his gun, they hurried the fellow off to town.

A warrant was very promptly issued for his apprehension, but he kept himself concealed in his favorite resort, a whore-house, until he found means to get away. . . . .

Affectionately,
B. Manly[27]

In the spring of 1836 George Lister was told to leave the college because he had been found to have intoxicating liquors in his room. He refused to leave the campus and "used language of abuse and defiance to one member of the faculty and offered personal violence to another." He was forthwith recommended to the trustees for expulsion, and because he had "assaulted a professor with a deadly weapon," he was bound over to the circuit court to be tried for assault and battery with intent to murder. This drastic action was given up, however, when Lister apologized, confessed, and promised to go home peaceably. He was not required to stand civil trial after that.[28]

Two other students, Wilson and Richard Walthall, got into trouble several years later, by threatening violence to members of the faculty, especially Professor Pratt, though it is not clear that they did more than threaten. Richard got into trouble when Professor Pratt caught him cheating in a Latin examination. After the examination was over the trouble began:

R. B. Walthall sought him, [Prof. Pratt] out and denounced what he had done . . . in language very offensive and insulting, at the same time, carrying his hand in his bosom, as if holding a concealed weapon. . . . During this interview W. J. Walthall [Wilson] stood nearby, uttering threatening sounds and brandishing a large stick. . . .

The faculty said that this was clearly "a combination with deliberate intention to overawe and insult an officer in the discharge of his duty," and they agreed that such an offense was "among the highest of which a student can be guilty." The Walthall boys were sent home and expelled by the trustees,[29] who only a few weeks later softened somewhat when they received a letter from Richard asking for readmission or for a letter of dismission. They did not readmit him, but they did say that if he went to another University they would not "pursue him with information of his conduct."[30]

If a teacher won the dislike of the students, his life was particularly miserable. A sudden fit of temper could cause an episode like that in which Thomas Jefferson Gordon in 1859 was expelled for an assault on Professor Mallet.[31] But only sustained and unrelenting dislike could bring the kind of experiences which cut short the career at the University of Alabama of Dr. Emmanuel Vitalis Scherb, graduate of Harvard and teacher of French. George Little gives an account of his persecutions:

He was a bachelor and very unpopular. He had a room on the second floor of Franklin Hall, right under the Erosophic Society Hall. One night the boys tied a rope to his door-knob and tied it to the banisters so that he could not open his door. They then went up into the Erosophic Hall and stopped up the fire-place and then went on top of the house and put a blower on top of the chimney to smoke him out. When, red-eyed and shaking, he found that he could not open his door he raised a window to get aid and the boys threw rocks at him.[32]

If punishment was meted out for this prank, it was halfhearted. The faculty did not like Professor Scherb either. He resigned at the end of his first year.

In spite of insult and in spite of physical danger the faculty valiantly struggled to enforce the rules through which academic order could be imposed upon the students. All the rules were difficult to enforce all of the time. And the rules which set up the rigid schedules of chapel, classroom, and study were a constant problem.

Compulsory attendance and decorous behavior at the chapel services which forced students out of bed by dawn or earlier was one unending struggle. In 1835 an attempt was made to regularize attendance at these services, at classes, and at study hours by a regulation known as the "Rule of Four." When a student was absent

THE OLD UNIVERSITY 211

more than four times in a month from any of these appointments, he was dismissed at the end of the third month.[33] Three students were penalized the first month this rule was in existence; they had been absent from prayers. Two months later two students were dismissed for violating the "four law" three times. Absence from prayers was part of their crime, though they may have missed other appointments also.[34]

The rule of four was not renewed when the laws were revised in 1838. But the faculty were enjoined to keep records of tardiness and absence and to deal with misdeameanors as they saw fit.[35]

They had, of course, been dealing with such misdemeanors all along. In 1836 one student was "seriously and publicly" reproved for disorderly conduct in chapel and warned that if he continued his behavior he would be "removed" from the institution.[36] In the years which followed, students were called before the faculty for a multitude of offenses, among which were: sitting out of place, moving out of place, being late for prayers, going to prayers in improper dress, coming into chapel with his hat on, noisy conduct, whispering, napping at chapel, reading a text-book, spitting on the chapel floor.[37]

Under the system of demerits in use in 1843, the penalty for improper chapel conduct was set at five demerits.[38] This system was abolished in 1850, but a book was kept recording all absences, tardiness, "egressions," and lapses from good deportment. The faculty were meticulous about these records. They formally decided that tardiness and sitting out of place in chapel were to be set down as disorders, whereas tardiness at recitations and "egressions" from them were to be reported under "punctuality."[39] Two years later, when Professor Tuomey and Mr. Henry were assigned to mark absences on Sunday mornings (members of the faculty with no morning classes were responsible on weekdays), a note was made that students must "leave the prayer room with due decorum" and that "jumping over benches" was to be marked as a disorder.[40]

A few special instances break the montony of the record. One student, dismissed from the University in 1835, shocked everyone by coming back and "appearing again in the Chapel and there offering abusive language to some of the Faculty." This was enough to prompt the faculty to ask the trustees to change his suspension to expulsion.[41] Most of the instances of discipline, however, are more routine: Guy S. Goldsby, senior, who had been absent from prayers "for some time" was spoken to in 1851. Walthall, junior, also a frequent absentee, was told that he must attend prayers or leave college.[42] If this was the same Walthall who insulted Professor Pratt, he very shortly was leaving college—for other reasons.

Regulations covering classroom behavior were even more strict and explicit. The first ordinances of the University prohibited, in lecture, recitation, or devotions, such disturbances as whispering, reading, or using a textbook in any recitation room unless required by the teacher.[43] And the laws of 1839 gave these prohibitions an even more ominous sound:

The Students are required to behave themselves toward all persons, specially toward the officers, with the utmost decorum and respectfulness. During recitation or any public exercise, they are particularly enjoined to avoid every mark of inattention or indecorum; and each officer is bound strictly to enforce the regulation. For gross or persevering violation of propriety, the offender may be forthwith dismissed from the room, if his instructor should think it necessary.[44]

The "gross or persevering violations" were many. Here are a few which won for their perpetrators censure or punishment: Physic Rush Elmore got five months suspension for beating on the doors and doorposts of recitation rooms while classes were in session.[45] Richard F. Inge was required to withdraw from the University because, among other things, he persisted in "groaning during recitations."[46] Gould was admonished for "shooting chalk" and told that he would be punished if he continued this practice.[47] John G. Dew tried the patience of the faculty to such an extent by his conduct in the recitation room that they accused him of "evincing an ungrateful spirit, after the repeated indulgences . . . granted him" and requested him to reform at once or face the consequences.[48] Low standing, frequent absences, and indecorous behavior in recitation all combined to bring students before the president for reprimand.[49]

Sometimes incidents occurred for which no one seemed responsible. One day in 1843 all the textbooks for the freshman class in ancient geography disappeared. Of course, no one knew who had taken them. They appeared again after "a due length of time," and then the faculty retaliated by allowing make-up recitations only for those who signed a statement that they had no part in making the books disappear.[50]

THE OLD UNIVERSITY   213

Sometimes the disturbances took on the character of an epidemic. February, 1852, was one of those times. However, most of the misdemeanors during that month were minor. James M. Fitzpatrick had a confidential chat with the president and promised not to "groan" in class any more. He got off without even having to apologize to Professor Benagh, whose classes seem to have been the focal point in the disturbances.[51] But John T. Grace and David R. George, who had evidently given their courage artificial stimulant before "disturbing" the class, were directed to leave school and were reinstated only on signing a pledge to abstain from all intoxicating liquors.[52] Edward F. Nott, who had been "murmuring" in Professor Pratt's classes, got off with the signing of the same pledge.[53]

"Emissions from class"—or just plain cuts in the modern student's vocabulary—were also severely frowned upon. At first, if a student persisted in being absent, he might incur penalties of "high punishments." Later this rule is not quite as definite. The 1831 rule read,

No student shall be absent from any exercise except by permission of the officer by whom that exercise is to be performed, unless he has obtained from the President leave of absence from the College.[54]

The laws of 1839 stated that:

An individual may be excused from attendance on a single exercise, by the officer with whom it should have been performed; but a class can not be excused except with the concurrence of the President; and no student shall absent himself from the University premises, without leave first obtained from the President.[55]

The "Rule of Four" was applied during the middle thirties more often to class truancy than to lapses in chapel attendance. Four students were admonished during November, 1835,[56] and ten during the following February.[57] Of the twenty-two admonished that March, four were second offenders.[58]

Letters home were used to enlist parental support for the maintenance of student regularity.[59] Seventeen of these letters had to be dispatched in the month of March, 1834, to the parents of students admonished by the president for excessive absences from class.[60]

Irregularity of class attendance and general neglect of study often went hand in hand. In 1834 Ezra F. Bouchelle, who had attended "only several" classes between January 15 and April 9, was asked to withdraw from the University. He did not go docilely, but added an insult to a teacher to his crimes, and so was recommended for expulsion.[61] Three students were sent home the following June for being "unjustifiably negligent,"[62] and a year later another was suspended for "habitual idleness, inattention to his studies, and neglect of college exercises."[63] Another student went home in 1842,[64] and three the next year were told firmly that at the present rate they were not likely to "overtake their class in geometry."[65] A student dismissed for "perserving [sic] idleness and impropriety of conduct," in March of 1844, was reinstated, with a warning, five days later.[66]

Parents of two students in 1847 were told that their boys were "not improving their time." One was advised to take his son out of college; the other asked to "apply a corrective."[67] The same message went to fathers in 1848, but one at least was ineffectual, since a son who was to have been "withdrawn" by parental action was still around the following month, and still being scolded for his low standing.[68] One student the following year, who was found many times "idly lounging and sporting away hours of study," was first talked to by the president and then advised to go home.[69]

The faculty showed an unwonted patience in 1852, when they found that Franklin S. Pate was not attending any of his classes. Pate, when talked to by the president, said that he was trying to make up his mind whether or not to stay in college. He was given a week to reach his decision, and then a second week because he could not seem to make up his mind. Nearly a month passed before Pate finally agreed to stay, provided he be excused from the study of geometry.[70] It is interesting to note that while Pate toyed with the idea of leaving college, three other students were dismissed for a "strong presumption of disorder" and continued inattention to college duties.[71] There was often little consistency in the application of discipline in the old University of Alabama.[72]

In an effort to do their utmost to discourage the "egressions" which caused so many of their troubles, the faculty voted in 1850 that any student "egressing without reciting" should get a deficiency mark for that day's recitation, whether or not his name actually came up in the drawing of the cards.[73] Two years later, however, four students reported as regularly absent from their mathematics classes were, for some strange reason, simply told that they could be excused from attending classes for the rest of the term.[74]

THE OLD UNIVERSITY 215

Cheating, regarded by the students as a perfectly legitimate strategy in their battle of wits, was another headache. This took many forms. One of the more dramatic was that used by two students who, in July of 1843, broke into the faculty rooms for purposes of bettering their grades. William Saunders was after papers in Mr. Foster's desk; Benjamin L. Whelan went for the book in which Professor Barnard, secretary of the faculty, kept records of student grades. The escapade put both boys beyond the need of grades; they were summarily dismissed.[75]

For the most part, however, the students used the time-honored methods of getting illegitimate help on recitations and examinations. Using a textbook during a recitation was common. They referred to a concealed paper on which needed information had been written, an act referred to as "papering" in the early faculty ledger. Prompting—the age-old expression of student solidarity—was also frequent.

Alexander Meek, the first student cited in the faculty records for cheating, was unlucky. He failed his senior examination even after resorting to "most unjustifiable means to sustain himself in that examination." But he was given another chance, because he apologized both for cheating and for using bad language when he found the cheating had done no good. He graduated with his class.[76]

In 1843 Robert Tait and Samuel S. Murphy received some help on an examination on the application of algebra to geometry. They had to take another test the next day. If the episode had repercussions, they came because Tait did not obey the faculty summons, not because he had cheated.[77]

But by 1847 the faculty were becoming less lenient. They ruled that students who cheated were not to be given a chance to redeem themselves through a second examination.[78] They really tackled the problem the following year, when a committee appointed for the purpose presented a set of rules that must have looked completely fraudproof:

1. That each student, on entering a recitation-room, shall deposit his text-book apart from his seat, and not have a book or memorandum near him, while the recitation lasts—except in the departments of ancient and modern languages, or in other departments occasionally by direction of an officer.

2. That each student, in reciting, shall advance to some vacant space designated by the officer, apart from his own seat or that of any student.
3. That recitations in all the classes requiring a text-book to be used, shall be made by the student advancing and using a book furnished by the University for that purpose.
4. That students at the black-board shall not wear a cloak.
5. That if any student at his seat or elsewhere, in a recitation room, assume a posture, or pursue any course which may justify the suspicion that he is using or seeking improper help, the officer will rate him at zero, whether called to perform or not—and inform the student at the close of the exercise that he has so marked him.
6. If a student persevere in attempts to evade the purpose and efficiency of these rules, or shall be detected more than once in seeking or using improper help, the Faculty will treat him with the severity which his disingenuous conduct merits;—even to final exclusion from the University, when the case seems to require extreme rigor.[79]

But these rules covered classroom contingencies alone. They were not fine mesh enough to catch Richard I. Hogan and John C. Houston, who committed so many plagiarisms in their compositions within three months of the passage of the new rules that they were directed to write them all over and to appear before the president for a reprimand before they could continue their classes.[80]

Rules for the conduct of written examinations were made more stringent in 1851. Among the new provisions devised to hold cheating to the minimum were these measures:

1. A number shall be assigned to each student (not that of the catalogue) by which he will be known.
2. This number is to be written conspicuously (enclosed in a circle) on every paper employed. . . .
3. Avoid all communication, by words, figures, writing, signs, or looking over the work of another.
4. Bring no book except required by the nature of the work, no atlas, portfolio, or other case of papers, Pens and ink, cap-paper (blank), slate and pencils. See that you have plenty before you begin:—no going out. Use no memorandum (previously made) of any kind. Margin to be ruled and left blank for binding.
6. If a question is to be asked for elucidation, it must be asked aloud; and the answer, if given, will be given *aloud by the officer.*
7. Any fact which gives rise to the suspicion of unfairness, or receiving aid, will subject a student to [a direct question] or to a re-examination, at the discretion of the examining officers.[81]

Rules may have helped, but rules did not cure the malady. Duncan Dew and Thomas W. Curry were charged with using "unfair means in recitation" in June of 1851.[82] And in the same year Walthall's difficulty with Professor Pratt started because Pratt accused him of using a translation in a Latin examination.[83] And by 1853 the faculty were ready to admit one of their few acknowledged defeats in the disciplinary area: they decided to give up written examinations entirely because it was impossible to "isolate" a student enough to keep him from cheating.[84]

It is, perhaps, interesting to note that stealing, unlike cheating, was apparently not a common vice among the students of the University of Alabama. The Hall boys, who were in college in the 1850's, twice mentioned experiences with petty thieves. Crenshaw Hall wrote his father in 1858:

The other night somebody entered one of the Sophs rooms while he was asleep, broke open his trunk in 3 feet of his head, and took $150 in notes and bank bills besides nearly all of his best clothes. Whoever it was, I suppose, stood out of doors and saw him put his money in the trunk, as the boys had heard someone walking around there 2 or 3 nights. I have not been robbed yet, and I hope I will not be. This robbery occurred in Washington Building.[85]

Bolling had earlier written his mother about two robberies. The first time, he said, only about eight dollars was taken; the second time, nearly $160.[86]

That there should have been no other instances of stealing in the early University is, of course, incredible. But there was not enough thievery for a faculty, troubled with many other matters, to be greatly alarmed.

If keeping order in chapel and classroom was difficult, keeping order in the dormitories was impossible. The struggles of the faculty at this point make other struggles pale in comparison. They were responsible for policing study hours, which, in practical terms, meant all the hours when students were not actually in the classroom. They did their best to perform those duties faithfully, to make the assigned round in room inspection, to check on absences, to reprimand for carelessness and noise, and to cajole and beseech and bully the students into conformity with the hated rules which governed them every moment of every day. It was no accident that the most celebrated mass student rebellion, growing out of an effort to turn students into regimented scholars, was the result of the room visitation and its infringement upon what the students chose to regard as their privacy.

In the very early years the students sometimes regarded the room visitation as a game of wits. It was fun for the students to hide when the professor trudged around on his tour of duty, to let him give an absence mark, and then to confront him with the fact that they had been in their rooms all the time. As early as 1837 the harried faculty took notice of such "impositions" which were "practiced on the faculty by representations that students were in their rooms when they were not." They said that henceforth "any student whose person is not seen, or his voice heard by the professor when he visits the room" should be counted absent flatly and finally. They also added that each professor should mark absent from his room any student found during study hours in an entry where he did not belong.[87] Wandering students were thus subject to double check; they might escape the notice of their own officer only to be caught by the inspector of some other entry or dormitory.

Many minor misdeameanors were recorded in the faculty ledger of those years. Students were admonished for throwing stones into the entry, for playing music in rooms during study hours, for firing pistols in rooms, for moving furniture in study hours, for carrying a bed across the campus, for congregating at the door of Jefferson Hall and throwing stones against the building, and for halloing when an officer was visiting the rooms.[88]

Most of the entries are fairly succinct. November 9, 1833, four students, absent from their rooms without satisfactory explanation, on Saturday evening, admonished and parents informed.[89] April 10, 1836, Lawrence E. Lister, previously cited for inattention to studies, absences from prayers, recitations, study hours, adds a four-day visit to town, without permission, to his list of misdemeanors; suspended for ten months.[90] June, 1842, John B. Ashford admitted disturbing study hour by shouting through a tin tube from his dormitory window; dismissed from the University.[91] May, 1842, five students reported for throwing water from dormitory windows; admonished privately by the president.[92] January 22, 1849, three students complain of noisy behavior in the room above them; offenders told they will be moved to a lower story if they are not quiet.[93] October 20, 1851. "Room No. 9 Jefferson, occupied by Fisher, Grace, and Atkinson is reported by Prof. Stafford for disorder upon Friday night last."[94]

Some of the misdemeanors uncovered by the prowling professors needed more discussion, either because the facts in the case were obscure or because students, in one way or another, resisted efforts to punish them.

Were the four students sitting around a table with a deck of cards on it, on March 6, 1834, actually engaging in the forbidden game, or were they not? The visiting officer who penetrated the "back room of their suite" was sure they were. Three of the students insisted that they were just "throwing the cards around" for fun; the deck was an old one they had found. The fourth student, however, betrayed the group; he said they were playing cards, and he added that it was not the first time they had played. The case was further complicated when one of the accused appeared before the faculty with a dirk in his shirt; he was withdrawn from school. Another student, who had a bad record of neglecting his studies, was also dismissed. The boy who confessed and the fourth card-player, who had behaved themselves very creditably in the past, were merely warned to mend their ways.[95]

The unpopular Professor Scherb had, in February, 1853, a stubborn case. He reported "the occupants of Rooms 13 and 18, Franklin College," for a list of offences including "disorderly noises, shooting, dancing, etc." The offenders were promptly notified that such conduct met the "serious disapprobation" of the faculty and must end at once.[96] A second official message three days later told the "inmates" of Rooms 13 and 18 that they would be assessed for damages done to the banisters in the north entry of Franklin Hall.[97] Professor Scherb had been forced to report to his colleagues at that meeting that the occupants of these two rooms had not only disregarded the faculty warning but were behaving worse than ever. He was sure that John J. Harris was one of the offenders; he had seen him in the act of misbehaving. He strongly suspected that William C. Comegys was one also. It is interesting that, in the face of Professor Scherb's eye-witness testimony, Harris was allowed to plead innocent, but the suspected Comegys was "required to withdraw."[98]

The episode may have been the one which caused the "smoking out" of Mr. Scherb described by George Little; the faculty minutes record that a month later he was again embroiled, when, at a late hour, his room was "assaulted" and "showers of stones were thrown in at the windows."[99] Although Professor Scherb was transferred to Jefferson Hall at the beginning of the spring term, his troubles continued. In May the faculty notified the students that the sixty cents paid to repair the lock on Professor Scherb's room would be assessed against the whole student body.[100] In all of these cases involving Scherb, there is a singular lack of faculty response; punishments, if inflicted at all, were usually light.

Card playing seems to have been a problem which recurred all through the period. One incident, which occurred in the spring of 1852, involved George Little and some of his friends. We have, therefore, two accounts of it which reflect the difference in point of view of students and teachers on some of these infringements of college rules. The faculty account has a stern ring:

It is reported to the Faculty that Burke, Comegys, Marlow, and Harris 2d (Freshmen) were seen playing at cards, during study hours, in the room of Marlowe and Little. The President is requested to send for them individually, and see what security they can give that the offence will not be repeated. The fathers of these students are also to be informed.[101]

Perhaps the president used his discretion about such instructions from his faculty, for Little, for himself at least, remembered no unpleasant consequences from the incident:

The students were also very fond of playing cards. One day four of us were enjoying a game in my room when Professor Milt Woodruff knocked on the door. I knew his knock, put my cards in my pocket, picked up my Horace and began to study diligently. He reported the other three—Willie Ormond, Malcolm Burke, and John Harris, and also Nicholas Marlowe, who happened to be in the room but was not playing. I was not reported. Very often these games were played for money.[102]

A policeman's lot is not a happy one. But that lot is rendered more miserable when those in high places suggest that the policeman is not adequately performing his duties. The faculty of the early University of Alabama—some of them at least—found room visitation exceedingly distasteful. They were, therefore, justly indignant when, in 1843, the committee on education of the senate of Alabama, inquired into the "causes which have tended to retard the prosperity" of the University and insinuated that lack of discipline enforcement by the faculty was one of these causes. The faculty responded with spirit:

> The Faculty would state . . . that within the hours defined by the documents submitted, embracing the greater part of the day, and all the evening, or night, the students are required to be present in their rooms, unless in attendance on their proper recitations; and that, to insure this presence, and the proper attention to study, they are liable to visitation at all hours by the Faculty, and are more or less frequently visited, as circumstances seem to require. . . . The Faculty, beyond exercising the right of daily, hourly, if they please, visiting the rooms of students, of requiring their presence whenever they may choose, individually in their own rooms, and of keeping a continual eye upon all the buildings and grounds, attempt nothing further in the way of direct government. They assume that, under these restrictions, and with this degree of surveillance, every student will conduct himself as a man of honor. They watch as closely for the prevention of evil as the officers of any college, in the United States, and all experience has shown, closer watching is attended with the aggravation of the evils it is intended to prevent.[103]

Even the "degree of surveillance" about which the faculty boasted was enough to aggravate the situation. That fact was thoroughly clear in 1854: student resentment against being watched and regimented every instant of every day broke into open rebellion.

The students by that time had devised their own way of handling the visitation rule. Whenever a professor started his inspection rounds, the first student to spot him set up the shout of "Wolf!" Other students took up the cry, as if by magic, all noise, card-playing, and forbidden activities stopped. The inspector found his boys studiously preparing their lessons as required by University rules. It might have been wise for the faculty to let the wolf game play itself out, but they thought otherwise at the time. They sternly announced that any student who gave this warning would be suspended. James M. Doby was the first victim, and thus raised himself to University fame. As soon as Professor Benagh had finished "visiting" Doby's room one spring day, the boy set up the wolf cry. Thereupon, he was promptly called before the faculty, and when he refused to deny the charge against him, was expelled.

His fellow sophomores were up in arms at once. They wrote an indignant statement to the faculty, declaring that they considered

Doby's action "unexceptionable" and announcing that they would attend no more college exercises until he was reinstated. When the thirty-three boys, who signed the communication were promptly suspended,[104] the indignation spread.

In protest several freshmen and juniors and even one senior withdrew from college, and only ten of the suspended sophomores ever returned to the campus. It is interesting to note that one of the boys who ended his connection with the University of Alabama in this student protest against faculty spying and injustice was Hilary Abner Herbert, who later became Secretary of the Navy under President Grover Cleveland.[105]

Newspapers throughout the state took up the cry. And the professors who, ten years earlier, had been under suspicion of being too lenient with their young charges were now pictured as Paul Prys, Dogberries, fat gliding ghosts, police spies, invading the sanctity of privacy of high-minded young men who were quite right in asserting their resentment of such tactics. Said the Mobile *Daily Register*,

It appears to us that the plan pursued by the Faculty of our University . . . of visiting the rooms of the students, at uncertain hours, as a species of police spies, is one that ought to be abandoned. There is nothing so offensive to a high-minded young man or to societies of such, as to be under a constant species of surveillance—to be treated as eye-servants—to have the lean tudor or the fat professor, in his soundless slippers, gliding ghost like through the passages about his door, or popping in, like Paul Pry, unawares upon his retiracy or social intercourse. Such conduct should not be systematically pursued even towards a child, by a parent.—There is a sanctity of privacy belonging to every one—and nothing can justify its rude invasion. We have known more disturbances in college life, on this account, than on any other, and we do not wonder that the student at Tuscaloosa shouted out "Wolf!" when grave professors were playing the part of Dogberries, and attempting stealthily to detect them in their peccadilloes.[106]

The "grave professors" must have smiled wryly at this expression of public opinion. They had tried manfully to impose upon undisciplined youth a pattern of scholarly life which they believed essential in the making of educated men. They had expected no thanks from the students—except perhaps in the retrospect of mature life. But from the adult public of the state, surely they expected to receive more understanding. The criticism of the *Register* was strangely inconsistent with the hue and cry which other newspapers were even then helping to spread about the shocking behavior of University students, the wild escapades that outraged decency and trampled on the rights of citizens.

Although the list of offenses, offenders, and punishments meted out is a formidable one, the University of Alabama was not unique in this chaotic state. In like manner schools throughout the South and other areas were experiencing the same problems in varying degrees.

The neighboring states of Georgia, Virginia, Mississippi, and South Carolina have evidence of similar behavior of students. According to Professor Francis Leiber, South Carolina was more fortunate in her students, for on May 15, 1837, he recorded in his journal that

"Not once have I appealed to their honor and found myself disappointed. If you treat them *en gens d'arme,* of course they not only try to kick, but you give zest to resistance."

Dr. Joseph LeConte, who was a professor at South Carolina after Leiber left, wrote in his *Autobiography* that in their college life they were the most honorable students with whom he had been associated.[107] LeConte previously had been a professor at Franklin College (University of Georgia). Not many professors held such a high regard for the students, for, as has been noted, professors suffered frequently through the actions of the students.

At South Carolina, Dr. Cooper's horse, Blanche, was often painted and her tail shaved. When the horse died, the students solemnly proposed as an honor a public burial and a holiday.

Problems of a more serious nature, that of bodily harm and assault, were not infrequent at other schools. Instances similar to those at Alabama are probably on record in most schools in existence during this period. Despite the sentiments of Professors Leiber and LeConte concerning the students of South Carolina College, a professor was burned in effigy, his house was attacked, and his family terrorized by those same "honorable" students. In 1822 Dr. Cooper, president of that college, wrote to Thomas Jefferson and gave him an account of the outbreak in which the professors

were threatened, pistols were snapt at them, guns fired near them, Col. John Taylor (formerly of the Senate from this place) was in company with myself, burnt in effigy; the windows under my bedroom have been repeatedly shattered at various hours of the night and guns fired under my window.[108]

An outbreak at the University of Virginia similar to Doby's Rebellion at the University of Alabama was the culmination of a series of "vicious irregularities" beginning on June 22, 1825, continuing on August 5, and reaching a climax about ten days after the last outbreak on September 19. These disturbances were directed against Professors Thomas H. Key and George Long. The boys, disguised with masks, shouted, "Down with the European professors!" Two other professors who attempted to break up the gathering were assaulted.[109]

In 1839 Gessner Harrison, the chairman of the faculty at the University of Virginia, was approached by two students, one recently expelled and the other suspended. One of the students, larger and stronger than the professor, seized and held him while the other vigorously horse-whipped him. Although approximately one hundred students gathered to witness the attack, only a few feeble and unsuccessful attempts were made to stop it. After being released Harrison denounced the two as cowards and was violently reattacked. After this the two fled toward Lynchburg, where they were overtaken. During the process one was shot in the shoulder.[110]

The most tragic of the Virginia riots occurred on November 12, 1840. Professor John A. G. Davis, a member of the faculty who had been very forbearing and firm with the students, was murdered. On hearing an uproar by a group of students, he stepped out of his quarters and attempted to remove the mask of one of the rioters. As he did so, he was fired upon, and in a few days he died of the wounds he had received. The students, shocked by this unexpected turn of events, helped to pursue and capture the assassin, Joseph E. Semmes, a student from Georgia, and his accessory, William A. Kincaid, of South Carolina. Semmes had no personal grudge against Professor Davis, but he had been heard to say that he intended to shoot the first member of the faculty who tried to unmask him. Although the circuit court refused to free him on bail, the court of appeals accepted a $25,000 bond. Semmes failed to appear for trial; later, in Texas, he died, a miserable human being. Kincaid returned from South Carolina to testify at Semmes' trial, and when it was postponed he decided to remain in Virginia until the second trial, in October. He was placed under bond, and he seems to have attended lectures at the University during several years after the murder. Apparently he was never brought to trial.[111] Another murder was committed at a college in Mississippi. After a heated discussion of the Compromise of 1850, a drunken student stabbed to death President Jeremiah Chamberlin of Oakland College.[112]

The problems of discipline which the officers of the early University of Alabama met as they tried to make the students conform to rules which rigidly governed every minute of campus life were many and difficult. But there were other disciplinary problems even more thorny. These came from the irrepressibility of youth and the eternal urge of boys to fight and roister and get into mischief. And they were complicated because these youngsters on the early campus were sons of the frontier.

CHAPTER X

Problems of Discipline:
Rebellious Youth

WHEN the young University, under its first president, faced the first crisis to be precipitated by the unruliness of its students, an investigating committee reported to the trustees its opinion of the causes of student unrest and rebellousness. Parents were considered partly to blame. The newly-prosperous cotton planters pampered their sons in childhood, gave them slaves to wait upon them, and sent them off to college equipped with an extravagant wardrobe, an extensive supply of dirks, pistols, bowie knives, and swords, and an unlimited credit in the town of Tuscaloosa. Small wonder that the boys "seemed to entertain the opinion that they were entering a theatre where they were to appear as men of the world." They could hardly be expected to do otherwise than "erect the standard of rebellion" at the first efforts of the faculty to discipline them.[1]

This analysis is valid for the whole period. And perhaps a later generation may add, in retrospect, that fathers who themselves were searching hearts and consciences to find answers to the problem of the duty of civil disobedience may not have been the best teachers of unquestioned submission to authority. The times were troubled; the spirit of defiance was in the air. In such a time even ordinary restraints became more difficult to enforce.

The key to the situation, however, lies in the investigating committee's note about standard student "equipment." Spoiled sons of wealthy parents came arrogantly to the campus, ready to resent and resist any effort at control. The essential marks of proud young men of the world made the difference between ordinary student episodes and the dangerous incidents which so scandalized the public that the reputation of the University was impaired.

The expressions of student rebellion were much the same in

the early University of Alabama as they are on school and college campuses today—with due allowance, of course, for the fact that the old University included students in their early teens as well as those we now consider "of college age." Close association and routine caused frictions then as now. Boys fought with each other and were destructive of property. They were known to bully the weak and defenseless and to dare to affront the representatives of authority. They tried to acquire sophistication by assuming the vices of "men of the world." But these proud possessors of dirks, pistols, and bowie knives could quickly and easily turn a rough-house into an assault, or a student mass meeting into a mob.

Possession of weapons was, of course, against the rules. Among the "high offenses" specified in the laws of 1839 was "keeping of wines, liquors, gun-powder, or any deadly weapon."[2] But the University authorities seem to have used their discretion in applying this law. The faculty ledger for the years 1843 to 1860 records comparatively few instances in which mere possession of weapons or even random use of them was considered worthy of note. One student was reported for shooting a gun at Franklin Hall, another for "using" a poker, a third for having a gun on campus, a fourth for shooting a bird on campus, and several for shooting during study hours. Among these last were Franklin Hall occupants, who disturbed the peace by firing pistols one Saturday morning.[3]

Some other cases were at least briefly discussed by the faculty in those meetings so well filled with problems of keeping students in order. One student caught carrying a sword-cane was suspended for five months. The faculty felt that the practice of carrying such weapons was "productive of the most serious evils."[4] Students returning from a hunting excursion in 1842 created a disorder by shooting their guns on the campus, but the faculty, noting that the boys had not intended to be disorderly or disobedient, released them.[5] General firing of guns or pistols on the campus was frowned upon. In fact, the president in June, 1847, warned the whole student body that such demonstrations had to stop, or the faculty would "take measures to correct the evil."[6]

Surprising leniency in cases of unintentional accidents was also shown. In December, 1847, the professors were undoubtedly disturbed that a student had been injured by a gun in the hand of another student. But as no one could find out who owned the gun and as the whole thing was clearly an accident, no action was taken.[7] The faculty were even known to reverse themselves if they found they had acted too harshly in such cases, as they did in 1851, when a student was accused of drawing a pistol in a quarrel with a "country-man." It was not the first time this student had been reported for shooting pistols, and the faculty felt "determination to treat, with stringency, the use of pistols by students." They asked the boy to withdraw from the University. But he managed later to convince his judges that the pistol in his hand when he argued with the "country-man" had been handed to him by someone else on the spot and that he had been wrongly accused of firing shots in his room. Upon "signing certain pledges," he was fully reinstated.[8]

It should be added that the faculty also, at times, extended the prohibition against "deadly weapons" to include arms probably not thought of by the drafters of the University laws. They banned "large spades and shovels" in 1853 and ruled that each student should be allowed to have only a small fire shovel and a poker.[9]

Of too frequent occurence were student fights which ended in the stabbing or shooting of one or both of the contenders. These combats always caused perplexity and concern in faculty meetings, and the penalties meted out seem to have depended, at least in part, on the general conduct record of the culprits. One very early and very "melancholy" incident is typical of the situations with which the early faculty had to deal.

The incident involved three students: Boling Smith, William B. Inge, and Samuel Inge, with the two Inge boys apparently against Smith. William had thrown a rock and had attempted to draw a knife on Smith; Samuel had stabbed him near the heart. But there is some evidence that Boling may have been the aggressor. The professors dealt with each boy separately. They told Boling that he had used "language forbidden by the laws of this Institution and proscribed by every well-ordered society and calculated to induce consequences the most disastrous." They told him that he had attacked a fellow student "without sufficient provocation." But they added that he had a general reputation for peace and order and that they would not dismiss him if he did not repeat his offense. Although both William and Samuel were publicly admonished, only

Samuel was dismissed from the University.[10] Boling did not justify the faith the faculty had placed in him. He bided his time, and at his next opportunity he tried to settle his score with the remaining Inge. He was suspended on March 9, 1833, for an "unprovoked attack" on William B. Inge.[11] The exact time of the first incident is uncertain, for the record in the faculty minutes is undated. However, Oran Roberts, who entered the University on February 13, 1833, wrote of being assigned to a room which had been vacated by Samuel Inge who had been dismissed.[12] It seems probable that the whole Smith-Inge feud extended over less than two months.

Roberts tells of another early episode which involved shooting and general disorder. This time it was a student prank rather than a quarrel, but it was a prank which students of any day might dream up to persecute an unpopular classmate. The victim was Franklin W. Bowden. Into his dormitory room one night came two students who engaged in a violent fight. One student appeared to be mortally wounded; the other fled. Bowden was left alone with what he believed to be a dying boy. Other students found him thus. They expressed their horror, told Bowden that he would most certainly be accused of murder, and volunteered from friendship to save him from the sheriff. Bowden protested, but his saviors hurried him off the campus, shooting their pistols, and reiterating their vows to protect him. They left a badly frightened boy at the edge of the woods.

This hoax, of course, was devised, Roberts notes, "to try his metal." But the panic-stricken Bowden out in the dark woods did not know that the fight had been staged. Presently he heard footsteps and voices. Thinking that it was the sheriff's posse he hid until the searchers had passed and then hastened to the sanctuary of home. The searchers were not sheriff's men; but they were students and faculty who had missed Bowden from his room and had come to find him.

After such an experience for Bowden to come back to the University required courage. But he did return about ten days later. When William L. Beale ventured to make fun of him about being so gullible, he promptly found himself in a fight. The faculty noted that this fight had taken place, but there is no record that any effort was made to discover or to punish the original pranksters.[13]

Sometimes the faculty attempted to discourage violent quarrels and disorder by requiring offenders to make formal and public apology. At least five students were given this treatment in the spring of 1833: Sidney Brown, Beaufort W. Brown, and Richard S. Johnson for a disturbance in Steward's Hall, and two others for a fight on the campus. All of the apologies bear the marks of having been dictated; none seemed to arise spontaneously from remorse and repentance. All humbly begged forgiveness for their "great impropriety" and promised future obedience to all University laws. Sidney Brown piously expressed the wish that his acknowledgement should be made "as public as was the offence." His letter may be taken as typical of those written, under faculty pressure, by many culprits during this period:

I acknowledge and regret the great impropriety of my conduct in the Steward's Hall on Munday morning, especially in resorting to the use of a deadly weapon for the purpose of injuring a fellow-student; and wish my acknowledgement to be made as public as was the offence. May I hope the Faculty will overlook this great error on being assured of my wish and purpose to obey all the Laws of this Institution.[14]

Mere words did not seem wholly satisfactory. The faculty went on record the same spring as determined to be more strict in enforcing the rules against fighting; they had shown, they said, too much forbearance.[15] To show their seriousness they suspended the next offender, Zebulon P. Davis, on June 1. He was charged with "an assault upon a Gentleman, in the presence of a member of the Faculty, though he afterwards made satisfactory apology as far as disrespect to said members of the Faculty is concerned."[16]

John Cochrane was asked to withdraw from the University the following year because he had had two fights on the campus. His opponents, Ephraim D. Connor and William D. Connor, were seriously admonished by the president, but were not otherwise penalized.[17]

When Hugh L. Clay and Aaron Jones in the spring of 1837, drew pistol and knife respectively, in one of their frequent fights, "their extreme youth" was given as reason for a light sentence— only ten days' suspension.[18] Two other boys, also presumably young as both were freshmen, were treated with similar leniency. John H. Greene and Peyton G. King, roommates, also had a fight on the campus. King said that Greene had "revealed a personal communication" of his. If this was true, the faculty and the president could see that King had provocation. So the president admonished Greene and told him to find another roommate.[19]

Greene was in trouble again within a year. At least, the sophomore Greene of 1844 may be presumed to be King's ex-roommate. This time the trouble assumed serious proportions, which may have made the faculty regret they had not taken a firmer course with the troublemaker the year before. Greene, according to the account, started the fight at dancing school when he "insulted" James M. Foster by running against him. Right in the ballroom Foster spoke to him angrily and drew his knife. Greene retaliated in the barroom after the class was over; he hit Foster with a stick, but he had his knife out and handy. While Foster was looking for his knife, Greene slipped away. A feud had been started, and before it had run its course, four boys had left the University, and two others had been publicly reprimanded.

Greene, knowing that Foster would attempt reprisal after that ignominious blow in the barroom armed himself and two of his friends, P. T. Herbert and Francis Ellis. Two other students, Alexander McDow and John D. Carpenter, were assigned the responsibility of seeing that there should be no interference in the expected fight, which was not long delayed. A few days later Foster attacked Greene, disarmed his enemy with ease, took his two pistols and threw them away. When Greene called for help, the real fight began. Herbert rushed at Foster with a dagger. The fact that McDow tried to head him off and was dangerously stabbed may have sobered the fighters, for the fighting appears to have ended abruptly at that point.

Retribution was prompt and stern. Greene and his two guards, Herbert and Ellis, because they had been armed, were indefinitely suspended; the trustees were asked to expel them. Carpenter and McDow got off with public admonishment. Foster was "allowed to withdraw silently."[20]

Such fights and knifings made very little stir on the campus. They were taken as a matter of course and of as little importance as a skirmish might be in a boys' school today. Bolling Hall, writing home in 1858, undoubtedly expressed the nonchalance with which the students, and even at times the officers, looked upon these episodes: "I have no college news to give you," said young Bolling, "except a little fight that took place yesterday." Then he describes the incident. Frank King, coming home from supper with some friends had passed Tom Mobley and twitted him about the girl he was in love with. Mobley "cursed" King and passed on. King, becoming angry, drew his knife and started after the disrespectful Mobley. There was a fight. "They were separated with some difficulty," Bolling commented, "when it was found that Mobley was pretty badly cut in two or three places. I suppose the matter will end here. King is not near as large as Mobley."[21] The inference here seems to be that King might have been punished if he had picked on some one smaller than himself.

Other schools in the South also had regulations against the possession of "deadly weapons," but they had as much difficulty in enforcing them as did the University of Alabama. At Virginia one young man declared in 1836 that he always carried a dirk because he might have good reason at any time for whipping it out. On May 20, 1836, a Virginia collegian was known to have been carrying both a pistol and a dirk about his person.[22] Georgia students were no exception, for they, too, were handy with these tools of destruction. During an argument between two students in 1836 both a pistol and a dirk were used. One student, who was stabbed near the heart, barely recovered. Another argument ran the following course: two students in disagreement with one another had a fight in which one was stabbed. They were expelled, but by petitions and promises they were able to get reinstated.[23]

College dining halls are traditionally centers for student demonstrations, and the steward's hall at the early University of Alabama was no exception. The "affray" for which Sidney Brown apologized so abjectly in 1835 was only one of many incidents when student fighting took place against the background of dining tables, where food and cutlrey and dishes could be used as missiles as well as the customary fists, knives, and pistols.

Robert B. P. McAlpine and William K. Barnes were suspended in July, 1835, for fighting in the dining hall. McAlpine must have come back after his sentence was over, for he was in trouble again the following year, this time for having an empty liquor bottle in his possession.[24]

A quarrel in the autumn of 1836 started when two Alexanders clashed over possession of a certain chair. Alexander J. Weissinger appears to have been the aggressor in the first place, for he was later "admonished" for using violence to get possession of Alexander D. Lalande's chair. Lalande, however, reacted with so much violence that he was suspended for four months. The faculty said that he had used abusive language, threatened violence, and drawn a deadly weapon, and they added that he had a quarrelsome disposition anyway. Lalande substantiated the last of these charges by refusing to obey the rule that suspended students must leave the campus immediately. He was, therefore, expelled in disgrace. Weissinger, meanwhile, was allowed to pay for the damage he had caused, to make satisfactory apology to the steward and his wife, and to publicly acknowledge his misbehaviour. But he stayed on the campus.[25]

Alexander Weissinger's brother James had already been in trouble with the steward that same year. On April 26, 1836, he was informed "that in consequence of the difficulty which he has had at the Stewards' Hall he cannot be allowed to return thither to board without the consent of the Steward." The same day another student, Physic Rush Elmore, was reprimanded for the "impropriety of his conduct at the Steward's Hall" and informed that he would have to mend his ways or face severe punishment.[26]

From the earliest days of the University until the middle forties, the faculty struggled with the problem of discipline in the dining hall. In 1833 and 1834 they were warning Thomas E. Matthews that he would have to "move his boarding forthwith" if he did not satisfy Mr. Taylor about his conduct there;[27] and telling William P. Givhan and John H. Marr that they would have to leave Steward's Hall unless they were able to convince the Steward's family that they would stop throwing food and fighting.[28] In 1843 they were dismissing Jeremiah E. Sanders from the University because of his "highly improper conduct in the Hall" and because his treatment of the Steward had been "grossly indecorous and insulting."[29] No amount of policing by the faculty kept order. It is small wonder that Steward's Hall was discontinued in 1847. But even after that, the dining rooms were focal points for trouble.

Between the fights in which students pommeled and even knifed and shot at each other the boys found other outlets for their energies. Teasing the University slaves was regrettably popular, and the teasing, like the fights, too often moved from harmless badgering to cruelty and physical injury.

Many of the boys who made up the student body came, of course, from slave-owning homes. As they were accustomed to exercise authority over servants, they were unprepared for the University campus, where servants were few and where these few were accountable only to the faculty. One such student was Henry M. Elmore, who in 1837 chastised a college servant as he would undoubtedly have done at home. When Elmore was called before the faculty, whose prerogatives he had usurped, he was required to sign an apology.[30]

Incidents became more frequent as the number of servants increased. The University authorities were not very severe in the penalties they inflicted for such offenses—unless the attack upon a Negro was particularly violent or accompanied by other rule-breaking, such as desecration of the Sabbath or the study hours. It is not clear, for instance, whether John P. Wallace and Joseph C. Guild, who were admonished in 1842 for "chasing a Negro through the campus with loud outcries during study hours," were being punished for the first or the second charge against them.[31] And the stiff sentences given to four students the following year after a disgraceful attack upon some slaves took into account much more than the episode itself.

Byrd Fitzpatrick, James M. Foster, William Saunders, and John L. Smith, who were involved, chose Sunday to stage a "riotous disturbance" around the home of one of the professors. That was the first count against them. In their rioting they had dragged some Negroes out of the professor's yard and maltreated them "professedly in sport, but considerably injuring and abusing one of them." Now there was a second count. The fact that they had done all of this "to the disturbance of the whole college, and especially of the families of the officers,"[32] resulted in a third charge, which was enough to justify suspending Fitzpatrick, Saunders, and Foster for the rest of the term. But Smith added other counts to his score when he told the faculty that he did not think that the deed was worse for "being done on the Sabbath, more than any other day." As he was the oldest of the group and had had previously a discreditable record, Smith was suspended indefinitely.[33]

Fitzpatrick and Saunders did not serve out their sentences. They literally found friends at court and came back the day after their

THE OLD UNIVERSITY 235

dismissal petitioning the faculty for reinstatement and backing their plea with letters from lawyers attending Supreme Court sessions in Tuscaloosa. Since these important men were willing to vouch for the future good conduct of their young friends, the boys were allowed to come back to college.[34] Smith, who also petitioned for reinstatement a few days later, manifested the "proper spirit," said the faculty, and his petition was granted.[35] Only Foster stayed away from the campus, as ordered, until the new term began.[36] He came back to college then and within four months was again in trouble for mistreating servants. With two other boys he so severely beat up a Negro belonging to the president that the poor fellow had to have surgical attention. Foster was dismissed at once for his "rude and disorderly disposition and course of conduct." This time he tried the tactics which had worked so well with his former partners in crime. He wrote a contrite letter, expressing "sorrow for the offense, and a disposition to make every reparation in his power for the wrong he had committed." The tactics worked. Foster was reinstated, though the faculty said sternly that they reserved the right to dismiss him "whenever his longer stay shall seem inexpedient."[37]

One slave named Moses seems to have had more than his share of trouble with the young ruffians of the campus. It was in the spring of 1845, when the first "Moses mishap" came; Benjamin J. Saffold pierced Moses' arm with a table fork. According to the faculty minutes, Moses was a hired slave and not the property of the University. As money was involved the University authorities were duly stern. They cited Saffold for presidential admonition, telling him that he must pay all doctor's bills and make good the University's expense for loss of the servant's time. If the injury should prove permanent, he was to be held accountable for all damages.[38] The bill for lost time, noted in the minutes a month later, came to $4.00.[39]

Moses had a second injury early in 1846. His right arm was disabled when A. P. Robinson hit him with a crutch because the slave refused to bring the student's food to him in his room. Robinson's only punishment was being required to pay $1.50 for the substitute hired while Moses' arm mended. But the faculty did take action on the incident. They refused to permit students to send University servants on errands, even to get food for them when they were ill. On February 20, the faculty voted that college servants were not allowed to render special services of any kind to students.[40] A week later they modified the regulation to permit errand-running if it did not interfere with regular duties.[41]

Perhaps it was the same Moses who was involved in a somewhat different escapade. When the president was informed that certain students had stolen some of his turkeys, the guilty students decided that the tattletale was Moses. At the first opportunity they waylaid him and administered a sound trouncing. Two of the students involved were suspended because they refused to admit their part of the beating. That suspension sentence did not hold either.[42]

The suspension of Milton J. Saffold for beating Sam over the head in June, 1845, did hold, but only because of the circumstances surrounding the episode. Saffold struck Sam for "presumed insolence" when the servant refused to scald his bedstead. As Saffold had beaten servants twice before that year, the faculty were incensed to such a degree that they told him he was indefinitely suspended and that he must "leave Tuscaloosa in the stage which departs for Selma this evening."[43] When the summer was over, the old pattern of petition for reinstatement began. From the boy's father came a letter enclosing one from Milton, begging to be allowed to come back to college. What action the faculty might have taken on this letter is unknown. In the same mail came another letter from Milton; this one, written without paternal prompting, stated that he did not want to return to school. The faculty, deciding that the college was better off without Milton, declined to readmit him "on general grounds." But they never told Saffold, Sr., about his son's duplicity.[44]

Moses was again the target of a mischievous group of students when on a Saturday night in June, 1850, a party of students consisting of Bugbee, Chapman, Glassell, Peck, Pharr, and Wynne, attended by Barnard's servant, Morgan, went into Moses' yard, took his fowls, and were troublesome generally. It was suspected by President Manly that this servant, Morgan, was delegated to an unusual task by the students, for he wrote as follows:

This boy, Morgan, acts as a Pimp to get out Barnard's women—especially the younger Luna; whom they use in great numbers, nightly.[45]

The general tone of faculty discussions on student violence toward servants suggests that the professors regarded these demonstrations as injury to University property rather than as attacks upon human beings. Also they had a long and troublesome struggle to keep the inanimate property of the school from too much ruination at the hands of destructive youth. Some of the damage to windows, locks, gates, fences, and furniture was undoubtedly accidental. Some of it was incidental, a by-product of the rough-house and fighting that made an important part of student life. Some of it was sheer mischief and wanton destruction of property.

When the culprit was known, property damage was charged to him, and he had to pay for repairs. When a room was damaged, the occupants of the room were held jointly responsible for the damage. Students in an entry or a dormitory as a whole, or even the entire student body, were assessed for damages where actual culprits were unknown. And there was always the contingent fund which took care of costs of repair when assessment seemed unfair or inadvisable. A few instances of student destructiveness, culled from the minutes of the faculty who dealt with them, will indicate the nature of these damages and the way in which repairs were handled.

One day in February, 1842, thirteen panes of glass were broken in the Rotunda by students throwing stones. The one student in the group who was caught paid that bill.[46] When the bellrope was cut and the ladder leading to the cupola damaged the following year, five students admitted their part in the prank; these five paid for repairs totalling $3.84.[47] That same autumn so many windows were broken that a committee on glazing was appointed; this committee collected from the entire student body $41.05 for window glass repair. The one student who refused to pay his assessment was debarred from recitation until he should do so.[48] However, the authorities were not unfair. Just a few weeks earlier they had ruled that a student whose windows had been broken by blinds during vacation need pay only half the cost of repairing them because he was not to blame for the damage. The contingency fund took care of the remainder.[49]

Windows were always getting broken. The faculty made a public announcement in 1847 that all windows and window fixtures removed by students must be replaced by the occupants of the rooms from which they had been removed.[50] The following fall new students were not required to pay for window repairs as these charges were made to the contingency fund. The replacement, however, of a second window broken in the Rotunda was charged to the students who were on the campus when the damage had occurred.[51] Two students assessed for window breakage in 1851 were refunded $1.70 when they proved that the panes had been broken by a storm, which blew out a sash on which a bead had been missing all the year.[52]

Boring holes through walls was also a favorite form of student destructiveness. In 1843 two students were charged for repair of a hole made through the partition between their rooms.[53] Two years later all of the occupants of Rooms 6 and 7 in Franklin Hall and Rooms 4 and 9 in Jefferson Hall were fined $1.00 to repair the walls between those rooms. Opportunity for exculpation was given in this case and in many other property-damage cases in which it was difficult to determine the offender by means other than confession.[54] And it is probably true that the exculpation law was as ineffective in most cases as it was in those described in the preceding chapter —the disappearance of the Bible from the Rotunda and the doorknobs from the Lyceum.

The middle entry of Franklin Hall was "disfigured by indecent writing" in 1846, and the residents of the whole entry shared the expense of whitewashing them.[55] When students defaced the walls of their own rooms, they, of course, paid for the repainting.[56] In 1846 two brothers who tore down their grate after a servant had repaired it were charged $1.50.[57] And two years later three students who took up a plank from the flooring of their room paid fifty cents each to have it put back.[58] In 1851 a student who had injured the roof of an entry to a dormitory cellar was reprimanded and fined $1.00.[59] In 1853 cellars were cleaned at the expense of the students and then nailed up at the expense of the University, but no reason for this division of expense is given.[60] A year later occupants of the north and south entries of Jefferson Hall paid $1.50 an entry for the repair of damaged banisters.[61]

Damages also occurred in spots other than the dormitories. One incident was somewhat unusual in that Professor Tuomey paid half of the repair bill for broken cabinet panes in his room; the University, the other half.[62] That may be the only case on record in

THE OLD UNIVERSITY 239

which a member of the faculty bore any expense of breakage. But probably they were careful men and seldom responsible for property damage. No one was held responsible for the damage done in February, 1849, when the Observatory was ransacked. Some of the furniture was removed, the clock was set ahead, mercury was spilled on the floor, and the terrestrial eye-piece of a small telescope was stolen. But the faculty apparently placed the blame on marauders; no effort was made to blame students.[63] When twenty-five examination boards (used in examinations when there were not enough desks) were taken from the president's room in 1853, however, the whole student body shared the expense of $7.50 for the replacement of the boards and for repair of some broken windows.[64] Damage to campus gates and other college property one night in early December, 1849, was also assessed against the whole student body, with opportunity given once more for exculpation.[65]

According to the earliest laws of the University, if "any student shall be guilty of profaneness . . . he shall be admonished, suspended, or expelled according to the nature of the offence." Included among the "high offenses" in later laws was "indecency or obscenity in language."[66] These strong rules were almost unenforceable. When tempers flared, tongues lashed out with the richest oaths of frontier vocabulary. But the profanity and blasphemy could seldom be separated from the circumstances in which it was used, and there seems to be no record of punishment meted out for an unruly tongue alone. In many cases "blasphemy" was a factor in the decision to inflict heavy penalties for misdemeanors. A student in 1834, making the routine apology for disturbance in the dining hall, declared himself "particularly mortified" because of his "indecorous language."[67] A student expelled in 1836 received heavy punishment for "insolent and profane language" as well as for other misdeeds.[68] Two boys were suspended in 1837 for using "very profane language" as well as for wielding a knife and pistol in a quarrel.[69] Grave, indeed, was a case in 1842 in which the culprit engaged in "loud blasphemy."[70] Such illustrations could be cited indefinitely, but it is impossible to say whether the boys on the University campus were freer with their profanity than were the men in the communities from which they came.

Innocent animals were frequently the victims of boyish pranks devised by the students. Two incidents, similar in nature but neither causing any material damage to University property, occurred three years apart. On January 19, 1848, a wagon belonging to Mrs. Eliza Perkins was brought to the campus and placed on the pavement of the Rotunda. In the wagon was Professor Tuomey's front gate. The harness, some fodder and a bench taken from the Rotunda were placed on the rostrum. A sheepskin was hung on the prongs of the lightning rod, and a large two-year-old calf was tied to a lightning rod on the apex of the Rotunda dome.[71] Three years later, on a Saturday morning in January, three calves were tied to the pillows on the rostrum. President Manly admonished the students for such unseemly conduct about a place of God's worship.[72] Some months later an old white horse suffered at the hands of the students. He was put into the Rotunda with the badges of the Sons of Temperance hung on him.[73]

On somewhat rare occasions students infringed upon a much more generally accepted rule of gentlemanly conduct—they were wanting in chivalry toward women. The furor growing out of the episode in 1845 when students insulted ladies on the campus by flashing lights in their faces with mirrors has already been described. The girls at Mrs. Stafford's school were sometimes the target for boisterous, though probably not uncomplimentary, demonstrations. In 1856 on Dr. Garland's complaint, Benjamin C. Adams was called before the faculty; he had shown disrespect to three young ladies leaving Dr. Mallet's classroom by singing to them a Negro song.[74] The general impression of these and scattered other incidents is that they were no more than might be expected of boys living shut off from feminine companionship in the man's world that was the University.

A harmless prank occurred in January, 1851, when the junior class, after finishing an examination in integral calculus, decided to honor this termination of studies in an unusual manner. Accompanied by music, about fifty students marched in procession, to the common in front of Professor Garland's house. There a funeral oration was delivered by William H. C. Price. With great solemnity a hole was dug, the textbook buried, and a little hillock with a head board was left. The demonstration was quiet and orderly with the exception of a few shouts and the noise of the funeral guns after the burial.[75]

Here and there in the old records appear accounts of somewhat unusual misdemeanors, some of them showing the painstaking care with which students of any generation will work out details of a prank or hoax. To originate the "grossly improper" fake commencement program, which appeared just before the commencement exercises in 1846, must have caused its perpetrators much burning of midnight oil. In embarrassment and consternation the faculty scurried about to stop the circulation of the program. They voted to withhold diplomas from all seniors who did not disclaim having any part in its preparation. Then they worried lest this action be interpreted as a "dare" and leave them with no class to graduate. They modified their decision, suggesting rather than ordering, that as a duty to himself each senior should exculpate himself from "any share in so discreditable a business."[76]

Two students were disciplined in 1854 for "assuming a disguise," which apparently consisted of blacking their faces.[77] In 1847 five were "seriously admonished" for being disguised and misbehaving in town.[78] That same year three students were reported for failing to join the student procession at commencement or at an exhibition.[79] Recorded in the faculty ledger in the 1850's are accounts of other unruly students: the student who annoyed Professor Tuomey by "pulling his nose in class"; the student who similarly affronted Professor Wyman by making a "gyrating motion of hand and nose"; the two students who injured a young tree on the campus; the student who rode a horse on campus; and the two boys who chased a mule.[80] Although these misdemeanors, singly, were youthful spirits, their continued occurrence presented problems for the officers who tried to keep those spirits in decorous repression.

In 1848 when James T. Killough accepted a challenge to fight a duel, he encountered an ordinance that could be enforced without "if's" and "but's." Edward G. Baptist and John Fleming were in Mr. Gould's recitation room when Killough came by and locked them in. Baptist then broke the lock and found Killough standing there. Brushing past him without saying a word, Baptist went into the class room and recited. Afterward Killough asked him what he meant by rushing past him. When Baptist replied that he would hold no communication with him, Killough said that his action showed him to be a "damned rascal." Baptist sent a challenge by Thaddeus H. Perry to which Killough returned an answer by Lucian

Martin, accepting the challenge and naming the conditions of the duel—that both should enter a room in Jefferson Hall, naked, and armed with bowie knives.

Baptist, the younger and the less virile of the two, went to President Manly and expressed the intention of handing Killough a pistol and telling him to defend himself. Upon advice procured from Judge Peck and Lawyer Vanhoose of Tuscaloosa, Baptist asked for an honorable dismissal.[81] This dismissal was granted together with a $15 loan to cover his expenses home. The next day Killough was called in, and after conversing with Manly, he, too, decided to take an honorable dismissal. He was desirous of returning to college, but the faculty thought it best to allow neither of them to return.[82] Despite the stand taken by the faculty in 1848, six years later, in 1855, the then Rev. Edward G. Baptist of Lewis Store, Virginia, was awarded an A.B. degree by the board of trustees upon the recommendation of President Manly.[83]

Duelling was not peculiar to the University of Alabama; students Baptist and Killough had their counterparts in schools all over the South. Although duelling was not uncommon in Virginia, the university in that state had strict regulations for repression. A student, B. F. Magill, while in Staunton on leave, escorted a young lady to a ball. A drunken guest at the ball asked the lady to dance, but she, acting upon the advice given previously by Magill, refused. On learning of her escort's advice, the drunken man called Magill to the door and, being the stronger of the two, gave him a severe beating. The student thereupon challenged his assailant to a duel the next day but was reported and arrested. When the faculty received the news, they expelled Magill.[84] And it was reported that in February, 1840, two students, Walke and Bell, fought a duel in the District of Columbia.[85]

Another instance of this form of combat took place between sons of prominent families in South Carolina. Two students, Roach and Adams, reached a stalemate when both grabbed the same plate of trout in steward's hall and neither would relinquish it. Presently Roach released his hold and glared fiercely at Adams. The ensuing quarrel resulted in a challenge being given by Adams and accepted by Roach. The strange part of the affair is that the seconds of both young men were prominent citizens of the state. General Pierce M.

Butler, distinguished Mexican War colonel who later became governor of South Carolina and Mr. D. J. McCord, a distinguished lawyer whose name lives in the judicial records of that state, were the two men who agreed to aid Roach and Adams. The students fought about ten miles out of Columbia. Both were courageous and fought with pistols at ten paces. At the count of one, two shots rang out simultaneously. Roach, although wounded seriously, recovered after a length of time,[86] but Adams received a mortal wound.

Dismissals for "general disorder" appear now and then in the record, but the lack of detail, in contrast to the meticulous description of the circumstances of most disciplinary cases, makes one wonder whether the faculty, giving a thought to the posterity which might read the records, felt that unsavory details of some of these cases were best left unrecorded.

As long as students worked off their excess energies on the campus, they did not greatly impair the reputation of their University. The town of Tuscaloosa was, however, near at hand and very alluring. While the students of the old University of Alabama did their full share in building the time-honored tradition of town-gown controversy, the townspeople regarded students as ruffians and students looked to the town as a free field for adventure.

When the University opened in 1831, the town and the campus were distinctly separate. The settled part of Tuscaloosa then extended roughly from the present Queen City Avenue westward to Thirty-Second Avenue and from the river to Fifteenth Street. The University, built on Marr's field, was almost a mile east of the town limits, on the Huntsville Road, now University Avenue.[87]

If the board of trustees thought that town and campus would be safely separated by the provision that faculty, as well as students, live in the University community, they very quickly discovered their error. By the autumn of 1831 rules began to appear which were designed to discourage and prevent students from going into town for any purpose. The definition of study hours and the regulation that students must be in their rooms during these hours was one of the first of these efforts.[88] Only on Saturday and Sunday was there any time when the boys could go to town without violating study-hour rules. The next faculty move was designed to raise the barriers still higher by setting extreme penalties for any student who visited town during study hours. He would be admonished for a first offense; after that his punishment might be whatever the faculty thought the case required.[89] By January, 1832, specific prohibitions had been added to cover attending the theater, the circus, the race track, or any public dancing party.[90]

Of course the students disregarded these laws. Tuscaloosa was their escape from the rigid rules of the campus, and to Tuscaloosa they went—legally when they could, illegally whenever they thought they could do so undetected. The University authorities did what they could to bar the way. In April, 1833, the faculty noted that it was "commonly reported that some students of this Institution are in the habit of resorting to town, particularly at night, to the great detriment not only of their own character, but of the reputation of this University, and of the honor of the whole State." They ruled that thereafter no students might be excused to go to town at night except upon application to the whole faculty; permission would be given by the faculty only for "urgent reasons."[91]

The students continued to go to town. It should be remembered that not all their excursions, not even most of them, were motivated by mischief. Boys went to town on perfectly ligitimate business: to see the sights, to shop in the stores, to call on the girls and go to private parties, and to attend concerts and lectures and even the sessions of the state legislature. But they went also to get away from rules and to sample and taste the vices and pleasures which would make them, in their own minds, truly sophisticated men of the world.

Those visits to town raised to major proportions one problem which might otherwise have been relatively minor, though it would most certainly have existed on the campus. This problem was drinking. It was the principal factor in many disciplinary cases both on the campus and off. It was the cause of disorders and even riots. Some of the disturbances resulted in unfavorable relations between the town and the campus and gave the University an unfavorable reputation throughout the state.

Some of the blame must rest on the town. Town merchants sold the liquor to the boys who came from the campus. In 1847 the General Assembly moved to check this practice by passing a law forbidding the sale of intoxicants to students of the University or any academy or school in Alabama. Fines for violation of this law ranged from $50 to $500.[92] A number of cases were brought in Tuscaloosa under this law, and fines ranging from $50 to $300 were imposed. In 1850 two men were convicted in the circuit court of Tuscaloosa County for selling spirituous liquors, "to-wit whiskey and brandy" on several occasions to University students.[93] They were fined $75 plus costs.[94]

University authorities did their utmost to keep the students away from liquor. Not only was the law of the school explicit and stern, but also the faculty gave as much encouragement as they could to the Sons of Temperance, which fostered a voluntary abstinence pledge among the students. Students brought up for first offense against the intoxication law were required to sign abstinence pledges.

But the faculty records contain many references to drunkenness, a problem which the authorities never really solved. The first instance was recorded in 1833, when a student was dismissed "with disgrace" for using profanity, being intoxicated, engaging in riotous conduct, and using disrespectful language to the faculty.[95] In 1836 when an empty bottle was found by the president on a student's table at eleven o'clock one night, the student was only reprimanded. He was told, however, that he would have been suspended except that he had presented clear evidence that "his having the spirits was accidental . . . that no other students participated, and that his company consisted only of two respectable citizens."[96] But the discovery alerted the faculty to the need for more drastic action. They served notice that since "the introduction of intoxicating liquors into the University would be attended with the most vicious consequences," volations of the rules against drinking would be punished henceforth by suspension for the first offense.[97] In fact, they suspended a student the very next day for having intoxicants in his room; they even recommended him for expulsion because of "abuse, defiance, and threatening violence" to a professor.[98]

In 1847 James T. Killough, who was later dismissed for accepting an invitation to duel, was required to take a total abstinence pledge. The faculty said that he was becoming addicted to liquor and that he had been guilty of improper conduct in town while he was intoxicated.[99]

The faculty reiterated in January, 1848, that it was an "unalterable rule" that students brought up for intoxication or for possession of "ardent spirits" be immediately dismissed.[100] But three months later, when they had occasion to make good this threat, they asked the president to talk with the offender to see whether it would ever "be proper to reinstate him." Having signed the total abstinence pledge,[101] he was back in his classes in less than a month.

In 1851 two students who signed this pledge and got similar relaxation of the "unalterable" rule were not sufficiently grateful for their reprieve. Within two months one of them, reported for disorder and disobedience in the classroom, was sent home.[102] Sometimes the faculty seemed to have been too weary of the perpetual problem to take action. In November, 1851, they heard, without doing anything about it, a report that some students had been drinking in town one Wednesday evening.[103] Perhaps the faculty detected one of the culprits a month later for they dismissed a boy who in one week had been drunk twice in town.[104] That same year reports of drunkenness during the Christmas holiday resulted in more reprimands and more signing of pledges.[105] And the faculty were duly shocked three months later when one of the same boys was again reported for intoxication. When the lad insisted, however, that he was taking liquor only for medicinal purposes, the professors solemnly let him off because he had violated his pledge "in the letter rather than in the spirit."[106] A second of the holiday-making group fell from grace almost a year after his initial offense. He admitted that he had been drinking but insisted that he was not drunk. The president, after discussing the case with the boy's father and with some of his professors, decided that he should be allowed to go on with his classes.[107] The faculty acquiesced in the presidential decision and then disposed of the next case in the usual fashion—a warning and an invitation to sign the pledge. In this instance the accused student showed spirit; he chose to leave the University rather than sign.[108]

All through the years the problem was too stubborn for the faculty. They kept their rules rigid, but they could not be inflexible in the enforcement of these rules. By 1858 the problem of drinking had become so serious that the grand jury of Tuscaloosa County issued a public report that warned of the serious consequences of students' continued use of intoxicants:

THE OLD UNIVERSITY 247

To the cause of the numerous crimes and misdemeanors brought to their notice, the Jury could neither be blind nor indifferent. They have no hesitancy in expressing the belief, as shown from the facts, developed before them, that nine-tenths of the offences brought to their notice, had their origin in the use of intoxicating liquors. The most discouraging feature connected with this spread of crime in our community is found in the fact, that a number of the Indictments at this term, are against minors, mere youth, students in our University, and public schools. . . . It can . . . be but cured by the strictest vigilance and watchfulness on the part of those who have the care of the youth, and by lessening both the facilities to procure and the opportunities of indulging in the use of ardent spirits.[109]

In spite of "strictest vigilance," it can safely be said that drinking accounted for at least nine-tenths of the trouble between the University and the townspeople.

The control of gambling was another problem complicated by the facilities which the town offered. Like drinking, this vice was frowned upon by some of the students as well as by the University officials, and they fought it with the same weapon, the pledge. The text of resolutions drawn up by twenty-one students who remained in the college during vacation of 1835 is as follows:

Resolved, That we view gambling as one of the most injurious and despicable vices, with which our country is cursed, and all gaming houses are nuisances, which ought not to be tolerated in any community.

Resolved, That we view gamblers as men utterly reckless of reputation . . . as men who ruin unthinking youth. . . .

Resolved, That we regard those men who are guilty of the infamous crime of robbing youth of our land, of their money, their character, their time, and their most valuable opportunity for education, and preparation for useful citizenship as unworthy of the countenance of a community which has any regard for the welfare of the rising generation.

Resolved, As we have been informed the gamblers have threatened not only to burn the town of Tuscaloosa, but like wise to use violence to citizens using the most laudable measures to put them down, that we therefore, most cordially second the resolutions passed by the citizens of Tuscaloosa on the 21st inst. and that we are ready and willing to support the committee of vigilence in the discharge of such duties as may devolve on them.[110]

Perhaps these paragraphs were written with burned fingers. It is worthy of note that names of the signers of these sentiments appear many times in the disciplinary records of the faculty. Perhaps it is also significant that in the same year the faculty agreed that they would alternate in visiting places in Tuscaloosa where students might be meeting for gambling.[111]

Also at most other colleges gambling was considered a major offense. In 1820 the favorite game of the students and hotel keepers was loo. In 1836 one student at the University of Virginia is known to have lost $250 in a game at one sitting, a considerable sum even at today's values.[112] A student at Georgia offered undeniable proof to President Waddel that he was not guilty of gambling as accused for he did not "know the ace of jacks from the nine of deuces."[113]

The problem of drinking also reared its ugly head in Virginia. As the taverns and bars were open on Sunday and as it was also the day of liberty for the students, most of the offenses occurred then.[114] Because of the ease with which the students were able to obtain the liquors, drunkenness came second in frequency among all the crimes committed by the students at the University of Georgia. Even President Waddel, a man of exacting conscience, found strong drink necessary to his good health.[115]

If there were other vices which students sought in town, the delicacy of the faculty suppressed the record of them. One brief, tragic case, appearing in newspaper and court records, indicates that the University boys did at least occasionally venture into parts of Tuscaloosa where they certainly should not have ventured. The student involved was W. B. Fulton. He and some of his friends "in mere sport" stood outside the house of Mrs. Nancy Johnson, "a common woman of the town" and annoyed her. She fired through a hole in the wall at her tormentors. Fulton fell with a load of buckshot in his head and died very soon. He was, said the newspaper writer, a very promising lad about seventeen years old.[116] When the case came to court, it was discovered that Mrs. Johnson had shot and wounded two other men before she killed Fulton. She was convicted of manslaughter and sent to the penitentiary for two years.[117]

Most of the town-gown brushes were relatively minor, but none the less annoying to the townspeople and embarrassing to the University authorities. As early as 1835 one student, Sydenham Moore, got into a fracas with H. L. Martin of Tuscaloosa. But the student said that he had acted only in self-defense after Martin had threatened him. He had, however, attended a party in town without permission. The faculty admonished him and extended the admonition at their next meeting to include sixteen other students who had gone to the party. But they did not punish Moore in any way for his quarrel with Mr. Martin.[118]

The president in 1846 reprimanded the whole student body for making a disturbance at a public lecture in town.[119] When in 1848 the farm of Mr. Comigys was robbed of some poultry, six students absent from their rooms that night were questioned about the theft. Four admitted their guilt and offered "to do anything in their power to repair the mischief of their foolish act." The faculty admonished three of them for not having good academic records, but they did not punish the confessed thieves for their crime against Mr. Comigys.[120]

The wharf on the river was the scene of a disorder on a Saturday evening in 1852. Three students were questioned. One said that he had been there only a few minutes and that he was trying to quell the disorder. The other two admitted that they were in the fracas and that they had been drinking but were not drunk; they had, they insisted, done no injury to property. The first of these boys, already on his honor not to drink, was dismissed for breaking his word. The others were allowed to stay in school upon signing the pledge of abstinence.[121]

Sometimes the faculty themselves helped to widen the rift between campus and town. Their reply to an invitation to unite with the city in a Fourth of July celebration in 1851 cannot have increased good will toward the college. The professors simply said that the members of the faculty had "already made such a disposition of their time for that day that they cannot attend."[122]

Once in a while major incidents occurred which had the town up in arms and which received state-wide publicity. The most famous of these were: the circus episode of the 1830's, the Doby Rebellion of the 1850's, already described, and the tragic killing in 1858 of Edward L. Nabers. All of them except the last stemmed from relaitvely minor causes and all were the occasion for the explosion of pent-up animosities against the University. They reflect a steadily worsening relationship, which hampered the University in its efforts to get public support.

Even before the circus episode had practically disrupted the college, a bitter battle was waged around a much tormented Mr. Dearing who had the misfortune to live in the first house which students passed on their way along the Huntsville Road from the campus into town.[123] Mr. Dearing had long been annoyed by students. As he said in the letter to the newspaper later:

> Night after night, and week after week, and at almost every hour of the night, companies of students came by my house, singing songs the most obscene, and using language the most disgraceful and offensive to decency.[124]

When one of Mr. Dearing's female servants disappeared, he was sure that she had been spirited away by these student ruffians and that she was even at that time hidden in one of the University buildings. He went out to the campus to find her. And here the accounts of the episode become confused and contradictory. The faculty, writing a circular letter to calm the fears of parents and trustees, inclined to blame Mr. Dearing for the disturbance which followed.

When Mr. Dearing came to the University to look for his missing servant, he asked a University officer to search a building where he thought she was hidden. Mr. Dearing, unable to find her, went away, but came back again with a search warrant, a sheriff, and a posse. Although coöperation had not been asked of the faculty, it was they who searched the rooms, again without result. The students quite properly resented the intrusion, for they thought that their "honor had been slandered." When a stone was thrown at the departing group, the retreat became a riot. The students, throwing brickbats and striking with canes, chased the running townsfolk; even some shots were fired. Although the faculty finally gained temporary control of the disturbance, the fight soon began again as a result of the "threatening warlike language" of Mr. Dearing. The students, under this provocation admittedly "so far forgot their duty and dignity" that they went around to Mr. Dearing's home a few nights later, took off his gate, attempted to steal his poultry, and got into a fight, in which firearms were used on both sides and in which one student was slightly wounded.[125]

At several interesting points Mr. Dearing's account concerning the servant girl contradicts the faculty's account. He said that he had gone to the campus in the first place because the boys had boasted to him that they had the girl in one of the University buildings and had defied him to release her. When he appealed to a faculty member to help him search, the professor, after looking in some of the rooms, said that the only place she could possibly be hidden was in one of the society rooms, where entry would require a search warrant. Mr. Dearing did nothing further until the servant had been missing for three weeks; then he took the advice given him and got a warrant. He, with the sheriff and his men, went first to Dr. Woods, who referred him to faculty members in charge of the Hall. But they refused to join the searching party. By that time the students had begun to gather, and Mr. Dearing assured them that he would be quite satisfied if the professors alone conducted the search. Mr. Dearing thought that Professor Bonfils really searched, but he was not so sure about Professor Hudson. While Dearing was standing talking to the president and the professors, he was suddenly hit on the head with a brickbat and attacked "in language and act." Then upon the faculty's advice, he went home. The missing servant came home later in the evening.

His account of the disturbance on the night of March 13, is also written from a quite different angle:

On the night of March 13th a company of Students coming from town, approached my house in a noisy and threatening manner. Some immediately came to my front gate, and broke it down; others entered the lane, in the rear of my dwelling, and advanced toward the poultry house, saying they would have some turkeys. One of them got near half way in the window of the house, but came out unsuccessful. Knowing their threats, and that they were well armed, I was prepared with my musket, and approached within ten or fifteen feet of them, requesting them to leave my premises. As soon as I spoke, I heard them cock their pistols. I instantly leveled my musket and ordered them to depart. After going a few steps, one or more of them fired upon me. I then fired in self-defense, and one of the party was wounded—to my great regret, the son of a particular friend.

He concluded his article with a comment which many men were to echo before the problems of discipline in the University had been solved:

Certainly I shall regard it as a calamity, if in consequence of the corruption of morals and the entire want of order and of discipline in this institution, or on account of the inefficiency, or incapacity of its presiding officer, I am compelled to incur the anxiety and expense, of sending to a distant college, a son whom I had hoped to educate, within sight of my own dwelling.[126]

The faculty were not entirely remiss in their handling of the episode. They suspended all classes during an investigation which resulted in the decision that firearms were so dangerous that they must be "extirpated" before classes could resume. After obtaining from the students involved in the fracas a pledge to abstain from the use of arms, they wrote to the parents and trustees. Their report, as has been already noted, gave a slant which shifted much of the blame to the abused Mr. Dearing.

Henry Tutwiler was the only professor who refused to sign this letter. Perhaps he considered that the white-wash was somewhat too apparent. His opposition did not improve his relations with his colleagues. Since Mr. Dearing had made a direct reference to President Woods' incompetency, the president, too, was less secure. The episode helped to bring to a crisis the agitation on the campus which, two years later, resulted in the almost complete change of staff. As for Mr. Dearing, he soon solved his problem by building a new home further south, away from the main line of traffic between the University and town.

By 1858 the strained relations between the University and the town had reached almost open warfare. Crenshaw Hall, writing home that spring, told of a student prank which had the sole purpose of stirring up the townspeople. Students had set a brush fire and then had waited for the townspeople and fire engines to answer the false alarm. The students' hostile attitude toward the town, Crenshaw observed, had been increased because President Garland had said that "two of the townspeople had told him that they would not come out if the college were to burn up."[127] Later in the same year Crenshaw was even more explicit in a letter to his father:

The break between the citizens and students is becoming wider and wider every day, and I cannot conjecture what will be the final result of the ill-feeling now existing between the two. . . . It would not do for a town fellow to crook his finger at a student now.[128]

The period between these two letters is marked by one of the most serious episodes of the early history of the University. The tragedy started as a campus affair, but because of the general feeling

THE OLD UNIVERSITY

in the community and in the state, drew to itself all the accumulated thunder and lightning of public resentment. On June 4, 1858, David A. Herring shot and killed Edward L. Nabers. Exactly how the tragedy itself occurred is still a mystery, but its background is clear. Starting in a boarding house fight, it involved, as so many lesser brawls had done, the use of forbidden firearms.

At the dining table Herring's mates twitted him because his home state, Mississippi, had repudiated her foreign debts. As Herring apparently was sensitive and easily tormented, the other boys at Mrs. Baird's boarding house pressed their advantage until life became so intolerable for him that, resolving to protect himself, he bought a repeater pistol.

On the morning of June 4, there was the usual banter around Mrs. Baird's breakfast table. The upshot was that Herring and Walter M. Gilkey went outside to settle in a "fair fight" a matter which seems to have involved an insult Herring had given to Gilkey the evening before. Eyewitnesses disagreed about what happened next. Some said that when Herring drew his pistol and started toward Gilkey, Nabers went to Gilkey's aid. Others said that Gilkey struck a blow with a stick before Herring drew and that Nabers, intervening, struck Herring on the head with another heavy stick. Still others insisted that Nabers rushed at Herring without provocation and that Herring drew in self-defense. But all agreed on one fact: Herring had fired his pistol—and Nabers was dead.

Herring took refuge from the rage of the students in the Battles' home until the civil authorities could get him safely out of town. He was tried on June 5, and acquitted on grounds of self-defense. He left town again at once.

The townspeople, on the whole, approved of the verdict. But the students did not. Their friend and classmate had been murdered; and his killer had gone scot-free because of the cold-blooded indifference of the courts. Many of the students, who could no longer stand being associated with a University where such things happened, went home. Bolling Hall describes both types of reaction in a letter to his father:

The citizens of Tuscaloosa when they heard the sentence, sent up a yell of joy. Never were my ears saluted with a sound so harsh, so inappropriate. It sounded more like the demonical yell of the savage as his victim in the last agony of death writhes under the scorching flames. Congratulations were heaped upon him. Even Brown, the Trustee of the college, congratulated him. Was ever such a premium paid for murder! What safety is there to a student at this place unless he can protect himself? Tuscaloosa is a shame upon the name of Alabama. The women of the place had declared that if Herring was put to bail they would go to sewing to pay him out, so great is their delight in seeing students murdered in cold blood.

Well, the effect is that about thirty of the most respectable students have already gone home. There are only four or five left in the Soph. class and they are, with the exception of one, not fit to associate with. Seven or eight Juniors have left and a good many Freshmen. Several of my class are going off as soon as the examination is over. . . . I do not think you ought ever to send another one of the boys here; not even ought Crenshaw to come back here next year.[129]

President Garland tried to pour oil on troubled waters by writing to parents, who were undoubtedly alarmed by letters like this. He sent them a statement of the court record and assured them that the storm would pass. "Like a troubled atmosphere, it will become more calm in consequence of the agitation which has swept over it," said the president.[130] It is probable that he only half believed what he had written. It was becoming increasingly evident to him, of all men, that the problems of discipline in the University were getting out of hand and that something must be done soon, to heal the breach between the school and its town and to restore the University's good name in the state.

Six months after the Nabers killing, the *Monitor,* a Tuscaloosa newspaper, ran a series of articles on the causes for the deplorable state of University affairs, for the reasons of decrease in enrollments, and for the general decline of the whole institution. These articles stirred wide comment; the state of the University had become a public issue. Many recommendations were made for reform and improvement, with the general agreement that something must be done. In these discussions the feud between the college and its community was highlighted again and again, the underlying annoyances and exasperations standing out clearly. The Livingston *Messenger* stated that the citizens of Tuscaloosa could, if they would, help to end the friction by efforts to "naturalize and domesticate" the new students arriving on the campus:

THE OLD UNIVERSITY   255

Any one who will mingle among the students of the University and the People of Tuscaloosa will soon discover that they form two distinct and almost belligerant communities. Who is in fault here we cannot say. We know, however, that a feeling of dislike for the people of the city of Tuscaloosa, has been handed down by a kind of apostolical succession from class to class, even to this day. Nor, so far as we can learn, has the deportment of the mass of citizens been such as to do away with this prejudice.

If they, upon the admission of a student, would seek him out, make his acquaintance, introduce him to their families, and thus in a measure naturalize and domesticate him, is it credible that he would rob their orchards, and poultry houses, take down their gates, and turn cattle on their shrubbery? Would he cut their well ropes; carry deadly weapons for their canine sentinels, and make night hideous by his yells and groans? Credat Judaeus Apella. Even we believe that Southern boys have too much chivalry in their constitution, to indulge in 'these boyish freaks,' as they are sometimes termed under these circumstances.[131]

It is interesting to observe that the journalist has managed in these paragraphs to suggest the nature of student pranks in a manner that served to spread farther the reputation for disorderly conduct the University endured.

Another suggestion in the same newspaper was that better relations between faculty and students would help the situation:

It may be true to some extent, that there is little community of feeling between the Faculty of the University and the students. We think ourselves there is too much distance between them; but we believe it attributable as much to the students as to anyone else. There seems to be among them a code of morals by which it is perfectly lawful to annoy the officers of the institution, and the citizens of the town. A Professor, desirous of breaking through the reserve and distrust of the students, and introduce them to the society of the place more fully, began giving a series of elegant parties, to the different classes in succession. The Senior class, as the oldest, came first. On the evening of the first entertainment, when the guests had assembled, and were engaged in the festivities of the evening, a number of chivalrous (?) Juniors, Sophs, and Fresh congregated in the vicinity and because they were uninvited, insulted the Professor, his family and guests, half of whom were their own college friends, with an outrageous and unearthly charivari. The Professor very properly discontinued his entertainments. If there is no community of feeling between the students and faculty, the former are at least as faulty as the latter.[132]

Dr. Garland, "the Professor" whose strawberry party had become a target for disorder, probably would have preferred that the episode be forgotten rather than be used to intensify the myth about the ruffians on the University campus.

A third analysis of the root of the trouble, published a few weeks later, concluded that the very location of the University, as well as its dormitory system, was conducive to all kinds of evil:

Prominent, however, among the grave defects of the University, we set down 'the manner of its location and its dormitory system.'

By the manner of its location, we mean its isolated position—apart from the community—outside the city—being a distinct community, not identified with, or assimilated to the neighboring population; but detached from it, and inevitably thereby, more or less antagonistic to it. The dormitory system is part of this isolation and is necessary to the present location, because there is not sufficient population contiguous to the University to furnish homes for students. By this plan, students are merely 'camping out'. They are simply congregated in houses instead of tents; but the evils of the camp, to a considerable extent, unavoidable, must be incident to their manner of life. Cut off from constant daily contact with families and the refinement of females, and unrestrained by the immediate prescense [sic] and influence of the public, they must, perhaps, sometimes unconsciously, fall into the loose habits of tented life; and, in those who are prone to dissapation [sic] and rowdyism, the cultivation of bad propensities is not a difficult matter under such circumstances.

If the University has [sic] been placed in the midst of our community, and its students compelled to seek their homes—sleeping and boarding—in families of citizens, and thus be caused to feel themselves a part of the community, it would have enjoyed better prospects for success.[133]

With all this discussion of University shortcomings as a background, efforts of the trustees to gain from the General Assembly badly needed financial relief were made more difficult. The University could not reform itself without funds. Apparently it could not get financial justice from the lawmakers until it had reformed itself. Matters had reached a crisis.

But President Garland had been thinking furiously ever since he stepped into the presidency in 1855. It took both shrewdness and daring to recognize that the cure for rebellion against discipline might be more discipline, that the evils of 'camping out' in dormitories, criticized by the newspaper writer, might be overcome by camping out in tents. But President Garland, having those qualities of shrewdness and daring, wisely turned the University into a military school. Boys who had rebelled and stormed in disobedience when their independence of action had been cramped by faculty rules snapped to salute under rigid military discipline and, in breathlessly short space of time, removed the tarnish from the name of the University of Alabama.

CHAPTER XI

The Military Years
1860-1865

AT THE STATE CAPITOL in Montgomery, in January, 1861, the governor and members of both houses of the General Assembly reviewed the Alabama corps of cadets. Something new had been added to the University, whose guidance had been part of the business of each legislative session for more than forty years and whose financial worries were even then a major legislative headache. More than a touch of skepticism must have been visible on the faces of the state officials as they waited for the drill to begin. When Dr. Garland had first proposed taking to Montgomery boys who had had only four months of military discipline, faculty members and parents alike had been doubtful. They pointed out the temptations of the journey and of the capital city, recalled the long tradition of headstrong unruliness, and prophesied that those who undertook such a venture would rue the day.

Colonel Caleb Huse, who had faith in his cadets, had been given the responsibility for making the decision. He had arranged for two steamboats to make the trip: one to take the corps down the Tombigbee to Mobile; the other to complete the journey up the Alabama to Montgomery. Later he wrote proudly that, even though there were open bars on these boats, no cadet even entered one.[1] The boys marched into the state capital and took it by storm. The stereotype of the wild and lawless university student with "dirk, pistol, and bowie knife" was destroyed.

In honor of the cadets Montgomery gave a ball, followed by a lavish banquet.[2] President Garland received more than twenty applications for appointments during the visit.[3] Everywhere, as the Tuscaloosa *Observer* reported when the trip was over, the University cadets won "golden opinions" not only for their splendid drill

THE OLD UNIVERSITY 259

but especially for their manly bearing and behavior when not on duty. "A new era will dawn upon the education of our young men," this paper declared, "if in addition to making them scholars, we can make them well-behaved and accomplished gentlemen."[4]

The men on the reviewing stand, their skepticism turned to open admiration, expressed in practical terms their new faith in the state's "institution of learning." On the day after the drill the legislature, suspending rules, rushed through both houses a bill raising the University endowment from $250,000 to $300,000 and the rate of interest from six to eight per cent.

This was the goal toward which Dr. Garland had been working ever since he assumed the presidency of the University. In 1862 he wrote to Governor J. G. Shorter about these years of effort. He had, he said, become convinced that the old collegiate system had been a failure and that the University, operating on this pattern, had done more harm than good. Under the old system the University had been sending out for each good student perhaps two who were drunkards or otherwise ruined in moral character. "It was to correct these evils," said Dr. Garland, "that for six years I labored to effect the introduction of the Military system—and it was for this purpose that the Trustees introduced it."[5] It may be added that there was more than a touch of the authoritarian in Dr. Garland's personality. By 1863 he was writing to Governor Shorter of his complete loss of faith in democracy:

The sooner we take the organization of the Military and I may add the Civil arm of the Govt. from the popular vote of the whole mass of the people, the more stable and wisely administered will our affairs be. The experiment on this continent has undermined my prejudice in favor of popular elections. This however is out of the record.[6]

President Garland's recommendations gained acceptance slowly. Several sessions of the legislature had considered them and rejected them. Admittedly, it might be useful to have a military school at the University if the mounting tension between North and South broke into war; but it would be an expensive innovation, and the University was in financial difficulties already. The trustees finally acceded to the president's request that he be allowed at least to visit some of the few institutions in the country where military discipline was part of the educational system. When he came back from his tour, which included Nashville University, The Citadel, in Charleston, Virginia Military Institute, and West Point Military Academy,[7] he was more convinced than ever that answers to the problems of the University of Alabama lay in the speedy adoption of a military system.

He reported his findings to the trustees. He told them that under the old system students were receiving a "hot-house culture" which encouraged rather than discouraged laxity of conduct and boorishness of manners:

Beyond a few regulations, prohibiting the entering of a public room with the hat on or attending chapel or recitation in deshabille—or spitting on public floors—or some infraction of the rules of propriety, but little is done in our colleges for the improvement of a student in manners, and in the neatness of his room and person.[8]

A properly organized military academy would give due attention to these things. It would solve the vexing problem of student control, he thought, and it would obviously be very useful in case of war as a training ground for soldiers.

The argument of military expediency undoubtedly had growing weight with the lawmakers and the trustees. When in 1860, by large vote of both houses, the Alabama General Assembly gave Garland the authorization he needed to go ahead with his plan, he moved quickly. Students returning to the campus in September, 1860, found their college transformed into an army camp. They donned uniforms patterned after West Point, took up the arms and equipment furnished by the state, and for four solid weeks lived in army tents and went through a rigorous military training and camp routine before they entered the academic life.[9] Even after classes began, the military aspect was predominate. They were now members of the Alabama corps of cadets, a component part of the state troops. When war came, they were given the status of enlisted men in the Confederate Army.

Military routine was followed night and day, even after classes were resumed. An early morning drill came before breakfast. The cadets marched and counter-marched to tunes played by a Negro fife-and-drum corps. Walking tours helped harden the fledgling soldiers. Rules were stiffened. A system of demerits took care of minor infractions of these rules; serious misdemeanors were tried by courts-martial.[10]

A military staff had been recruited from older military academies to supplement the teaching faculty. Dr. Garland himself was "superintendent" and commander-in-chief. He donned the regular grey uniform of a colonel and held reviews and inspections "with the soldiery precision of a West Point Superintendent."[11] Caleb Huse, recommended by the superintendent of West Point, was the first commandant. Three graduates of Virginia Military Institute made up his staff: Major James T. Murfee, assistant commandant; Captains Charles L. Lumsden and James H. Morrison, instructors in military tactics. Much credit for the immediate success of the experiment belongs to Caleb Huse, a first lieutenant in the United States Army at the time of his appointment. Just after he had returned from a six month's leave of absence spent in Europe, the War Department extended that leave to May, 1861, to enable him to direct Alabama's new military school. Before his duties began, the governor of the state commissioned him a colonel.

With the assumption of his duties, his troubles began, for Caleb Huse was a Yankee, Massachusetts-born and bred. And sons of a state more and more conscious of the mounting antipathy toward things Northern were prepared to resent and oppose him. Three weeks after the military department was organized, the cadets told Dr. Garland that a mutiny was brewing in his camp, and that the cadets were prepared to run the "Yankee" out of the state. The leaders in the movement, who had been among the trouble-makers in the old University, were boys who could carry out such a threat. When the president informed Huse of the situation, Huse asked whether his resignation was wanted by the faculty and trustees. Assured that it was not, he calmly continued his duties. The threatened mutiny never materialized; within a surprisingly short time all such danger had disappeared, for the boys had learned quickly to respect and admire their Northern commandant.[12]

Huse seems to have been unaware of the tenseness of the North-South situation when he accepted the post in Alabama. Years later he wrote his conviction that the militarization of the University and the secession movement in Alabama were quite unrelated:

The introduction of military drill and discipline at the State University had no connection whatever with any secession movement in Alabama, and the fact that a Massachusetts born man and of Puritan descent was selected to inaugurate the system, will, or ought to be, accepted as confirmatory of this assertion.[13]

Huse may have come to the University of Alabama with Southern sympathies. It is certain that he left the University a fully adopted man of the South, for in the spring of 1861, instead of returning to the United States Army, from which he was on leave, he joined the Confederate Army and went to Europe to buy military supplies for the Confederacy.[14] Students who had flouted the relatively mild regulations of the old regime to prove their spirit and independence made an amazingly quick adjustment to military discipline. They became "brass button conscious,"[15] and adopted, as soldiers, all the restraints that were unbearable before. They developed habits of order, punctuality, obedience to authority, and personal neatness. The new order was conducive to study, and study to higher standards of attainment. The prestige of the University rose; the institution assured its existence by proving its worth.

As early as November, 1860, one cadet wrote to his uncle

I remember that you did not seem to like the idea of introducing the military into the University when you and I were talking about it in the summer.

But I hope you have changed your opinion, as I have. There is a complete change for the better in all our movements.

Drunkenness and card-playing, said this cadet, had dropped from the list of student amusements. Days were devoted to study. No noise disturbed the barracks. Students were deprived of every pretext by which a lazy boy could escape study. "It will be a fine college—from this time forward," was his conclusion.[16]

In general his enthusiasm was shared by the cadets, but more so, it may be supposed, by the citizens of Tuscaloosa. A few indulgent parents raised objections to guard duty at night, on the basis that such duty was injurious to the boys' health; these parents received a firm reply from Dr. Garland. The officer of the day was required to see that each sentinel who went on duty was adequately dressed. Although sentinels were allowed to stand inside the Round House and keep watch through its glass windows when the weather was bad, parents continued to worry about the young sentries. Garland's answer to them was stern:

take off guards from post after 10 o'clock at night, and wherein have you altered the old system? . . . To preserve the morals of Cadets primarily and their health incidentally, is then the object of the rules.[17]

In Dr. Garland's mind from the first, one other object had been even more important than the preservation of the morals of the cadets—the preparation of Alabama youth for the war he thought was inevitable. That war came within months of the September day when the first Alabama cadets began their drills on the campus training ground. Feeling was running high in Alabama that autumn, but so quickly had the new discipline asserted itself that the University campus was one of the calmest spots in the state when November brought the news of Lincoln's election. Instruction went on as usual; drills continued; there was no excitement and no disorder, "much to the satisfaction of every one and especially to the citizens of Tuscaloosa."[18] The following January no hysteria or panic was evident in the orderly demonstration for the legislators in Montgomery. In the very shadow of a catastrophe the young men who would most keenly feel its force showed little realization of the imminence of that catastrophe.

Two months after the Montgomery trip, the storm broke. When the "irrepressible conflict" began its shooting stage, many of the cadets drilled on the campus of the University abandoned their books and their drill manuals to join the Confederate Army. In June, fifty-five cadets signed this communication to Governor A. B. Moore:

We, the undersigned, members of the Alabama Corps of Cadets, feeling the responsibility which our native State has taken upon herself in withdrawing from the Federal Union and assuming an independent position among the nations of the earth, hereby tender our services, through you, to her, ready & willing to go, at any time and to any place, her honor and independence may require.[19]

Many cadets resigned to join companies being formed in their home communities. Others were detailed by the governor to train volunteer companies; by June of 1861, nine such companies had been drilled in this manner.[20] The University became, in truth, the "nursery" of the Confederate Army.

The swift course of events created both opportunity and problems for the leaders of the University military school. Immense increase in prestige came as the drills on the campus took on the aspect of grim reality. More students flocked to the spot where they could prepare for their part in patriotic duty while they studied. But students who came were restless, impatient to take their places as fighting men. The student turnover was tremendous. And as war tempo increased, all the problems of equipping, provisioning and maintaining the school became more complicated and more bewildering.

Dr. Garland had to recognize that in war time military necessities took priority over the gentler forms of education. He wrote his conviction to his friend Governor Shorter, saying, "The military state of the Corps must be considered as more important than its scholastic, during the period of our struggle for independence."[21] But he never lost sight of the values fostered and developed in the academic departments of his school. In June, 1861, he published a message to the people of Alabama. Many literary institutions, he said, had disbanded and closed their doors for the duration of the war. The University of Alabama would continue its regular curriculum. To compensate for loss of enrollmnet of boys above eighteen, the University would admit boys fourteen years old and would provide preparatory instruction for them.[22] Three years later he was still struggling to keep the flame of learning alive within the University walls. That same year (1864) Dr. Garland wrote Governor Watts a letter in which he expressed his concern over the decline in education under the pressures of war. "Among the greatest of the calamities inflicted upon the country by this unrighteous war," he said, "is the interruption of our educational facilities." He was grieving because the older men were passing from the public scene; the middle-aged were dying on the battlefield; and the young boys were going off to the army with the merest rudiments of education. Soon the country would be "destitute of cultivated intellect." The war's end would find the state with no "supply of educated talent to meet the demands of the learned professions." "In this state of things," he declared, "one could suppose that the whole country would feel the peculiar interest in the success of the University."[23] Garland fought for the continuity of the intellectual life as valiantly as he did for military discipline. In consequence, when other schools dropped academic courses for total military preparedness,[24] boys at the University of Alabama continued to study the classics between drills and to ponder philosophical problems as well as military tactics.

Enrollment in the Alabama corps of cadets rose to 158 during the academic year 1861-62, as compared with 81 the year before.[25] New cadets far outnumbered the old ones because so many boys had enlisted at the first opportunity. Colonel Huse himself had gone off to active service for the Confederacy, but his second in command, Colonel J. T. Murfee, had succeeded him and was showing qualities of leadership rivaling Huse's own. That March the governor again called upon the cadet corps to drill about 12,000 volunteers, who composed some thirty regiments of infantry and cavalry and a number of battalions and batteries in twelve encampments throughout the state. Writing to General Gideon Pillow, Dr. Garland spoke proudly of the performance of his cadets. He said that their efficiency and skill had won them the utmost favor of both the government and the people, and that the corps was overwhelmed with applications as a result.[26]

However, an "overwhelming" number of applications was needed to keep the corps in existence. Many of the cadet instructors who answered the governor's call never came back to the University campus. They became, instead, officers of the companies they trained. When the corps went into camp in September, 1862, there were hardly enough old cadets to fill the posts of cadet officers, and when they resumed their studies nearly all the noncommissioned officers were new recruits. That year the senior class had no members, and the junior class had only three students.

Dr. Garland reported to Governor Shorter that same fall about the state of the military school. He noted the parallel academic and military staffs. In the former, of which the president was head, Rev. J. W. Pratt was professor of logic, rhetoric, and oratory; George Benagh, professor of natural philosophy and astronomy; André DeLoffre, professor of modern languages; W. S. Wyman, professor of ancient languages. John W. Mallet, nominally professor of chemistry, was on leave to "assume the duties of Genl. Superintendent of the Laboratories of the C. States," and Mr. W. L. Boggs was substituting for him. The chair of mathematics, left vacant when Major Murfee became commandant of the corps, was still unfilled, but two of the military staff were giving instruction there. William J. Vaughn was assistant professor of ancient languages. Two quite new posts appear on the list: principal and assistant instructor in the "Academic Department," the two jobs being filled respectively by E. R. Dixon, and H. M. Somerville.

The military staff consisted of seven officers: "L. C. Garland, Col. & Superintendent," Major J. T. Murfee; Captain D. Poyner; Captain H. H. Murfee; Captain E. A. Smith; Captain John F. Gibbs, quartermaster; and Major John B. Read, surgeon. Three employees without military rank were attached to the military staff: John P. Boyle, superintendent of repairs; William H. Gossage, tailor to the corps; and James T. Pierce, steward. The total of the two staffs was thus nineteen.

Dr. Garland reported an enrollment of 197 cadets and said that there was a waiting list of 55. Applications were coming in from all the Confederate states except the Carolinas and it was evident that the enrollment could go to 400 if there were room for that many. He spoke with pride of the success of the plan he had worked so hard to establish:

This enlarged usefulness of the University must be very gratifying to its friends and to the public generally. Its present prosperity seems to be based upon a sure foundation. In the first introduction of the Military System, the circumstances were favorable to its success; but the effeciency of the System, and its decided superiority to any other for the training of our youth, will ensure to it the abiding confidences of the public. When the war shall have closed, I look for the continued prosperity of the Institution.

He did not speak as glowingly, however, of the condition of the equipment with which his cadets were training. As there was "very great destitution" at that point, he begged the governor for help:

The drill and discipline and spirit of the Corps are very good, and it would be a pity to dampen its enthusiasm and blunt its efficiency by the lack of means to carry its military instructions beyond the school of the Soldier.

Furthermore, Garland told the governor that he had investigated complaints about the mess hall and had found them to be "misrepresented and greatly exaggerated." An inexperienced steward, who probably should have been discharged, was at fault, but finding a replacement was difficult. The president asked the governor to recommend a new steward.[28]

The question about out-of-state applications evidently was one to which Dr. Garland gave some thought. Just two weeks after he filed his report, he wrote the governor a second letter asking for instructions of policy at this point. He said,

> Applications for admission into the University continue to be made. Quite a number of them come from other States, and it is a Question which I submit to your decision, whether the appointment must be restricted to applications from Alabama. If we could accommodate all, it would of course be a satisfaction to extend the benefits of the University to other states—and it would be extending the area of intellectual cultivation from which a harvest might be reaped in more peaceful times. . . . The *Institution itself* would therefore, as it seems to me be benefitted. . . . But the question of justice to the youth of Alabama springs up.—and it is by no means clear that the Institution should prosper to the detriment of the native-born youth of the State.[29]

The open-door policy which Garland suggested was apparently not adopted. Alabama applicants were given preference over those of any other state throughout the period.[30] However, the number of out-of-state cadets increased steadily. There were six in 1860-61, ten in 1861-62, twenty in 1862-63, and forty-eight in 1863-64. Most of them came from Mississippi and Georgia.

During the war, problems of administering an institution increased. It was difficult, for example, to get food and equipment. As new problems arose, Dr. Garland grappled with them all with vigor, ingenuity, and tenacity.

In September, 1863, the corps was filled to its limit of 200, and on the waiting list were still 140. Garland, deciding to let 100 more enroll in October,[31] ordered additional tents for them.[32] As food could not be thus easily obtained, the regulation to the effect that each new cadet was to bring two hundred pounds of bacon from home was made and enforced. "Bacon is an indispensable condition to the reception of your son," Dr. Garland wrote one parent.[33] He firmly told another that he would consider it an act of bad faith to receive cadets without being able to feed them: "What can I do, in a market which is not offering a single pound for sale, except in the way of barter for salt, or thread, or something else which I cannot command?"[34]

The University steward became a traveling buyer, who went not only all over the state but into neighboring states as well to find the food he needed. He succeeded reasonably well. The mess hall served abundant meals, but they were plain and probably lacked variety. The daily fare consisted chiefly of bread, rice, beef, potatoes, molasses, milk, and coffee. Bacon was on the menu twice a week, and other foods, including vegetables, appeared when they were available.[35] The cadets complained, of course, like any other students and like any other soldiers. On at least one occasion Dr. Garland lost patience with a complainer. He wrote a parent,

Your son says he cannot stand our discipline and our fare. The discipline is that of West Point, or the Virginia Military Institute or any other state Military Academy of high grade. The fare is better than my own or than three fourths of the families in the city of Tuscaloosa. . . . He has determined to desert his post and I have paid him $50 to bear his expense home.[36]

When cloth for uniforms was scarce, sheets and calico curtains from home were pressed into service for lining coats and trousers.[37] The problem of shoes Dr. Garland met by setting up a cobbler shop on the campus. He persuaded General Gideon Pillow to detail an experienced shoemaker to take charge.[38] The University bought beef supplies on the hoof so that hides could be used for shoes.[39]

Governors and army officers were constantly urged, implored, and even slightly bullied to furnish the equipment for the cadet corps which the commandant considered the due of his fledgling troops. The president told Governor Shorter that the muskets available were poor in quality and often practically useless for want of repairs.[40] A year later he reminded the governor of this lack and in the winter of 1863 he followed his complaint with an even more detailed one, adding that the cannons still had not been supplied. No ball cartridges had been made for the muskets the governor had supplied because all the local supply of lead had been exhausted for more than a year. "There are about 1000 pounds on a vault in this vicinity in which I have had an eye in case of necessity," said the resourceful commander, "but it is the vault of the late Capt. Wm. T. King, whose wife's grief at his loss is such as to preclude the propriety of speaking to her on the subject of dismantling her husband's tomb."[42]

Horses for the crops were as hard to get as bullets. When the president's request for horses for his artillery company was flatly refused, he went to the citizens of Tuscaloosa and entered contracts with those who were willing to let the cadets use their horses for drill or to repel raids.[43]

The greatest problem of all for the indefatigable Dr. Garland was that of desertion. As enrollment boomed, so did the rate of turnover. The total number of cadets in 1862-63 was 266, though the limit that year was at 200. More than half of those enrolled that year deserted or resigned to join the army. Every device was used to stem this tide of desertion, even though it was desertion with the loftiest of patriotic motives.[44] Of course, applicants who sought merely to escape conscription were not wanted; they were discouraged by a system which gave preference to those applicants asking to enroll for the longest terms. On the other hand, applicants more than twenty-one years of age or those lacking post-graduate work were rejected except in special cases.[45] The lowering of the conscription age to eighteen made further difficulties for Dr. Garland. Some eighteen-year-olds with suitable army substitutes were admitted to the corps; those who were already enrolled were allowed to remain. The average age of the cadets on the University campus during the war years was approximately fifteen or sixteen.

As the war progressed, the problem of desertion became increasingly serious. The reasons are not difficult to find. Some boys became restive under strict military discipline. Others walked out because they could not endure being taunted with accusations that they were in the corps to escape conscription. Still others, fired with patriotic zeal, felt only enlistment in active service could bring them peace of mind. A few undoubtedly forced their own dismissals to avoid the stigma of desertion. Young Griffen was one of these. When Professor Pratt finally sent him home, the professor wrote to the boy's father about his son's strange behavior. After he had been warned concerning accumulated demerits, he had calmly accumulated more. He had been absent from drill. He had visited the city without permission. He had broken arrest twice and when tried by court martial had pleaded guilty to every charge without offering any defense. "He seemed to covet demerits," said Professor Pratt mildly.[46] Young Griffen had, however, not been secretive about his purposes. He had announced a few days before he went on his one-man rebellion that he was soon to join the army.

Dr. Garland fought the tide of desertions with all his might. He was convinced that the future of culture in the state of Alabama, if not in the whole South, lay in the continuation of the kind of education being given to the Alabama cadets. He fumed when as many as sixteen deserted in a single day. He did more than fume when a Tuscaloosa citizen came to him with the report that about one hundred cadets were on the point of deserting. From the dais of the Rotunda he turned out the whole corps and addressed them upon the dishonor involved in desertion. To give his remarks proper emphasis, he repeated the process the next day. Again the cadets were assembled; again their commander-in-chief "enforced upon them the obligations that should hold them to their duty here." Garland's eloquence was at least partly effective; only twelve deserted after he had talked with them. Several others petitioned the governor to be permitted to resign.[47]

Over and over, Garland labored with restless and impatient boys and berated their elders who countenanced their desertion of posts "to which they are held by parental advice, by a state commission, by a written pledge of honor, and by every private and public interest." He said that boys who came to the corps only long enough to learn how to drill a company were receiving nothing and giving nothing in their brief stay on the campus. He was scornful of the way in which deserters were feted and hailed as patriots and heroes by a "world insensate . . . enough to justify the means by the end."[48] After each desertion he wrote an order dismissing the cadet from the corps for violation of his word of honor, pronouncing his disgrace as a soldier and declaring that his name would not only be reported at once to the commander-in-chief but would be published in the catalogues of the University as that of a deserter.[49] And no deserter was ever allowed to repent and return. "These are not the materials we want," declared the stern disciplinarian who commanded the unit.[50]

This very same disciplinary firmness prevented Dr. Garland from any leniency in law enforcement. Delinquencies and infringements of University rules brought demerits according to their seriousness. A cadet who accumulated one hundred or more demerits in four consecutive months was sent home. No consideration for the stability of the corps ever softened Dr. Garland at that point. And when the trustees seemed to him to be adopting an unduly lenient policy in regard to the reinstatement of dismissed students, he told them so. In May, 1864, in addressing a communication on this point to the board, he said that they were weakening the discipline of the corps. He insisted that if the delinquencies for which demerits were given were ignored, the whole system would break down, leaving not one solitary feature of superiority over the "let-alone" system under which the University had formerly operated and suffered.[51]

Justice tempered the sternness in these dismissal cases. Garland wrote to each parent a careful letter, telling him that his son was being dismissed for delinquencies "each in itself small, and not affecting his moral character in the ordinary sense of that word."[52] Encouraged by the moderate tone of such a dismissal letter, one parent wrote to ask Garland's advice about the future of the dismissed student. Dr. Garland replied that the boy should be put in some other good school and started on the rudiments of useful and entertaining knowledge under a skilled teacher. Furthermore, he insisted on two conditions in the boy's instruction: "1st, never to suffer him to pass over anything he does not fully comprehend; and 2nd, Never to leave it until it has been made, so to speak, a part of the mind itself." Then the wise doctor added a further comment which is always good educational doctrine:

. . . in nine cases out of ten, boys come to hate their books, from a consciousness that they are deriving from them neither improvement of mind nor practical knowledge. The desire of knowledge is natural to every one—but it must be *knowledge*—something real, something that can be appreciated and valued.[53]

Garland's determination to keep his Alabama cadet corps and his University serving the future as well as the present for his state brought him from time to time into spirited conflict with Confederate officials. Defiance of conscription officers was used when necessary, and some important people connected with the war effort found that the soldierly scholar had carried the doctrine of states' rights farther than they found convenient.

Early in the war Governor Shorter assured Dr. Garland that the state would not permit the enrolling officers of the Confederate states to conscript the cadets. In February, 1863, he went farther and commanded the University president to resist such enrollment, if necessary, by his military power.[54] Dr. Garland had no hesitancy in exercising this authority. He believed that his cadets would be better soldiers if they completed their University course. He saw no "necessity for hurrying off, when by staying and availing themselves of their opportunities of improvement, they may finally go prepared to serve their country with much greater efficiency."[55] He told his cadets that he was under orders from the governor to protect them from premature conscription and that he intended to carry out these orders and would "suffer no conscribing officer to interfere with the rights and privileges of the Cadets."[56] He notified boys accepted for cadetships that they were under such protection and advised them to appeal directly to the governor of Alabama if anyone tried to interfere with them.[57]

Garland's first real conflict with the conscription officers came in 1864 after a law had been passed that drew principals into the ranks. One enrolling officer tried to conscript four cadets over eighteen years of age who had furnished acceptable substitutes for the army and had received official exemptions before they entered the Alabama corps of cadets. President Garland was outraged. Here was a violation not only of the rights of his University but also of the rights of his state. He wrote indignantly to Governor Watts,

It is probable that the Action of Congress may render it necessary to procure from the proper Authority, the exemption again of Cadets over 18 years of age. But be that as it may, the highest authority I recognize is the Executive of the State of Alabama. Our present difficulties have come upon us, by the doctrine [that] the Federal Govt. is superior to that of the State. We are fighting for the sovereignty of Alabama, and there is no power on earth that I acknowledge to be above that of my State. The allegiance I owe to the Confederate Govt. is *under* that I owe first to Alabama—and where the two authorities collide, my obedience shall be rendered to that of the State. Therefore, it is my desire to have your instructions in the matter, and they shall be my law.[58]

The Governor responded promptly to this declaration of allegiance. He requested the Confederate Secretary of War to issue orders to protect the Alabama corps of cadets from interference by enrolling officers. If the four cadets in question were conscripted, he argued,

THE OLD UNIVERSITY 273

all others who had become eighteen since joining the corps would also be subject to the same procedure. The Alabama corps would be dissolved and all study at the University made impossible.[59] The four boys remained with the corps. Several months later the same controversy arose in a slightly different form. Another new law had been enacted, lowering the age limit for enrollment to seventeen years. Again enrolling officers were threatening students, to Dr. Garland's "great annoyance and perplexity."[60] And again, Dr. Garland turned to the highest authority he acknowledged, the governor of his state. He reminded Governor Watts that since the state military institution in Louisiana had fallen into the hands of the enemy, there were only four such schools left in the Confederacy. The preservation of these four was definitely in the public interest:

> It seems to be as much to the interest of the Military affairs of the Gov't. as of the Civil that these institutions be allowed to receive all they can accomodate.[61]

Difficulties in getting needed supplies for his corps added to Dr. Garland's worries and increased his impatience with the high officials of the Confederacy who, in his opinion, so sadly underestimated the function of the University military school as a training ground for officers and fighting men for the army. "The great blunder in our Confederate Government," he declared, "has been the conceit of a short war."[62] He felt that a recognition that the war would be "long and protracted" would bring realization that the Alabama cadet corps was an integral part of the Confederacy's military organization. The quartermaster department of the military school would then be allowed to buy government supplies that could be spared from the army.

In this fight, too, Dr. Garland fiercely maintained his position in regard to states' rights. Once he urged Governor Watts to impress for the state a woolen factory near Tuscaloosa before it was taken over by the Confederate government.[63] When Confederate authorities, in the spring of 1864, took steps to take over the horses for which Dr. Garland had contracted, he wrote a sharp letter to General Polk:

> I hope, Sir, that you will furnish me with an order, to any officer on such service, to leave the horses of this Battery unmolested, and not drive me to the disagreeable necessity of protecting them by force.[64]

The letter got results, at least for a time. Impressing officers were forbidden to interfere with the cadet battery. In the last weeks of the war, however, the long-disputed horses were impressed under orders of General W. H. Jackson, of Forrest's army.[65]

From the first, Dr. Garland, more than most men, appears to have recognized the seriousness of the struggle in which North and South had engaged. He was convinced that every Union victory brought danger nearer to the gates of the University. The enemy, knowing well the aid and support given to the Confederacy by the University of Alabama, would certainly destroy that institution if they could. He was convinced also that the danger of slave insurrections was much greater than the general public recognized and that adequate safeguards against such uprisings were not being set up.

As early as October 31, 1862, he poured out his fears in a confidential letter to Governor Shorter. He spoke of the shortages which kept him from adequately equipping his cadets and then stated bluntly his expectation that the corps would see active service after the first of January "in suppressing insurrectionary movements among our slaves along the borders of our navigable rivers." He explained his reasons for fear:

Lincoln's proclamation means nothing unless he puts arms into the hands of our slaves . . . and that he is inhuman enough to do this, we cannot for a moment doubt. Now suppose he should get possession of all our navigable streams—then what? We have not the means of repelling such an invasion—I doubt if the Confederate Govt. can help us, and the damage which may result from the seizure of property—from the removal of slaves, and especially from arming and organizing them into bands of midnight assassins is beyond our calculation appalling.

He agreed that the quietness and "subordination" which the slave population had shown thus far was heartening. It was "the most striking display of Divine interposition" and "an occasion of the most devout gratitude to God," but he added that it was "the part of wise men to prepare for the worst":

and the worst certainly is the midnight conflagrations of our houses and the butchering of our wives and children. Lincoln knows that any general insurrectionary movement in the slave states would dissolve our armies. Our soldiers would fly to defend their firesides from a domestic foe, and our regiments on the border would melt away like snow before a summer's sun.

He looked for "gigantic efforts" on the part of the abolition forces to "penetrate by water into the heart of every state" to make contact with their potential allies, the slaves scattered on plantations along the rivers "with scarcely a white man to direct their quiet labors." He asked, "What shall protect them from the demoralization of a contact with Lincoln's minions?" And he made his own proposal:

I hereby submit the question, whether provision ought not *now* to be made for the removal of all the males between 15 and 60, into cantonments far in the interior, where they may be guarded by a comparatively few soldiers, and if necessary marched out of the reach of Lincoln's troops. . . .

The only safe alternative to such a plan would be the mustering, arming, and training of the white men in every township exposed. If neither plan were followed, all would be "wild confusion" should an invasion occur.

Dr. Garland finally outlined the role of his cadets in case of emergency:

Whilst the Cadets should not be needlessly exposed to destruction in an assault against superior numbers of the enemy, yet in the event of insurrectionary movement any where in the dense slave population of the middle counties, I shall not hesitate to fly as rapidly as possible to the defense of women and children.

Thus he justified his plea that arms for his corps be sent at once. "I am no sensationalist," he added, "but I want no preparation to make when the time for action comes."[66]

As the war moved on, however, the prospect of an enemy raid on Tuscaloosa seemed more probable than a slave insurrection. Here was an even more direct threat to the safety of an institution which Dr. Garland cherished. In May, 1863, he wrote to the governor,

If the enemy should ever reach this place, they would not leave at this University one brick standing upon another. At Oxford, Miss., they totally destroyed buildings, Library, and Apparatus and the private residences of the Officers. Yet that was not a Military Institution. If they did that in the *green* tree what will they not do in the *dry*?[67]

A false alarm, reaching Tuscaloosa in the same month that this letter was written, gave Dr. Garland occasion to be proud of the boys he was training and yet more apprehensive than ever about the ability of the community to resist raids from the enemy. The report came that fifteen hundred "abolitionists" were on the march toward Tuscaloosa from the direction of Elyton, county seat of Jefferson County. Dr. Garland had his corps provisioned for three days and on the march within six hours. "It was gratifying," he said, "to witness the ardor and enthusiasm with which they marched to the anticipated conflict."

He told the governor that no similar ardor and enthusiasm had been forthcoming from the townspeople. Although he had offered to receive fifty men into the ranks and arm them with guns and ammunition, less than a dozen had responded, and more than half of those were school boys under sixteen years old. He had tried to get horses so that his cadets could be mounted and move quickly to a strategic spot where they could either stand and defend the town of Tuscaloosa or reinforce the defenders of Selma according to the developing emergency. After he had searched the town, and had found only eight horses and four mules, the rest were being used by owners running away from the threatened city.[68]

This experience made him surer than ever that the Alabama corps of cadets, young and inexperienced as they were, constituted the only available force against raids if they occurred. His letters to Governor Shorter at this time, though full of apprehension and indignation, suggested proposals for meeting new raids strongly and effectively. "These raids are a disgrace to us—Any of them can be stopt before they penetrate the State 50 miles if the citizens will do their duty."[69] When he made a trip to Columbus, Mississippi, in May, 1863, he planned his itinerary so that he could "see prominent and active men in every neighborhood" through which he passed, and "endeavor to get them to organize their means of defence—and to hold themselves and their neighbors in readiness to act upon a moment's warning."[70]

The plan of defense which he urged upon these men was simple. He firmly believed that a few hundred cavalry could be prevented from penetrating very far into the interior if every man who had a gun would "backwhack," falling upon his neighbor, and those in one neighborhood back upon the next, until they could be met by the corps of cadets to form a nucleus for defense. Garland told the governor that another object of his scouting trip to Columbus was to set up a line of couriers between that city and Tuscaloosa. A raid on

Tuscaloosa and the University was almost certain to come from that direction.[71]

By autumn of 1863 the Federals had taken possession of northern Mississippi. General Bragg, retreating to Chattanooga, had abandoned the defense of the Tennessee Valley. Dr. Garland's fears mounted still higher. With a careful analysis of the danger and of the steps to be taken to meet this danger he again turned to Governor Watts. When all efforts to get official coöperation in setting up adequate defense measures had failed, Dr. Garland wrote him a long letter, dated January 22, 1864, to shield himself, he said, "from the possible reproach that may hereafter be cast upon me in the event that the University buildings are destroyed."[72]

According to Dr. Garland, Tuscaloosa was in a particularly vulnerable position. Should the enemy try to destroy the valuable factories, mills, and railroads centered in and near Selma, only three routes would be open to them—and two of these passed through Tuscaloosa. Tuscaloosa was, moreover, an important target in itself; and the University, by its services to the Confederacy, had certainly made itself the object of enmity from the northern forces. The country between the Tennessee Valley and Tuscaloosa afforded no protection against enemy incursions. It was full of "tories" and deserters ready to aid the enemy. As long as the Tennessee Valley was in Union hands, Tuscaloosa would be in danger.

In considering how the danger could be met, Dr. Garland continued, he had been forced to discount all possibility of effective resistance on the part of Tuscaloosa citizens. The majority of the voters of the county had originally been anti-secessionists; moreover, they had given abundant proof of their unwillingness to volunteer their services at a time when prospects of Confederate victory were much brighter. It was clear, Dr. Garland insisted, that Tuscaloosa's only hope for victory lay in the Alabama corps of cadets. They did not lack patriotic spirit, but the spirit alone could not repel an enemy attack. The campus was only an open plain, and an infantry unit of 260 boys would have little chance of defending it against 1,000 to 1,500 Federal soldiers.

Fortification of the University grounds seemed the only solution. Dr. Garland reasoned that since raiders were in a hurry, they seldom took the time and effort to lay seige to a place even feebly fortified. He had, he told Governor Watts, explained this to his predecessor, Governor Shorter, who had indeed ordered that fortifications be built around the campus. He had even commissioned an agent to impress 150 laborers in the community for a period of six weeks. Provisions had been bought, cabins built, and thousands of pickets felled and hewed.

Governor Watts himself was responsible for stoppage of the important undertaking. On December 28, 1863, he had received a petition signed by 101 Tuscaloosa citizens, urging that he revoke Governor Shorter's order. The petitioners argued that the tools and laborers being used on University fortification were badly needed for work on crops. They had insisted that the proposed fortifications would give little protection against bombardment, and they had declared themselves "thoroughly convinced that the proposed call is both unnecessary and unavailing."[73] The governor had listened to these petitioners and had ordered that hired laborers be substituted for impressed ones.

Dr. Garland reminded Governor Watts of this decision and reminded him also of the clear fact that hired laborers at any price could not be had. The order from the governor had been, in effect, an order to discontinue the work of fortifying the University. The governor must recognize his responsibility for this decision. With this letter off his conscience, Dr. Garland turned again to making his cadets into a force of which he and his state could be proud.

Major General S. G. French and two brigadier generals visited the campus in the spring of 1864, giving Dr. Garland a golden opportunity to show off his boys. The gallery which assembled to see the review was not altogether friendly. When the cadet section of artillery took position to fire the salute at Major General French's appearance, there was more than a little heckling. "Those babies can't handle the guns . . . they don't know how to load!" But taunts changed to cheers when the salute rang out rapidly and precisely. One of the generals with French remarked later that he had seen all the "crack corps" of Europe and the cadet corps at West Point drill, but had never seen anything to excel the wheel of the battalion in double ranks, six companies front, at double-quick, that closed the Alabama cadets' exhibition drill of that day.[74]

The corps had its first baptism by fire that same year. When the school term closed in July, the cadets started for a fifteen-day furlough with orders to reassemble at Selma. The governor, meanwhile, had received dispatches informing him that Rousseau's cavalry raid was heading toward Montgomery. He hurried to that city and issued a call for all cadets in Montgomery or those passing through that city to report for duty. Fifty-four responded. They were promptly made a temporary company, under command of Lt. George E. Redwood, C.S.A. With Lockhart's battalion and a company of conscripts from Camp Watts they met the enemy several miles east of Chehaw, July 18, 1864. The cadets formed the skirmish line in that battle, repulsing the enemy and giving chase as far as Auburn. Then the cadets returned to Montgomery and continued on their furlough. Two cadets were wounded in this fight.[75]

Another taste of the rigors of war came to the cadets when, their furlough ended, they assembled at Selma. They were ordered to Blue Mountain, near Anniston, to the station at the northern end of the Alabama and Tennessee Rivers Railroad, and from there to the east bank of the Coosa River, where the railroad crossed that stream. But by the time they had their camp ground cleared, they were ordered to move on to Pollard and then on to Montgomery to be reviewed by the governor. They got into camp eventually at Saluda Hill and spent a month there. Many cadets were elected company officers in various Alabama commands, but many others received another kind of war decoration—they were stricken with pernicious fever. With no hospital available and limited medical supplies, this outbreak was serious. It would have been worse had it not been for the efficiency of Dr. John B. Read, the University surgeon, and the corps officers. No cadets died.

From camp the remnant of the corps, under the command of State Captain Eugene A. Smith, was moved back to Montgomery again, via Pollard. The governor gave orders to the quartermaster general to supply them with everything they needed. Cadet Captain Samuel Will John, acting quartermaster of the corps, eagerly accepted that invitation. His requisition, which included everything down to replacements for medical supplies of quinine and morphine, was filled promptly.[76]

Raids and rumors of raids increased as the Federal troops came nearer. In the spring of 1865 the Alabama cadets were called out a number of times for guard duty. Several times in March they crossed the river to Northport and beyond to protect approaches to the bridge. News of "Wilson's Raid," designed to cut deep into the heart of Alabama, heightened the tension and the impatience of the cadets on the campus. The opportunity to defend their University was coming closer every day, and they were ready, in valor at least, for the crisis.

Yet, in spite of Dr. Garland's Cassandra prophecies and in spite of his efforts to build watchful protection and to foresee every eventuality, the attack when it came was a complete surprise and a complete disaster.

On the night of April 3, 1865, taps were sounded as usual at the University. The cadets went to bed with no foreboding of danger, but before the dawn of the next day, they had been aroused from sleep, had seen the city of Tuscaloosa surrendered to the enemy, and had found themselves in heartbreaking retreat from the University they had hoped to save. As they paused for breakfast on the Huntsville Road, they heard the explosion of the reserve ammunition on the campus and saw the smoke of burning buildings. Dr. Garland, watching with his cadets as the flames devoured his life work and his life hope, must have grimly remembered that he had foretold down to the last detail the disaster that now engulfed him.

CHAPTER XII

The Destruction of the University

MAJOR-GENERAL J. H. Wilson reached Elyton by March 30, 1865. Tuscaloosa, sixty miles away, was then within easy reach of his raiding armies. His order to Brigadier General E. M. McCook was terse and definite:

Detach one brigade of your division, with orders to proceed rapidly by the most direct route to Tuscaloosa, to destroy the bridge, factories, mills, university (military school), and whatever else may be of benefit to the rebel cause. . . .[1]

General McCook chose General John T. Croxton to carry out this mission:

. . . You will march with your brigade in compliance with the foregoing order, and report in person to General Wilson for further instructions.[2]

General Croxton's first attempt to fulfill this mission was thwarted. Moving quickly along "the most direct route," he reached the northeastern part of Tuscaloosa County on Friday, March 31. The next morning, however, he suddenly came in contact with the rear of General W. H. Jackson's command, which had just turned off the Tuscaloosa road into the Centreville road. Jackson reversed his column and the Battle of Tryon began. All day the two armies fought in the fields of a farm; then Croxton retreated toward Elyton. He had lost two officers and thirty men.[3]

To drive through to Tuscaloosa along the route first chosen would mean more battles and more losses. Jackson's troops, Croxton estimated, numbered about 2,600; he had in his command only 1,500 men. Jackson could count, moreover, on support from the home guards and the University cadets. "I determined, therefore," Croxton wrote in his report of the operation, "to effect by stratagem what I could not hope to accomplish directly."[4] He decided to enter Tuscaloosa from the north side of the river.

In a forced march over mountainous and rugged country, the Federal troops came, on April 1, to Johnson's ferry, on the line of Tuscaloosa and Walker counties. One flat boat was there available to carry the men, as well as the many Negroes who had joined them, across a river swollen by spring rains. The horses were forced to swim. All day Sunday, April 2, the slow crossing continued.[5] Not until Monday morning, April 3, was Croxton's army ready to begin the forty-mile trek along the "Watermelon" Road to Tuscaloosa.

As they moved forward, advance scouts picked up all men and boys who might spread the alarm. One important Confederate scout was captured twelve miles from the Tuscaloosa post.[6] At nine o'clock that evening they had reached the outskirts of Northport, where they dismounted. They avoided Confederate infantry pickets by moving through the fields with Negro guides. Then Croxton and 150 picked men of the Second Michigan cavalry moved down to the bridge.

Croxton intended to put his picked force in ambush near the bridge and wait for daybreak to make a quick, decisive raid on Tuscaloosa. His army, weary and exhausted after their long march, would be able to fight better in the morning. As the General moved toward the bridge, however, he saw that the handful of old men and boys who guarded it were beginning to remove the wooden flooring.[7] They had evidently learned that the Federals were approaching. Delay, even for the night, was impossible. Croxton must strike at once. He opened rifle fire on the home guards. From behind the bales of cotton on the covered bridge came answering fire, but it was feeble. Again Croxton's men fired, killing a retired Confederate captain and severely wounding a young boy. By ten o'clock, even the feeble resistance had ended. The Federals held the bridge and the road to Tuscaloosa was open.[8]

When Croxton's spies, who had preceded him into the city, reported that two six-pound cannons had been stored in a livery stable for use of the home guards and the cadets,[9] Croxton sent fifty men to seize these important defense weapons. Another detail crossed the bridge and set fire to the hat factory, which had manufactured gray wool hats for the Confederate Army. The following morning many Negroes were seen wearing hats that had been snatched from the fire.

Advance scouts preceded the main body of Croxton's troops into Tuscaloosa itself. As the evening of April 3 wore on, they became both bold and boisterous, roaming the streets quite openly. Some wore gray uniforms. Renegade Southerners, dressed in Yankee uniforms, joined them. Dr. Garland had been right in distrusting some of his Tuscaloosa neighbors. As many of the roisterers were very drunk, looting was widespread.

At the home of Dr. S. J. Leach on 4th Street, a wedding party attracted the attention of one group of maurauders. Emily Leach had just been married to Captain James Carpenter, and carriages of the wedding guests lined the street. With a whoop, the invaders overturned the carriages, frightened away the Negro coachmen, and dashed for the house, shooting as they ran. Mrs. Leach, who bravely stood on the front porch and tried to reason with the uninvited guests, narrowly escaped one bullet which pierced the brick wall beside her. The dignity of manner with which she and Dr. Leach received the invaders may have somewhat quieted the soldiers, who, even though they put the men in the wedding party under arrest, allowed the bridegroom to say goodnight to his bride before they sent him to Croxton's main camp for the night. Ladies in the party had quickly hidden watches and jewelry in their capacious bustles when the raid started, and there is no record that these valuables were disturbed. After household Negroes had hurried the family silver to safe hiding places, they watched "with disgust" as the soldiers ate up the wedding supper, the remains of which the servants themselves had hoped to enjoy. Mrs. Leach finished the episode in a grand manner. When the prepared food had disappeared under the greedy onslaught, she brought out homemade wine and other delicacies and served them herself to the men who had wrecked her reception.[11]

The roistering in the streets had reached a brisk pace before any one thought of notifying the young defenders of Tuscaloosa, who were asleep in the University dormitories. It was the supervisor of the Insane Hospital, Dr. Bryce, who carried the alarm, at midnight or shortly thereafter.[12] At about twelve-thirty Dr. Garland ran through the campus shouting, "Tell them to beat the 'long roll'; the yanks are in town!" From the guard rooms the Negro drum corps responded. Almost instantly they began "cording down" the drums, and sleepy-eyed cadets heard the "long roll" they had been waiting for with young eagerness. The time had come for them to save their University and their town.

In less than five minutes Company B, the color company, reported to Colonel Murfee. Company C drew up to the right; Company A, to the left of the standard-bearers. Colonel Murfee moved them to the corner of the campus nearest to Tuscaloosa. Then a platoon from Company C, placed under the command of State Captain Murfee, were deployed as skirmishers and moved toward the city. The main body of the corps and some of the professors followed.[13]

Down the muddy road at "double time" went the boys who had drilled and waited for just this moment. They were ready and willing; their plans were carefully drawn and sound. But they were beaten before they started. The squad of cadets detailed to get the artillery from its livery-stable repository came face to face with the Federals, who had reached that cache first. The cadets were put under immediate arrest. The main body of the corps, reinforced by a small group of home guards, waited in vain for their cannons on the brow of River Hill, chosen because it was an excellent vantage point for the use of these cannons.

Dr. Garland, who waited with them, had a grave countence. He learned that the cannons were already in enemy hands. He learned also, from some citizens who had been taken prisoners and then paroled, that the Federal troops far outnumbered the defenders of the city. He realized that to order his cadets to stand and fight would mean yet more young lives sacrificed in a battle they could not hope to win. Looking with pride and pity at his cadets, he ordered a retreat.[14]

The battle, which never was a battle, was over by one o'clock. Republican Mayor Obediah Berry and Father William S. McDonough, a Catholic priest, carried the white flag to the river bank[15] to signify the official surrender of Tuscaloosa.[16] In capturing the city, the Federals had suffered twenty-three casualties; sixty men had been taken prisoner. Also, three pieces of artillery had been seized. The only wounded man on the Confederate side was Colonel Murfee's brother. He was shot in the foot.[17]

Dr. Garland and his disappointed cadets did not wait for the end to come. Quickly they retreated along the road they had come, back to the University. There was time for some hasty destroying of stored ammunition to keep it from falling into enemy hands. But Dr. Garland, determined that his cadets should not be taken prisoners, ordered them to prepare for a forced march. As the boys got their overcoats and filled their haversacks, Negro cooks packed up the food which was to have been the breakfast for April 4.

The Federal troops were almost on their heels as the cadets started their journey along the Huntsville Road. From a bridge where the boys stopped to rest and eat, the sound of exploding ammunition on the campus came clearly through the morning air. The boys saw the smoke of the burning buildings of the University they would have given their lives to protect. Then they gathered their haversacks and marched on.[18]

Meanwhile, the men of Croxton's command had reached the campus and were fulfilling Dr. Garland's direst prophecies by wantonly destroying this institution which had given such valiant service to the Southern cause. Almost the whole plant went up in flames; some of the professors' homes nearby also caught fire. The explosion of the stores of powder which the cadets had been unable to destroy could be heard for miles around Tuscaloosa. The Federals had laid a train from the magazine to a distance of about forty feet before they applied the torch to it.

At the Rotunda, Professor André DeLoffre made a brave attempt to save the library, of which he was custodian. He appealed to the officer in charge of the raiding squad to spare one of the finest libraries in the whole South. The officer himself must have had some appreciation for books. He restrained his men while he sent to General Croxton a message asking whether it was imperative for this excellent library to be burned. The General replied curtly that his orders left him no discretion; the library must go. The officer then entered the library, selected for himself a rare copy of the Koran, and ordered the building burned. Explosive torpedoes thrown on the roof and through the open doors started the conflagration. It was a dry day and the flames spread rapidly.[19]

286   *THE DESTRUCTION OF THE UNIVERSITY*

According to unrecorded reports, two ladies of the University family were somewhat more successful than the language professor was in staying the hands of the destroyers. At the President's Mansion, Croxton's soldiers met their equal in Mrs. Garland, who, with only her servants, was left to defend her home. Dr. Garland was off marching with his cadets; the children were safe at Bryce Hospital. The soldiers piled the furniture in the center of the building and set fire to the beautiful mansion. Mrs. Garland and her Negro servants stood by. As fast as the flame caught, they stamped it out. Mrs. Garland kept repeating that she had every intention of remaining in her own home. The officer who witnessed this strange battle of the soldiers pitted against this determined woman must have been moved by genuine respect for her courage. He not only ordered his men to put out the fires and to replace the furniture but also assured the president's wife that she would be molested no further.[20]

The enemy met another feminine defender at the observatory. The outcome of that skirmish was a compromise, for although the apparatus was destroyed, the building was left standing.[21] Perhaps there is evidence that the ladies won more in the encounter than the soldiers knew, for one of the important pieces of apparatus, the telescope lens came to light many years later. It had been hidden under a pile of rubbish. Also discovered years later, by Dr. W. S. Wyman and Trustee Willis Clark, were University records which some unknown persons must have saved and tossed into the Observatory basement on the night before the fire.[22] In saving the shell of the building the ladies had saved at least a few of the papers important in the history of the University.

Only four buildings survived the destruction of that April day in 1865: The President's Mansion, the Observatory, the Gorgas Home, and the Round House. It is ironical that this Round House, built for cadets on guard duty and the only building erected for military purposes on the old campus, should have been left untouched by the invading forces bent on taking revenge for the military activities cradled in the University of Alabama.

General Croxton reported on April 4 that his mission was complete:

April 4, destroyed the foundry, two niterworks, the military university, a quantity of stores, and supplied command with all the rations we could carry. Spent the day resting men and animals. . . .[23]

But the same General Jackson, who had so inconveniently made him change his plans as the mission started, prevented his making the dignified withdrawal from Tuscaloosa that would have befitted a conqueror. On Tuesday, April 5, while his men were resting and eating their lunch, they heard a clatter of horses' hoofs down Greensboro Avenue. Spurring their horses to full gallop, the riders came on. They were waving their hats and yelling: "Hurrah for Jackson! Jackson is coming!"

Croxton had no wish to encounter Jackson again. He gave quick orders. "Boots and Saddles" was sounded. Croxton's army headed for the river, crossed it, and, to make doubly sure they would not be pursued by the redoubtable Jackson, burned the bridge behind them. They acted in such haste, in fact, that they left one company on the wrong bank and forced it to go down the river to Saunder's ferry before it could cross to safety.[24]

Out at the barricaded bridge on Hurricane Creek, Dr. Garland, on the day of disaster, had gathered his cadets around him for early morning prayers. Then he and his boys had moved toward Centreville, with Montgomery as the ultimate goal. Near Scottsville the corps learned that Wilson's raiders had destroyed the bridge across the Cahaba and had taken Selma. So they headed for Marion, instead, where news reached them that the Confederate cause was hopeless.

Dr. Garland could do nothing at this point but disband the corps whose base of operations had been destroyed and whose usefulness in a lost war was at an end. He furloughed the cadets until May 12, with orders to reassemble at such place as might be designated.[25] The boys made their way home as best they could. Some, however, tried to join the fast crumbling armies of a lost cause.

The order to reassemble was never issued. Before May 12, news had come to Alabama of Lee's, Johnston's, and Taylor's surrenders. The war was over, and "the ex-cadet doffed his gray and went to work as diligently as he had drilled and studied."[26] For one more year Dr. Garland remained the nominal head of a University which had perished in flames. Then he, too, moved on to other fields of activity. The University of Alabama, like the Southern cause, had gone down in defeat.

Three tablets on the University campus are memorials to the proud cadets of the 1860's. The first two commemorate "deserters" whose impatient patriotism worried their "Colonel" as he tried to hold his military school together. One of these calls to remembrance the Captain Charles P. Storrs Cadet Troop, made up of University cadets and young patriots from Montgomery, which fought battles at Johnsonville, Henryville, Mount Pleasant, Columbia, and at many other places, and laid down its arms at Gainesville, May 14, 1865.[27] The other one commemorates an escort company of cavalry which was formed by Captain Bascom T. Shockley, nineteen University students, and twenty-nine other Alabama youths and it served with Brigadier General Dan Adams through the last year of the war.[28]

The third tablet holds in memory all the students from the University who served their state in the war. The University of Alabama gave to the Confederacy 7 general officers, 25 colonels, 14 lieutenant-colonels, 21 majors, 125 captains, 273 staff and other commissioned officers, 66 non-commissioned officers, and 294 private soldiers, making a grand total of 825. "Recognizing obedience to the state . . . they loyally and uncomplainingly met the call of duty, in numberless instances sealing their devotion with their life blood." Eighty-nine of them were killed in action; 21 died of wounds; 58 died in service; and 4 died in federal military prisons.[29] In addition to those who lost their lives, many of the survivors of battle were maimed for life. To commemorate this heroic record a Memorial Stone with a bronze tablet was erected on the campus by the Alabama Division of the United Daughters of the Confederacy on May 13, 1914.

But the University gave something more to its state and to the region suffering the aftermath of a tragic war. It gave the ability and courage and perseverance which would, in a comparatively short space of time, rebuild and reconstruct the "institution of learning" which had played so important a part in the growing period of the state, and which would be an even more important force in the century ahead.

Part Two

REBUILDING THE UNIVERSITY

CHAPTER XIII

Reopening the University
1865-1871

LANDON C. GARLAND, President of the University of Alabama and Commandant of the Alabama cadets, was not easily defeated. Standing with his boys around him on the Huntsville Road that April day in 1865, he watched the smoke rise from the fires consuming his life work and hope. The disaster which he had foreseen but had been unable to avert was a reality. It was a moment even more bitter for him than for the boys who had so eagerly trained themselves for a battle lost before its start. Yet as he turned away from the tragic glow in the sky, as he guided his cadets to safety and dismissed them on furlough, Dr. Garland's mind was already busy with plans for the new University which should rise from the ashes.

With the executive committee of the board of trustees, he worked out the details of those plans during the summer months. The University would reopen on October 1. It would admit sixty or seventy students. There were no dormitories for these students, of course, but that could be arranged. The President's Mansion, gallantly saved from the flames by Mrs. Garland, would accommodate a number of boarders. Dr. Garland would move into a house formerly occupied by one of his professors to make room for the boys. Board and lodging for other students would be found without difficulty in private homes near the campus. A small faculty would have to serve the University in this emergency period. Dr. Garland himself could handle mathematics as well as his administrative duties as president. Three other veteran professors would provide for the other curriculum essentials: Professor Mallet for chemistry; Professor Wyman for Latin and Greek; and Professor Pratt for logic, rhetoric, and oratory. Anticipation of tuition fees coming in by October 1 would enable Dr. Garland to buy essential apparatus.[1]

When autumn came, however, it was apparent that Garland and the trustees had been too optimistic. Only one student, a son of ex-Governor Thomas H. Watts of Montgomery, presented himself on the date set. And only two of the four professors were at their posts. Professor Pratt had moved to New York, and Professor Mallet was now at the medical college of Louisiana. The executive committee bowed to the inevitable. They reversed their decision to open the University, since it was obvious they did not have a University to open. They told Professor Wyman they had no immediate need of his services. But they retained their president, instructing him to try to get help for the University from the legislature and to report to the full meeting of the trustees in December.[2]

When the board met on call of Governor Parsons, December 7, plans for rebuilding the University plant occupied the first place on the agenda. The University must have some buildings before it could hope to attract students. Someone would have to direct the arduous task of getting the buildings erected, and the task of assembling not only bricks and wood but also funds to finance the program. The trustees turned again to Dr. Garland. They made him president and general superintendent of the University for an interim period beginning January 1, 1866, and ending October 1, 1867. They voted him a salary of $3000 for this period, in addition to traveling expenses; and they gave him, rent free, the use of the house in which he was living. Dr. Garland accepted the position and went to work.

Before the trustees adjourned this meeting, their instructions to their new "Superintendent" had been worked out in detail. Dr. Garland was to obtain plans and estimates on the necessary buildings and submit them to the board. As soon as a plan was approved, he was to advertise for bids on the construction and, with the advice of the board, enter into the building contracts. With the advice of the executive committee, he might buy a steam engine, build a saw mill on University land, and organize a force of workmen to saw the lumber for the new buildings.[3] He might also organize workmen to make bricks if by so doing he could save money. While the building program was going forward, the trustees said, some attention should be given to the academic equipment needed. Dr. Garland should have philosophical and astronomical instruments repaired

ALVA WOODS
First President, 1831-1837

BASIL MANLY
Second President, 1837-1855

LANDON CABELL GARLAND
Third President, 1855-1865

WILLIAM RUSSELL SMITH
President, 1870-1871

NATHANIEL THOMAS LUPTON
President, 1871-1874

CARLOS GREENE SMITH
President, 1874-1878

JOSIAH GORGAS
President, 1878-1879

in so far as possible. He should put forth every effort to assemble a new library. When the possibilities of salvage and donation seemed exhausted, he might buy the instruments and the books which were absolutely necessary.[4]

The new superintendent was also to be, in effect, the treasurer of the University. Money might be drawn from the state treasury on his warrant, countersigned by the governor. Garland was required to furnish bond of $24,000, with two securities approved by the governor. He was empowered to issue to creditors of the University certificates of indebtedness when their accounts had been settled and the amounts due accurately ascertained.[5]

One other item of business appears in the December 7 minutes, and Dr. Garland's eyes must have gleamed as he heard it. A memorial should be presented to the United States Congress, the trustees voted, for indemnification for the losses sustained by the University when General Croxton's raiders burned its buildings. One can imagine the alacrity with which Dr. Garland accepted the request that he prepare this memorial, gather the supporting evidence, and see that it was properly presented in Washington.[6]

For a few months the plans made by Dr. Garland and the trustees moved forward smoothly. The General Assembly gave practical encouragement to the planners in February, 1866, when it voted a loan of $70,000 "for the purpose of rebuilding the University of Alabama and furnishing it with the means of imparting a thorough education." One-third of this loan might be drawn from the state treasury in 1867; one-third in 1868; one-third in 1869.[7] One week after the passage of this act, the board of trustees set up a permanent building committee to work with Dr. Garland. Colonel R. Jemison, Jr., was made chairman, and Judge P. King, W. S. Mudd, and J. H. Fitts were the other members. The power to countersign the warrants issued by the superintendent had formerly been left in the hands of the governor but was now given to the building committee chairman.[8] The program was progressing in a most satisfactory manner.

By spring, however, new financial worries had appeared, and even the weather was conspiring to slow down the reconstruction work. The legislature had voted a loan, but, as the governor reported to the trustees in February, the state of the Alabama treasury was such that interest due on the University fund could not be paid.[9] Ready money was essential if bricks for the new buildings were to be made. The trustees voted to borrow $7000 for the 1,000,000 bricks they needed. The building committee negotiated this loan with R. & J. McLester, merchants of Tuscaloosa. The McLesters agreed to advance $2000 to the committee and to furnish them with 500 bushels of corn at $1.65 a bushel and 3,400 pounds of meat at ten per cent above actual cost. They also undertook to pay the wages of the brickmakers, to an amount not to exceed $700 a month, until January, 1867. The members of the building committee were to give their draft on the comptroller of public accounts as soon as funds were in the treasury, and they were to pay eight per cent interest on all cash advanced and supplies purchased.[10]

Dr. Garland's problems were not so easily handled. In May he reported to the board that he was having difficulty carrying out their order that wood for the burning of brick should, if possible, be obtained from University lands.[11] Much of the timber on these lands had already been stolen, Dr. Garland said, and he was quite powerless to prevent further pillage. Even when a trespasser was caught, little was gained. He probably had no property subject to the operation of a judicial process. Take, for instance, the case of Peters, a squatter who was abusing University land. Although he had been told to leave, he was still there.[12] The trustees responded to Dr. Garland's tale of woe by ordering that Peters be notified that if he did not go away he would be prosecuted for damages and indicted for trespassing. They agreed that, in the future, indictments should be sought against people like Peters. And they promised each other that they would work individually to prevent depredations from occurring.[13]

May also brought other bad luck. Up to that month, as Garland wrote Governor Patton in April, the "business of brick making" was being carried on "with every prospect of confining the cost within the limit (seven dollars per thousand) imposed by the Trustees."[14] Then it began to rain. There were seventeen rainy days in May. Work had slowed down. Human nature as well as the weather was disappointing that spring and summer. While Dr. Garland was on a business trip north in July, the building committee discovered that a large quantity of corn and meat entrusted to the brickyard superintendent, J. W. Massey, had disappeared. Massey was promptly discharged and tried for embezzlement. It appeared at his trial, however, that his sins had been those of carelessness, waste, and inefficiency rather than dishonesty. The committee decided not to press for criminal prosecution. The culprit was discharged with a severe reprimand for gross neglect of duty.[15]

That neglect, however, probably added to the cost of the bricks made under his supervision. In November the trustees estimated that they had about half the bricks they needed and that the final cost would be more than eight dollars a thousand. This was at least a dollar more than the limit originally set, but it was still under what it would have cost to buy the bricks from the only brickmakers in Tuscaloosa. Moreover, time had been saved. The trustees were eager to start building.[16]

They took careful stock of their position before deciding to break ground and start actual building operations. The finance committee reported that the University owed $19,854. This could be cancelled out by the $20,000 which was due to come to the University from the state in January. There would then be some $50,000 available in the next two years from the legislative loan. There were some 500,000 bricks ready to be put into use. If the building committee moved promptly, the University might well be ready for a limited number of students in the fall of 1867.[17]

The building committee received its formal authorization to proceed the next day, November 21. They were to adopt plans, get bids, make contracts, and move as rapidly as they could with the reconstruction work. They were authorized to employ an architect to superintend the work at a salary not to exceed $4000.[18] But it was clear that the building program made necessary some cutting of corners. The purchase of chemical and philosophical apparatus and books for the library would have to be postponed. Perhaps the buying could be better done when a new faculty was available to advise and consult. The book publishers who had so generously offered to sell the University books at one-half retail price could probably be persuaded to extend the time of their offers.[19] Getting the buildings under way was the important thing now. The other essentials of a university could be added later.

Dr. Garland chose that moment to resign. Just why he did so

is not clear, since his contract with the trustees had nearly a year more to run. Perhaps he considered that his job was, at least temporarily, at an end, that the services of a trained architect would be more useful than his own services at this point. Perhaps he, with his perceptions sharpened by experience, saw the shadow of politics beginning to creep toward the University that he loved. He could have been aware at last that reopening that University was still a far-off event.

The trustees accepted the resignation with appropriate regret, recording their respect for Dr. Garland as a man of integrity and a teacher of great ability. They invited him to go on living rent free in his house. They told him they would be calling upon him for services when they needed him and that they confidently expected that when the University was opened again he would be back in a position commensurate with his high character and attainments. They appointed a committee to wait upon Dr. Garland with these resolutions and to invite him to continue attending board meetings.[20]

They made no attempt, however, to fill the vacant post of president. They turned the fiscal affairs of the University over to J. H. Fitts & Co., authorizing them to take charge of such funds as might be committed to their charge through warrants drawn by the governor on the comptroller of the state or as otherwise might come to the trustees on account of the University.[21]

By December, J. H. Fitts and Robert Jemison, Jr., of the building committee had hired an architect. He was Colonel James T. Murfee, former commandant of the military school, now an architect in Tuscaloosa. He was voted a salary of $4000 for the year beginning December 1, 1866, and he was made responsible for furnishing drawings, specifications, and estimates.[22] Three months later, in March, 1867, the contract for the actual building was given to G. M. Figh & Company of Montgomery. Under a bond of $20,000, this company undertook to put up the building, later to be known as Alva Woods Hall for $63,367. They agreed to complete the central part of it by January 1, 1868, and the wings by the following June.[23]

Excavation began at once and by April 12, 1867, the first masonry was laid. The walls of the central building were up by June and progress was being made on both wings.[24] Then the supply of bricks began to run short. The trustees and the builders had thought that enough bricks could be salvaged from the ruins and added to the stock of new bricks on hand to complete the new building. But the yield from the ruins was disappointing, many of the bricks being too damaged to use. And somehow it appeared that there were fewer new bricks than the estimates called for. The builders asked more time to complete their work, and the building committee granted them an extension. It was no fault of G. M. Figh & Company that the bricks had run short.[25] Neither was it their fault when further delays were caused by bad weather and by the breaking of a saw at the sawmill.

Extending the building time made it necessary to extend also the term of employment of Mr. Murfee, architect. He took a reduction in his pay for the second year, but agreed to serve to December 1, 1868, for $3000.[26]

In April, 1868, the building committee reported to the board that the total amount spent on the building, including the cost of brick-making, was $54,614.85.[27] This was $22,000 more than the funds in the hands of the fiscal agents. If the Figh Company was to buy furniture and stoves and do the painting, another $7000 would be needed. The board then adopted a resolution that the comptroller of the state might be drawn upon for his warrants on the state treasury in such sums as the president might specify for the interest due the University. J. H. Fitts & Company, as fiscal agents, would use these warrants in the settlement of University liabilities.[28]

The contractors finished their work in July.[29] The new building could house 180 students; its kitchens and dining room could feed 500. Only $30,000 of the state loan had been used to finance this first post-war building of the University of Alabama.[30]

While the builders put the finishing touches on the new University, the trustees turned their attention to the selection of the faculty which would give it life. They met in April, 1868, for the first time since the fall of 1866, and discussed reorganization plans.[31] In June the committee on organization appointed in April was ready with a system of rules which the board formally adopted. Then they looked back to the early University leaders and decided to invite Henry Tutwiler to serve as president. They also called back Professor Wyman and Dr. Garland. Wyman was to have the post of ancient languages unless Tutwiler refused to serve as president, in which case the presidency would go to Wyman. Dr. Garland was to teach philosophy. J. T. Murfee would go back to his old duties as commandant. John H. Forney would teach mathematics, and A. Q. Thornton, modern languages. The president would be paid $3000; the professors, $2000. Houses rent free would be the perquisite of all the faculty.[32]

That faculty never assembled. The trustees had reckoned without the politicians. And politicians, with or without carpetbag, were firmly entrenched in those troubled postwar days. On November 5, 1867, a state convention assembled at Montgomery had written a new constitution for Alabama. The government of the University of Alabama had, by this constitution, been taken from the hands of the trustees and given to the elected board of education which, when dealing with University affairs, was to be called the board of regents of the state University. Power to appoint the president and the faculty of the University was vested in the regents; the University president was an ex-officio member of the board, but he had no vote in its proceedings.[33] The door was wide open for the use of University positions as patronage plums, and the door remained open for eight years. Toward the end of this period, the Tuscaloosa *Times* bitterly criticized the system. When the University was governed by a board of trustees, chosen by joint vote of the two houses of the General Assembly, this paper stated, its affairs were "steadily administered upon the platform of a complete political neutrality," and the University "was never regarded as constituting a portion of the official spoils which were to be lost or won in a political campaign." Under the board of regents, however, the University became "a coveted portion of the official spoils" of each election with results that were deplorable:

. . . And when the election closes, one party or the other has achieved a political victory in electing a majority of its partisans as members of the Board, and reaps the reward of victory, in the power and the right, to govern the affairs of the University and to distribute its chairs and offices among its friends . . . . the stability of the tenure of office in the Institution is entirely destroyed.—The Professors hold their chairs at the will of the Board of Regents, and are liable to be displaced, with or without cause, or at the mere caprice of the Board. Every change in the policy or the political complexion of the Board, exposes them to the danger of removal.[34]

The first board of regents, which came into power in the summer of 1868, showed quickly the worst features inherent in the new plan. It was a Radical board, composed, according to the Montgomery *Mail*, of "four scalawags and four carpet baggers."[35] It held its first meeting at Montgomery on August 5, and promptly undid all the decisions the University trustees had made two months earlier by declaring all University offices vacant. The resolution was not passed without protest. Three members of the board of regents, all Southern-born, voted against it and entered a solemn resolution of their opposition to it, saying that it was illegal, unjust, and disastrous to the interests of higher education.[36] They were a minority, however, and the board overrode their protests and picked the kind of faculty they thought the University should have.

The Reverend R. D. Harper and the Reverend A. S. Lakin, both Northerners, were the principal nominees for the presidency. Harper had been connected with the Freedmen's Bureau and had organized Negro schools in northern Alabama. Lakin had been active in recruiting Alabama Negroes into Loyal leagues and influencing them to vote the Radical ticket. After these names had been placed in nomination, one of the native Alabamians on the board executed a maneuver which almost gave the University an able and loyal president: he nominated Professor Wyman. His move was successful beyond his hopes. On the first vote, Professor Wyman got the votes of the three dissenters but neither of his opponents had a majority. By the third ballot two more votes had swung to Wyman: his count was five to Harper's three. Reluctantly the board had to concede his election.[37]

Turning to the other appointments, the regents voted to retain Gen. John H. Forney as professor of modern languages and to give the chair of rhetoric and oratory to H. S. Whitfield. Wyman, Forney, and Whitfield would be generally approved by the people. They were sound men. But, having made that much of a concession to the popular wish to have competent educators at the University, the board decided that it really ought to balance the slate with some good Radicals. Three Ohio men got those jobs. David Humphries, chosen professor of ancient languages, formerly editor of a Radical paper in Decatur,[38] had been having a hard time getting himself placed in a political job. He had tried, at the opening session of the legislature at Montgomery, to get himself elected as clerk, enrolling clerk, engrossing clerk, and doorkeeper. He had been successively defeated for all these jobs, the last time by a Negro.[39] T. M. Goodfellow, appointed commandant, said cheerfully that he knew nothing about military science, but he "guessed" he could learn.[40] J. M. Geary, elected professor of mathematics, completed the list.

By the next day the board had half its job to do over. Wyman and Whitfield had both refused to serve, and there seemed great probability that Forney would also decline. The board gave up trying to please the Conservatives and educators. It replaced the three who would not serve by appointing the Reverend A. S. Lakin of Ohio, president, and Jasper Callans of DeKalb County and Joseph Kimball of Ohio to the professorial chairs Whitfield and Forney did not want.[41]

Dr. Wyman had, however, just begun to fight. He thought that the action of the board of regents in declaring the University offices vacant was illegal. In September when President Lakin, accompanied by the state superintendent of education, arrived at the University he was met by a stubborn professor who held on to the keys of the University and would not let them go. The *Independent Monitor* was only too glad to publish Wyman's statement that he would not deliver the keys to Lakin "or to any other man who recognized him as the rightful President" and his defiant ultimatum: "I shall retain them until I am required by due process of law to give them up."[42] The *Monitor* had been fighting its own battle against Lakin since his appointment.

Ryland Randolph, editor of the *Monitor,* had already become a standard-bearer in the bitter fight against "scalawags and carpetbaggers." He was one of the first Alabama members of the Ku Klux Klan and in 1868 was elected leader of the Tuscaloosa Klan.[43] In his dual capacity of editor and cyclops, he had ideal opportunity to harass Radical members of the University faculty, and he made good use of that opportunity, bringing to the task all his considerable gifts for searing invective.

When the board of regents announced their University appointments, Randolph had issued a flat warning. "If these scoundrels expect to live quietly here, and draw their salaries, extorted from the sweating brows of the toiling tax-payer of Alabama," he said, "we tell them, they are mistaken. This community will be too disagreeable for them, and the sooner they resign the better."[44]

Lakin and N. B. Cloud, state superintendent of education, arriving in Tuscaloosa a few weeks later, had ample reason to believe that Randolph was not joking. The *Monitor* celebrated the coming of the University's new president with a cartoon and a threat. The cartoon, a crude woodcut, showed two grotesque figures hanging to a tree. One of them carried a carpetbag labelled "Ohio." The text under the cartoon left no doubt as to its intent:

Southern society—the carpetbagger and scallawag—if found in Dixie's land after the break of day on the 4th of March next. . . . The contract for hanging will be given to the negro who, having mounted the carpetbagger and the scalawag on the mule that he *didn't draw* at the elections, will tie them to a limb and, leading the said mule from under them, over the *forty acres* of ground that he also didn't get, will leave the vagabonds in mid-air.

With this violence brewing around them, Lakin and Cloud decided, quite reasonably, to leave town. Wrote the *Monitor's* fiery editor:

Scallawag Cloud of Montgomery and Carpetbagger Lakin of Nowhere arrived here Thursday. . . . On Friday afternoon Lakin incontinently departed, by way of the Huntsville Road. On Saturday morning Cloud also "made tracks" in the direction of Montgomery. . . . Every fellow they met on the streets appeared, to their alarmed fancies and guilty consciences, to be Ku Kluxes in disguise.[45]

Lakin's resignation was before the regents when they next met.[46] Randolph had won the first round of his battle. In so doing, he had, of course, provided excellent copy for the Northern press, which gave wide circulation to the incendiary cartoon and editorial to prove how the spirit of lawlessness prevailed in the South. Even some Southern Democratic organizations formally denounced Randolph; he was, they said, a rabid extremist, doing more harm than good.[47]

Randolph was impervious to such admonitions. He watched while the regents tried to rebuild the faculty, and then he declared that the new appointments were "just as bad, if not worse than the first choice." His particular target was the Reverend R. D. Harper, the president-elect, who, he declared, would be no more welcome in Tuscaloosa than Lakin had been:

We expect to hear of his namesake, of *Harper's Weekly* notoriety, being shocked once more because of the terrors of Ku-Klux outrages at the Alabama University. Disreputable Harper is destined to soon turn gray through "sudden fears", if he ventures to occupy the respectable mansion of the President of the University. . . . Lakin's chances of security would have been infinitely better.[48]

Other faculty appointees came in, however, for their share of terrorization. Those selected in December, 1868, were a completely new group. The conservatives appointed four months earlier had promptly refused to serve, and the welcome accorded President Lakin had apparently frightened off the Radicals—Goodfellow, Humphries, as well as Geary.[49] President Harper was given just one Northern comrade on the new faculty; he was J. De F. Richards of Vermont, then representing Wilcox County in the Alabama senate.[50] The five other teachers were all Alabama-born.[51] Three of them, however, were Radicals. So the fight Randolph was waging had plenty of targets.

When the steamboat "Jennie Rogers" arrived in Tuscaloosa in February, carrying furniture belonging to Professor Loomis and Vernon H. Vaughan, the letters K.K.K. appeared mysteriously on each article before the boat landed. When Professor Callans tried to sound out opinion toward himself in the town, Randolph ridiculed him in the columns of the *Monitor:*

Callans has been consulting several of our citizens as to his safety here—having heard much about that branch of the Ku-Klux-Klan, stationed in Sipsey swamp. . . . Our opinion is, if these University harpies . . . "except the siterwation" (to use the classical language of Callans) of entire social ostracism . . . and do not cross the paths of the Sipsey swampers . . . they may . . . desecrate the Professors' mansions without immediate . . . Hinderance.[52]

The Reverend Mr. Harper went down before Randolph's barrage as the Reverend Mr. Lakin had before him. In March the *Monitor* gleefully announced that Harper had "wisely resigned his office."[53] Some hardy souls must have braved Randolph's roar, however, for, on April 5, 1869, the University did actually open its doors with Professor J. De Forest Richards as acting president and twenty students ready to be taught.[54]

The *Independent Monitor* commented on July 5, 1870, with regard to Richards' administration:

This impudent, hoary-headed, Yankee, arch-scoundrel has, along with his mate and cubs, been occupying one of the University houses ever since he was removed from the position of President *pro tem,* and, by the aid of horses belonging to the University, is rearing a large crop of grass and a small one of corn on the broad field pertaining to the President's mansion to which he has no more right than has the meanest negro, or any other being superior to himself, in town.

According to the *Monitor*, N. R. Chambliss served as president during the remainder of that year, 1868-1869. This periodical states that Chambliss "commanded a Spartan band of three scallawag cadets at the close of last session."

By this time, more newspapers than Randolph's *Monitor* had begun to heckle the University regents. The Democratic press cried out that politics had brought the University to utter ruin. The Montgomery *Advertiser* advised the professors who were still on the job to show their self-respect by resigning. The paper contended that the University should be turned into a school for freedmen if it could not be reorganized under the direction of the white sons of Alabama:

It is worse . . . than a mistake, looking to the true educational interests of Alabama, to place, for political reasons of the lowest sort—to provide mere offices for a number of impecunious persons, this Institution, under the control of those who have not the confidence of the people in the important matter of education.

Even if the Faculty, or Board of Professors, were competent in the sense of learning and science, they should not wish, after the experience of the past year, to remain connected with the University. But when personal, political, and educational reasons all conspire to demand their resignation and when they must be conscious of the real grounds, without a moment's hesitation. We are clearly of the opinion that the University should be at once converted into a School for Freedmen, or else that it should be organzied under the auspices of the native white population of the States.[55]

The *Monitor* took up the cry that University affairs must be divorced from politics. In July, 1869, it ventured to offer positive advice to the regents whose actions it had hitherto so bitterly—and successfully—opposed. The writer declared that the board should "ignore party politics entirely" when it met in August to elect a new president. They should choose a man acceptable to the people of Alabama—a man such as "their own fellow-citizen—Admiral Raphael Semmes." That would be a non-political appointment, the *Monitor* insisted. The Admiral had "withdrawn himself entirely from politics" since the war.[56]

Before the regents had had time to consider the *Monitor's* nomination, it was rejected firmly by the Republican press. If Mr. Harper should be succeeded "by any of the men whose names are prominently mentioned as likely to be his successor," warned the Radical *Weekly State Journal* of Montgomery, "it will be better for the University to be locked up and its key thrown into the Warrior River. We want no new school of secession politics under heroes of the lost cause, inaugurated in Alabama under the guise of a school of letters."[57]

The board of regents, meeting in August, took reasonably conservative action. They again chose a Northerner for president, inviting Cyrus Northrop, then a professor at Yale, to accept that position. But they elected Major N. R. Chambliss of Selma as professor of mathematics, and they retained all the members of the faculty which had had charge of the University during the preceding year.[58] The Democratic press wailed, of course, at their failure to make a Southerner president. "They can certainly expect to do no better in the future than they have done in the past," said the *Monitor* in its most lugubrious manner.[59] Even Mr. Northrup's refusal of the presidency did not cheer up the *Monitor's* editor. His warning to the regents that they had one more chance to re-establish the University in the affections and confidence of the people has a pessimistic ring:

There are too many first class institutions in the other Southern States, and in many of the Northern States, free from the offensive and mischievous ideas of Radical party teachings, and which are easily and cheaply approached by Railroad communications, to make it possible, or even probable, for Southern parents to prefer a Radical school to a more generous and enlightened one.[60]

A second decision made by the regents at the August, 1869, meeting aroused even more controversy than had their choice of another Northern president. They voted unanimously to move the University away from Tuscaloosa "at the earliest moment practicable."

Whereas the best interests of the State University and its future success demand its removal from its present site in Tuskaloosa and located elsewhere;

Therefore, be it resolved by the Board of Regents, that it is their purpose to remove said University at the earliest moment practicable;

REBUILDING THE UNIVERSITY

Resolved 2nd, That it is the wish of the Board to carry out the will of the people of Alabama in the location of the University, and to that end solicit proposals to state explicitly the amount of aid that will be guaranteed whether in money, lands or other property, in consideration of the permanent location of the University—in such City or towns.[61]

A committee of three was appointed to receive proposals and to make recommendations to the board in November.

The *Weekly State Journal* praised this decision. It would serve the people of Tuscaloosa right to have the University, which brought them business valued at a hundred thousand dollars a year, taken away from them:

The people of Tuscaloosa, in olden times, were glad to have in town an institution which caused the expenditure of money in their midst to an amount that made it estimated as worth at least a hundred thousand dollars a year to the town. They have abundantly shown that they do not want it there any longer.[62]

The "people of Tuscaloosa" meanwhile had already discounted the news. There had been rumors that the regents would take this action. The *Observer* had shown its indifference by declaring that the University had failed "for reasons entirely unconnected with men and things in Tuscaloosa."

There is not a spot on the green earth, where it could have been a success, under its present administration.[63]

The *Monitor's* editor, shrewdly guessing that one reason for the proposed move might be to get away from his vitriolic pen, dashed any such hopes that the regents might be entertaining:

We understand that the Board of Regents are discussing the propriety of removing the University from Tuskaloosa. They propose to locate it at Selma or Montgomery, providing one of those cities will agree to put up a suitable building. We also hear that it is the home of the editor of this paper . . . . he intends to follow up the University. . . . He is determined to establish the *Monitor* wherever the University may be located.[64]

Whether Randolph's warning that moving the University would not rid it of his persecution had anything to do with the dropping of the proposal or not is a matter for conjecture; there is no record of the report of the site committee, and obviously, the University remained where it was.

Randolph's campaign of vituperation did, however, backfire once during this period. He drove Professor V. H. Vaughan a little too far and almost paid for his fun with his life. An innocent bystander, William Byrd, got the bullet intended for Randolph, and the editor himself escaped with a scratch on his back and a wound in his left leg.

Professor Vaughan did not attempt to tackle Randolph alone. When he could no longer stand being called a "scallawag," "drunkard," and "upstart ignoramus" by Randolph, he turned for help to a twenty-five-year-old student, William Smith. Smith was the son of G. A. Smith of the board of regents. He had served several years in the Union Army and he was a member of the Radical party. He hated Randolph on principle, though he did not know him personally. And he was doubly willing to aid Professor Vaughan because that professor had intervened to keep him from expulsion when he was suspected of stealing from the commissary department.

The conspirators worked out their plans in careful detail, and on April 1, 1870, they were ready to put those plans into operation. In order to check their arrangements they had one final talk at Vaughan's home. With two large dueling pistols and a double-barreled shotgun hidden away at the bottom of a small wagon, Vaughan and a Negro driver rode toward town. He left the carriage on Main Street, but, as he paced up and down, he never moved more than forty or fifty steps from that base of operations. On a corner about 200 yards away, Randolph, while talking with friends, noticed his old enemy and was, perhaps, entertained to see that Vaughan's hands were firmly clasped on two loaded pistols in his pockets. While Randolph watched Vaughan and speculated on whether the professor would actually dare to bring the pistols into action, Smith assumed the role he had agreed to play. With one hand on the cocked repeating pistol in his pocket, the student jostled Randolph suddenly and roughly.

Randolph's reaction was quick, but not unexpected; he slapped the boy briskly. Smith, quickly drawing his pistol from his pocket, fired, but the shot went wild. The fight was out in the open then, and one of Smith's shots killed William Byrd. Randolph, who now had his pistol out, shot at his fleeing assailant; however, the bullet glanced and inflicted only a slight wound. As his gun was now empty, he threw it at Smith, who recognized the gesture as a signal that he had regained his advantage. He turned and shot Randolph in the left leg. But Randolph, before collapsing to the sidewalk, managed to draw his knife and inflict enough damage to cause his assailant to run away.

Vaughan had stayed discreetly on the sidelines during the fight. But when the sheriff's posse discovered Smith hiding in Vaughan's home, his part in the conspiracy became known. He went to jail along with Smith. The professor was charged with instigating the assault which led to the murder of Byrd. Fears of Randolph's terrible Ku Klux Klan haunted the prisoners as they waited for their trial. The sheriff was persuaded to provide them with a guard of federal soldiers.

When the case came up for preliminary hearing on April 20, the court let Vaughan go. That decision was not wholly welcome to the badly frightened professor. The K.K.K. was still more dangerous than the law. Vaughan went straight from the jail to the headquarters of Captain Mills, commander of the federal soldiers stationed in Tuscaloosa, and begged him to detail a squad of men to protect him. Captain Mills refused his request, and Vaughan spent an uneasy night listening for Randolph's avengers. The next day he left town on horseback, with several cadets giving him protection as he fled along the Huntsville Road.

Smith was left in jail, without bond, to wait indictment for Byrd's murder. A guard of federal soldiers stood outside his cell. On the morning of April 27 the prisoner disappeared. The sheriff called up a posse to chase him. The trail was clear enough at first. Smith was heading for Shelby County and another student, named Osborne, was with him. Then the pursuers lost the scent completely. Smith had made good his escape. Governor W. H. Smith telegraphed Sheriff Pegues, urging that the search be continued; a reward of $400, the highest amount authorized by law, would be paid for Smith's capture. Captain Mills locked up the soldiers of the guard suspected of complicity in Smith's escape. But Smith himself had vanished into thin air.

This was Ku Klux in reverse. One wagster said as much in a wire to Alabama's Senator Willard Warner:

William A. Smith (Loyal) who killed Byrd (Rebel) in attempting to assassinate Randolph (Rebel), was released from our jail last night by parties unknown to the Federal soldiers who were guarding his door. He has "gone where the woodbine twineth." The lock was forced from the outside by invisible "Ku Klux." Another "Ku Klux outrage"! Inform the Government and Senator Spencer. Send along your "Melish."

Senator Warner spoke to President Grant about this. According to reports filtering back to Tuscaloosa, the president advised him to refuse to pay charges on the wire and to ignore the whole thing.[65] The episode was closed. Randolph was still at large, however, to continue his crusade against the board of regents.

That board was getting more and more thoroughly bogged down trying to run the University. Only a handful of students were going to classes, and the problem of finding a president who would stay was as far from solution as it had been when the regents began work two years earlier. In 1870 Professor N. T. Lupton was elected president, but he promptly resigned when the regents failed to live up to their promise to give him a faculty free of political influence.[66] When the school term closed that September, there were six students in the University and five professors.[67] One more president, William R. Smith, served a part of the year 1870-71. He resigned when the new enrollments showed only ten students, four of them sons of faculty members. The board of regents were forced to admit that only a complete reorganization could save the University from ruin.

At this crucial point the alumni came to the rescue. In the summer of 1870 graduates living in and near Tuscaloosa had met to talk over the deplorable state of affairs on campus. They were, they said, "deeply pained at the languishing and prostrate condition of their *Alma Mater*," and, therefore, felt a "common impulse" to offer their help "in raising and elevating it to that proud position it was wont to occupy in days of yore." The *Independent Monitor* published the text of the alumni offer on June 28:

The aid and influence of the Alumni are freely tendered to any laudable effort to reorganize the University upon such a basis as will command the respect and confidence of the citizens of Alabama. Those participating in that meeting can be prompted by no sinister motives—they can only have in view the prosperity of the institution. The purity of their intentions no one can call in question. Deeply pained at the languishing and

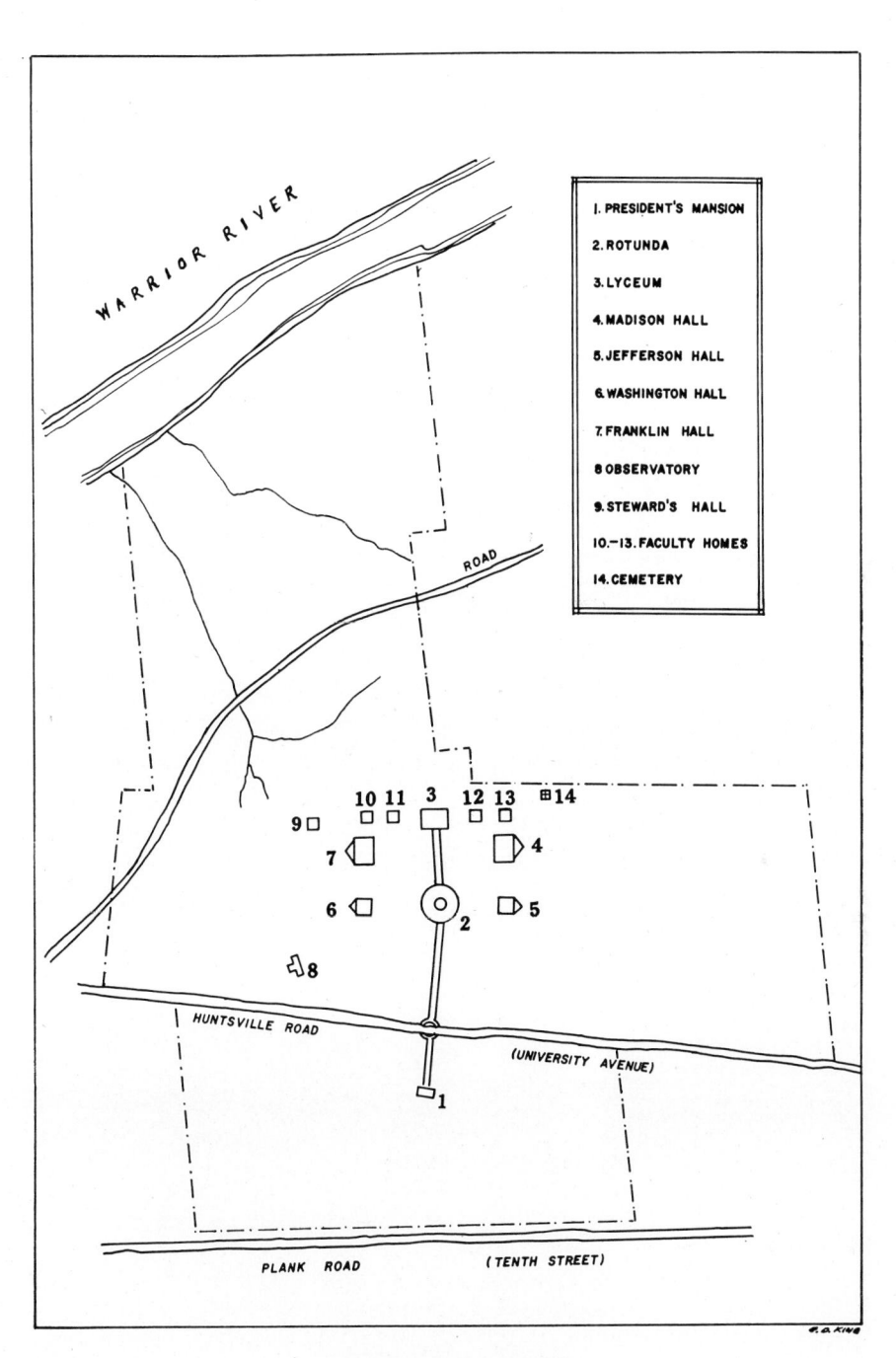

THE CAMPUS IN 1852

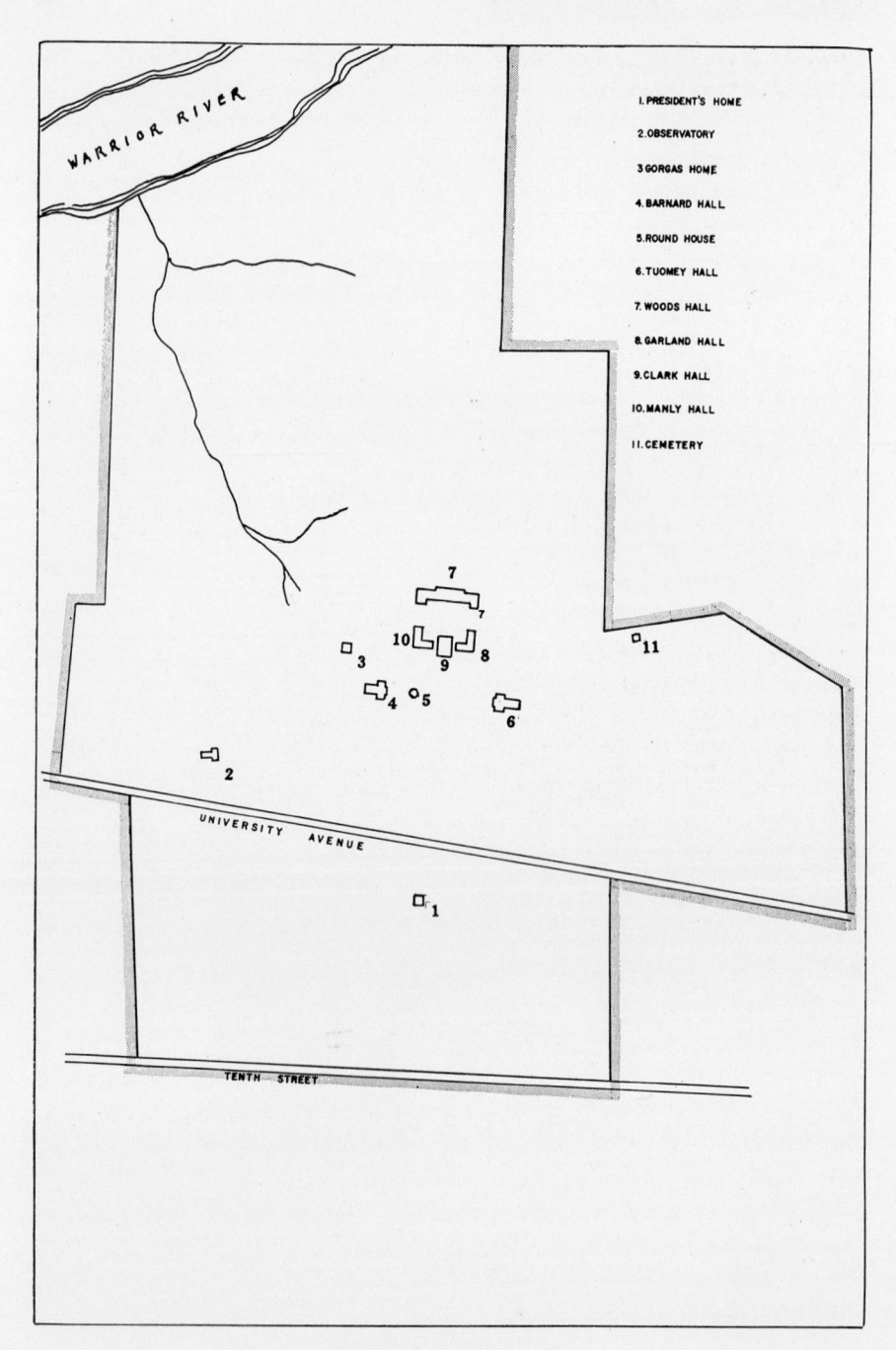

THE CAMPUS IN 1888

prostrate condition of their *Alma Mater* to which they are bound by the tenderest ties of affection, a common impulse has seized its sons to make an effort to assist in raising and elevating it to that proud position it was wont to occupy in days of yore.[68]

The regents did not at once grasp the helping hand thus extended. But when Presidents Lupton and Smith had gone the way of all the other presidents-elect and enrollment had dropped almost to the vanishing point, they turned at last to the men who knew and loved the University best—its alumni. In the spring of 1871 the board sent out a formal call, inviting the alumni of the University to meet with the regents on Commencement Day:

We enter upon the duty assigned to us [that of reorganizing the University] the more willingly, because we believe that your cooperation will be accorded any effort which has for its object the rebuilding of our University. The Board knew well your powerful influence, and wisely judged that this honest appeal could not fail to awaken in you a lively interest in the affairs of the University.

Your efforts, united, as we hope they will be, with those of the Board, cannot fail of success; and we know we do not ask too much, when we demand your aid as a debt of gratitude which you owe to an institution which has lavished its treasures upon you in its days of prosperity. . . . We invite you, therefore, to meet us at Tuskaloosa, on the commencement day in June next, and let us place the University high up among the institutions of learning in our land, so that, like the sun at meridian heights, she may cast her rays backward, reflecting honor on you, and forward, giving cheering light to the coming sons of Alabama.[69]

This handsome olive branch was almost universally admired. Even the *Daily State Journal* was ready to admit that the University was in dire need of reorganization. It was ready to go even further in frank admission that "so far, in the ranks of the Republican party in Alabama, men of the proper grade as men, scholars of the proper tone and finish as scholars, to fitly and successfully fill the different chairs of the University, have not been developed."[70]

In this pleasant atmosphere of willingness to forget personal and political difference for the good of the University, the reorganization took place. The June meeting of alumni and regents fulfilled the hopes of its planners. It was a victory for the conservative elements, but it was also a piece of good educational planning, with positions assigned on the basis of proved ability, not political affiliation.

Commodore Matthew F. Maury, elected president, had been suggested for that post by many conservatives. Professors Meek, William J. Vaughn, and Wyman, returning to the University they had served before the war, were well loved and highly respected as men and scholars. Professor Peck's mathematical ability seemed to justify his retention as the only survivor of the old Radical faculty.

The complete list of the appointments made at the reorganization meetings included the following: Matthew F. Maury, President; Reverend Telfair Hodgson, Professor of Moral Philosophy and Metaphysics; W. A. Parker, Professor of Greek; W. S. Wyman, Professor of Latin; D. S. Peck, Professor of Pure Mathematics; B. F. Meek, Professor of English Literature and History; J. G. Griswold, Professor of Modern Languages; W. J. Vaughn, Professor of Applied Mathematics and Astronomy and Civil Engineering; N. T. Lupton, Professor of Chemistry; E. A. Smith, Professor of Mineralogy and Geology; G. P. Harrison, Commandant of Cadets and Professor of Military Engineering; and Dr. A. S. Garnett, Surgeon. The salary of the president was to be $5000; each professor was to have $2500.

Before adjourning, the reorganization meeting dealt with one other item of business. Peyton Finley, Negro board member, presented a resolution requesting the superintendent of public instruction to seek from the United States Congress grants-in-aid for public education and, especially, for the establishment of a University for the education "of the colored race of this State." Finley's resolution carried a flat statement that his fellow Negroes had "no desire or intention . . . to interfere with the action of the State University." It may have helped to set an atmosphere of confidence by calming some fears of Radical intentions.

Whereas: The public good demands the establishment in this State, of a University for the education of the colored race of this State, etc.

Whereas; The Present financial condition of the State University is such as to prevent much aid to the University for colored people for some time to come, and

Whereas, The colored race have no desire or intention, nor would they under any circumstances, attempt to interfere with the action of the State University by any claim or pretext of right thereto, Be it Therefore
Resolved, That the Superintendent of Public Instruction be, and is hereby authorized to make application at Washington, to urge upon the

Congress of the United States, at its next session, in behalf of this Board and the people of Alabama, for a grant of public lands in aid of such a University, and an additional grant in aid of the public schools of this State.[71]

The Regents accepted Finley's resolution.

At last the board of regents had managed to take an action pleasing to the Democratic press of the state. Most of the conservative newspapers praised the newly selected faculty and expressed gratification that the regents, with their Radical majority, had pushed politics aside and had chosen scholars sure to command the respect of the people of Alabama. The one harsh note in the universal song of praise was sounded by the *Southern Argus,* whose editor was less impressed with the dazzling array of ability brought together by the regents than he was by the size of the faculty—for a college which had been able to attract only a handful of students—and by the handsome salaries the regents had set. "We are by no means satisfied," he remarked, "that the re-organization has not been effected upon a scale not warranted by either the endowment or the prospects of the University."[72]

Commodore Maury had other misgivings about the University whose presidency he had agreed to accept. By September he notified the regents that he wished to resign. He reminded them that his acceptance of the office had been contingent upon the provision of "means necessary for properly setting up the University, and furnishing it with needful apparatus and appliances." That condition had not been met. The "existence of the pecuniary embarrassments by which the University [was] . . . surrounded" also caused him great concern. The Commodore was, however, a considerate man. He told the board that he desired "to throw no hindrance in the way of the preparations that are going on at Tuskaloosa." Therefore, he had moved to provide his own successor; he had called a faculty meeting in July and set in motion plans for reorganization. Wyman, Vaughn, Meek, Garnett, Griswold, Lupton, and Smith had been present at this meeting, and from these men Wyman, Lupton, and Peck had been appointed an executive committee to perfect organization plans. When he had made up his mind to resign, Maury turned again to his faculty leaders and asked them to hold a meeting to elect a chairman "who by regulation is authorized to serve in place of the President" pending confirmation by the regents. "He will have been chosen ere this reaches you," President Maury concluded. "I therefore can be of no further service and beg to retire. . . ."[73]

Wyman, Peck, Meek, Vaughn, and Lupton attended the faculty meeting Maury had called. They chose Professor Lupton as chairman. Two weeks later the full faculty confirmed their choice.[74] The University opened on October 4, 1871, with Professor Lupton in the president's chair.

News that the University, which had been operating with great difficulty for three years and more, was now in a position to step forward with sure and confident step was welcome in the homes of Alabama. The sons of the state had been going far beyond the limits of Alabama in search of education as the clouds deepened around their own University. Parents who had reluctantly sent their boys to the colleges of Virginia or North and South Carolina rejoiced that they could now keep them closer home. Students caught the new spirit of adventure in the rebuilding of their own University; they wanted to have a part in its restoration. In October, 1871, they flocked back to the old campus. By November the enrollment had reached a postwar high of seventy-five students, and it was confidently expected that enrollment would increase steadily in the following terms.[75]

Thomas C. McCorvey was one of the students who helped to reopen the University that autumn. Twenty years later, he still remembered the unique flavor of campus life as "vigorous young blood" was being "infused" in the veins of an institution which had been dead but was now alive again. In the yearbook of 1893, he set down his memories:

When the University threw open its doors in 1871, it found a clever body of students ready made to hand—students who had already seen something of college life under a variety of conditions. There was material for all the college classes; for several young men who elsewhere had been advanced to within one year of graduation were eager for a diploma from Alabama's University. I can now look back and see how excellent a thing for this institution was this bringing together of students from a number of other colleges. We were all "taken out of ruts." The traditions of no one college were here set up in student life; but our intellectual habits as well as our college slang and our college customs was a

REBUILDING THE UNIVERSITY

composite of the varying phases of student life at a score of other institutions. . . .

As with students, so with Faculty. In the reorganization of that body a variety of vigorous young blood had been infused into the college life. Wyman and Vaughn and Meek, then young in years, but old in experience, remained from the former Faculty to pass on to the new organization the traditions of a glorious past. Lupton and Parker and Smith, trained in the great universities of the Old World, introduced new habits of thought and methods of work; while in Garnett and Hodgson and Griswold and Peck, we had men of affairs as well as scholars—men who knew the great world outside the college walls.

It would be hard to estimate the stimulating effects of the conditions mentioned upon the ambitious student.[76]

Much remained to be done before the University could be restored even to its pre-war strength. It would take years of hard and patient work to put it again in a position of educational leadership. There would be many obstacles to overcome. With the growth of the University, financial problems would increase. Press and public would offer their gratuitous criticism; the clergy would cry out against the godlessness of youth. There would be temperamental teachers and rebellious students. There would be all the frictions which human beings generate as they rub shoulders in a narrow world. There would be problems of political influence and political control. The road would always be stony.

But, in the autumn of 1871, the atmosphere was one of hope and confidence. The University of Alabama had risen from ashes; no crisis the future could hold would ever threaten so deeply the foundations of its life.

CHAPTER XIV

The Presidents
1871-1901

NATHANIEL THOMAS LUPTON was the first of eight men who served the University of Alabama as president during the important three decades between 1871 and the turn of the century. All of the eight were Southern born, except General Gorgas, and he had, as the *Gazette* remarked when he was chosen, "done all that a good and sensible man could to remedy the youthful indiscretion" of Northern birth by marrying a daughter of Alabama and by serving the Confederacy loyally during the war. All were mature men: Lupton, moving into the office at the age of forty-one, was by far the youngest of the group; Smith, Gorgas, and Clayton were about sixty at the time of their appointments; and Wyman, by the time that he sat in the presidential chair in his own right instead of as an interim substitute, had reached the age of seventy. Four of the presidents—Lupton, Carlos G. Smith, Powers, and Wyman—were professional teachers; three—Lewis, Clayton, and Jones—were lawyers; Gorgas, with West Point training, was, first and last, a soldier. Four were alumni of the University of Alabama, and all of them, before they left office, carried that University's honorary LL.D. Each, in his own way, left his mark on the growing University.

President Lupton, a scientist by training and experience, was thrust into administrative office by the same force of circumstance that had earlier made him a teacher instead of a lawyer. He was born in Winchester, Virginia, December 19, 1830. He chose Dickinson College in Carlisle, Pennsylvania, for his pre-law studies, and was graduated there in 1849. He had hardly begun his serious study of law when a flattering offer of a teaching post changed the course of his career. By 1857 he was professor of chemistry at Randolph-Macon College. A year later he came to the new Southern University just opening at Greensboro, Alabama. Opportunity for travel and for study abroad were incidental to this new position. He went to Europe to buy scientific apparatus for the new university, and he studied under Bunsen for one year at the University of Heidelberg. He was still at Southern University when the war came. Then he became chemist of the Nitre and Mining Bureau of the Confederate States. The three years Lupton spent as administrative head of the University of Alabama formed only an interlude in his life's work as teacher of science. Eleven years at the newly organized Vanderbilt University in Nashville, Tennessee, and eight more as state chemist and professor of chemistry at the Alabama Polytechnic Institute at Auburn rounded out his career. Lupton died in 1893. He was, stated the *Corolla*, "an enthusiastic student and teacher, as well as a fine executive officer."[1]

The problems which fell upon Lupton's shoulders when he assumed the presidency of the reorganized University in the autumn of 1871 were many and heavy. And during his first weeks in office he felt none too secure in his own tenure. Although he was the choice of his faculty colleagues, the board of regents could easily set aside the faculty vote if they chose to do so at their November meeting. The faculty gave their chosen leader full and active support. They petitioned the regents for confirmation of his election and went so far as to suggest that future University presidents be chosen in the same way, by vote of the faculty from among their ranks. The regents did not warm to the suggestion of giving up their prerogative of selecting University presidents, but when they met in Montgomery in November, they called into consultation Professor Wyman, already recognized as the natural leader of the University, and they confirmed President Lupton in office. Back on the campus, the rest of the faculty drew a deep breath of relief and voted that a letter of thanks be sent to the regents.[2] The first crisis in the life of the reorganized University had been safely passed.

The University was desperately in need of funds; it could not operate long on enthusiasm alone. When President Lupton took office, he was confident that some of the financial need could be met by combining the proposed new agricultural college with the University. Congress had acted in 1862 to provide land grants for states wishing to build colleges devoted to the agricultural and mechanical arts. But Congress had also ruled that no portion of the money realized on land sales could be used to buy or build a college plant. Governor Patton had pointed this fact out in 1866. He had said: "The financial condition of the State, and the poverty of its people, do not justify the appropriation of any money out of the public treasury for the erection of such buildings"; and he had recommended that, following Georgia's example, the agricultural college be made a part of the state University.[3] President Lupton thought this a very practical plan, as he stated in his first report to the state superintendent of education:

Our University, with its able Faculty, magnificent buildings, ample Military Department, meets all the requirements of the Congressional grant, leaving the interest of the fund free for the employment of additional Professors in the schools of Practical and Agricultural Mechanics, and Practical and Agricultural Chemistry.[4]

The plan never materialized. Tuscaloosa, Florence, and Auburn were all in the race to get the agricultural college. Auburn was able to offer the building and property of the East Alabama Male College, a Methodist school. In 1872 that offer was accepted.[5]

Equally disappointing were efforts to secure from the federal government indemnity for the burning of the University in 1865. When one of the Tennessee colleges got similar relief in 1874, Congressman Charles Hays made another attempt to get action on Alabama's claims,[6] but his bill was never passed. The financial problems of the University continued to mount.

Problems of personnel, like those which had plagued his predecessors before the war, also faced President Lupton. It was hard to keep the faculty together. Professors Hodgson and Griswold resigned at the end of 1872, their departures being duly "regretted" in the faculty minutes.[7] Hodgson's work in moral philosophy was then taken up by Joshua Hill Foster; and Hampton S. Whitfield, teacher of mathematics and astronomy from 1870 to 1871, was brought back to fill the other gap—though Professor Griswold's field had been modern language. In the spring of 1873 there was a real campus battle. Commandant George D. Johnston disagreed with Lupton over a decision which, the General said, had been taken over his head and which had "jeopardized his just authority." When the faculty supported their president, Johnston resigned. Professor Eugene A. Smith took over his duties for the rest of the term,[8] and then Thomas C. McCorvey became commandant. Mathematics Professor William J. Vaughn turned in his resignation, also, in the spring of 1873.[9] And a year later the faculty had before it the resignations of Professor Peck and of President Lupton himself.

Of the ten teachers who made up Lupton's faculty in 1871, only four were left: Professors William Stokes Wyman, Benjamin Franklin Meek, William A. Parker, and Eugene A. Smith. But in loyalty and devotion these four represented a sound foundation for any faculty. Professor Meek would be at his post until he died, in 1899; the others would serve even longer, well into the twentieth century. That they were, on the whole, well satisfied with their first venture in president-making is attested by the tone of the resolutions with which they bade Godspeed to their colleague President Lupton. Those resolutions were, the record reads, "in appreciation of the uniform courtesy, great fidelity, and signal ability" with which President Lupton had "ever performed the duties of his high and responsible office."[10]

The board of regents was faced again with their old problem of getting a president for the University. When they met on June 29, 1874, things went with surface smoothness. They quickly elected Henry Tutwiler, of Greene Springs, Alabama, one of the first faculty members of the old University, to take over the chair left vacant by Lupton in July. He was to have a salary of $2,700, the use of the President's Mansion, and stated tenure for five years. There must have been some dissent, however, for the regents first safeguarded their appointment by providing that Tutwiler could be impeached by a three-fourths vote of the regents for "any felony or misdemeanor involving moral turpitude,"[11] and then on the following day rescinded Tutwiler's election. They were, perhaps, unwilling to commit themselves for that five-year term, even with their right to impeach protected. It is possible that the tenure provision was a condition which Tutwiler himself had insisted upon.

General W. H. Forney was the second choice. He was notified by telegraph of his election, and by telegraph he refused to serve. The regents then considered three candidates: Basil Manly, General Stephen D. Lee, and Dr. Carlos G. Smith. A vote of 7-2-2 gave the office to Smith, who was willing to serve.[12] It had taken the regents only a few days this time to get a new president.

Dr. Smith was a close friend and associate of Henry Tutwiler.

He had taught for a time at Tutwiler's school in Greene Springs, and both men had married daughters of Paoli Pascal Ashe, first steward of the University, back in 1831. Smith, a doctor of medicine, was sixty-one years old when he came to the University of Alabama; he was distinguished in his career as teacher and administrator. He was born of Virginia parents in Oglethorpe County, Georgia, December 18, 1813, and most of his childhood was spent in his parents' home state. When the family moved to Tennessee in 1831, Carlos went to the Clausell school. After teaching for several years, he then entered the University of Nashville in 1837 and was graduated from that school the following year. The next nine years of his life were partly devoted to teaching ancient languages and mathematics at his alma mater and at Hume Academy, and partly occupied with medical studies. The M.D. which he received at the University of Pennsylvania in 1847 was the only earned doctorate held by any of the University of Alabama presidents in this period. There is no indication that Dr. Smith ever practiced medicine. Instead, after he had taught under his brother-in-law at the Greene Springs School, he turned more and more to school administration. For a time he was principal of the Greene Academy, at Huntsville, after which he established his own school, the Mountain Home Academy, in Lawrence County. The burning of that school during the war sent him back to Huntsville, where he was living when he was called to the presidency of the University.[13]

Before President Smith had been on the job more than a few months, it was evident to all that the regents had discovered a man with a genius for public relations. That October the Huntsville *Democrat* declared,

He has gone vigorously to work to build up the fallen fortunes of the University, by advocating its claims to the support of the people of Alabama, in person and by letter. He has already received promises of many new students, and hopes to visit many prominent towns in Alabama, and, by personal application, considerably increase the number. . . . We deem it a most fortunate circumstance for the interests of the University that it has secured a President, whose personal character, learning, ability and experience, challenge full public confidence, and, under his auspices, we confidently expect for it a new and brighter era.[14]

There was need for a publicity expert in the president's chair.

The promise of rapid growth for the reorganized University had failed to materialize; only fifty-two students were enrolled the year Smith took office. The president went to work vigorously to turn the tide. Copies of the University catalogue and circulars extolling University advantages went out broadside through the state. Newspapers ran advertisements in unprecedented volume. "Intelligent and influential men" began to receive personal letters from President Smith asking for their support of the University and to find the indomitable president himself waiting on their doorsteps for personal interviews.[15] He asked for their moral support and interest in their own institution of learning. Above all, he wanted their sons as students.

Alabama was too small to contain President Smith. He mapped out a recruiting itinerary which included Mississippi, Louisiana, "and other contiguous states," as well as Alabama, and by the summer of 1875 he had persuaded the regents to give him $500 for travel expenses and all the time he wanted in which to canvass for students.[16]

Enrollment boomed. There were 74 students enrolled by the end of Smith's first year, 179 by 1878. Meanwhile the faculty was strengthened. Professor Henderson M. Somerville came in 1872. In 1875 Professor John M. Martin joined the law school and Professor Horace Harding taught civil engineering. Two years later Professor John C. Calhoun came to teach Greek. When Smith's term of office ended in 1878, various campus improvements were under way. The new gas lights for laboratory and mess rooms were almost ready for installation.

The stumbling-block over which President Smith fell so unceremoniously and suddenly in the summer of 1878 was put in his way by the Alabama legislature when, in 1876, that body took the government of the University away from the regents and gave it back to a board of trustees. The members of this body were now nominated by the governor and confirmed by the senate.[17] It was a wise move, one which freed the University from the hampering influence of party politics. But it gave to President Smith a new set of masters, who went about their jobs with all the thoroughness of a new broom.

Messrs. W. G. Clark, H. A. Herbert, John A. Foster, N. H. R. Dawson, W. C. McIver, Enoch Morgan, Marion Banks, James Crook, and Edward C. Betts made up the board that took over University administration in 1876, with the governor and the Superintendent of Public Instruction as ex-officio members.

When this new board took charge of the University in 1876, it divided itself into standing and special committees for more efficient administration. After that date the following standing committees functioned: finance; university property; salaries and fees; instruction, rules and regulations; and quartermaster. On June 30, 1877, the committee on organization recommended the appointment of the following standing committees, of three members each to be appointed by the president pro tem at each annual meeting of the board of trustees and to act until the next regular meeting:

1st. On Finance. The finance committee shall have general oversight of the financial affairs of the University, examine the Treasurer's report and vouchers, and make such suggestions from time to time in relation to income and expenditures as may occur to them.

2d. On University Property. Who shall have charge of the Buildings, land and other property of the University, make recommendations for repairs improvements, alterations, and extension of the buildings, the leasing of lands and report upon all matters relating thereto which may be referred to them.

3rd. On Salaries and Fees. Who shall consider and report at each session of the Board what changes (if any) are expedient or necessary in the salaries of said Professors and others, the rates of Tuition and incidental charges for Cadets, and on such other matters as may be referred to them by the Board.

4th. On Instruction, Rules and Regulations. Who shall consider all alterations of, and additions to, the course of Instruction or the regulations of the University, that may be suggested by the President and Faculty, or may occur to them and make report to the Board.

5th. On Quartermasters Department. Who shall examine the report of the Quartermaster, compare and audit his vouchers, recommend any changes they think desirable in the management of the commissary department, and make report thereon to the Board.

Other important standing committees were added when needs arose—for example, executive, judiciary, and education.

The special committees were many and varied in the nature of their duties. Some of these were as follows: committee to audit the treasurer's report; committee on legislation; committee on cadets' petitions; and committee on fraternities.

After working with President Smith for two years, the board of trustees apparently came to the conclusion that his business methods simply would not do. They did not fire their executive. Instead, they failed to reappoint him, passing over his name without mention and voting to invite General Josiah Gorgas to become the University's new president.[18]

This high-handed treatment of a man who had increased University enrollment some 240 per cent in four years naturally drew a storm of public protest. Henry Tutwiler sprang at once to the defense of his brother-in-law in a letter to the Selma *Times,* a letter which was promptly copied by the Tuscaloosa *Gazette*. He recalled the circumstances of Smith's election by the regents, dwelt on his fine qualifications for the presidency and the many sacrifices he made in accepting the post:

He gave up his school [in Huntsville], sold his apparatus and a portion of his property, at a sacrifice, and at great expense removed to Tuscaloosa. . . .

The steadily increasing enrollment figures, Tutwiler said, formed a record that President Smith could be proud of:

That much of this increased patronage was due to Dr. Smith is evident from the fact that the University has had the same Faculty, with the exception of the Prof. of Greek, elected a year ago, as it had before his connection with it.

Although it was hard for Tutwiler to accept as wise the board's decision to remove Smith, it was impossible for him to condone the manner in which the removal had taken place. The trustees had not even shown the elements of courtesy:

The election of the new President took place on Thursday, July 4th, but Dr. Smith had no intimation of it until Friday, July the 5th when he learned of it by a note from a friend. . . . Before the adjournment of the Board on Thursday, the Board passed a resolution that their Secretary should not disclose the result of the election till 12 M Friday. The Trustees then left, some on Thursday evening, others on Friday morning trains. . . .

Tutwiler became indignant at the thought of the shocking conduct of the board:

They had given Dr. Smith no notice of any complaint or dissatisfaction, and therefore no opportunity of defense. If there was any investigation of charges against him, it was conducted in secret and without his knowledge. The meanest criminal is entitled to a notice of the charge against him, and has the right of meeting his accusers . . . face to face. But here is a gentlemen of high culture, pure character, and distinguished reputation, summarily ejected, without notice, from a high position which he had filled four years with credit to himself and benefit to the State. A vote of thanks . . . would have been much more appropriate.

Smith's defender knew that some people would attempt to justify the trustees' action by blaming the president for a fatal fight between two of the University cadets the previous February. He said,

Every one familiar with colleges and universities knows that no amount of vigilance can prevent such occurrences. In this case not a single member of the Faculty knew or suspected any misunderstanding between the two cadets. . . .

The least the trustees should have done, Tutwiler insisted, was to give President Smith the privilege of resigning:

Everyone acquainted with Dr. Smith knows that he would not have retained his place a single day if the Board had given him the least intimation of a want of confidence. He is now turned adrift suddenly and unexpectedly, without timely notice to seek a home and means of support for a large and helpless family.

In closing his letter, Tutwiler hinted that other members of the faculty were said to have received similar treatment by the board, and he paid his personal tribute to an old friend:

I write this as an act of simple justice to a friend whom I have known longer and more intimately than I have known any man in the State, and whose high Christian character and eminent abilities have been the object of my warmest love and admiration.[19]

The *Gazette* editor was not sure that Tutwiler acted wisely in stirring up controversy over Smith's dismissal:

We sympathize deeply with Dr. Smith; but think that the discussion that will follow . . . will result in no good to Dr. Smith or the University. Dr. Tutwiler we think puts too fine a point, if he considers the action of the Board a reflection upon Dr. Smith's Christian character or ability as a teacher. We do not approve of the manner of his notification,—more delicacy and tenderness and sympathy might have been used. But the policy of the Board of electing for the one year (which is questionable) was known to the whole country.[20]

In a matter of weeks the rumors of campus riots as justification for the dismissal were being widely discussed, as Tutwiler had foreseen they would be. The Tuscaloosa *Gazette* picked up such a story from the Selma *Argus* on August 8. Disclaiming any disposition to "increase existing bad feeling," and granting that it was "most natural" that Smith and his friends should feel aggrieved, the editor ventured to express his opinion that the trustees had acted for the best:

> It is possible, of course, that the wisest thing has not been done . . . but it is certain the condition of the institution the past year was not satisfactory. . . . The muffled reports of rows, riots, dissipation, and lawlessness among the students . . . excited such distrust in the minds of parents and guardians that the future of the school was seriously imperiled; and those charged with the protection of its interests would have been false to their trusts if they had failed . . . to take cognizance of the fact. . . . It is but fair to presume that, with all the facts before them, they made an intelligent and disinterested effort to prevent a recurrence of disorders that would inevitably destroy any educational institution. They have acted . . . upon information not wholly before the public, and it will be soon enough to condemn them when their work results badly.[21]

Reading the trustees' terse minutes of the unhappy controversy, one surmises that they did indeed act on "information not wholly before the public." But it seems evident, too, that this information had to do with matters fiscal rather than disciplinary. President Smith had his own way of handling money, a way which the trustees considered unbusinesslike, to say the least. When their efforts to make the president follow their financial regulations failed utterly, they apparently got tired of trying to work with him. The dismissal which stirred such bitterness may have had as simple an explanation as that.

Dr. Smith, for example, was accustomed to draw the full amount of appropriations as soon as they were voted, to convert the state warrants into cash, and then to use the cash as he needed it. The trustees thought it better practice to draw the money only as expenditures were made and bills incurred. The money which went into Dr. Smith's pockets did not always come out again for the purposes for which it had been appropriated. The finance committee pointed out that only $44.05 of the $151.43 appropriated for repairs to the

President's mansion had actually gone into such repairs. The $56.07 set aside for repair of University fences and grounds seemed to balance against the amount spent. But Dr. Smith had cashed the $500 contingent fund for $466 in currency and had spent all but $3.33 of it. He had, moreover, not only exceeded by some $90.80 the $400 which the trustees had appropriated for advertising but he also had completely disregarded instructions about the papers in which such advertising was to be bought. Perhaps the most annoying performance the finance committee had to report related to the $500 the trustees had appropriated to repair University buildings and other property. President Smith had promptly turned the appropriation into $475 in cash and had spent $335 of it. Instead of going into building repairs, however, the money had purchased a miscellaneous assortment of stoves, chairs, coffee pots, pans, bedsteads, castors, surgical alcohol, spoons, plates, scales, buckets and dippers. Although granted the trustees agreed that these were much needed articles, these purchases could hardly be called building repairs, and it was for building repairs that they had voted the money.[22] The publicity-minded Dr. Smith could be a most annoying fellow.

Whatever the reasons for the trustees' decision, Smith's connection with the University ended. For some years he directed a normal college for girls at Livingston; then, in 1886, because of failing health, he retired to Palatka, Florida, where he died in 1892.[23]

The trustees had been fortunate in the choice of Smith's successor. Anticipation of the arrival on campus of General Josiah Gorgas, military hero, took the edge off the public concern over the departure of Smith. The Tuscaloosa *Gazette* nicely caught the spirit of the-king-is-dead-long-live-the-king in an editorial published on August 1:

From what we know and have heard of him [General Gorgas]—if the trustees made a mistake in making a change, they certainly acted sensibly in selecting a man who comes as near "filling the bill" as any they could have found. He is represented to be a highly educated gentlemen of fine executive and disciplinarian ability. . . . the Greensboro *Watchman* complains that an Alabamian was not chosen. This we think also falls to the ground, inasmuch as it was no fault on the part of General Gorgas; unless he gave some intimation of a repugnance to such a nativity. But he has done all that a good and sensible man could to remedy this youthful indiscretion, by marrying one of Alabama's fair daughters, whose father Alabamians delighted to honor.[24]

The "fair daughter" of Alabama who had rescued the West Point second lieutenant of ordnance from his handicap of Pennsylvania birth was Amelia Gayle, daughter of Governor John Gayle. She had married her Yankee in 1853 and had so thoroughly transformed him into a good Southerner by 1861 that Captain Gorgas of the United States Army resigned his position to join the Confederate forces. He was chief of ordnance during the war, and in 1864 he rose to the rank of general. After the war was over, General Gorgas had, for a time, managed the iron works at Briarfield, Alabama, but when the call to the University of Alabama came, he was vice-chancellor of the University of the South at Sewanee, Tennessee. Born on July 1, 1818, he had just passed his sixtieth birthday when that call reached him.

There was good reason behind the trustees' choice of a military man to head the University. The post-war glamor which public opinion sees around the military heroes could be counted on to help insure General Gorgas a warm welcome. His army experience qualified him to handle strongly and wisely the disciplinary problems which still plagued the campus. And the General turned out to be more than a soldier. He was a warm human being, who, in his tragically brief association with the University, left an unforgettable impress upon its life.

By February, 1879, the Montgomery *Advertiser* predicted that General Gorgas would be "the most popular President . . . that the University has ever had." He was winning the confidence of the boys and he was handling them with wisdom and "exact justice":

It is a most pleasant fact to note the growing popularity of Gen. Gorgas, with the "boys" at the University. A new commander is, generally speaking, in camp phrase, unpopular, until he leads "the boys" in a fight,— and after they see him under fire, and how coolly he manages his troops, then their admiration begins to show itself by the troops calling him "pet names," and it is then they will "follow him to the death." Gen. Gorgas is not an exception to the rule. . . . The "boys" who, a short time ago, shook their heads with ominous forebodings, are now fairly exuberant in praise of his wise administrative ability,—his exact justice; . . . we predict, that, in twelve months, he will be the most popular President, with people and students, that the University has ever had. We say this . . . because it is simply deserved commendation of his entire fitness for the position he holds as an experienced educator and a man of rare executive ability.[25]

Even as the *Advertiser* was making this happy forecast, General Gorgas was giving up the reins of his office; he was too ill to carry the work any longer. Professor Wyman's report to the board of trustees when they met in July indicated how quickly Gorgas had won the confidence of his faculty:

Under his wise and discreet guidance the business of the University was conducted quietly and prosperously to the close of the First Term. The President fell sick a few days after the beginning of the Second Term, to wit on the 23d of February, and he has not, since that time, felt able to discharge the duties of his office.[26]

General Gorgas offered his resignation at that time, but the trustees were reluctant to let him go. Surely a summer of perfect quiet and freedom from care would restore his health. They offered him a leave of absence on a professor's salary, with such deductions as might be necessary to provide help for Professor Wyman. They invited him to continue to live, rent-free, in the President's Mansion.[27]

It seems to have been a foregone conclusion that Professor Wyman would serve as preisdent pro tem while General Gorgas's health was rebuilding. He did so, ably and quietly, for another year. By the summer of 1879, however, it was apparent that the General would never be able to take up again the heavy duties of the presidency. Reluctantly the trustees set about choosing another president: Burwell Boykin Lewis.

Even then they did not let Gorgas go; they offered him the newly created position of librarian, a position which he accepted at a salary of $400 a year. Mrs. Gorgas was also put on the payroll, as supervisor of hospital care for the sick cadets. And it was at this point that the Gorgas family moved into the old steward's hall, which had survived the war and which was now to be the University's first hospital. The building still is known as the Gorgas Home.[28] Having provided for the economic security of the Gorgas family, the trustees recorded their affection for the General in terms that must have touched his heart:

Resolved: That in view of the continued ill health of General Gorgas, which compells a severance of his relations with the Board as President of the University, we desire to place on record some expression of our high appreciation of his character and services; of the rare tact and ability which characterized his administration, until he was stricken by disease; of the great improvement he effected in the order and discipline of the Cadets; and particularly, of the admirable system and method which he observed in keeping his books and accounts; and of the clearness and correctness of his business reports to the Trustees. He carries with him into retirement our highest esteem and confidence, and our earnest wishes that he may soon be restored to health, and that many years of happiness and usefulness may yet remain to him.[29]

The General apparently had none of the faults of his predecessor.

General Gorgas died May 15, 1883. The trustees voted $100 toward his funeral expenses "inasmuch as he was in full discharge of his duties at the University as President when stricken with the malady that ended in his death after years of suffering."[30] Again they spread upon their record a memorial of their esteem and affection for his life and work.[31]

Moving to select a new president in September, 1879, the trustees had before them twelve possible candidates: Rev. Dr. Joseph R. Wilson, Gen. D. H. Hill, Dr. George Little, Rev. Dr. A. J. Battle, Dr. John Massey, Col. Samuel H. Locket, Gen. Stephen D. Lee, Dr. John W. A. Sanford, Hon. Burwell B. Lewis, Dr. John W. Mallet, Gen. Kirby Smith, and Col. James T. Murfee.[32] It is interesting to note that four of these candidates—Battle, Massey, Mallet, and Murfee—had previously served on the faculty of the old University. Five of the men were graduates of the University: Little, Battle, Massey, Sanford, and Lewis.

With such an array of talent to choose from, general discussion was impossible. The board wisely left the sifting of the names to a committee and confirmed unanimously that committee's choice of Lewis.[33]

Prior to this election the trustees had been under some public pressure to select a president from within the state—preferably from within the University itself. The Mobile *Register* had stated the case for such appointment that summer:

The President should be chosen from the ranks of professors, from those who for nine years past have labored faithfully for the restoration of the University. There is no reason and no necessity for going beyond the University and to other States for material for a President. The experience which has been acquired by Wyman, Parker, Meek, Eugene Smith, and other learned men of the faculty who have shed lustre upon the

University, fits each one of them for the executive chair. We understand perfectly well the reluctance with which one of the so-deserving men would consent to step above the others, but such modesty should give way to the good of the institution. The day is past for going to Europe for some brilliant theological luminary to light the fires of learning with a torch from the parent altars. The people are no longer dazzled by the name of military leaders whose claim upon our gratitude are no stronger than those of the man with the knapsack. If the trustees should, in their search for a President, go outside of Alabama and select a military man, while within the State and within the faculty are men competent for the place, we apprehend that such action will not meet with the approval of the people. The University cannot afford to make a mistake in this matter. Auburn is already cutting ground from around her.[34]

Lewis was not a member of the faculty. But neither was he a "theological luminary" from abroad nor an imported military hero. He was a native son of Alabama, born in Montgomery on July 7, 1837. He had farmed with his uncle, Judge Shortridge, in Shelby County, as a boy. He entered the University of Alabama at the age of sixteen and graduated with distinction in 1857. He studied law in Selma, gaining admission to the bar in 1858; and after practicing in partnership with Colonel Storrs, in Montevallo, and R. W. Cobb, who later became governor of the state, he established his own good law practice in Tuscaloosa. Just before the war broke he had married Rose Garland, daughter of the greatly respected University president. He had served in the Confederate Army during the war, and, since peace had been restored, he had twice represented his county in the state legislature. He had just been re-elected for his second term in the United States Congress when he was made president of the University.[35] The trustees had chosen well, and the newspapers lost no time in congratulating them and lauding young Burwell Boykin Lewis. According to the Eufaula *Times and News,*

The position could not have been conferred upon one who was more competent to occupy the exalted station, or one who could command so much influence in the interest of the institution. Col. Lewis has devoted his life to the study of the classics and the science of government, and in both branches he is an accomplished scholar. . . . He is a pure, upright, Christian gentleman, commanding the respect and esteem of all with whom he is brought in contact. He is a friend to the young man and encourages him in his efforts for success. . . . While he has excellent faculties for discipline, he will never have to resort to rigidity to enforce his laws, because it will be a pleasure to obey the wishes of such a man. . . . The Trustees have made a wise selection and we congratulate the State upon the result of their conference and choice. . . . The son has returned to his ALMA MATER to show his filial love for her kind rearing.[36]

The Tuscaloosa *Gazette* reprinted this glowing editorial and echoed its sentiments:

The friends (and they are legion) of Hon. B. B. Lewis will not be surprised to learn that he has been called . . . to the Presidency of the State University. . . . If there be any surprise, it will be that he has yielded to the desire of the people of Alabama, and laid aside his present honorable position in Congress, to serve his people in a less fascinating, less ambitious, but really a higher and more important and responsible sphere—the education of the youth of Alabama. . . . His practical wisdom, his native good sense, his youthful vigor, his true moral courage, with his splendid intellectual attainments and Christian purity, combine to make the prerequisites of a President over such an institution complete. We congratulate the people of Alabama upon having Burwell B. Lewis at the head of the State University.[37]

The six years of President Lewis's administration came close to justifying such enthusiasm. They were eventful years. Not only did the state legislature, under the determined prodding of the alumni, vote a grant of $50,000 to the University but the United States Congress, belatedly making amends for war losses, tossed into the laps of the trustees new land grants, with all the advantages and problems such grants would bring. The University embarked upon a new building program, made important improvements in its grounds, and became the proud possessor of telephone connections with the outside world.

Some of the rigid restrictions on student activities were eased while President Lewis had his firm but gentle hand on the helm. Fraternities, so long under the cloud of administrative disapproval, came back to the campus as open, legitimate student organizations. Dances, including a fine commencement hop, were held under University auspices. Such laxity in discipline was, of course, not without its critics. In view of the emphasis placed on President Lewis's unimpeachable Christian character at the time of his inauguration, it is entertaining to read the record of his controversy with the Reverend W. C. McCoy, who suspected him of condoning the reading of Ingersoll by some of the students.

This administration, which held so much promise, came to an abrupt, sad end. On October 11, 1885, President Lewis died. Once more the trustees turned to Professor Wyman and made him acting president at a special meeting that November. The faculty had already indicated their wish for this appointment. Also, they had volunteered such complete coöperation in taking over Professor Wyman's classes that the trustees were able to give to Mrs. Lewis the money which might have been spent on substitutes and to leave her, for the time being, in possession of the President's Mansion.[38] In the months that followed, the students invited the townspeople of Tuscaloosa to help them raise money for a suitable memorial to their beloved lost leader by supporting a memorial concert. This concert, held on May 21, included in its program music by Chisholm's Orchestra, vocal music, recitations, and a performance by the University "Bottle Corps."[39] When the tablet was presented in June, the Board of Trustees accepted it "with unfeigned pleasure and satisfaction."[40]

At that June meeting the trustees would have liked to appoint their acting president as Lewis's successor. They were deterred from doing so only because of Professor Wyman's "modesty and plea of infirm health." Before they took up the matter of electing a new head of the University, however, they recorded in their minutes a resolution of gratitude to Mr. Wyman. They desired to express

their high appreciation of the admirable ability, faithfulness and success with which Dr. W. S. Wyman has discharged the onerous and responsible duties of President of the University during the collegiate year just terminated . . . and to assure him of the continuance of their confidence in the attainments and qualities which, but for his modesty and plea of infirm health, would have made him the choice of the Board for the permanent President of the University.[41]

The board of trustees turned to General Henry DeLamar Clayton as the possible successor of President Lewis. He was born March 7, 1827, in Pulaski County, Georgia. General Clayton was a graduate of Emory and Henry College, Virginia, in the class of 1848 and received license to practice law in Alabama in 1849. General Clayton had just failed to win nomination for Governor of Alabama. He was a highly respected public servant, having twice been a member of the Alabama legislature before the War, and having filled with distinction the post of Judge of the Third Circuit Court since 1880. His war service had given him prestige which the Alabama public had not forgotten; he had served as aide-de-regiments as they arrived at Pensacola; he had won his rank on the battlefield through the brilliant performance of his brigade.[42] Here was a man with all the qualities the University needed for its sound administration and for its prestige in the community. The trustees conferred on General Clayton the honorary degree of Doctor of Laws and gave him the keys to the University.[43]

The Tuscaloosa *Gazette* set its stamp of approval on the appointment in an editorial bristling with Latin tags. General Clayton's "administrative abilities and business sagacity" would "make him *facile princees* of College Presidents." "His popular manners,—his frankness,—his *suaviter in modo,—fortier in re*," would most certainly breed confidence and respect on the campus and off:

He who can weld a heterogeneous mass of citizen soldiery into a homogeneous bank of fighting patriots . . . can certainly bring to the highest vantage ground of usefulness and power for good the fortunes of our dear old University. . . .[44]

That President Clayton commanded the complete respect of the board of trustees was evidenced by their willingness to put into his hands more power than any of his predecessors had enjoyed. In 1888 they specifically empowered him to replace quartermaster, commandant, or post adjutant if the incumbent showed inefficiency or negligence. The presidential appointees would be subject to confirmation of the board, but, in the interim between board meetings, the decision to hire and fire was firmly in the president's hands.[45] Two years later the board increased his authority over the teaching staff. If he found an assistant professor "guilty of intoxication, card playing, or any grossly immoral conduct" on the campus or in Tuscaloosa, he might suspend him for the first offense and discharge him if he did not mend his ways. Replacement for an assistant instructor thus fired was to be made by the faculty. The culprit's salary was to stop on the date of his suspension or discharge.[46]

In further evidence of their pride and trust in General Clayton, the trustees sent him to San Francisco in July, 1888, to represent the University at the National Education Association convention. This was the first time that the University of Alabama had sent an official representative to a national meeting of educators. The trustees voted their emissary $150 for expenses—or as much as might be necessary of that sum.[47]

President Clayton fared well, also, in getting his trustees to recognize that the duties of the president, increasing as the University grew, necessiated more clerical and administrative help than had hitherto been provided. Since 1877 an appropriation of $200 a year had been made for such help.[48] In 1888 the board authorized the appointment of a post adjutant, at a salary of $300 and board, "to discharge such duties, largely secretarial, as might be required of him by the President."[49] And the following year the president was authorized to work out plans, within the $300 limit, to give himself two assistants instead of one. He might, said the trustees, "at his option . . . employ two young graduates, one of whom shall receive $50 in consideration of his acting as Law Librarian and the other $250 and board as Post Adjutant and clerk in the President's office."[50]

Important as these administrative changes were, they probably made less impression on campus life than did another occurrence during President Clayton's regime—the opening of a gymnasium. Physical education had made its appearance on the campus and competitive sports were just around the corner. Marcellus T. Hayes became director and instructor in the gymnasium. He was to be directly responsible to the president in regard to the examination of the students by the surgeon, "which should be frequent and imperative," and in regard to the whole gymnasium program.[51]

The transfer of Commandant Thomas C. McCorvey to the newly established chair of history and philosophy in June, 1888, was the most important faculty change in President Clayton's regime.[52] Captain James Courtney Hixson, of Union Springs, just graduated from the University, took Colonel McCorvey's place as commandant.

Once again death ended a sound and useful presidency. General Clayton died on October 13, 1889, after a short illness. Once more, Professor Wyman attended the funeral services of a superior officer, watched the honor escort of cadets accompany the General's casket on the start of its journey to Clayton, where the old soldier would be buried, and then took up, as a matter of course, the executive bur-

REBUILDING THE UNIVERSITY

dens of the president's office. The procedures followed after President Lewis's death were put into force again. Professor Wyman was given the president's salary. His own stipend as professor of Latin was available for Mrs. Clayton and her family because the faculty had again arranged among themselves to help teach Wyman's classes. The trustees, knowing that the University was in good hands, made no move to choose another president until the next June.[53]

During this interim, advice from the press was freely given. The Tuscaloosa *Gazette* made thinly veiled reference to the "slurs . . . continually flung at this institution from over the State," suggesting that "the thrusts have had concealed in them the insinuations of too much politics." The fact that people were referring to the University commencements "as seasons for political concoctions and 'slate making' . . ." was doing the institution no good. The University was worth about one million dollars now; soon its income should make it independent of state aid. This was the time for the appointment of a real statesman:

> We need a Thomas Jefferson, who will plan so wisely and disinterestedly, as to lift it above all political soiling, and make it stand, as the University of Virginia. Its finances, which from now on will become more and more available so that its income will be ample, ought to make it an institution of pride and trust to the State and the whole South.[54]

When the trustees met in mid-June, 1890, the *Gazette* again admonished them with an impassioned plea that they lift the bedraggled reputation of the University by giving it a president truly worthy of the great future it ought to have:

> As the time draws nigh for the Trustees of the University to elect a President, the people all over the State become more and more anxious. They look forward to their action as one of the most important events that has transpired in the history of our college. The University lies near to the hearts of the people of Alabama. Their nearest and dearest interests are involved in its future destinies. They are justly proud of what it has done in the past but look forward to future achievements that will eclipse and overshadow the past—to a time, when the past will be remembered as the '"day of small things," and though not "despised," will be cherished only as a savor of better things.
>
> The great wealth of mineral lands that the people of Alabama, through the agency of their government, have recently bestowed upon their college makes it one of the richest institutions of learning in the South; and,

hence, the people have a right to expect corresponding blessings to flow back to them for their munificence and liberality. It is a rich legacy they have provided for their children—that is all—and they expect it to be so managed and directed and guarded by those entrusted with the control of its affairs as that the greatest possible good will come to the greatest number of people—as that our children and future generations may rise up and call us blessed for providing them a great university that will justly merit the endearing name of "Alma Mater."

In a large measure it is to the President of the University that the people must look for this wise management and its corresponding beneficial results. It is but natural then that we be casting around in our minds for the man who is possessed of the rare combinations of character the Trustees are supposed to be looking for.[55]

When this editorial appeared, on June 19, the trustees had already, on the previous day, completed "casting around in their minds" for the man "possessed of the rare combinations of character" the *Gazette* referred to. Apparently, they had asked General Cadmus M. Wilcox to do some preliminary sifting of candidates, for it was upon his recommendations that the board acted that day. The full record of the election in the board minutes is interesting, partly because the name of Professor Wyman appears again. This time the office of president was not directly offered to him:

Resolved—that the election of a President be had by a viva-voce vote and in open session. The resolution was adopted. . . . The hour—Thursday morning at 10 o'clock—for the special order having arrived, the election of a President of the University was then taken up. The reading of recommendations being called for, the Secretary proceeded to read those of Gen. Cadmus M. Wilcox. On motion the reading of further communications was dispensed with and the Board proceeded to the election of a President, no nominations being made. Mr. Webb offered the following resolution: Resolved—that Dr. W. S. Wyman be and he is hereby elected President of the University of Alabama and Professor of Latin at a salary of $3500.00 this election to be for the year 1890-91. The resolution was lost by a yea and nay vote:

 Yeas: Clark, Webb, Rhett   3
 Nays: Palmer, Foster, Dawson, Crook, Seay, and Brown 6

A vote was then taken which resulted as follows:
Jas. K. Powers, 1; Wm. S. Wyman, 2; Rich. C. Jones, 2; C. M. Wilcox, 1; Jno M. Martin, 1; Jno. W. Bishop, 1; J. H. Byson, 1.
No one having received a majority of the votes cast, a second vote was taken, which resulted: Powers 1; Wyman, 3; Jones, 5.
Mr. Palmer then moved to make the election of Gen. R. C. Jones to the

REBUILDING THE UNIVERSITY

office of President unanimous, which was seconded by Mr. Webb and carried.

Thereupon Gen. Jones was declared to be elected President for the unexpired term of the late Gen. Clayton.

Messrs. Webb, Brown, and Rhett were appointed a committee to notify Gen. Jones of his election.[56]

In selecting Jones the trustees had again given the University an alumnus as president, and they had also again confirmed their predilection for Confederate generals and lawyers. Richard Channing Jones was born in Brunswick County, Virginia, on April 12, 1841. However, when he was only three years old, his family had brought him to Camden, in Wilcox County; so he was next door to being a native son of Alabama. He was only eighteen years old when he was graduated from the University of Alabama and still under twenty-one when he answered the call to the colors and went with the state troops to Fort Morgan. Since the war, he had practiced law in Camden and had served two terms as state senator in the General Assembly.

From Camden came the new president's telegram of acceptance.[57] The *Gazette* acknowledged that the trustees had chosen "a man of marked ability, high character, and last but not least . . . a thorough Christian gentleman."[58]

The faculty which greeted President Jones on his arrival on the campus was, in the main, a mature, stable group. The days of rapid upheaval and quick turnover were passed. In this period when no president served for more than six or seven years, the teaching staff of the University provided an important continuity. Professors Wyman, Meek, Parker, and Smith were the ranking veterans. They had served since 1871 or longer. Professor Joshua H. Foster, who had come in 1872, was still teaching philosophy and astronomy; he would resign in 1892. Professor Thomas C. McCorvey, who came as commandant in 1873, still occupied the chair of philosophy, political philosophy, and history. Professor John Caldwell Calhoun had been teaching Greek and Latin since 1877 and would remain until 1897. Mrs. Amelia G. Gorgas, who had taken over her husband's duties as librarian, was still at her post—and would be until 1907. Among the newcomers were Robert Hardaway, who had become professor of civil engineering in 1882; Professor Thomas W. Palmer, professor of mathematics since 1883; Professor William B.

Phillips, just arrived to teach chemistry and mineralogy; John J. Harris, who had become quartermaster in 1882; and Andrew C. Hargrove, who had returned in 1889 to teach again the classes in equity-jurisprudence which he had taught in 1885 and 1886. Phillips and Hargrove would resign during President Jones's administration; the others would still be at their posts when he left.

To this faculty, General Jones added Professor George M. Edgar in philosophy and astronomy; Adrian S. Van de Graaf, in the law school; James M. Pickel, in chemistry and metallurgy; and Ormond Somerville, in the law school. The president himself, like his predecessor, President Clayton, taught classes in international and constitutional law.

Two dramatic "firsts" marked the administration of this president: football was introduced; and the first women students were admitted. Either achievement should have been enough to insure his lasting fame and to give him secure standing with the students of his day. Yet it was, apparently, imperfect relationships with his students that helped to place President Jones under investigation, a procedure which was not uncommon in the early life of the institution.

When the board of trustees met in June, 1896, they felt compelled to consider complaints coming from the senior and sophomore classes. The basis of the petition of grievances was probably irritation with the military system which had been growing more and more unpopular. But the boys made a complete sweep with their accusations. The president and the professors were, they declared, grossly incompetent and should be removed at once. President Jones himself came in for specially vigorous attack.

The trustees voted to dispense with "the charges preferred specifically against President Jones," but they set up two committees to go thoroughly into the other complaints. One committee was to investigate "what changes shall be made in [the University's] government and its faculty," to decide "whether the military feature shall be dispensed with," and "to make inquiry as to what changes if any shall be made in the personnel of the faculty." This committee was to report to the full board at the next annual meeting or at a specially called meeting if either the committee itself or the president of the board thought such a meeting advisable. The other committee was to deal with "the complaints against the Professors" and was to report to a called meeting of the board by October 1, 1896.[59]

Investigations make good newspaper copy. The press of the state tried the case while the committee worked, unhampered by any knowledge of the facts the committee had before it. The Mobile *Register* was fair enough to point out the dangers of unfounded rumor. A large part of the reports in circulation "alleging actions on the part of the faculty and particularly regarding neglect of duty on the part of members of the Faculty" were, this paper insisted, "gross exaggerations of the statements made to the committee."[60]

The Tuscaloosa *Gazette* also took a moderate wait-and-see attitude. The mere fact that some students were discontented did not prove that the whole University was "rotten" and needed "remodeling from top to bottom." Students had been known to exercise very bad judgment. On the other hand, a wise man smelling smoke does look carefully to see if there is a fire. And the smell of smoke, the *Gazette* believed, did hang over the University:

It will not be denied by anybody that there is a rift in the University lute somewhere. The appearance of a committee of the corps of cadets before the trustees with charges against the faculty is evidence sufficient of some discontent or trouble and a lack of harmony between students and professors that is to be greatly deplored. . . . The voice of the people is not always right by any means. What the boys want and ask for is not always best for them and they realize it later on. For instance, one of the complaints made against one of the professors was that he excused his classes too often. Judging from personal experiences it is reasonable to conclude that the very men who made that complaint were foremost in strenuous efforts to get that same professor to excuse them on any and all occasions. The fact that the students have gotten into a state of discontent is by no means assurance that the whole University is rotten and needs remodeling from top to bottom.

But when the smell of smoke is discovered in a man's house, if the man be prudent, he looks for fire even though he is confident that none exists. So in this case the Trustees should give this matter the most careful consideration.

It would not do for them to be ready to sit in judgment on the faculty, many members of whom have been with the Universiy from its struggle up to its present prosperous position. Neither should they disregard the student body. . . .

Whether justly or not, the University boys seemed to feel for some time that the trustees and the faculty . . . were not in sympathy with them. Petitions have been absolutely disregarded and on one occasion the boys openly avowed their belief that the Trustees failed to meet because they did not want to pass on a question the boys regarded as vital. On the other hand they have not failed at times to interpose when the faculty could much better have managed things.[61]

The committee chosen to investigate and report included Willis G. Clark, chairman, of Mobile; James E. Webb, of Birmingham; and M. L. Stansel, of Pickens County.[62] The report which they wrote completely vindicated the faculty and the president. The University staff, said their investigators, were "learned and efficient." The departments of chemistry, physics, and geology deserved special commendation. The whole trouble, they thought, was simply a great deal of public misunderstanding and "misapprehension":

After a most laborious investigation which covered almost every conceivable detail of University life, the administration of the affairs of the Institution, the committee finds that there has been a vast deal of misapprehension on the part of the public of this commonwealth in regard to this noble institution. Misapprehension, which results in a great degree from a lack of information, and in some instances from wilful perversion of important truths.

The committee also felt that the charge of "infidelity" among the professors was in no way justified. But it would be easier for a president to handle cases of neglect of duty if he had the right to remove the negligent professor:

They recommend the giving to the president of the executive power which should necessarily be his: power of removal for cause a member of the faculty; and that he be made an ex officio member of the Board of Trustees with a vote on questions pertaining to the management.

Furthermore, in the opinion of the committee, the trustees did not meet often enough. They should meet oftener than once a year, and they should provide a "board of control to consist of the president and two citizens of Tuscaloosa elected by the alumni" to carry responsibility between trustees' meetings. This board of control should really take over the practical management of the University:

The board of trustees ought to exercise purely a revisory authority, and at their annual meeting . . . review in a general way the actions of the President and board of control. . . . The executive head of any institution, financial, commercial, or educational, should have power and authority, commensurate with his responsibility, and the unanimous voice of those who are informed upon the present status of the University seems to be that the president is too much restricted in the prerogatives that should attach to his position. . . .

The committee had not been able to resist the temptation to do a little curriculum planning, some of it well within their charter, some definitely beyond it:

The president should not teach in the Law School or any department. A Dean should be appointed with a salary of $2500 or $3000, and be required to devote all his time to the school. . . . The course of instruction should be extended to two years. . . . Perhaps the greatest need, and one which most strongly impressed your committee, is the necessity of more practical business methods in the administration of the financial and economic affairs of the institution. . . . The committee thinks the faculty too large. They suggest to the trustees that much might be saved by uniting two of the chairs as now constituted. For instance, we think that one able Professor could well fill the Chair of Ancient Languages and Literature, as one learned gentleman now fills most acceptably the Chair of Modern Languages. While we may be treading on dangerous grounds here, we still feel constrained to express the opinion that one professor could very well fill the Chair of History, Philosophy, and English. . . .[63]

This is the Tuscaloosa *Time's* account of the report, and it is difficult to determine whether the editor has interpolated some of his own comments, and whether he has, by judicious omission, made the findings of the committee more completely favorable to the administration than they were. Certainly, there is little in the newspaper record which explains why President Jones should, almost immediately after the committee reported, notify the Governor that he would not be a candidate for reappointment in June, 1897.[64] He resigned after an eventful seven years in office. General Jones then returned to his former home in Camden and resumed the practice of law. He died September 12, 1903.

The trustees elected James Knox Powers to succeed General Jones. Powers was a native son of Alabama, having been born August 15, 1851, near Oakland in Lauderdale County. He had had valuable administrative experience as President of the State Normal

College at Florence before assuming his new duties. He was a graduate of the University in the class of 1873, and he was recognized as a leading educator in the state, having served in 1891 as President of the Alabama Education Association.

It should have been an auspicious time to take over the direction of University affairs. The alumni had once again successfully persuaded the legislature to grant funds to the University, and there were great possibilities of growth and development. But the unsolved conflicts of President Jones's regime were still rumbling. When, in 1900, discontent broke into open rebellion against President Powers and Commandant West, Powers tendered his resignation to become effective on June 30, 1901.[65] He returned to Florence, Alabama, and was later reelected President of the State Teachers College. He died in Florence on August 15, 1913.

Again the trustees tendered the presidency to the man who had, through all this troubled period, done more than any other individual or group of individuals to keep the institution steady on its course. And this time, Professor William Stokes Wyman did not refuse.

Said the Tuscaloosa *Gazette:*

. . . the duties of President will be discharged by Prof. W. S. Wyman, the Nestor of the University, than whom no one is more faithful and competent. . . . No one fills his chair and sphere better than he, and the duties of President are performed with an ease and grace, with that earnest fidelity to duty which characterizes his every act. It detracts nothing from the other members of the Faculty to give Prof. Wyman due credit for zeal, competency and fidelity.[66]

Dr. Wyman was seventy-one when he took office as the duly elected President of the University in 1901. He had been connected with the University, almost without a break, since the day when, an eighteen-year-old boy with one year at Harvard behind him, he had come back to his native Alabama to enter the University, then younger than he was himself. His life and the life of the school he loved had so interwoven themselves that the story of one became the story of the other.

In the Old University, young Wyman had been graduated in 1851, and had returned almost at once to tutor in Latin and Greek, and had risen to the rank of Professor by 1860. He had helped build

WOODS HALL

Named for the first president of the University, Woods Hall was the principal University building from 1868, when it was constructed, until 1886, when Clark and Manly halls were built. The ground floor of Woods has been occupied at various times by classrooms, dining hall, student store, literary society rooms, offices, and laboratories. The upper floors contained dormitory rooms until 1945, when the building was converted to classrooms and faculty offices for use by several instructional departments.

CLARK HALL

Named for Trustee Willis G. Clark when it was completed in 1886, Clark Hall housed the University library and the auditorium for many years. It is now occupied by the main art gallery and by the administrative offices of several divisions of the University.

REBUILDING THE UNIVERSITY 341

up the library of which the University was so justly proud and had seen its treasures devoured by flames on an April day in 1865. When President Garland doggedly returned to the ruined campus that October, Wyman was at his side. When the first board of regents arrogantly tried to foist upon the University a president hated and distrusted, it was Wyman who met the interloper at the gates and quietly refused to surrender the keys. When the sadder and wiser board turned at last for help from alumni and faculty to save the University from total ruin, it was Wyman who headed the committee appointed to perfect organization plans, and Wyman who negotiated with the board the appointment of President Lupton.

Three times before this 1901 election, Wyman had sat in the president's chair. When General Gorgas became too ill to serve, as well as when Presidents Lewis and Clayton died in office, he had been able to hold the University together. He carried on the heavy administrative responsibilities in a manner which won the respect of the trustees, of his colleagues, and of all who valued the University.

He had served in countless other ways as well. The new library as well as the old had his interest and his conscientious work. He was acting librarian through most of the 1870's. When the collection had grown large enough to warrant the employment of a regular non-teaching librarian, he continued his watchful and helpful interest in library affairs. It was under his direction that the first card catalogue was started in 1896.

Since he was University historian, too, the board of regents probably could not have made a better choice when, in 1872, they decided that their institution should have a man especially delegated "to collect and arrange all documents and facts which refer to the past history of the University;—and to collect and preserve all current facts and publications connected with the University."[67]

From 1870 to 1872 he had even found time to serve the cause of education in the General Assembly. Of that term in public office, an admirer of Dr. Wyman's who wanted to see him sent as delegate to the constitutional convention in 1899, wrote:

Dr. Wyman is a statesman of broadest and most comprehensive views and knowledge, as well as one of the most profound thinkers and most finished scholars of any age.

I happen to know that he is the author of the "Educational Article" in our present constitution, which would be an excellent law, but for the bad amendments after it left Dr. Wyman's hands. . . .

Dr. Wyman is responsible for the phrase "Public Schools" instead of "Free Schools" which saved the state from adding to the overwhelming debt which had been piled up under the republican convention of 1868. Indeed, when Hargrove saw that the article was in danger of being distorted he wired Dr. Wyman to come at once to Montgomery and assist him to prevent it. But, despite their efforts, the amendments were adopted and hence the imperfections in the school law under which we are now working.[68]

Librarian, historian, statesman, administrator—Dr. Wyman was all these. But he was first, last, and always a teacher. His excursions into administrative work were always reluctantly made because they took from him at least part of the work that was a constant delight to his mind and soul—the teaching of Latin to generation after generation of University boys. When he finally accepted the presidency in his own right in 1901, it was on condition that he might continue his teaching. And when he discovered, as he did within a single year, that the double load was too heavy for his frail health, it was the presidency, not the professorship, that he relinquished. He went happily back to his classroom and taught another several years before his retirement. It is interesting and gratifying to note that in 1908 he and his colleague Dr. W. A. Parker were given the first pensions the University ever paid; they were voted the sum of $600 a year by the trustees "in view of their service to the institution in the past."[69] Dr. Wyman was a loved and familiar figure around the University until his death, in 1915. He is buried in the family plot in Evergreen Cemetery in Tuscaloosa.

Few institutions in any time or place can match this record of more than fifty years of devoted and able service. From 1871 to 1900 eight men sat in the president's chair at the University. Each one was at some time aided and strengthened by the gentle and unassuming professor of Latin. The University of Alabama in the three last decades of the nineteenth century was, in a unique sense, Dr. Wyman's University.

CHAPTER XV

Business Management and Campus Development

1871-1901

THE UNIVERSITY Endowment Fund, set at $300,000 by the General Assembly just before the War Between the States and by the Constitution of 1875, was the main source from which income to maintain the University was derived. An interest rate of eight per cent brought a relatively steady payment of $24,000 a year throughout this period. For several years payments dropped below this figure, and in 1869, 1871, and 1873, the University appears to have been fortunate enough to draw more than the stipulated eight per cent. Income from student fees was always negligible. The University, as it started its post-war life, was hard pressed to find the money to pay its faculty, to maintain its plant, and to provide the equipment necessary for the development of a first-rate institution of learning.

The decade between 1871 and 1881 was particularly difficult. One disappointment had been the failure to establish the new agricultural college at the University. By 1872 the hope of securing in this way the use of grants made by Congress for an agricultural school had completely vanished. Congress still disregarded pleas that the University be indemnified for war losses. Three years after the failure of the Hays bill in 1874, the trustees made another determined attempt to get Congress to act,[1] but this appeal, too, was ignored.

Even the courts of Alabama seemed to ignore the financial plight of the University. At least they stopped the board from saving $830 in 1876 by repudiating an obligation recognized by its predecessor, the board of regents. That obligation arose out of the claim presented by Washington Moody for the Tuskaloosa Insurance Company, asserting that the University owed him $830 for services as fiscal agent during the war. He claimed that he had received and paid out for the University from $300,000 to $350,000 a year during that period. The board of regents had recognized the debt in June, 1871, and had authorized the president to settle it. But the matter was still pending in 1876, when the board of trustees came back into control of University affairs. Moody presented his claim again. The board told him that the board of regents, which had made the agreement to pay, was no longer in existence. Moody then brought suit in the circuit court of Tuscaloosa and obtained a judgment against the University for the $830. The trustees appealed, contending that they should not be bound by actions taken by the regents. The Alabama Supreme Court thought differently, and in 1878 this court handed down its decision: the corporation known as the University of Alabama, according to this court, had been in continuous existence since 1820; therefore the board of trustees succeeded to all the debts incurred by the board of regents.[2] It was discouraging to have this sum taken from the already inadequate funds of the University.

By 1881, however, under the strong guidance of President Lewis, University affairs took a definite turn for the better. The trustees faced their problem squarely in their July meeting that year. The one dormitory and classroom building was filled almost to capacity. It was certainly "unreasonable to expect, without increased facilities, any considerable increase in the number of students and in the usefulness of this Institution."

It was almost a stroke of genius that the trustees, probably at the suggestion of President Lewis, turned to the Society of Alumni for help. They appointed a committee to work with representatives of that society on plans for lobbying relief legislation through the General Assembly.[3] The alumni responded with vigor and alacrity. The joint committee appointed J. H. Fitts as its chairman and prepared to move in on the lawmakers.[4]

They moved slowly at first, but by 1883 they were ready to press the claims of their alma mater in Montgomery. The special committee, journeying to Montgomery that June, had mapped strategy that would have been a credit to any lobbying group. They met first with some twenty legislators known to be friendly toward the University. To this meeting they invited the superintendent of public instruction and several well-known educators. That caucus decided upon the general provisions of the relief bill and on the plan for its introduction. They agreed that the report of the board of trustees should be printed and distributed to all Assembly members. As soon as this report had been formally received, bills appropriating $60,000 to the University should be quickly introduced in both houses. There was plenty of opposition, of course. While the debate went on in the legislature, it went on also in the newspapers. Some editors called the measure a "shameful fraud" on the tax payers of the state. The 400,000 school children of Alabama would get nothing out of it. It was "based on lobby pleas" and "begged out of a foolish . . . Legislature," said the Hayneville *Examiner*.[5] Other editors were quick to side with the University. Said the Greenville *Advocate*,

the cry that the State should give all the aid she can to the common schools and let the University go a-begging, is raised in defiance of right and justice. In most cases, it is the demagogical howl of professional politicians or of sensational newspapers . . . seeking to curry undeserved favor with the "dear people." No matter how greviously the common schools may need assistance from the State . . . the people feel that the University too has claims which should not be disregarded. . . .[6]

Some of the opposition was softened when an appropriation of $30,000 for the Agricultural and Mechanical College at Auburn was added to the bill. Now, there were proponents of two institutions pushing for its passage. A further obstacle to enactment was removed when the trustees of both institutions signed an agreement that no part of the appropriation would be drawn from the state treasury until provision had been made for payment of the interest on the state debt due July 1, 1884. The governor signed the bill in June,[7] and the trustees rejoiced with President Lewis that at last an expanded building program was possible.

Success bred success, apparently. The University had scarcely embarked on plans to spend the money which the alumni had wrung out of the legislature when news came that the lawmakers in Washington, too, were waking up to the claims of Alabama's institution of learning. In April, 1884, a new grant of 46,080 acres of public lands was voted by Congress in "An Act to Increase the Endowment of the University of Alabama from the public land in said State." The act stated that revenue from these lands was to be used for new buildings as well as for the restoration of the library and scientific apparatus which had been destroyed by fire.[8]

Like their predecessors in the 1820's, the members of the board of trustees were again forced, quite happily it may be supposed, to become large-scale real estate operators. This time the state was no longer pioneer soil. The work of the board was complicated by this fact, but it was also possible now to handle the important business with better methods than the older board had been able to devise.

Governor E. A. O'Neal lost no time in appointing Eugene A. Smith, A. C. Hargrove, and J. Burns Moore to serve as land commissioners for the selection under the grant. It was necessary to move quickly, for there was a land "boom" in Alabama and investors and speculators were rapidly taking up the most valuable mineral lands. By June, 1885, the commissioners' report was heard by the trustees.

Messrs. Smith, Hargrove, and Moore had tried first, they said, to determine what public lands would be most valuable to the University. They had soon discovered that there was little or no available farm and timber land as valuable as land in some of the mineral regions. Investigating further, they had found that the most valuable iron lands had already been taken up by private interests. That left the coal fields as the most promising possibility for University acquisition.

The commissioners had proceeded wisely after making this tentative decision. They had hired experts to test for coal, to trace coal developments, to bore "with a diamond drill." They had studied private investments and had looked into the prices being paid by corporations and individuals for coal land. Then, on the completion of this basic survey, they had procured from land officials certified plots in a large number of townships and had made their initial selections of about 30,000 acres of coal land.

All this they had done by November, 1884. They had intended to pause at that point and wait about a year before choosing the rest of the land. They would know then where some projected railroads would be built and would be able to choose land made valuable by its nearness to transportation facilities. However, at about that time, Congress passed not only the "Morgan Land Bill," offering Alabama mineral lands for public sale, but also the "Newell Bill," making them available for homestead entry. When new competitors came into the field, the commissioners decided that they should move quickly. They continued, therefore, to make other selections, completing them by January, 1885.

In May the Secretary of the Interior approved 42,253 acres proposed by the commissioners; approval on the other 3,827 acres was pending. The lands which the University thus acquired were in the Warrior and Cahaba coal fields in the counties of Walker, Jefferson, Shelby, Bibb, and Tuscaloosa.

With justifiable pride the commissioners pointed out that these lands contained some of the richest coal deposits in the state, and they cautioned the board to move slowly and carefully in disposing of its new wealth. It would be better to wait for prices to rise, as they were sure to do, than to throw the lands upon the market at the small prices they would bring before the region around them had been developed.[9]

While the commissioners had been at work, the trustees had been working astutely, also, to safeguard their new grant against any inroads which an unfriendly legislature might be tempted to make upon it. A committee appointed to study the matter reported its conviction that the act of Congress that gave the lands to the University could not properly be construed so as to permit the state legislature to recover, from the income on those lands, money advanced to the University. To make doubly sure that the $60,000 appropriated in 1883 could not be taken back by the State from land sales receipts, however, legislation was framed to constitute a relinquishment of any claims the State might have. The measure passed the lower house without opposition of any importance, but it was almost defeated in the senate. One senator tried to reverse the bill entirely by offering an amendment that the University be required to repay the $60,000 to the state out of land sales. Fortunately the amendment was voted down, and the bill in its original form passed on February 5, 1885.[10]

In that same legislative session regulations for the administration of the land grant were set up. Title to these lands was to be vested in the board of trustees, who should dispose of the University holdings in accordance with the purposes stated in the act of

Congress. Lands were to be sold for at least four dollars an acre, and at least one-half of the purchase money must be paid in cash at the time of the sale. The balance might be paid in installments. The treasurer of the state was to keep money from land sales in a separate account. When the purposes directly stated in the act had been fulfilled, proceeds from land sales were to be added to the University endowment. They might then be invested by the trustees in national and state securities, preference being given to the bonds of Alabama.[11]

The way was now clear for the operations which would convert the land into money. The trustees, meeting in June, 1885, deliberated carefully on the best procedures. They heard a detailed report from the committee which had met in Mobile in May to draw up a land policy. The committee had called in experts on Alabama mineral lands for consultation. The thorniest problem before it had been this: Was the boom in mineral lands at its height? If it was, the wisest course would be to offer the entire grant for sale at once, accepting a moderate price for all the holdings. But if land prices could be expected to continue rising, such a course would mean that the University would lose the possibility of considerable gain in the future. The committee satisfied itself that the speculative chances of land appreciation were good. They noted two things: a growing tendency to invest in mineral lands and "the high repute of Alabama as offering the best field for such investments." If the speculative risk looked good to private capital, it must be, reasoned the committee, equally good for the University:

If any syndicate could afford to buy the land and pay taxes and other expenses and hold them for a "rise," . . . certainly the University, which had no taxes to pay and would have little expense otherwise, can afford to keep all over the amount necessary or desirable to be sold to meet immediate needs.

They recommend, therefore, that the lands be sold only as money was needed for buildings and improvements. They estimated that $50,000 would meet such needs for the current year.[12]

The board accepted this recommendation. Then it established a committee on the University land grant to direct the work of the land commissioner. This committee was made up of three members elected annually by the board. Duties of the land commissioner were also defined at this time. He was to negotiate for the sale of lands, prevent trespasses, bring suits for the possession of lands unlawfully occupied, and rent or lease any lands which might properly and profitably be so handled. Mindful of the difficulties which laxity in record keeping had caused their predecessors in the early days of the University, the trustees also instructed the land commissioner to keep suitable maps showing all University lands, to bind these maps in permanent form, and to record on them when final payments had been made on lands sold. These maps were to be kept under the direction of the land committee, and that committee would have access always to the other records the commissioner was required to keep. He must keep a complete register of lands contracted or leased giving the names of all purchasers and lessees, the dates of sales or leases, the prices agreed upon, the times of payments, and all other information necessary to give a complete and accurate picture of the condition of the University's holdings. He must not sell any land for less than $4.00 an acre. When enough land had been sold to realize $50,000, the minimum price would rise to $10 an acre.[13]

Advertisements in newspapers announced that the land committee was ready to transact business.[14] The first buyer was the Pennsylvania Mobile Coal Company, which, on December 7, 1885, bought 800 acres in Walker County for $4800. By the following June, some 3,880 acres had been sold. The University was richer by $38,280, receiving an average of $9.85½ per acre.

Land Commissioner A. C. Hargrove, reporting to the board at that time, recommended that they revise their action of the previous year to allow the sale of another $50,000 worth of land. Prices for coal lands that were not close to lines of transportation probably would not rise rapidly in the near future, he said. And, meanwhile, the operation of the provisions of the Morgan Bill might force prices down to $1.20 an acre and hold these prices low for many years. He also expressed his opinion that the flat minimum of $10 an acre was too rigid. It would be better, he thought, to sell some of the land for $5.00 an acre than it would be to let some other tracts go at the $10 minimum. The board expressed its confidence in its commissioner by voting to permit him to sell lands to the amount of $100,000 and to make adjustments in the minimum price with the unanimous consent of the land committee.[15]

Commissioner Hargrove did not use the permission to adjust

the minimum in the following year. The price of the 4,587 acres sold in that period was high enough to bring the average price of each acre on the 7,967 acres disposed of to $11.53. The total proceeds from these sales had mounted to $91,843. Offers on some of the lands in Bibb County had run as high as $20 per acre. The land committee was confident that very little of the University land would bring less than $10 an acre; much of it could be sold for $20 or more. The Morgan Bill had not made as much trouble as they had feared it might. Demand for mineral lands was so great that the committee even felt that there was a possibility of price inflation. Therefore, it seemed advisable for the University to continue to sell while the market value of land was high.

The trustees showed their approval of this advice by authorizing the sale of yet more land, up to one-third of the University holdings. But they ruled that land must bring the $10 minimum except in very rare instances where small lots, detached from other lots, were sold. They ruled also that the unamious consent of the land committee must be obtained before any sales were made. That committee must inform itself fully about the location, character, and surroundings of the land in question before making a decision to sell.[16]

Another 2,623 acres were sold by June, 1888, all at $15 an acre. About one-fourth of the University holdings had been disposed of, and there were still some sales pending.[17] Then, as it was obvious that most of the desirable lands had been marketed, the board halted sales. Except for some parcels which clearly would never appreciate in value, better return to the University could be obtained, the trustees thought, by selling rights of way to railroad companies on such terms as seemed advantageous.[18]

The trustees instructed Commissioner Hargrove to proceed along these lines. Then they tossed into his lap a problem at least fifty or sixty years old. They told him to make a study of the leases on the land which was the original endowment of the University, to report whether these leases were all valid and binding, and to determine whether the University should and could regain possession of any of the leased land. For a number of years the standard leasing period on these holdings had been five years, until the decision had been made, in 1881, to allow some ten-year leases. It was presumed that such short term leases would be manageable. It was hoped that something could be done about lands that, according to earlier laws, had been leased for ninety-nine years. The trustees requested Mr. Hargrove to look up the meager records and make a report.[19]

Only the patient help of Professor Wyman enabled Commissioner Hargrove to carry out this assignment at all. When he came before the board in the summer of 1889, he told of the deplorable state of the old records. The record book had been so torn and mutilated during the carpetbag days that it was indecipherable. While Professor Wyman was digging through piles of old rubbish, he had found some valuable papers. But even with these in hand very little could be done. Among these papers, for example, was an old lease made by Edmund King. In 1824 King had bought about 188 acres in Shelby County, and in 1832 had converted his purchase into lease. He had paid no rent since 1839. It was unlikely that the University could recover anything from King after this long lapse of time. The same situation obtained in regard to all the old leases. They would be better forgotten.[20]

The boom of the 1880's had almost run its course by 1890. The trustees recognized that it would be better to lease the University lands during the period of falling prices. They formally recorded their policy that it was against the judgment of the board to sell at ruling prices more than one-third of the total mineral land grant, and they instructed Commissioner Hargrove to see whether he could not increase the University income by making royalty arrangements on coal mined from leased lands. He was authorized to go ahead with such leases and royalty agreements if it was found practical to do so.[21]

This decision was made in February, but no leases had been made by the following June. At that time the board with unanimous approval of the land committee, authorized the sale of an additional 10,000 acres.[22] At this meeting they also surveyed the whole record of the land grant. Of the 46,080 acres provided by the grant, some 12,889 acres had been sold for $159,938.43, an average of about $12.34 per acre, not including what had been received for timber, rights of way, and rents.[23] The University had completed its part of the land selection, but there still remained some parcels which had not been approved by the Secretary of the Interior. The final approvals on some of these tracts were not forthcoming until 1899.[24]

The timing of the grant had been fortunate for the University. A financial depression was spreading through the country in the early days of the 1890's. Land, even good Alabama mineral land, was a drug on the market. Only 40 acres were sold in the year 1890-1891. Inquiries had been made about other tracts, but the prices offered had been too low to consider. It was becoming hard to collect on past due land notes, and no applications for leases for mining purposes had come in during the year. At the beginning of 1890 the building fund was down to $14.88, and no help could be expected from the land fund. Many needed improvements had, of necessity, been postponed.[25] The fact remained, however, that the University had realized a rather handsome sum on its lands in the lush days of the 1880's.

In 1892 the board made another attempt to promote land sales. They told the land committee to sell enough to bring in $100,000, which might be added to the University endowment. The land committee, however, was not to reduce the University holdings below 20,000 acres, and it was not to sell for less than $10 an acre. It was all very well to vote to raise $100,000 by selling land; actually converting the land into money was another matter. Only 923 acres had been sold by June, 1892. The price of $15 an acre on this land had been good, but the total had been too small to invest.[26] The land committee was discouraged about prospects.[27] And the land commissioner took the occasion to rap the board for being so unwise as to attempt to realize $100,000 on land in a period of depression:

I deem it dangerous to make plans for the use of large sums of money, in the near future, with the expectation of selling lands at such prices as they should command.[28]

The picture was not all black, however, even at that meeting. The land committee said that arrangements for transporting coal to the Gulf had given new impetus to the coal industry. A large appropriation in the River and Harbor Bill would make possible the construction of three locks in the Warrior River near Tuscaloosa. If mines were then opened up along the upper Warrior River, there would be new demand for University land.[29] The University had already done its part to help this project along. It had voted in February to convey to the United States Government all the necessary lands and rights-of-way for dams, locks, and other works in Tuscaloosa County; it also had placed some two and one-half acres at the disposal of the federal government for a lock site and a quarry.[30]

By June, 1893, a total of 1,326 acres had been sold; this money was to go into the proposed $100,000 fund. Price per acre had been $15 for half the lot; $10 for the other half. The lands that were sold for $10 an acre had been scattered and were probably not worth more than they had brought. No attempt had been made to invest proceeds from the sales in bonds for the endowment fund.[31] A year later the land committee turned in a report of no sales. They were, however, making studies which would be useful when times improved.[32] Some 31,904 acres of the land grant remained in the possession of the University, but they seemed to have temporarily lost their convertibility into money needed for University development.

The hoped-for upswing began to appear in the middle of the decade. There were no land sales to report when the board met in June, 1895, but a tract of 600 acres in Bibb County had been placed on ten-year lease for mining purposes. The Cahaba Southern Mining Company agreed to pay a royalty of seven cents a ton on the coal mined there.[33] Within two years this royalty agreement was bringing in an income of $3600 a year.[34] A similar arrangement with the Aldrich Coal Mining Company was averaging $400 a month in 1898.[35] Small wonder that the trustees were enthusiastic about the revenue possibilities of such leases. They were eager for more, and they were also willing to make important concessions to railroads which might open up new mining possibilities.

A tract of land in Bibb County was sold to the Mobile & Ohio Railroad, in 1897, at the legal minimum price of $4.00 an acre. The projected railroad, the land committee reported, would be completed within a year, with cars running from Columbus, Mississippi, through Tuscaloosa, to Montgomery. The route would pass through some of the best coal lands the University owned and would greatly enhance the value of that land.[36] This policy of granting rights-of-way to railroads which might increase the value of University lands was continued in the following years; in 1902 the executive committee was authorized to grant such rights at its discretion.[37]

Thus, the federal land grant had proved a fruitful source of revenue for the University. From 1886 to 1900, the receipts for sale of land and timber and for rents and royalties had amounted to more than $200,000. This was an annual average supplement to the state appropriation of more than $14,000 a year. These additional funds enabled the trustees to erect Garland, Tuomey and Barnard halls and to make many other needed improvements.

The executive committee had taken over the duties of the land committee in February, 1896. Land Commissioner Col. A. C. Hargrove died in December, 1895, after ten years of service. The land committee had, thereupon, carried on without a commissioner for more than a year. Then, in March, 1897, C. B. Verner was chosen commissioner, and the board decided that a special committee on lands was no longer necessary.[38]

Two problems of land management engaged the attention of commissioner and trustees at this point. One had to do with the old problem of squatters on University lands; the other with a moot question whether the University should or should not "body up" its land by trading isolated parcels for tracts contiguous to University holdings.

In June, 1898, the board told Commissioner Verner to apprehend trespassers, to bring suits against them if the executive committee thought best. At any rate he was to get rid of them and prevent damage to University property.[39] The commissioner seems to have been a man of rare common sense. He worked out his own plan with the squatters, a plan that was both unique and effective. He simply made the trespassers regular University tenants, issuing formal leases to them at $1.00 a year. Then he impressed it firmly upon their minds that the University, as their landlord, had a right to expect that they would treat the land with respect, that they would cut no more wood than they needed for fuel, and that they would not increase the clearings. Seldom did the commissioner collect even the nominal $1.00. But, what was far more important, he had stopped almost completely the depredations which were impairing the land. The squatters cheerfully recognized the rights of their landlord when they knew that this landlord recognized their extra-legal rights as squatters.[40]

The problem of land consolidation was not so easily solved.

REBUILDING THE UNIVERSITY 355

Professor Eugene A. Smith, state geologist as well as faculty member, thought consolidation important. The executive committee so reported to the board in the summer of 1898, adding that they had not proceeded on Dr. Smith's advice because no advantageous offers had been received.[41] The policy of working toward such consolidation appears to have been followed for several years without much question. The Birmingham *Ledger* explained to the public the rationale of the policy:

Here in Alabama we have but begun the work of developing our coal lands and the university has but begun to lease its lands. All of the coal will be leased and taken out on better and better royalties.

To work these lands advantageously they must be contiguous for no one wants to lease small bodies of coal lands. For that reason the sales and exchanges and purchases should be made until the university lands are as well together as possible. Then the lease will come easier and more profitably.[42]

The soundness of arguments such as this was challenged in the June, 1900, board meeting;[43] and in May, 1905, land commissioner A. B. McEachin made a determined effort to reverse the policy. There was more profit, he insisted, in a number of small leases than in a very few large ones. The University, for example, was getting $50 minimum royalty per month from one lease of 40 acres; its income from leases of 320 acres was only $320. Evidently the executive committee did not agree with its commissioner, for they asked authority to continue exchanges. And the board sustained them.[44]

In 1899 the University almost allowed 4,400 acres of its most valuable mineral land to be sold for much less than its worth. Only the vigilance of the alumni kept the Sloss-Sheffield Company from owning all of it. The board policy of leasing rather than selling was well established by this time, but, in September, 1899, Governor Joseph F. Johnston called a special board meeting to consider the Sloss-Sheffield Company's proposal to buy this tract in Jefferson and Walker counties for $56,000. Five of the nine members of the board came to the meeting and quickly set their stamp of approval on the sale.[45] The alumni seriously objected. They felt that disposing of this valuable land at $12.50 an acre was "unfortunate, and not in harmony with the best interests of the University." They insisted that the sale should be vacated and set aside.[46] In a special meeting that December the board heard Dr. Eugene A. Smith express his opinion that the lands in question were worth $150 to $250 an acre. They then voted six to two to instruct the executive committee to take legal steps to annul the deed.[47]

The executive committee instructed Commissioner William C. Fitts to retain title to the land for the University.[48] Suit was brought to enjoin the terms of the sale from being carried out. The Sloss-Sheffield Company entered a motion in the chancery court to dismiss the bill for want of equity. This motion was overruled; the chancellor held that the bill did contain equity. The Sloss-Sheffield Company appealed. The Supreme Court, acting on April 1, 1901, sustaining the action of the lower court,[49] permitted the University to keep its land.

An adjustment with the Sloss-Sheffield Company closed this controversy. An exchange of land was negotiated. The Sloss-Sheffield Company received from the University 2,520 acres of the lands they wanted, but gave to the University an equal number of acres of other mining lands. On about 1,120 acres of the University's acquisition, only mineral rights were transferred. Therefore, the Sloss-Sheffield Company agreed to pay $3,920 in lieu of the transfer of surface rights and to give the University also the sum of $5000.[50]

By 1905 some 22,340 acres of the land grant of 1884 were still held by the University. Transfers had been made to consolidate these holdings and the University now had 1,040 acres in Tuscaloosa county; 1,140 acres in Bibb County; 640 acres in Shelby County; 9,360 acres in Jefferson County; and 10,160 acres in Walker County. Some of the richest coal seams in the state were located in these lands.[51] The leasing policy was working even better than had been expected. The first lease, made in 1895, had netted the University $32,453 by 1903, a revenue of about $54.09 an acre. Leases were being made on a ten-year basis, and royalties were running from five to eight cents per ton.[52] The gift from the government had indeed increased the University assets.

As soon as the General Assembly passed the appropriation bill in 1883, new buildings for the University became possible. With income from land sales also earmarked for development, the University was in a position to get old buildings repaired, new facilities constructed, and a whole list of modern improvements introduced

MANLY HALL

Manly Hall, built in 1886, is remembered by generations of former students as a dormitory and administration building. It was named for Rev. Basil Manly, the second president of the University. Like Woods, Garland, and Clark, Manly Hall was painted yellow from 1912 until 1949, when the paint was removed and the brick uncovered.

GARLAND HALL

Completed in 1888, named for President Landon C. Garland, this building provided quarters for the museum of natural history, the geological survey, and the trustees on the first floor, and dormitory rooms on the upper floors. Garland on the southeast, Manly on the southwest, Clark on the south, and Woods on the north from the "old quadrangle." In 1945-1949, Garland, like Woods and Manly halls, was renovated.

to the old campus. The decade of the 1880's rang with the sound of hammers. The University entered that period with a single, somewhat shabby building erected since the war. It emerged with five new halls, telephone, waterworks, and electricity, and with a "modernized" plant.

In the summer of 1883 the building committee went to work on plans.[53] By September brick-making had begun.[54] And at its November meeting the board accepted the building plan prepared by W. A. Freret of New Orleans.[55] In the spring of 1884, shortly before two buildings were scheduled for completion, the question of names came up in a trustees' meeting. They decided that the first post-war building, completed in 1868, should bear the name of the University's first president: it should be called Alva Woods Hall. The new west-wing building would take the name of the second president; it would be Manly Hall. For the central building, however, the trustees decided to honor one of their contemporaries, Willis G. Clark, who had been instrumental in getting aid from the legislature and who had worked hard on plans for the building program. Clark Hall would commemorate such services. The east-wing building, when erected, was to be called Garland Hall, in honor of the third president of the University.[56]

The memorial stone for Clark Hall was laid on May 5, 1884, "a day ever to be remembered in the history of the University of Alabama." Exactly fifty-two years before, the cornerstone of old Franklin Hall had been put in place. The blend of memory and hope which characterized the present occasion surely justified the emotion that made the chronicler of the event feel inadequate and helpless to express his thoughts:

Here is a subject on which a philosopher might express deep thoughts; a poetical person might here write a poem; an eloquent person might here wax of the event . . . partly because others have done it before us, and partly because we, like they, would prove inadequate to the attempt, and would do the occasion injustice, Therefore, we simply give the order of the exercises. . . .[57]

Bad weather early in the evening had curtailed plans for a great procession, but it must have cleared sufficiently to allow a formidable program of speech making. The head of each University organization made a speech. The senior captains of the cadets spoke for the corps. The president of the Alumni Society spoke for the graduates; the president of the University for the faculty; the governor of Alabama for the trustees.

Then the ceremonies began. Professor Wyman slowly placed in the box to be sealed in the cornerstone the articles and documents which would preserve the memory of the day for generations yet unborn. Mr. Clark, at his side, described each article as Professor Wyman put it in its place:

1. Historical sketch of the University—by W. S. Wyman.
2. A report of measures taken by the Board of Trustees and Society of Alumni to enlarge the University—the success of their efforts in that direction and the progress made thus far.
3. A parchment copy of the Act of the General Assembly appropriating $60,000 to the University for the purposes stated. The act is written on parchment and bears the great seal of the State.
4. The roll of Alumni of the University, comprising the names of all the graduates from the first commencement to the present time.
5. A copy of the Act of Congress, known as the Morgan Bill, donating 46,080 acres of the public lands in Alabama for the uses of the University.
6. Letter from John A. Foster, expressing regret at his inability to be present and explaining the cause of his absence.
7. Letter of Hon. Wm. H. Forney to Hon. N.H.R. Dawson in relation to the bill donating lands to the University.
8. Report of the Superintendent of Education for the State of Alabama for the year ending September 3rd, 1883.
9. Blank diploma of the University with the signatures of all the officers present at the laying of the Memorial Stone.
10. Boat song by Samuel Minturn Peck, of Tuskaloosa, dedicated to Mrs. Mary C. O'Neal.
11. A silver dime taken from the corner stone of Franklin Hall of the old University, laid May 5th, 1832, just fifty-two years ago—date, 1821.
12. Copy of present laws and regulations of the University.
13. A copy of the University *Monthly* for May, 1884.
14. A silver dollar coined in 1799, presented by J.H. Fitts & Co. Also a nickel coined in 1884.
15. A programme of the Memorial exercises.
16. A copper plate with the names of the present Sophomore engineering class engraved upon it.

The governor and Mr. Clark laid the stone, with its treasure load, in its place. Then the Hon. H. C. Armstrong, superintendent of education, made "a few very appropriate remarks . . . in behalf chiefly of the large crowd of ladies present." And the exercises were closed, as they had begun, with prayer by the Reverend J. S. Dill. Colonel Dawson had presided at the ceremonies, and Chisholm's famous orchestra had furnished the music.[58]

Weather slowed up the work on the buildings as it had threatened to slow up the cornerstone ceremonies. The winter of 1884-1885 was cold and wet. In February some of the freshly laid upper walls fell to the ground, carrying with them expensive terra-cotta work. Although the weather was partly responsible for this disaster, the contractor, too, was at fault. He had not taken steps to protect his freshly laid wall; he had not even put a plank across it to keep the mortar from washing out. The trustees pointed out this fact to him when they refused his claim that he should be paid for the crumbled wall as well as for its replacement.[59] Despite difficulties both Manly Hall and Clark Hall were finished by June, 1886. These halls had cost the University $70,959.73.[60]

An immediate start on a third new building was authorized that summer.[61] It was to bear the name of Landon C. Garland, who had served the University faithfully as professor and president and commandant.

Garland Hall, finished in March, 1888, cost $22,550.[62] Two other halls being constructed on the campus that spring were made possible by the revenues coming in from the sales of University land. The trustees did not name these two until a year later. Then they honored two great professors of the old University: Michael Tuomey and F. A. P. Barnard.[63] Tuomey Hall was completed in May, 1888, at a cost of $10,150.[64] Barnard Hall was just about completed when the trustees held their June meeting that year; it had cost $9,574.[65]

These changes in the campus landscape in the lush days of the 1880's were by no means the only alterations those years brought. As new buildings rose, the shabbiness of the old ones was accentuated. The trustees took note of this fact in the summer of 1885. There was Alva Woods Hall, new only in its name. It had, presumably, had some repairs in 1876, when an appropriation of $700 had been voted to fix up that building and the President's Mansion. But apparently the money had run out before a thorough job had been done:

The appearance of the front walls which have never been painted is certainly very bad and is daily growing worse and contrasts greatly with the new building . . . the floor and joists of the front stoop in every story are rotten and decaying and the flagstones on the ground are so badly worn as to need replacing at once.

The board voted $300 to correct this situation.[66]

They did not, however, seriously consider the needs of the President's Mansion until 1888. By that time the old building, which had survived the fire, was in dire need of attention. The front gallery of the second floor had sunk three or four inches because the brick arch on which it rested was crumbling. Plaster had fallen in a number of places and the outside stairway needed new iron railings. An appropriation of $500 was made to take care of these repairs.[67]

There is no indication that the board found it advisable to spend money on a third building, the Fowler House, whose condition was the subject of discussion in several board meetings. The quartermaster had been allowed to manage this house since 1876. He had been allowed to put half the rent he derived from it into repairs that year. After that, rent money from the Fowler House had gone into the University fund.[68] In 1885 the trustees, noting that the property was in bad condition, remarked:

> The Fowler House is rapidly decaying and before a great while will not be habitable.[69]

The rapid expansion of the University plant was making such makeshift quarters as the Fowler House of minor importance.

New conveniences for the students and faculty were added during this period; some had come even earlier. A bowling alley—almost the first recognition the board had given to the need for the student sports activities—had been built in 1879.[70] There had been a brisk little squabble over this affair, for, when the work was finished, the trustees attempted to withhold $20 from the $250 they had agreed to pay contractor Maapen, contending that he had not lived up to the terms of his contract. But when Maapen threatened to sue, the money was finally paid.[71] Fire protection may have been installed before the '80's began. In the summer of 1879 the board had appointed a committee to "inquire into the propriety" of equipping the University building with "not less than three nor more than five" of the well-known "Babcock's fire extinguishers."[72]

But in the middle of the decade of land-sale prosperity, the trustees gave the institution really fascinating additions. Some were relatively small: in 1882, the $75 organ, which was so eagerly welcomed by the choir and glee club;[73] in 1887, the flagpole which went up over Clark Hall;[74] and after 1875, the fireproof vault in which important records were kept.[75] Other additions were of such nature that they must have greatly simplified the business of living on the campus.

In 1887 a laundry for use of the students was opened; it was hailed as a great convenience. The following summer the townspeople were offered the use of its facilities during vacation. The trustees said that the machinist would be on the job any way, and the laundry should not stand idle.[76] Three other items of living convenience were dealt with in the June, 1888, meetings. The board made an outright appropriation to build a barn and dairy so that the University could have its own supply of butter, milk, and cheese; some $350 was set aside for the construction of the buildings and another $450 to buy cows.[77] The board referred to its building committee a recommendation that a mess hall and kitchen be built at a cost of not more than $5000.[78] And the board recommended that steps be taken to employ a University tailor, a University shoemaker, and a University barber, who would, as members of the regular staff of the institution, set up shops on campus and serve the students and the faculty.[79]

Improvements on the grounds were also made in this period. Some $300 was set aside in 1884 to make a good sidewalk from the University to the city of Tuscaloosa and to transplant shade trees.[80] A new fence was put around the grounds in 1887, the trustees appropriating $500 for this purpose. Because iron was too expensive, the fence was to be made of wood, but the plan was to replace one side of it with iron fencing each year.[81] The trustees said that their purpose in building this fence was to mark out the boundary lines of University property. That it had other aims, too, is indicated in a resolution which the board passed that same session: that something had to be done to keep the livestock from running at large on the campus.[82] The land commissioner, acting under instructions of the executive committee, also made his contribution to campus improvements by buying up properties contiguous to the University grounds. In 1890 the 29 acres immediately back of Woods Hall had been acquired for $2000;[83] later, the "Leatherwood, Quinn, and Donoho property" would come into University possession for a total of $1,950, leaving only one improved lot outside the University holdings.[84] The commissioner reported that this lot could be bought for $350.

A good deal of attention was given to sanitation. Drainage pipes were laid from the new buildings in 1887, and the "defective sanitary arrangements" of Woods Hall had been corrected. The board noted, at its June, 1887, meeting, that this undertaking had seemed so important to the health of the students that the board had been circularized by letter between regular meetings to get the needed authorization.[85] Even earlier than that a special committee, appointed in 1883, had done what it could to abate the nuisance of "an offensive odor" caused by the open sewer from the Asylum. The committee had conferred with the superintendent of the Asylum and had asked that the sewer be covered. It had also superintended the removal from the University grounds, to "a convenient place on the stream immediately below the bath house," of the privy whose "offensive exhalations" were thought to be "productive of sickness."[86]

The University was becoming modernized, the old primitive ways were disappearing. The most interesting notes in the record of the trustees' deliberations on University development during the period have to do with this modernization.

Gas was probably installed on the campus around 1877. In that year the trustees asked a special committee to investigate the possibilities of installation. The committee was to find out if gas should be piped in from the Asylum, if it should be made of coal, or if the process of converting rosin to gas should be tried. The committee thought the rosin process was worth attempting. They recommended that, for a start, pipes be run into the laboratory, the mess hall, and perhaps into other first-floor rooms of Woods Hall, at a cost of about $1,500. Extensions could be made later.[87] After the committee made a further investigation, they said that the rosin process was not desirable. There was danger that it would gum up pipes and burners, and it would probably not produce enough heat for laboratory purposes. The committee finally decided that it would be wiser to get the gas from the Asylum, after all. The trustees concurred with this judgment.[88]

By 1888 the board had moved from the gas to the electric era. They had before them that June various proposals from the committee that had been studying the matter, and, before they adjourned, they had appropriated $5000 for the installation of electric lights and had given the committee permission to secure power from a local company as soon as such a company was formed.[89]

The first telephone appeared on the campus in 1883. It was a battery-run affair, with a little crank to help its operation. The trustees proudly set aside $25 for the expense of operating it during the year 1883-1884.[90] The telephone proved its expansive powers quickly. The trustees were shocked to note that their telephone bill had doubled in a single year. They had to vote $70 for the service in their next meeting.[91]

In 1887 the trustees were negotiating with the Tuscaloosa and Castle Hill Land and Manufacturing Company, which wanted a right of way through University property for a streetcar line. The request was granted on condition that the company pay all expenses incurred in building the line and that the land assigned could revert to the University whenever the trustees wanted it back.[92]

Earlier boards had considered the problems of water supply and heating. In 1879 the trustees had asked the president to find out if reservoirs built on top of Woods Hall would be adequate to give the cadets an abundance of pure water, and also to get estimates on the cost of building such reservoirs and the pipes to distribute the water through the building. There should be, said the board, sufficient facilities for the "winter baths" which were so essential to the health of the boys. The president should also, the trustees said, look into the possibilities for heating the building with steam and warm air. Perhaps a furnace could be run in connection with the cooking range.[93]

Perhaps nothing came of this study. The trustees were still concerned with the problem of water supply when they met in June, 1887, so much concerned, in fact, that they directed the building committee to inspect the new waterworks the Asylum was building. The University might be able to get a water supply there. The building committee thought that this would be an unsatisfactory plan; besides, the University had money enough to build its own water works. The trustees, in agreement with this idea, voted $8000 for this purpose, stipulating that bath rooms and a steam laundry be built in connection with this project.[94]

By the time the flow of money from the new lands began to dry up, temporarily, in the early 1890's, the University had brought itself beautifully up to date. Perhaps it was this very fact which necessitated in the 1890's curtailments that the enthusiastic alumni found difficult to accept. Their alma mater still needed improvements. If land sales were slow, then it was the responsibility of the legislature to meet the need and meet it generously. By 1896 the Society of Alumni had launched another lobbying effort, to increase the University fund to a point where it would yield more than the $24,000 annual interest which had been forthcoming for some thirty-six years. They had appointed J. H. Fitts, treasurer of the University for a quarter of a century, as their chairman and spokesman. They had invited, and received the coöperation of a committee from the board of trustees.[95]

Chairman Fitts' report, entitled *An Appeal from The Alumni of the University of Alabama To The Legislature of the State, for an Equitable Adjustment of the Claim of their Alma Mater Against the State of Alabama,* reopened a quarrel which had been started in the days of the old University, long before the Civil War.

He compared the endowment and annual income of the University of Alabama with that of other state universities, using figures which had appeared in the New York *Evening Post* in 1890. Only one institution was lower in the list than the University of Alabama, and that institution had not yet converted its public lands into money.

He drew a sad picture of the way in which the University had been hampered and crippled since its birth. It had lacked essential money to provide buildings, and to form and develop professional schools. Because of these handicaps, it was a university in name only. Only the law and engineering departments worked in the graduate field which was a proper area for a University. The University of Alabama was little more than a college.

In order to show how this deplorable state of affairs had come about, Mr. Fitts turned back the pages of history at this point and reviewed the whole record of the University's original land grant. The state government, he declared, had by "gross negligence and misappropriation" cheated its state University out of at least $2,-000,000. The "arbitrary" settlement which was reached in 1848 was "an attempt of the Legislature of Alabama to play the part of the unjust step-mother to an institution solemnly entrusted to its guardianship and care" when Alabama became a state. The University had been "struggling for a bare existence" at that time; threats of repudiating the University debt were being made "and the policy of doing so strongly advocated by some." The trustees had been forced by circumstances to relinquish all the other claims of the University, including those based on losses due to relief laws, and to accept the compromise which gave it $250,000 of the $300,000 due from the State Bank. The agreement had been made under coercion; it was never just. Although the legislature had increased the endowment fund to $300,000 in 1860, that had been done only "under the incentive to engraft a military department upon the institution."

The combined appropriations of the General Assembly and the federal government for the new Agricultural and Mechanical College exceeded that of the University. In 1900 that institution was receiving an annual income of over $50,000, though it had been in existence less than thirty years. The University of Alabama, after sixty-nine years of service to the state, was drawing only $29,000.

The appeal closed with an impassioned plea that the General Assembly repair the great wrongs that previous legislatures had done the University: that the debt of $2,000,000 be at last acknowledged, that bonds to this amount, bearing 3 per cent interest, be issued, that justice be done at last.[96]

The General Assembly could not ignore this appeal from a large and influential body of citizens, especially a body which had, less than a score of years earlier, enforced its will on the legislators of that day. A commission of three members was set up to make an investigation of the charges. The governor appointed John J. Mitchell; the trustees, James W. Lapsley; the Society of the Alumni, Eugene A. Smith.[97]

By a vote of two to one, the commission exonerated the state from any responsibility for University troubles. Their report declared that the relief act of 1834 had been designed to encourage purchasers to pay for otherwise forfeited land at an equitable valuation; it was "wise and proper legislation." The losses suffered by the University had been due to "general depreciation in value, rather than . . . favoritism in the Legislature." The wisdom of the men who made those decisions many years ago, the commission added, was not to be questioned lightly. They had acted on information no longer completely available, and "the settlements themselves are very persuasive of the justice of what was then solemnly agreed upon." The state was not, therefore, in the opinion of the majority of the commissioners, "justly or equitably indebted to the University in any amount" above the recognized endowment fund.[98]

Governor J. F. Johnston transmitted this report to the General Assembly. He called the attention of the lawmakers to the high caliber of the commissioners:

Their character and ability, and the research and labor given by them to this subject entitles their judgment and conclusions to the confidence of every citizen. . . .

He noted that the report was not unanimous, that a minority report had been filed. He expressed surprise that neither report had made a point of the fact that the state had, for some time, been paying eight per cent interest on the University fund "when it could have floated bonds and have paid off the principal of the debt at a cost in interest of one half that paid."

The governor found the report exceedingly valuable. He commented on the "thoroughness of research, clearness of statement, and correctness of conclusion" which it displayed:

It shows that the State has never betrayed the trust reposed in it and has been just and liberal to the University and frees that institution from asserting any claims against the State other than those that appeal to the highest and most patriotic impulses of the people.

Then he advised the General Assembly to have the report printed in the journal of one house in order that it might "be permanently preserved." And he reminded the lawmakers that when they set up the commission to investigate the alumni charges, they had provided that half their compensation should be paid by the state and half by the University, but had failed to set the amount of this compensation. That matter should be attended to without delay.[99]

REBUILDING THE UNIVERSITY

To all of this Eugene A. Smith, representative of the alumni on the commission, vigorously dissented. He had been connected with the University for thirty-eight years and he had heard too many reports on the early mismanagement of University funds to be willing to whitewash those early lawmakers as his colleagues had done. To say that all the acts of the legislature bearing on the University had come up to the full measure of justice and equity would be, he remarked, attributing to that body qualities "more than mortal." He disagreed with his colleagues' findings in regard to the old relief acts; they were, on the face of them, designed for the relief of purchasers, not to help the University. When the University had accepted the settlements of 1848, they had done so under the pressure of necessity. But they had questioned the justice of the settlement even then:

That these settlements were accepted in good faith by the then authorities of the University, we have recorded proof that they were even at that time not considered equitable by all friends of the University we have also convincing evidence; that they have been accepted by all, in succeeding years, is negatived by the very existence of the present commission.[100]

The General Assembly, quite understandably, accepted the majority report and did not increase the endowment fund. But they may have felt Professor Smith's disapproving presence at their elbow, for, even while the controversy was going on, they voted a special grant to the University—$10,000 for 1898; $10,000 for 1899.[101]

When the new state constitution was adopted, in 1901, the University made one more small but significant gain. The new law provided that income on the University fund should be at least $36,000. It was expressly stated that this amount should not be decreased even if it were found advisable to discontinue the military system.[102]

The University thus entered the twentieth century with slightly better financial position than it had had during the previous thirty years. But increased income was always more than offset by increased expense as the University forged ahead to take its rightful place in the world of education.

The University was forced to operate on meager resources throughout the entire period, 1866-1901. The average annual state appropriation was $24,000.[103] Beginning in 1886, there was an average yearly supplement of $14,000 derived from lands. In 1897 the General Assembly made an additional appropriation of $10,000 a year, for the next four years.

The accompanying table shows the principal expenditures for the period.

THE RECOMMENDED EXPENDITURES, 1876-1901

Year	President's Salary	FACULTY RECOMMENDATIONS Other Administrative Expense	Number of Professors	Combined Salaries	LAW Number of Professors	Combined Salaries	Commandant
1876-1877	$2,750	..	6	$13,500	2	$1,000	$1,600
1877-1878	2,500	..	7	12,600	2	1,000	1,400
1878-1879	2,500	..	9	13,100	2	1,000	1,600
1879-1880*	2,500	$1,600.00	9	13,400	2	1,300	1,400
1880-1881	2,500	2,095.00	10	15,200	2	1,300	..
1881-1882	2,500	2,520.00	9	14,800	2	1,300	..
1882-1883	2,500	4,863.55	7	14,900	2	1,300	..
1883-1884	2,500	5,383.20	10	16,800	2	1,300	..
1884-1885	2,500	3,540.20	11	18,500	2	1,300	..
1885-1886	2,500	2,876.00	13	18,600	2	1,300	..
1886-1887	2,500	2,389.15	11	17,400	2	1,400	..
1887-1888	2,500	2,749.00	11	17,400	2	1,400	..
1888-1889	2,500	2,459.25	12	17,000	2	1,400	300
1889-1890	2,500	2,694.90	14	17,400	2	1,700	900
1890-1891	2,500	3,422.00	14	19,500	2	1,700	1,500
1891-1892	2,500	3,585.00	15	20,150	2	1,700	..
1892-1893	2,500	4,225.68	10	18,000	2	1,700	..
1893-1894	2,500	11,019.06	12	18,800	2	1,700	..
1894-1895	2,500	9,627.96	12	18,450	2	1,700	300
1895-1896	2,500	11,246.53	12	18,450	2	1,700	800
1896-1897	2,500	10,815.78	12	18,450	3	1,900	300
1897-1898	2,500	13,078.75	12	20,300	2	3,100	300
1898-1899	2,500	8,466.41	12	21,000	2	3,100	675
1899-1900	2,500	14,828.93	11	19,800	3	4,100	675
1900-1901	3,000	8,081.43	14	23,400	2	4,500	1,200

* Figures off $450

THE RECOMMENDED EXPENDITURES, 1876-1901

Quarter-master and Steward	Chemical and Philosophic	Library Expenditures	Equipment and Supplies Purchases	Maintenance and Improvements	Total
$1,500	$1,000	$ 550	..	$2,100.00	$24,000.00
1,300	200	..	..	..	19,000.00
1,400	..	..	..	..	19,600.00
1,500	100	200	$ 75.00	1,215.00	23,290.00
1,000	250	400	1,425.76	1,150.00	25,320.76
..	200	400	189.00	950.00	22,859.00
..	300	450	475.00	200.00	24,988.55
..	350	100	125.00	1,800.00	28,358.20
..	100	400	..	750.00	27,090.20
1,500	100	400	60.00	1,800.00	29,136.00
1,500	100	400	37.70	1,100.00	26,826.85
1,500	100	1,500	..	1,481.50	28,630.50
1,500	100	500	450.00	600.00	26,809.25
1,500	..	1,800	1,800.00	800.00	31,094.90
1,500	..	500	5,000.00	5,975.00	41,597.00
1,500	300	1,500	..	600.00	31,835.00
1,500	..	500	5,400.00	6,100.00	39,925.68
1,500	..	1,500	..	2,750.00	39,769.06
1,500	..	500	..	1,550.00	36,127.96
1,500	..	1,000	22.00	2,743.89	39,962.42
1,500	..	500	95.00	1,282.30	37,342.08
1,500	..	500	250.00	1,300.00	42,828.75
..	..	500	1,450.00	1,860.00	39,551.41
1,800	..	500	350.00	5,471.36	50,025.29
..	300	500	2,227.93	3,710.00	46,919.36

The records of the expenditures of all departments of the University between 1868 and 1876 were so incomplete that an accurate estimate of these expenditures is impossible. During that period the University was under a board of regents consisting of carpetbaggers and scalawags, whose members were elected by popular vote, and, for some reason, failed to keep an accurate system of records.

In the foregoing table an analysis of the recommended expenditures for the University (not including those for buildings) during the years 1876-1901 reveals several interesting things. First of all, the president's salary is surprisingly stable. From 1877 to 1900 it did not change at all. In 1900 it was increased from $2500 to $3000. Other administrative expenses varied more than this; however, up until 1893 they remained at a fairly consistent low figure, varying between $1600 and $5400. In 1893 they jumped to $11,019 and thereafter remained in a much higher bracket than before, never going lower than $5000, and usually being well above this low figure. The most interesting point about faculty salaries is that in the early part of this period the law professors were paid very low salaries, being expected to supplement their earnings by their Tuscaloosa law practices. It is also interesting to notice the increased number of faculty members, from the low figure of eight in 1876-1877 to a high of sixteen in 1901. The combined salaries of faculty members increased in almost the same proportion as the number of faculty members. This increase shows, however, that faculty members were only slightly better paid in 1901 than they had been in 1876.

An interesting "sign of the times" is the treatment of the commandant's salary. In the early part of the period he was considered to be an especially important person on the campus, something of a "commander-in-chief" and, as such, was set apart from the rest of the faculty and paid from a separate fund—as was, for instance, the president. Later, as the military functions of the University became less and less important, the commandant was put on a more or less equal basis with the rest of the faculty and his salary came out of the same fund as theirs. The quartermaster and steward received the same treatment, probably for much the same reasons.

The library expenditures follow a rather stable pattern. In 1876-1877 the amount was $500, and nothing was spent for years. In 1880 the appropriation was apparently set at $400, at which figure it remained until 1888, except for two years. In 1888 the library appropriation seems to have been raised to $500, where it remained until 1901. During these years four exceptionally large appropriations were made, ranging from $1000 to $1800, otherwise the $500 appropriation was the rule.

The appropriations for "Equipment & Supplies" are quite varied. The increases and decreases appear to be without any particular pattern and are undoubtedly the result of particular needs

REBUILDING THE UNIVERSITY

at particular times. These appropriations reach a "high" for the period in 1892-1893 at $5400, and a "low" in 1895-1896 at $22, if we except the several years during which no appropriations were made at all.

The appropriations for "Maintenance & Improvement" show little change over the years, remaining, in general between $1000 and $5000 per year. The year in which this appropriation was the lowest was 1881-1882; the year 1899-1900 was the highest.

If plotted on a chart, the total expenditures for each year would show a steady upward trend, in spite of ups and downs along the way. The peak year for total expenditures is 1899-1900, with expenditures of $47,000 shown. This is a ninety-eight per cent increase over the base year of this period, 1876-1877, when the total expenditures were $23,950. Four of the first five years following this base year showed decreases in expenditures: 1877-1878 showed a twenty-two per cent decrease (the lowest total expenditure during the period 1876-1901); 1878-1879, an eighteen per cent decrease; 1879-1880, a four per cent decrease; and 1881-1882, a five per cent decrease. However, 1880-1881 showed a five per cent increase. After 1881-1882, expenditures were never lower than the base year (1876-1877) and, as we have noted, climbed steadily.

The study of income and expenses leaves one wondering more than ever how so much progress was possible with such slender resources. The University drew heavily on the wealth of loyalty it possessed in its faculty and its students in those days when money was not easily obtained.

CHAPTER XVI

The Schools and Their Teachers

WHILE the trustees labored to perform faithfully their duties as stewards of University funds and University land, and while they were developing a campus which should be an adequate setting for their institution, the faculty were building the educational foundations which were fully as important. They were a small group of men, almost never, during this period, more than a dozen strong. They were inadequately paid and greatly overburdened. They had not only most of the problems which still trouble educators today but also many problems which have now disappeared from campus life. Even so, they made up in zeal for the limitations of circumstance, and they moved the University forward so that its intellectual life kept pace at least with its physical growth.

When the reorganized University opened in 1871, work was offered in eleven independent schools, in addition to a normal department. The following year these schools were grouped under the general designation of The Academic Department. The normal school and the newly organized school of law became the nucleus of the Department of Professional Education. A third department had catalogue status that year and the next, but apparently never went into actual operation. The aims of the Preparatory Department were set forth in the *Catalogue:*

This Department, which has not yet been organized, is intended to prepare boys thoroughly for entrance upon any of the courses in the Academic Department. An introductory class will be formed, if necessary, of young men over fifteen years of age who are not fully prepared in all the studies required for admission into the Bachelor of Arts course.[1]

The division into academic and professional departments continued until 1898, when, following the educational trend of the times, the courses were re-aligned in two large classifications: the College, where undergraduate work led to degrees of B.A. or B.S.; and the University, where academic work on the graduate level and work in the professional schools led to advanced and specialized degrees.

In the Academic Department of 1872 students were offered work in the following subjects: Latin, Greek, modern languages, English language and literature, moral philosophy, pure mathematics, applied mathematics, chemistry, geology and mineralogy, natural history, military engineering and political economy. As the years went by, the names of some of these subjects were changed and there were a few additions and a few consolidations; however, the emphasis on classics, philosophy, mathematics, and science remained strong throughout the period.

The schools of Latin and Greek remained nominally separate and distinct all through the thirty years, but there was a natural interchange of teachers as need arose. Latin was Professor William Stokes Wyman's special province. From 1871 until his retirement he handled practically all the courses given, with little more than tutorial assistance except during the periods when he was filling in between presidential regimes. At first he was professor of Greek also, but after 1875 he was willing to turn that work over to others. Warfield Creath Richardson held the chair of Greek from 1876 to 1877. John C. Calhoun, who took over at that time, served for twenty years. William B. Saffold was in the chair when the century ended. He was an alumnus and M.A. of the University, and he had received his Ph.D. from Johns Hopkins just before coming back to his alma mater to teach.

Professor William A. Parker directed the school of modern languages from his arrival on the campus until well into the twentieth century. He, also, was a son of the University of Alabama, a graduate in the year 1855, an M.A. three years later. The only change in the organization in this department came in 1898 when it was divided into the School of German and the School of Romance Languages.

The chair of English language and literature belonged to that stalwart pillar of the University, Professor Benjamin F. Meek. He, as well as his colleague, Professor Wyman, could remember the old days on the campus before the war. He received his A.B. in 1854, his A.M. in 1858. He had, no doubt, worked with young tutor Wyman in those days and had served under young Professor Wyman as a teacher of ancient languages from 1863 to 1865. Until his death, in 1899, Meek handled the work in English practically single-handed. After that, Professor Charles H. Barnwell, South Carolina College, A.B. and A.M., Harvard Ph.D., began his comparably long term of service on the University of Alabama faculty.

A war-time alumnus, Professor Eugene A. Smith, gave the School of Geology and Mineralogy both continuity and distinction. Smith had graduated from the University in 1862, and he had traveled farther than his colleagues for his graduate study; he had received his Ph.D. from Heidelberg in 1868. The year after he came back to his alma mater to teach geology, he married Jennie Garland, daughter of the University's wartime president, Landon C. Garland. That made him brother-in-law to one of the presidents under whom he worked, for President Lewis had also married one of the Garland daughters. Dr. Smith combined his teaching with service as state geologist during a large part of the time when he was on the University faculty. The School of Natural History was combined with Dr. Smith's department in 1874. Prior to that time the courses in natural history had been taught by Dr. Algernon S. Garnett, surgeon of the cadet corps. Warfield Creath Richardson (1877-1878) and William B. Phillips (1890-1892) conducted some of the work in mineralogy during these years. The "natural history" appendage to the name of the school was dropped in 1891.

In contrast with these four schools where personnel was stable and where courses developed rather than shifted, the other schools of the University's academic department underwent many alterations during the period and were served by many different teachers.

Some of the most interesting changes took place in the school of moral philosophy. The very evolution of its name is significant. In 1876 it became the school of mental and moral philosophy; in 1879, the school of mental and moral phiolsophy and political economy; in 1888, the school of history and philosophy; and in 1899, the school of history and political economy. Two fields of study to become of increasing importance in the modern university curriculum thus slipped into the University of Alabama almost by a back door. Traditionally, the chair of moral philosophy had been occu-

REBUILDING THE UNIVERSITY

pied by the president, but only presidents Lupton and Smith continued this tradition after the reorganization of 1871. Professors Telfair Hodgson (1871-1872) and J. H. Foster (1872-1874) taught the work in the early days of the period. When history became an important subject in the school, Col. Thomas C. McCorvey, who had been commandant of the cadets ever since his graduation from the University in 1873, was given the job of teaching it. He had more than military qualifications for the position. In the fifteen years since his graduation he had added to his Bachelor of Philosophy degree, the degrees of Bachelor of Laws and Master of Arts. Through his marriage to Netta Tutwiler in 1880, he belonged to one of the early families of the University. He remained in the University family until he had rounded out a full half-century of service.

Mathematics also showed interesting and significant changes. The schools of pure and applied mathematics were combined in 1872. Work formerly offered as applied mathemaics was included in the program of the new school of natural philosophy in 1873. Astronomy, added to the school of mathematics program for a two-year period between 1874 and 1876, drifted over to the newer school after that; it became the school of natural philosophy and astronomy. By 1897 "Philosophy" was dropped here also. The school entered the twentieth century as the school of physics and astronomy. Four professors worked in mathematics: David L. Peck (1871-1872), Hampton S. Whitfield (1872-1878), William James Vaughn (1878-1882), and Thomas W. Palmer (1883-1904). Vaughn, who had been an alumnus of the old University and a member of the pre-war faculty, and his fellow alumnus Hampton S. Whitfield taught astronomy and physics as well as mathematics. Whitfield had been superintendent of schools in Tuscaloosa County before he joined the faculty in 1872. The real Nestor of the School of natural philosophy, however, was Joshua H. Foster, graduate of the class of 1839, A.M. in 1842. Having been at several times mathematics tutor in the old University, he came back in 1872 and stayed for twenty years. He was successively professor of moral philosophy (1872-1874), professor of natural philosophy (1874-1892), and professor of astronomy (1876-1892). He was seventy-three years old when he retired. Professor George M. Edgar carried the work from then until 1898; Dr. Herbert A. Sayre began his teaching that year.

Chemistry, which had been one of the proudest departments

in the old University, appears to have been less well served in the new. The work in this field was handled for the most part by tutors and by professors whose major interest lay elsewhere. President Lupton taught chemistry from 1871 to 1874; Geologist Eugene Smith from 1874 to 1890; Mineralogist Phillips from 1890 to 1892; Metallurgists Pickel and Persons during the rest of the period.

In 1872 the school of military engineering became the school of military science and then dropped from the list of schools of the Academic Department until 1892, when it reappeared as the school of military science and tactics. Military science was taught, however, all through the period, but it was taught on the drill field as often as in the classroom.

The faculty and trustees experimented to some extent in adding new schools as well as in combining the old. There was a School of Mining and Metallurgy, authorized as early as 1887, but not actually staffed until Dr. James M. Pickel was appointed in 1892. The work in mining and metallurgy continued, but the identity of the school was lost. Augustus Persons succeeded Dr. Pickel, teaching the work in the School of Chemistry. The mining courses were transferred to Dr. Eugene Smith. In 1899 a School of Pedagogy and Psychology was established, with the hope that it would attract more mature students to the University.[2] There was a move, which apparently came to nothing, to establish a chair of elocution.[3]

The most significant additions, beyond those which came through the evolutionary process, were the Department of Physical Culture and the chair of biology.

The first of these innovations came into existence in 1889. The building of the University waterworks about that time probably made it possible for the first time to equip a gymnasium with "approved contrivances for physical exercise and development, also with locker rooms, hot and cold water, shower and sponge baths." But the University authorities were not content with having a place where students could exercise. They set up examinations and classes to see that they did so. Physical examinations were given at the beginning of each session:

The strength of the muscular system, to a certain degree, is ascertained by a series of tests and anthropometrical measurements, after which suitable exercises are prescribed.

All students were required to go to gym classes at least twice a week:

Each class (numbering not more than twenty) has its special hour for systematic development of the body. In addition to the class drills, individual practice, under the supervision of the instructor, is permitted. Those who desire to gain the best body development possible to their physical condition, should exercise regularly from one to two hours a day. The course includes, also, lectures given by the instructor, on the best method of physical culture and of preserving health.[4]

Dr. William O. Somerville, surgeon of the cadets, was one of the men who acted as lecturer in hygiene.

Physical education was noncontroversial then as now, but this was not so with biology. As early as 1883 the suggestion had been made that such a school, which would include physiology and hygiene as well as biology, be established. It was voted down by the trustees.[5] In 1897 the board was bolder; it decided to go ahead with the establishment of the chair.[6] It did not do so, however, without providing for a special committee to screen candidates. The committee came back with the recommendation that Dr. John Graham be given the post. The committee reported that it had written many letters and considered many names and that Dr. Graham, because he had made biology his life study, seemed the best candidate for the job. They outlined Graham's background. He had been graduated from Princeton in 1892 and had returned to that University on a fellowship to serve as assistant in biology. He had spent his summers in Woods Hole, Massachusetts, carrying on his biological research with other scientists of note. He had studied three years in Germany and had received his Ph.D. from the University of Munich, *magna cum laude*. He had also studied at the Russian Zoölogical Laboratory in France and at a zoölogical station in Italy. He knew thoroughly such subjects as zoölogy, botany, geology, palaeontology, physiology, embryology and understood both laboratory and field work. He could handle pre-medical courses as well as straight academic work.

The trustees must have listened respectfully to this long and laudatory report. But they probably sat forward more eagerly in their chairs when the committee proceeded to assure them of Dr. Graham's moral qualifications for the position. He would be not only a competent but a safe influence on the campus, the committee insisted. "He comes from a staunch Presbyterian Ancestry," they said, "and we are assured by those who write to us in his behalf that he has given loyal adherence to the faith of his fathers." And they brought forward a letter from Graham himself to prove the point. Graham had written,

I am a member of the Presbyterian Church and hold firmly to the teachings of Protestantism. I realize fully the responsibility that rests on a teacher of science as to his attitude toward Theistic belief.[7]

With these reassurances that the new man would not increase the charges of godlessness against the University, the trustees inaugurated the study of biology in their curriculum.

Civil engineering wavered between the Academic and Professional departments during this whole period and underwent many shifts and changes in so doing. It was a two-year course in the School of Applied Mathematics in 1871. It dropped from sight from 1872 to 1874 and then reappeared as a division in the Department of Professional Education, although much of the work which went into the course was under the direction of the professor of mathematics. For three years, 1878 to 1881, the civil engineering course disappeared again, and it was then once more re-established under the professor of mathematics. That time it became permanent, however. It ran up a large enrollment; a chair of civil engineering was established. In 1897 the school became simply the School of Engineering. For the work in civil engineering the University drew on a surprising number of graduates of other institutions. Of the six men who were professors of civil engineering between 1875 and 1900, only Professor Vaughn, who combined work in this field with his work in mathematics, held an Alabama degree. Horace Harding occupied the chair from 1875 to 1877; President Gorgas taught civil engineering briefly before his illness; George S. Wilkins, Princeton graduate with graduate study at the School of Mines in Paris, came in 1897; and a second Princeton man, Charles R. Kellerman, was acting professor in 1899-1900.

Among the eleven, more or less, schools of the academic department, students might choose their way to no fewer than six degrees, according to the curriculum of 1871-1872. A student might specialize in one school and come out with a certificate of graduate of that school. To do this he had to pass examinations in all the studies in the school of his choice, except that he did not need to complete analytical chemistry and civil engineering to get his chemistry or mathematics certificate. And he could get that certificate in a single modern language without taking all the courses offered in all the modern languages.

The degree of Bachelor of Philosophy required a wider range of study. It was available to boys qualifying for graduation in the schools of French or German, English, Moral Philosophy, Applied Mathematics, Chemistry, Geology, or Natural History if they could present also certificates of proficiency in junior and intermediate mathematics. If such a student presented certificates of proficiency in junior or intermediate Latin, instead of mathematics, he was given the degree of Bachelor of Science.

The Bachelor of Arts degree indicated that the student had a certificate of proficiency in junior and intermediate mathematics and graduation in Latin, Greek, one modern language, English, moral philosophy, chemistry, geology or natural history, and applied mathematics.

To earn the Master of Arts degree, the student had to be a graduate of all the schools except that of Military Engineering.

A degree of Civil Engineer was open to those who were graduated in mathematics, applied mathematics (including civil engineering), chemistry, mineralogy and geology, French, and English.[8]

The qualifications for degrees and, to some extent, the degrees themselves underwent modification as the years went by. The degrees open to academic department students, according to the *Catalogue* of 1872-1873, may be summarized as follows:

Graduate in a School: for satisfactory attainment in all the leading subjects in the curriculum of that school.

Bachelor of Arts: for graduation in Schools of English, Latin and Greek, Mathematics, German or French, plus "distinctions" in the Schools of Chemistry, Mineralogy and Geology, Natural Philosophy, and Moral Philosophy.

Bachelor of Philosophy: for graduation in Schools of English, French or German, Chemistry, Mineralogy and Geology, and Natural Philosophy, plus distinctions in the Schools of Latin and Moral Philosophy.

Bachelor of Science: for graduation in the Schools of English, Mathematics, Modern Languages (French and German), Chemistry, Mineralogy and Geology, Natural History, Natural Philosophy, and Moral Philosophy.

Bachelor of Letters: (same requirements as for the degree of Bachelor of Arts, with the omission of Mathematics)[9]

Civil Engineer: for graduation in English, Mathematics, French, Natural Philosophy, Chemistry, Mineralogy and Geology, Mechanical Drawing, Shades, Shadows and Perspective, and Practical Engineering.

Master of Arts: for graduation in all schools required for the A.B. degree, including those schools in which distinctions alone were sufficient for the A.B. degree.[10]

In 1876 this maze was greatly simplified. The Civil Engineering degree was being given in the professional school and only the Bachelor of Arts and the Master of Arts degrees were left as goals for Academic Department students. Students could still be content with the certificate of graduate in a school. They could earn an A.B. by graduating from any two schools if they had also completed a general course in other departments laid out with the advice of the faculty. The schools were organized to meet this requirement; each had two courses, one required for graduation in the school itself; the other including courses which would supplement graduation in other schools. For an A.M. degree students had to do one year of graduate work and qualify for graduation in three schools. They must have their A.B. degree, and they must complete the master's work within three years.[11]

Work leading to the A.B. degree was soon divided into two different courses: the classical and the scientific. Students in both courses followed the same program for two years. They took Latin, mathematics, English, and Greek or two modern languages. Then the classical students went on to work in Latin, Greek, English, modern languages, chemistry and physics, with mental and moral philosophy figuring prominently in their fourth year, whereas the scientific students dropped the classics and worked in modern languages, chemistry, and physics, with geology added in their fourth year. All were required to study English composition and declamation straight through the course. In 1888 courses in history were added to the requirements for both classical and scientific students; they continued through the full four years of both programs.

Prior to 1897 the courses leading to engineering degrees swayed on the borderline between the Academic and Professional departments, but they seem to have been regarded as belonging more truly to the first of these. They were undergraduate courses, and they offered alternatives for those who did not wish to take either of the programs leading to the A.B.

In 1882 a course leading to the degree of Bachelor of Engineering was mapped out. For a short time its first year was the same as the first year in the A.B. course, but after that Latin and Greek were ruled out from the start for the building engineers. English, mathematics, physics, and drawing made up the first year's course. The second year carried these forward and added engineering, mechanical drawing, and modern languages. The third substituted chemistry for physics and left out English. The fourth offered engineering, drawing, German, and geology. In 1887 the language requirement was dropped for the last three years.

The engineering work was divided into two branches five years later. It was then possible to become a Bachelor of Engineering or a Bachelor of Mining Engineering. Students working for a B.M.E. were not allowed to take any Latin or Greek. They devoted the first year to English, mathematics, physics, and drawing; the second, to English, mathematics, engineering, drawing, and chemistry; the third, to mathematics, physics, engineering, drawing, chemistry, and mining; the fourth, to such technical subjects as chemical analysis; assaying, metallurgy and ore dressing; mining laboratory, exploitation, and mining machinery; general and technical geology. The last mentioned subject included field work; excursions to mines and technical works were part of the required program. Candidates for this degree had to spend one month of the summer between their junior and senior years at work in mines or furnaces—and write a thesis on their experiences. Students who wished to take the degree of Mining Engineer also had to spend the summer after their graduation in practical research laid out by the professor of mining, geology, and metallurgy.[12] Then they could finish work for the advanced degree in a year by studying analytical chemistry, exploitation of ores, and other subjects in the fields of chemistry, geology, and engineering.[13] Some of these boys must have been gluttons for work, for a note in the *Catalogue* of 1889-1890 states that students whose standing warranted it might take in connection with engineering courses "any or all of the following modern languages: French, German, or Spanish."[14]

382   THE SCHOOLS AND THEIR TEACHERS

The old degree of Bachelor of Letters was revived in 1891. To qualify for this degree, students took English, Latin, Greek, physics, drawing, and history the first year; English, Latin, Greek, chemistry, and history, the second year; and in the two final years, followed the course prescribed for the classical A.B. students. There were then five undergraduate courses in the Academic Department: the classical course, leading to a B.A.; the scientific course, leading to a B.S.; two engineering courses; and the revived B. Litt. course.

Some changes were made in requirements for the master's degree. In 1879 a University graduate could get it by staying on for a year after graduation and taking subjects approved by the faculty. He had to make a grade of 90 or better on his final examination, but there was no other formality.[15] Then the faculty decided that an examining committee of three should read those final examination papers and that, in each case, the chairman of the committee should be the professor of the field in which the candidate offered his major work.[16] The next year the requirement went into effect that candidates should work in three schools and take at least three recitations a week in each of them.[17]

The course which the faculty laid out for L. C. Pratt, in 1897, gives an indication of the work an A.M. candidate was supposed to cover. Pratt, who had just received the degree of B.S. from the Agricultural and Mechanical College at Auburn, wanted to work in the schools of History and Philosophy, English Language and Literature, and Physics and Astronomy. The professors of these schools laid out his course: three hours a week with the sophomore class in general history; one hour a week with the junior class in constitutional and political history of the United States; one or two hours a week in a post-graduate course in institutional history (with Woodrow Wilson's *Historical and Practical Politics* as textbook); two hours a week with the senior class in English literature; one hour a week with a post-graduate class in Anglo-Saxon; five hours a week in senior astronomy. That made thirteen or fourteen hours in the classroom. In addition he was to work from original sources to prepare a thesis on some subject in American history, to do some careful editing of some English classic; to write three essays, and to perform whatever graduate work in astronomy and physics his instructor might assign.[18] The days when the A.M. degree was almost automatically bestowed on graduates who wanted it after three years were a long, long time past.

A graduate degree in civil engineering, to match that in mining engineering, was introduced in 1882.

Some indication of the growing maturity of the University is given in the crystallizing of these courses, their increasing definiteness and sense of direction. Other indications of the same growth are found in the unfolding programs of the schools of the Academic Department themselves. Comparison of the offerings of 1879-1880 with those of 1898-1899 shows clearly the progress made and some of the directions of that progress:

I. SCHOOL OF LATIN

1878	1898
Review elements of Latin Grammar, and read 21st and 22d books of Livy, the Odes and Epodes of Horace, and a brief treatise on Roman Mythology. Exercises in turning English into Latin.	Livy, Book I; Readings in Legendary History of Rome; Selections from Odes and Epodes of Horace (about 1,000 lines); Studies in Greek and Roman Mythology. Review in forms and principles of syntax, together with the practice of Latin Composition.
Higher syntax, Cicero's Offices, Horace's Satires and Epistles. Latin Composition and Roman History will be taught.	Selected Letters of Cicero; Selections from the Satires and Epistles of Horace; systematic study of Latin quantity and laws of Latin verse; the Syntax of the Compound Sentence with practical exercises in Latin Composition, studies in the life and times of Cicero; Readings in Roman Antiquities; Studies in the Life of Horace and the History of Roman Satire.
Juvenal's Satires and selections from Anals of Tacitus. Training in advanced Latin Composition and lectures in Roman Archaeology.	
Terence or Plautus and Pliny's Letters. Lectures in History of Roman Literature and Latin Etymology.	
	Selections from the Elegiac Poets; The Annals of Tacitus; Study of Lyrical Metres; outline history of Roman Literature (to be filled up by study of works in the University Library); practice in sight reading.
	The Pseudolus of Plautus; The Andria and the Phormio of Terence; the Roman Drama and the Roman Theatre (lectures); Elements of the Science of Language (lectures); Cicero de Oratore, Book I; Quintilian, Book X; Rapid Reading from late Latin Authors (Aulus Gellius, Petronius, and others); Extemporaneous Composition with Lectures on Latin Rhetoric and Style.

II. SCHOOL OF GREEK

1878

Goodwin's Greek Grammar, in connection with White's First Lessons in Greek, and Boise and Freeman's Selections from Greek Authors.

Homer's Iliad, Demosthenes, and Jones's and Boise's Exercises in Greek Prose Composition, in connection with Godwin's Greek Grammar.

Thucydides, Plato and Euripedes, and Greek History, with longer exercises in Greek Composition.

Sophocles and Aristophanes, and the History of Greek Literature.

1898

Review of Forms and Syntax; Xenophon (Anabasis), Prose Composition.

Xenophon (Cyropaedia) or Herodotus; Lysias (Select Orations); Prose Compositions; Syntax by Lectures and Recitations; Mahaffy's "Old Greek Life."

Homer (Selections from the Odyssey); Lucian (Select Dialogues); Prosody; Jebb's Introduction to Homer; History of Greek Literature; Lectures on the origin and development of the Dactylic Hexameter; Essays on topics connected with subjects under discussion.

Thucydides (Selections); Sophocles (Antigone); Demosthenes (Select Orations) or Plato (Apology and Crito); History of Greek Literature; Prosody; Syntax by lectures and recitations; Essays upon topics connected with the subjects under discussion.

III. SCHOOL OF THE ENGLISH LANGUAGE AND LITERATURE

1878

The studies in this school embrace: the history, grammatical structure, and philological peculiarities of the English language; composition, rhetoric, and criticism; logic; history of English literature; principles of oratory; modern history; Anglo-Saxon and Early English. (No division into courses by years given in the catalogue)

1898

1. History and structure of the English Language; English literature, including selections from Goldsmith, Scott, and other authors with critical and philological notes; private reading of selected books; English composition; exercises and essays; letter writing.

2. Rhetoric; English Literature, including the classical authors, with critical and philological notes, and private reading of selected books; English Composition and Elocution.

3. Logic, Argumentative Discourse; English Literature, reading of classical authors from Chaucer to Tennyson and private reading of selected books; English Composition in various kinds of discourse; Elocution, Preparation and delivery of orations.

4. Anglo-Saxon and Middle English; including reading of representative authors and English philology; English literature, American literature, Southern literature, Alabama literature, including reading of representative authors and private reading; English composition in various kinds of discourse; Theses: Preparation and delivery of orations.

REBUILDING THE UNIVERSITY

IV. SCHOOL OF MODERN LANGUAGES

1878

1. French: French Principia, Otto's French Reader, Noel and Chapsal's Grammaire Francaise, Lamartine's Graziella or Erckmann-Chatrain's Conscrit.

1. German: Ahn's German Grammar, Whitney's German Reader, Whitney's Grammar and Reader.

2. French: Noel and Chapsal's Grammaire Francaise and Exercises, Lacombe's Histoire du peuple Francais, Moliere's Misanthrope, Corneille's Cid.

2. German: Whitney's Grammar and Schiller's Wallenstein's Tod; Goethe's Wilhelm Meister.

1898

1. French: Whitney's French Grammar and Otto's French Reader.

1. German: Whitney's German Grammar and Whitney's German Reader.

2 French: Three of the following; Le Cid, Le Misanthrope, La Mare au Diable, Graziella, Le Conscrit, L'Abbe Constantin, Un Philosophe sous les Toits, La Belle Nivernaise.

2. German: Three of the following: Egmont, Nathan der Weise, Wallenstein's Tod, Immensee, Die Braune Erica, Der Geisterseher, Der Zerbrochene Krug, L'Arrabbiata.

V. SCHOOL OF CHEMISTRY (AND METALLURGY)

1878

3. Lectures with experiments, three times a week upon chemical physics, descriptive chemistry or the elements and their compounds, and elementary principles of theoretical chemistry. Barker's College Chemistry used as text. Six hours a week devoted to laboratory work with instruction in chemical manipulation, qualitative analysis, and quantitative analysis.

4. Two lectures a week in organic and technical chemistry and mineralogy. Six to nine hours a week in laboratory with instruction in quantitative analysis and practical determination of minerals.

1898

1. General Inorganic chemistry, two lectures and two hours of laboratory per week.

2. Qualitative Chemical Analysis, six hours of laboratory or one lecture and four hours of laboratory per week.

3. Organic Chemistry, with a shorter course of two terms, each with two lectures and two hours of laboratory per week.

4. Quantitative Chemical Analysis, with shorter and longer course as in Organic Chemistry, each with six hours of laboratory a week, or one lecture and four hours of laboratory.

5. Metallurgy and Industrial Chemistry with a shorter course of one lecture and four hours of laboratory for three terms and a longer course with two lectures and eight hours of laboratory for three terms. Includes metallurgy of iron, steel, and gold; chemistry of building materials, of steam raising, of lubricants and lubrication, of sources of energy (wood, charcoal, coal, coke-by-product ovens, gas, electricity).

6. Medical and Pharmaceutical Chemistry.

VI. SCHOOL OF GEOLOGY AND NATURAL HISTORY (1878)
SCHOOL OF MINERALOGY AND GEOLOGY (1898)

1878

Le Conte's Elements of Geology used, in addition to such instruction in the elements of natural history as may be necessary to the full appreciation of the paleontological portions of the text.

1898

1. Mineralogy and Petrography, four hours a week of lectures, demonstrations, and laboratory.

2. General Geology, three hours a week of lectures, recitations and excursions to localities near Tuscaloosa.

3. Economic Geology and Geology of Alabama, including instruction in modes of occurrence and distribution of metallic ores, coal, limestone, cement, clays, phosphates, ornamental and building stones, especially as occurring in Alabama.

4. Geological Excursions, field trips to places of geological interest around Tuscaloosa to study geological formations, mines, quarries, etc.

VII. SCHOOL OF NATURAL PHILOSOPHY AND ASTRONOMY (1878)
SCHOOL OF PHYSICS AND ASTRONOMY (1898)

1878

1. Mechanics

2. Physics, embracing Hydrostatics, Pneumatics, Sound, Magnetism, Electricity, heat, Lights, and Meterology, by lectures and experiments.

3. Astronomy, by lectures and text-books, and observations.

1898

1. General course including units of measurement, kinematics, mechanics of solids, liquids, gases, acoustics, heat, optics, electricity, and magnetism.

2. Advanced treatment of mechanics, optics and electricity.

3. Astronomy, facts and principles and use of instruments. Practical instruction in observatory.

VIII. SCHOOL OF MATHEMATICS

1878

1. Complete Algebra, study Trigonometry and Geometry.

2. Complete Trigonometry, study Conic Sections and Calculus.

1898

1. Algebra.

2. Plane and Solid Geometry

3. Plane and Spherical Trigonometry, and Analytical Geometry

4. Analytical Geometry and Calculus

5. Calculus and Determinants

IX. SCHOOL OF MENTAL AND MORAL PHILOSOPHY (1878)
SCHOOL OF HISTORY AND PHILOSOPHY (1898)

1878	1898
One course given in senior year, using Haven's Mental Philosophy, Peabody's Moral Philosophy, and Fawcett's Political Economy as textbooks.	1. Advanced American History and History of England. 2. Oriental and Greek History, History of Rome, and Medieval and Modern Europe. 3. Polticial and Constitutional History of the United States. 4. Psychology, Ethics, and Economics.

X. SCHOOL OF BIOLOGY (CREATED IN 1897)

1898

1. General Biology

2. Comparative Anatomy of the Vertebrates; Cytology; Normal Histology.

3. General Embryology.[19]

While the Academic Department was laying the foundations for a sound and modern college curriculum, the Department of Professional Education, which was to become the nucleus of the Graduate School or University proper, was also making progress. It was always, in this period, more loosely organized than the Academic Department. Often, as for example in the engineering courses, the boundaries between the departments were blurred.

The Department of Professional Education included two schools when it was organized in 1872: the School of Law and the Normal School. By 1897 it had drawn into its orbit the Medical School and School of Pharmacy, both located in Mobile, and the School of Engineering was definitely related to it at last.

The Normal Department, organized in 1871, was short-lived. The hopes and aims of the faculty as it started are indicated in the faculty minutes of an October meeting in 1871:

In this Department, which is designed for the preparation of Teachers, instruction is given by each professor as to the best manner of imparting knowledge of the subject taught in his School, and at stated times the students are required to put into practice the principles taught, by teaching a class under the direction of the Professor.

The President of the University will deliver a course of general lectures on the art of teaching and conducting schools, with special reference to discipline.

Certificates of proficiency will be given to those who leave the University for the purpose of teaching, setting forth their qualifications, which will, without examination, admit them into the Public Schools.[20]

The *Catalogue* for that year outlined admission requirements and the prescribed course of study for a three-year period. Those wishing to enroll were to be at least sixteen years old and had to pass examinations on the "elementary principles of Arithmetic, Geography, and English Grammar." Here, as in the old University, admission requirements for the teachers' course were far less exacting than for the regular courses of the University.

The three-year course offered the following work:

The *Junior Class* studies Arithmetic, English Grammar, Physical Geography, Book-keeping, and Penmanship.

The *Intermediate Class* studies Algebra and Geometry, Composition, Rhetoric and History, Logic and Natural History, including Physiology, Zoology and Botany.

The *Senior Class* studies Trigonometry, Surveying and Analytical Geometry, Mental and Moral Philosophy, Natural Philosophy, Chemistry, and Lectures on the Art of Teaching and conducting schools with special reference to discipline.[21]

Twenty-one students were said to have entered the school that year, and others were taking special courses in it.[22] By 1874, however, the Normal Department had disappeared. It was not until 1899 that a School of Pedagogy and Psychology would again try to meet the needs of future teachers.

The Law School, organized in 1872, started off on a much higher professional plan than that of its predecessor in the old University. By 1899 its curriculum had developed both depth and strength. The *Catalogue* for 1872-1873 gave the prospectus. The time needed for completion of the course was one and a half years, "or three terms of four and a half months each." That meant that, by diligent application, the course might be completed in nine months. Textbooks and lectures were to be "judiciously combined" for the best possible instruction, and practice in "Moot Courts" was an advertised feature of the program. The law professor would draw on eminent attorneys "in full practice and of proper acquirements" to help with these courts. The textbooks announced as the basis for the course included: Walker's *American Law;* Kent's *Commentaries* (4 volumes); *Stephens on Pleading;* Greenleaf's *Evidence* (3 volumes); Blackstone's *Commentaries* (select portions); Adams' *Equity; Parsons on Contracts* (3 volumes); Roscoe's *Criminal Evidence;* and the *Revised Code of Alabama.* Collateral reading would be "encouraged when the student has the requisite time."[23]

From the very first it was promised that graduates of the law school would be entitled to practice in all Alabama courts "on mere motion and without examination."[24] The *Catalogue* of 1879 called special attention to the fact that holders of the University's LL.B. might practice before the supreme court of the state:

The superior advantages to be derived from being educated in the State of the student's intended residence are too frequently overlooked, until learned in maturer manhood in the school of experience. To no one does this truth apply with so much force as to the young law student. The acquaintance formed and the friendships cemented by him during a University course, pursued in his own state, are capable of the most pleasant and profitable utilization. These are too numerous and self-evident to the reflecting mind for elaborate mention.[25]

The LL.B. degree was conferred only on students who had completed the entire course and who had passed written and oral examinations "in the presence of the Faculty." Students might combine law studies with work in the Academic Department "under regulations prescribed by the Faculty."[26]

The budget of the Law School, always kept separate from that of the Academic Department, is an indication that the University expected its law professors to derive the major part of their income from their own practice and to work in the classroom as a service to youth. This fact is probably one reason why the University, in search of teachers of law, relied almost wholly on its own alumni, men who had already achieved professional distinction. Of the eleven men who taught in the Law School between 1872 and 1901, only President Clayton did not hold an Alabama degree.

Henderson Middleton Somerville, who was the first professor of law and who remained on the faculty until 1890, served for part of his term as an Associate Justice of the Alabama Supreme Court. In 1856 he was graduated from the University and in 1859 received his A.M. there. He had brief experience teaching mathematics in the old University from 1862 to 1865. John Mason Martin, who came in 1875 to teach equity-jurisprudence, was president of the state senate at the time of his appointment. Later, from 1885 to 1887, he served as congressman from Alabama's Sixth District. He was a classmate of Somerville and both had earned their A.M. degrees in the same year. A third member of that class of 1856, Andrew Coleman Hargrove, came in 1885, and, with the exception of the two years from 1886 to 1888, remained until 1895. He had gone to Harvard for his LL.B. degree. His extra-curricula interests, like those of Professor Martin were in the political field. He had been a member of the Alabama Constitutional Convention of 1875, state senator from 1875 to 1884, and representative in the General Assembly at the time of his appointment to the University law faculty. He was president of the Alabama senate from 1888 to 1892, continuing his law teaching all through this period. John David Weeden, also an old University graduate, joined the staff the same year that Hargrove did. He had earned his A.B. in 1858 and his A.M. the year before his appointment. He taught statute and common law during his first year on the faculty; after that he served as professor of equity-jurisprudence until 1889. He was a trustee of the University from 1883 to 1885.

Three University presidents—Lewis, Clayton, and Jones—were members of the law faculty while they were in office. Lewis taught international and constitutional law from 1880 to 1885. Clayton filled the same chair from 1886 to 1889; Jones from 1890 to 1897.

By the late 1880's the law school was beginning to draw on its own graduates for its teachers. A Tuscaloosa attorney, Sterling A. M. Wood, B.A. and LL.B., 1877, was the first of these. He held for one year, between the regimes of Clayton and Jones, the chair of international and constitutional law. Adrian S. Van de Graaf, who was appointed in 1891 to teach statute law and common law, had done his undergraduate work at Yale. But he was an Alabama Law School graduate of the class of 1884, and he had married Professor Hargrove's daughter the year before he joined her father's faculty. In 1896 Judge Somerville brought his own son, Ormond Somerville, to the faculty. Ormond had received his A.B. in 1887 and his LL.B. in 1890, and he had been tutoring in Latin and English for part of the time since his graduation. He was professor of statute and common law for one year; then he served as professor of law until 1909.

The relationship between the School of Law and the University as a whole was not always clear. The action of the trustees in 1886 to make the president of the University also chancellor of the law faculty may have helped to define the lines of authority. The chancellor was to have general supervision of the law department. With the coöperation of the professors in both the law and the academic departments "acting as one body," he would enforce the same rules of discipline on the law students as on the other students. The law students were still exempted from military drill, however.[27]

By 1897, however, the Law School considered itself sufficiently "of age" to have its own administrative officer in the person of a dean. A committee of the trustees was appointed in March to "correspond, select, and report . . . for the approval of the Board a suitable person to be elected Dean of the Law Faculty." The committee included Hon. J. E. Webb, Judge Thorington, and Judge Richardson.[28] It is interesting to note that this committee did not look beyond its own membership for candidates. They came back to the board in July with the recommendation that Judge Thorington be given the post. Mr. Webb and Mr. Richardson signed the report. The committee suggested that the dean be given a salary of $2500 and his residence, "with the expectation and intention" that a salary increase would be speedily granted if the number of students in the Law School "increased above the number of 30." They suggested a term of three years for the dean and continued the one-year term for the assistant professor of law.[29]

William Sewell Thorington, who thus became first dean of the Law School, was a pre-war student in the University. He is listed as a graduate in 1865, the year when the University closed and many students were unable to complete their courses. He had served as city attorney for Montgomery and had also been Judge Advocate General. He had been a member of the board of trustees for nineteen years at the time of his appointment. He resigned from the board, of course, when he became a faculty member.

The curriculum of the school was growing with its faculty. By 1875 its work had been divided into a School of Common and Statute Law and a School of Equity-Jurisprudence.[30] A third school, the School of International and Constitutional Law, was added in 1879.[31] In 1888 the course was changed to cover two full years of work, though some allowance was made for students who came in with some previous study of law.[32] By 1899 students were following a stiff course, outlined in the *Catalogue* thus:

First Year
- The Law of Persons; Personal Property (including Sales)
- Domestic Relations
- The Law of Contracts
- The Law of Torts
- Constitutional and International Law
- Mercantile Law

Second Year
- The Law of Evidence; Pleading and Practice in Civil Cases
- The Law of Corporations
- The Law of Real Estate
- Equity-Jurisprudence and Procedure
- The Law of Crimes and Punishments

The Code of Alabama was to be studied in both years and "leading cases" were to be part of the subject matter covered.[33]

As the School of Engineering developed into an integral part of the Department of Professional Studies, its curriculum, too, took on greater rigor. The *Catalogue* for 1875-1876 notes that English composition, rhetoric, algebra, geometry, and plane trigonometry were prerequisites for this course and that students deficient in any of these subjects would be required to "pursue them in the Academic schools." Two courses—a regular course and an advanced one—are described:

The regular course (two years) will comprise the study of Surveying and Mensuration, Mechanics (theoretical and graphical), Strength of materials, Conic Sections, Analytical Geometry, and Construction, including roads and railroads, roofs, bridges, arches, retaining walls, locks, dams, etc. In order to fix in the mind the principles taught and enable the pupil to apply them readily, much time will be devoted to field and office practice.

REBUILDING THE UNIVERSITY

The advanced course (one year) for those proficient in the preceding will comprise French, Chemistry, Geology, Mineralogy, Spherical Trigonometry, Calculus, Geodetic Surveying, and an extended course of Engineering principles and practice with the designing and estimating for different kinds of Engineering structures.[34]

By 1899 separate courses in civil engineering and mining engineering were being given. It seems possible that the acquisition by the University of coal lands may have had its effect on the emphasis in this school. The purely engineering subjects taught that year included the following: surveying; mechanical drawing; topographical drawing and mapping; railroad engineering; highway engineering; properties and manufacture of materials of construction; hydraulics; mine surveying and mapping; structures; water supply, sanitary and irrigation engineering; materials, masonry, foundations and tunneling; machinery and machine design; and photography. Mining students also included, in their third year, a special "engineering" course: drilling and boring; breaking ground and blasting; shafts, tunnels and drifts; timbering; methods of mining; ventilation; pumping; illumination; mining machinery; extraction and treatment of mining products; ore dressing machinery.[35]

The Medical College of Alabama, founded in 1859, was always technically a part of the University of Alabama, although it was located in Mobile. The act which incorporated the College stated this explicitly:

"The Medical College of Alabama" hereby incorporated, shall constitute a department of the University of the State of Alabama, and upon dissolution of said corporation from any cause whatever, all the property real or personal belonging to the corporation hereby created or held in trust for it shall incur to the benefit of and vest in the University of the State of Alabama.

From the first, however, the two institutions had separate budgets and separate boards of trustees. On the matter of funds, the act stated:

That nothing in this act . . . shall be so construed as to authorize the application of any portion of the University fund or any fund or property which may hereafter belong to the University of Alabama, to the use or purposes of the corporation hereby created. . . .

A tenuous relationship between the College and the University was established in the provision that the president of the board of trustees of the Medical College should be an ex-officio member of the University board of trustees.[36]

The first steps to make this relationship more than nominal were taken in 1889. In that year the University trustees invited the Medical College trustees to join in setting up a committee, representative of both institutions, which should consider "whether it is expedient to establish relations between said College and the University; and if they shall decide affirmatively, then . . . to prepare and report to this Board a plan by which said relationship can be practically effected."[37] President Clayton and Messrs. Clark and Thorington were the University representatives. The Medical College apparently received the invitation with favor and appointed its representatives for the joint committee.[38] Nothing came of the deliberations, however. And it was eight years before another attempt at merger was made.

Professor Wyman brought the matter up at a faculty meeting in January, 1897. His motion that a committee be appointed to "prepare a memorial" on the problem of closer relationship between the University and the Medical College was approved, and Professors Wyman, Smith, and Edgar were asked to serve. Dr. Moody of the Medical College was to be advised of this action.[39]

Two months later the committee reported. They thought it "desirable" that "the closer union of the two [institutions] be effected, so as to make the Mobile Medical College in fact what it was designed to be . . . the Medical Department of the University of Alabama." They saw no serious obstacle to such a merger, and they urged that the board of trustees be requested to take necessary action "if possible, during the present scholastic year." They had several suggestions regarding the methods of working toward union.

1. That the President of the University of Alabama, be recognized as the President of the Medical Department at Mobile, attend the Commencement exercises . . . and sign the diplomas. . . .
2. That the Dean of the Medical faculty of the Mobile College, and other members of the faculty and of the board of trustees, be invited to attend the Commencements of the University of Alabama, as official representatives of the Medical Department.
3. That the Calendars and Catalogues of the two institutions be published together in a single pamphlet, each institution paying (if

thought desirable) its proportionate share of the expense. . . .
Or, if it be deemed better to publish independent Catalogues, then in a full Catalogue of the one institution there shall be printed a Condensed Statement of the Courses, etc., of the other.
4. That . . . a special committee be appointed, consisting of the President, and one or more members of the faculty of the University, for the purpose of conferring with a similar committee from the Medical College, in regard to the adjustment of the courses of study . . . and other details.[40]

The board of trustees and, apparently, the officials at Mobile, also, were favorably disposed toward these faculty recommendations.[41] The joint committee was appointed: Dr. Moody represented the Medical College; Messrs. Clark and Smith, the University. The plan of merger, presented in a faculty meeting on April 5, 1897, had the following main points:

1. The Medical College had sent in material for inclusion in the University Catalogue and was going to send similar material on the Department of Pharmacy. The University was in process of preparing its material for the Medical College Catalogue. It had been agreed that each institution would pay for its own catalogue. Both schools were holding publication of their catalogues until after Commencement, so that names of new officers could be included in both.
2. Accredited students from the University were to be admitted to the Medical College after their Junior year, without having to take again the prescribed work in Chemistry and Physics. The same privilege would be allowed to University students entering the Course in Pharmacy; they would be given credit there for one full year of work.
3. Exchange of representatives at Commencements would be put into immediate operation, and the two institutions would exchange "samples of Diplomas with seals and ribbons" with the thought that greater uniformity might be achieved here.[42]

The trustees receiving this report from the faculty found nothing revolutionary in it. Their comment shows that they did not feel that any drastic steps had been made to consolidate the two institutions, but they were content to leave well enough alone. They said,

Although the departments seem to be intermingled in the catalogue, yet, in law and in fact, the Medical Department is independent and self-sustaining. Indeed, the Trustees of the Medical College have really no more control over the Faculty of that College than have the Trustees of the University—the law gives the Faculty full power over the internal management of the College; to regulate its educational system, elect and dismiss its members, reduce or augment its teaching force at pleasure, it is in fact a self-perpetuating body. On the other hand, it must be self-supporting as well, and has no power to impose, even on its own Board of Trustees, any financial obligation or responsibility. It collects the fees it imposes but must pay its own debts and provide for its own salaries. The reputation and high character of the members of the Faculty and their pride in their own work are ample guarantees of their fidelity and devotion to the College.

The trustees noted, however, that, in view of the closer relationship developing with the College at Mobile, it seemed wise to give up any idea of developing a School of Pharmacy at the University. The board would, instead, adopt the already existing department at the Medical College.[43]

It was another ten years before the nominal union of the two state institutions became more than a matter of joint catalogues and reciprocal arrangements regarding admission of students. In 1907 the General Assembly dissolved the board of trustees of the Medical College and the merger became a reality.[44]

The first faculty of the Medical College, in 1859, had included Dr. J. C. Nott, professor of surgery; Dr. J. H. Heustis, professor of anatomy; Dr. W. H. Anderson, professor of physiology and pathology; Dr. George A. Ketchum, professor of theory and practice of medicine; Dr. F. A. Ross, professor of materia medica and therapeutics; Dr. F. E. Gordon, professor of obstetrics and diseases of women and children. Dr. Anderson served as dean of the faculty, but Dr. Nott was apparently the prime mover in college affairs. Years later the *Corolla* wrote of him:

The eminent and lamented Dr. J. C. Nott was, perhaps the leading spirit in the conception and inauguration of [the Medical College] . . . . Possessing a vigorous and broad intellect, and entertaining comprehensive views on all subjects, manifesting throughout his professional life a generous devotion to the science of medicine and a princely courtesy for those engaged in the practice and study of it . . . he was preeminently the man to take the lead in founding and organizing an institution of medical learning.[45]

The institution had had only a few years of development before war closed is doors. It had reopened in 1868. Apparently, its curriculum went through at least two major reforms before the end of the century. The *Corolla* indicates that one took place about 1885:

The Faculty now felt the necessity of a radical reform in their requirements of study. Experience had taught them that attendance on two courses of lectures was quite inadequate to prepare students for the duties and responsibilities of the medical profession. Actuated by these convictions . . . the Medical College of Alabama was among the foremost in suggesting and organizing the Southern Medical College Association, which has for its object the elevation of the standard of medical education . . . .[46]

The *Corolla* is more definite about exactly what improvements were made in 1893-1894. The changes in the curriculum are described as follows:

First, the requirement of better preliminary education. Second, the lengthening of the College session to six months. Third, the lengthening of the College term to three years. Fourth, attendance on courses of instruction in each of the special laboratory departments, to wit; Histology and Bacteriology, Chemistry and Operative Surgery. . . .

While utilizing all clinical material to the best advantage, didactic teaching is neither underrated nor lost sight of. From five to seven lectures are given daily at the College during the session. . . .[47]

The *Catalogue* of 1896-1897 lists the following courses required of graduates in the Medical School: anatomy; physiology; chemistry; materia medica and therapeutics; theory and practice of medicine; surgery; obstetrics, gynaecology, pediatrics; ophthalmology, otology and laryngology; microscopy, histology, and bacteriology; dermatology; and physical diagnosis. Listed in the School of Pharmacy that year were the following courses: general physics; inorganic and organic chemistry; pharmacy; toxicology; materia medica; botany; microscopy; vegetable biology; and medical jurisprudence.[48]

Of the original faculty, only Dr. Ketchum remained by the close of the century. He was dean of the school and professor of theory and practice of medicine. Others who had come to the teaching staff by that time included the following: W. H. Sanders, professor of ophthalmology, otology and laryngology; Charles A. Mohr, professor of chemistry and medical jurisprudence; T. S. Searles, professor of surgery; W. B. Pape, professor of physiology and hygiene and clinical medicine; Rhett Goode, professor of regional anatomy; H. A. Moody, professor of materia medica and therapeutics and clinical medicine; E. D. Bondurant, professor of mental and nervous diseases and of histology, pathology, and bacteriology; T. H. Frazer, lecturer on dermatology; H. B. Mohr, lecturer on descriptive anatomy; P. J. Acker, demonstrator of anatomy; Ruffin A. Wright, adjunct to chair of ophthamology, otology and laryngology; and James F. Harrison, demonstrator in chemical laboratory. All were doctors of medicine; Charles Mohr was also a graduate pharmacist. Only Dr. Owen, Dr. Acker, and Dr. Wright were alumni of the University of Alabama.

Reorganization in 1898 which divided the University into the College and the University helped to clarify the relationship between undergraduate and graduate or professional courses. The College had two undergraduate courses leading, respectively, to the degrees of B.A. and B.S. It still had its eclectic students, who were admitted on condition that they carry at least eighteen hours of work if they lived in the University halls and that they satisfy the faculty that they had ability to work profitably in the college. There were still students qualifying, not for a degree, but for a Diploma of Graduation. The regulations regarding these students did not change during the years between 1871 and 1901:

Students who, from inability to remain long enough at the University, or for other sufficient reasons, are unable to complete all of the studies of one of the regular courses, are allowed to select a course of study, on the following conditions: first, they must take at least three Schools; secondly, they must satisfy, by preliminary examinations, the Professors of the Schools they wish to enter, of their ability to study with advantage the subjects taught in the classes of those Schools that they desire to enter. These students, upon the completion of the Course of Study in any School, are entitled to a Diploma of Graduation in that School, and are enrolled as Alumni of the University.[49]

The University proper now included the graduate courses leading to the M.S. or M.A. degrees, and also the following professional schools: the Department of Engineering, giving the degrees of C.E. or M.E.; the Law Department, giving the degree of LL.B.; the Medical Department at Mobile, giving the degree of M.D.; and the Department of Pharmacy, also in Mobile, giving the degree of Ph.G. In 1890 there had been discussion of the advisability of mapping out a program toward a Ph.D. Mr. William B. Phillips had brought up the subject, but the faculty considered it inexpedient to act upon his suggestion.[50]

Courses in the College were modified somewhat in this reorganization. Scientific students had some choice in electives in their senior year. Those who wished to study engineering did so as a branch of their scientific course and received the degree of B.S. along with their fellows instead of receiving the specialized engineering degree.

In the University, requirements for the master's degree became somewhat stiffer. The course of study had to embrace at least two schools, and candidates had to present one major and two minor subjects. All of the work in the major field had to be on the graduate level and had to be at least equal to the amount of time spent in the two minor fields. One minor had to have relationship with the major field. The work was thought of as covering one year. Candidates had to be holders of A.B. degrees. They were required to submit the subject for their thesis by December 1 and their finished thesis by May 1. After that they were ready for the examinations, which were held in the last week of May. Candidates for the M.S. degree followed a similar plan.[51]

To encourage graduate work of this kind and "to make the University a center of scholarship and culture," the trustees established a series of post-graduate scholarships, one for each of the following groups of schools: Latin, Greek, and Modern Languages; English, History, and Philosophy; Mathematics and Physics; Mineralogy, Geology, and Chemistry; and Civil and Mining Engineering. The scholars, selected by the trustees on recommendation of the faculty, received free tuition and free living. They were not subject to military discipline. Scholarships were awarded on this basis from 1892 through 1896. Then their place was taken by five fellowships, which carried the same privileges. The fellows were appointed by the president of the University.

Forty-two men, as members of the faculty from 1871 to 1900, helped to develop this steadily improving curriculum for their University.[52] Twenty-two of them had received their degrees from the University of Alabama. Few of them had advanced degrees, unless perchance the University itself chose to honor them during their term of service.

The forty-two did not, however, compose the whole academic staff of the University. The role of the tutors—of whom there were fifty-four in this period—was also important. They were usually young graduates of the University of Alabama—only three of the fifty-four tutors, instructors, and assistants were graduates of other institutions. Many of them were studying for their master's degrees. In two departments, tutors carried the whole load of teaching in the days before 1900. Gymnastics, introduced in 1889, was taught first by Marcellus T. Hayes and later by Eli Abbott. Hayes had been a student at Randolph Macon College from 1887 to 1889. He studied law while he was teaching in Alabama; he received his LL.B. in 1892. Having first attended the Agricultural and Mechanical College of Mississippi, Abbott was enrolled as a special student in the University of Alabama in 1893, the year before he became teacher of gymnastics. The work in pedagogy and psychology was taught during 1899, the year of its introduction, by Jacob Forney. He had been graduated from the University of Alabama in 1889, had received his A.M. in 1892, and had served as president of the State Normal College at Jacksonville for six years before he came to the new department as instructor.

Some departments leaned very heavily on these young men to supplement the work of over-burdened professors. The Department of Chemistry used fourteen tutors; the Mathematics Department, ten; the English Department, eleven; the Civil Engineering Department, eleven; the Latin Department, eight; the Physics and Astronomy Department, six. They, as well as the men for whom they worked, deserve credit for the progress made in thirty University years.

A few experiments reflecting trends of the time or foreshadowing developments of the future complete the story of the curriculum planning in the University of Alabama between 1871 and 1901.

In 1898 the faculty suggested to its committee on instruction that some provision be made for students who wanted business training.[53] In the classics-saturated curriculum of the nineteenth century, business subjects found little foothold. However, there had been a course in bookkeeping announced in the program of the Normal School in 1872.[54] And in 1878 President Carlos G. Smith, oddly enough, in view of his own informal business methods, was enthusiastically working toward the establishment of "an Extended Course of Commercial Education" in 1878. He reported to the trustees that Professor Richardson was teaching, at the president's request, "a large class in Bookkeeping." It is a little strange that the course appears in the Department of English Language and Literature, but perhaps Professor Richardson was the only member of the faculty who had the requisite knowledge to teach such a course. President Smith hoped that Professor Richardson's class would be the nucleus of something much bigger:

I am much gratified to be able to report that this Small Beginning has been at last made in the direction of Commercial Education—for which there has been, from time to time, much demand from many patrons and Students of the University during my Connection with it. I trust, it may please Your Hon. Board to order that instruction on Book-Keeping be continued in the University. . . .[55]

Apparently his plea was disregarded. In 1880 the faculty rejected a request that a class in bookkeeping be established.[56] They did, however, grant permission the following year for Cadet T. H. Smith to teach shorthand on Saturdays.[57] There is no indication that the committee on instruction made any report on the assignment given them in 1898. The school of commerce as a recognized part of a university was still in the future.

Extension work, on the other hand, had become a small but important part of the University program by 1900. From the first it was called by the name under which it would later have more broad development. Stated the *Catalogue* of 1898-1899,

The University has become a "Centre" in a circuit of University Extension work, thus providing six lectures in successive weeks, to which all students are admitted free of charge. The course in 1898-'99 was delivered by Professor J. G. Carter, on the Great Novelist of the Nineteenth Century—Scott, Dickens, Thackery, Hawthorne, Eliot, and Stevenson, in the order named. These lectures gave a great stimulus to literary work in the University as well as in the city of Tuscaloosa.[58]

Professor A. H. Merrill of Vanderbilt University was appointed the following year to give four "lesson-lectures" on "Elocution." "Instruction was varied with recitations, thus combining pleasure with profit."[59] That same year the Honorable E. L. Russell of Mobile lectured on "The Practice of Law" and Dr. A. H. Moody of the Medical Department gave an address on "The Legal Status of the Medical Profession."[60]

Also in 1899 a determined—though unsuccessful—effort was made to establish a summer school. This bright idea originated with the board of trustees, who ordered that such a school be offered in the *Catalogue* of 1898-1899 and that the faculty draw up suitable regulations for it.[61] A reluctant committee of professors went to work. The plan which they developed called for a six-weeks session in the summer of 1899. The session was designed especially for teachers, students preparing for college, and undergraduates who had deficiencies to make up. Three professors had expressed willingness to teach in this school; the president was to appoint others if he felt that this was necessary. The professors were to be given the tuition fee of $10 and any required laboratory fees:

The Fund accruing from the tuition fees shall be kept by the Treasurer separate from the general funds of the University; shall be called the summer school fund and shall be paid, on certificate of the President, to the Instructors who have conducted the course, in proportion to the number of pupils in each course.

A course was to consist of five recitations a week, and no course would be given unless there were at least five students registered for it. The library would be open for two hours once a week to serve summer school students.[62]

Having obeyed the trustees' orders and produced a summer school program, the teachers thought themselves justified in expressing a mild protest against the whole idea. Instead of saying boldly that they did not want to give up their vacations, they offered the following objections for the consideration of the board:

1. To induce students to attend a summer school a course of Pedagogy would be necessary, which we are not now prepared to offer.
2. That owing to the putting in force of the new school law in regard to the examination of teachers, the vacation energies of the teachers will be exhausted in preparing for such examinations.
3. That one of the necessary conditions for a successful summer school would be an adequate advertising fund.[63]

These predictions and warnings proved justified. President Powers mentioned the summer school when he reported to the trustees in June, 1900:

Up to this time, though the School has been extensively advertised, there has not been any indication that the attendance will be large.[64]

But there is no record of summer school registrations in the two years of the experiment; perhaps there were no registrations to record. The University would need an enlarged faculty and an enlarged budget before it was ready to extend itself in the direction of summer courses.

Contrasts between that University of fifty years ago and the University of today are many and obvious. The significant fact, however, lies not in the differences between the two periods but in their continuity. The schools of the University of the late nineteenth century held, at least in embryo, the materials which would develop into the complex curriculum of the mid-twentieth century. The teachers who served in that period were forbears of which any faculty in any time can be proud.

CHAPTER XVII

The Library

THE VITAL importance of a library in enriching and strengthening the work of schools and departments had always been recognized by the trustees and teachers of the University of Alabama. They had been justly proud of the old library, housed in the Rotunda, in the days before the war. They had considered its destruction one of the most serious losses the University sustained at the hands of Croxton's raiders. They had also regarded its restoration essential to the very life of the new University.

When President Garland met with the discouraged trustees in December, 1865, the priority rating given to the library was clearly shown. The board instructed the president not only to take steps to get a building under construction as quickly as possible but also to see at once to the re-assembling of a library. Only as the difficulties in reopening the University became evident did the board reluctantly decide that it would be more practical to let the library wait until there was a faculty to help in its selection.

A Library depends more upon its character, than its number of volumes. Our means are too limited to purchase a large library, and [since] it must necessarily be small, it becomes of first importance that the selection should be judiciously and economically made. The selection of books for a college library should devolve upon the faculty, that the Trustees might have the benefit of their consultation and advice. If we had a faculty now we surely would call upon them to furnish us with a catalogue of books, necessary or desirable. . . .[1]

The re-assembling of the library came only with the reorganization of the University in 1871.

There has been some questions to whether there was any nucleus of a library at that time. Legend has it that the only book saved

REBUILDING THE UNIVERSITY

from the flames in April, 1865, was a rare Koran which a book-loving Yankee officer slipped into his pocket before he gave orders to fire the building and which he later returned to the University. But William R. Smith, acting president of the inactive University, reported to the regents in January, 1871, that the library consisted of some 1,200 volumes. "This," he said, "is the remnant of the burnt library."[2] And Clark, writing the *History of Education in Alabama,* estimates the number of books salvaged at about the same figure.[3] There had been a few donations since the war. One gift from Senators Warren and Spencer and Congressman Pierce "and others" was noted by the regents in an 1869 meeting.[4]

Whether the library of 1871 consisted of a single rare book or of a miscellaneous assortment of charred books snatched from the fire, however, there is no question that it was completely inadequate for any university which had pretentions to scholarship. Fortunately, on the faculty of 1871 there were men who were willing to work patiently and steadily to restore, almost book by book, the library the University had so tragically lost. A library committee, including Professors Smith, Wyman, and Garnett, went to work at once. Professor Smith agreed to serve as librarian, and any library equipment that could be assembled was housed in the observatory building.[5]

For the next eight years the library operated without a paid librarian. From 1871 to 1874 Professor Smith was both librarian and teacher of geology. Professor Wyman performed the same duties from 1874 to 1879, except for one year (1875-1876) when Chemistry Tutor Thomas W. Clark served in that capacity and one year (1876-1877) when R. Emmett Pettus, also a chemistry tutor, worked under his direction. In September, 1879, the board made provision for a paid librarian, at a salary of $400.[6] Later that same year, the ailing President Gorgas, resigning from the presidency, was moved into the newly-created post. Mrs. Gorgas succeeded to this position when her husband died in 1883.[7] And when Mrs. Gorgas resigned, in 1907, her daughter became librarian.

During much of this period, even after Mrs. Gorgas began her work, the library was, in a very real sense, Professor Wyman's library. He helped to make the first library rules. He helped to choose and buy the books for its shelves. He undertook in 1896, with the aid of his colleague, Professor Smith, to give the library an up-to-date card catalogue for its "13,000 to 15,000 volumes." He even bought a typewriter with his own money for this work, though it is pleasant to record that the trustees voted the following summer not only to reimburse their cataloguer the sum of $100 but to allow him to keep the machine "in consideration of his valuable services in making said catalogue."[8] The year before, they had set aside $450 from the land fund to pay for cases for the cards, for clerical help, and for supplies needed for the project.[9] Professors Wyman and Smith had worked with such economy that there was a balance which made generosity possible.

It took about three years for the library to outgrow its observatory quarters. Then Professor Wyman[10] and his library moved to the room which had been used by the professor of natural philosophy in the "barracks," later known as Woods Hall.[11] Then new steps had to be taken to safeguard the books; a room in the barracks was much more accessible than the old room had been. Professor Wyman was told that he might buy a lock for the door and have twelve keys made so that each member of the faculty and the quartermaster might have one. Wyman was authorized to keep any remaining keys.[12] There could not have been more than three, for probably the commandant and the surgeon were accommodated, also.

Less make-shift quarters for the growing collection were made possible when, in 1886, Clark Hall was finished. President Clayton had taken particular interest in planning the alcoved library room on the first floor of this new building.[13] But he had underestimated the library needs in his planning. When the trustees met in June, the president submitted plans for a new shelf-space; these plans were approved by the building committee. They were modelled after the alcove arrangement in the Supreme Court Library in Montgomery.[14] Apparently the library remained in Clark Hall for the rest of the century.

The library collection grew steadily: 6,000 volumes by 1879; 8,000 by 1886; "13,000 to 15,000" by 1896; perhaps 20,000 by 1905. This increase had three sources: books bought with the comparatively meager amounts collected in library fees, books bought with appropriations made by the trustees, and books given to the library by friends of the University.

Money came slowly for the first ten years and more. Of the 658 volumes acquired in 1873, 243 had been bought out of library fees and 415 had been given.[15] A year later, after a particularly good season of gifts, the faculty found $200 unexpended in the library fund and appointed Professor Wyman a committee of one to spend it. He was specifically told that he might buy three copies of Shakespeare.[16]

There seem to have been no direct appropriations until the regents were superseded by the trustees. Then, in 1876, the library was given $500 for books and $50 for periodicals. One hundred dollars of the book appropriation was to go for books in German and French, to be chosen by Professor Parker.[17] In 1879 the board authorized a $200 purchase, the Universal Biography.[18] In 1882-1883, $450 was spent on periodicals;[19] and the following year, $100 was allowed for the binding of worn books.[20] It is not clear whether any of these sums were direct appropriations; it is probable that most of them came out of the student fees which the library itself collected.

Then, in the late 1880's, the Library received funds from a new source. The terms of the act of Congress seemed to the trustees such as to warrant channeling some of the land revenue to the library. In 1887 the board made a general appropriation of $1000 for the library proper and $500 for the law library.[21] Since it looked as though the library would not have to depend in the future on student fees, the library fee of $2.00 was dropped at that time.[22] Several times during the next decade similar appropriations were made. When the trustees had money in the treasury, they were disposed to be generous with their library.

More touched with personality than the outright purchases were the gifts which helped fill the library shelves and which expressed the love and loyalty of friends old and new. Some of the gifts were valuable and welcome; some, no doubt, were worth little more than the spirit which prompted the gift. One of the first packages—consisting of 120 volumes—came from the widow of the late Samuel N. Stafford, a professor in the old University. The books arrived in 1874, and the faculty, thumbing through them noted that many were rare and valuable and that many were "enriched" with notes in Professor Stafford's handwriting.[23] Almost 200 books from other donors were added to the library that same year.[24]

In 1877 two alumni, Thomas M. Henley and Captain John C.

Henley, gave a collection of 600 books that were "especially rich in philosophy and classical literature."[25] The gift reminded the faculty that there was a growing number of treasures on the shelves. They ruled that any student mutilating a book or "scribbling" in it should be debarred from library privileges.[26] Gifts in 1878-1879 came from Dr. Josiah C. Nott, who led the Medical College development; from two ex-presidents—Rev. Basil Manly, Jr., and Dr. Landon C. Garland; from Rev. Telfair Hodgson, once professor of moral philosophy; from Hon. Percy Walker, from Dr. John F. Innerarity, of Mobile; from Mrs. Stafford; and from Joel Munsel, of Albany, New York.[27]

More rare books came in 1880 from Hon. T. C. Clarke, of Greene County; Enoch Morgan, of Eutaw; Judge Thomas Peters, of Lawrence County; and Hon. M. L. Stansel, of Pickens County. The gift from Judge Peters caused particular excitement among the faculty. It included not only books on botany but also a choice collection of plants "preserved and prepared in a scientific manner by himself." And the Judge had cast down a challange to the University savants by writing his letter of gift in Latin. Not to be outdone, the faculty appointed Professors Smith and McCall to write a letter of thanks, also in Latin, on parchment stamped with the seal of the University, telling Judge Peters that the collection would be kept in a separate case and "forever known" as the "Thos. M. Peters Collection."[28]

When Professor Meek died in 1899, his library of 654 volumes was willed to the University. That same year Col. and Mrs. B. L. Hibbard, of Monroeville, established a collection as a memorial to their son, John Leslie Hibbard, who had been a member of the class of 1893, editor of the first *Corolla,* and who had died suddenly a few months before he was to have been graduated. Some 350 volumes formed the nucleus of this memorial library; by 1901 it contained more than 1,000 books. That year the trustees conferred the degree of Bachelor of Arts *post obit* on Hibbard, "in consideration of the very high scholarship which he had throughout his course maintained." They assured his parents that the John Leslie Hibbard Memorial Library would be kept in cases especially provided for its preservation.[29]

The library grew also by the acquisition of collections which had been accumulated elsewhere. As early as 1873 Professor Wyman began to negotiate with the Alabama Historical Society about the possibility of using the University library as a depository for the society's library and archives. He felt that such a move would be a service to the society and would also enrich the University collections.[30] In 1887 an alcove was set aside for the use of the Alabama Historical Society, because, said the trustees, the University was appreciative of its duty "of encouraging and aiding in the preservation of the Historical reminiscences and Data of the State."[31] The collection may have outgrown its alcove by 1891, for in that year the trustees directed the building committee to find a suitable room for a historical museum and to invite donations to it.[32] The present large Alabama Collection in the Amelia Gayle Gorgas Library is an outgrowth of the collection thus begun.

In 1886 books on law were separated from the general collection and became the foundation of a specialized law library. Thereafter, appropriations were made separately for the two libraries, and gifts were solicited and received by both. The law faculty was permitted to buy reports as well as text books out of their annual appropriation.[33]

The designation of the library as a depository for the publications of the United States government made it necessary very early to establish a separate document room. By 1900 this document room contained over 10,000 volumes, an almost complete collection of government documents published since the War Between the States.[34]

The periodical room, another adjunct to the library, had its special appropriations. Students fortunate enough to have leisure moments frequented this room. Current newspapers were on file there, as were copies of both serious and popular magazines. In 1896-1897 the newspaper list included the following: Union Springs *Herald,* Troy *Standard,* La Fayette *Sun,* Shelby *Sentinel,* Tuscaloosa *Sunday Times,* Tuscaloosa *Daily Gazette,* and *West Alabama Breeze.* At about the same time, subscriptions were being carried for the following magazines:[35]

North American	$ 4.05
Forum	2.55
Century	3.55

Atlantic	3.25
Littell's Living Age	5.55
Popular Science Monthly	4.55
Cosmopolitan	.90
Review of Reviews	2.50
Harper's Weekly	3.30
Life	4.30
Puck	4.05
Judge	4.05
Book Buyer	.85
Scientific American	2.55
Total	$46.00

The list was more readable and more sophisticated than the list of periodicals which had once graced the tables of the old Library. Here were all the leading literary magazines of the day. Here also was humor. The presence of *Life,* and *Puck,* and *Judge* shows how far the faculty had moved in fifty years toward a reasonable and humane attitude about what students should read in their spare moments.

The trustees seem to have been well content to let the faculty, led by Professor Wyman, manage library affairs. They heard the librarian's annual report with sentiments similar to the ones they had expressed in 1877, when they told Librarian Wyman that his expenditures had been "judicious and necessary and of a character calculated to add permanent value to the library and its furniture."[36] It was the faculty who deliberated on lists of books to be bought. In 1895 they noted particularly that books on general literature, essays, fiction, poetry, biography, popular science, popular history, and travel were the great library needs of the year. They asked each professor to hand in a list of recommended books, not to exceed the amount of $50.[37] In 1879, when the library of Mrs. Goldsby, of Selma, was placed on sale, it was the faculty who recognized and purchased two important books in the collection. That same year the faculty set up a special committee, including Professors Meek, Foster, and Calhoun, to study a rare book catalogue for possible selection of new volumes for the University collection.[38]

It was also the faculty who made and enforced the library rules. The first post-war set, probably drawn under Professor Wyman's direction, were very similar to those of the old library. They described the duties of the librarian: to keep the library neat and clean; to register books bought or given; to collect fines; to call in all books one week before vacations or commencement. They provided that the library should be open at least once a week during term time. They stated that the privilege of using the library should be given to regents of the University, contributors who gave $100 or more, officers of instruction, resident graduates, and students. (No graduate was to be considered "resident" unless he actually lived in a college hall.)

Then the rules became more detailed about procedures and penalties. Listed are some of the provisions which the faculty approved in its meeting on November 7, 1871:

Students could draw out no more than three books at a time and keep them for two weeks, unless, in connection with work toward a public exhibition, they got special permission from the librarian to take more.

The system of fines established graded amounts due for late books according to the size of the book.

If a book was lost or damaged, the student might replace the volume or set or pay for it. He had to pay double the value of a defaced book, three times the value of a lost book.

Students must not take down or displace books.

Students who did not "observe order and decorum" while receiving books from the librarian were subject to fines, up to fifty cents, or other punishment.

Books "valuable for their plates, their rarity or their antiquity, or of a character fitting them for consultation rather than reading" could be withdrawn from circulation by the librarian.

No book taken from the library might be used as a text book.

No books might be loaned to anyone outside the University, nor carried out of the immediate vicinity of Tuscaloosa. Officers of instruction "employed abroad in scientific research" were exempted from this rule.

Failure to pay fines forfeited library privileges.

No diplomas were to be issued to library defaulters.

All officers had to return the library books they held at least twice a year—January 1 and July 1. If they did not do so, they incurred the same penalties as applied to students.

The Faculty was responsible for the enforcement of the rules, even when faculty members or Regents were involved.[39]

Some additions were made to these rules during the next ten years. In 1879 the faculty ruled that the library would be open from one to two o'clock daily and from two in the afternoon until Retreat on Saturday. From the wording of this resolution in the faculty minutes it appears that the trustees had intended that the library should be open to students at all times—a very impractical arrangement, the faculty thought.[40] Special permission was given at this time to professors who wanted to use encyclopedias or other reference books in their rooms instead of in the library. They might take them for one week if they first reported to the faculty that they were doing so.[41]

A much more succinct set of rules was presented for faculty approval during the period in which General Gorgas was librarian. They bear the date of April 29, 1881:

I. Cadets and law students shall have access to the library only between the hours of 12 M and 2 P.M. on every day except Saturday. They may remain as long as they desire between these two hours.

II. They shall take no books, papers, magazines, or other documents from the Library until charged in a book by the Librarian.

III. They shall open the doors of no cases without the consent or direction of the Librarian.

IV. The Officers of instruction and government shall have access to the Library at any hour.

V. They shall take no books, magazines, papers, or other documents from the Library, even for the shortest time, until the same are charged to them. Magazines and papers may be charged upon the slate suspended in the room. No cyclopaedias or other works of general reference shall be kept out of the library for a longer period than two days; no other books longer than two weeks; provided, that this rule shall not apply to the use of books by a Professor, for purposes of instruction, and that the Professor shall make, to the Faculty, a report of books thus used.

VI. No magazine shall be kept out of the Library, by any one, longer than twenty-four hours, and no paper longer than twelve hours.

VII. Conversation (except in a whisper) shall not be carried on in the Library at any time when there are others present besides those engaged in conversing.

VIII. It shall be the duty of the Librarian at least once a week to report violations of these regulations, by Cadets, to the Commandant, and violations by others, to the President.

REBUILDING THE UNIVERSITY

IX. It shall be the duty of the President and the Commandant, on learning of any violation of these rules, to call the attention of the violator to the same.[42]

When the faculty, having approved these rules, referred them to the trustees, that board had one important revision to make: the words "except in a whisper" in Section VII should be struck out.[43]

Not until 1905 were the library hours set at the familiar nine-to-five, seven-to-nine in the evenings, which many generations of students later came to know. The library remained closed on Sundays and holidays even then.[44]

To students on the University campus for the quarter century between 1882 and 1907 the library stood less for rules and regulations than it did for a person—a very gentle lady, who checked books in and out, distributed the students' morning mail, and, as she did so, became the friend of every boy on campus—Amelia Gayle Gorgas.

Years later Tom Garner, then editor of the Tuscaloosa *Times-Gazette*, put in words a picture he carried in his heart:

The alumni remember her as she sat day after day, in the library, a frail little woman always clad in black, with snowy hair covered with a little cap of lace, with luminous young eyes and a gentleness of manner that won their devotion.[45]

Amelia Gayle Gorgas looked back on a full and interesting life when, in her early fifties, she first took her place behind the library desk. She was born in Greensboro, June 1, 1827, the daughter of Judge John Gayle of the Alabama Supreme Court. When she was four years old, her father was elected governor and the family moved to Tuscaloosa. Governesses and tutors gave Amelia Gayle her early schooling; then she went to a school for young women in Columbia, Tennessee, and was graduated there with honors. Years of sparkling life in Washington with her father, then Congressman Gayle, came next. Amelia was one of two women to sit on the platform when the cornerstone of the Washington Monument was laid.

She was twenty-six years old when, on a visit to Mobile, she met and later married Josiah Gorgas, of the Ordnance Department of the United States Army. Their life together took them to army posts in South Carolina, Maine, and Pennsylvania. When war broke, Captain Gorgas joined the Confederate forces to become General

Gorgas, Chief of Ordnance. After the war, General and Mrs. Gorgas spent a few years in Briarfield, Alabama, where the General was in charge of the iron works. They had been at the University of the South since 1869, when the call came which made the General president of the University of Alabama in 1878.

Life became difficult then for Amelia Gorgas. Within six months her husband's health failed. In 1883 he died, leaving her to carry on without him as the years moved along, and she became the white-haired little old lady that Garner remembered. She died in 1913, at the age of eighty-six, in the same house she had occupied for thirty-four years.

Her years in the service of the University library had had their compensations, however. Chief among them was the love and comradeship of generation after generation of students, who strove to express their affection and their admiration with all an undergraduate's sincerity and vigor. One student wrote an article about her library in the *Corolla* of 1894:

The library is open from 11 o'clock until 4 o'clock, during which time you can see a good many boys reading current periodicals with which its tables abound. Those desiring to read books usually draw them and carry them to their rooms, where they can keep them no longer than two weeks. As it was only a few minutes until drill when I walked in, I hastily glanced at the latest *North American Review,* also *Puck,* and went over and took my seat by Mrs. Gorgas, the Librarian, for a few moment's chat. In after years, such chats as this will be among my most pleasant college remembrances. In fact I would consider my college course well spent had I gained nothing else outside of my association with her. Should you ever wish to tame the boisterous cadet, to find the *Open Sesame* of his heart, to make him your true friend, simply speak her name. . . .[46]

Students a couple of years later dedicated the *Corolla* to Mrs. Gorgas:

Conforming to the unanimous desire of the ALABAMA CADET CORPS, and thus, in a measure, expressing their filial love, THE COROLLA of 1896 is dedicated to MRS. AMELIA G. GORGAS, whose tender ministrations to the sick, motherly counsel to the wayward and erring, and words of incentive to all, have made her the good angel of their college home.[47]

An editorial note explains the dedication:

Recognizing the influence for good upon us all of that which is truest and noblest, a Southern woman, and knowing that the highest type is combined in "OUR LIBRARIAN," Mrs. Amelia G. Gorgas, who has been to us always tender, thoughtful, unselfish—a mother—to her the most revered and beloved person of the University, we dedicate this our best effort.[48]

Amelia Gayle Gorgas was, perhaps, the first woman to set the imprint of her personality on the growing University. It was appropriate that her memory should live on in the library she helped to build. The present Administration Building of the University was called the Amelia Gayle Gorgas Library during the years when it housed the library. Today the Amelia Gayle Gorgas Library stands as a memorial to her.

CHAPTER XVIII

Scholastic Standards

ANY UNIVERSITY curriculum has validity only as a process by which young minds are trained and tempered. Selecting the human material for this educational process and devising the means for testing the stages of that material's transformation presented many problems for the University of Alabama, especially in the years just following the reorganization of 1871. The promising enrollments of the first two years of the new University, as "exiled" sons of Alabama came home gladly to their own institution of learning from study in other states, dwindled alarmingly by 1873. There were only fifty-two students that year. Certainly, the University could not be maintained without students. Certainly, also, the uneven standards of secondary school education did not produce a very large pool of well-prepared young men. In the decade of the 1870's the University screened its applicants with a wide-mesh screen. Only as conditions on the campus and conditions in the educational environment improved was it possible for the University educators to put into effect the scholastic standards they felt essential.

Candidates for admission in 1871 were apparently welcomed with a minimum of formality. To enter the freshman class a boy had to be at least fifteen years old. He was expected to produce a sheaf of credentials that testified to his good moral character and his worthiness to be admitted to the University. A certificate from his last teacher or a certificate of honorable discharge from a chartered college or university established his scholastic standing. If the trustee from his home district vouched for him, that was enough in itself.[1]

Presumably, even in that year, applicants were examined by the faculty before admission, but it was not until April, 1872, that the

REBUILDING THE UNIVERSITY

teachers set down in their minutes the exact content of these entrance examinations. Prospective students, they then decided, must pass certain examinations:

1. English, covering grammar, modern geography, and Hart's *First Lessons in Composition and Rhetoric*.
2. Latin grammar, including prosody; Latin composition; three books of Caesar's *Gallic Wars;* four books of the *Aeneid* of Vergil; and six orations of Cicero.
3. Greek grammar and Jacob's *Greek Reader*.
4. Mathematics, including arithmetic, algebra through equations of the first degree, and three books of geometry (Davis's *Legendre*)[2]

The traditional classical emphasis was still as strong as it had been in the early University.

The trustees and faculty took a very realistic view of these admission requirements. They would be an insurmountable barrier for many would-be students—and the University needed students. Let everyone come who would, they said. And they set up special classes to give students the preparation in Latin, Greek, and mathematics which other schools had failed to provide. Professors Hodgson and Vaughn had "sub-junior" classes in Latin that first year of the reopened University; Professor Parker taught "sub-junior" Greek; and Professor Peck, "sub-junior" mathematics.[3]

The contemplated Preparatory Department, of which these special classes were a part, never went into full operation and was dropped soon from the catalogue announcements. But from time to time, discovery that unprepared students had slipped through the meshes of the entrance tests made it necessary to form tutorial classes. The year of 1879 was such a year. In the fall, enough students deficient in mathematics had enrolled to form a class in arithmetic under Tutor McCall. At the beginning of the second term Mr. McCall had to undertake, also, the tutoring of students who were deficient in Latin. He had to drop a junior English class to do this; Professor Meek then taught the English class.[4]

Exceptions to the admission rules regarding age were frequent, especially in the days of desperate struggle for enrollment. In 1873 R. A. Ashley, aged fourteen, was admitted because he had an older brother in the University.[5] The faculty recognized the precedent set in this and similar cases when they ruled, in 1880, that applicants younger than the required age might be admitted if they had an older brother on the campus or if they had "unusual preparation." At this time the admission age was raised to sixteen years.[6] An entry in the faculty minutes, in 1874, reads: "Paoli Smith (under age) was by vote of the Faculty admitted."[7] Paoli, who was fourteen, did not have an elder brother in the University—but the fact that he did have a father who was the president must have seemed at least the equivalent.

Some effort was made in these early years to enlarge the enrollment by attracting students who were beyond the customary college age. Young men "of suitable age and character" were allowed to attend classes in the "literary departments" without being subject to military discipline, provided that they did accept regulations made for them by the faculty and that did not live in the barracks.[8] In this 1875 ruling "suitable age" was understood to mean twenty-one years of age.[9]

There is no record of the disposition made of one exceptional admissions case in 1873, when a Creek Indian wrote to ask that help be given him so that he could study at the University that year.[10] Admission requirements were probably not quite elastic enough for that stretch.

By 1879 enrollment figures had felt the magic touch of Publicist-President Carlos G. Smith. They had climbed from 74 in 1873-1874 to 179 in 1877-1878. It was time, said the trustees, to clarify and stiffen entrance requirements.[11] The faculty presented the requested plan. It was not greatly different from that which had been in force since 1871, but it did establish the entrance examination as a requirement for admission.

All applicants for admission to the University must present testimonials of good moral character. The certificate of the last teacher is especially desirable. If the applicant comes from any chartered University or College, he must present a certificate of honorable discharge from the same. All candidates for admission to the first, or Freshman class must pass an approved examination on the following Subjects:
I. Department of English
English Grammar, including Punctuation and Prosody, the elements of English composition and Modern Geography.
Butler's *Practical Grammar* and Swinton's *School Composition* are recommend as text books.

II. Department of Mathematics
Arithmetic and elementary principles and operations of algebra
III. Department of Latin
Latin Grammar including Prosody, and the writing of Simple Latin Sentences; Four Books, Caesar's *Gallic War,* Six Books of the *Aeneid* of Vergil and Six Orations of Cicero.
IV. Department of Greek
For the academic year beginning in October, 1879, there will be no entrance examination in Greek; but for the year beginning Oct. 1880 and thereafter the applicant will be examined in the Forms of the Greek Language and the Simpler Rules of Syntax. He must also have such a facility in reading Greek as may be acquired by the careful study of two or three Books of Xenophon's *Anabasis.*

Applicants for admission to a higher class must, besides passing in these preliminary examinations, pass an approved examination in all the Studies previously pursued in the Class they wish to enter.[12]

Scientific students were not required to pass the Greek examination. And an "irregular" student had to take only the examinations which showed him capable of working in his chosen department.[13]

When the faculty proposals were discussed by the board of trustees, Professor Wyman, acting as president because of the illness of General Gorgas, stated clearly the dilemma in which the University was placed. If the board approved of the new requirements, he said, even if the granting of free tuition was extended to cover all students, there would probably be no great increase in enrollment. Students who wanted to come would be debarred by the stringency of the examinations. On the other hand, if tuition fees were progressively lowered or eliminated and the terms of admission kept easy, so many students would flock to the University that they would quickly overflow the barracks built to accommodate no more than 150 cadets. That would mean the development of a "privileged class" of students, since the overflow would have to be taken care of off the campus and off-campus students could not be under regular military discipline.[14]

The first part of this analysis was proved sound within a year after the introduction of the new plan. In July, 1880, Acting-President Wyman called this fact to the attention of the trustees:

The preliminary examinations established by you at your last meeting deterred many young men who had not accomplished the studies required for admission, from applying for admission, who, but for these preliminary examinations, would have entered. About 20 were advised not to become applicants for admission. I had ascertained by correspondence with them that they were not yet ready to pursue a college course profitably. Six were rejected after coming up to the University for examination. . . .

The total enrollment for the year would have reached at least 180, Professor Wyman estimated, if the new bars had not been put up. It had actually reach 158, but withdrawals during the year had left only 132 students at the year's end. Nevertheless, that was the best record for any year since the reopening of the University.[15]

The new requirements had, however, had the result of improving scholarship, Professor Wyman said:

In the matter of scholarship the results of the year's work have been more Satisfactory than those of last year, mainly, as we believe, because our new Students came to us better prepared for college.[16]

With only minor changes the entrance requirements adopted in 1879 remained in force through the rest of the period under discussion. In 1882 a slight relaxation in the classical requirements is indicated in this *Catalogue* statement:

The quality of the student's knowledge of Latin and Greek will be more regarded than the amount of Latin and Greek he has read.[17]

More and more students were coming in without being required to prove their classical knowledge. Greek was optional in the scientific course. Students enrolling in engineering omitted both Latin and Greek. The same exemption applied to students in mining and metallurgy when that department was established in 1886.[18]

English examinations, meanwhile, became increasingly difficult. After 1883 each candidate was required to write a composition of not less than two hundred words to prove his knowledge of spelling, punctuation, capital letters, division into paragraphs, syntax, and expression. For several years the *Catalogue* announcement stated that the theme for this composition would be drawn from Anderson's *Popular History of the United States* or Defoe's *Robinson Crusoe*. Goldsmith's *Vicar of Wakefield* was added to the list in 1886. Both Goldsmith and Defoe were dropped two years later, and Anderson's *History of England* was added, along with two novels by

Sir Walter Scott—*Ivanhoe* and *Quentin Durward*. The Ginn editions of the Scott books were recommended for study.[19]

Character requirements were always taken seriously. One student who celebrated his arrival in Tuscaloosa too exuberantly almost failed to get into college at all. He was denied admission by the faculty because he had been seen on the streets "in a state of intoxication." He barely managed to squeeze in on probation when the faculty indignation had cooled somewhat the next day.[20]

Age requirements, on the other hand, were administered with the same leeway as in the very early days of the reopened University. In 1887 two fourteen-year-olds, P. W. White and John Parker, were admitted "on account of thorough preparation." Young White was placed under the special supervision of the president, young Parker under that of his professor father.[21]

Compared with other schools in Alabama at the time, the entrance standards of the University were high—too high, some newspapers thought as they compared enrollments at the University with those of denominational colleges throughout the state.[22] Many of these colleges were little more than preparatory schools, but their more liberal admission policy provided serious competition for a University in search of students. It was to the credit of the University of Alabama that the determined effort to raise standards continued in spite of such competition.

The routine of entrance examinations in 1881 was described by President Lewis in his report to the board:

The first three days of the Session were occupied in the examination of applicants for admission, and in the Classification of new Students. On Monday, Oct. 11, recitations and lectures began and were proceeded with regularity thereafter. Two or three applicants were found unprepared to pursue with profit any course of instruction here prescribed and were not admitted; but in every instance where it was found practicable to give an irregular course to applicants who were not prepared for the regular curriculum, such a course was prescribed and the applicant admitted.[23]

Spring entrance examinations were given a trial in June of 1887, partly to relieve the pressure at the beginning of the academic year and partly to give students an opportunity to make up deficiencies by summer study. The results of the first experiment were not very promising. Only two boys showed up for the examinations June 17 and June 23: Monroe Roseneau and J. P. Clayton. They were passed for entrance to the freshman class in the scientific course on condition that they write an approved composition on one of the subjects listed among the English requirements in the *Catalogue*.[24]

By 1889, however, the idea had caught hold. Some nineteen boys took examinations that June. Eight of them were flatly refused admission because of lack of preparation; eight were unconditionally admitted; one boy who tried to enter the sophomore engineering class was told that he would have to go into the freshman class; and two were admitted with conditions in one or more subjects.[25] Fall examinations were, of course, also given. That same year, 1889, thirty-five young men presented themselves for examinations in September. Twenty-four were unconditionally admitted; five, unconditionally refused; the others came in with work to make up in one or more courses.[26]

All this screening and examining of candidates, under the constant pressure to admit as many young men as possible, made a great deal of extra work for the faculty members. The work increased as enrollment grew and as the University began to establish firmer standards. For several years there seemed to be no alternative to the entrance examination system. As the development of public education under state supervision gradually raised the standards of secondary schools, however, the professors on the University campus began to realize that they could put reliance on the soundness of work being done in more and more of the secondary schools. The first discussions regarding admission by certificate are recorded in the faculty minutes of 1890.[27]

Although the trustees thought well of the proposal made by the faculty, they proceeded to establish an elaborate system for the accrediting of schools. They proposed that a three-man board of visitors should be appointed by the faculty to visit the schools annually to see which were worthy of being accredited.[28] That meant more work, not less, for the overworked professors. They protested, asking that they be allowed to work out for themselves the details of a simple and practical plan.[29]

Apparently the board acquiesced, for in July, 1892, they readily adopted Professor Benjamin Meek's "resolution governing the establishment of University Auxiliary Schools":

1. Any school, in the state of Ala. for boys and young men, whose course of study comprises the requirements for admission into the Freshman Class, in any of the Courses of the University, the text-books announced in the Univ. Catalogue, or similar ones approved by the Univ. Faculty, being used—may, upon written application of the Principal submitting curriculum of study, be declared by the President and Faculty of the University, *A University Auxiliary School*, and be awarded a Certificate to this effect.
2. Any young man, of the age required for admission into the University, shall upon presentation to the President of the University of a certificate signed by the Principal of a University Auxiliary School, be admitted into the Freshman class, of the Course desired, without examination.
3. The Certificate from the University Auxiliary School shall be in the following form, printed forms being furnished by the Secretary of the Faculty to all Auxiliary Schools.
To the President and Faculty of the University of Alabama
Mr.............................. of ....County, a young man......years of age and of good moral character, has been a student of............................for...................
He has, in a satisfactory manner, pursued the following studies:.....,
........, ... which are substantially in accordance with the requirements for admission into the Freshman Class of the...........
Course, of the University of Alabama, and he is recommended for admission into this class.

                              ....
                              Principal of..................
                          ....
                        A University Auxiliary School.[30]

The first list of auxiliary schools was published in the *Catalogue* for 1892-1893:

Marengo Military Academy, Demopolis, *W.A.McLeod, Principal*
Verner Military Academy, Tuscaloosa, *W.H.Verner, Principal*
Livingston Military Academy, Livingston, *J.M.Dill, Principal*
University School, Montgomery, *J.M.Starke, Principal*
Greenville Public School, Greenville, *J.R.Smith, Superintendent*
Brundidge High School, Brundidge, *Horace Carlisle, Principal*
University Military School, Mobile, *Julius T. Wright, Principal*
South Highland Academy, Birmingham, *James White, Principal*
Butler High School, Butler, *J.M.Watkins, Principal*
State Normal College, Florence,
Millwood School, Anniston
Snowden Academy, Snowden.

The matter of accrediting schools never became a mere formality. It was not enough to apply for recognition as a University auxiliary school. The faculty at the University made careful and painstaking effort to be sure that these schools actually did meet exacting standards. They examined the curriculum of the city schools of Uniontown, for example, and decided that it would give adequate preparation for the "Scientific and Latin Scientific courses," but that Greek must be added before Uniontown students could be admitted on certificate to the University's classical courses. They definitely rejected the public schools of Eufaula and "Brettieru's, Citronell and Fruitdale School Co." because the catalogues of these schools did not indicate scholastic standards that were high enough.[31]

After schools were approved, they had to keep up their standards or run the risk of being dropped from the auxiliary school list. The State Normal School at Florence, the Millwood School at Anniston, and the Snowden Academy at Snowden had all been dropped by 1899. But nine of the schools originally listed were still in good standing, and twenty-seven others had been added. The additions to the list included the following schools:

University Military School, Clanton, *E.Y. McMorries, Principal*
Huntsville Male Academy, Huntsville, *Frank Puryear and John E. Wiatt, Principals*
Prattville Academy, Prattville, *M.M.Smith, Principal*
Birmingham High School, Birmingham, *J.H.Phillips, Supt., and J.B. Cunningham, Principal*
Mt. Willing High School, Mt. Willing, *John Knight, Principal*
Boy's High School, Anniston, *Samuel C. Pelham, Principal*
State Normal School, Jacksonville, *C.W.Daugette, Principal*
Cuba Institute, Cuba, *W.P.Pierson, Principal*
Furman Academy, Furman, *J.T.Adams, Principal*
West Alabama Agricultural School, Hamilton, *G.T.Howerton, President*
Gaylesville High School, Gaylesville, *A.P.Lowry, Principal*
Carrolton Academy, Carrolton, *L.V.Rosser, Principal*
Union Springs Institute, Union Springs, *J.B.Murphy, Principal*
Alabama Normal College for Girls, Livingston, *Miss Julia Tutwiler, Principal*
Boyd High School, Ramer, *B.H.Boyd, Principal*
Pollock-Stephens Institute, Birmingham, *Mrs. E.T.Taliaferro, Principal*
Tuscaloosa District High School, Berry, *H.A.McKinnon, Principal*
York Academy, York, *W.H.Altman, Principal*
Uniontown High School, Uniontown, *A.M.Spessard, Superintendent*
Eufaula City Schools, Eufaula, *F.L.McCoy, Ph.D., Principal*

Bessemer High School, Bessemer, *G.M.Lovejoy, Principal*
Citronelle College, Citronelle, *N.R.Baker, Principal*
Decatur City Schools, Decatur, *R.R.Harris, Principal*
Robert Donell High School, Gurley, *Rev. H.L.Walker, President*
Spring Lake College, Springville, *W.C.Griggs, Principal*
Knott High School, Mobile, *Miss Knott, Principal*.[32]

When the University of Alabama became a member of the Association of College and Preparatory Schools of the Southern States, in 1897, further standardization of entrance requirements was in active operation. The University adjusted its own requirements to meet those set by the association. To do so it had to enlarge its requirements for reading, but did not have to make any basic curriculum change.

Even with the auxiliary schools and the increasing standardization of secondary school courses, certificates could not completely eliminate the need for entrance examinations. Of ten students admitted on one day in the fall of 1897, four came in by certificate; the others took the regular entrance examination and came in with such conditions as their performance in that examination indicated they deserved.[33] Something of the breadth of knowledge expected of applicants is shown in this sample examination which was given on the campus of the University of Alabama in October, 1899:

Entrance Examinations

N.B. In the grading of papers, special importance will be attached to spelling, punctuation, sentence and paragraph structure.

English
I.

Write a paragraph (about one hundred words) on each of the following topics:
1. The Contest between Palamon and Arcite
2. The Story of Alice Pyncheon
3. Sir Roger at the Play

II.
1. Write a brief character-sketch of Macbeth
2. Give Carlyle's estimate of Burns as a Poet
3. Write an outline of Milton's life from 1660 to 1674
4. Analyze the following passage, and parse the italicized words:
   "The raven *himself* is *hoarse that croaks*
   the fatal *entrance* of Duncan *under* my
   battlements."

American History

1. Name the oldest city in the United States, and tell when, by whom, and under what circumstances it was founded.
2. Give some account, with dates, of the events that marked the beginning and the end of the Revolutionary War.
3. Give a short sketch of the life and public service of Andrew Jackson.
4. State the circumstances which led to the "Compromise of 1850"; and give the terms of that compromise.
5. Name the four presidential tickets in the field in 1860, and give the results of the election in that year.
6. Give the events, with dates, that are usually taken to mark the beginning and the end of the Civil War.

Geography

1. Name the capitals of the German Empire, the French Republic, and the Kingdom of Spain.
2. Mention the two great rivers of India and the bodies of water into which they respectively flow.
3. Name the mountain range which bounds Italy on the north, and the range which extends down the Italian peninsula.
4. What country forms part of the Southern boundary of the United States.
5. Name the five great American States lying north of the Ohio River and east of the Mississippi River.

Algebra

1. Factor:
   (a) $a x^3 + x + \frac{1}{2}$.
   (b) $4(xy - ab) - (x^2 + y^2 - a^2 - b^2)^2$
2. Solve:
   $x + ay + a^2 = 0$
   $x + by + b^2 = 0$
3. Find the square root of
   $25 a^4 + 9 b^4 + 4 c^4 + 12 b^2 - 20 c^2a^2 - 30 a^2b^2$
4. Solve:
   $x^2 + xy + y^2 = 133$
   $x + \sqrt{xy} + y^2 = 19$
5. Solve:
   $2x^2 - 4x + 3\sqrt{x} - 2x + 6 = 15$

Geometry

Prove the following theorems

1. The sum of the interior angles of a polygon of n sides is equal to n-^{2} straight angles

2. The tangents to a circle from an external point are equal, and make equal angles with the line adjoining the point to the centre.
3. If two circles are tangent to each other, the common internal tangent bisects the two common external tangents.

Latin

I.

1. Translate Caes. Bell. Gall. I, 24
2. Give principal parts of *advertere, sustinere, complere,* and *conferre*.
3. Decline in the singular number *Caesar, equitatus,* and *acies*.
4. Why is the subjunctive used in *sustineret?*
5. Why do you translate *in summo jugo* by the words, "on the top of the hill"?
6. In what case is *hominibus?* Why not *ab hominibus?*
7. In what respect is the Gerund a noun?
   In what respect is it a verb?
8. How do the constructions of names of towns differ from those of common nouns?

II.

Translate Verg. *Aen.* II, 243-247
What does the second book of the Aeneid tell about?
What was the *fatalis machina?* Who was *Cassandra?*

III.

Translate Cuc. in Cat: III, 3
What became of Catalene after he left the city?
Tell very briefly how Cicero obtained positive evidence against the conspirators

IV.

Translate into Latin:
Caesar because his camp was not far from the enemy's camp, instructed Labienus to withdraw his forces from the top of the mountain, and to form his line on the top of the hill. Labienus, when he saw that the Helvetians were approaching, (appropinquare), resolved not to wait for the arrival of Caesar. But having seized the hill he sent his cavalry to check the enemy's advance, while he himself refrained from battle.[34]

Measuring the progress of students after they had passed such entrance examinations and had taken their places in the classroom required careful and ingenious planning on the part of their teachers. The faculty gave careful thought to a system of grading when they met in November, 1871, shortly after the University had reopened.

All departments, they decided, should be equal in their relations. In all classes a maximum mark for recitations and examinations should be 100 and the minimum of passing mark 60. Each professor would keep a memorandum on the daily recitations of the students in his classes. He would reckon the final standing for each student by averaging the examination grade with the average grades for the term. Reports of term standing and examination grades were to be sent to parents and guardians. At the end of the second term a list of graduates would be published with names alphabetically arranged. Honors lists could be published, also, if that seemed advisable. Honor students were those achieving the "Excellent" standing of 90 or over. Other grades were to be called "Very Good" (75 to 90), "Good" (60 to 75), and "Disapproved" (below 60). Delinquencies and demerits were not to affect the scholarship grades. Every Saturday morning at prayers, the list of honor students for the preceding week was to be read, together with the list of those students whose standing was "disapproved." These lists were to be designated as the "plus" list and the "minus" list.[35] Preparation of these lists was to be a part of the regular business of the faculty meetings. Each week the secretary of the faculty called the roll of students, noting opposite his name the number of times he had been absent, late, unprepared, or otherwise delinquent. Unless delinquencies announced in chapel brought immediate written excuses, demerits were to be duly entered in the record book.[36]

The system of grading was somewhat modified and refined as the years went on. In 1875 the gradations between the perfect rating of 100 and the "disapproved" rating of under 60 were changed: 60 to 75 was made a "passable" grade; 75 to 85, good; 85 to 95, very good; 95 to 100, excellent.[37] In 1893 there was lively debate in faculty meeting about raising the passing grade from 60 to 75 to promote the "interests of higher education in Alabama." A committee, which included President Jones, Professors Edgar, Wyman, Parker, and McCorvey, debated this proposal and decided against the change.[38]

Parents and guardians of students continued to get frequent reports of the work their boys were doing, but the students themselves often had to be content with very general information. Even the chapel announcements of those students with very high or very low standing may have been eliminated by a ruling of 1879:

REBUILDING THE UNIVERSITY 429

The publication of the Honor Roll at Commencement shall be the whole of the information communicated to students as to their standing, except in the case of those applying for degrees. These latter may be informed if they have sustained themselves in examination.[39]

The rules adopted in 1887 called for the "publishing" to the cadets through the commandant of "plus" and "minus" lists at two-week intervals.[40] Perhaps this running check on progress was never really dropped. Students who, with or without due warning, fell below the passing grade in half their studies or more were automatically dropped back into the next lower class when term grades were sent in.[41]

The professors, however, were never allowed to forget for an instant the importance of accurate grading of the work done in their classrooms. The rules which they adopted in 1887 indicate the vast amount of bookkeeping they made for themselves:

1. By three o'clock on the afternoon of the first Monday of each month, all Professors and Assistant Professors shall make, on rolls provided for that purpose, reports of the Standing of all Cadets during the preceding month. In making these the Symbols for grades shall be used, never the exact figures.
2. At the faculty meeting on Monday, Nov. 15 and every alternate Monday thereafter, each Professor and Assistant Professor shall hand to the Secretary a list of all the Students in his department, who are *plus* or *minus* for the preceding two weeks. These lists Shall, on the next day after retreat, through the Commandant, be published to the Corps and returned to the President's Office to be filed.
3. At the faculty meeting on the first Monday in each month, the entire roll of Students shall be called, and cases deserving of Special attention shall be considered by the President and the Faculty.
4. At this faculty meeting every Professor and Assistant Professor shall present to the President *in writing,* the names of any Cadets who, from fault or failure of any kind, Should be seen by him, and Shall accompany each name with the necessary remarks for the information of the President.
5. At this faculty meeting all the officers of instruction must be present unless specially excused by the President.[42]

A near rebellion in a faculty meeting two years later may have been the exasperated reaction of men trying to follow this exacting set of rules. A resolution asking the trustees to abolish all grades except passable and deficient and so to make graduation the only honor of the University divided the faculty four to four. Professor Wyman broke the tie in favor of the resolution.[43] There is no indication that the trustees paid any attention to it. The rebels went even farther at that meeting. They reached a second tie vote on a motion to abolish commencement exercises and all public exercises. This time Professor Wyman, in his capacity of chairman, broke the tie in favor of the conservatives.[44]

A more practical method of relieving teachers of book work was adopted in 1894, when the position of registrar was established. The new officer was to take charge of reports on grades turned in by the professors, to record them in books provided for the purpose. He was to keep, also, a complete record of the names and addresses of all graduates, "full, honorary, or in a department." At the end of each session faculty members would hand over to the registrar numerical grades for class work and for examinations. The task of compiling these grades and ascertaining the standing of each student would be left to the registrar. Changes of reports once recorded in the registrar's book were to be made only by faculty action. Professor Palmer was chosen by his colleagues to serve as the first registrar of the University.[45]

Through all their struggles with the grading system the faculty and the trustees never lost sight of the fact that such a system was merely a means to an end. That end was a standard of scholarship of which the University could be proud. A resolution adopted by the trustees in 1887 reflects this attitude:

Resolved:—That a high standard of scholarship and morality in her Alumni is of more importance to the University than mere numbers, and it is the wish of the Board of Trustees that the Faculty should bear in mind the importance of maintaining a high standard of scholarship, and that the standard of scholarship may be raised as opportunity offers.[46]

There was also a sane and liberal recognition of the inadequacy of any system of grades as a final test of education in a resolution passed by the faculty in 1888:

It is resolved that the Standing of the Student Shall depend upon his Knowledge of the Subject; That it is the business of each professor to find out for himself as best he can what that Knowledge is; That it is Evident that of two students who are fairly matched in ability, the one who is most diligent and regular in attendance on recitations, will know most about the Subject taught. This fact Should be impressed upon the Students. That the recitations and Examination papers made by individual Students shall be regarded by the Professor *not* as the *Sole* means of ascertaining the Student's Knowledge, as has been the theory heretofore.[47]

Examinations, however, continued to loom very large in the nineteenth century student's life. Small ones were held daily in the section rooms. General examinations at terms' end were major events, though they were no longer, as in the old University, made the occasion for Roman holidays, when townspeople from miles around came to witness the ordeal of the squirming students.

Rules for the general examinations were set up in 1872, and the faculty worked over these rules, revising and modifying them, all through the thirty years which followed. The 1872 rules provided that all examinations be held in the presence of the examining officer and two other members of the faculty. They were to be given at the end of each term on the subjects studied that term. The examining officer might decide whether an examination should be wholly written or partly written and partly oral, but he might not order an examination which was entirely oral. Examinations were then scheduled from 8:30 to noon; and from 2:00 to 5:30 in the afternoon. The examining officer was responsible for enforcing the many rules. No book or paper might be brought into the examination room without special permission from the officer in charge, and no communication among cadets during examination was permissible. Examination papers had to be written in ink "in a fair and legible hand." Each completed paper had to be accompanied by an honor statement:

I hereby certify that I have neither given nor received any assistance during this examination.

All cadets were required to remain in the examination room until their papers were handed in.[48]

The examination hours set in these rules were modified in 1879, probably with groans from the students. The examining period lasted until one o'clock then, instead of ending at noon.[49]

In 1887 the number of general examinations during the year was cut from three to two. It was decided at that time to hold one examination at the end of the first term, but to combine the examinations for the second and third terms. The standing of an individual student would be determined by combining the two examination grades, the first counting one-third and the second, two-thirds.[50] Later the timing of the two examinations was shifted; they were given at the end of the second and third terms instead of at the end of the first and third.[51]

Special examinations were established in 1874 and given each June until 1878. These were for students graduating in a school, and they covered all the work of that school. A grade of 80 was required for passing. Students taking the special examinations were excused from the generals in subjects covered in the specials. The professor of the school, with two of his faculty colleagues appointed by the president, made up the examining board.[52]

The schedule of examinations given in the spring of 1872 is typical of the period:

Monday, June 10, Senior English, Senior Mathematics, Junior German
Tuesday, June 11, Senior, Intermediate, and Junior Latin
Wednesday, June 12, Chemistry, Natural History, Senior Greek, Senior German
Thursday, June 13, Intermediate and Junior English
Friday, June 14, Moral Philosophy and Applied Mathematics
Monday, June 17, Senior French; Intermediate and Junior Mathematics
Tuesday, June 18, Junior French; Intermediate, Junior, and Sub-Junior Greek
Wednesday, June 19, Sub-Junior Latin
Friday, June 21, Sub-Junior Mathematics.[53]

Questions regarding the validity of the whole examination system were raised from time to time. The board of trustees called upon Professor Wyman, in 1889, to answer some of the objections being raised to the system. They must have been playing with the idea of introducing some features of the English educational system, for Professor Wyman, in the course of his defense of examinations as something that "could not be dispensed with," also enlightened the trustees about "the differences between English cramming and what is known as cramming in the United States."[54] By the end of the century, however, an effort was being made to minimize the importance of the term examinations and to put greater stress on the testing that went on through the year. Stated the *Catalogue* of 1899-1900,

In addition to the daily recitations and exercises in the section rooms, written examinations are held at the close of each term. It is believed that short and frequent examinations will conduce to regular habits of study, and place more stress on attendance and class work. Long examinations at long intervals have a tendency to encourage idleness during the term and cramming for a pass during the closing days of the session, whereas frequent examinations stimulate daily preparation. The final examinations immediately precede Commencement Week. Each examination is conducted by the Professor of the School to which the class belongs, in the presence of at least one other officer, designated by the Faculty.[55]

A system of incentives developed slowly as the University endeavored to encourage young students to show their mettle as young scholars. An increasing number of prizes were awarded for outstanding accomplishment in various fields. There was the honor, always cherished, of being chosen as a commencement orator. There was the recognition of earned merit through the Roll of Distinguished Students. The third of these was most closely related to the system of testing and checking through which the University judged the quality of its product.

The Roll of Distinguished Students was established in 1874, with rather lenient requirements. All students who made seventy-five per cent or better on their general examinations had their names listed in the *Catalogue* and announced at Commencement. The faculty must have quickly recognized that they had set too low a standard, for the qualifying grade was raised to 90 in 1875.[56]

The competitive motive came into the picture ten years later. In 1886 the experiment was tried of listing as distinguished students the two in each class of the three courses in the Academic Department who achieved the highest marks, provided that these "highest" marks were 90 or better.[57] That was apparently too strict a limitation, for the following year the number to be chosen from each class of the Academic Department was set at "not more than eleven nor less than nine."[58] There were four courses in the Academic Department then, and each was entitled to representation on the honor roll in proportion to the number of students in each class. Students placed on the roll then had to have a ninety per cent overall average, and a ninety per cent grade in at least three departments. Only students taking regular courses were eligible. Law students became eligible for the Roll of Distinguished Students in 1887.[59]

By 1891 this rather complicated system had been given up and the trustees had ordered that all students with grades of 95 and over were to be named as honor students. Four years later, after a committee headed by Professor Wyman had studied the subject of honors carefully, a new plan was adopted, a plan which had again developed complexity.

According to this plan all students with grades of 95 or better in any school or schools were to be listed on the General Roll of Honor, unless their standing had fallen below 75 in some other school during that period. The Roll of Highest Honors was to be made up of students completing sophomore and senior years. At the end of his sophomore year a student with an average grade of ninety-three per cent in all the schools in which he had taken full courses was entitled to Second Year Honors. At the end of his senior year, if he was a candidate for a titled degree and had an average grade of ninety-three per cent in all the schools he had worked in, he was entitled to Final Honors. The list of Second Year and Final Honors was to be printed in conspicuous type on the first page of the Commencement Program, and included in the *Catalogue* under the title: HIGHEST HONORS OF THE UNIVERSITY. The General Honor Roll went into the Commencement Program, too, but "near the end" of that publication.[60]

Once more the plan proved too complicated. It was revised in 1899 into a somewhat more manageable form, and it was tied to the new organization plan of the University which now recognized the "College" and the "University." In every college class all candidates for titled academic degrees who attained the ninety-five per cent average in all their full courses received Highest Honors and had their names duly printed in the Commencement Program and the *Catalogue*.[61]

Looking over the old records, one is struck with the patience and persistence with which the faculty and trustees worked to establish a firm educational foundation for their University. By 1901 they had come through the years of experiment and the years when expediency forced admission of large numbers of unprepared students. They had established the standards for a truly modern institution of learning.

CHAPTER XIX

Faculty Problems

WHEN class work at the University was resumed in the autumn of 1871, after the miscellaneous students had been welcomed, examined, and enrolled in regular and special classes, the newly constituted faculty met to set up the rules under which they would work. These rules, formulated while the professors awaited confirmation by the regents of their choice of Professor Lupton as their leader and president, dealt in somewhat general terms with the responsibilities of the faculty as the body "charged with the immediate government and direction of the University." They were more specific about the procedures for weekly faculty meetings "for reviewing the state of the College," about the records to be kept, and about the code of ethics which individuals were expected to observe.

The faculty minutes of November 7 include the regulations agreed upon at this time:

Government of the Faculty

I. The Faculty are charged with the immediate government and direction of the University, and have authority to make all By-Laws, Orders and Regulations necessary for carrying into effect their powers and duties, not inconsistent with the laws of the Board of Regents.

II. The Faculty shall have weekly meetings, for reviewing the state of the College and considering such cases as may be brought before them. One of their number, annually, shall be elected their Secretary, who shall keep a fair and full record of their proceedings, in a well bound book, which shall be at all times subject to the inspection of the Board of Regents.
No action of the Faculty which is not recorded in the Faculty-book, shall be considered valid.
The decision of the Faculty shall be by a majority of voices. In

case of a tie the presiding officer shall have the casting vote. The presiding officer may call meetings of the Faculty whenever he may deem necessary.

III. The President is the chief executive officer of the University. He shall have the power to visit any classes, or attend any recitation in the University at will; and give such directions, and perform such acts generally (not inconsistent with the laws of the University) as shall in his judgment, promote the interests of the Institution. In case of the absence of the President, the senior Professor present, shall take his place, and perform the duties of executive officer.

IV. Each officer shall keep a Roll or Numerical Statement of the Proficiency, etc., etc., of each Student reciting to him: in which shall also be marked every delinquency or misdemeanor he may observe in any student.

Twice, at least, in each year, the Faculty shall cause a proper abstract from these Rolls to be transmitted to the parent or guardian of each pupil.

V. Each officer shall lay before the Faculty, at its earliest meeting, all well-sustained complaints made by him, against a Student, and all facts affecting the moral character of a Student, which may have come to his knowledge.

VI. No officer shall seek, either directly or indirectly, to mitigate any censure passed upon a Student, or to procure his admission into any other Institution, without express permission of the Faculty.

VII. The opinion or vote of any member of the Faculty shall not be made known, directly or indirectly, to any one who is not a member of the body; except when express permission shall be given to that effect by a unanimous decision of the Faculty.

VIII. A member of the Faculty shall not be a sitting member of any Society of Students.

IX. No law of the University, nor act of the Faculty, nor of an individual member thereof in his official capacity, nor any question connected with the government or discipline of the College shall be debated by any officer in the presence of a student.

X. At every annual meeting of the Board of Regents, the President of the University shall present to the Board a list of the names of all the students, together with the time of admission of those received since the last annual meeting: also an account of the course of studies which have been pursued by the several classes,—under what officers they have studied,—what textbooks have been used, and how much has been accomplished.[1]

In those regular weekly faculty meetings, as in the faculty meetings of the pre-war period, the problems and performance of indi-

BARNARD HALL

Barnard Hall, built in 1888, was named for Professor F.A.P. Barnard. Originally it contained classrooms and laboratories for the physics department in the main structure, and the first University gymnasium occupied the west wing. The ROTC department used Barnard Hall as an armory for many years; it is now the Air ROTC headquarters.

TUOMEY HALL

Named for Professor Michael Tuomey, Tuomey Hall was constructed in 1888, for instruction in chemistry. After the department of chemistry became a school and occupied a new building, it became the headquarters and classroom building of the ROTC.

vidual students in a still small university could be dealt with on a personal basis. The teachers could, and did, consult together about this boy's failure in his studies, or about that boy's habits. There is an intimacy about the record which has disappeared from most of the records of present day faculty meetings.

One important contrast stands out as the faculty records of 1871 to 1901 are placed beside those of the old University. Problems of discipline—the problems over which the teachers of the thirties and forties and fifties regularly worried—had moved into relative insignificance. The commandant of the cadet corps had become the disciplinary officer, and, except in rare cases, apparently he was able to cope with the problems assigned to him without finding it necessary to refer them to the full faculty.

Lessening of the police function made it possible for the faculty to put more of their time on matters directly related to scholarship, to work out the careful plans for making and recording grades analyzed in the preceding chapter, and to give shape and direction to a developing curriculum. While that curriculum was in a fluid state, with a bewildering number of schools, courses, and degrees spread out before the students, one of the most time-consuming jobs in faculty meetings became that of granting or refusing student requests for transfer from one course to another. The following excerpts are typical; all the cases came up in a single month in 1881:

Worthington's application to take Engineering Course instead of Classical Course approved. He is allowed to substitute his Latin and Greek for Modern Languages.[2]

The application of Cadet Johnson, to be allowed to take *two* years courses in *one* year, in *Chemistry,* which with Junior French and German together with any work the Faculty may see fit as a post-graduate course for Master of Arts, "granted."[3]

Resolved—that Cadet A. Jones be allowed to change from Scientific to Engineering Course and to substitute his standing in Ancient Languages for one of the Modern Languages if he finds that he has not time for both.[4]

Patiently, one by one, cases of students who wanted to drop one course or take another, cases of students who wanted to be excused from making up recitations missed through illness, cases of students who wanted rules waived for their convenience were processed by their teachers. Patiently the secretary of the faculty wrote down his "fair and full" record in the "well-bound" book. His record of November 7, 1886, is very similar to what he wrote week after week throughout the year:

Nov. 7, 1886

After reading the minutes of last meeting the President reported that T.A.Dickson had withdrawn his request to change his course and that Messrs. Todd and Otis having shown permission from the proper authorities had been transferred to the Scientific Course. Showalter was allowed partial Senior Privileges, i.e., relieved of guard duty and permitted to visit town one evening in every two weeks.

Petitions of Messrs. Wilson, Booth, and Earle to be excused from making up recitations missed by Sickness were returned that they may procure the proper certificate from the Surgeon.

Mr. Freret's petition to be allowed to make up certain recitations missed in English was referred to Prof. Meek.

Petitions of Messrs. Patton and Fry, E.M., to be excused from making up recitations missed by Sickness, being accompanied by proper certificates, are granted.

Petition of Mr. Compton in reference to dropping German and Substituting Spanish therefor was referred to Profs. Parker and Calhoun.

Petition of Mr. Quarles in reference to his Status in regard to Final Honors in his Class was referred to Profs. Meek, Calhoun and Palmer. Prof. Wyman read a Communication from Hon. W. Coachman of the Indian Territory in reference to his Son entering the University. Prof. Wyman was directed to write to him and State that his Son could take an Eclectic Course composed of English and Such other Studies as would occupy his time.

After recording the grades of the Students for the month of October, on motion a Committee, composed of Profs. Meek, Smith, and Hardaway, was appointed to consider and report at the next Faculty meeting the best method of making reports hereafter as to the progress, etc., of the Students.

Faculty adjourned. J. C. Calhoun, Secretary[5]

One move to simplify the business of faculty meetings was made by Professor Edgar in 1896, when he offered a resolution that students should not be allowed to transfer from one course to another "except in extraordinary cases and then only without conditions."[6] The faculty accepted this proposal and presumably got some relief from mind-changing students by so doing. Direct relief for the secretary of the faculty came about the same time. The faculty had petitioned the board of trustees in 1889 for permission to appoint a secretary from the ranks of the instructors or assistants and to pay him "proper" compensation for extra work.[7] They had repeated that request in 1891.[8] There is no record that the trustees responded to the idea of "proper" compensation, though they paid the secretary of the board $250. But they must have given permission for the appointment of a secretary of less than professional rank, for in 1893-1894 Daniel Holt Smith, instructor in chemistry, was serving as secretary to the faculty, and for several years thereafter assistants in the chemistry department also held this job. The professors took it under their own wing again in 1897-1898. Professor Palmer was secretary that year; Professor Graham, the following season.

During these years the faculty began to reach out beyond the limits of their own campus toward the associations with colleagues in other colleges and universities which would later become so important to the intellectual life of faculties. At a meeting in May, 1895, they discussed a communication from Vanderbilt University about the formation of a Southern Association of Schools and Colleges. They were cautious and conservative in their response. They would, they said, send a delegate to the proposed convention if it was not held before July. Although they favored the general idea of an association, they wanted to await the report of their delegate to the convention before they committed themselves about joining.[9] When, in October, the matter came up again, the Alabama teachers voted to send to the Atlanta Convention of the Southern College Association one delegate from the Scientific Department and one delegate from the Classical Department.[10] The delegates could not have brought back a report of unmixed approval, for Dr. Parker's motion that the University join the association failed to pass in January.[11] Nearly two years elapsed before an invitation to send delegates to the annual meeting of the Association of Southern Schools and Colleges at Knoxville, Tennessee, opened up the question of affiliation with a regional educational association again.[12] The matter was discussed at several meetings. By October 27, it was agreed that affiliation would meet with approval "if practicable"; by November 15, Professor Saffold was able to announce such affiliation as an accomplished fact.[13]

Weekly faculty meetings were time-consuming, but to the earnest staff they were secondary in importance always to the daily work of the classroom. If the faculty in the last three decades of the nineteenth century was small in relation to the number and variety of the curriculum offerings, it was not too badly out of proportion to a student body which did not number 250 until after the turn of the century. That the teaching load which faculty members carried was reasonable is apparent from reports submitted by department heads to President Carlos Smith for the year ending July 1, 1874.

Professor Meek reported that he was carrying eight hours of recitations and lectures each week in addition to supervising declamations and essays. His four classes, each meeting twice a week, had a total of forty-two students: twelve freshmen, eleven sophomores, fourteen juniors, and five seniors.

Professor Parker was meeting his elementary French class of fifteen students three times a week; his second French class of eight students, twice a week; his first German class of ten students, three times a week; his second German class of nine students, twice a week. That gave Professor Parker a total of forty-two students and a teaching load of ten hours a week.

Professor Smith said there were seven students in his classes in mineralogy and geology. He did not specify the number of hours he taught, but his load must have been light enough to allow him plenty of time for his job of state geologist.

Professor Foster had sixteen students enrolled in a miscellaneous assortment of classes which included philosophy, mechanics, astronomy, and bookkeeping. He was teaching eleven hours a week, in addition to frequent laboratory sessions with astronomy students who were making telescopic observations at night. Two seniors, meeting three times a week, made up the class in mental and moral philosophy. Three students, meeting three times a week, had been taking "mechanics" the first term and astronomy the second term. Seven students in natural philosophy had met three times a week. Four students had had two bookkeeping lessons a week in the second term.

Professor Whitfield was the only one of the group who reported a really heavy class schedule. Fifty-four students and sixteen classroom hours a week was his record. His regular algebra class of sixteen students met five times a week, and he was giving an "irregular" class three times a week to help three students make up the regular class work. He was also teaching arithmetic to eleven students three times a week; trigonometry to twenty students three times a week; and analytical geometry to four students twice a week.[14]

Professor Whitfield's schedule may have become more typical as the years went on and the curriculum developed. Certainly the schedule handed to Colonel McCorvey in 1888 would have been cause for complaint if other faculty members by that time had not come to spend more hours in the classroom. Colonel McCorvey had two freshman classes in history and political economy that year; each class met three times a week. He also had two recitations a week with classical sophomores; three with classical juniors and one with scientific juniors; five with classical seniors and one with scientific seniors. He was spending nineteen hours each week in the classroom.[15]

If the faculty of that day ever discussed in their formal meetings teaching methods and classroom procedures, they left little record of such discussion in their minutes. The picture of what went on in those classrooms has to be built in imagination on the meager foundation supplied by the *Catalogue:* "The Mode of Instruction in Both Departments is by Lectures and Recitations from Text Books, accompanied by daily examinations, oral and written."[16] Obviously, each teacher was given wide latitude for working out his own methods.

A few joint decisions were made. Professor Foster once inquired about the custom of his colleagues in regard to permitting the use of books and paper in recitation, but the content of the discussion is not recorded and the final agreement was to permit each teacher to do as he pleased about this matter.[17] Perhaps the discussion was responsible for the rules adopted the following month that students should "remain in their Seats in silence except when called upon to recite" and that they might not "refer to any book or paper not relating to the recitation of the hour" under penalty of being reported to the officer of the day.[18] On another occasion an argument arose over the right of individual teachers to decide if an examination should be given. It was finally agreed that teachers had this right, but that they should notify the full faculty or the committee on examinations if they decided to omit a scheduled examination.[19] For the most part, however, the teachers apparently struggled with their own problems, and such references in the minutes are oblique.

Adequate equipment was one of these problems. As late as 1887, the faculty petitioned the board of trustees to supply the recitation rooms with desks.[20] Even that essential could not be taken for granted, it seems. Easing of financial stress made it possible to grant more and more of the requests for equipment coming from the departments and the individual teachers, and some of these requests show a creativeness at work and the kind of imagination that makes good teaching.

Professor Parker was given a special grant of $25 in 1879 so that he could subscribe for two daily German newspapers.[21] German had a better chance of becoming a living language in classroom after that. In 1892 the $50 purchase of a "magic lantern" or stereopticon must have added zest to the classes in geology and history.[22] A set of plaster-of-paris models for the Geology Department was bought that same year for $75, and the History Department got a full set of historical maps.[23] The library was an increasingly valuable resource; the historical museum was growing.

Textbooks were always a problem. In 1879 the trustees were so concerned about the high cost of books that they appointed a special committee to see what could be done about lowering that expense, which of course, was an expense borne by the students. They even considered the idea of having the University operate its own bookstore. The committee reported that the prices of the textbooks did not seem unreasonable to them, that the recent establishment of a new bookstore in Tuscaloosa would probably take care of the problem by introducing competition. They advised strongly against having the University attempt to buy and sell its own textbooks. That action would lead, they feared, to a large accumulation of "dead stock" and would mean pecuniary loss to the University. The trustees were not wholly satisfied with this report. They asked a new committee to go into the problem further, to determine if the University should undertake to furnish textbooks to the students without charge. The plan which this committee was asked to consider had unhappy possibilities. The faculty would submit to a committee a

REBUILDING THE UNIVERSITY 443

list of the books they wanted to use in their classes and the number of books they would need. Once this list had been adopted no teacher might change a textbook without consent of the trustees.[24] The matter was apparently dropped before the trustees involved themselves in such an arrangement.

The textbooks in general use were always listed in the catalogue announcement of courses. Some of these, which were more or less standard through the years, are listed in the description of courses in the chapter "The Schools and their Teachers." The books used in the recurring courses in political economy and economics indicate the manner in which the University was moving toward modern thought. Fawcett's *Political Economy,* as a textbook, and Mills' *Political Economy,* as a reference book, were the cornerstones of the course Colonel McCorvey gave in 1879. By 1889 Smith's *Wealth of Nations* and two volumes by Walker had been added to the list. In 1898 the course "intended to give an outline knowledge of the accepted theories in Economic Science" which McCorvey was giving had for its textbook Walker's *Political Economy.*[25] And when, between 1887 and 1890, a course of study for a master's degree in political economy was offered, the *Catalogue* description outlined it thus: "Readings upon Values, Prices, Free Trade, and Labor and Labor Unions—Prof. Cairnes being considered the best authority on these subjects; and readings in Socialism, Communism, the Rights of Property, Money, and the Tenures of Land—J. Stuart Mill being considered the best authority on these subjects."[26] Course outlines and course readings were beginning to have a decidedly twentieth century ring.

More and more field work was brought in by progressive faculty members to enrich the classroom studies. The old Observatory, survivor of the war, was used to its fullest extent by astronomy students. Astrological phenomena were one of the few causes for relaxation of military rules for cadets. When something happened in the heavens, cadets were allowed out of their dormitories at most unusual hours. For the "Transit of Venus" in 1882 a schedule was posted: juniors might watch it at eleven o'clock; freshmen and seniors, at twelve; sophomores, at two in the morning.[27] Students enrolled for the scientific course worked three hours a week in the laboratory and made an increasing number of field trips. Engineering students visited mines, factories, and furnaces as their professors sought to make real and practical the theories of the classroom. Some of these excursions involved a considerable amount of time and travel. As early as 1873, Professor Whitfield's surveying class had to be excused from regular classes between eight o'clock in the morning until noon twice a week so that they could be out applying their knowledge in actual surveying.[28] In 1889 Colonel Hardaway took his senior class to visit the furnaces in Birmingham, a long and tedious journey for those days.[29] In May, 1891, the junior class in engineering was given permission to be absent from the University for the first nine days of June to locate a railroad line "to run from the terminus of the Tuscaloosa Northern Railroad to connect with the Mineral Branch of the Louisville and Nashville Railroad at Brookwood."[30] The trip must have been a success, for, when the trustees met that June, they approved a plan to make such survey tours annual events, with the University providing the three wall tents and other camping equipment the students would require.[31]

Education was coming out of its "ivory tower" at the University of Alabama. The classical scholars were still there, pouring into their work the vitality of their own love of learning. But beside them now worked, just as zealously, men bent on training youth for the practical service of their own day. The improved teaching methods established in the last three decades of the century were hammered out through experiment.

The atmosphere of security which is now assumed essential for the best working of the academic mind was almost wholly lacking on the University campus. All through these years the men who taught felt the constant uncomfortable pressure of inadequate salaries and the equally uncomfortable necessity of winning reappointment each year they served.

The reorganizers of the University in 1871 had ambitious ideas on the subject of salaries. To attract high-calibered men they were willing to pay salaries which, by the standards of the time, were generous. Matthew Fontaine Maury, the new president who resigned promptly after his inaugural address, was voted a salary of $5000. The professors who served with him were to have $2500 each. A very extravagant budget, asserted the *Monitor*, especially in view of the fact that it was voted when no students had actually registered for the fall classes.[32] The public, reading this and other newspapers, shook its head in disapproval and foreboding.

The resignation of President Maury changed the situation. Professor Lupton, chosen by the faculty as their leader, was already on the payroll at the $2500 figure. He did not have to be lured by promises of a princely salary. The actual salaries paid to the teachers in the reorganized University cannot be determined, because the records of the board of regents for the years 1869 to 1873 have not been found.[33]

The listed salary rates and the amount of money which found its way into the professors' pockets in those early years did not always correspond. Salaries were paid monthly,[34] but, except for a small prorata dividend of currency from student fees, they were paid in state certificates. When a teacher cashed his certificate, he was usually forced to do so at less than its face value. His salary was cut in this process, no matter what the records of the University treasurer showed. President Carlos Smith was gravely concerned about this situation in 1874. He urged that University salaries be paid in currency. The regents told him that University professors were on exactly the same footing as other employees of the state, that all state salaries were paid in certificates, and that it would be unfair to give special treatment to the University faculty.[35]

In fact, said the regents at this meeting, the University salary scale was too high. A proposal to cut those salaries to $1600 was voted down, but there was heated discussion about what to do for teachers who lived in University houses. Some argued that those who provided their own housing should get $200 above the base rate; others argued that those who had homes furnished for them should be paid $200 less than that rate. No conclusions were reached in this argument; the matter was finally tabled without clarification of policy.[36] President Smith may have won a slight concession in the argument at that time, for it appears from the regents' minutes a year later that tuition fees, divided share and share alike among members of the faculty, were allowed to constitute a token salary bonus that year.[37]

With the transfer of the University control back to a board of trustees, better records of University business were kept. Salary scales can be followed with more accuracy. The scale adopted in 1876 was as follows:

President	$2750	with house and grounds
Academic Professors	2250	with house and grounds
Commandant	1600	
Quartermaster & Steward	1500	(one person)
Law Professors	500,	together with tuitions not to exceed $25 per pupil.
Civil Engineering Professor		such fees as he may collect from students.
Mechanic		amount not to exceed $50 per month.[38]

This schedule did not stand long unchanged. Funds were low the following year, and the professors took a cut of $250. The $200 concession for teachers who could not be assigned to University houses, about which the regents had wrangled three years earlier, was finally granted. The civil engineering professor had apparently become a recognized part of the regular faculty by this time, for no mention is made of the special fee basis for his remuneration. The salary of the mechanic, who had enjoyed the prospect of a maximum of $600 a year, was cut back to $400.[39] Even those reductions did not solve the budget problem. In July, 1878, the trustees did a little more slashing. When they finished, the president's salary had dropped to $2,500, professors' salaries to $1,800, with only $150 allowed for commutation of rent; and the quartermaster's pay had become $1,400.[40] The scale adopted at that time remained in effect through the rest of the century.

Only in the Law School was there an upward salary trend. The $500-plus-fees arrangement of 1875 disappeared the following year. The two professors in the law department were to get a flat $650 for their services. In 1888 differentiation between the two men in the school was indicated in a ruling that one professor of law was to have $1,000 a year; the other, $400.[41] The following year the trustees voted a salary of $1,300 to the professor of equity-jurisprudence, but held the salary of the professor of statute and common law at $400.[42] This action stabilized the salary scale for at least seven years: in 1896 the trustees noted that Professor Van de Graaf, succeeding

Colonel Hargrove, who had died, would have a salary of $1300 and that Professor Somerville, who became acting professor of statute and common law, would get $33.33 per month.[43] Recognition of the growing importance of the Law School brought an important budget change in 1897. The position of dean of the Law School was created, and the new officer was placed on equal footing with the president of the University: he was to have $2500 and his residence.[44] The assistant professor of law got a $200 raise that same year;[45] by 1900 his salary had gone up to $1200.[46] Law salaries were always budgeted separately during these years, and it should be remembered that they were low in comparison with other faculty salaries chiefly because it was expected that the men who taught in the Law School would supplement their pay from the University through the practice of law in Tuscaloosa.

If salaries for men of professorial rank were low, those received by assistants and instructors were so much lower that it is hard to see how the teachers of lesser rank managed to get along at all. In June, 1884, the trustees noted that their three assistant professors were getting $600 each.[47] They hired an additional instructor the following year for $400 plus board. At that time someone had an impulse of generosity and recommended that J. B. Little, assistant professor of chemistry, be given a salary raise to $750. The proposal was voted down promptly. Mr. Little would be contented with $600, or the post would be given to Daniel Webster Langdon.[48] Apparently, Mr. Little accepted the ultimatum and even took a cut later, for when he resigned in 1887 he was getting $500. The two boys who took over his work, both students, divided that princely salary between them.[49] An indication of what the University expected in return for the $600 standard salary paid its assistant professors is given in the faculty minutes in 1886. It was noted that Mr. Little was teaching ten hours a week in chemistry and six hours a week in physics, while Mr. Gilbert was putting in ten hours of mathematics teaching and six of English.[50]

Instructors got even less than assistants, but their low remuneration was partly justified because they were usually young graduates working toward their master's degrees, needing only enough subsidy to make this graduate study possible. Sometimes undergraduates were given tutorial jobs to eke out their resources and enable them to complete their courses. There was little standardization in the arrangements made at this academic level. Combinations of jobs and salaries were possible; so were divisions of the jobs on shared salaries. When Surry F. Mayfield, for instance, declined an assistant's position in the department of physics and astronomy in 1888, Messrs. Francis and Sibert were allowed to divide the job between them and, also, to divide the $200 stipend which Mayfield had refused. Since both these men held assistant professorships carrying salaries of $300 plus board, they had bettered their financial position by a rather substantial proportion.[51] Mr. Sibert, especially, had made a substantial gain since the year before when, as an undergraduate, he had been an instructor in freshman drawing at a salary of $10 a month.[52]

The gymnasium instructor occupied a place in the scale somewhat above the other instructors, but far below the professorial staff. In 1890, finding it difficult to make ends meet on his regular stipend of $500 and board, he petitioned the trustees to allow him the expenses of light, fuel, and laundry. The trustees not only granted this request but also, at their next meeting, raised his salary to $800,[53] at which figure it remained at least through 1897.

Looking over the salaries paid assistants and instructors in 1889, the trustees noted that assistant professor Langdon was getting $600; instructor McKenzie, $300 plus board and washing; instructors Beeson, Crook, and Somerville, $100 plus board and washing.[54] Each was expected to spend ten hours a week assisting the professor to whom he was assigned.[55] The discrepancy in salary rates must have concerned the members of the board, for the following year they adopted a standard rate of $300 for tutorial salaries.[56] In 1899 a burst of generosity at the formation of a new staff for a pedagogy and romance language department brought instructors' salaries, at least in that department, to a new high: $1300.[57]

In the military department the commandant's salary, set at $1600 in 1876, was briefly cut to $1500 in 1879, but the trustees restored that cut within two months. The quartermaster, however, got dropped from $1500 to $1000 that year, and apparently that cut was not restored.[58]

Once in a while, especially in the early years of the period, discrepancies between the scale and salaries paid troubled the trus-

REBUILDING THE UNIVERSITY 449

tees. A committee studying salaries in 1878-1879 reported that some professors had been getting only $1500 instead of the $1800 which was then standard.[59] Presumably the board intended to equalize the scale at that time.

With due consideration for the needs and preferences of their teaching staff the trustees had ruled that all salaries should be paid in twelve monthly installments. This was a convenience for the teachers, who thus had a regular income during vacation months. But it was an opportunity for Professor D. W. Langdon to put the board into a most embarrassing position. Langdon accepted appointment as an assistant professor in June, 1889. He drew two months salary and then resigned. The trustees demanded a refund; he had done no work during the vacation months. Mr. Langdon refused to make such a refund. And the judiciary committee of the trustees sustained his action:

Mr. Langdon had the legal right under the terms of the contract of employment to draw the two months pay and . . . this Board could not require him to refund the same. No services were rendered by Mr. Langdon during the time for which the pay was drawn for the reason that none were required of him at that time, nor contemplated by the terms of his employment. . . .[60]

So Mr. Langdon kept his money, but the board, determined not to be caught that way again, adopted a new policy of paying salaries in nine installments during the academic year.[61]

Pressure for increased salary rates was, quite naturally, constantly brought to bear on the board through all this period. President Lewis, in his Annual Report of 1881, tried to soften the hearts of the men who held the purse strings and to make them understand that $1,800 was an inadequate compensation for men who were serving the University as faithfully as were the faculty of that time:

I hope also that I shall be pardoned if I mention the fact that since the salaries of the Professors were reduced to Eighteen hundred dollars each, that there has taken place a general rise in the prices of all the necessaries of life; and that $2000.00 would now scarcely exceed in purchasing power the sum of $1800.00 when that sum was previously fixed as the amount of a Professor's Salary. Nothing is so essential to the Continuous, cheerful, and efficient work of an instructor, as the assurance that his pay is sufficient to relieve his mind of all anxiety for the maintenance and support of his family in a manner suitable to their condition in life—to say nothing of the hope of being able to save some small pittance annually for providing a fund in behalf of his loved ones for the night that "Cometh when no man can work." It is not for any personal consideration that I make this appeal; but from a deep sense of conviction that you could do nothing that could be of any greater service to the University than to place its Faculty beyond the harrassing uncertainty of their ability to live within their incomes. I am satisfied that the education of their children and the increased costs of living make $1800.00 insufficient to secure this desirable end on behalf of some of them.[62]

Later in the same report, President Lewis reinforced his convictions, this time with special tribute to the men who worked under him:

It affords me pleasure to bear testimony to the zeal and efficiency of all officers of instruction during the past session. . . . I hope I shall be pardoned for calling again the attention of your honorable body to the inadequacy of the salaries of the professors. I trust that should you find that the best interests of the University will justify it, you will make such increase in their pay as your judgment may dictate. Especially would I urge that the pay of Assistant Professor McCalley be increased. He has given several years of faithful work to the University for which he has received no *adequate* compensation.[63]

The trustees rejected President Lewis's plea and other similar pleas in the years that followed. In 1883 they did rule that the order that teachers living in University houses pay for all repairs on those houses was too burdensome and should be rescinded.[64] A move to raise salaries in 1888 faded out. Only Mrs. Gorgas, the librarian, was granted a raise. She had been getting $400 plus the use of one of the University houses; she was given a raise of $100.[65] The trustees did not yield on the point of salary. Even when funds through land sales became available, such money could not be used for the increase of salaries. The professors at the University of Alabama before 1900 never lost the sense of "harassing uncertainty" about money, a condition which President Lewis so much deplored.

The trustees were adamant also on another matter which gravely troubled the teachers and which added to their sense of insecurity—the question of tenure. The board insisted that they could best perform their duties to the University if they kept firm control of their right to review annually the work done by the faculty and to reappoint or fail to reappoint the teachers on the basis of this review.

REBUILDING THE UNIVERSITY

The faculty insisted that they could do their best work only if they had a feeling that their appointments were relatively permanent. The tug-of-war went on steadily from the time that the reorganized University opened its doors.

President Lupton spoke for his faculty colleagues when, in 1873, he addressed the regents:

Permanence and stability are essential to the prosperity of public institutions and especially institutions of learning. As long as the idea prevails that the Faculty will be annually reconstructive, and that the mode of discipline is liable to essential change at every meeting of the Board, so long will young men hesitate to see the advantages and honors of the University and turn their footsteps to more firmly established seats of learning.[66]

The board of regents, however, had its own convictions on this matter. A committee charged with setting policy in this and other areas had stated these convictions quite clearly:

What shall be the tenure of office for professors? Shall the professor's tenure of office be limited to four or six years, or some other fixed period? The usual—in fact, almost universal plan has been to elect professors to serve indefinitely, the power of removal being left with the regents or trustees. Practically this power is seldom used, even when it ought to be . . . . there are few institutions which have not suffered from retaining men not sufficiently capable. Positive action is required when a removal is to be made, and no one wishes to initiate it.

Men are retained in their places as professors from this reluctance of Boards to act, who, with the same incapacity or want of highest capacity, if in any business house or establishment could not, for any considerable time, hold their positions. This is a very great evil and drawback upon our institutions of learning. There is hardly an institution in the country which does not, to a greater or less extent, suffer from it.[67]

The case for and against tenure could hardly be better stated.

The organizing committee had recommended to the regents a plan of limited tenure:

Your Committee recommend that the professors who are to be elected at the present session of the Board, be elected for two years, and that their successors be elected every four years.[68]

It is interesting to note that these provisions were never put into effect. The regents and, later, the trustees preferred to elect the whole faculty at each annual session of the board. Moreover, the governing body retained the right to remove at will any professor who at any time during the year seemed to them to be doing unsatisfactory work.

President Lupton's warning to the regents in 1873 that this system of arbitrary removal was causing "uncertainty and consequent uneasiness" which was working "injuriously" both on the campus and throughout the state,[69] impressed the board so much, however, that they almost reversed themselves on this important point. Four days after President Lupton's report, the regents had before them a resolution making faculty appointments permanent for life or during good behavior and requiring six month's notice before the dismissal of any teacher.[70] But the resolution was never acted upon. Within another four days the conservatives were able to rally support again for the old system; all faculty positions were declared automatically vacant at the year's end, and the right to reappoint or to fail to reappoint was firmly in the hands of the board as it had been before President Lupton spoke.[71]

President Lupton had understood the difficulties which teachers face under such direct and autocratic control. Professors at the University of Alabama in those days worked with a constant sense that they were being watched by members of the governing body. They feared that a change of policy or teaching method, the infliction of discipline, or the firm handling of the son of an influential father might at any moment bring down upon their heads the disaproval of the regents or trustees, and might even cause them to be summarily dismissed from their posts. Their discontent made itself heard whenever the governing body met, usually through their friends on the board who were aware of the injustice and instability of the situation. Scarcely a board meeting passed without some discussion about the thorny problem of tenure.

In 1876 the board of trustees reaffirmed the position taken by the regents: faculty appointments were for one year; faculty members could be removed during the year "for cause."[72] The next year they found it necessary to defend this policy, but not to change it. They were well aware, they said, that it was important to retain competent professors. They knew as well as anyone that professors became increasingly useful to the University as the years of their

BURWELL BOYKIN LEWIS

President, 1880-1885

HENRY DELAMAR CLAYTON

President, 1885-1889

RICHARD CHANNING JONES

President, 1890-1897

JAMES KNOX POWERS

President, 1897-1901

THOMAS CHALMERS McCORVEY
Commandant, 1873-1888
Professor of History and Philosophy, 1888-1923

WILLIAM STOKES WYMAN
President, 1901-1902
Acting President, 1879-80, 1885-86, 1889-90

service multiplied. But they would, nevertheless, continue to make one-year appointments "with the view of retaining in their hands the power of removing them by declining to elect, whenever the interests of the University, in their judgment, requires it."[73]

A resolution, introduced in July, 1879, called for the establishment of a three-year term for faculty appointments, with the condition that professors might be removed at the will of the board "without conditions or assignment of cause." Apparently no action was taken on this proposal.[74] In 1885 a radical resolution that faculty members be elected for life was voted down. This time, however, a concession was made. It was agreed that the faculty and officers should be elected for three-year terms.[75]

The three-year term remained in force, at least in theory, for the remainder of the period under discussion. In 1888 an effort to change tenure from three years to "the will of the Board of Trustees" merely resulted in the reaffirmation of the three-year policy.[76] Nearly ten years later, however, when faculty elections were before the board at a June, 1897, meeting, the minutes showed that professors and tutors were to be elected for a one-year period, the president for a term of three years.[77] The will to control the lives of the teaching and administrative staff through control of their jobs died hard.

A conspicuous example of the working of these controls was the decision by the board not to reappoint President Carlos Smith in 1878. For lesser men on the faculty, the annual anxiety over reappointment must have been a source of great discomfort. Life on the University campus was no sinecure for the harassed professors trying to build a great institution of learning.

CHAPTER XX

Student Life

THE YOUNG MEN who came home to school when the University opened in 1871 gave to the life of the campus a flavor blended with traditions and accents of colleges and universities far outside the limits of their home state. The customs and the college slang of the University of Virginia and the Virginia Military Institute, of Washington and Lee and Randolph-Macon, of Chapel Hill and of Davidson, Erskine and of Wofford, of Athens and of Mercer mingled to form the beginnings of student tradition at the University of Alabama.[1] Yet that tradition was always rooted in Alabama soil and built by Alabama youth.

The University grew in three decades from an enrollment of 107, in 1871-1872, to an enrollment of 261, in 1900-1901. It averaged 128 students a year in the 1870's; 201 in the 1880's; 196 in the 1890's. And throughout the period, nearly all of the students enrolled were young men of Alabama. The peak of out-of-state enrollments came in 1887-1888, when 25 of the 238 students were from states other than Alabama. Mississippi had at least one representative on the campus through the period; Louisiana was nearly always represented; there was a scattering of students from other southern states; but only an occasional individual from farther afield—from Nevada, Pennsylvania, New York, California.

Professor Wyman seemed to have been almost alone in his opinion that this ingrown quality of the University was unfortunate, that effort should be made to attract to the campus young men of other states. In 1894, when admission requirements were under discussion, Wyman urged that thought be given to modifying those requirements "so as to open the doors of the University to a large number of the young men of the state, and of other states, of suitable

REBUILDING THE UNIVERSITY

age, who are by existing conditions of admission debarred from entering even the lowest class."[2] His allusion to "young men . . . of other states," however, was tentative and in no way influenced his colleagues to think of their University as more than a state school for state citizens. Throughout the period young men of Alabama were favored by admission rules. The certification system admitted, without examination, graduates of many Alabama schools. Advantageous, also, was a system of fees developed during these years.

It cost $130 to send a boy to the University of Alabama for a term, or half-year, in the early 1870's. This sum included tuition, board, fuel, lights, attendance, and incidentals.[3] Special students paid $38 a term,[4] a figure which must have been almost wholly for tuition. These fees were high enough to embarrass some applicants and their parents. The faculty recognized this fact in 1873 by voting to accept a down payment of $30 at the time of admission, allowing two months for the completion of payments.[5] At least one faculty member took advantage of this provision and received an extension of time for the payment of his son's fees.[6] Enrollments may have been held down by the fees, for the slump in student numbers in the middle years of the decade was sharp enough to alarm the trustees and to cause them to make drastic cuts in the fee schedule. Total expenses were reduced to $95 a term in 1876, a saving of $70 a year for parents of University sons.[7] Fees were reduced again twice during the next ten years: to $83 a term in 1879,[8] to $76.50 in 1883.[9] But, by that time, the trustees apparently decided that they had overstepped the line of good policy. In 1884 the fees went up again, to $96.[10] This fluctuation continued in the 1890's. In 1891 all term expenses, including board, lodging, washing, fuel, lights, attendance, surgeon's fee, hospital and medicine fee, and incidental fee totalled $80.50;[11] in 1894 they were as high as $96.25;[12] in 1897 they had dropped to $65.00,[13] exclusive of tuition.

Not all students paid these full fees. When the board of trustees resumed responsibility for University administration in 1876, they noted the authority given them by the legislature to admit tuition-free three students from each county. They would, they said, exercise that power with "judicious liberality."[14] Two years later they even extended that power by voting to admit without payment of tuition sons of ministers, of faculty members, and of the quartermaster.[15] The following year seventy-three students, slightly more than forty-four per cent of the whole student body, had been exempted from payment of tuition fees, either because they were trustee appointments from the counties or because they were sons of ministers or teachers.[16] In 1879 a new class of tuition-free students was established when the trustees authorized the appointment of one student from each congressional district. The scholarship in the case of these favored young men included not only tuition but all other charges except the costs of textbooks and clothing. That meant that some counties in the state could now have more than three young men in the University under special scholarship provisions.[17] More than half the students who entered the University that year, some seventy-eight in all, came in under some waiver of tuition fees. Expenses of the free cadetships came out of general tuition receipts, and in 1879 those expenses totalled $418.30.[18]

All these provisions favored Alabama youth, and, in 1887 the trustees gave even more sweeping advantage to the boys of the home state by eliminating tuition fees in the Academic Department for all students from Alabama. Home-state students then paid a contingent fee of $5.00 into the University fund,[19] as well as the expenses of board, lodging, washing, fuel, lights, etc. But out-of-state students paid all these fees and expenses plus a tuition fee of $40 a year. The University continued to give the advantage to sons of the state it was founded to serve.

Plain living and strictly regimented living was the portion of students on that early campus. For the first fifteen years after the University reopened, the only living quarters provided were the "barracks," not even, in those days, dignified by the name of Woods Hall. An iron bed and small table furnished by the University were the only equipment in the rooms. Students brought their own sheets, blankets, pillowcases.[20] Student comfort received little or no consideration from the University authorities until the middle 1880's, when money from land sales was making it possible for the University to expand its plant and to look with less Spartan eye upon the bodily needs of the cadets. In 1886 a committee inspected and reported the condition of the barracks in which the boys were living:

There were no closets in the cadets' rooms used as sleeping apartments and no wardrobes. The bedsteads and work stands were not satisfactory.

REBUILDING THE UNIVERSITY 457

It was almost impossible for a cadet to keep his clothing in a small trunk and if hung on nails about the room it gave the room an untidy appearance which was not in keeping with military discipline and which impaired the formation of habits of neatness and orderliness.[21]

Sam Friedman, who attended the University between 1885 and 1889, remembered that the expanding cadet corps outgrew the barracks by 1887 and made necessary the building of additional temporary barracks, which must have been equally uncomfortable:

In about 1887 the normal corps of Cadets, being about 125 or 150 strong, was augmented to 175 and the University was forced to build a long line of wooden one-storey rooms, joined together, and located about where the old engineering building now stands. Several years later these rooms were torn down.[22]

When Garland Hall was completed the trustees decided that it might be good policy to allow cadets to earn, by good conduct and seniority, some amelioration of their living conditions. They decided to set aside rooms for seniors in Garland Hall and to furnish them more attractively than the barracks rooms. They could, they thought, favor seniors in this way without causing jealousy, since every lower-classman could look forward to achieving this senior privilege. The plan would, in fact, encourage lower classmen to stay with the University long enough to become seniors, and would put a premium on "gentlemanly deportment." They said,

. . . the Juniors of this year would have an additional strong incentive to return to the University and become Seniors next year, while the Seniors would be complimented by the additional consideration shown them and be induced thereby to be more gentlemanly in their conduct.[23]

Glamor was added to the privilege they were about to bestow on the gentlemen of the senior class, the trustees noted a trifle pompously, because these favored young men would be housed under the same roof as were visting members of the board of trustees. As plans for Garland Hall had progressed, the board had directed that "suitable rooms" be provided for members of the board to occupy "when officially visiting the University."[24] Six rooms on the third floor of Garland Hall had, accordingly, been reserved for use by trustees. These rooms were furnished "not elegantly nor luxuriously, but comfortably and pleasantly, with the design to make the rooms as attractive, at least, as the trustees would be apt to get at the Tuscaloosa hotels.[25] The building committee had taken thought for trustee comfort in selecting the third floor, where rooms would be "cooler and more retired" than on the lower floors. The committee thought that "when the hall was filled with students it would be pleasanter to be above rather than below them."[26] Whether the seniors who came to live in Garland Hall actually felt that having an occasional trustee moving about in the rooms above them added "dignity and consequence" to the privilege is not a matter of record.

Underclassmen continued to live in Woods Hall barracks, where the forty-six rooms were often overcrowded in the 1870's and 1880's.[27] But, even there, some service for the more menial tasks was always available. Two "stoop boys" carried coal to the rooms, removed ashes, and brought buckets of water. By special permit from the commandant they were allowed to scour the floors for a fee of not more than thirty-five cents,[28] to be paid by the student. An errand boy carried mail to and from the postoffice until 1886, when a University post-office was established on the campus.[29] Gradually, the erection of new and more modern buildings and the installation of such facilities as gas, electricity, and running water took the starkness out of campus living. But luxury was never a mark of student life in these three decades.

The austerity of the daily routine matched the austerity of living quarters. The University had been a military college when war interrupted it. It was a military college when it reopened in 1871. Furthermore, it continued to be a military college, in spite of growing student restlessness and rebellion, until the twentieth century.

The reveille horn, sounding forth at six o'clock, started the student's day. Room inspection came at six-thirty. Breakfast was at seven, and prayers came immediately after that. From eight o'clock until one the guard in the quadrangle saw that there was no visiting or disturbance in the barracks. The studious silence was broken only by the bugle, which, five minutes before each hour, signaled students to form in line ready to march into the classrooms. At one o'clock, the bugle blew for dinner. From two to four the business of studying and reciting was resumed. After classes came the daily military drill, and then an all-too-brief "release from quarters," during which students might relax and stroll around the campus. Supper was served at six, and at seven "call to quarters" sounded the beginning of the evening study period. When "tattoo" was signaled at nine-thirty, the student was free to lay aside his books. He could retire as soon as the sergeant inspected his room, or he could read or study for another hour. When "taps" sounded at ten-thirty, however, lights went out and the day was over. At eleven o'clock the officer of the day began his rounds to see that all was quiet and that the cadets were safely and silently in their rooms.[30]

Each student entering for the first time his barracks room found there a copy of the rules and regulations of the University.[31] He was expected to memorize these rules, and he was warned that they would be enforced by strict military discipline. Most of the rules were carried over from earlier University codes, and included the same effort to foresee all the misdemeanors which might occur to student minds and the same resort to generalities to take care of unpredictable mischief. Students were enjoined to "abstain from all vicious, immoral or irregular conduct," and to "conduct themselves with the propriety and decorum of gentlemen." They were to respect and obey the duly constituted authorities or run the risk of dismissal. They were to treat their fellow students with consideration: they must not insult a sentinel "by word or question"; they must not use "reproachful or provoking language or gestures" to another student; they must not "wantonly abuse" each other—by "unjustifiable tricks"; they must not be party to any move to ostracize a fellow student; they must remember that state laws as well as University laws would be invoked if student fights became violent.

As in the earlier pre-war formulations of University laws, the lawmakers attempted by fiat to tether restless feet to the University grounds. Special permission from the president was required before a cadet might leave the campus or even be absent from his room for more than half an hour. He might not even leave that room during study hours without special permission. Visiting any "house of entertainment" was forbidden. "The strictest attention to study and all other duties" was emphasized, and the cadet who could not present satisfactory written excuses for absences was judged guilty of "a culpable neglect of his duty" and might be dismissed.

Cheating in the classroom or on an examination was subject to heavy penalties. The rules indicated some of the possibilities the rule-makers foresaw: no student should "utter a falsehood" by answering for another at roll call or "commit a fraud" by engaging another to answer for him. Foreseen damage to University property was guarded against in rules which forbade students to "damage wantonly" his room or to "loose, damage, destroy, sell, or otherwise dispose of the arms, accoutrements, books, instruments, or other public property" in his possession. Cooking in the dormitory rooms was forbidden, and "entertainment" in those rooms could be given only with special permission. No student might keep a servant, a horse, or a dog.

Rules which guarded student morality were strong and explicit. No student was to drink or have in his possession any "spiritous or intoxicating liquors." Without special permission, no student might go to any inn, public house, or place where liquor was sold. Playing cards or "any other game of chance" was strictly prohibited, and a student found with the cards "or materials used in those games" in his possession faced certain punishment. Proper observance of the Sabbath, including reverent church attendance, was required, and penalties were provided for students who misbehaved at divine service or who used "any profane oath" or "execrated or profaned the Sabbath."

Most explicit of all were the regulations against the use of firearms. As in the old University, students coming to the University in the 1870's still signed this pledge before they were admitted:

Having become a member of the University of Alabama, I do hereby acknowledge my obligation to obey all its laws and regulations. And I do further pledge myself *on honor,* that I will not have in my possession or carry a pistol, bowie knife, sword-cane, or any other deadly weapon, except such arms as are furnished by the military department, so long as I am a cadet of the University, during term time, or while I remain at the University during vacation, without the consent of the President or Faculty.

The old injunction against taking part in duels was also carried over from the older codes. Students were forbidden to send or accept challenges, "written or verbal." It was also against rules to "upbraid another for declining to fight." Students were to report to the president at once if they heard of any duel in the making.

On and on the list of regulations extended. It is evident that the authorities did not want to leave a single loophole; they added at the end a blanket clause:

All immoralities, disorders, misbehaviors, or neglect of which cadets may be guilty, to the prejudice of good order and military discipline, though not herein expressed, are to be punished according to the nature and degree of the offence.

By the laws of 1873, punishments for infringements of laws minor and major were classified into three grades: (1) privation of recreation, extra tours of duty, or reprimand; (2) arrest or confinement to room or limits; and (3) suspension, dismissal with the privilege of resigning, or public dismissal. Enforcement of the laws was a matter for the military authorities, who had the coöperation of the academic faculty.

Everything in and about the University was strictly military. . . . All infringement of military rules was penalized by demerits and grave offenses placed you under arrest and confinement to your room, although of course you still had to attend classes and other calls.[32]

Rules and routines which provided for the students the religious training and expression which the trustees and faculty considered vitally important were somewhat less strict in the new University than they had been in the 1840's and 1850's. Chapel, however, was still part of each day's required schedule, though students did not have to sit through the prayers with empty stomachs; they could breakfast before they prayed. Chapel services were held in the barracks until the completion of Clark Hall, in 1885, and a new and suitable place was provided in the new building. Naturally, the students grumbled about compulsory chapel. The more devout among them protested in the name of their piety, protesting that "optional" chapel attendance would more truly foster a spirit of devotion. Said one student critic in 1887,

. . . morning after morning we see the students enter the chapel with identically the same feeling, as they go to the discharge of any other college duty. They regard it as a task to be performed and to be gotten through with as soon, and with as little inconvenience as possible. The call that summons them to prayer is the same as the call that summons them to drill. After they are in the chapel, I dare say, it does not occur to half of them, even that they are in a house of worship. This is not on account of the irreligious tendencies of the students, but because worship is lowered to the plane of a routine college duty. . . . There seems to be but one other plan, and that is to make chapel attendance optional. . . .[33]

With the general public eyeing the University with suspicion because of the "godless tendencies" fostered there, the authorities could not afford to listen to such reasoning. They continued to require students to attend chapel daily and also to be present at the Sunday services conducted on the campus by a clergyman from Tuscaloosa. Exemptions from attendance at these latter services were allowed for students who presented requests from their parents that they be excused "on the grounds of religious scruples."[34] But, presumably, even these dissenters were required to attend with regularity the church of their choice in Tuscaloosa on Sunday morning. Each student indicated the church he preferred when he enrolled, and, thereafter, each Sunday, he lined up with his fellow religionists in a church section which was marched to the place of worship and delivered into the hands of the church wardens. Attendance at Sunday school was optional. And students who wished to go to evening services had to get special permission to do so.

Students attending these formal services were under careful scrutiny. Their church manners did not always satisfy the critics. A reporter from the Tuscaloosa *Gazette* watched them while they listened with "marked indifference" to a baccalaureate sermon in 1881, and then wrote an editorial about the occasion. The students, he said, sat with "stolid unconcern" and looked on "like the spectators at a show, at the devotions of others around them." They seemed to take no interest in the service designed chiefly for their benefit.[35]

Yet by 1887 the Young Men's Christian Association, founded by Professor Wyman in the fall of 1881, boasted a membership of two-thirds the student body.[36] Its meetings came after supper on Sunday evenings and perhaps had the fellowship and informality which students missed in the compulsory religious services. Usually the president of the association or some member appointed by him conducted the meetings; once a month a minister from town was invited to conduct the service.[37] After women were admitted to the University, Y.M.C.A. meetings took on an even more attractive aspect; the girls were often called upon to furnish music for the Sunday meetings.[38]

REBUILDING THE UNIVERSITY

Bible study as a regular course in the curriculum was not introduced until 1897. Several classes under Professor Palmer were offered that year.[39]

If the University authorities were slightly less concerned than they had been before the war about the spiritual health of the students, they were much more deeply and practically concerned than they had been then about their physical health. The days when sick boys depended on their roommates for care during illness had disappeared completely. When the University reopened, in 1871, the University physician was given an office in the old "Roundhouse." By 1879 the trustees had provided small infirmary space where students could be cared for. Two upstairs rooms of the "Pratt House," later called the Gorgas Home, were set aside as a "hospital." At a cost of $150 they were fitted up in a manner "acceptable and satisfactory to the Surgeon and President of the University." Should these two rooms prove inadequate, the trustees said, the president might spend up to $100 to equip the other two rooms on the same floor, to isolate them from the basement rooms, and to make them "conducive to the quiet and comfort of the sick."[40] At this time the surgeon was authorized to select a matron. She was to receive up to $3.00 a day and board while she was on duty.[41] When the illness and retirement of General Gorgas brought before the college authorities the problem of easing the financial situation of this loved president and his family, the post of matron of the new infirmary seemed tailor-made for Mrs. Gorgas. She was installed in that position in Septmeber, 1879.[42]

The four rooms in the "Pratt House" must have been completely inadequate when epidemics swept the campus, as they did rather frequently. An epidemic of measles in February and March, 1878, affected about forty students. Some of the cases were very severe.[43] Tonsilitis, gastric fever, and mumps caused much illness among the students during the winter months.[44] Malaria was common, and in the winter of 1881-1882 there were eight cases of malarial fever. Since the infirmary was crowded at that time, the two students considered by the president to be most dangerously ill were cared for at the President's Mansion. The overworked college surgeon had to call a consulting physician in the most serious cases. When President Lewis reported to the trustees in June, he reminded them of the burdens the physician had carried. And commended the doctor for the faithfulness with which he had answered calls day and night, during the "cold and rain of winter."[45] Another epidemic, in 1882, frightened the trustees because it seemed to be typhoid fever. The committee appointed to investigate this epidemic was reassuring: the disease was not really typhoid, though it had many of the same symptoms. They could find, they said, no local cause for the epidemic, and they assured the board that everything possible had been done to prevent its recurrence.[46]

Apparently, the University at first assumed the costs of medicines prescribed by the University physician. These costs were minor when students were enjoying normal good health, but they mounted steeply during the time of epidemics. In 1882 President Lewis spoke to the trustees about this problem. He suggested that the surgeon be required to keep on hand in his office a few medicines "proper for ordinary cases of indisposition." Dosages from this stock could be furnished at the expense of the University. But when the surgeon found it advisable to prescribe for ailing students drugs not in his stock, prescriptions should be filled at the expense of the patient.[47] The trustees accepted this recommendation[48] and ordered the surgeon "to keep on hand a sufficient supply of leading medicines for use in ordinary cases of sickness among the cadets."

As early as 1874 some students were urging that the University begin to provide health-building as well as health-restoring services for its students. They wanted a gymnasium. One student editor voiced this opinion in the University *Monthly:*

. . . encouragement [is] now given to physical culture in the majority of our Colleges and Universities. . . . The symmetrical form of the broad-shouldered, brawny armed youth, has taken the place of the enfeebled bookworm, and we venture the assertion, that the standard of scholarship has not been lowered thereby. . . . Notwithstanding what "old fogies" may say, a well-equipped gymnasium is about as essential to good recitations as is the "midnight oil," and generally the successful man is the man of muscle as well as of brains. . . .[49]

It was fifteen years before the trustees heeded this admonition from youth. But when Barnard Hall was built, provision was made for a gymnasium,[50] and after 1889 faculty and trustees alike encouraged students to take plenty of exercise in the gymnasium. They even took this activity from the realm of military duty and set up a new department of physical culture, which distinguished itself through exhibitions on the campus and at the Tuscaloosa music academy and opera house, where the "brawny-armed" youth of the University showed off their prowess in sparring matches, dumbbell drills, club swinging, high kicking, and Roman ladder statuary.[51]

Scholarship came first on the old University campus. There was never any question about that. For more than nine hours of every day, attention to books and classes was prescribed by rule and enforced by the quadrangle guard. The standard student load was four courses each year, and most courses called for five recitations a week. Some students eagerly added courses above the required minimum and became too involved in class work to adjust to University life. The faculty recognized the dangers of such zeal, particularly for new students, when they ruled, in 1881, that new students might take no more than twenty-one hours a week.[52]

Even such technical limitations could not prevent professors from urging extra work upon their classes, nor students from overburdening their own schedules. By 1890 the teachers had become so zealous that it was necessary for the faculty to make a rule that no professor might, without consent of the faculty, require any class or any individual student to do more work than that provided for in the recitation scheme. Colonel McCorvey must have been one of the prime offenders who made such action necessary. The faculty ruled expressly that he might let his senior class sections complete the extra work he had given them, but that his junior classes were to be relieved of it forthwith.[53] Student petitions to take extra work were frequent. In 1887 W. E. Griffin, a student, asked permission to take concurrently the law course and the academic course. He thought that the added work would not be too much if he could be excused from taking his turn as officer of the day. The faculty said that he might take the two courses together if he liked but that there was to be no interference with "his *Academic* and *Military* duties."[54]

Scientific students and, particularly, students in civil engineering carried much heavier loads than students in classical and literary courses. In 1892-1893, for example, classical students had from sixteen to nineteen classroom hours a week in addition to five themes each term; in some years they had declarations as well. Literary course students had approximately the same load. But scientific students had twenty-one hours of recitations in the first two years. Although they had only thirteen or fourteen hours of recitation in the last two years, they made field trips and worked three or four afternoons a week in the laboratory. And seniors taking civil engineering not only went to class twenty hours a week but had a constant round of field[55] trips as well. By June, 1897, the trustees felt that an equalization of loads in various departments was in order.[56] The faculty tried to carry out this directive the next fall by ruling that no student might carry less than eighteen hours a week in the Academic Department unless his work was restricted on the advice of the surgeon.[57]

Rigorous as the classroom schedule was, old graduates who remembered college days in the late nineteenth century recalled enough humorous incidents of those classrooms to dispel any idea that they were really the sober and serious intellectual workshops the professors wanted to make them. Mr. Sam Friedman, who lived in Tuscalooca, had a rich store of these reminiscences. He remembered "Little Doc" Eugene A. Smith, not much more than five feet tall and full of enthusiasm for athletics. He remembered his colleague "Saph" Calhoun, who was known to favor members of his own fraternity when it came to handing out marks. He remembered particularly the fat and formidable Benjamin F. Meek, six feet and three inches tall and, according to the students of his day, so near sighted that he once bumped into a cow in the street, lifted his hat, and said, "Excuse me, Madam." Mr. Friedman's thumbnail sketches of Professor Meek in action help to bring to life the classroom where students of another day learned more than the English classics:

Many were the stories and many were the jokes played on Dr. B. (Benny) F. Meek, Professor of English. He was an unmarried man between 50 and 60 years old, about 6' 3" in height and *extremely* fat. His eyes twisted and winked in every direction and he was extremely near-sighted. At the same time he was a kindly gentleman and a splendid instructor. However, his manner and mannerisms scared his students out of their wits. It is said that one young man on his entrance examination was so scared he was unable to name the Capital of Alabama.

If you wanted to get "excellent" in oratory, all you had to do was to declaim: "Look not on the Wine when it is Red," a poem written by Dr. Meek's brother, the Poet Laureate of Mississippi.

One day I was in his class room and suddenly an alarm clock attached to a long string and held by a student in the room just above, swung through the open window past the Doctor's ear, with a loud buzz, then continued to swing back and forth past the Doctor's ear, and every time it passed, the Doctor struck at it thinking it was some enormous bug.

In class one day the Doctor had sent a number of cadets to the blackboard with examples in English. Later when the cadets had finished, on going around to examine their work, he came to a blank space with no name above it. He turned around to the class and said: "Young man, I do not know who you are, but I am going to give you a zero anyway."[58]

Professor Meek was by no means the only teacher to find himself the butt of classroom jokes and pranks. There was the kindly astronomy professor, Dr. Joshua H. Foster, who started every sentence "with a whistling sound."

The observatory, containing about an 8" telescope was located about a quarter of a mile southwest of the barracks. One day one of the boys climbed up on the roof and placed a small spot on the object glass of the telescope, and the next night the Doctor, on looking through his telescope was very much excited, thinking he had found either a new planet or a new comet. . . . [59]

For students living the cloistered life of the barracks the only touch of home was often their contacts with the families of the married professors who lived on or near the campus. As hard as these men must have tried to keep their personal affairs out of the classroom, they did occasionally let family crises encroach on those sacred premises, though seldom with the dramatic and memorable effect produced by the advent of Mrs. Parker's triplets. Mr. Friedman told this story:

Dr. William A. Parker was professor of French and German. His residence was located on the campus not very far from his class room. On one occasion, he was holding class when one of his young sons rushed in excitedly and whispered in a loud voice, "Papa, mama is having a baby." The Doctor replied, "I will be over very shortly." A little later the young lad came back and said in another loud whisper, "Papa, mama is having another baby." "I will be right over," answered the Doctor. After another few minutes, the same lad came rushing over and said to the Doctor, "Papa, mama is having another baby." "Class dismissed," the Doctor said, "I will have to go over and put a stop to this."[60]

Few loopholes for recreation were left when the faculty arranged the regimented life of the University of Alabama students.

But in the rare and precious free hours, as well as on the holidays which the faculty decreed according to their whims, those students managed to have a surprisingly good time and to lay the foundations for the extra-curricular life which many of the students of a latter day would consider by far the most important factor in a college education.

Saturday afternoons and Sundays an exodus from the campus occurred. The cadets went calling. Sam Friedman, looking back to the '80's remembered with pride that the "town boys did not have much chance with the home girls on Sundays."[61] Those girls could sit at home confident that some of the roving bands of University boys would ring their doorbells, ask respectfully for "Miss Annie" or "Miss Grace" or "Miss Ella" (to drop the "Miss" was considered the height of bad form),[62] and come in for talk, laughter, and probably home cooking. Some boys, jingling the munificent sum of $2.50 in their pockets, were able to vary the calling routine by inviting a girl to go driving. "A girl, boy, horse, and a thin buggy, on a fall or spring afternoon (never at night) was just about the acme of entertainment," one student of the gay nineties still remembers.[63]

There were other attractions in Tuscaloosa, too. They ranged from Sunday school picnics to the more sophisticated offerings of the Academy of Music, where, according to Hill Ferguson of the class of 1896, road shows brought an occasional breath of Broadway. Mr. Ferguson writes,

I recall the Woodward-Warren Company (Bessie Warren of Tuscaloosa fame) which played week stands with popular 10, 20, and 30 cent prices. Some years later, Bessie Leach (Hayden) played "Little Lord Fauntleroy" in this company with great success. Fields Ministrels, Louis James, and occasional visits from John Temple Graves I, and other lyceum lecturers are entertainments I recall. . . .[64]

He remembered also the songs which boys of the gay nineties sang, hummed, or whistled as they went back to the campus after an excursion to a music hall or theatre in town:

Annie Sercy singing, "That's The Sweetest Story Ever Told"; Grace Kennedy with "Sweet Bunch of Daisies"; and other of Samuel Minturn Peck's songs. She also sang, "O Promise Me," and other of DeKoven's songs from Robin Hood, the Highwayman, and other light operas of the day. Bob Boyle with "Afterward"; Moulton Smith, bearing down on

"Sunshine of Paradise Alley"; "Puss" Cochrane forced to sing, "She Was Only A Bird In A Gilded Cage" over and over again. Vernon Hope with "My Best Girl's A Corker"; dear old "Brother John" Milner with his hymns at the YMCA—all stand out in my memory. "White Wings" held over from the '80's; "After the Ball"; "Annie Rooney"; "Bicycle Built For Two"—and the Stephen Foster and Gilbert and Sullivan songs—were very popular. "Washington Post," "King Cotton," "El Capitan," and other of John Philip Sousa's marches, were also at the height of popularity.[65]

Featured among the picnics which marked the spring and autumn months was the one Mrs. Peter Bryce gave annually for the students.[66] Permission to go to such picnics was solemnly granted—or withheld—by the president and the faculty, as was permission to attend the other events which Tuscaloosa offered. When the circus came to town, the University authorities no longer attempted to declare it out of bounds as they had in an earlier day. Students were allowed to go with official blessing, but they had to go "in section."[67] The annual street fair, held in October, was always on the student calendar. The cadets flocked into town not only to examine the exhibits with a critical eye but also to cut holes in the prize pumpkins and "swipe" the sugar canes.[68] Singing schools in churches provided more decorous entertainment, and chess and checkers had their earnest devotees on the campus.[69]

The most important holiday of the school year was Christmas. At Christmas time with permission of the parents or guardians of the students, a vacation of from ten days to two weeks was usually declared. But that vacation could not be taken for granted. In 1878, for example, the president sent a circular letter to all parents and guardians advising them that no leaves of absence would be given for Christmas that year.

Thanksgiving brought suspension of classes, but students were allowed to leave campus that day only in such formations and on such permits as were issued on Sunday. New Year's Day was a holiday when special permission for calls in town was given. Classes were usually suspended on Memorial Day and on the afternoon of the annual Day of Prayer observed in February by all schools and colleges of the state. Probably in self-defense, the faculty, for many years, declared April Fool's Day a student holiday.[70]

Special celebrations were occasionally added to the list of declared holidays. Students were permitted to attend the ceremonies connected with the completion of the M. & O. Railroad on May 12, 1898.[71] They also were dismissed for a peace celebration in October of that year.[72] But they seldom received permission to attend celebrations farther afield than the town of Tuscaloosa. The faculty let them go to the Confederate veteran reunion in Birmingham in 1894,[73] thereby upsetting a long precedent. For in 1872 an invitation to students to attend the Mobile Agricultural and Horticultural Fair had been politely refused,[74] and in 1884 the faculty had deemed it "inexpedient" for students to go to Birmingham for a music festival sponsored by the board of trade.[75]

Throughout this period dancing headed the list of forms of entertainment preferred by students. And the controversy which centered around the "hops" sanctioned by the University sent its echoes far beyond the campus walls. Pressure of public opinion and public criticism led the trustees from time to time to try to outlaw University dances, but the students' will to dance was irrepressible.

Soon after the University reopened, the University hop made its appearance. Students were allowed to give dances in the mess hall and to invite young ladies from Tuscaloosa to these parties. Usually they were held during the Christmas holidays under watchful faculty supervision, but they did not escape the attention of the moralists of Tuscaloosa. Dark hints of the "night revelling" on the campus appeared in the local press, and there were grossly exaggerated reports of "Lawn, Shooting, Round and Kissing Parties by moonlight," and of masquerade balls "all besmeared with wine and laughter."[76] Students must have laughed at these rumors. They thought the campus dances were all too tame. In 1879 they petitioned the faculty for permission to attend dances in town, where supervision would be less onerous.

Although the faculty did not see its way clear to remove the ban on town dances, the student petition was received with consideration. A more liberal policy in regard to campus dances was adopted. The president and the commandant were directed to decide how often and in what manner student dances should be held. The students were reminded that they must not expect to be excused from classes because of entertainments on the campus.[77] And the Commencement Hop, which became the climax of the social year, was sanctioned and inaugurated.

Those Commencement hops were gala affairs, according to the memory of men who were cadets at the University in the 1880's. Girls came from all over the state to attend them. Said Mr. Friedman,

Although Commencement was in June, all cadets were compelled to have their tight-fitting coats completely buttoned up, and I remember how dripping wet we were within ten minutes after the beginning of the dance.[78]

Smaller dancing parties during the year were often decided upon by majority vote of cadets willing to help pay expenses.[79] The senior class found the commandant increasingly willing to give permission for mess hall dances. It was better, the commandant once told his faculty colleagues, to let such parties go on where he could watch and control them than it was to let the students go off to town for their amusement.[80]

Outside clamor against the godlessness of this liberal policy at the University continued to mount. University critics, especially strait-laced churchmen, found in the dances held under the aegis of the University faculty, confirmation of their worst fears regarding the moral tone of the institution. The clamor had reached such a pitch by the late 1880's that the trustees could no longer ignore it. In June, 1889, a special committee solemnly reported to the board its disapproval of the laxity of discipline evidenced by the frequent permissions given for campus dances during the school year. This practice, said the committee, could "serve no good purpose." It was, on the contrary, "subversive of Discipline and detrimental to the proper discharge of Academic duties." There should be no such diversions from the main business of the University. The committee disapproved of even the Commencement Hop. They felt that since students were "discharged from all restraint and discipline" at the close of Commencement exercises, no good purpose would be served by letting them stay around the barracks instead of leaving promptly for home. The trustees listened to the committee report and approved it. By resolution they forbade dances during the academic year in University buildings. By the same resolution they outlawed the University hop.[81]

The students did not take this action without protest. In June, 1890, they were before the trustees with alumni re-enforcements. They failed by one vote to get the Commencement Hop reinstated.[82]

The next year another committee investigating campus entertainment succeeded in getting the trustees to reaffirm the stern policy toward dances. The board resolved:

That the President may permit such entertainments on the University grounds or in the buildings during Christmas holidays, and the closing of Commencement days as may be approved by him and the faculty, but no such entertainment shall be construed, [or] understood as to mean a Hop or dance: and no such entertainment shall be permitted until application in writing is first made to the President describing the character of the entertainment and giving the names of the managers, and specifying the hour when such entertainment will begin and the time it will close.[83]

The trustees were fighting a losing battle, however, against the lively wills of the dance-loving cadets. By 1893 the Commencement Hop, thinly disguised as "University Reception," was back on the Commencement program again;[84] and the faculty were once more granting permissions for dances during the school term, though they often changed proposed dates from week-days to week-ends, and they shortened proposed hours. Students who thought they should be permitted to dance until two o'clock in the morning were fairly sure of having that part of their plan vetoed.[85] By the end of the decade there were even two dance clubs—"German" clubs—on the campus; one supported by seniors and law students, the other by underclassmen. They gave regular dances once or twice a month. The term "German" applied both to a dance step and also to a dance at which the girls chose their partners.[86] But the ban against dancing in town or at any public place remained in full force throughout the whole period,[87] though Hill Ferguson's recollection of the popularity of fraternity, class, and club dances held at the City Hall, the Washington Hotel, or the "L.T.F." hall, indicates that this ban, too, was weakening.[88]

When the trustees gave up trying to prohibit the Commencement Hop, they apparently decided to give full support to this colorful climax for the University year. From time to time they even made appropriations toward the expenses. Probably they themselves shared some of the undergraduate thrill when the mess hall blossomed forth with pennants of crimson and white, and DeLow's Band, from Birmingham, struck up a grand march. The University Reception began at half past nine and lasted until one o'clock, at least an hour later than the standard closing hour for other University dances. The program which the Tuscaloosa *Times* announced for the dance of 1893 is probably typical, it recalls the graceful, stately rhythms which marked dancing before the advent of jazz:[89]

Grand March	Waltz
Waltz	Lancers
Polka	Polka
Waltz	Waltz
Mazourka	Polka
York	Waltz

If the rhythms of those dances echo unfamiliarly on student ears today, however, the financial problems attendant upon the occasions still have a familiar ring: Transportation was a big drawback, as a hack cost $5.00, and even $2.50 each for two couples was high. The girls didn't like to ride on the "dummy line."[90] The high cost of taking one's girl to a dance is no modern invention.

The campus was a man's world throughout the nineteenth century. The University student was thought of in the masculine gender and the life of the campus was geared to the needs of young men. The University of Alabama was a man's school; it was, furthermore, a military school. Girls had their place in the recreational schedules of the cadets, but not in the classroom. By the middle nineties, however, the first scouts of the advancing army of coeds had begun to edge their way into the sacred precincts. By the turn of the century they had opened the way for the University to become in fact what it had always been in theory, a co-educational institution.

It is somewhat strange that women students were so slow in coming to the University campus. Other universities throughout the country had been admitting women for many years before the first coeds were admitted to the University of Alabama. Yet the founders of the University had expressly provided for the establishment of a "female" branch of their institution of learning:

And be it further inacted, That the said Trustees shall have the power, and it is hereby declared to be their duty to select a site for a female institution; which institution shall be considered as a branch of the University of the State of Alabama, and shall be governed by the same laws, so far as the same may be applicable.[91]

It took seventy-two years for this open-door policy toward women to become a reality. In the idea of co-education the University of Alabama had been a pioneer. It had the authority to admit women more than ten years before Oberlin College, in 1833, admitted men and women alike and started a movement which spread slowly throughout the country. But, as Northern colleges joined this movement—Wisconsin in 1867, Michigan in 1870—the University of Alabama, like most Southern schools, lagged behind.

There had been good and practical reasons for this slowness to take advantage of legislative authority. Governor Israel Pickens discovered some of the obstacles in the way during his term as governor. He had been an early enthusiast for the idea of co-education. In 1821 he had told the state senate,

In the application of this literary fund to the establishment of an institution, where our sons may be instructed in all the branches of literature, it is believed neither to be inconsistent with the object of the act of national munificence, which has given us these means, nor with the generous and refined sentiments of the age in which we live, to apply a portion of them to female education.[92]

Two years later, he spoke even more seriously:

Although female education has ever been one of my favorite objects, and particularly so as connected with the proposed establishment; neither the state of the funds nor the immature condition of our settlements require nor justify the precipitate organization of these branches.[93]

The war and the problems it brought further postponed the realization of the idea of the founders. It was enough to struggle to rebuild a broken University on its old foundations. To cope with an expansion which would allow the admission of women was too difficult a task. Yet for twenty years between the reopening of the University and the admission of the first coed, the subject of co-education was never far from the minds of those responsible for the policy and administration of the University of Alabama.

The board of regents, in 1870 or 1871, received a report from Joseph Hodgson, Joseph H. Speed, and Thomas A. Cook, who had constituted a committee to help plan for the reorganization of the University. The question of the University's responsibility for the education of women in the state was sharply raised:

Your Committee find themselves face to face with the great question of the day. Why is not the State equally bound to provide University education for its women as for its men? In Missouri they first admitted female students to the Normal college of the University. They were not at first admitted to worship in the chapel at the daily convocation nor to recite with classes in the University building. At length the chapel doors were open to them, and they were permitted to join their voices in the morning song of praise. Then, as they were prepared, recitation and lecture rooms were one by one opened to them. This was done without the formal vote of either the Board of Curators or the Faculty.

It was found that they did no harm. Women are now admitted, in the limited numbers that come, to all the advantages of most of our Universities precisely as are young men.

The professors, without exception, bear testimony that this has been done with decided advantage to the good order and proprieties of the whole body of the University students.

We are not prepared to meet this question fully; but while waiving it for the present, your committee asks for it the serious consideration of this Board and of the people of Alabama. A host of our women, born in luxury, but growing up in poverty, stand ready to become Teachers in our Public Schools. Shall we not at least give them an opportunity to attend our Normal Department, and our theoretical and practical horticultural classes?[94]

The emphasis on the new need of Southern women for vocational education is interesting here. But apparently the board of regents, like its committee, was "not prepared to meet this question fully."

Eight years later the resourceful President Carlos G. Smith, working out an elaborate home-study extension plan, suggested that one argument in favor of such a plan was that it would "give a *reality* and *dignity* to the higher education of young ladies, utterly unattainable in Alabama." Bringing women to the campus, President Smith thought, had certain drawbacks, but his plan would meet the growing demand of women for college education.

And I may add, that this System, is in some respects preferable to the Co-education of the sexes, as it does not force young girls into Companionship with young men while in attendance at recitations and lectures, and does not Compel them to reside at a distance from home. They may pursue their studies at home or in whatever Schools they please and offer themselves as examinees to the local committees just as young men do with precisely the Same advantages, and are entitled to the Same Academic honors or Certificates, if successful in their examinations. . . . Nothing has contributed more to raise the Standard of the education of women, wherever this System has been introduced than the opportunity it affords young ladies of obtaining precisely the Same Academic honors that young men receive at the close of their College or University Courses of study. And I may mention another very great advantage under the operation of this System. It takes the matter of Conferring diplomas upon Young Ladies out of the hands of the utterly irresponsible, often incompetent, and unworthy private individuals and places it where it properly belongs—in the hands of a body of Trustees and Professors acting under the authority of the State; and makes such Honors, *State* Honors, as they ought to be, that are really worth something to the young ladies, that obtain them.[95]

President Smith left the campus abruptly, on request of the trustees, before he could develop his home-study plan either for men or women. But the subject of co-education continued to be hotly argued on the campus and off for the next decade and more. The Philomathic Society, in 1884, chose as the subject for its public debate: "Should Co-education be Prohibited?" The society attempted to choose its judges fairly. "Owing to the character of the subject . . . two ladies, Mrs. Lewis and Mrs. Bryce, were put on the committee with Rev. A. Monk, Capt. McEachin, and Prof. A. Hill, for the purpose of deciding the question."[96] The affirmative side won, but there is no indication whether or not the decision represented a three-to-two split, along sex lines, by the panel of judges.

The press took up the controversy. By 1890 the *Alabama Christian Advocate* was accusing the state and its University of ignoring its responsibility for the higher education of women and of "throwing its responsibility upon the church and upon private enterprises":

Our girls must be educated. The future demands it. . . . One thing, however, is settled, the coming woman will have a head as well as a heart. Brain power is the scepter of the future, and our women are finding it out. Wifehood means more than a pretty face and affectionate manners, and motherhood means more than statesmanship. . . . Our women will never ask or hold a seat in our general conference; will never fill our pulpits; will leave the ballot box in the hands of their husbands; will not seek notoriety; will be as modest as in ante-bellum days; and yet she will not be a hot-house flower. Hers will be a practical character. She will know how to cook a biscuit as well as to read Virgil and talk French and paint in water colors.[97]

However inaccurate the *Advocate* editor was in his prediction that women would not overstep the bounds he set for them, he was right in his guess that women were getting impatient of the debate. They were demanding action.

At the University of Alabama this demand for action was embodied in Julia Tutwiler, daughter of one of the University's first professors. When the board of trustees met in June, 1892, Mr. James E. Webb rose to say that he was offering "by request" a petition from Miss Tutwiler asking that the doors of the University be opened for women. Miss Tutwiler put the facts plainly and cogently. She reminded the board that the federal lands had been given to provide education "for the youth of the state." She insisted that half the youth of the state had been deprived of their just share of the benefits of the grant quite long enough. Nowhere in Alabama, she reminded the trustees, could an intelligent girl get the equivalent of a university education. It was certainly time something was done about it.[98]

The trustees had great respect for Miss Tutwiler. They listened to the petition respectfully and then sent an invitation to its author to come and discuss with the board her views on co-education "as she viewed the situation in light of her many years of experience as a teacher of girls." Miss Tutwiler came before the board two days later. She made, the records note, "a strong and eloquent appeal in behalf of this movement." She was gratified, she said, at having been allowed to speak "in behalf of the women of Alabama."

She must have been persuasive as well as eloquent. Before she left the room, Mr. Northington had introduced a motion, which was seconded by Mr. Crook that "young women of not less than eighteen years of age and good character and antecedents who are able to stand the necessary examinations be admitted to the sophomore class or any higher class of this University, provided that suitable homes and protection have been provided for them."[99] The matter was then referred to the committee of instruction, rules and regulations, with orders for the committee to report at the next meeting of the board.

The odd provision that women should be admitted only to the three upper classes is explained by one contemporary writer as prompted by the trustees' desire not to appear to compete with various girls' colleges of the state. Those colleges were, it seems, hardly more than preparatory schools. They might be induced to raise their standards somewhat if, by including in their curriculum the first year of university work, their graduates could enter the University with advanced standing.[100]

Miss Tutwiler's encounter with the trustees opened the floodgates of campus discussion. In the year between the board meetings the faculty tackled the question for themselves. President Jones and Professors Wyman, Edgar, Parker and McCorvey were appointed a committee to determine "whether the University should be opened to young ladies, and, if so, under what limitations."[101] It took that committee about three weeks to conclude its report. The faculty then voted to "welcome the admission of young ladies to the University when the Board of Trustees can make appropriate provision for their reception."[102]

With this expression of faculty approval the trustees were in a position to act promptly and confidently. On June 28, 1893, they called up the motion on co-education that had been referred the preceding year to the committee on rules and regulations, added to it the clause "under such rules and regulations as may be prescribed by the President in consultation with the Faculty," and then put their stamp of approval on co-education for the University of Alabama.[103] Within a matter of days a faculty committee, including President Jones and Professors Meek and Palmer, was able to report that satisfactory classroom arrangements had been made for the newcomers: the professors of English and mathematics had agreed to exchange rooms with other teachers when they met classes in which young ladies were enrolled. Just why such exchange was necessary for these two departments and not for Latin and modern languages is somewhat puzzling. All these recitations were held in Woods Hall, whose upper floors were used as student dormitories. The president was requested to make arrangements for board, room, and supervision of the women students.[104]

For a number of years the rate of matriculation for women was slow. Miss Anna Byrne Adams and Miss Bessie Parker, both of Tuscaloosa, were the first. They were admitted as special students in 1893 and the following June were recognized as among the honor students with average grades of ninety-five per cent or better.[105] Stated the *Corolla,*

The city has sent, from the bosom of its honored families, many young men to the University. . . . It has also sent of late two of its gifted daughters. . . .[106]

In the same yearbook the picture of the staff of the *Crimson-White* shows the two girls among the six associate editors of that publication.[107] The newcomers had lost no time in identifying themselves with the extra-curricular life of the campus.

Miss Annie F. Ziegler of Mobile, admitted without condition to the sophomore class in 1894,[108] apparently never actually got to the University. Perhaps she could find no satisfactory living quarters. Miss Adams was the only woman actually on the campus that year. She studied English, German, philosophy, and history in the Academic Department, and again she made the honors list at the end of the year. She was listed in June, 1895, as a graduate in the Schools of English, German, Philosophy and History, thus becoming the first woman graduate from any of the schools of the University of Alabama. Her picture, with the somewhat cryptic subscription "E Pluribus Unum," appeared in the *Corolla* among those of the other seniors,[109] though her status was still given in the *Catalogue* as "special student." She had succeeded also with her editorial assignment. The picture of the *Crimson-White* staff showed her as again an associate editor.[110]

Miss Parker seemed to have been absent from the campus that year, but she was back again in 1895-1896. She was studying chemistry, geology, mineralogy, French, and German, and when the year ended she was included as "Graduate in Schools" in those schools. She was also on the honors list and the winner of the J. C. White Prize in Mineralogy.[111] She was back again for her honorary M.S. degree, which was conferred in 1901. Her "senior" picture in the *Corolla* was inscribed: "A maiden never bold; of spirit so still and quiet."[112]

The campus, just getting accustomed to a one-by-one trickling in of coeds, was startled when no less than five young ladies marched in at the start of the year 1896-1897. Mary Carter Hill, of Tuscaloosa, Lucy Grace Archer Martin, of Birmingham, and Alice Searcy Wyman, of University came in as special students; Annie Ross Searcy and Alyce Wildman, both of Tuscaloosa, enrolled as eclectic students.[113] All five of them were on the honors list the next June.

The pictures of all five illustrated a fable, entitled "The Maidens," which graced the *Corolla* that year. Miss Martin, "Graceful alike with tongue and pen," and Miss Wildman, an "illustration of the blessedness of being little," got their pictures also in the senior lists.[114] Miss Martin apparently carried on the tradition started by her two predecessors that there should be a woman on the *Crimson-White* editorial board. She was pictured as the only girl in the group of eight sitting around the editorial table. Three of the boys with her were in cadet uniform; three were more formally dressed, with wing collars and bow ties; the seventh, somewhat in the background, wore a four-in-hand.[115]

The University was fortunate in its first coeds. The first seven young women to enroll succeeded, in a remarkably short time, in convincing the University authorities that they and girls like them would be an asset to the campus. By 1897 a committee of the trustees was willing to call the experiment a complete success and to recommend certain changes in rules and in facilities to encourage more women to come to the University.

The experiment of the instruction of young ladies at the University has formed a subject for inquiry by your Committee, and we are gratified to be able to state that the unanimous expression of the Faculty and students is highly favorable both as to their exemplary conduct and the progress made in their studies and the stimulating and highly beneficial effect that their presence has had upon the cadets and other students both as regards studiousness and deportment.

There are only five young ladies at present in attendance and they have had to contend with discomforts and disadvantages which ought to be remedied. We believe that the attendance of young ladies should be encouraged and that suitable provision should be made for their convenience and accommodation. It is believed that a moderate expenditure, a slight change in the regulations and a suitable publicity of the advantages offered by the University will cause a large increase in attendance for this desirable class of students. We therefore recommend that from the commencement of the next session young ladies should be permitted to enter the Freshman Class, and that the age limits be reduced to seventeen years. We further recommend that suitable provision be made for a study room in Garland Hall, and that the Class rooms of English and Mathematics be removed from Woods Hall to suitable rooms on the second floor of Garland Hall.[116]

However, not all the trustees shared the enthusiasm of this committee. When, in July, 1897, the motion to admit women to the freshman class was introduced, an attempt to table it was lost by a 7 to 4 vote. Judge Richardson then moved that co-education of the sexes be prohibited in the University of Alabama. Friends of co-education were able to table that motion by a 6 to 4 vote and then to get majority approval for the original proposition.[117] Beginning in 1897 women eighteen years of age and over, "of good character," were admitted to all rights and privileges of any class in the University. Women had finally come to the campus.

Fifteen girls were among the students the following year. Three —Julia Trent Royall, Abbie Searcy, and Lucy Wilson—had enrolled as regular members of the sophomore class, and Miss Searcy and Miss Wilson had been elected first and second vice-presidents of that class. Twelve were special students, eight of them from Tuscaloosa, and one each from Talladega, Birmingham, Northport, and University.[118] The *Corolla* recognized the significance of the mounting invasion by publishing a full-page spread of their pictures, showing them in the picture hats and frilly blouses of the day. The same yearbook contained couplets about each of fourteen of the coeds; a two-page article on "Co-Education"; and a less serious article, "How Co-Eds Study in Their Boudoir," purporting to reveal all kinds of frivolities going on in the ladies' study hall.[119]

The presence of ladies on the campus occasionally embarrassed an officer intent on "bawling out" an unruly cadet. In 1898 President Powers reported to the board of trustees that Commandant James Baylies was guilty of using "some very emphatic, improper, profane language" in the process of reprimanding Cadet F. S. White. And the president added: "To make matters worse, the young ladies passed within a few steps of the party during the altercation . . . ."[120]

For the most part, however, the routine of the University seemed to have been changed surprisingly little when women became part of campus life. Annie Searcy remembered in later years that she and her fellow coeds had been treated with respect and solicitude by the teachers, but that special favors were few. They were seated alphabetically in classes, mixed with the cadets as their names happened to come. They were questioned in recitations in order. Between classics they walked and talked with the cadets in the quadrangle just as girls have been doing ever since.[121]

By 1898 it was apparent that living arrangements must be made for the increasing number of young women who wanted to enter the University of Alabama. The trustees that year agreed to admit "at the discretion of the faculty" girls as young as sixteen if they lived at home.[122] But the board also listened to Miss Tutwiler when she told them that a number of graduates from the Alabama Normal College would come to the University in the fall if there was any place for them to live. They authorized the president to set aside the Harris House as a women's dormitory and to call it the Julia S. Tutwiler Annex.

The *Corolla* of 1899 contained a complete history of the opening of this Annex:

When the University opened, ten young ladies, all graduates of the Alabama Normal College, entered the University and took up their abode in this residence. Miss Sallie J. Avery, for many years a principal teacher in the Alabama Normal College, accompanied them as chaperone and superintendent of the Annex. These students entered for the most part as special students, taking studies in various classes; however most of their studies were in the Sophomore Class. The Alabama Normal College had been admitted as an auxiliary school to the State University some months before.

The names of the first resident girl students of the University of Alabama are as follows: Misses Alma Bishop, Mamie Bullock, Augusta Cleary, Mary DeBardeleben, Kate Horn, Fannie Ingersoll, Rosa Lawhon, Leila McMahon, Sadie Mason, Annie Turk. From their first day they have taken a high stand in their classes; their professors say that their influence and example have raised the standard of study in their classes.

The *Corolla* also commented on the coöperative system of housekeeping which these young women adopted:

These young ladies are acting as pioneers in showing to the girls of Alabama the compatability of "plain living and high thinking." They have divided among themselves the work of their household and have dispensed entirely with outside service, except for their laundry work. By this means, the annual expense of each member of the houshold has been less than one hundred dollars. This includes college dues and purchase of books as well as their board and washing. Alabama will some day be proud of the women who will be developed from such girls.[123]

Miss Tutwiler arranged that supervision for the Annex during its first year should be provided without cost to the University. At

REBUILDING THE UNIVERSITY

the close of that year the experiment was working so well that the president urged the trustees not only to take over the supervisory expense but also to enlarge the building so that at least ten more students could live there another year.[124]

Nineteen other students that year were living at home in Tuscaloosa or in boarding houses in the town. Julia Trent Royall, Abbie Searcy, and Annie Greer Turk were regular juniors. Six others were regular sophomores; the rest were listed as special students. The *Corolla* again reflected the friendly curiosity of the campus in the emphasis it gave to news and comment on the coeds. One article on "The University Co-Ed," apparently written by one of the girls, contained a generous reference to the town girls who must have been eyeing with some concern the advent of rivals on the University campus:

The Tutwiler Annex . . . has certainly proved a success, and a peep into it would be highly interesting to anyone who might wish to see how well girls can do "bacheloring," and, indeed the students there do show . . . that practice in the culinary art is by no means detrimental to the study of mathematics, the classics, or the languages. We must not, however, fail to mention our town girls, who are admirably sustaining the reputation already acquired.

We have been enjoying for the last few months our delightful study room. It is conveniently located in Manly Hall, and while we never failed to appreciate the many kindnesses shown us by our "Mother Superior" during our stay in the library, we are exceedingly grateful for "Co-ed Boudoir," a room of our very own, where we can come and go as we please.

Again, the year 1899 marks an epoch in the history of the University in that it is the first year that the young ladies of the Sophomore Class have been permitted to appear on the rostrum of Clark Hall at the Annual Sophomore Exhibition.[125]

Of the eight full pages of the yearbook given over to the feminine side of University life, one full-page was reserved for the picture of the girls in the Annex. Quips similar to the following were scattered here and there:

Rules of Conduct: Rule 3: The student that goes to the books in the secretary's office to look up the age of a co-ed is bound to be found wanting in some essential qualities.[126]

There was an account of the Sophomore Exhibition, when Miss Augusta Harrison Cleary gave an oration on "The American Flag"; Miss Mary Christine De Bardeleben discussed the "Fate of Virginia"; Miss Leila Wood gave a "Tribute to a Confederate Soldier"; Miss Sadie Mason talked on "A Voice from the Poor House"; Miss Leila St. Clair Mason spoke on "The Changed Cross"; and Miss Lula Knox Powers gave her oration on "Courting and Science."[127] There was the boast of the junior class historian that his was "the first class to be honored with full-course co-eds" and was "the first class to have them among its graduates."[128] Included was even a poem entitled "Cooking at the Annex."[129]

Similar editorial interest in the ladies reached the local press that year. The Tuscaloosa *Times* headed one article: "Coeducation in Earnest at the University this Year." That editor was especially impressed with the uniform adopted by the young ladies who lived in the Annex. Those "mortar board caps, white waists and black skirts" were "neat, economical and attractive." The writer even suggested that it might be a good idea for the Tuscaloosa girls to "adopt the same whenever at the University or on the way to and fro, with the initials 'UA' on the caps."[130]

Another kind of community interest and support was evidenced that spring, when the Woman's Club of Birmingham established a scholarship for a young woman from Jefferson County and saw to it that a place was reserved in the Annex for that scholar when she was chosen.[131]

Four more women were graduated in various schools in June, 1899: Lollie Eddins, Abby Hogan, and Mary Washington Moody, of Tuscaloosa; and Laura Scott McGehee, of Northport. Six "irregular" sophomores and other special students were on the honors list.[132] The coeds were holding the pace that the first women on the campus had set. When in June, 1900, Miss Rosa Lawhon, of Livingston, stepped up to the dais on graduation day to receive her A.B. degree, she became the first woman ever to receive a title degree from the University of Alabama. By that time women had even entered the graduate departments of the University. Susie Fitts Martin Mayfield, "M. E. L. Arkansas Female College," was doing graduate work in French that year. And in 1904 Anna Trott Hunter was granted the first earned Master of Science degree, for which she submitted a

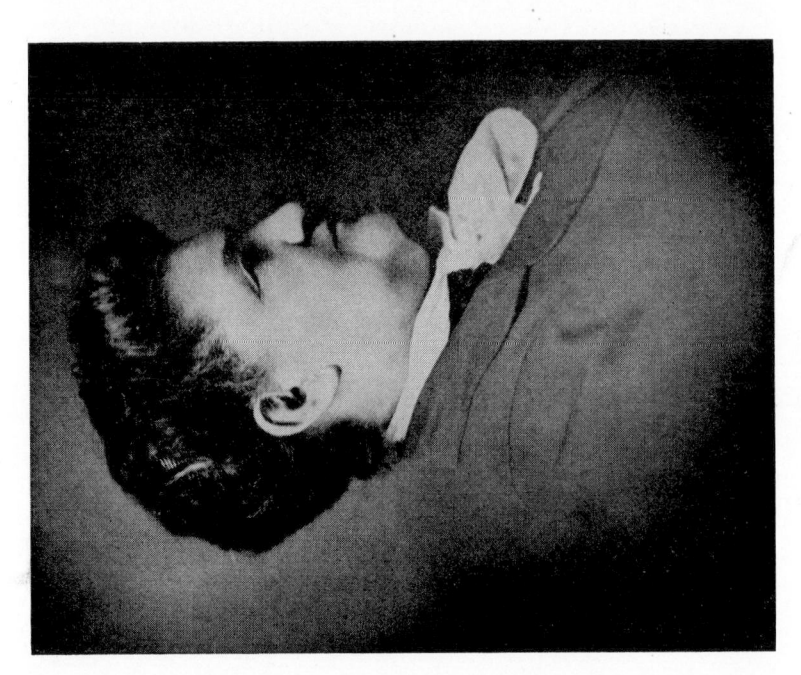

JULIA STRUDWICK TUTWILER
Advocate of Co-education

AMELIA GAYLE GORGAS
University Librarian, 1882-1907

DRESS UNIFORM, 1890

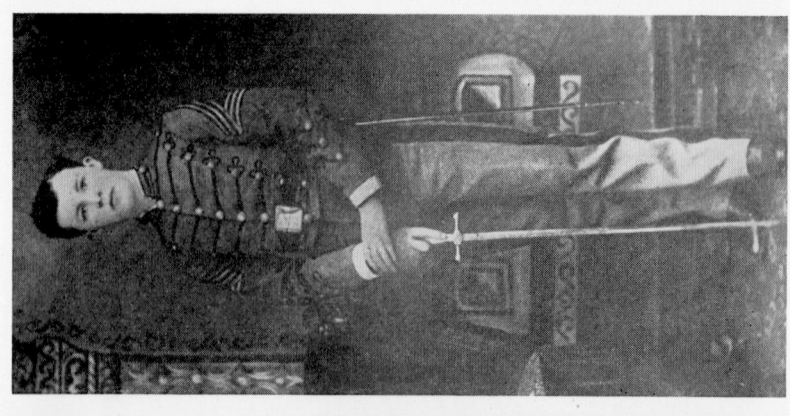

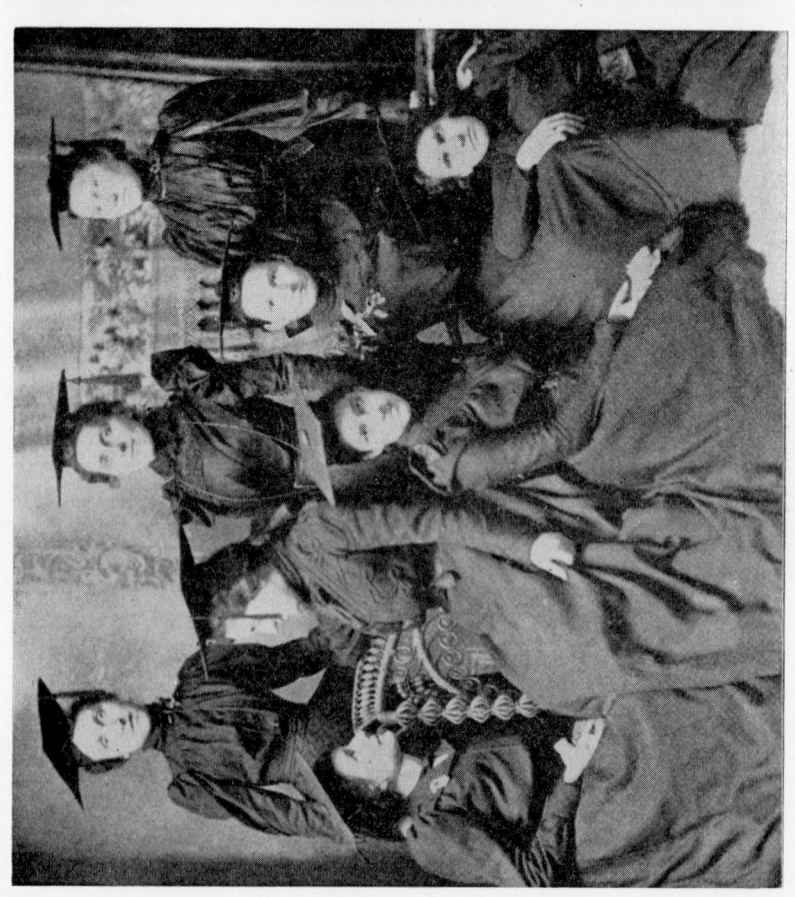

THE COEDS OF 1899

thesis on "A Mathematical and Experimental Study of Compound Harmonic Motion."[134]

Women had made a surprisingly quick adjustment to the life of the campus. They had especially taken a prompt and helpful hand in the development of the extra-curricular life which was beginning to proliferate at the University and which was giving to it the flavor and tempo of a twentieth-century university. Women were at the University of Alabama to stay.

CHAPTER XXI

Military Discipline

THE OUTWORD and visible sign of belonging to the University of Alabama was the trim grey uniform which the student donned after arrival on the campus and did not abandon until, diploma in hand, he emerged an educated gentleman. In material, color, and cut the uniform was reminiscent of West Point. It was worn with a light forage cap of blue cloth.[1] It was a source of both pride and annoyance to the cadets who wore it. It was a symbol of the military discipline and organization which persisted on the University campus until the early years of the twentieth century.

Each cadet was required to furnish his own uniforms, but the purchase of the uniforms was in the hands of the president, who was instructed by the trustees to buy them at the lowest possible cost.[2] This arrangement, together with the practice developed among the cadets of handing down uniforms from class to class, resulted in more than occasional misfits. On one occasion the trustees found it necessary to appoint a special committee to investigate complaints that the cadet uniforms were so tight that they were "injurious to the health" of the boys who wore them.[3] That buttoned-up discomfort was probably increased by bulky underwear of that day. Hill Ferguson wrote of that underwear with something approaching a squirm, fifty years after he was a wearer of it on the University campus:

A cadet at the University, with his uniform, wore just about the same clothing that a boy in military school would wear these days, with the following exceptions:

The "coat shirt" had not been invented. All shirts were put on over the head, and taken off in the same manner. . . .

Underwear of union suits or shorts did not come into use until after

1900. In our time, home-made drawers had tapes around the bottom to tie around the ankles. Store bought, or "Scrivens", drawers had an inch seam of jersey cloth down the sides to make the garment less binding, and an anklet of similar material to insure a neat fit under the socks. . . . We wore sock supporters, or pinned the socks to the drawers with a safety pin. . . .[4]

If the clothes pinched, so, also, did the cost, which Ferguson remembers as one reason for the brisk trade in secondhand uniforms. About $35 a year had to be budgeted for these uniforms unless one could get this equipment from a graduating senior. A Tuscaloosa "military tailor & clothier," advertising in 1884 his ability to supply cadet uniforms of "the best 'West Point Government Standard' Goods," indicates the items which made up the total equipment and the total bill: "coatee, $10.50; pants, $5.50; cap, $1.75; dress cap and pompon, $4.00; fatigue, $9.00; and vest, $4.00.[5]

Some changes in the uniform were made before it was given up entirely. In 1892 the trustees voted to substitute a cheap white cork hat for summer wear in place of the cap previously required; to change the pattern of the blouse so that it conformed more nearly to that worn at West Point; and to require that plain black cravats, worn with standing collars, take the place of the many-colored ties then in use.[6] In 1900 they made a further concession to climate, ruling that the summer uniforms were henceforth to be blue serge coats, white duck pants, and campaign hats. The trustees thought that this uniform would be more serviceable and more dressy. They did, however, show consideration for the finances of the cadets and their parents by allowing the use of the old uniform except for drill or parade.[7]

Drill and parade had sufficient glamor to give the military system a certain hold on the cadets in a period when the basis of the system was being increasingly challenged. One hour of drill a day was the rule until 1891, when the trustees cut it down to three hours each week. Dress parade, at which all cadets had to be present unless excused by the President, was specifically continued even after that time.[8] Commencement programs featured competitive drills by companies of the cadet corps. Large crowds turned out to watch and to cheer the captains of the winning company as they received their prizes from the hands of the trustees.[9]

On rare occasions some chosen company of cadets was permitted to venture off the campus to compete with other military units. Considering an invitation for such participation in the Cotton Centennial Exposition in New Orleans in May, 1885, the trustees cautiously voted permission on condition that each cadet get written consent from his parent or guardian and that the cadets be accompanied on their tour by a member of the faculty. They must have felt that this expedition was worth while when news came that Company E of the Alabama corps of cadets had walked away with the first prize in the drill competition, winning $500 and a gold medal. On that occasion the winning company was commanded by Cadet Captain Louis V. Clark, later Brigadier General of the Alabama National Guard. Captain Clark and the three cadet lieutenants who were his aides were presented with swords by Governor E. A. O'Neal and were officially commended by the U. S. Army technicians who judged the contest for the "accurate, careful, and elegant manner" in which Company E had performed. The best of the units from other Southern colleges, including Auburn, South Carolina, and Louisiana State, had taken part in the competition, and the University cadets had surpassed them all. Small wonder that shouting and hilarious crowds celebrated the return of the heroes of Tuscaloosa.[10]

The roll of Company E included Captain Louis V. Clark, Lieut. Oscar L. Gray, Lieut. John R. Vidmer, Lieut. Henry R. Dawson, Sergt. Wm. J. Boothe, Sergt. Thomas P. Brown, and Privates John M. Anderson, William E. Booker, Burwell L. Boykin, William W. Campbell, Julius M. Clements, Newton N. Clements, Jr., Elisha B. Cottingham, Lawrence P. Dawson, George W. Feagin, Alston Fitts, George H. Forney, Glenn Foster, Alexander M. Garber, Thomas E. Gary, William D. Gay, Oliver A. Hobdy, John L. Horn, William T. Lenoir, Charles E. McCord, A. S. J. McCoy, William P. Nelson, William B. Oliver, John C. Pugh, William W. Quarles, Thomas M. Stevens, Henry P. Williams, Henry F. Wilson, Jr., and Bernard A. Wood.

The military system was not all drills and parades, however. There were other routines which galled the students. Said one young cadet serving guard duty in 1871, "If this is *playing* soldier, what must the *real thing* be?"[11] Said another, two years later, "Of all the boring things which have ever been written of, spoken of, or

REBUILDING THE UNIVERSITY 489

thought of, the most boring is that of being 'O. D.' on Sunday."[12] The sense of imminent danger, which had made the cadet of 1860 accept eagerly the military routines of that day, had faded out by now. Although the cadets still liked to march and drill, they were bored with playing soldier, and their boredom deepened into rebellion before the century closed.

The system which President Garland had instituted as a means of discipline and of training patriots for a conflict he believed to be inevitable had lost that reason for its being. But it had retained the function which Garland had regarded as secondary: it was still the instrument for the enforcement of campus discipline.

The commandant had become the chief disciplinary officer of the college. With the aid of his quartermaster, he had lifted the disciplinary burden almost wholly from the shoulders of the faculty, which could now devote its meetings less to the meting out of punishments and more to matters academic. The commandant was, however, still directly responsible to the president of the University.[13] One serious dispute resulting from this curtailment of absolute military authority occurred in 1873.

The commandant, General George D. Johnston, for reasons which seemed adequate to himself, imposed extra guard duty. President Lupton vetoed the order, removed the extra guard, and was sustained in his action by a six to two vote of the faculty. The commandant submitted his resignation, saying that the action of the faculty, "in failing to sustain my just authority as Commandant of the University has put it out of my power to be of any further service to the Institution."[14] He carried his case to the board of regents, and that board, after listening to him and to President Lupton, appears to have taken a somewhat ambiguous position. It assured the aggrieved commandant that it" appreciated the motives and feelings" which had led him to resign. It assured the president and the faculty that it "intended no reflection" on their conduct.[15] The commandant's resignation was not withdrawn. Dr. Smith was made acting commandant, and Maj. T. C. McCorvey became assistant commandant, at a salary of $1200 and soon became commandant.[16]

Perhaps a feeling that the delicate balance of authority between the academic and military departments of the University could be held best when the commandant belonged to the University family actuated the faculty when, about this time, they recommended that military appointments be made, in so far as possible, from among cadets who had acquitted themselves well in the Academic Department of the University.[17] Thomas C. McCorvey, appointed commandant the following July, met this requirement; he had just received his Bachelor of Laws degree.[18] Colonel McCorvey served as commandant from 1873 to 1888. He was succeeded by James Courtney Hixson, who at that time had just received his A.B. degree from the University. In 1890 Mr. Hixson became a Bachelor of Laws. He acted as commandant until 1891. He later served as United States Consul at Foochow, China, and as a volunteer in the Spanish-American War, becoming a lieutenant in the United States Army in 1901.

The idea that a military man should direct a military academy was always strong, however. During this period the trustees worked hard to get a real soldier into the post of commandant. Their first effort in this direction was made in 1879, when a special committee carried on an unsuccessful correspondence with the War Department. The committee asked that an army officer be detailed to serve as University commandant. He was to be paid by the United States Government, but he was to work under the direction of the faculty.[19]

Ten years later the trustees made an even more determined effort to get a regular army man on the campus. This time they sent Colonel N. H. R. Dawson, a member of the board, to talk matters over with the Secretary of War. According to the Colonel's report, the Secretary of War said that in the assignment of army men for campus duty the land grant colleges came first and that there were more applications from such colleges than there were officers available. An application to the Secretary of the Navy, Colonel Dawson said, had been answered in the same way.[20]

Perhaps Colonel Dawson's good offices were more effective than they appeared to be. In 1891 the War Department assigned Lieutenant Tredwell W. Moore to duty on the University of Alabama campus, to succeed Mr. Hixson. The board of trustees quickly appointed him commandant, but thought it necessary to explain the appointment as motivated by "considerations of economy and the promotion of discipline and good government under the supervision and control of the President of the University." No regular army lieutenant must be allowed to think that he was not under academic orders. The board formally resolved that it had neither the intention of extending or emphasizing the military system, nor the thought of making military government a "prominent or permanent" feature on the campus. [21]

Lieut. Moore was followed by three regular army officers: Lieut. Walter L. Taylor, 1893-1894; Lieut. William G. Elliott, 1894-1895; and Lieut. James Baylies, 1895-1898. A return to civilian commandants was made in 1898, when Erle Pettus, A. B., held the office while studying for his degree of Bachelor of Laws. Peyton Herndon Moore, another University of Alabama Law School graduate, acted as commandant in 1899-1900. Lieut. V. M. Elmore, Jr., was appointed in June, 1900, to the position but did not actually appear on the campus until April, 1901, on his return from service in the Philippines with the 29th Volunteers. During his absence the post of commandant was first held by the unfortunate James W. West, who resigned following the student rebellion of 1900; next by J. R. Forman, who served about a month; and then by Major William J. Parkes, B.C.E., who served from January to April, 1901. Colonel Elmore was ordered away for active duty in February, 1902, after his appointment as a second lieutenant in the regular army. Samuel H. Sprott, A.B., '98, finished out the year. Alto V. Lee, Jr., completed the roll of commandants. He received the sum of $300, plus board, laundry, and law tuition, for his services from September, 1902, to June, 1903. At that time the military system was abolished at the University.

Whether the commandant was drawn from civilian or military ranks, the officers, commissioned and noncommissioned, working under him were always chosen from among the cadets. The first of these company officers to be appointed when the University reopened were boys who had come back to Alabama from schools outside the state. Four had attended the Virginia Military Institute; one had received military training at Bingham, North Carolina.[22] After that, the cadet corps was in a position to train its own officers. Here again the dual authority of the academic and military departments asserted itself. The commandant appointed the corps officers, but he appointed them on recommendation of the faculty, which designated the students to be made officers and stipulated the rank which each should hold.[23] Recommendations were made after weighing carefully the student's academic standing, his military record, and his general conduct and character. In 1892 the trustees set down with great exactitude just how much emphasis should be given to each of these three factors. Academic standing was to count 45; military standing, including length of service, 35; and general character and deportment, 20.[24] Until seniors were allowed to become non-military students, in 1896, all commissioned officers were chosen from the senior class.[25]

The commandant and his cadet officers were the law enforcement body on the campus. Cadet officers who were convicted by court-martial of having failed wilfully when on duty to report any cadet for violation of the laws and regulations of the University were reduced in rank.[26]

Students in the University community before the turn of the century seem to have been as lawless—and as law-abiding—as average students on any campus. Although the "crimes" for which they sustained court-martial, accumulated demerits, and risked dismissal ranged from sheer mischief to murder, minor misdemeanors far outnumber instances of malicious wrong-doing. And the general impression is of a community as well-behaved as could be expected if one remembers the youth and high spirits of its citizens and the repressive nature of its laws, some of which seemed made to be broken.

As in any military organization, "insubordination" and "disrespect to officers" had a high percentage in the calendar of crime. Sometimes the non-military officers of the University thought they weighed too heavily in the scales. President Carlos Smith told the trustees as much in 1878, but his plea for presidential power to revise demerit lists went unheeded. President B. B. Lewis had better luck four years later. He told the board that he believed that the president of the University should have the power to scale down demerit records when, in his judgment, such action was advisable. Students, he said, could run up two hundred demerits in five months and thus be subject to dismissal, without having "manifested any thing vicious or immoral" in their conduct or character.[27] The trustees found his request reasonable and gave him permission to remit a sufficient number of demerits to prevent the necessity of dismissal if a large proportion of these demerits had been given for "military delinquencies" of an unimportant character.[28] Three years later the trustees balanced this action by ruling that students who received as many as one hundred demerits for misconduct could be confined to quarters or put under arrest for not more than one month.[29]

The strict rules concerning absences from barracks were, of course, subject to frequent violation. Entries in the faculty minutes in the 1880's are typical. In 1880 two students not only went to a school exhibition in town without permission but did not behave very well while they were there: they got three weeks of "confinement."[30] One Saturday night in 1882 three students absent from barracks from a quarter past eleven o'clock until two-thirty in the morning ran into stiffer penalties. Two were sent home; the third was confined to his room for a month and required to perform ten extra tours of guard duty.[31] The two who were dismissed were later allowed to come back and undergo the same punishment as their companion.[32] Five years later a boy who tried to slip in a six-day stay in Tuscaloosa between his leaving home and his arrival at the University was suspended and sent home for three weeks. At the end of the suspension period his father was asked to certify that his son had actually stayed at home during the three weeks.[33]

Parents of University sons were sometimes called upon to help enforce the discipline of the campus. They were often warned by letter that their boys were coming close to the danger point in the collection of demerits. The sons themselves were sometimes given a "two-weeks warning" under these circumstances. Often the letters home contained additional comment which could not have been welcome to parents. One parent learned, in 1878, that his son was a "waster of money"; another was informed that his boy was "becoming demoralized."[34] A decade later one letter home advised that a troublesome student be kept under the paternal roof the next session because "his presence as a student is not beneficial to him and is hurtful to the institution."[35]

The boys on the old campus showed typical student ingenuity in discovering loopholes in the rules and wriggling through them. One of the earliest disciplinary cases after the University reopened had to do with three boys who noted that all school fees except those for tuition and hospital were refunded to students who were dismissed during term time. They promptly went about the business of securing for themselves a dismissal with refund. Two of them succeeded in getting dismissed for gross insubordination by a unanimous vote of the faculty; the third was ordered to stand courtmartial. But the expected refunds were not forthcoming. The faculty ruled that students dismissed thereafter would be given only enough money for travel expenses home. Their parents were to be notified that the balance due would be refunded on their order.[36]

Hazing was a perennial problem. The practice was as current at the University of Alabama as on most campuses of this period and showed the usual tendency to go to excess. In 1898, after a number of students had been dismissed for their part in disorderly hazing, the students themselves took steps to end the custom. Resolutions condemning hazing and promising to abolish it were adopted by the six fraternities collectively and by the four classes separately.[37] The classes followed up their resolution by petitioning the faculty for release of the students then under arrest for hazing and for the reinstatement of those who had been dismissed.[38] The University authorities granted the petition. They also issued a statement, signed by the president, expressing gratification at the stand taken by the fraternities and the classes. "In eliminating hazing from the University," said the president, "they have justified the confidence of the faculty and of the state in their future."[39] The students also hailed the bright new day when the freshman was able to walk about "with the dignity of a Senior."[40] And both students and faculty appear to have been over-sanguine in these expressions. By 1901, less than three years after the "reform" had taken place, it was again necessary to suspend nineteen students for hazing.[41]

Old patterns of mischief, reminiscent of the Old University before the war, reappear in the record: disorder in the dining hall, ungentlemanly conduct off campus, and even disrespect to ladies all continued to bring public censure and disciplinary action. In 1874 the editors of the *Monthly* received a letter signed "Critic" which expressed grief and disappointment that the students, "though very polite and gentlemanly most of the time, occasionally forget themselves, and do things which they ought not." Critic then told of one undignified episode. Several ladies, he said, had stopped at the

University to watch the evening parade. When someone from the galleries "commenced to laugh and halloo," they were "perfectly surprised, knowing as they did the reputation of the Cadets for gentlemanly conduct." The ladies thus affronted had "immediately left the campus, returning to town by the outside road." That was no isolated incident, Critic added. A citizen from Tuscaloosa could hardly set foot on the campus without being assailed with cries of "Rat," "Fresh," "Fish"![42] The disposition to annoy the ladies, who were still all too rare in campus life, seems to have persisted throughout the period. In 1902 the *Crimson-White* commented that many students were guilty of "a grievous breach of etiquette" when they congregated in front of the McLester Hotel on Sunday mornings to stare at the ladies and to make audible remarks about their personal appearance.[43] In 1889 a special committee appointed by the trustees to visit the University was shocked at the confusion, noise, and disorder in the mess hall. Students shouted at the waiters. They shouted at their officers and at each other. They were boisterous and disorderly. And, so far as the gentlemen of the committee could see, their officers made no attempt to keep them in order. What they saw with their own eyes, taken with what they had heard from other sources, said the committee, seemed evidence that the general discipline of the corps had not been kept up to the proper standard. They were especially concerned about disorders during commencement week and about such other breaches of discipline as shouting on the campus, answering roll call in a "boisterous" tone of voice, exploding bombs on the grounds, and keeping untidy and disordered rooms.[44] Perhaps the grave representatives of the board may have expected too much decorum from boys who needed some safety valve for high spirits kept in check by the rigid rules of the University.

New patterns of mischief appeared also. Electric lights, which came to campus in the 1880's, remained a challenge to pranksters for at least a decade. When three students—Dent, Pettway, and Renfro—engaged in a scientific experiment with a fellow student named Westmoreland, forcing his fingers into an electric light socket so that he got a shock, the University authorities were themselves shocked. Captains Dent and Pettway were reduced to ranks; Renfro was turned over to the commandant and president for discipline.[45] The practice of sticking bayonets into electric sockets was common enough to receive notice in the yearbook of 1896.[46] And, as late as 1900, a minor mystery developed when light bulbs in the barracks were broken at a surprising rate and no one could discover who was responsible for the breakage.[47]

The records are sprinkled with references to disciplinary action for misdemeanors not always too well-defined. At least one student was dismissed for "profane swearing,"[48] and another, found guilty of "sending an obscene message through the mail on postal cards" and using "obscene language" at the table in the mess hall, was put on probation for a month and threatened with dismissal if he did not mend his ways.[49] One student was dismissed because he had committed "two offenses of disorderly conduct" on hop night and had deserted his church section.[50] "General bad conduct" caused the forced withdrawal of some students.[51] Not even seniors on the eve of graduation could count on leniency. There are several instances in which diplomas were withheld from seniors who dared to engage in "disorderly conduct" during commencement exercises.[52]

More definite and, in the main, more serious are the records which deal with the efforts of the University to protect student morals and to punish student violence. Here, also, the faculty and the commandant grappled with relatively few new types of misdemeanor. Cheating and petty thievery appeared from time to time. Drinking remained a major problem, and the smoking of cigarettes was becoming one. The outlawed pistol and knife still figured in an occasional campus prank or serious brawl. The authorities were still bending every effort to throw "every possible safeguard" around "the morals of cadets." Even the rule against playing cards was "rigidly enforced,"[53] at least in the earliest decade of the period.

Thefts in the barracks were dealt with in a very practical way, by minimizing temptation. When, in 1882, President Lewis suggested to the trustees that they forbid students to keep more than $3.00 in their rooms overnight, the trustees accepted his suggestion. Monies over that amount were to be deposited with the treasurer and drawn upon as required. A "small check book" was to be provided for this purpose.[54]

In the late 1890's cases of cheating on examinations came up for special attention. In 1896 two students reported by fellow students for cheating were dismissed from the University. Later, however, they were allowed to come back and take their final examinations. When the trustees were asked to approve degrees for these culprits, they expressed some doubt that the students should have been reinstated. But, they said, there might have been "circumstances within the knowledge of the faculty, not known to the trustees," and therefore they authorized the degrees.[55] Three years later, when Professor Barnwell reported that certain freshmen had been cheating during a "written recitation," the faculty requested the president not only to warn the offenders but also to admonish the whole student body of the seriousness of the offense.[56]

The original rules of the reopened University made drinking any amount of any intoxicating beverage a crime for which a student risked dismissal. By 1879, however, University authorities were recognizing that the strict enforcement of this law ran counter to human nature and to the customs and sanctions of the day. A new rule, adopted in that year, sought to draw a distinction between drinking and drunkenness:

Any Cadet found drunk or under the influence of wine, porter, or any spirituous or intoxicating liquors or brandied fruits, shall be dismissed or otherwise less severely punished.[57]

The faculty and the commandant now had the problem of deciding at exactly what point drunkenness set in. Soon after this new law was passed five cadets, found by the commandant under the influence of liquor, escaped dismissal because their case appeared "not very vagrant" and they "all declared that they had been unwittingly betrayed into excess, and seemed to be sincerely repentant." Instead, they had been confined to quarters for six weeks, given six extra tours of guard duty, and reduced to ranks. In reporting this episode to the trustees that June, the president was inclined to think that too much leniency had been shown. The boys had been more disorderly than he had realized at the time. They had been "quite boisterous" while returning to campus in a carriage the Saturday afternoon of the occurrence. Yet, since "it might be said that they were not drunk in the proper sense of the word," he supposed that the discipline meted out to them was technically correct.[58] He had already told the students, however, that similar cases would be more sternly handled in the future.[59] The following year the faculty asked the president to refuse to matriculate a young man who had been seen drunk on the streets of Tuscaloosa before his arrival on the campus to apply for admission.[60]

In 1882 President Lewis expressed his belief that the problem of drinking among students had been pretty well solved. He told the trustees as much in his annual report:

No case of drunkenness has come to the knowledge of the University officers, and it is believed that this vice—unfortunately too common among young men—does not exist here at all.[61]

He spoke too soon and too confidently. Within the next year one student was dismissed for drunkeness, and another, having been found in company with drunken persons, though there was no positive proof that he had been drinking, was ordered confined to his room.[62]

Smoking was frowned upon rather than banned. In 1879 the trustees asked the president to prohibit "segar stands" on the campus.[63] In 1892 they admonished him to do what he could to suppress the tobacco habit, "especially the smoking of cigaretts."[64] But apparently smoking was never actually banned. Boys smoked briar pipes and the newer cigarettes.[65] Each New Year some of the smokers, in an effort to reform, swore to give up smoking along with other bad habits; they reminded themselves of the new life they intended to lead by inscribing their resolutions on the walls of their rooms.[66]

Commenting on the morals of the students on the campus in the 1890's, Hill Ferguson has this to say:

It is very difficult to compare the manners and morals of one generation with those of another, but some conclusions may be drawn. . . . Women were much better behaved in the 90's than they are half a century later. The "feminist movement" was only in its beginning. Some of the old women dipped snuff, but I never saw one of them smoke, and smoking among young women just wasn't done.

The same rule applied to liquor. The men did their drinking off to themselves, and the little drinking among the girls, if at all, was done with no ostentation.

The automobile, with its parking, petting, road houses, tourists camps, and other demoralizing influences, was not even dreamed of in the "gay nineties". Opportunities for moral laxity were very limited.

REBUILDING THE UNIVERSITY

The men and boys of that period seeking amorous adventure, were confined almost exclusively to the professional class—white and Negro. "Smoky Row," which was all that the name implies, was one of Tuscaloosa's popular institutions in the '90's.[67]

Although the years had probably cast a haze over the campus of the '90's in Mr. Ferguson's mind, it is true that the coeds coming to the campus in that decade presented few disciplinary problems. As for the discipline meted out to cadets for visits to Smoky Row, the delicacy of the day apparently prevented the faculty from writing unsavory details into their records.

The old problem of the deadly weapon in the hands of high-spirited youngsters had around it no such taboo of silence. The swashbuckling spirit which had marked the old University was on the wane during the three decades of the late nineteenth century. However, student quarrels were still apt to flare into violence, and the disciplinary machinery of the University was still brought into play to restore order and to punish the offenders. There were probably more fights among the students than ever reached the official records, but the records are full enough to indicate that the weapons so explicitly banned by University law appeared with some frequency in angry student hands.

The most tragic shooting affray of this period came in 1878, when Kibble J. Harrison shot and killed William W. Alston. The quarrel arose originally on a point of Southern chivalry, and Harrison appears to have been the offender. He had, his fellow students reported, made some "defamatory" remarks about Alston's cousin, and Alston had warned him that he would whip him "as soon as the cut on his hand got well." The matter came to a head on Friday, February 22, 1878. Harrison was planning to leave the University that day, but he had no intention of seeming to dodge a fight with the aggrieved Alston. After he remarked to his friend Spraggins that he supposed he would have to "wind up his career in College with a fight with Alston," he went out of Spraggins' room in search of that fight.

Alston apparently recognized the day as his last chance to extract an apology from the insolent Harrison. He had been laughing about it, his friends said later, and was confident that he could get the retraction he demanded. His friends told him that Harrison would shoot if attacked, and they advised Alston to be ready to defend himself. Alston said he would take his pistol along, but that he would use it only in self-defense. What he wanted, he said, was to have a "fair fight" with Harrison, with his fists. Then he asked one of his friends, named Fitts, to go with him to see that there was fair play and to prevent Harrison's friends from entering the fight. Fitts wanted to take a pistol, but Alston persuaded him not to do so.

Alston found his adversary on the second stoop of Woods Hall. He went up to Harrison and put his arm across his shoulder. The two boys walked to and fro together while the preliminaries to the fight were disposed of. Alston asked Harrison if he had made certain remarks about his (Alston's) cousin. Harrison replied that he did not care to say whether he had or had not. Alston warned him that he would have to take the consequences. When Harrison replied that he was willing to do so, Alston struck his opponent full in the face. Harrison staggered, but not so much that he could not draw his pistol. He shot Alston in the breast. Alston threw up his hand to the wound and then quickly withdrew it to grasp his own pistol and fire. There was a brisk gun battle. Harrison emptied his pistol and dashed back into Spraggins' room for another. At that point, Alston, shot in the breast, the neck, and the hand, collapsed across the banister. He died within a few minutes. Harrison was wounded in the shoulder and the right arm, but his wounds were minor.

If the reports of eye-witnesses picked up by the newspaper are to be trusted, what happened next was more shocking than the shooting itself. Triumphant yells from the Harrison faction greeted Alston's fall. "Trot out another man," shouted the victor's roommate. "We have killed one and will kill another!" Someone else shouted, "Hurrah for 47!" (the number of Harrison's room) "It is ahead again!" The Tuscaloosa *Times* found in these bloodthirsty expression evidence that secret societies on the campus had divided students into hostile groups.

Harrison was, of course, arrested. At the hearing which took place four days later, he was charged with voluntary manslaughter and bound over to the grand jury under bond of $5,000.[68] A year later, when his case came up for trial, the jury returned a verdict of not guilty.[69]

A CADET COMPANY IN 1893

Seal in Use 1822-1865

Seal in Use 1872-1905

OFFICIAL SEALS OF THE UNIVERSITY

The incident shook the campus to its foundations. Four students were dismissed for their share in the episode. Enrollment dropped off as the news of the tragedy traveled around the state. Blame for his supposed share in the lack of discipline which made the incident possible was one factor causing the dismissal of President Carlos G. Smith the following June, though the president vehemently disclaimed any responsibility. "As long as I live," he told the trustees, "I shall deeply regret, that I got no clue to it, and had not even a suspicion of it, till all was ended.—If I could have received the slightest intimation of it, before hand, it might have been easily prevented."[70]

The trustees made their own investigation of the Alston shooting and of the general state of discipline at the University during the two years since the board of trustees had resumed control of its affairs.[71] The investigating committee brought in its report in July. The investigators had discovered, they said, "prevalence to a reprehensible degree of personal combats between students" and irrgularities of conduct "assuming in several instances the character of riots." Clearly, students were violating their pledge not to possess weapons; this was a "most injurious imputation against the moral tone" of the students. They found some grounds for the rumor that the Alston affair was, in part at least, caused by ill feelings between members of different secret societies which had been "smouldering ever since, breaking out from time to time into personal collisions between the more prominent members of the several factions." They concluded with the observation that the Alston affair could have been foreseen by anyone aware of the general state of disorder on the campus and that unless the laws of the University were more efficiently enforced, there was "something more than a probability that this shocking affair" might be repeated.[72]

The trustees listened gravely to the committee's report; then they ordered the faculty to enforce strict observance of the laws. They were to "suspend, dismiss with the privilege of resigning, or publicly dismiss any student guilty of gambling, profanity, drunkenness, carrying concealed weapons, engaging in fights and broils, and stirring up such between others, or any gross immorality." The faculty was to be held to a "strict accountability for the prompt, vigorous, and impartial performance of this duty."[73]

A year later Acting-President Wyman brought to the board a reassuring report. He said that although the "smothered fires of faction" had threatened to "burst forth anew" at the beginning of the year, the commandant had succeeded in effecting a reconciliation between the leaders of the two factions. Peace had been preserved. The students themselves, Professor Wyman observed, seemed "resolved to bury the past." There was every evidence "that the deplorable spirit of faction which seemed, at one time, likely to perpetuate itself," had died out.[74]

This did not mean, however, that the students had actually and finally foresworn their cherished weapons. Mention of those weapons appears again and again in the disciplinary records straight through the period. In 1880 one student was reported to the board of trustees for expulsion because he had cut another student in an affray.[75] The following year two students were cited for "wilfully killing a dog, with a rifle taken from Barracks." The faculty not only put the offenders under arrest for four weeks and ordered them to pay $10 damages to the dog's owner but they wrote a new rule also: that any student who had in his possession cartridges or other ammunition without the consent of the president or commandant risked dismissal.[76]

One fracas in February, 1898, involved disciplinary action for the commandant as well as for a number of students. The commandant had attempted to order off campus a former student named Thornton Parker. Frank White, a senior, had come to Parker's defense, and, "clubbing his gun," had hit the commandant with it. The commandant, somewhat pardonably it would seem, had then used language which shocked some ladies who happened to be passing by. White was suspended for two weeks. Other students in any way connected with the incident were reprimanded and letters were sent to their parents. As for the commandant, the president, remarking that his use of profanity had "seriously impaired, if it did not end, his usefulness," suspended him indefinitely.[77]

The general and exuberant impulse of students to fire guns on the campus seems to have lessened with time. But there is at least one instance on record where the old urge to make noise asserted itself. In 1888 some students decided that the advent of the last month in the school year, June, should be properly saluted. At a secret meeting they decided that a salute of twenty guns should be given. Plans were carefully laid. It was decided that the students who were to fire the salute would use guns belonging to other students, so that the authorities would have difficulty in determining which were the real culprits. Shortly before midnight on the chosen day the conspirators gathered "on the middle of the third stoop." They loaded their borrowed guns, fired twice each very quickly, dropped the guns, and ran for the shelter of their rooms. At the court of inquiry the next day the commandant questioned all the boys who did not have guns in their rooms shortly after the firing. All except one of the witnesses showed clearly that they were as much mystified as the commandant about the missing guns. But one boy, who refused to testify, upset the careful plans of the conspirators. He had overheard some of the planning and had hidden his own gun. The real culprits were in a dilemma. They did not want an innocent man to be expelled for refusing to testify. Furthermore, they were not quite sure whether that man would steadfastly keep silence under threat of expulsion. At a secret meeting the guilty students decided that the wisest course, under the circumstances, was full confession. The president, who received this confession, was reported to have been faintly amused by the whole episode. Nevertheless, the celebrating seniors were all placed under arrest and kept under arrest until the day of their graduation.[78]

Rebellion against the stern discipline of the University took the form of persistent objection to the military system which enforced it. The University of Alabama was the only military school in the state at the time of its reorganization,[79] and it was perhaps natural that the students should be restive under restraints which they knew to be unique on their own campus. Efforts to abolish the military system recurred all through the period, coming to a climax in the student rebellion of December 7, 1900. But the University authorities were too convinced of the value of the system to listen to the arguments of disgruntled students.

As early as 1873 the board of regents had before it a resolution that the military system be discontinued. The resolution was considered, however, against the background of a report made by a special committee which had visited the campus and had been much impressed with the military system in operation. One curious argument this committee advanced was that such a building as the barracks was unfit for a university unless the military system were maintained to enforce discipline. Since funds for a new building were not available, it was clear that the military system would have to be kept. The board took a half year to think matters over. Then a special meeting was called, to which alumni and faculty were invited. At that meeting it was decided to postpone indefinitely further discussion regarding the abolition of the military system.[80] President Carlos G. Smith apparently agreed with this action. He told the regents, in his annual report that year, that the more he saw of the workings of the military system, the more convinced he became of its superiority over every other type of school discipline. Abolition of the system would be disastrous, he insisted. Even the "agitation of that measure during the present session," might have results injurious to the University.[81]

But the first breach in the system came at just about this same time, in spite of President Smith's enthusiasm. The first non-military student came to the campus in November, 1873,[82] and the following year the faculty ordered that the "Round House" be fitted up for the use of one of the non-military students.[83] In 1875 it was agreed that young men "of suitable age and character" might take University work without being under military discipline if they lived off campus and submitted to such regulations as the faculty deemed appropriate.[84] The phrase "suitable age" was defined as meaning twenty-one years of age and over.[85] The Tuscaloosa *Times* thought this "a wise and timely arrangement." It commented that "the friends and the opponents of the military feature of the University have, in this judicious arrangement of the Faculty, a compromise of their conflicting views, which will enable them to share equally in all the academic privileges and advantages of the Institution."[86]

President Smith's enthusiasm for the military system had been dimmed somewhat by 1878. Reporting to the trustees that year, he reiterated his support for the system in principle, but asked that its operation be limited. He requested that the board give him power to grant temporary relief from military drills if it seemed advisable for him to do so. The military system, said President Smith, should be regarded as a means of maintaining good order, but it should not

REBUILDING THE UNIVERSITY

be allowed "in the slightest degree, to interfere with the Student's Academic duties."[87]

In the 1890's the students themselves seem to have entered this controversy. In February, 1891, the senior class petitioned the faculty to be excused from military duty for the remainder of the academic year. There was a lively discussion. One professor moved that the petition be approved provided that the seniors remove themselves from the barracks. Another suggested that the military feature had been abolished at the University of Tennessee, at Knoxville, without any detriment to discipline at that school. Others warned that disaster would follow such a course at the University of Alabama. Some believed that increased University expenses would be one of the consequences. The petition was refused by a vote of seven to four, and the president was instructed to report the petition and the action of the faculty to the trustees at their next meeing.[88]

The trustees upheld the faculty action, and, in so doing, incurred the ire of the students. On commencement day, 1891, after the seniors had safely tucked away their diplomas, a pamphlet entitled *Senior Battery* started circulating among the commencement visitors and the student body.[89] It was a blast against the refusal of the trustees to listen to the student plea for relief from the military system:

The petition of the Senior Class to the Board of Trustees for ex-military has been disapproved, and we have seen our fondest hopes for both ourselves and our Alma Mater dashed to the ground. . . . The fact that the petition was signed by every member of the Senior Class except three shows that there is something radically wrong with the military system and if the Trustees had the good interests of the school at heart they should have given our petition more careful consideration.[90]

Admittedly, said the student pamphleteers, publication of such criticism of the action of University authorities would be considered a breach of University law. But what right had the University authorities to make such a law?[91]

For the next five years the subject was tossed back and forth by special committees of faculty and trustees. In general, the authorities stuck firmly by the military plan in spite of increasing pressure from the students. But some concessions were made.

In 1893 a faculty committee reported "that the interests of higher education in the University would not be promoted by the abolition of the Military as a compulsory feature."[92] In 1894 the senior class again petitioned for exemption from military duty.[93] The petition was again refused, but the commandant was directed to drill as infantry officers all members of the senior class who were not commissioned officers, instead of continuing the practice of drilling senior privates as an artillery corps.[94] In 1895 the board of trustees, by a narrow margin of four to three, voted down a resolution which would have empowered a committee to consider the advisability of exempting seniors and juniors from the military system.[95]

The seniors gained their freedom from military service in 1896. In that year the trustees voted that they should be made "ex-military" and that they should be removed from the barracks. The general provisions that, upon enrollment, all students became members of the Alabama Corps of Cadets remained in force, but the faculty were authorized to permit young men "of any of the lower classes, of suitable age and character" to remove themselves from the barracks and from the military controls if, in the opinion of the faculty, such action seemed advisable.[96] The trustees noted that taking the seniors out of the barracks would be a good thing in itself. It would mean that the cadets would be on a more equal footing than they had been. The many rights and immunities which set seniors apart from underclassmen would not be so evident under the new arrangement. And, because none of the seniors had drilled in battalion except the commissioned officers, the new plan would not materially decrease the size of the battalion.

Evidently not all seniors welcomed this release, for in 1899, on the recommendation of the president, the trustees voted that seniors might elect to put themselves under military discipline, with the understanding that once they had done so they might not change their minds and withdraw from the corps except with the consent of the faculty.[97] The following year the president reported that four seniors had availed themselves of this privilege. They had, he said, served as captains and adjutants for the corps and had added to the efficiency of the organization "through their advanced age and maturity." He noted also that city cadets now had their own day quarters in Manly Hall. Their separation from the military students resulted in better discipline.[98]

REBUILDING THE UNIVERSITY 507

These arguments about the military system were merely the rumblings of a storm which broke in full fury in 1900. A large-scale student revolt, which lasted a week before it was brought under control, left the system so weakened that its abolition a few years later was a foregone conclusion.

John D. McQueen, a leader in the rebellion, writing, in 1947, his reminiscences of that exciting week, puts the blame squarely upon James West, who had arrived to take over the post of acting commandant that fall and who apparently had delusions of grandeur and an excess of zeal in the performance of his duty.

Soon after the opening of the 1900 term, it became apparent that the Commandant, Mr. West, on account of the inequality of punishment meted out by him for minor infractions of the military rules, was not the man who should have been entrusted with the duties of Commandant. At times a more severe punishment would be placed on some students for violating a rule than was placed on another student who had at about the same time violated the same rule. This condition continued through the Fall months of the year 1900, and by the first of December, 1900, Mr. West had become very unpopular with the student body, and there was an undercurrent of feeling among some of the students that they would like to take Mr. West down "a peg or two" by demonstrating to him that he was not quite as big or important as he seemed to feel his office as Commandant made him.[99]

There was nothing spontaneous about the demonstration. It was planned in careful detail by a little group of ringleaders which, according to Mr. McQueen, included himself, W. R. Chapin, W. Earl Drennen, Fred G. Stickney, C. H. Young, W. J. Conniff, and J. R. Forman. The strategy adopted was that of creating a disturbance which the commandant could not check and which would, therefore, discredit his authority. The matter had to be handled so that those participating could not be identified and punished. To this end, a round robin was circulated. All the residents of Woods Hall swore themselves to secrecy, promised to refuse to answer questions after the disturbance, and promised to resign and go home if any of their fellow students should be dismissed for a share in the episode. Every detail of the assault was carefully planned:

One group of students was detailed to secure barbed wire . . . and . . . to stretch it across the four flights of stairs which then led up to the first stoop of Woods Hall, so as to prevent anyone from entering the

Barracks when the demonstration started. Other groups were detailed to secure a supply of fire works, cannon crackers, tin pins. . . .

The students who were on that day, respectively, Officers of the Day and Sergeant of the Guard . . . by pre-arrangement retired to their respective rooms, and the doors of these rooms were . . . fastened from the outside so that these two officers might truthfully say they could not get out of their rooms when the noise started.[100]

The plot was a dramatic success. At the given signal the fun started. The commandant, aroused by the illegal din of fire crackers, rushed out to stop it and was himself checked by the barbed wire. When coal and other missiles rained down upon him, he beat a hasty retreat. In a few minutes he was back again with President Powers, but even the august presence of the University's executive did not curb the noise or curtail the showers of coal. Toward morning the racket subsided gradually and there was peace on the campus again.

The next morning the University authorities tried the standard methods of discipline. They placed all students under arrest and set up a military court of inquiry, but they soon discovered that student solidarity made such action futile. The students were quick to seize their advantage when the court adjourned without acting and when the order went out that classes might be resumed. At a mass meeting they carried the rebellion one step further by instituting what was, in effect, a student strike:

At this meeting all of the students who had signed the round robin pledged themselves not to perform any military duties, or to answer any military calls for so long as Mr. West was retained as Commandant; . . . . the said students pledged themselves thereafter to maintain perfect order, and to protect the University property; to attend all classes promptly, and regularly, and each student pledged himself to study with unusual diligence. . . .[101]

Another result of the mass meeting was a petition which was duly presented to President Powers. The faculty minutes record a statement of grievances submitted on December 6. Apparently the students presented, however, more than one petition before they were through with the matter. Mr. McQueen remembers that he and his fellow conspirators also demanded the dismissal of the commandant and even the disciplining of the president.

REBUILDING THE UNIVERSITY

The resolutions which the faculty considered indicate some of the points at which the military system galled the cadets:

To the Honorable Faculty of the University of Alabama, through the President:
We, the Alabama Corps of Cadets in Mass-meeting assembled, do respectfully request that the Faculty take action on the following resolutions,—
1st. Whereas we believe the call of "tattoo" to be a nuisance, and detrimental to study; Resolved that the aforesaid call be abolished.
2nd, Whereas we know tour-walking to be a *torture,* not a punishment, also to be inhuman; Resolved, that this mode of punishment be eliminated from the punishments inflicted by the authorities.
3rd. Whereas, the Catalogue states that the Corps drill three hours per week, and this has been the custom for some years, and whereas we have been forced to drill from three and a half to four hours each week, two hours during the week and the remaining one and a half to two hours on Saturday morning; Resolved that three Special hours be designated for drill. . . . We have had the restrictions placed upon us as long as men could honorably do so, and when the climax was reached by putting men on the quadrangle for visiting and other petty affairs then and not till then did we adopt measures to recover our rights.[102]

The faculty attempted to maintain its dignity in the face of such onslaughts. They said that in this case the students' exercise of their right of petition should have been directed to the military authorities.[103] But the students had the bit in their teeth now. There were further mass meetings, further threats of more demonstrations to come. In the Philomathic Hall on Sunday afternoon, Professor Palmer, who had the consent of the president, attempted to reason with the cadets. But they listened unmoved.[104] The next day the faculty relented enough to appoint a committee to hear the student complaints, though there were three members of the faculty who protested such action and asked that they be recorded as objecting because "to hear anything from students while they are in a state of insubordination is an utter subversion of all discipline."[105]

By this time the students knew they had the upper hand. Mr. McQueen writes of the growing confidence of the cadets as they, enforcing their own strict discipline to challenge a discipline they were determined to destroy, became aware that they had the faculty and the University officers completely on the defensive. When the hearing set by the faculty was held, the cadets were there with charges against the commandant and against the president as well. The president had, they insisted, been guilty of favoring sons of influential families in such matters as permissions to attend football games, dismissals, and letters home.[106]

President Powers had already had one brush with the rebels. He had attempted to expel from the University the board of control which was directing strategy for the rebellion and maintaining better order on campus than the military had ever achieved. He had been told that if he made such a move, the whole student body was pledged to resign and go home.[107] Seeming to accept the student censure, he made no attempt to answer the charges when they were made, but on the following day at a meeting of the faculty, he thought it necessary to say positively that he was not guilty of favoritism and to outline his policy in the enforcement of University rules.[108]

Commandant West, called before the faculty on Wednesday evening of the rebellion week, seems to have made at least an attempt to dismiss lightly the charges made against him. He said that the accusations were too flimsy to deserve consideration and that students were all too prone to resort to petitions on the slightest provocation. He recalled one instance in which the junior class had petitioned him to allow them to wear gold cords on their caps. Although he had told them that he would give the matter consideration, no one had ever come back to follow up the request. He insisted that students were like that.

By this time the faculty were in no mood to try to gloss over the charges. They questioned the unhappy Commandant West about the charge that general permits were not being issued. The commandant admitted that he had received no instructions to discontinue them, but he added that permits to go to town on Sunday were invariably granted and that he considered such permits very necessary. It was most unwise, he insisted, to allow students to go to town just to loaf on the streets, or about hotels and other popular places on general permits.

When Commandant West was asked to explain about the tattoo call, he explained that he had talked that matter over with the president before instituting this rule that was so obnoxious to cadets.

REBUILDING THE UNIVERSITY

The main object was to remove the temptation to be absent from barracks at night. He said that no one had ever complained about the rule before.

As for the extra drill hours, the commandant assured the faculty that those hours had been carefully arranged. As a matter of fact they had been instituted for the accommodation of football players so that they could make up on Saturday drills missed during the week.

The faculty inquisition took up the charges point by point. Commandant West admitted that he had made a mistake, as charged, in adding up demerits. He had become aware of this mistake when he found that unusually large numbers of students were required one afternoon to "walk tours." He said that he had at once rechecked his records and had found that the post adjutant had made a number of mistakes. He had done his best to rectify the error and thought that he had done so. He denied that he had put boys "on the quadrangle" for such petty offenses as visiting, but he added that he was certainly in favor of doing so. He ridiculed the idea that "tour-walking" was an inhuman form of discipline. Auburn, Howard, and West Point were all using this system; it was standard practice in most military schools. The faculty listened to his testimony and then resolved to turn the whole thing over to the trustees.

On the same day that the faculty held these hearings, the trustees at the request of President Powers, acted also. The executive committee had considered the problem first, but the full board did not meet until Friday. The perfect strategy and timing of the student board of control becomes more evident at this point. As the trustees laboriously interviewed individual members of the faculty, trying to sift evidence and get their own picture of the rebellion, a student messenger arrived with a figurative white flag, a resolution which read:

To the Honorable Board of Trustees of the University of Alabama, in mass meeting assembled, having brought our grievances to the attention of the Board of Trustees, and believing in their wisdom and integrity do hereby resolve that we return to all Military duties dating from "Tattoo" December the 14th, 1900.[110]

The trustees responded the next day with their own resolutions:

Resolved that, in view of the resolution adopted by the Corps of Cadets and which has just been presented to this Board of Trustees, the Students of the University who were engaged in the outbreak on Friday, December 7th, 1900 and those who have been engaged since that time in resistance to the military authorities be and they are hereby absolved from punishment for those offenses upon their compliance with the terms of the said resolution of the Corps of Cadets.

Resolved further, that this lenient action upon the part of the Board of Trustees is not in any wise to be construed as a precedent to govern in like offenses in the future.[111]

The trustees' minutes of that day imply that leniency was granted because of a generous request by President Powers. Mr. McQueen, however, remembered that a considerable amount of behind-the-scenes diplomacy had paved the way for the final compromise. Mr. Tenant Lomax and other members of the board had met with student representatives and had worked out the terms for the surrender message. There had been some attempt to force the student board of control to apologize, but the attempt was quickly abandoned when the students stood firm.

Mr. McQueen remembers, too, what the formal record omits, that the offensive Mr. West tendered his resignation as soon as the scrap was over and that the resignation of President Powers, effective the following June, was accepted at the same time.[112]

The nominal victory was in the hands of the trustees, for the students had backed down and had gone back to their military duties. Although discipline had been restored, the military system would be little more than an empty form from that day on. The students had successfully challenged that form of discipline. The real victory was theirs. And the fruits of that victory came when, on March 3, 1903, the Alabama legislature formally authorized the board of trustees "at any time they deem proper" to "abolish the military system at said institution or reduce the said system to a department of instruction." The University of Alabama ceased to be a military academy soon thereafter, and not until World War I brought the ROTC did the campus ring again with the tramp of soldierly feet and the sharp commands of the drill officers.

The rebellion of 1900 marks the end of one disciplinary era. It also has this further significance. It was evidence of the growth of student solidarity, which would be so important a feature of college and university life in the first half of the twentieth century. The boys on the University campus were learning to organize and to use their organizations to accomplish a multitude of ends, of which a measure of self-discipline and self-government was one. The story of those developing expressions of group life deserves a chapter to itself.

CHAPTER XXII

Extra-Curricular Activities

TWO student organizations of the old University rose Phoenix-like from its ashes. Classes were hardly under way in the autumn of 1871 before the Erosophic and Philomathic literary societies were again holding their four-hour meetings on Saturday evenings, debating the burning issues of the day. The faculty and trustees alike approved of this intellectual and genteel form of student activity.[1]

The student body was about equally divided between the two societies, and for a decade and more inter-society and intra-society rivalries were the principal feature of campus life outside the classroom. Each society had its own hall and library, where young orators solemnly debated such weighty subjects as "Is the abolition of slavery wrong?"[2] "Ought the farmers of the South to plant more grain and less cotton?"[3] "Ought a man to pledge himself to total abstinence?"[4] "Are public amusements beneficial?"[5] "Ought the immigration of the Chinese into the United States be prohibited?"[6] Woman's suffrage was a favorite topic for these debates, and now and then a lighter note was struck, as when the Philomathic Society earnestly debated the question: "Is single blessedness more conducive to happiness than married life?"[7]

Once a year, under careful faculty supervision, the leading orators of the rival groups matched wits with each other for the honor of their respective societies. The subject for an inter-society debate had to be approved by the president of the University, and the speeches, limited to 1,200 words, were carefully scrutinized in advance by the professor of English.[8] Once a year, also, each society sent out formal invitation cards for its anniversary program. Large audiences from town and campus attended these anniversaries, which usually featured a guest speaker and music as well as a debate.

Under this smooth and elegant surface, however, forces were operating to undermine the influence of the literary society on the campus. One of these forces was a spirit of faction which operated not only between the rival groups but within each society. The societies elected all representatives for public celebrations, and so important were these elections that they often caused a party split within the groups. Sometimes the bitter feelings thus generated could be dispelled with relative ease, as when, in 1881, the Erosophic Society members buried their election hatchets at an ice cream supper.[9] Sometimes the rift was so wide that only reorganization of the society could bring the factions together. In 1897 Professor T. W. Palmer was instrumental in effecting such a reorganization of the Philomathic Society. The revived society, with a membership of fifty students, united to gain a difficult victory in a debate with the law class the following April.[10] The Erosophic Society, impressed with the new spirit of the Philomathics, put itself through a similar reorganization soon afterwards.

Looking with concern at the disruptive effects of the society elections, the trustees decided in the early 1880's to take the privilege of election from the groups and to put into the hands of the faculty the duty of appointing representatives for public occasions. This only made matters worse. In 1884 the societies were in a flourishing condition and a third group of twenty-five members organized the Peithonian Literary Society,[11] But by 1891 this society had been dissolved,[12] and the Jones Literary Society, organized the following year by fourteen seniors, had an even briefer life.[13] Even the return of the elective franchise to the societies in 1892 failed to stem the decline.[14] The Philomathic and Erosophic societies had brief renewals of energy at the start of each school year, but they, too, were losing their hold on the students.

In 1888 a committee of the board of trustees brought in a report on the deplorable condition of the halls in which the three literary societies met. In the Erosophic Society room they had found a very shabby carpet on the floor, four desks, about twenty-five chairs, four common benches, three small pictures, and a presiding officer's stand. The books in the small library were thrown about in disorder, and the walls of the room were marked with notations of books that had been taken out and returned. The Philomathic Hall was in only slightly better condition. The carpet was not quite so worn. There were about fifty chairs, and a small library housed in a separate room. The Peithonian Society had no carpet, no library or collection of books, no president's stand; its only furniture consisted of two small tables, twenty-five chairs, one old slatted bench, and two pictures. The carefully guarded privacy of the club rooms had disappeared; the doors stood open so that anyone could enter. The atmosphere of culture, appropriate to literary societies, had vanished. All this, said the committee, was deplorable. These societies were "the pulse of literary life in every institution of learning." Something should be done to make that pulse beat more strongly.[15]

The trustees responded to this appeal with a special appropriation of more than $3000.[16] Alumni, also, came to the rescue. By 1898 the Philomathic Society, which had supplemented such gifts by sponsoring a lecture by Governor Taylor, of Tennessee, could again boast that it had one of the finest halls in the South.[17] The old literary societies long continued as a feature of campus life, but after 1885 they did not again hold undisputed sway over student loyalty.

The newer pattern of student organization, the secret fraternity, had made its appearance in the old University, but it had never received official support and it was, at best, merely tolerated by trustees and faculty. The men who rebuilt the University were determined to keep the fraternity from their campus if they could possibly do so. The students were just as determined to move with the times.

As early as 1874 the faculty voted to refer to the board of regents a student petition to establish a secret society on the campus.[18] Apparently the regents took no action on this request, but there is evidence that secret societies were in clandestine operation during that decade. The baneful influence they exerted was rumored to be one cause of the fatal shooting of young Alston, in 1878. By that time these groups were definitely and officially outlawed. Students had, for the preceding year, been required to sign a pledge that they would join no such group. In 1879 the pledge was revised and strengthened. It read,

I do further pledge myself, on honor, that I will not so long as I am a student of the University, either in term time or in vacation, or form or hold, without permission of the Faculty, any connection with, either directly or indirectly, any secret club, society, fraternity, or other organization or attend the meetings of, or wear the badge of any such secret organization, and that I will not so long as I am a student of the University, enter into any obligation or understanding, express or implied, direct or indirect, to join any such society after I shall have graduated.[19]

Two students who had violated their matriculaiton pledge were dismissed from the University the same month that this new statement was adopted,[20] and the trustees gave warning that the same fate lay in store for others guilty of the same offense. They were determined to enforce the ban.

Apparently the words "during term-time or in vacation" had been inserted in the pledge of 1879 because of faculty experience with resourceful student evasion of a less explicit phrasing. Apparently, also, some students failed to note that one loophole had been thus stopped up. In 1881 nine boys sent a respectful note to the faculty. They had, they said, failed to notice the new wording of the pledge, and they had joined fraternities. When their attention had been called to the words they had actually subscribed to, they had voluntarily severed their connections with the secret societies. They asked that the faculty pass a resolution relieving them from "the imputation of having wilfully violated their matriculation pledge." The faculty, moved by this evidence of a delicate sense of honor, passed the desired resolution.[21]

By 1885, however, the tide in favor of fraternities was running too strongly to be ignored or checked by official pledges. In that year the board of trustees received a petition signed by many cadets and by members of the law class, asking that the law against secret societies be rescinded.[22] The board responded with an ordinance which, under certain safeguards, opened the campus to fraternities:

Be it ordained that it shall be lawful for "the usual college societies" to be organized among the students of this Institution. *Provided* it be shown to the Faculty, that all such societies, whenever desiring to be established here, are of good standing in the colleges where they originated or have their parent chapters; and *Provided further* that all elections to any office or honor of a student or students which shall entitle him or them to appear on University Rostrum before the Public be held by the Faculty, *Provided further* that no publication shall be made in the University Monthly or elsewhere of any officers elected or any honors conferred by the Societies.[23]

This action was by no means unanimous. A strong minority held out against fraternities and insisted that its opinion be officially recorded in the minutes. This group feared the secret nature of the new organizations, whose meetings would take place without faculty knowledge or supervision and whose members would be "withdrawn from the surveillance of the officers and from the university discipline" during fraternity meetings and while engaged in fraternity activity. They feared also the disruptive influence of the secret society: it would "disturb the general harmony, unity and fraternity of feeling." They feared the introduction of a new loyalty which crossed state and regional lines: since fraternities had chapters on other campuses, they would tend to destroy enduring local ties and break up strong state feeling. They feared most of all, perhaps, the setting of a dangerous precedent. If a student petition could secure such a reversal of the board's long-standing policy, what would prevent campus youth from coming back with other and even more dangerous requests which would be "subversive to order and good discipline"?[24]

The will of the majority prevailed, however, and the faculty set about the task of drafting the rules under which fraternities could organize as accepted parts of undergraduate life. By October these regulations were in full force. A formal petition to the president was the first step required for any group wishing to form a fraternity chapter at the University. This petition must state the name of the fraternity, the names of the members, and names of the institutions in which the fraternity already had chapters. It must designate the place it planned to hold its meetings. It must include a pledge by all the members that they would faithfully observe the rules and regulations of the University of Alabama. With this petition before them, the faculty would decide by majority vote whether to admit the fraternity applying. Once a fraternity had been accepted, its presiding officer, at the beginning of each term, was required to file with the president a list of undergraduate members. The faculty were to have access to this list.

Fraternity meetings might be held on the campus or in the town of Tuscaloosa, but, in either case, formal approval of the faculty was required before a meeting-place could be designated. Fraternities which met in Tuscaloosa might not choose halls or lodge rooms "over or adjoining" places where "spirituous or malt liquor" was sold. Fraternities meeting on campus might meet on Friday nights or any time after inspection on Saturdays; those with town headquarters were limited to meeting on Saturday afternoon. Boisterous or disorderly conduct during these meetings would be proper cause for the suspension of fraternity privileges until the next annual meeting of the board of trustees.[25]

These makeshift meeting arrangements were not wholly satisfactory to the promoters of the new fraternities. They attempted to strike for full fraternity privilege while the iron of trustee approval was hot. In November, 1885, they were asking that they be permitted to build fraternity houses. But the trustees had gone as far as they would; they turned down the petition.[26]

Misgivings about the wisdom of opening the doors for fraternities kept coming up in trustees' meetings for years. In 1888 a resolution, adopted by a narrow margin of six votes to four, instructed the president and faculty to do what they could to "discourage the continuance" of these organizations.[27] It was too late to reverse the earlier decision by that time. Six fraternities were already in full operation. Two of them were revived chapters of fraternities which had come to the University before the war: Delta Kappa Epsilon and Sigma Alpha Epsilon.[28] Four were new on the campus: Sigma Nu, Kappa Alpha, and Alpha Tau Omega, established in 1885;[29] and Phi Delta Theta, established in 1887.[30] By 1902 two others had been added to this list: in 1899, a chapter of Kappa Sigma;[31] in 1901, a chapter of Phi Gamma Delta.[32] The latter fraternity had been a part of the pre-war University.

Literary societies and the newer fraternities were not the only forms of student organization during the last three decades of the nineteenth century. Each class had its own debating society, and the interest in debating generated in these clubs and in the literary societies reached beyond the campus limits. When the Gulf States Inter-Collegiate Oratorical Association was formed in 1902, the University of Alabama was one of its organizers, the others being the University of Georgia, the University of Mississippi, Louisiana State University, and Tulane University. H. W. Roberts of the University of Alabama was the first president of this association.[33]

Music and drama had their own devotees, though the organizations built around those interests appear to have had little continuity. There was a glee club with twelve members and a director on the campus in 1885.[34] By 1895 it had changed into the University Mandolin, Glee, and Guitar Club.[35] A University Quartette was featured in various campus programs,[36] and a quintette, consisting of two mandolins and three guitars, had at least a brief life span.[37] A Shakespeare Society was in operation in 1885,[38] but a more formal effort at student dramatics awaited the formation, in 1901, of the University Dramatic Club, under the direction of Professor James A. Anderson. It had a membership including eight men, four coeds, two "specialists," the manager, and an advance agent. Running true to the student tradition of the day, its first major performance, presented at the hospital in Tuscaloosa and at Greensboro, was "The Private Secretary."[39]

Perhaps the first of the organizations built around professional interest was the Kent Club, named for the legal commentator. This club, in 1898, provided for members of the junior and senior law classes opportunities for social, literary, and legal improvement.[40]

The newly reorganized University was not long without that important mark of a modern campus—the student publication. The idea of a student monthly occurred first to the leaders of the Philomathic Society in the autumn of 1873. The faculty, lacking foresight of the problems of student journalism, thought the idea an excellent one, and willingly appointed a committee to plan with the students for the first University magazine.[41] The University *Monthly* made its appearance that December under the joint sponsorship of the two literary societies. For the first twelve years of its life, its subscription price was $2.00; after that it was reduced to $1.50.

The plan of operation adopted by the organization committee called for the election of associate editors from each society. Presumably the chief editorial chair was to be held in turn by representatives of these societies. Thomas H. Watts, Jr., member of Philomathic, was the first editor-in-chief, and when he left the University in June of 1874, W. C. Jemison, of the Erosophic Society, was chosen by the editorial board to take his place for the last issue of that year.[42] Difficulties in the smooth operation of the elective process may have appeared about this time, for there is no record of another editor-in-chief being elected until 1886.

The faculty, well aware of the ill feeling generated in the editorial elections, had lost patience with the whole process by June, 1877, and they ordered the suspension of the four-year-old magazine.[43] The students' protest probably affected the faculty's decision in October to permit publication to be resumed, subject to certain conditions. The faculty reserved the right to choose two editors from each society. And they insisted that no article be published in the *Monthly* until some professor had seen and approved it.[44]

That was the beginning of a ten-year struggle. Again and again the faculty tried to ban the publication; again and again they were persuaded to try new organization methods which would permit continuation of its life. A joint committee from two societies persuaded the teachers to lift the ban imposed in the fall of 1879. But the teachers requested the president to appoint a censor from among the faculty for each issue of the *Monthly* thereafter.[45] In 1882 the faculty enlarged the editorial board: four of its members were to come from the societies; a fifth, from the law class.[46] In 1885 one member of the new Peithonian Society was given a place on the board of editors.[47] In the following year the board was reduced to three editors, one from each of the literary societies. The editor-in-chief was to be chosen from these three, and he was not only to preside at editorial staff meetings but also to serve as liaison man to keep the faculty in touch with proceedings.[48] The order made in June, 1887, to discontinue publication of the *Monthly*[49] was formally set aside, in a six to four faculty vote, three years later.[50] But the student victory was, this time, merely nominal. The *Monthly* was never published again. Its last issue bears the date of May, 1887.

The place held by the old *Monthly* was briefly filled by the *Journal,* which was established in January, 1891.[51] The control by literary sociteies had been broken now; the editors were chosen from members of the senior class—and they were chosen by the faculty.

Three years later the *Journal* slipped into oblivion to make way for a much more modern publication, the *Crimson-White,* in the beginning a four-page, four-column, weekly paper of campus news.[52]

The faculty was strict in its supervision of this new publication. It selected all members of the editorial staff: the editor-in-chief, the six associate editors, the business manager, and the general soliciting agent. It appointed a professor to act as censor.[53] But this watchfulness did not, apparently, prevent items of questionable propriety from getting into the new paper's columns. After six months of struggle, the faculty ruled that it was "inexpedient" to continue the publication of the *Crimson-White*.[54] This prohibition lasted through one full year before the faculty relented and authorized the re-establishment of the newspaper, making, however, some stern conditions about censorship. No article was to be published until it had been approved by a member of the faculty. Moreover—and here probably experience spoke—no words should be left out or inserted if these omissions or insertions changed the sense of copy which had been approved. The editors were notified that violation of this rule would result in permanent suspension of the paper.[55]

Either the student editors were more careful after that or the professors were less exacting. When President Powers told the faculty, in February, 1896, that the editors of the *Crimson-White* were violating their agreement to publish only that which was approved officially, the faculty voted not to punish this "first offense."[56] By the following autumn they were willing to give up direct censorship of the paper. Hereafter, they said, the editors themselves would be held responsible for any matter harmful to the University. The editors were invited to submit to a member of the faculty any article about which they were doubtful. If the faculty member was himself in doubt, he was to consult the president.[57] The *Crimson-White*,[58] had quickly come of age as a college journal.

Fully as important as the weekly paper on the campus in the nineties was the college yearbook, the souvenir of college days which the graduate bore proudly home with him after commencement and which served for a lifetime to revive memories of youth. By 1892 students of the University of Alabama were petitioning for permission to publish their own annual. A faculty committee helped supervise the organization of the editorial board and the planning of the first yearbook.[59] It was to be a joint enterprise of all four classes: seniors would elect three of the editors; juniors, two; and sophomores and freshmen, one each. The first yearbook made its appearance the following year. It was called *Corolla*, "a term suggestive of flowers, wreaths, garlands, and pleasant feelings," and its editors announced that their aim had been to present a picture of "the fads, the fancies, and the foibles of the college boy."[60] Only a researcher turning the old pages for the color and brightness of student life can fully appreciate the value which that picture has in the present day.

Although the expansion of student organizations and the beginning student publications were notable campus developments in the three decades of the nineteenth century, perhaps the most significant extra-curricular innovation of this era was the arrival on the campus of Athletics—with a capital "A."

Interest in organized games and athletic contests, almost wholly lacking in the old University, came early to the new campus. A new type of college student—"the symmetrical form of the broad-shouldered, brawny-armed youth,"[61] was making its appearance on campuses all over the country, and the students of the University of Alabama were quite aware of the trend. They begged for, and got, a gymnasium and a physical education department; and they launched a program of competitive sports which, before the turn of the century, had expanded into intercollegiate athletics.

Baseball was being played in the mid-seventies. The baseball club was even allowed to play match games on Friday afternoons. However, players who had recitations during game time were required "double lessons."[62] Some students played on Tuscaloosa teams as well. In one important game in 1882 the Hiawathas, made up of University students and Tuscaloosa boys, played the Selma Pastimes and lost 26 to 22.[63] Class teams rivaled each other also in tennis, swimming, track, fencing, and boxing.

By 1891 an athletic field day, corresponding closely to the present "A" Day celebrations, had become a part of the student calendar. Hundreds of people came from far and near to see the wrestling, sparring, tumbling, dumbbell drills, fencing, horizontal bars, club swinging, mat work, Roman statuary, German horse, and other events which gave evidence of the athletic prowess of the Alabama cadet. The faculty, impressed by the success of the first field day, officially declared it an annual event in 1892,[64] and by the following year the array of cups and gold medals to be awarded as prizes was already beginning to be dazzling.[65] In 1894 students from other colleges were invited to take part in the contests. Tulane boys were among those who accepted, and they put up stiff competition for the Alabama students. One of them walked off with the medal for the best all-round athlete; three won prizes in individual contests.[66]

About the time when the first Field Day was being organized, a truly campus-shaking event occurred. Bill Little came home from a year at Phillips-Andover, in New England, bringing with him the canvas clothes, the cleated shoes, and the pigskin balls which he had used there in playing the great new game which was sweeping the country. Football had arrived at the University of Alabama in 1892.

Admiring boys crowded around the gridiron hero, fingered the trophies he had brought with him, and began to plan for their own team. The University Athletic Association was born then. Burr Ferguson was made its first president and William M. Walker, its first vice-president.[67] A call for subscriptions went out, and enough money came in to hire a trainer, Eugene Beaumont, to teach the rudiments of the game to eager students.[68]

Bill Little, the heaviest man on the team, was the natural captain. His weight of some 220 pounds was considerably above the team's average weight, which was only 162 pounds. The lightest man on it weighed only 135 pounds.[69] But the boys tried to make up in enthusiasm what they lacked in brawn. In a surprisingly short time they were ready to challenge all comers and to start their University on its first schedule of intercollegiate sports.

Birmingham was their first point of call. To get permission for the trip, the players had to file with the president written permission from parents or guardians.[70] Defeat, by a narrow margin of 5 to 4, was the result of that first game with the Birmingham Athletic Club,[71] but the Alabama University players staged a comeback and trounced this team 14 to 0 in a second game. Other games that year had similar uneven scores. The University team beat Birmingham High School 56 to 0, but lost their first game with Auburn 32 to 22.[72] The first team included W. G. Little, captain and left guard; R. E. L. Cope, right guard; H. M. Pratt, center; F. M. Savage, right tackle; Eli Abbott, left tackle; D. A. Grayson, right end; Burr Ferguson, left end; W. M. Walker, quarter back; G. H. Kyser, right half back; D. H. Smith, left half back; W. B. Bankhead, full back; substitutes: A. G. McCants, D. B. Johnson, T. Sydney Frazer, R. E. Boyle, C. C. Nesmith, M. P. Walker, Bibb Graves, S. W. Henderson.

REBUILDING THE UNIVERSITY 525

Getting a foothold in the intercollegiate sports world was discouraging at first. Apparently some of the other Southern colleges had a slight advantage over the University in the new game, for when the players of the University sought opponents in 1891, they found some of these schools unwilling to meet them. The *Journal*, of January, 1893, had an explanation for this. It was that "a victory over us would have added but few laurels to their wreaths (bare enough, some of them, already), while a defeat would have cost them much."[73] The formation that year (1892) of the Southern Inter-Collegiate Athletic Association probably helped to regularize this situation. Vanderbilt, Sewanee, and Alabama were in the Southern division of this new association; St. John's, Virginia, Johns Hopkins, North Carolina, and Wake Forest, in a Northern division.[74]

Baseball players felt that if the football team could range over the countryside in search of competitors, the baseball club should have the same privilege. The trustees thought that the argument of the baseball players was reasonable and authorized the faculty to let them play out-of-town games, provided, of course, written consent from parents or guardians was duly filed.[75] In February, 1892, the faculty gave permission for the team to play five games away from the University; expenses were to be paid by the clubs visited. The faculty expressly stated, however, that this permission was conditionally given; the president and teachers reserved the right to decide later whether such trips were really for the best interests of the University.[76]

Sparked by the football and baseball teams, interest in campus athletics boomed at the University. A tennis club and a track team were soon organized,[77] and tennis became so popular that a number of new courts had to be built for its devotees.[78] Even a boat club was organized by the physical education instructor in 1893.[79]

Townspeople were, in the main, delighted with the new developments. The firm of Friedman & Loveman expressed this general approval in their gift to the Athletic Association of a flag of the college colors.[80] That flag is interesting, for the whole idea of University colors seems to have been a by-product of football.

Just where the crimson and white combination originated is almost impossible to determine. Zipp Newman and Hill Ferguson state that they were adopted as the colors of Cadet Company E of

1885, in compliment to Mary Fearn, the company's sponsor, who wore crimson, white, and grey. They said,

Mary Fearn, a slender, beautiful brunet of New Orleans, selected the University of Alabama's colors of Crimson and White. And wore them for the first time in 1885 as sponsor of Alabama's Company E crack military corps in competition in New Orleans.

The governor of Louisiana introduced Miss Fearn, the daughter of Walter Fearn, U. S. minister to Greece, to Louis V. Clark, captain; Oscar L. Gray, first lieutenant, and John R. Vidmer, second lieutenant, at an exhibition drill of Company E in Mobile.

"Miss Fearn asked us what were the University of Alabama's colors," said John R. Vidmer, one of two living members of Company E, in a long-distance conversation from Mobile. "We told her that Alabama didn't have any official colors. She then asked us the colors of our uniforms.

"I told her our caps were black, our coats grey and our trousers white. Miss Fearn said 'black is too funereal, and gray was neutral.'

"She proposed crimson, white and gray. This was after we had asked her to be our sponsor in New Orleans."

When Alabama dropped the gray is not known. But ever since they have had a football team at the university since 1893, the colors have been crimson and white.[81]

The Journal of November, 1892, carried a comment which suggests that the University colors may have been chosen from year to year:

Crimson and white were our colors last year, and as we were very successful in them, they will be used again. Cheer for the white and "red," boys, as you would for Dixie.[82]

The Journal of January, 1893, carried an editorial in which the editor attempted to console the students who were discouraged as a result of an unsuccessful football season, and indicated that the colors may have been changed from the preceding year.

Let us, then, not be discouraged, but let us take care that we put a team on the field next fall which will win games for the crimson and gold, and add new lustre to the name of our university.

However, crimson and white had evidently gained great headway, and campus traditions grow fast. Within a few months, the crimson and white had become the accepted badge of the University. Says the *Journal*, reporting a spring dance:

Almost an infinite amount of crimson and white, the University colors of which we are all so proud, was draped from one end of the hall to the other, and hung in graceful folds over the heads of the gay revelers.[83]

Adoption, by silent consent, of University colors caused no controversy. But when the new interest in athletics resulted in the establishment of a chair in physical education at the University, many conservatives throughout the state were concerned about the future of the institution. Mr. M. T. Hayes, director of the gymnasium, felt moved to answer such critics in an article in the Tuscaloosa *Times*. He pointed out that the University of Alabama, in giving emphasis to physical education, was following the lead of most of the reputable colleges in the country.[84]

In 1896 new regulations for the use of the gymnasium were adopted. Seniors and law students, for whom gymnasium work was non-compulsory, might use it from four o'clock until seven o'clock on Mondays, Wednesdays, and Fridays. All students could use it from nine until four every day except Sunday. From four until seven on Tuesdays, Thursdays, and Saturdays, it was reserved for cadets, and only cadets could have the privilege of using it after seven in the evening.[85] New enthusiasm for athletics may have prompted this apportionment of time. Some outsiders used the gym, too; non-students could come into the classes on payment of a five-dollar fee.[86]

By the middle nineties the athletic schedule had become the pivot around which campus life revolved. From the first week in October until after Thanksgiving, the varsity football team was the center of interest. A schedule of class games filled the time between Thanksgiving and Christmas. After the holidays the gymnasium team worked toward its March exhibition. March to June was baseball time. Some time in May came the annual Field Day. Even the interclass games, overshadowed now by intercollegiate contests, had their enthusiastic rooters. On one memorable occasion, large crowds turned out to watch, in pouring rain, while juniors and sophomores played a game on a field partly under water.[87] Visiting teams were always an exciting novelty; in 1893, baseball guests from Sewanee were given a gala dance in the mess hall.[88]

The football teams, which had started all this burst of activity, were slow in coming into their own. It was hard, in those days, to get a coach with enough knowledge of the relatively new game to be effective. The one hired in 1892 was so unsatisfactory that he was quickly fired, and the team carried on under the direction of its captain.[89] The team that year was unusually light, even for the University of Alabama; the players averaged only 149 pounds.[90] Not withstanding an inefficient coach and light men, the team won two games and lost two during the first season.[91] The following schedule will show the games played between 1892 and 1901, the score of each game, the names of the captains, managers, and coaches, and the institutions from which the coaches came:[92]

Games Played in 1892-1893
Eugene B. Beaumont (University of Pennsylvania), Coach
William G. Little, Captain; F. T. Bush, Manager

November 11, Birmingham
Alabama, 56
Birmingham High School Stars, 0

December 10, Birmingham
Alabama, 14
Birmingham Atheltic Club, 0

November 12, Birmingham
Alabama, 4
Birmingham Athletic Club, 5

February 22, 1893, Birmingham
Alabama, 22
Auburn, 32

Games Played in 1893
Eli Abbott (University of Pennsylvania, and Alabama), Coach
G. H. Kyser, Captain; J. S. Webb, Manager

October 14, Tuscaloosa
Alabama, 0
Birmingham Athletic Club, 4

November 11, Birmingham
Alabama, 0
Sewanee, 20

November 4, Birmingham
Alabama, 8
Birmingham Athletic Club, 10

November 30, Montgomery
Alabama, 16
Auburn, 40

Games Played in 1894
Eli Abbott, Coach
S. B. Slone, Captain; J. R. Dewberry, Manager

October 27, Jackson, Miss.
Alabama, 0
Mississippi, 6

November 15, Birmingham
Alabama, 24
Sewanee, 4

November 3, New Orleans
Alabama, 18
Tulane, 6

November 29, Montgomery
Alabama, 18
Auburn, 0

Games Played in 1895
Eli Abbott, Coach
Henry M. Bankhead, Captain; S. R. Prince, Manager

November 9, Columbus, Ga.
Alabama, 6
Georgia, 30

November 18, Baton Rouge
Alabama, 6
L. S. U., 12

November 16, New Orleans
Alabama, 0
Tulane, 22

November 23, Tuscaloosa
Alabama, 0
Auburn, 48

Games Played in 1896
Otto Wagenhurst (University of Pennsylvania), Coach
S. B. Slone, Captain; Champ Pickens, Manager

October 24, Tuscaloosa
Alabama, 30
Birmingham Athletic Club, 0

November 14, Tuscaloosa
Alabama, 20
Miss. A. & M. College, 0

October 31, Tuscaloosa
Alabama, 6
Sewanee, 10

Games Played in 1897
Allen G. McCants (Alabama), Coach
Frank S. White, Captain; George T. Bestor, Manager

Tuscaloosa
Alabama, 6
Tuscaloosa Athletics, 0

No team in 1898

Games Played in 1899
W. A. Martin (University of Virginia), Coach
T. W. Wert, Captain; J. W. Stickney, Manager

October 21, Tuscaloosa
Alabama, 16
Tuscaloosa Athletics, 5

November 24, Jackson, Miss.
Alabama, 7
Mississippi, 5

November 11, Tuscaloosa
Alabama, 16
Montgomery Athletic Club, 0

November 25, New Orleans
Alabama, 0
Southern Athletic Club, 21

Games Played in 1900
Malcomb Griffin (University of Virginia), Coach
W. E. Drennen, Captain; A. H. Wellborn, Manager

October 21, Tuscaloosa
Alabama, 23
Taylor School of B'ham, 0

November 17, Montgomery
Alabama, 5
Auburn, 53

October 26, Tuscaloosa
Alabama, 12
Mississippi, 5

November 29, Birmingham
Alabama, 0
Clemson, 35

November 3, Tuscaloosa
Alabama, 0
Tulane, 6

Games Played in 1901
M. H. Harvey (Auburn), Coach
W. E. Drennen, Captain; J. D. McQueen, Manager

October 26, Tuscaloosa
Alabama, 41
Mississippi, 0

November 16, Tuscaloosa
Alabama, 45
Miss. A. & M. College, 0

November 8, Montgomery
Alabama, 0
Georgia, 0

November 28, Birmingham
Alabama, 6
Tennessee, 6

November 15, Tuscaloosa
Alabama, 0
Auburn, 17

An examination of the foregoing schedule of games shows that the university's football teams played 34 games between 1892 and 1901. The teams won 15 games, lost 17 games, and tied two. Alabama scored 425 points while the opposing teams scored 402 points. Alabama did not win a game in 1893 and in 1895, but won three of the four games that were played in 1894, including the all-important game with Auburn.

There was a great turnover in the number of coaches employed during the period 1892 to 1901. Seven were employed and only one, Eli Abbott, remained more than one year. Abbott coached the teams during the years 1893, 1894, and 1895. Inadequate material, facilities, and compensation were perhaps too discouraging for most of them.

In spite of meager material—the squad often numbered only fifteen or sixteen men—the building of a University team went on. Each new year a stronger team challenged the traditional rivals: the Birmingham Athletic Club, Georgia, Tulane, Tennessee, Auburn, Sewanee, and Birmingham High School.

By 1895, however, certain evils in the system of intercollegiate athletics were beginning to worry the college authorities. The conflict between scholarship and sport was becoming evident. Also, the dangers of the game as played in the rugged nineties were becoming more and more apparent.

At first the faculty took only mildly repressive action. They expressed their belief that college athletics, properly conducted, were conducive to the good morals and physical development of students. But sports could not be allowed to overshadow the main business of the University. They ruled that all players must be regularly matriculated students who had enrolled within three weeks of the beginning of the fall term or within ten days of the beginning of the winter or spring term. They also ruled that leaves of absence for intercollegiate matches must not exceed six days in the college year for either the football or the baseball teams. They ruled that neglect of studies or absences from class would disqualify a player.

Then, having safeguarded the academic standards of the school, they turned attention to the safety of the students. Before a student might play on any athletic team, he had to be examined and approved by the University surgeon. No student under twenty-one years of age might be a member of a team unless he had special written permission from his parent or guardian. In addition, no off-campus games were to be permitted except with teams of other institutions of learning.

The faculty felt that football need not be the killing sport it had been in its first days. It was their opinion "that the injuries sustained by any football players are, in nearly every case, the result of slugging and other forms of foul play." The problem, then, was to prevent such foul play. If that could be done, "the game of football will not be attended with any more danger to life and limb than baseball or any other sport, especially since the mass plays of former years have been abandoned." They had a suggestion regarding the manner in which the necessary safety could be attained:

In every game of football, there shall be an umpire, a referee, and two linesmen appointed, who, in addition to their regular duties shall be required to report all cases of slugging or foul play coming under their notice, and any player found guilty of foul play shall be ruled forthwith out of the game.

They invited Vanderbilt, Cumberland, Sewanee, North Carolina, Georgia, Auburn, Mississippi, and Tulane to join with the University of Alabama in forbidding intercollegiate football until the adoption of this rule or a similar one, "looking toward the removal of danger from the game."[94]

The provision that no off-campus games should be played with non-educational institutions brought strong student protest. In 1896 the faculty noted that "match games" with Tuscaloosa teams might be played on the campus.[95] They set up a committee to determine whether similar permission might be granted in regard to the Birmingham Athletic team; the committee was instructed to look carefully into the reputation of that team before granting the permission.[96] They took one further step toward insuring the safety of their players by asking the University surgeon to attend the games whenever he could do so.[97]

That year was an unsuccessful one, for the football team failed to win a single game. The baseball team, on the other hand, boasted that it would have won the pennant for the third successive year if there had been any such trophy in the Southern colleges.[98]

The trustees went into action in June, 1897, with a ruling which all but wiped football off the University map. No more games, they said, either of football or baseball might be played off the campus.[99] President Powers announced the decision promptly, so that new students coming to the University would not do so under a wrong impression. A storm of indignation broke over his head before he had time to establish the fact that he was the spokesman for the board and not for himself. The students groaned and grumbled. One of them burst into impassioned verse in the *Corolla* by describing the "Moaning of the Tied," the implication being that Alabama's team was indeed "tied" by the new ruling.[100] The Tuscaloosa *Times* questioned the decision, also. To be sure, said this editor, it was a moot question as to whether athletics were beneficial. But even if they were the evil some people thought them to be, they were "a necessary evil" and no prominent college could afford to be without them.[101]

Interest in athletics dwindled. Few students bothered to come out for football practice. New men trying out for the team were no longer excused from drill. The Athletic Association suffered financial loss as interest in the game declined. Only one varsity game was played that year. Alabama won that, with a score of 6 to 0 over the Tuscaloosa Athletics, but there was little enthusiasm over the victory. Interest in class games declined, too; a series of games was arranged, but only one was actually played. The gymnasium exhibition was omitted that year; military drill kept students away from needed practice.[102]

The slump lasted two years. Then the board of trustees, dismayed, perhaps, at the results of their effort to control University athletics, voted to give back to the faculty the right to regulate sports. The action was taken when one of the two members of the trustees' athletic committee said, in a board meeting, that "after careful examination of the subject of athletics for more than three years," he had modified his views on football and baseball. He thought such questions as the right of teams to travel should be decided, not by the trustees, but by the faculty. His colleague on the athletic committee dissented vigorously; he was adamant in his opposition to allowing teams to travel. But the board appeared only too glad to shift to the faculty the responsibility for finding a way out of the difficulties made by the ruling of 1897.

If the faculty thought best, said the board, they might, by a two-thirds vote, suspend the ordinance forbidding teams to travel, but they were to limit the travel of football and baseball teams to not more than two games or series of games during a year. They were also to see that a traveling team was accompanied by an officer of the University and that rules were devised for "the preservation of a high standard of order and decorum."[103]

The faculty acted promptly on their new authority. But, as they suspended the prohibitory rule against travel, they took the occasion to impose new eligibility rules. No student with more than one condition against him was to be eligible for the football or baseball team. Any member of any athletic team might, by vote of the faculty, be removed from that team if two or more professors reported that he was not doing passing work in their subjects.[104]

Rejoicing over the lifting of the travel ban was mingled with some impatience that the trustees and faculty had not gone far enough. The *Corolla* for 1900 published a sketch of a statue "Commemorating the Emancipation of Athletics—June, 1899";[105] but it also voiced a general sentiment that this emancipation was still incomplete:

For the past four years our Athletic teams have been kept at home like naughty children, but this year the guardians of the University have allowed them to visit twice a year in the charge of a nurse to keep them from harm.[106]

A slight relaxation in this rule came a year later, when the faculty transmitted to the trustees a request from the manager of the football team asking that his team be allowed to play three off-campus games. The request was based partly on financial considerations: the team was about $75 in debt and needed the income from off-campus games to make it solvent. But the manager also reminded the trustees that the baseball team was being allowed six days for its off-campus games to make it solvent. At the recommendation of President Wyman, the trustees granted this request.[108]

When one reads accounts of the old game of football, one does not blame the trustees and the faculty for being apprehensive about it and for trying to keep the students from too frequent exposure to the dangers of the game. Thomas Wert, one of the players in the late 1890's, remembered and wrote for the centennial issue of the *Crimson-White* what it was like to be a football player before the game had developed the niceties of the twentieth century.

The trustees of the University had refused to allow the team to leave the campus for several years, but in '99 they took the lid off since the teams had gone from bad to worse. . . . We managed to get up a pretty good team, and we got a game with the University of Mississippi. We played at Jackson, Mississippi, in back of the old Capitol, and the odds were 5 to 1 against us. But we played like veterans and won 7 to 5. . . . in those days football wasn't a lady's game. When one of the Mississippi players tried to move the ball after it was dead, I fell on his neck with my knee. I hadn't done so before the entire grandstand was empty and people came down on me with umbrellas, walking canes, and the like, and if it hadn't have been for a bunch of policemen surrounding me, I'm afraid I would have been knocked out myself. . . . The next day we left for New Orleans to play the Southern Athletic Team. They had prizefighters, dockhands, and everybody else on their team. . . . They kicked me, trampled on me, and sometimes bit me all at the same time. In all my experience I had never taken a minute out of the game until this one, but I took plenty out for this one. . . . Frank White had been knocked out and I was left to do the kicking. . . . I remember returning to the Hotel on the street car. Cy Brown's

REBUILDING THE UNIVERSITY

nose was about as big as his fist. I had two black eyes, my nose was larger than Cy's, and I was also lame. . . . We got beat that day, 22 to 0.[109]

Although it was a rugged game, it was on the campus to stay. As the new century began, the University of Alabama was one of nineteen members of the Southern College Athletic Association it had helped to found. That group now included the following schools: Georgia, Central University, Tulane, Clemson, Furman, Cumberland, Vanderbilt, Nashville, Sewanee, Tennessee, Texas, Alabama, Mercer, Auburn, Kentucky State, Georgia Tech, Louisiana, Mississippi Agricultural and Mechanical College, and Southwestern Presbyterian University.[110]

And on the University campus the trustees were hearing for the first time a plea by their president which would be echoed on hundreds of different campuses, in hundreds of different tones, as the new century moved ahead: the University must have a new gymnasium.[111]

CHAPTER XXIII

Commencements and Honors

PLANNING the first commencement after the University reopened was a relatively simple matter. There were only two candidates for titled degrees in 1872: George Hamilton Bradfield and John Warren King, though there were a larger number of boys qualified to receive diplomas of graduation in the various schools. The faculty and regents were not yet ready to resume the granting of honorary degrees. Yet even the simple preparations occupied University officials over three months of faculty meetings.

The schedule that was finally worked out followed closely the pattern developed before the war. Junior Prize Declamations opened the celebration, Friday evening, June 21. On Sunday the Reverend D. W. Gwin, of Montgomery, delivered the baccalaureate sermon. Monday offered the double attraction of the Intermediate Exhibition in the morning and military exercises in the late afternoon. The literary societies engaged J. W. Taylor, of Tuscaloosa, to present the Anniversary Oration on Tuesday morning, and the Alumni Oration given in the evening by Colonel Sam M. Meek, of Mississippi, rounded out that day. Military drill filled the late hours that same afternoon. Commencement itself came on Wednesday, with orations by the graduating class, an address by President Lupton, and the conferring of degrees.[1]

The senior orations presented no problem that year. One of the two graduates was assigned the task of presenting the valedictory address in English; the other delivered the Latin salutatory.[2] The question of the baccalaureate sermon, however, was more troublesome. As early as March the faculty had decided that ministers from various Protestant churches would be invited to perform this service, and they had avoided any charge of favoritism by drawing lots to determine the order in which invitations should be issued. The results of that drawing, noted in the minutes, brought the Baptists into first place, with Episcopalians, Presbyterians, and Methodists following in that order.[3] Commencement was only ten days away when a delegation of clergymen from Tuscaloosa requested the faculty to hold the baccalaureate service in a Tuscaloosa church instead of in the University chapel. The faculty acceded to this request, but not without disagreement: Professor Griswold specifically asked that his vote against the proposed change be recorded in the minutes.[4]

At the eleventh hour the question of where the faculty should sit at the various commencement events came up for decision. The agreement reached may give an indication of the relative importance of the parts in the ceremonies. During the Junior Prize Declamation, the faculty might sit either on the platform or in the audience; for the Intermediate Exhibition, they were expected on the platform. They might do as they pleased for the Anniversary and Alumni orations, but they were expected to present themselves in a body to sit on the platform for the commencement exercises themselves.[5]

Never again would commencement planning be as easy as it was that year of 1872. After that at least three constantly recurring problems had to be grappled with year after year: the matter of the baccalaureate sermon, the matter of choosing orators from the graduating class, the matter of keeping the commencement festivities within reasonably short time limits.

The baccalaureate services came back to the campus in 1874. But getting a preacher willing to deliver the sermon became a major problem. Bishop Wilmer, of Alabama, was the faculty choice for baccalaureate preacher in 1874. They issued their invitation in March.[6] In April, having been turned down presumably by the bishop, they issued a second invitation, this time to Henry Niles Pierce, of Arkansas.[7] In May, after another refusal, they tried the Reverend R. H. Cobbs, of Greensboro.[8] Unsuccessful there, also, they appealed for help to the president,[9] and, under presidential persuasion, the Reverend P. A. Fitts was finally prevailed upon to deliver the important sermon.[10]

A similar situation occurred in 1875, though the faculty that year had tried to avoid disappointment by naming both a first choice and an alternate. They decided that if Bishop George Pierce could not preach the sermon, they would settle for Dr. D. C. Kelly.[11] Both men declined, however.[12] The next man approached, Mr. George W. F. Price, agreed to come,[13] but changed his mind several weeks later.[14] Finally, the Reverend B. F. Larrabee, of Tuscaloosa, was invited and, according to the Commencement Program printed in the *Catalogue,* he did deliver the sermon that year.[15]

In the 1880's things were somewhat better. Getting a baccalaureate preacher in 1883 involved only three invitations. Dr. E. L. Loveless was invited in February[16] and Dr. W. P. Harrison in March, and both declined; but before March had ended, Dr. A. S. Andrews had agreed to come.[17]

The clergy were inclined to look disapprovingly at the University in those days. That may have been one explanation of their reluctance to accept baccalaureate invitations. But, as one reads the record of official decisions regarding the remuneration of those preachers, an even more cogent reason suggests itself. Travel expenses were usually forthcoming. Dr. Basil Manly was granted $60 for his trip in 1876,[18] the Reverend R. H. Cobbs was paid $50 in the following year,[19] and the Reverend Joseph R. Wilson, who came from Wilmington, North Carolina, received $100 in 1878.[20] But when, in 1879, the sum of $25 was appropriated as a fee for the Reverend Mr. Brandon, of Tuscaloosa, the finance committee of the board of trustees protested. His services as baccalaureate preacher, said the committee were "in the line of his duty as a Christian minister." He would be "put to no expense or inconvenience" to preach the desired sermon. The committee thought that if the University started paying fees to local men, it would set a precedent "pernicious to the interests of the University." So Mr. Brandon's fee was canceled.[21] The board went back to its practice of getting baccalaureate preachers from far enough away so that the unquestionable travel honoraria could be paid. The Reverend Dr. Tucker was paid $50 in 1880;[22] and Bishop Harris of Michigan came the following year for $100.[23]

By 1875 there were so many candidates for degrees that commencement exercises had to be extended to one full week, in order to give each boy his chance to orate. The program that year was as follows:

Friday night, June 28 — Intermediate Prize Exhibition
Sunday, June 30 — Baccalaureate Sermon
Monday morning, July 1 — Anniversary Oration before the Literary Societies
Monday night, July 1 — President's Reception
Tuesday morning, July 2 — Exercises of the Law department
Tuesday night, July 2 — Alabama Historical Society
Wednesday morning, July 3 — Orations by the Bachelor of Arts candidates
Wednesday night, July 3 — Alumni Orations
Thursday, July 4 — Orations by the Master of Arts candidates and the Valedictory Oration.

The faculty made their first attempt that year to set limits to student eloquence. No bachelor's or master's oration could be more than 960 words long. The valedictorian, to be chosen by the faculty from among the A.B. and A.M. candidates, might use 1400 words for his important address. Some adjustment in the Wednesday and Thursday schedules might be made, the faculty agreed, when examinations were over and they knew how many graduates they had in each category.[24]

Similar word limits for orations were adopted the following spring.[25] In 1877 the limits were stated in minutes rather than words: the valedictorian could have fourteen minutes, others had nine minutes.[26]

By 1879 the faculty had to face the fact that, even with careful timing, they could not provide enough minutes for all graduates to orate. They solved this problem simply at first, decreeing that the commencement orators should be the eight students who had the highest average in all their studies, from their entrance into the University until the end of the first term of their senior year. Then more complicated plans were devised. One scheme provided that the highest scholars in each course should be chosen in proportion to the number of candidates in that course. Later it was decided that all candidates for graduation whose averages up to the third term of their senior year were 90 or higher should be eligible to contend for a place on the commencement program. A committee of the faculty heard uncorrected orations from those who wished to compete and chose the orators, who then had to work with the professor of English to correct and polish their speeches before commencement day. Candidates who did not deliver orations were required to write graduating theses under the rigid supervision of the faculty.

Limiting the number of orators allowed time for each speaker. Speakers were given a limit of 1,080 words in 1881,[27] but in 1883 an over-all time limit for orations set at an hour and a half brought the allotment for each speaker down to eight minutes.[28]

There were other suggestions for shortening the commencement program. President Lewis recommended, in 1881, that Law Day be abolished and that representatives of the law department be included in the commencement exercises. This would cut the festivities back to their original length; they could close on Wednesday instead of running on into Thursday.[29]

Even with these efforts at compression, commencement week remained full. And orations of one kind or another continued to be the principal feature of that week. The underclassmen started off the talk fest. The sophomores exhibition honored the second-year men with the highest standing in elocution, but no student could take part whose grades had fallen below 60 in any department during the first and second terms of the year. In a competition similar to that used in choosing senior orators, seven members of the junior class were selected to take part in the junior exhibition.

Guest orators for the literary societies, the alumni, and the Historical Society swelled the volume of oratory as the week progressed. But it was the seniors who really capped the climax with their marathon of oration on commencement day itself. Listed in the Tuscaloosa *Times,* for June 27, 1883, the oration and thesis subjects of that year are a formidable array:

Order of Exercises

ORATION	The Heir of all the Ages	*Phares Coleman, Greensboro*
THESIS	The Mississippi River Problem	*William F. Andrews, Selma*
THESIS	Capital Punishment	*William P. Brothers, Calhoun County*
ORATION	Self and Success	*Joseph B. Earle, Birmingham*

Music

ORATION	The Alabama Law of Married Women	John Manly Foster, Tuscaloosa County
THESIS	Society and the Fanatic	Benjamin J. Fitzpatrick, Montgomery
THESIS	The Race Problem in the South	Andrew W. Hayes, Bibb County
THESIS	The Fate of Reformers	Charles Hopkins, Mobile
ORATION	Stability of Republican Government	Benjamin H. Hardaway, University of Alabama

Music

ORATION	Westminster Abbey and its Occupants	Richard C. McCalla, Jr., Tuscaloosa
THESIS	Influence of Public Opinion	Charles P. Liddell, Gadsden
THESIS	Darwin and His Influence	John B. Little, Butler County
ORATION	Illiteracy and the State	Roscoe McConnell, Birmingham

Music

ORATION	Oratory	Isaac Oliver, Tuscaloosa
THESIS	It Might Have Been	James Allen Loughridge, Marlin, Texas
THESIS	Heroes and Hero-Worship	Robert M. Marks, Montgomery
ORATION	Alexander Hamilton Stephens	Walter D. Seed, Tuscaloosa

Music

ORATION	The Scholar in Politics	Percy R. Somerville, Tuscaloosa
THESIS	The Duke of Wellington	Wolsey R. Martin, Tuscaloosa
THESIS	Lessons from the Life of Peter Cooper	R. H. Miller, Denton, Texas
THESIS	The Leaders and the Led	Henry F. Reese, Demopolis
ORATION	Alabama	Alfred M. Tunstall, Greensboro

Music

Even if the theses had been delivered by title only, this would have made a long program and the audience would have been weary with sitting before time came for the conferring of degrees, the baccalaureate address by the president, more music, and finally the benediction.

Trends in students' thoughts are reflected in the oration topics. It is interesting to watch the hold of philosophy and the classics gradually weaken, giving way to the newer interest in science. The program for 1893 clearly shows that trend:

Mental Growth in the Nineteenth Century   *Bibb Graves*
Science and Civilization   *David Allison Grayson*
The Dawn of Electricity   *James Thaddeus Holtzclaw*
Agriculture, a Success   *Thomas Harris Maxwell*
Manhood and True Education   *Hugh Morrow*
The Nicaraugua Canal   *Ray Phillips Saffold*
Marvelous Advance of Science in the Nineteenth Century
                                              Daniel Holt Smith
Edgar Allen Poe   *Richard Council Wooten*
Robert Browning   *Joseph Darlington Wright* [30]

But the commencement exercises consisted of more than orations.[30] There were prizes to be awarded and honorary degrees to be bestowed. Most of the prizes were allied with oratorical prowess, and in the early years they reflected the strong classical influence. As early as 1872 a junior prize in declamation was awarded a gold medal for distinction in the composition and delivery of an oration. A prize for excellence in Latin composition was available to members of the intermediate class, and one for similar achievement in the senior class. In 1879 the board of trustees established its own prize for commencement oratory. It was $25.00 "or the equivalent in a badge or other suitable testimonial."[31] The trustees apparently felt that prize-awarding was their prerogative, for that same year they prohibited the offering of prizes by professors unless the teachers had specific authority from the board.[32]

Prizes established by friends of the University also appeared early. The Early English Text Society and the New Shakespeare Society of Great Britian prizes were offered by Professor F. J. Furnivall, the famous British scholar, who sought thus to stimulate both the study of Shakespeare and the study of pre-Chaucerian literature. These prizes made their first appearance at commencement in 1878 and were still being given in 1893.

A somewhat ingenious prize, known as the Ready Writer Prize, was established by the Reverend Wallace Carnshaw, rector of Christ Church, in Little Rock, Arkansas, and first announced in the *Catalogue* for 1883-1884. This prize was to be awarded for the best English essay written by a member of the senior class. The theme was to be announced after the competitors entered the examination room. Two subjects cited in the *Corolla* indicate the nature of the improvisation required of the competitors: in 1892 they wrote on "Evidence of a Divine Plan in the Unconscious Combinations of Human Energies, as Illustrated in Modern History"; in 1893, on "Excessive Self-Consciousness the Root of Pessimism and Loyalty to God the Remedy."[33] Whether the Reverend Mr. Carnshaw himself set these somewhat astonishing subjects is not stated.

Science prizes first appear with the award offered by Mr. J. C. White, of Bisbee, Arizona, for the most distinguished student in the field of mineralogy. This J. C. White Prize was first awarded in 1890. The following year the trustees, probably as part of their effort to stimulate new interest in the literary societies, set up the Trustee Prize for the best society oration. Two orators from each of the three literary societies were to compete for this in a special contest.[34]

The practice of conferring honorary degrees had been well established in the old University, and it was not long before the revived institution was again awarding such honors with a rather lavish hand. The trustees were particularly generous in creating Masters of Arts. In the thirty years between 1871 and 1901 they added 131 holders of that degree to the list of 56 that had been given before the war. The practice of giving that degree almost without question to graduates of three-year standing who had done some study or research since graduation persisted for many years. The M.A. degree was also a convenient way to give dignity to a professor or instructor who had not earned a graduate degree before appointment. Among these teachers who became honorary M.A.'s of the University in which they taught were the following: Horace Harding (1876), Thomas C. McCorvey (1880), James C. Hixson (1890), Reuben M. Searcy (1892), Ormond Somerville (1890), Martin Sibert (1889), Edward B. Anderson (1889), James R. Burgett, Jr. (1894), Henry McCalley (1879), Benjamin Hardaway (1886), Samuel Lapsley (1886), John B. Little (1886), Carlie B. Gibson (1886), John Daniel (1886), John M. Francis (1889), William B. Saffold (1890), and Jacob Forney (1891). Most of these men received the degree after appointment to the teaching staff.

By the early 1890's, however, the trustees were becoming aware that granting as honorary degrees those which should be earned was questionable practice. This applied not only to the degree of M.A. but also to the degree of Ph.D., which the University had given six times. A committee appointed to study the matter recommended that the giving of both these degrees on an honorary basis be discontinued:

Believing that the conferring, *honoris causa*, of the academic degrees Master of Arts, Doctor of Philosophy, and all others that are usually attained after completion of a prescribed course of study, tends inevitably to discourage the pursuit of advanced study in this University, to lower the degrees in the estimation of the public, and to discredit the institution conferring them, the faculty hereby most earnestly requests the Board of Trustees that they adopt a rule that hereafter academic degrees like Master of Arts, Doctor of Philosophy, etc., be conferred only upon those who have completed a prescribed course of study in a manner satisfactory to the Faculty.

The committee was willing to make one concession, however, in fairness to graduates in classes prior to 1892 who had not applied for the honorary Master of Arts degree, which some of their classmates had received:

Inasmuch, however, as many members of classes previous to that of 1892 have already, upon application, received the honorary degree of Master of Arts, it might be only fair to extend to the others of these classes the same privilege.[35]

The trustees apparently accepted this recommendation in its entirety. No more honorary Ph.D.'s were given, and after that, with one exception,[36] graduates given honorary M.A.'s were members of classes from which some graduates had already received that degree.[37]

Of the more definitely honorary degrees, the trustees' favorite seems to have been that of Doctor of Laws. This degree was given thirty-two times between 1871 and 1901. All eight of the University presidents of that period were so honored. Two veteran professors— William A. Parker and Henderson M. Somerville—received similar recognition of service to the University. Among other recipients were Peter Bryce, the first head of the Alabama State Hospital (1882); James Massey, president of the Alabama Central Female College of Tuskegee (1879); Oran Roberts, governor of Texas (1881). Massey and Roberts were both alumni of the University.

REBUILDING THE UNIVERSITY 545

Doctors of Divinity were created nearly as fast. The University had given that degree twenty times before the war; it now added twenty-nine names to the list. In 1892 there was heated controversy in the board as to whether the giving of this degree should be discontinued. The decision was made, reconsidered, and made again that the board would "decline to confer the Honorary Degree of D.D. on any one."[38] The decision failed to hold, however: two D.D.'s were conferred in 1892, one in 1894, one in 1897, and one in 1900.

These were the most frequently given degrees, but there was a scattering of others. Seven young men were made honorary Bachelors of Law. The School of Engineering set up its own requirements and its own degrees:

Any civil, mining, or mechanical engineer who has graduated in the Course of Engineering, having taken the Bachelor's Degree in the University of Alabama, and who may have been in active and successful practice for four years, and had had responsible charge of work as Chief of Division, Superintendent or Resident Engineer, may be advanced to the full honorary degree of C.E., M.E., or Mech. E of his academic course, upon the recommendation of the Professor of Engineering and endorsement of five honorary graduates of the University of Alabama in the Course of Engineering. And the diploma therefor, signed by the President of the University and the Professor of Engineering will be issued on the payment, in advance, of a fee of three dollars.[39]

The requirement of five endorsements was not always insisted upon. Charles F. Wheelock, Jr., received his honorary C.E. in 1899, even though he had not submitted such credentials.[40]

Screening the applicants for degrees became increasingly difficult as the years went on. Recommendations were made to the trustees by members of the faculty, members of the board, friends of the University, and in some cases, even by the candidates themselves. Mr. E. Y. McMorries was one of those who presented his own claims without false modesty. President Carlos Smith was non-committal when he transmitted the application to the board:

At his [Mr. McMorries'] request, I recommend his application to your favorable Consideration. His letter will explain the grounds of his application for the degree of "Ph.D". I have not personal acquaintance with the gentleman. His application rests upon his own representations, and those of his friends who may have Communicated with Members of your Honorable Board.[41]

The following June,[42] Mr. McMorries received the degree he wanted.

Candidates did not always fare as well as Mr. McMorries, even when they had friends on the campus. In 1879 the faculty formally requested honorary masters' degrees for two men: Henry McCalley, assistant in chemistry, and Edward N. Jones, who, in 1858, had left the University because of poor eyesight. Although he had not finished his course, Jones had since become "a useful citizen of Wilcox County" and a successful lawyer. The trustees voted to confer a degree upon McCalley, but not upon Jones.[43] And when, in 1896, the twelve members of the law class of 1885 were recommended for honorary M.A.'s en masse the trustees decided that that was too much.[44]

The trustees showed a praiseworthy disposition to hold down the length of their honors list. As early as 1879 the board ruled that no more than three honorary degrees might be awarded at any commencement, except for the degrees given to graduates of the University.[45] That rule remained in operation for ten years, though it was suspended in 1882 to allow the granting of three LL.D.'s, one D.D., and two M.A.'s.[46] In 1889 the ruling was repealed.[47] Honorary degrees that commencement numbered fifteen! But the trustees, at the same time, tried to set up other safeguards against a proliferation which would cheapen the honor. They ruled that all applications for honorary degrees higher than that of Master of Arts should be referred to the committee on instruction, rules, and regulations[48] and that the recommendations of this committee might be accepted by a three-fourths vote of the board.[49]

Most of the men honored in these early commencements were sons of Alabama, but occasionally the trustees looked beyond the borders of their own state. In 1877 Dr. James Little, of the Medical College of Atlanta, Georgia, was given an honorary M.A. In 1879 Reverend Samuel S. Harris, bishop-elect of the diocese of Michigan, alumnus of the class of 1859, was made LL.D. In 1887 Professor Meek referred in faculty meeting to "a communication received from a gentleman in Arkansas relative to conferring *Honorary Degree* on a certain person in that State."[50] The only honorary degrees given that year went to John D. Leland, class of 1860, then living in Texas, and to a Mr. Alonzo Monk, whose address is not

REBUILDING THE UNIVERSITY

given. Mr. Monk, honored with a new D.D., may have been the "certain person" to which Professor Meek referred to.

Only once did the trustees in this period resort to the questionable procedure of granting an honorary degree to one of their own members. The exception was John D. Weeden, class of 1858. He had served on the board from 1883 to 1885, resigning to become professor of law in the University. Mr. Weeden was made honorary M.A. in 1884. Two other honorary M.A.'s were added to the board after they had received their degrees: Hubert Davis, M.A., 1883, came on the board in 1898; Alto V. Lee, M.A., 1885, did so in 1890.

Perhaps the only instance of the granting of an honorary degree to a man who had not completed his undergraduate work occurred in 1893, when Herbert A. Sayre, who had stopped school after his junior year, in 1885, was given the degree of "Bachelor of Engineering *Extra Ordinem*," because he "more than accomplished the work required of the Senior Class and is now pursuing an advanced course of study."[51] That advanced course of study, at Johns Hopkins, brought Mr. Sayre his Ph.D. two years later. He then came back to Alabama in 1898 as professor of physics and astronomy.

Presumably the trustees themselves defrayed expenses for the diplomas given to recipients of major honorary degrees. In 1890 they requested the president to work out a new form for these diplomas and to have one hundred copies made.[52] In 1876 the faculty had voted to pay the person preparing diplomas $2.00 apiece for them. Certificates for graduates in schools were to be obtained for $1.00 each.[53] Very shortly, however, the expense for these and, probably, also for the diplomas given to run-of-the-mill candidates for honorary M.A.'s was shifted to the recipients. Students paid a fee of $3.00 for the coveted paper. In the early years they were written in Latin and signed by all members of the faculty and by such trustees as were able to be present.[54] After 1885 students had their choice of a diploma written in Latin or one written in English.[55] And by 1899 the faculty had grown to such an extent that it was agreed that only the names of the president of the board of trustees and the president of the University need be signed to the document.[56]

One diploma of those old days hangs in the Alabama Collection. It is of particular interest because it marked the first appearance of a woman on the commencement platform. Anna Byrne Adams, the first woman to graduate from the University in any school, received it on June 19, 1895:

> The Academic Senate of the
> UNIVERSITY OF ALABAMA
> Tuscaloosa
> To the friends of Literature and Science, greeting:
> Be it known, that we declare
> *Anna Byrne Adams*
> a *Graduate* in the Schools of
> *English, German, Philosophy* and *History*
> In Testimony whereof, the names of the President and of the Professors in the said schools are hereby subscribed, this, the *nineteenth day of June, A.D. 1895.*
> Richard C. Jones, *President*
> Benjamin F. Meek, *Professor of*
> *English Language and Literature*
> Wm. A. Parker, *Prof. Mod. Lang.*
> Thomas C. McCorvey, *Prof. of History*
> *and Philosophy*[57]

Important as were the orations, the prize awards, and the conferring of the degrees, commencements in the late nineteenth century did not want for glamor. The military drills were still a colorful feature of the celebration. The Commencement Hop, except in the few years of its eclipse, was the high point of the student year. And, if there was talking in abundance, there was first-class music in almost equal profusion.

The trustees seem to have been very willing at all times to budget generously for commencement music. In 1879 the corps of cadets asked the board's help in paying for this important item, and the board promptly gave them $150.[58] The next fall the board indicated its willingness to pay half the expenses for commencement music, but suggested that the cadets and the faculty should confer with Board Member W. G. Clark, of Mobile, so that the best possible contract should be made.[59] Mr. Clark made arrangements with the Alabama Regiment Band that year to furnish all "field, orchestral, and dance music" needed during commencement week for $195, of which the board paid $120.[60] During the next few years, however, even under Mr. Clark's watchful eye, music expenses climbed to $260, and the board decided that a committee, made up of the president of the University and board members in Mobile and Montgomery, should assume the responsibility of getting music at a more reasonable price.[61] Some saving was effected; music cost about $200 from 1883 to 1887. By that time the cadet drum corps was ready to play for all except the ceremonies of commencement day itself. A band from Selma performed on that day for $96, a fee which covered both the commencement exercises and the ball. The cadet corps was given $100 for playing during the other events.[62] These fees were scaled down two years later. The cadet orchestra got $40 for playing at commencement exercises; an outside band provided music for the hop for $50. Since there was an item of $4.10 spent on telegrams about these arrangements, the total cost of commencement music that year was $94.10.[63]

The local press always gave considerable space to the University's commencements. And in the old accounts some of the color and excitement, the pomp and circumstance of the celebrations, is preserved down to our own generation; for example, the *Gazette* reporter wrote in 1876,

We are gratified to report that the Exercises at our State University during the recent Commencement season were peculiarly entertaining and instructive. The prize declamation by the Second Class, on Friday, 30th ult., attracted a large audience, and too much praise cannot be bestowed upon the performance.—The young gentlemen all did well, and reflected great credit upon their instructor, Prof. B.F. Meek. The prize is bestowed by the Professor, and in this instance, Mr. Ed. R. Morrissette, of Wilcox, was the fortunate competitor. His Excellency, Gov. Houston, reviewed the Cadets on Saturday evening, and was evidently gratified at all he saw and heard.

On Saturday night, a paper, exhibiting great research and study, was read by Mr. Thomas Maxwell, under the auspices of the Alabama Historical Society. We hope our citizens may have an opportunity of reading and fixing in their minds the valuable historical information spread out before them by Mr. Maxwell.

Rev. D. Basil Manly, Jr., delivered the Commencement sermon, and it is not too much to say, that it was made up of noble thoughts, wise suggestions, and excellent advice, and found an instant lodgement in the hearts of his youthful hearers. Old and young were alike delighted and felt nearer to the loved and honored minister, after its delivery, than ever before. The Hon. Peter Hamilton, of Mobile, delivered the Anniversary address before the Law Department of the University, on Monday, at 10 o'clock, winning golden opinions from every one. The address was philosophical in the strictest sense, yet the subject was so carefully unfolded, that no one failed to follow him and enjoy every word of it. He had selected "Law" as his theme, and before he had done with it, we were, one and all, disposed to think it one of the grandest fields for discussion and oratorical display to be found anywhere. So highly was his effort appreciated, that the University conferred upon him her highest distinction—the degree of Doctor of Law.

Monday afternoon was devoted to Military Exercises, when Col. McCorvey and his Corps sustained themselves in the handsomest manner.
These exercises were followed by the Reception at the President's Mansion. Of the many bright and beautiful things said and heard on that occasion, we are not fitted to speak. Enjoyment and gratification distinguished the occasion, and everyone was loath to leave the scenes of so much pleasure. The Junior Exhibition followed on Tuesday. The large audience were charmed by the graces of oratory and sparkling thought, and the high encomiums bestowed upon Prof. Meek must have filled his heart with sincerest gratification.

After tea, everybody repaired to the old Hall of the House of Representatives, so kindly furnished by President Lanneau, of the Central Female College, to hear the address before the Society of the Alumni by Professor B.F. Meek. We are not willing at this time to attempt an outline of this chaste, beautiful and eloquent speech. It was all that the occasion demanded, and all that an accomplished rhetorician could make it. His subject was: *The Duties and Responsibilities of the Alumni of the University of Alabama,* and when he had done with it, there was nothing left unsaid.

Commencement day came at last, and every one, not confined by sickness, seemed determined to enjoy the intellectual repast. Such an audience was never before assembled at the University. All did well, and bore with them, in parting from us, the heartfelt good wishes of our entire community.

Among the most interesting features of this very successful commencement was the graduation of eight young men in the School of Law. . . . Upon these young men the degree of LL. B. was conferred after an examination which for extent and thoroughness equalled that of any law school in the country—an examination which the young lawyers stood with great credit to themselves and to their accomplished instructors. . . .

At an early hour of the evening, the University building was brilliantly illuminated, and young hearts were all impatient for the "Hop" to begin. Such beautiful ladies, such noble, majestic married ladies, and such exquisite toilets, we are powerless to describe.[64]

The same exuberance and pride sounds in an account of the 1883 commencement which appeared in the Tuscaloosa *Times*. That reporter was particularly interested in the array of oration themes and in the distinguished visitors from near and far who crowded into the "Hall" for the ceremonies:

On Wednesday morning, the Hall was crowded with the patrons and friends of the University, from all portions of the State. At the appointed hour, the procession, headed by His Excellency, Gov. E. A. O'Neal, and President Lewis, and composed of the Trustees, Faculty, Students, and Cadets of the University, the Alumni Association, distinguished citizens of the State, marched in, and were seated upon the Rostrum and front seats which had been reserved for that purpose.

After delightful music by the splendid Mobile Band, the Exercises were opened with prayer by Rev. Dr. Andrews of Selma. . . .[65]

For the better part of a week each summer, the University thus put its best foot well forward, spreading before its friends and its critics alike abundant evidence of scholarly soundness and social grace. During that brief period critics were politely silent, and friends were more than usually disposed to extravagant praise of the University as it was and even more extravagant visions of the University as it might be in the future. As the stirring music of the band and the shouts and laughter of youth mingled with the sonorous oratory, those who loved the University could forget the nagging undertone of criticism and censure which, on other days, grated harshly on their ears.

CHAPTER XXIV

Secular and Sectarian Opposition

THE STEREOTYPE of the University student as a drunken and dissolute wastrel, ready with knife and pistol, which had developed in the 1830's before President Garland brought order out of chaos with his military system, did not reappear when the University reopened in 1871. Yet the University and its students struggled forward through the closing decades of the nineteenth century under a barrage of criticism which sapped its strength and undermined its influence. This criticism may have been less lurid than that of pre-war days, but it was all the more effective because it was, in the main, more sophisticated and more skilfully aimed at the prejudices of the public.

The University was vulnerable at two points, It was a state institution, supported by taxpayers who could, under the proper touch, be made to scream loudly against new appropriations which would come out of their pocketbooks. It was, also, a secular institution, and, as such, it was in competition with struggling denominational colleges whose partisans could see in their strong rival all the features of Sin personified. The two-pronged attack continued into the twentieth century; it had its elements of humor, especially in retrospect, but it hindered and hampered the growing University.

The attack began before work on the new campus was well under way, and its nature was indicated in the early 1870's in two statements which introduced the themes on which succeeding years would develop variations. One of these statements was, oddly enough, the Alumni Address, which J. J. Garrett, '56, delivered in June, 1873; the other was a long and ostensibly friendly article in the Tuscaloosa *Times*, April 1, 1874.

Mr. Garrett began on a note which must have struck a respon-

REBUILDING THE UNIVERSITY

sive chord in the mind of his hearers. He deplored the General Assembly's decision to establish the Agricultural College at Auburn instead of combining the new institution with the University. He reminded his listeners of all the cogent reasons for the consolidation and then remarked that those reasons had "either escaped a majority of the General Assembly, or were outweighed in their estimation, by those of a personal and local or less worthy nature."[1] Few friends of the University, then or now, could disagree with this position. In its struggle for adequate support the University would always have to contend not only with a reluctant legislature and a wary public but also with a second state institution competing for whatever appropriations were available. Mr. Garrett was right in his recognition of the consequences of this fact.

But surely some of his listeners must have questioned his good taste and common sense when, turning upon the leaders of a university celebrating only its second commencement since it had risen from the ashes, he charged that the University of Alabama had "never been a university in fact" and that, moreover, it was not even "what it once was, the most vigorous and exacting college on the continent." Granted that it had turned out some hundreds of disciplined minds, said the orator, its graduates did not, after a lapse of forty years, number one in a thousand among the state's white population. It had prepared none, Mr. Garrett charged, for entrance into any profession other than teaching, and it had given few degrees higher than the lowest in the arts. Never, in all its existence, had it succeeded in enrolling more than one-twentieth of one per cent of the population to which its doors were open.

Mr. Garrett was willing to admit that the General Assembly was partly to blame, because it had failed to foster the institution as it should have done. There were other external causes in operation also: the remoteness of the location and the fact that many parents wanted to have their sons educated in their home states. But the major fault, he insisted, rested with the University. At this point he took a vigorous swing at the "needless and endless regulations and restraints" imposed through the military system, which he considered incongruous to the spirit and temper of the South.

Mr. Garrett's speech may have been eloquent, but it could hardly have warmed the hearts of the alumni, who, only two years earlier, had put aside political and personal feelings to work with the regents to make the reorganization of this so-called worthless institution a reality.

The *Times* analysis was more temperate and more searching, though the writer took for granted that a "chronic depression in the fortunes of the University of Alabama" had existed "from its first establishment down to the present hour."[2] According to the *Times* the causes for this depression had to be discovered in the very early history of the institution. People had not yet forgotten the bitter and prolonged controversies over the first land sales. This was evident in the fact that little patronage for the University came from those parts of the state where University lands were located. And now that this old prejudice was dying out, another circumstance had arisen even more subversive of public trust in the University: the University had been converted "into a sort of political football, to be tossed to and fro in the successive games of competition between rival parties for supremacy in the state." In the old days, when the board of trustees was chosen by a joint vote of the two houses of the General Assembly, an era of political neutrality had kept "political passions and prejudices" from entering the administration of the University. The popular election of the board of regents was giving to the University boards that were almost totally unfit for the administration of its affairs. The election of the professors themselves could hardly do more harm.[3]

This part of the *Times'* criticism would soon be outmoded, as the legislature was about to restore control of the University to the hands of the trustees. It may well have been vigorous press criticism which helped to bring about this important reform. The other sections of his analysis, however, remained true and significant for many years after they were written.

Rumor—jealous rumor started by University enemies, political rumor fostered by men seeking political advantage, selfish rumor circulated by people fearing increased taxes, malicious rumor irresponsibly passed from mouth to mouth—was the real root of the University's trouble. The writer told of the whispering campaign and its inconsistencies:

Numerous objections or charges . . . many of them malicious fabrications of ignorance or enmity, others possessing only a shadowy plausibility, and none having any real merit or solidity, were invented and circulated against the University by its enemies. It was charged with being the foster-mother of indolence and bad morals in its students. Its discipline was arraigned as being either too lax or too rigid. . . . The University was denounced as an Institution organized and administered for the benefit of the rich and not for the poor. The tax-payers of the state were irritated and misled by the statement that they were burthened with the support of an Institution that devoured their substance, and returned them no compensation in the education of their children.

Who, then, was to blame? The *Times* did not hesitate to put its finger squarely on the real architects of the University's misfortune: the Alabama public.

The people of Alabama are themselves the responsible authors of its mutilated fortunes and hopes. It is their groundless prejudices against it, that have been the chief architects of its misfortunes in the past, and of its comparatively unprosperous condition in the present.[4]

Having fixed the blame, the writer closed his series of articles with a plea that the people of Alabama begin to appreciate and support their University. They should, he urged, discontinue the inconvenient and expensive practice of sending their sons out of the state for their education; they should support the University of Alabama and take pride in doing so. The press was reproved for its lack of interest in the University. Most of the newspapers in Alabama seemed "utterly indifferent to its fate." The press of Alabama was urged to launch at once a "prolonged effort to resuscitate the fortunes of the State University."[5]

The newspapers of the state did not respond to this clarion call. Only controversial situations turned their attention to the University, and when such a situation arose, there were, on the whole, more brickbats than bouquets tossed in the direction of the campus.

Usually the occasion for a burst of University publicity was related to money. When, for example, the embattled alumni were fighting in the lobby of the legislature to get the $60,000 appropriation that they won in 1883, such newspapers as the Hayneville *Examiner,* the Montgomery *Advertiser,* the Eufaula *Times,* the Fort

Payne *Journal*, the Birmingham *News*, and the Birmingham *Age* fought bitterly against the grant, while the Greenville *Advocate*, the Mobile *Register*, and the Tuscaloosa *Gazette* eagerly came to the defense of the right of the University to adequate support from the state.

That battle was still raging when the legislature had granted the money and the alumni lobbyists had gone home happy.

The Hayneville *Examiner* called the action "a shameful fraud upon the taxpayers of the state." Furthermore, they insisted that it was grossly unfair "to give 300 students $90,000 ($300 each) and to give 400,000 children at the common schools only $230,000 (57½ cents each)."[6] Declared the *Examiner*,

> . . . the legislature should not have voted $90,000 out of the state treasury to the colleges at Tuscaloosa and Auburn. An impoverished soil and a people struggling with a debt, are not in a condition to be generous before they are just. Colleges do not educate the masses, and it is the money of the masses that is taken to build up these two schools. It is a discrimination against the Howard, the Judson, the Seminary, St. Joseph, the Greensboro Southern, and all the other colleges and high schools of the state as well as against the 400,000 children at the common schools who will never get a cent of this appropriation.[7]

Editor Tom Baine of the *Examiner* was an Alabama graduate. An article like the foregoing one from his newspaper suggested treason. Friends on the University campus were indignant. The *Gazette* voiced their indignation:

> We can understand why some papers, to court favor with their Patrons under the guise of economy by saving the people's money, can make such assertions, but when the Hayneville *Examiner* asserts such trash we are astonished . . . for him [Baine] to turn upon his alma mater seems like a peevish ungrateful boy striking his mother.[8]

That did not faze Baine in the least. He remarked that he had paid all his University debts, some $250 a year, and owed nothing to the University. He had, he said, the same gratitude for the University as he would have for any merchant from whom he had bought something.[9] And he went on with his campaign for the cause of "the people" and the common schools.

Baine got support from the Eufaula *Times:* "Editor Thomas Baine . . . is on the right side—the side of the great people; and one of these days the people will be heard."

The *Times* indignantly added, "Common schools are neglected; the colleges are enriched. Sons of rich men are assisted; sons of poor men must whistle for their education."[10]

Other newspapers took up the cry. The Fort Payne *Journal* rang the changes on the theme the *Times* had stated. People who could afford to send their sons to the University could send them elsewhere if the University was full. They could, without noticing the expense, send those sons to colleges which never got a dollar of state aid.

Alabama takes care of the education of her sons with a vengeance, when she robs the poor people to provide for the education of rich men's sons. . . . The most humiliating feature of the whole affair is that there are newspapers who defend and uphold such a system, and who forget their duty to the masses, the people who need protection against the encroachments of wealth and power.[11]

Some editors even took the position that a state university, or even a college education in any form, was an unnecessary luxury. Said the Montgomery *Advertiser*,

There is such a thing as education run mad. Popular and universal education is becoming a veritable hobby. The idea seems to be fast gaining ground that nothing else is necessary to secure a young man's future but to give him a collegiate education.

The *Advertiser* felt that a college career was a waste of time for all young men except those preparing for the learned professions. Why should boys be sent to a university "merely to stuff them with Horace and Thucydides and Euclid" instead of to teach them "what poor men must do to live"? The writer painted a picture of the University as he saw it—or perhaps as he knew his rural subscribers wanted him to see it:

It takes a raw boy of 15 years and turns him out four years later with inflated and visionary views of what he is to do; and it takes at least four years more of contact with the details of life—if you can ever get him down to them—to knock such unfortunate stuffing out of him. There is in this region of the state nothing to do, as a general thing, save to plant corn and cotton; and it is rarely the case that a youth who has gone through the common collegiate course does not prefer to starve in a professional office to soiling his face with the sweat of his brow. Hence, when you educate a boy now . . . you may as well buy him a railroad ticket to the nearest town, or state, for you lose him forever from your fireside, unless he becomes a loafer on you.[12]

The Ashville *Aegis* echoed the cry that universities were "useless and unnecessary" and that the classics had ruined the character of most college boys. But it based its opposition to the state university on economic rather than moral grounds. "We are opposed to state colleges because they require legislative appropriations," said the editor. "Such appropriations we regard an actual fraud on the masses."[13]

There were, of course, voices raised on the other side. The Greenville *Advocate* declared that "the cry that the state should give all the aid she can to the common schools and let the University go a-begging, is raised in defiance of right and justice."[14] The Mobile *Register*, chiding Editor Tom Baine, said that the argument that common schools were harmed by the University was sheer nonsense, for the state needed teachers for these schools. And how should men be trained for the professions and political life without the University?

The University is intended to offer to any and all that liberal education which is the backbone of the intelligence and necessarily of the wealth and prosperity of the State.[15]

The Tuscaloosa *Gazette*, in addition to its brush with Baine, was extremely critical of all the newspapers that opposed "the wise forethought to make provision for the annually increasing numbers that come up from the common and high schools."[16]

The tempest over the special appropriations had almost spent itself by the opening months of 1884, when the *Sunday Morning Chronicle* of Birmingham stirred up a minor gust by inquiring, "in no spirit of faultfinding," why the University lacked "that enthusiastic support which a state institution should have." So few students applied for admission to the University, said the *Chronicle*, that the authorities were obliged to fill up its hall with boys who should have been in preparatory schools. Yet the denominational colleges, charging full rates, had no difficulty in attracting students. Why this unpopularity?[17]

Again the Tuscaloosa *Gazette* rose to the defense of its neighbor. It denied flatly that students of preparatory school level were being admitted to the University. Those who came in before they had reached college age did so only because of full preparation. As

REBUILDING THE UNIVERSITY   559

for denominational schools, everyone knew that they had no entrance standards at all; many of them were only preparatory schools disguised as colleges.[18]

Editor Tom Baine was not the only editor who ventured ill-tempered criticism of his alma mater. In 1888 an article in the Birmingham *News* alluded to the University as "a second or third rate semi-military little institution, unknown outside of Alabama."[19] It was evident, said the Montgomery *Dispatch,* that Editor Rhodes of the *News* was a newcomer in the state and had not been around long enough to "learn about things that Alabamians were in the habit of denominating 'second class'."[20] On the contrary, declared The Birmingham *Age,* Editor Rhodes had spoken no more nor less than the truth. It was "indeed a reproach to the State that its chief university should be a 'semi-military' establishment."[21]

The *News* was still clamoring for University reform eight years later, as a new alumi drive for legislative aid was once more drawing the fire of the press. "For years the University of Alabama has commanded little respect at home or abroad as an educational institution," said the *News*. The trouble had been ascribed to many causes, the popular cry being that there was too much politics in the management and too much military nonsense in the school.

The *News* knows it voices the sentiments of the friends of education in Alabama when it urges the trustees to make the university a live, up-to-date, genuine educational institution. The weak points in the faculty should be strengthened. A high curriculum and thorough instruction should be insisted upon. The University of Alabama should again become the pride of Southern scholars and its diplomas mean that its possessor is a fairly well educated man.[22]

To such criticism of educational standards was added censure of the conduct and morals of the students. This line of attack must have been ably taken by a writer for the *State Herald* who signed himself "Well Wisher," for the Mobile *Daily Register* went to some pains, in January, 1897, to refute his argument and to deny his charges. Well Wisher had asserted that "among the causes that have led to the university's downfall is the fast life that young men have led there." A boy who went to the University, he said, had to attend the germans and play football and baseball or risk being thought "a back number." He proposed for the University a thorough housecleaning: "every man from the president to janitor should be asked to resign—not that they are not capable, honest, good men, but new blood should be infused into it."

Indignantly the *Register* insisted that "Ill Wisher" would have been a more appropriate signature for this article. The charge of fast living among University students was both unjust and untrue:

If reference is made here to young men in general, he is very much mistaken. We, however, candidly admit that some have led a fast life during their course at the university, but where is the institution in which some few have not led fast lives? Where is the institution whose student body is composed exclusively of the highest type of men—quiet, orderly, noble, and upright? Even in denominational schools, the writer has heard of men leading fast lives—but he thinks it very unjust and unfair to judge the whole student body in any institution by the character and reputation of a few.

The charges of frivolity the *Register* dismissed as trivial. Certainly an athlete was popular among his fellow students. But it was unreasonable to think that any boy was looked down upon just because he was not qualified for athletics or fond of dancing. As for the housecleaning suggestion, that was ridiculous. "Would not the same causes that he [Well Wisher] assigns for its decline operate as strongly against it under new management?"[23]

When it came to censure on the moral level, however, the secular press took second place to the voice of denominational publications as the *Alabama Baptist* and the *Alabama Christian Advocate,* the official organs of the Baptist Church and the Methodist Episcopal Church, South, in Alabama. Leaving the field of academic and economic argument to the newspapers, these church papers and the men who backed them and read them kept up a constant fire against "the godlessness fostered within the gates of the state University."

Some of the criticism from the churchmen was sincere. The men who made it firmly believed that education without religion was no education. They had established denominational colleges because of this conviction. Most of them neither asked nor wanted public funds to help those colleges to grow; separation of church and state was part of their creed. But it did seem to them unfair that the state should put the weight of its support behind a secular university, where, they thought, atheism and infidelity were sure to grow, and thus create for the struggling denominational schools a competition they were ill able to meet.

However great their creedal differences, all denominations agreed on one point, the argument of which the *Methodist Quarterly Review* set forth ably in 1880. The school house was unquestionably, the article stated, the only answer to the problem of evil in both North and South, but it must be the school house firmly founded upon religion:

> But it is the school house built upon the foundation principles of morals and theistic religion, it is the school house where God is recognized and the Bible revered, and where the teachings of the world's noblest and best men are permitted to exercise unrestricted influence.

To attempt, as secular schools did, to dissociate the ethical and the intellectual, the Bible and the grammar, was an "unwise, unphilosophical and unsafe procedure." The theory of pure secularism in education ran counter to the whole philosophy and history of education:

> Is it the part of wisdom and statesmanship to smite it with paralizing force by one full revolutionary blow from the destructive hand of atheistic secularism?

It was abundantly evident to the Christian philosopher that academic and collegiate education could not safely be surrendered to the state, even if the state were willing to take control.[24]

Secular institutions of learning were certainly not the place for sons and daughters of Christian men, said the *Alabama Baptist*.[25] And from the great Roman Catholic Church came the voice of Bishop John J. Keane insisting that the "experiment of secular education" had resulted in a large increase of "indifference and skepticism."[26]

Two lines of action suggested themselves to the churchmen: they must check wherever they could any move to strengthen the secular university through state aid; they must appeal to the faithful to make financial sacrifice to give their sons a Christian education. They worked along both lines with persistence and vigor.

The prospect of free tuition at the University was a great blow. "Then what is to become of the Methodist and Baptist colleges in our State?" queried the *Alabama Baptist*, in June, 1885. Howard

College, for example, had no endowment except its buildings. How could it compete for public patronage with a university where tuition was free? Few fathers, the *Baptist* said mournfully, would "pause to ask whether what they save in money they lose in quality." They would send their sons where education would cost least. "Few men stop to think that moral training is far more important than intellectual in the very formulative period of life."[27]

Bishop H. N. McTyeire, writing to the *Wesleyan Christian Advocate* that same year, was even more vehement. The state university, their "powerful neighbor," would certainly draw students away from Methodist colleges if it offered free education.

How can a few hundred itinerant preachers, whose salary does not average $700 per annum, and the voluntary contribution of a few hundred members, compete with a great State, gathering its hundreds of thousands of revenue by the strong arm of taxation?

For the state to offer students a free classical or professional education, said the bishop, was just plain "communism or agrarianism." The state might just as well give them a farm or set them up in business! It was poor political economy for the state to try to do what "religious zeal and private munificence can and will do as well and even better."

"The anti-church sect," the bishop insisted, "is the most bigoted and intolerant of all the sects." But certainly they should not be subsidized by the public in their effort to undermine religion:

These gentlemen have a way of getting into the management of all public trusts, and of dispensing or enjoying the patronage. If they wish godless and unsectarian colleges and universities, this is a free country; let them build and run them at their own expense. It is asking too much of a Christian people to do it for them.

It would be far better if the state would get out of the "University business" entirely. But, if it must remain in it, it should at least be willing to compete on equal terms with the colleges it had chartered which deserved to be "protected and encouraged rather than crippled by its hand." It could at least charge for tuition.

The bishop digressed long enough to blast the "bad moral atmosphere" that had infected state universities before denominational colleges had "shamed them into propriety," to hint darkly of infidelity, drunkenness, and profanity among professors as well as students. Then he swung back to his main attack against free tuition. In a state where free common schools could hardly run four months in the year, such an idea was a "preposterous absurdity." And it was even more preposterous when one realized that free tuition would benefit most of those who needed it least. "Agrarianism this of an uncommon sort!" he declared. "It robs the poor for the benefit of the rich."[28]

The tax argument, which the secular press had used to good effect, and which Bishop McTyeire had voiced with a new twist, was echoed in other church papers. "Multitudes of all denominations," declared the *Alabama Baptist,* "prefer private schools, and so have to submit to double taxation."[29] It was grossly unfair to require such persons "to pay their pro rata tax to meet the tuition of those who attend the State University, and then pay the tuition of their own sons at their own institutions."[30]

As such arguments failed to check a liberal tuition policy at the University, churchmen made strong appeals to the loyalty of their flocks. The *Alabama Christian Advocate,* in 1888, after bemoaning the "strange and increasing craze for 'higher education' by the state" and urging that steps be taken to relegate state education to its legitimate area of the elementary school, put final responsibility squarely up to the parents. "One thing is certain, Methodists can not afford to entrust the state with the education of their children and the preparation of them for the great battle of life."[31] Baptists made similar appeals. Children sent to Baptist academies and colleges, stated the *Baptist Quarterly Review,* would get just as good an education as they could get anywhere, and probably a more practical one. Moreover, they would be protected against the danger, "as unfortunate as it is unnecessary," of forming social and marriage relations outside their denomination.[32] Christian parents made a sad mistake, declared the *Alabama Baptist,* when they sent their children to colleges not distinctly Christian. The spiritual welfare of the child was far more important than the few dollars that might be saved on education at such secular institution.[33]

Argument at this level was interesting and, perhaps, effective in good church homes, but it was not exciting. When the churchmen and moralists turned shocked and reproachful eyes upon campus scandal, real or imaginary, they were able to stir up controversies that echoed through newspaper columns and, doubtless, in homes and meeting places throughout the state. One such episode, in 1885, involved the popular and upright University President, B. B. Lewis and a traveling Methodist minister who objected to the works of Thomas Ingersoll.

It all started when the Reverend W. C. McCoy, traveling agent of the Southern University, a Methodist College at Greensboro, speaking at the Gainesville Methodist Church, made certain uncomplimentary remarks about the University of Alabama. If he had confined his speech to the usual charges—that it actually cost more to educate a boy at the University than at Southern and that the University was a rich man's college, though rich and poor alike were taxed for its support—little attention would probably have been given to the attack. But when Dr. Lewis received two testimonials from Gainesville telling him that Mr. McCoy had also warned Christian fathers and mothers not to send their sons to "that hot bed of infidelity" at Tuscaloosa, he bristled with indignation, accused the minister of slander, and demanded a retraction.

Mr. McCoy promptly obliged, and, in doing so, added fuel to the flames. He had not, he declared, used the words "hot bed of infidelity." What he had said was simply that "students had access to Ingersoll's works, and that in some instances young men, the sons of Methodist fathers and mothers, who went there consistent Christians and church members, had returned home unbelievers, and that, in the estimation of these young men, Ingersoll's books were considered choice literature."[34]

President Lewis was a Methodist himself. Perhaps that is why this accusation from a fellow Methodist touched him to the quick. He denied flatly that Ingersoll's books were allowed at his university. He said that, two years before, he had heard a rumor that students were keeping those books in their rooms. Then at a called meeting of the student body, he had spoken on Ingersoll and his doctrines, and had appealed to the students as men of honor to tell him if they possessed any of these books. One student confessed that he had a copy—the only copy on the campus. "At my request," said Dr. Lewis, "he sent it home by express, and from that day there has never been seen a copy in the University by students or professors."

Very, very interesting, said the Reverend Mr. McCoy, but apparently the good Dr. Lewis was not quite as omniscient as he thought he was. And the minister produced a letter from the superintendent of the Selma Printing Company to show how little President Lewis knew about the reading habits of his own students:

In the month of May, 1884, I received from a student of the State University, at Tuscaloosa, Alabama, two packages of infidel literature to be bound in book form. One of the packages was Ingersoll's works; both were infidel. They were bound, paid for, and returned to the student at Tuscaloosa.

"This proves," McCoy insisted, "that these infidel books have been in the hands of the students of the State University since his famous 'speech' was delivered two years ago." And, he added, "The speech is said to have been an excellent one, but it should have been repeated with emphasis in May, 1884."[35]

Dr. Lewis must have been troubled enough by that disclosure to do some investigating on his own campus. He went directly to the student who in 1883, had confessed ownership of the "infidel" books. Within ten days he was able to publish that student's explanation of the appearance of the Ingersoll books at the binders. The student wrote,

I am the student who, more than two years ago, sent home, by express, at your request, Ingersoll's writings. Towards the close of the last session, I did send them to a Selma Printing Company to be bound, but they were kept in the bottom of my trunk until I carried them home. I further state that I came here from another College with my faith in the Christian religion unsettled; but that I am now a firm believer in the Christian religion.

Dr. Lewis added that he had questioned not only the students but also the officers who inspected the barracks daily. The officers had assured him that there were no books by Ingersoll anywhere in those barracks. The president felt that the minister was grievously at fault in trying to create the impression that Ingersoll's works were in free circulation on the campus, and he soundly berated him for such conduct.[36]

The tone of the argument being conducted between the two good Methodists in the public press now became more acrimonious and more personal. It gained in spice what it lost in dignity. When

Mr. McCoy said, "Now, Dr. Lewis has compelled me to show his ignorance of the condition of things in the school over which he presides," and accused his opponent with utterances "unworthy of his position," the goaded president could not resist a thrust at McCoy's past.

"The best way to judge men is not by their professions, but by their antecedents," he remarked, adding that Mr. McCoy, "if he is willing to accept this criterion," would "not derive himself much consolation from it."[37]

Mr. McCoy's answer to this remark was made two weeks later:

. . . whatever I have been in the past, I consider myself too much of a Christian gentleman to indulge in unmanly thrusts in a controversy of this sort. This whole controversy has been unpleasant to me, and I would not have engaged in it if my own sense of honor had not compelled me to do so.[38]

Just why Mr. McCoy did feel honor bound to start and continue this "unpleasant" controversy is not easy to determine. He claimed that he had no thought of injuring the University—an obviously insincere statement, said Dr. Lewis. He had, on the other hand, Dr. Lewis charged, violated a promise given to a citizen of North Port that, in consideration of a gift from that citizen to his college, he would not speak against the University when he appeared in Gainesville. Why had such a course been taken in spite of the promise? Why had he so eagerly prolonged the controversy?

Just as the fight seemed to be ending, in late April, a Greensboro citizen, in a letter to the Tuscaloosa *Gazette*,[39] ventured an explanation: McCoy was personally ambitious. The writer of the letter said that he was moved to write because he did not want it thought that all the people, even in Greensboro, were "in accord with this selfish move of Mr. McCoy's." He himself had heard Mr. McCoy say that he had weighed consequences with great care before he stirred up the fight. When Dr. Lewis's first letter had come, McCoy had gloated that the University president had walked right into his trap. "If the University (Southern) builds up," McCoy had remarked, "I build up with it." The unscrupulous attitude shocked the writer. He was proud of the Methodist college in his home town, he said, but he believed there was room for that institution and for the University as well.[40]

REBUILDING THE UNIVERSITY

The Greensboro *Beacon* wrote the official "finis" to the controversy on May 12. That paper, said the editor, had given both the warring gentlemen a full hearing in its columns. No good could possibly result from continuing the argument. The *Beacon* was disposed to consider the episode closed and should prefer to publish nothing more about it.[41]

Dancing was, of course, frowned upon by most of the churches of that day. It was inevitably linked with drinking, gambling, immorality, and all the other sins against which preachers pounded their pulpits on Sunday. The University dances, including the Commencement Hop, were, therefore, a fair target for the churchmen critics. And these moralists did, in fact, succeed in stopping the University's public dances for a period of several years.

Mr. J. J. Garrett of Birmingham, who had early in the University's renewed life made that astonishingly bad-tempered Alumni Address, was still clamoring for University reform in the nineties. In 1893 he went to the North Alabama Conference of the Methodist Church, in Talladega, and there, contrasting the University with the fine Methodist school at Greensboro, he denounced the immorality on the University campus in words which went echoing through the newspapers all over the state:

Send your boys to Tuscaloosa and they learn to dance the German— hugging set to music—to drink and to gamble. If I had a boy to send to school, I would wear patched clothes to send him elsewhere than Alabama University.

This remark, it was said later, was a little too strong for the ministers at the conference; there was only mild applause. The Tuscaloosa *Times* was indignant:

One would infer from Colonel Garrett's remarks that the University of Alabama . . . was a den of infamy and vice where Satan held high carnival and the contagion of whose impure atmosphere parents with sons to educate should shun as the leper is shunned.

Nothing could be farther from the truth. There might be some unruly students, the *Times* admitted, but "the allegation that they, as a body, are given to immoral practices to a greater degree than students elsewhere, is absolutely without foundation in fact."[42]

A year later the Reverend C. L. Chilton, Methodist minister in

Auburn, was even more vigorous than Mr. Garrett in his attack on dancing at the University, though his article in the *Alabama Christian Advocate* had a dignity which the layman's speech had evidently lacked. The University hop was his special target.

To begin a commencement occasion with a 'sermon' and end it in the licentious dance is the acme of inconsistency, and to 'open the exercises with a prayer' and close them in revelry is a travesty upon religion.

The state authorities should put a stop to such a travesty; they had constitutional responsibility to see that morality was taught and enforced in the schools:

This may be contended for in spite of atheists and infidels, inasmuch as it is a function of the State itself, through its police power, to compel decency and good order.

All good citizens would agree, Mr. Chilton thought, that it was wrong to "turn a college into a dance house and thus allow the 'world' a set time and opportunity to propagate and practice an evil which the creeds of the greater part of Christendom condemn, as subversive of good morals." Every church, he said, condemned dancing, and with good reason. Had it not been proved by statisticians and others "that the modern dance leads thousands to ruin"? People who knew that dancing was sinful constituted the majority of the taxpayers of the state. In justice to them, the state should act to keep this pernicious practice from the University campus:

It is a fact that the schools of the State are supported and patronized by those, the majority of whom believe that the modern dance, as practiced, (whatever may be said of its 'athletic exercise') is wrong in principle and in fact, and, such being the case, I maintain that the State betrays a solemn trust when she fosters, encourages, and allows it.[43]

With such clouds of criticism billowing over the campus, the University officials and, especially, the law makers could not safely ignore the possibility of fire beneath the smoke. In 1897 a special joint committee of the legislature did a complete and thorough job of looking into "almost every conceivable detail of university life." That committee made short work of the charge that the moral tone of the campus was low. Such an idea was the result of lack of information or, in some instances, "wilful perversion of important truths." The committee branded as "absolutely false and without foundation" whispered reports that "infidelity and skepticism were more than winked at and even suggested in instruction." Only four members of the faculty were not active and prominent members of orthodox Christian churches; and even the four non-church members were of high moral character and went to church punctually and regularly. The youth of Alabama could not have better leaders.[44]

Having disposed of infidelity with a wave of the hand, the committee had dug into the real weaknesses of the University. They were then able to make some constructive suggestions which could be used to strengthen administration and to expand the effectiveness of the institution.

Some of these suggestions are noted in a summary of the report which the Tuscaloosa *Times* published on February 3, 1897. The president should be given greater executive power: he should be able to remove a faculty member for cause; he should be an ex-officio member of the board, with a vote on matters related to administration; he should have a free hand in managing University affairs, in consultation, perhaps, with a small board of control, consisting of two citizens of Tuscaloosa chosen by the alumni. The board of trustees should meet oftener than once a year to review actions of the president, but they should be prepared to give to the executive "power and authority commensurate with his responsibility." The alumni should have a voice in electing trustees.

The president should be relieved of his Law School teaching and a dean for that school be appointed with a salary of $2500 to $3000. The dean should have two assistants from the local bar. The law course should be extended to two years.

The military system should be abolished as soon as it was practical to get rid of it.

Consideration might well be given to the establishment of some new schools: a chair of biology, a department of dentistry, a school of electric engineering, and, perhaps a school of pharmacy.

Student fees should be reduced; they put the University at a disadvantage in its competition with other schools. It would be quite possible to reduce fees so that total student expenses could be reduced from $172.50 to $150. That would, in the committee's opinion, make a great difference in the enrollment.

Certain business practices needed to be changed. One of the members of the board, for instance, had disbursed University funds to a total amount of $190,000 over a long period of years, "on his simple check," without vouchers and without bond. Since the death of Land Commissioner Hargrove, the president of the board had been carrying on his work, in spite of the fact that the law specifically provided for the election of a land commissioner to reside at the University. That, also, was a matter calling for prompt rectification.

Some savings might be effected (here the committee was on admittedly dangerous grounds) by reorganization of the faculty and the combining of chairs in various subjects.

The most important discovery the committee made, however, was a simple one: the University needed more money. Dr. Eugene Smith had presented them with a careful report showing the relation of enrollment to endowment. He had called their attention to the fact that attendance at the University of Alabama was 6.1 for each $1000 of income, whereas the figure for large universities throughout the country was only 2.5 to 5 per $1000. The University was doing amazingly well on its limited resources. "If we get more money, we will get more boys," said Dr. Smith.

The *Times* thought that the challenge to the General Assembly implied in this report was clear and ringing:

Now, in conclusion, need we say that a great responsibility rests upon the General Assembly of Alabama with reference to this school, to foster and maintain it, in accordance with the trust reposed in its members by all of our people, for the good of those who are with us. The moral, intellectual, social, and lastly, the pecuniary welfare of our great State depends upon the education of her people. Yes, and even more than this, the very liberties of those who are to follow after us in the ages to come depend upon it. For, as the sun insists upon light and gladness, so does intelligence insist upon liberty. But as at night when the sun is gone, poor nature loves to weep; so when education and intelligence are no longer with us, we, too, will weep in chains and slavery in the darkness of ignorance.[45]

To raise itself above the carping of critics both secular and sectarian, the University of Alabama needed to grow. It needed to develop its plant; it needed to draw students by the thousands instead of by the hundreds; it needed to enrich and extend its curriculum. It needed the moral and financial support which would make such progress possible. Like any public institution, it would never be—and, indeed, should never be—free from just criticism from the public whose creation it was. But as the nineteenth century drew to a close, the hopes and dreams of University leaders were closer to realization than they dared to believe. The day of the Greater University was about to dawn.

Bibliography

A. Official Documents

1. FEDERAL

Records Of The War Of The Rebellion, 70 vols. Washington: Government Printing Office, 1880-1901.

United States Statutes At Large, 67 vols. Boston: Little and Brown, 1789-1947.

2. STATE

Alabama Constitutions, 1819, 1868, 1875, 1901.
Acts of Alabama, 1819-1911.
Alabama House and Senate Journals, 1819-1901.
Alabama Digest, 1820-1937.
Alabama Supreme Court Reports: Minor's Reports, 1820-1826; Stewart's Reports, 1827-1931; Stewart and Porter's Reports, 1831-1834; Porter's Reports, 1834-1839; Alabama Reports, 1840-1911.
Aiken, John G., *Digest Of The Laws Of Alabama.* Philadelphia: Alexander Tower, 1843.
Clay, C. C., *Digest Of The Laws Of The State Of Alabama.* Tuscaloosa: Marmaduke J. Slade, 1843.
Ormond, J. J. et als., *The Code Of Alabama* (1852). Montgomery: Britton and De Wolf, 1852.
Toulmin, Harry, *Digest Of The Laws Of The State Of Alabama.* Cahawba: Ginn and Curtis, 1823.

3. COUNTY, MANUSCRIPT

"Circuit Court Minutes Of Tuscaloosa County," Vol. 1, 1874-1880. Spring Term, 1879.
"Circuit Court Minutes, State And Civil Cases," Book II, 1856-1867.
"Minutes And Records Of The Circuit Court Of Tuscaloosa County," 1848-1855.

4. CITY

"Minutes of the City of Tuscaloosa," 1853-1911.

B. *University Records*

1. FACULTY RECORDS

"Minutes Of The Faculty Of The University Of Alabama," beginning October 31, 1831, and ending May 29, 1835.

"Minutes Of The Faculty Of The University Of Alabama," beginning June 5, 1835, and ending June 27, 1837.

"Faculty Minutes," 1837-1841, Missing.

"Minutes Of The Proceedings Of The Faculty Of The University of Alabama," beginning December 15, 1841, and ending May 16, 1854.

Minutes, 1854-1871, Missing.

"Proceedings Of The Faculty Of The University Of Alabama," beginning July 17, 1871, and ending May 9, 1879.

"Minutes Of The Faculty Of The University Of Alabama," beginning October 1, 1878, and ending June 25, 1886.

"Minutes Of The Faculty Of The University Of Alabama," beginning September 21, 1886, and ending June 5, 1893.

"Record Of Faculty Proceedings Of The University Of Alabama," beginning June 12, 1893, and ending October 9, 1899.

"Minutes Of The Faculty Of The University Of Alabama," beginning October 14, 1899, and ending September 3, 1906.

2. TRUSTEE RECORDS

"Journal Of The Proceedings Of The Board Of Trustees Of The University Of Alabama," beginning April 4, 1822, and ending December 22, 1832.

"Ordinances And Resolutions Of The Board Of Trustees Of The University Of Alabama," beginning April 4, 1822, and ending December 16, 1841.

"Record Of Ordinances And Resolutions Passed By The Board Of Trustees Of The University of Alabama," beginning December 12, 1842, and ending July, 1855.

Trustees Records, 1855-1866, Missing.

"Minutes Of The Board Of Trustees Of The University Of Alabama," beginning April 2, 1866, and ending June 12, 1868.

"Minutes Of The Board Of Regents Of The University Of Alabama," beginning August 1, 1868, and ending August 24, 1869.

"Minutes Of Board Of Regents," 1869-1873. Missing.

"Minutes Of The Board Of Regents Of The University Of Alabama," beginning November 26, 1873, and ending July 2, 1874.

"Minutes Of The Board Of Regents Of The University Of Alabama," beginning November 21, 1874, and ending July 8, 1875.

"Minutes Of The Board Of Trustees Of The University Of Alabama," beginning June 28, 1876, and ending June 20, 1888.

"Minutes Of The Board Of Trustees Of The University Of Alabama," beginning June 16, 1888, and ending June 19, 1895.

"Minutes Of The Board Of Trustees Of The University Of Alabama," beginning June 15, 1896, and ending June 11, 1901.
"Minutes Of The Board Of Trustees Of The University Of Alabama," beginning May 30, 1901, and ending May 27, 1907.

3. "REPORTS Of The Presidents To The Board Of Trustees Of The University Of Alabama," beginning July, 1878, and ending September, 1882.

4. LEDGERS
"General Ledger Of The University Of Alabama," 1861-1865.
"Ledger Of The Malphathalian Society," beginning September 8, 1836, and ending November 6, 1837.
"Quartermaster's Ledger Of The University Of Alabama," beginning June 13, 1885, and ending June 19, 1886.
"Record Book Of The University Of Alabama," containing the names of students and graduates, beginning April 18, 1831, and ending December, 1837.
"Record Book Of The University Alabama, Containing The Names Of Students And Graduates," beginning February 1838, and ending in 1865.

5. THE PAPERS OF PRESIDENTS
Copies Of The Official Letters Of President Landon C. Garland, beginning September 7, 1862, and ending June 16, 1864, 2 Vols.
Papers Of Burwell Boykin Lewis, In Duke University Library. Microfilm copy in Alabama Collection.
Diary Of President Basil Manley, 1834-1855. 4 Vols. In The Alabama Collection.

6. MILITARY RECORDS
"Ledger Of The Military Department Of The University Of Alabama," beginning February 19, 1873, and ending June 18, 1873.
Ledgers, 1874-1901.
"Copies Of Letters Of E. H. Murfee, Commandant, Concerning Military Discipline Of Students," beginning October 21, 1871, and ending November 24, 1871.

7. LETTERS
"Governors' Answers To Letters," beginning November 6, 1861, and ending May 13, 1863.
John Weems Holiday Letters. In Evans Memorial Library, Aberdeen, Mississippi.
Letters From Clement C. Clay, Jr., To His Father, February 28, and April 17, 1834. In Alabama Department Of Archives And History.

Letter From Dr. Basil Manley, October 27, 1851. In Private Possession.
Letter From Russell C. Davis, Reference Librarian, Union College, Schenectady, New York, January 20, 1948.
Letter To Professor John F. Wallis From John Gayle, Governor Of The State And President Of The Board Of Trustees, August 14, 1834.
Letters From Bowling Hall To His Father And Mother, 1857-1859. In The Alabama Department Of Archives And History.
Letters From Crenshaw Hall To His Father And Mother, 1857-1860. In The Alabama Department Of Archives And History.
Letter From Gurdon Saltonstall, December 22, 1832.
Letter From Frederick W. Thomas To The Board Of Trustees, March 20, 1847.
Letter From E. B. Thompson, Student At The University, To His Uncle, November 26, 1860.
Letter Written At La Grange, Alabama, November 11, 1840, From Henry Tutwiler To Dr. Basil Manley.
Letter Of Professor John F. Wallis To The Board Of Trustees, August 14, 1834.
Letter From Governor Thomas H. Watts To Confederate Secretary Of War, February 1, 1864. In Alabama Department Of Archives And History.
Letter From D. Woodruff Of Smith And Woodruff, Tuscaloosa, Alabama, To President And Board Of Trustees, University Of Alabama, June 18, 1830.

8. MISCELLANEOUS PAPERS

Bill Of Sale, Morgan, Chambers & Company, December 5, 1853.
Bill Of Sale, J. E. Rial, January 7, 1845.
Manuscript Papers, "Old University File," Tutwiler and Wallis vs. Woods.
Statement Rendered By Benjamin Whitfield, December 9, 1839.

9. ALUMNI MINUTES

"Minutes Of The Alumni Of The University Of Alabama," beginning July 8, 1850, and ending June 17, 1897.
"Minutes Of The Alumni Of The University Of Alabama," beginning June 21, 1898, and ending June 2, 1914.

C. Printed University Records

1. *A Register Of The Officers And Students Of The University Of Alabama,* 1831-1901. Edited by Thomas W. Palmer. Tuscaloosa: Published By The University, 1901.
   Corollas, 1893-1901.

Catalogues Of The University Of Alabama: 1837, 1842, 1844, 1845, 1846, 1849-50, 1853, 1854-55, 1855-56, 1857, 1857-58, 1858-59, 1859-60, 1861-68 Missing, 1869-1901.

D. Newspapers and Magazines

1. NEWSPAPERS

Advertiser And State Gazette, Montgomery, August 7, 1850.
Alabama Baptist, Birmingham, 1835-1951.
Alabama Christian Advocate, Birmingham, 1881-1901.
Alabama Journal, Montgomery, February 17, 1841.
Beacon, Greensboro, July 5, 1861.
Birmingham *Age,* 1881-1888.
Birmingham *Ledger,* 1896-1901.
Birmingham *News,* 1888-1901.
Centennial Edition Of The *Crimson-White,* 1931.
Crimson-White, 1894-1901.
Daily State Journal, Montgomery, February 16, 1872
Dallas *Gazette,* Cahawba, November 18, 1859.
Democrat, Huntsville, 1832-1850.
Eufaula *Times And News,* 1874-1890.
Flag Of The Union, Tuscaloosa, 1836-1843.
Greenville *Advocate,* 1861-1901.
Hayneville *Examiner,* 1868-1889.
Independent, Gainsville, 1856-1859.
Independent Monitor, Tuscaloosa, 1837-1872.
Intelligencer, Tuscaloosa, April 24, 1837.
Jacksonville *Republican,* 1837-1860.
Mobile *Register,* 1866-1911.
Montgomery *Advertiser,* 1866-1901.
Montgomery *Dispatch,* 1885-1889.
Selma *Times,* 1865-1913.
Southern Advocate and Huntsville Advertiser, 1825-1851.
Southern Argus, 1869-1882.
Spectator, Northport, February 24, 1874. 1871-1874.
Sunday Morning *Chronicle,* Birmingham, 1883-1890.
Tuscaloosa *Gazette,* 1872-1901.
Tuscaloosa *News,* 1910-1951.
Tuscaloosa *Observer,* 1847-1872.
Tuscaloosa *Times,* 1872-1896.
Tuscaloosa *Times-Gazette,* 1888-1901.
Weekly State Journal, Montgomery, 1867-1877.
Wesleyan Christian Advocate, Nashville, 1885.
West Alabamian, Carrollton, March 6, 1861.

2. MAGAZINES

Clinton, Thomas P., "The Military Operations Of General John T. Croxton In West Alabama," *Transactions Of The Alabama Historical Society*, 1899-1903, Vol. IV.

John, Samuel Will, "Alabama Corps Of Cadets, 1860-65," *Confederate Veteran*, January, 1917.

Journal, 1891-1893.

Landon, Cabell Garland, "The Prince Of Southern Educators," *Bulletin Of Vanderbilt University*, Vol. XXXVIII, No. 2, January 15, 1938.

Mallet, John W., "Redetermination Of The Atomic Weight Of Lithium," *The American Journal Of Science And Arts*, Vol. XXII.

McCorvey, T. C., "Henry Tutwiler And The Influence Of The University Of Virginia On Education In Alabama," *Transactions Of The Alabama Historical Society*, 1904, V. 87.

Methodist *Quarterly Review*, Nashville, Vol. 62, 1880.

The University Of Alabama Monthly, December, 1873-June, 1887, 14 Vols.

Transactions Of The Alabama Historical Society, 1899-1904, 5 Vols.

Vanderbilt Observer, Nashville, Vol. XVII, No. 6, March, 1895.

E. Published Books

Bruce, Philip A., *History Of The University Of Virginia*, 1819-1919, 5 Vols. New York: The MacMillian Company, 1922.

Clark, Willis G., *History Of Education In Alabama*, 1702-1889. Washington: Government Printing Office, 1889.

Coulter, E. Merton, *College Life In The Old South*. New York: The MacMillan Company, 1928.

Edson, James S., *History Of The Crimson Tide*. Montgomery: The Paragon Press, 1946.

Elliott, Edward C., and Chambers, Merritt M., *The Colleges And The Courts*. New York: The Merrymount Press, 1941.

Fitts, James H., *An Appeal From The Alumni Of The University Of Alabama*. Tuscaloosa: Burton and Weatherford, 1896.

Fulton, John, *Memoirs Of Frederick A. P. Barnard*. New York: MacMillian and Company, 1896.

Garrett, William, *Public Men In Alabama*. Atlanta: Plantation Publishing Company's Press, 1872.

Green, Edwin L., *History Of The University Of South Carolina*. Columbia: The State Company, 1916.

Horn, Stanley F., *The Invisible Impire, The Story Of The Ku Klux Klan; 1866-1871*. Boston: Houghton, Mifflin Company, 1939.

Jordon, Thomas and Pryor, J. P., *Campaigns Of Lieut-Gen. N. B. Forrest's Cavalry*. New Orleans: Blalock & Company, 1868.

La Borde, Maximilian, *History Of The South Carolina College*. Columbia: Glass Printing Company, 1859.

Lawrence, Arnold W., *Classical Sculpture*. London: J. Cape, 1929.

Longfellow, Samuel, *Life Of Henry Wadsworth Longfellow*, 2 Vols. Boston: Houghton, Mifflin and Company, 1893.

Lyell, Sir Charles, *Second Visit To The United States Of America*, 2 Vols. New York: London J. Murray, 1850.

Massey, John, *Reminiscenses*. Nashville: Publishing House Of The M. E. Church, South, 1916.

Meek, Alexander B., *An Oration Delivered Before The Society Of Alumni At Its First Anniversary*. Tuscaloosa: The Ciceronian Club, 1838.

Memoirs Of George Little. Tuscaloosa: Weatherford Printing Company, 1924.

Smith, Edgar F., *Experiments Arranged For Students In General Chemistry*. Philadelphia: P. Blakiston's Son & Company, 1904.

Smith, William R., *Reminiscenses Of A Long Life*. Washington: W. R. Smith, Sr., 1889.

Verner, Clara L., *Amelia Gayle Gorgus*. Montgomery: The Paragon Press, 1937.

Weeks, Stephen D., *History Of Public Education In Alabama*, United States Bureau Of Education, Bulletin No. 12, 1915. Washington: Government Printing Office, 1915.

Wiley, Bell I., *The Life Of Johnny Reb*. Indianapolis: The Bobbs-Merrill Company, 1943.

Woods, Dr. Alva, *Baccalaureate Address*. Tuscaloosa: W. W. & F. W. McGuire, 1833.

B. Unpublished Works

Anderson, J. A., "Military History Of The University Of Alabama," n.d.

Boucher, Morris R., "Factors In The History Of Tuscaloosa, Alabama, 1816-1846," M. A. Thesis, University Of Alabama, 1947.

Davis, William C., "The Philomathic Society." Material Collected by Roy L. Thomas.

Gayle, Sara Haynesworth, The "Journal or Diary" of, In Private Possession.

Huse, Caleb, "Personal Reminisces And Unpublished History Of His Life," 1904.

Knight, E. W., "What Constitutes A Good History Of A College," In Private Possession, 1948.

Owen, Thomas M., Jr., "The Genesis Of The University Of Alabama," n.d.

Ray, Mary C., "A History Of The Chemistry Department Of The University Of Alabama From 1831 to 1865." M. A. Thesis, University, Alabama.

Richardson, J. C. M., "College Memories." Hand Written Manuscript Of The Response To A Toast At The Alumni Banquet, University Of Alabama, June 20, 1899.

Enrollment of Students and Graduates by Years, 1831-1902

Year	Total Students	Gradutes	Year	Total Students	Gradutes
1831	94	0	1872-73	135	5
1832	111	1	1873-74	52	12
1833	98	7	1874-75	74	10
1934	101	11	1875-76	111	19
1935	105	8	1876-77	164	29
1836	158	12	1877-78	179	41
1837	101	1	1878-79	163	20
1838	38	8	1879-80	160	31
1839	61	10	1880-81	158	38
1840	73	9	1881-82	154	29
1841	63	7	1882-83	166	36
1842	86	6	1883-84	209	45
1843	87	9	1884-85	225	45
1844	114	18	1885-86	241	53
1845	99	11	1886-87	212	57
1846	92	17	1887-88	238	52
1847	101	18	1888-89	208	40
1848	102	14	1889-90	206	49
1848-49	104	18	1890-91	220	56
1849-50	80	15	1891-92	167	43
1850-51	91	9	1892-93	164	50
1851-52	126	19	1893-94	166	42
1852-53	117	14	1894-95	180	38
1853-54	121	15	1895-96	185	46
1854-55	112	23	1896-97	167	50
1855-56	128	15	1897-98	200	19
1856-57	144	19	1898-99	214	38
1857-58	112	19	1899-00	253	54
1858-59	83	26	1900-01	261	61
1859-60	95	11	1901-02	231	62
1860-61	137	20			
1861-62	154	8			

UNIVERSITY MEDICAL DEPARTMENT
(at Mobile)

Year	Total Students	Gradutes
1862-63	156	1
1863-64	341	3	1896-97	134	40
1864-65	296	8	1897-98	129	26
1869-70	54	0	1898-99	147	28
1870-71	21	?	1899-00	148	47
1871-72	107	2	1900-01	152	49
			1901-02	165	23

Notes

INTRODUCTION

1. *Spirit of the Age* (Tuscaloosa), April 16, 1831. Quoted by W. G. Clark, *History Of Education in Alabama, 1902-1889*, pp. 47-48.
2. W. R. Smith *Reminiscences Of A Long Life*, p. 210.
3. Clark, p. 37.
4. *Southern Advocate* (Huntsville), April 23, 1831.
5. Clark, p. 37.
6. *Southern Advocate* (Huntsville), October 9, 1830.

CHAPTER I

1. 3 *United States Statutes at Large*, 466-467.
2. *Ibid.*, p. 489.
3. Toulmin's *Digest*, p. 931.
4. *Acts of the General Assembly of the State of Alabama* (1820), pp. 60-65.
5. *Senate Journal* (1819-1820), pp. 7-17.
6. *Acts Passed at the Second Session of the General Assembly of the State of Alabama* (1820), pp. 4-6.
7. *Acts Passed at the Third Session of the General Assembly of the State of Alabama* (1821), pp. 3-8.
8. *Ibid.*
9. *Ibid.*
10. *Acts Passed at the Fourth Annual Session of the General Assembly of the State of Alabama* (1822), pp. 26-32.
11. *Acts Passed at the Annual Session of the Assembly* (1843), pp. 57-58.
12. *Acts of the Sixth Biennial Session of the General Assembly* (1857-1858), p. 279.
13. *Acts Passed at the Third Annual Session of the General Assembly* (1821), pp. 3-8.
14. *Acts Passed by the Fourth Annual Session of the General Assembly* (1822), pp. 26-32.
15. *Register of the Officers and Students of the University of Alabama, 1831-1901*, pp. 18-19.
16. *Acts Passed at the Annual Session of the General Assembly* (1843), pp. 57-58.
17. *Senate Journal*, December 19, 1821, pp. 164-167.
18. *Acts Passed at the Third Annual Session of the General Assembly* (1821), pp. 3-8.

19. *Acts Passed at the Fourth Annual Session of the General Assembly* (1822), p. 57.
20. *Acts Passed at the Extra and Annual Session of the General Assembly* (1833), p. 20.
21. *Acts Passed at the Third Annual Session of the General Assembly* (1821), pp. 3-8.
22. *Senate Journal* (1823-1824), December 18, 1823, p. 98.
23. *Acts Passed at the Second Session of the General Assembly* (1820), pp. 4-6.
24. *Senate Journal* (1821), pp. 2-12.
25. *Ibid.*, pp. 27-34.
26. *Acts Passed at the Third Annual Session of the General Assembly* (1821), pp. 3-8.
27. "Ordinances and Resolutions of the Board of Trustees," 1822-1841, June 11, 1823, pp. 17-18.
28. *Acts Passed at the Fourth Annual Session of the General Assembly* (1822), pp. 26-32.
29. *Senate Journal* (1823), p. 95.
30. *Ibid.*, 1824, pp. 107-108.
31. "Journal of the Proceedings of the Board of Trustees," 1822-1832, p. 71.
32. *Acts Passed at the Seventh Session of the General Assembly* (1826), p. 3.
33. "Journal of the Proceedings of the Board of Trustees," 1822-1832, p. 107.
34. *Ibid.*, p. 264.
35. *Acts Passed at the Twelfth Session of the General Assembly* (1831), pp. 56-57.
36. *Southern Advocate* (Huntsville), January 1, 1831.
37. *Ibid.*, May 1831; "Ordinances and Resolutions of the Board of Trustees," 1822-1841, April 16, 1831, p. 114.
38. *Southern Advocate* (Huntsville), May 7, 1831.
39. Mobile *Commercial Register*, April 30, 1831.
40. *Southern Advocate* (Huntsville), May 7, 1831.
41. Mobile *Commercial Register*, May 9, 1831.
42. *Southern Advocate* (Huntsville), September 17, 1831.
43. "Ordinances and Resolutions of the Board of Trustees, 1822-1841," p. 162.
44. *Ibid.*, January 17, 1832, pp. 146-147.
45. *Ibid.*, January 21, 1832, p. 149.
46. *Ibid.*, August 30, 1833, p. 187; August 15, 1834, p. 199.
47. *Commercial Register and Patriot* (Mobile), January 29, 1834.
48. *Southern Advocate* (Huntsville), September 24, 1833.
49. *Commercial Register and Patriot* (Mobile), January 29, 1834.
50. *Ibid.*
51. 5 *Stewart and Porter*, 17.
52. Aiken's *Digest*, pp. 653-655.
53. *Annual Report of the Trustees to the Senate and House of Representatives*, 1833.
54. *Senate Journal* (1898), pp. 1050-1052.
55. *Annual Report of the Trustees of the Senate and House of Representatives*, 1859.
56. "Ordinances and Resolutions of the Board of Trustees," 1822-1841, July 13, 1848, pp. 35-36.
57. *Acts Passed at the Fourth Session of the General Assembly* (1822), pp. 26-32.
58. *Senate Journal*, 1823, p. 95.
59. *Acts Passed by the Fourth Session of the General Assembly* (1823), pp. 26-32.
60. *Southern Advocate* (Huntsville), January 18, 1826.
61. *Commercial Register and Patriot* (Mobile), January 29, 1834.

62. *Ibid.*
63. *Ibid.*
64. *Ibid.*
65. *Acts Passed by the Extra and Annual Sessions of the General Assembly* (1833), pp. 60-61.
66. Tuscaloosa *Flag of the Union*, January 13, 1837.
67. *Ibid.*
68. *Alabama Journal* (Montgomery), December 14, 1842.
69. *Senate Journal* (1847-1848), pp. 12-29.
70. *Acts Passed at the First Biennial Session of the General Assembly*, held in Montgomery, 1848, pp. 137-138.
71. *Senate Journal* (1859-1860), pp. 11-28.
72. *Acts of the Seventh Biennial Session of the General Assembly* (1860), pp. 25-26.
73. *Acts of the Called Session of the General Assembly* (1861), pp. 56-57.
74. "Annual Report of the Trustees of the University of Alabama," 1833.
75. *Flag of the Union* (Tuscaloosa), January 26, 1842.

CHAPTER II

1. "Journal of the Proceedings of the Board of Trustees," 1822-1832, p. 91.
2. *Ibid.*, p. 5
3. *Senate Journal* (1821-1822), p. 7.
4. *Senate Journal* (1827), pp. 5-12.
5. "Journal of the Proceedings of the Board of Trustees," 1822-1832, p. 91.
6. *Senate Journal* (1827), December 29, 1827, pp. 101-110.
7. "Journal of the Proceedings of the Board of Trustees," 1822-1832, pp. 129-130.
8. *Senate Journal* (1828), pp. 99-101.
9. "Journal of the Proceedings of the Board of Trustees," 1822-1832, March 18, 1828, p. 123; March 24, 1828, p. 132.
10. "Ordinances and Resolutions of the Board of Trustees," 1822-1841, March 24, 1828, pp. 54-55.
11. "Journal of the Proceedings of the Board of Trustees," 1822-1832, December 13, 1828, pp. 145-148.
12. *Southern Advocate* (Huntsville), October 9, 1830.
13. "Ordinances and Resolutions of the Board of Trustees," 1822-1841, January 21, 1832, p. 155.
14. *Ibid.*, December 27, 1832, p. 163.
15. *Ibid.*, December 20, 1838, p. 262; December 16, 1839, p. 274.
16. *Ibid.*, December 20, 1838, p. 264.
17. *Ibid.*, December 22, 1840, p. 286.
18. J. A. Anderson, "Silhouettes of a Century," pp. 42-43.
19. "Record of the Ordinances and Resolutions of the Board of Trustees," 1842-1855, July 14, 1853, pp. 56-57.
20. *Ibid.*, April 14, 1831, pp. 106-107.
21. *Ibid.*, January 5, 1832, p. 140.
22. "Journal of the Proceedings of the Board of Trustees," 1822-1832, p. 363.
23. "Ordinances and Resolutions of the Board of Trustees," 1822-1841, January 21, 1832, p. 149.
24. *Ibid.*, December 28, 1832, pp. 158-159.
25. *Ibid.*, January 3, 1833, p. 161.
26. *Ibid.*, August 14, 1834, p. 196.
27. "Record of the Ordinances and Resolutions of the Board of Trustees," 1842-1855, December 19, 1845, p. 14.

28. "Ordinances and Resolutions of the Board of Trustees," 1822-1841, August 12, 1835, p. 207.
29. *Ibid.*, November 23, 1835, p. 213.
30. *Ibid.*, July 13, 1837, p. 237.
31. *Ibid.*, July 17, 1838, p. 239.
32. *Ibid.*, December 18, 1840, p. 281.
33. *Ibid.*, December 18, 1840, p. 283.
34. *Ibid.*, December 22, 1840, p. 285.
35. "Record of the Ordinances and Resolutions of the Board of Trustees," 1842-1855, December 19, 1843, p. 14.
36. *Ibid.*, December 27, 1844, p. 17.
37. Clark, p. 66.
38. "Ordinances and Resolutions of the Board of Trustees," 1822-1841, December 31, 1828, p. 67.
39. *Ibid.*, April 14, 1831, p. 111; December 20, 1832, p. 161.
40. "Faculty Minutes," 1831-1835, October 14, 1833.
41. "Ordinances and Resolutions of the Board of Trustees," 1822-1841, December 20, 1838, p. 261.
42. *Ibid.*, December 15, 1842, p. 2.
43. Bill of Sale, Je. E. Rial, January 7, 1845.
44. Bill of Sale, Morgan, Chambers & Co., December 5, 1853.
45. Letter from George Benagh, Lynchburg, Virginia, to Henry A. Snow, Treasurer, University of Alabama, August 21, 1860.
46. Statement rendered by M. D. Williams, April 14. 1831.
47. Statement rendered by Benjamin Whitfield, December 9, 1839.
48. "Record of the Ordinances and Resolutions of the Board of Trustees," 1842-1855, December 15, 1842, p. 2.
49. *Ibid.*, July 13, 1848, p. 37.
50. Receipt of Payment, Alex Baird, December 4, 1850.
51. Receipt of Payment, Mrs. J. C. Buchannan, May 18, 1839.
52. Statement rendered by Cook & Romegay, November 28, 1839.
53. Warrant drawn by L. C. Garland, September 26, 1860.
54. Old University Records, n.d.
55. Note given by D. Manly, January 10, 1840.
56. Note given by George Benagh, January 1, 1858.
57. Letter from F. A. P. Barnard to Board of Trustees, July 15, 1851.
58. Statement rendered by Dr. Reuben Searcy, 1857.
59. President Basil Manly's "Diary," 1848-1855, p. 219.
60. *Ibid.*, January 13, 1851, p. 105.
61. Quoted in *Dallas Gazette* (Cahawba), November 18, 1859.
62. President Basil Manly's "Dairy", 1848-1855, October 14, 1850, p. 95.
63. "Ordinances and Resolutions of the Board of Trustees," 1822-1841, December 15, 1837, p. 254.
64. *Ibid.*, December 20, 1838, p. 264.
65. "Record of the Ordinances and Resolutions of the Board of Trustees," 1842-1855, December 26, 1844, p. 18.
66. *Ibid.*, December 25, 1845, pp. 20-21.
67. *Ibid.*, December 26, 1845, p. 22.

CHAPTER III

1. Smith, *op. cit.*, p. 206.
2. *Ibid.*, pp. 206-7.

3. *Ibid.*, p. 212.
4. *Ibid.*, p. 213.
5. *Ibid.*, pp. 228-229.
6. *Ibid.*, pp. 206-7.
7. M. C. Ray, "A History of the Chemistry Department of the University of Alabama from 1831 to 1865," pp. 14-15.
8. "Journal of the Proceedings of the Board of Trustees," 1822-1832, January 2, 1829, p. 172.
9. *Ibid.*, January 5, 1829, p. 177-178.
10. *Ibid.*, January 9, 1829, p. 182.
11. *Ibid.*, December 16, 1829, p. 188.
12. *Ibid.*, December 18, 1829, p. 192.
13. *Ibid.*, December 19, 1829, pp. 195-197.
14. *Ibid.*, December 21, 1829, p. 201.
15. *Ibid.*, December 22, 1829, p. 203.
16. *Ibid.*, December 23, 1829, pp. 210-11.
17. *Ibid.*, January 7, 1830, p. 219.
18. *Ibid.*, July 1, 1830, p. 259.
19. "Ordinances and Resolutions of the Board of Trustees," 1822-1841, July 2, 1830, p. 192.
20. *Ibid.*, November 21, 1830, p. 195.
21. "Journal of the Proceedings of the Board of Trustees," 1822-1832, November 25, 1830, pp. 276-8.
22. *Ibid.*, January 15, 1831, p. 299.
23. Clark, pp. 47-48.
24. Letter from Russell C. Davis, Reference Librarian, Union College, Schenectady, New York, January 20, 1948.
25. Ray, pp. 14-15.
26. "Journal of the Proceedings of the Board of Trustees," 1822-1832, June 30, 1830, p. 253.
27. *Ibid.*, July 1, 1830, p. 258.
28. Smith, p. 203.
29. T. M. Owen, Jr., "The Genesis of the University of Alabama," Typewritten manuscript in Alabama Collection.
30. "Ordinances and Resolutions of the Board of Trustees," 1822-1841, April 14, 1831, p. 111; January 2, 1832, p. 311.
31. "Journal of the Proceedings of the Board of Trustees," 1822-1832, April 11, 1831, p. 310.
32. *Southern Advocate* (Huntsville), April 23, 1831.
33. "Ordinances and Resolutions of the Board of Trustees," 1822-1841, April 13, 1831, p. 109.
34. Smith, pp. 205-6.
35. "Journal of the Proceedings of the Board of Trustees," 1822-1832, January 18, 1830, pp. 241 and 244; July 1, 1830, p. 256.
36. *Ibid.*, December 7 and 20, 1830, pp. 281 and 286.
37. *Ibid.*, January 8, 1831, p. 290.
38. "Ordinances and Resolutions of the Board of Trustees," 1822-1841, January 2 and 15, 1831, pp. 100 and 106.
39. "Journal of the Proceedings of the Board of Trustees," 1822-1832, January 15, 1831, p. 299.
40. "Ordinances and Resolutions of the Board of Trustees," 1822-1841, April 13, 14, 1831, pp. 110 and 111.
41. *Ibid.*, December 23, 1831, p. 139.

42. "Journal of the Proceedings of the Board of Trustees," 1822-1832, December 21, 26, 1831, pp. 336-346.
43. *Ibid.*
44. "Ordinances and Resolutions of the Board of Trustees," 1822-1841, December 28, 1832, p. 165.
45. *Ibid.*, August 11 and 16, 1834, pp. 192 and 201.
46. *Ibid.*, August 12, 1835, p. 208; December 21, 1836, p. 226.
47. "Ordinances for the Government of the University of Alabama," April 16, 1831, Chapter II, Sec. 1, pp. 4-7.
48. "Ordinances and Resolutions of the Board of Trustees," 1822-1841, January 2, 1832, p. 143.
49. *Ibid.*, January 17, 1832, p. 149.
50. "Faculty Minutes," 1831-1835, December 26, 1831.
51. *Ibid.*, 1835-1837, October 16, 1833.
52. *Southern Advocate* (Huntsville), October 23, 1830.
53. "Ordinances for the Government of the University of Alabama," April 16, 1831, Chapter V; *Laws of Transylvania University*, August, 1829, Chapter V, pp. 8, 9; *Laws of Harvard College*, Cambridge; printed at the University Press, by Hilliard and Metcalf, Chapter VI, "Of Misdemeanors and Criminal Offenses," 1820, pp. 19-25.
54. Clark, p. 43.
55. *Baccalaureate Address*, December 17, 1836, pp. 3, 5.
56. Letter from Charles W. Tait to his Grandfather, University of Alabama, June 20, 1832.
57. Letter from G. Saltonstall, December 22, 1832.
58. "Journal of the Proceedings of the Board of Trustees," 1822-1832, December 14, 1832, p. 381.
59. Manuscript Papers, "Old University," in Alabama Collection.
60. "Ordinances and Resolutions of the Board of Trustees," 1822-1841; December 28, 1832, p. 165.
61. "Notes from the Journals or Diary of Sarah Haynsworth Gayle," March 5, 1834.
62. Letter from Clement C. Clay, Jr., to his father, February 28, 1834.
63. Letter from Clement C. Clay, Jr., to his father, April 7, 1834.
64. "Ordinances and Resolutions of the Board of Trustees," 1822-1841, August 14, 1834, p. 194.
65. Manuscript Papers, "Old University," Tutwiler and Wallis vs. Woods.
66. Letter to professor Wallis from John Gayle, Governor and President of the Board of Trustees, August 14, 1834.
67. Letter of Professor Wallis to the Board of Trustees, August 14, 1834.
68. "Ordinances and Resolutions of the Board of Trustees," 1822-1841, August 15, 1834, p. 198.
69. See Chapter on Disciplinary Problems.
70. "Faculty Minutes," 1835-1837, December 21, 1836; p. 61; February 6, 1837, p. 63.
71. "Ordinances and Resolutions of the Board of Trustees," 1822-1841, December 14, 1832, p. 159.
72. "Faculty Minutes," 1831-1835, April 30, May 15, 1832; June 16, 1833.
73. Smith, p. 208.
74. "Faculty Minutes," 1831-1835, April 7, 1835.
75. Roberts, p. 15.
76. "Faculty Minutes," 1835-1837, April 26, 1836, pp. 42-43.
77. Roberts, pp. 15-17.
78. "Faculty Minutes," 1835-1837, April 29, 1836, pp. 43-44.
79. *Ibid.*, April 30, 1836, p. 44; May 9, 1836, p. 44.

THE OLD UNIVERSITY

80. "Statement from a Committee of the Suspended Students to the Trustees of the University of Alabama," *The Intelligencer* (Tuscaloosa), April 24, 1837.
81. "Faculty Minutes," 1835-1837, April 12-20, 1837, pp. 69-74.
82. *Ibid.*, July 29, 1837, p. 79.
83. "Ordinances and Resolutions of the Board of Trustees," 1822-1841, July 17, 1837, p. 240; December 11, 1837, p. 245.
84. Smith, p. 210.
85. W. Garrett, *Public Men in Alabama*, p. 47.
86. Original letter bound with *Addresses of President Alva Woods*, in Alabama Collection.
87. Ray, pp. 14-15.

CHAPTER IV

1. Clark, pp. 77-8, quoting from Dr. Boyce's *Funeral Discourse*, p. 66.
2. *Ibid.*, p. 46.
3. Ray, pp. 20-21.
4. "Ordinances and Resolutions of the Board of Trustees," 1822-1841, August 11, 16, 1834, pp. 192 and 201.
5. *Ibid.*, August 12, 1835, p. 208.
6. Sketch of Professor Brumby in LaBorde's *History of the South Carolina College*, Columbia, 1859, quoted in Clark, p. 68.
7. Clark, p. 80.
8. G. Little, *Memoirs*, p. 13.
9. Ray, pp. 3, 37-41.
10. *Ibid.*
11. Smith, pp. 234-236; 242-245.
12. *Ibid.*, p. 245, quoting from Garrett, *Public Men in Alabama*.
13. Clark, p. 73.
14. President Basil Manly's "Diary", 1834-1848, May 20, 1841, p. 228.
15. *Ibid.*, 1847-1857, August 12, 1847, p. 34.
16. *Ibid.*, 1848-1855, September 30, 1854, p. 276.
17. J. Fulton, *Memoirs of Frederick A. P. Barnard*, pp. 195-196.
18. Clark, p. 135.
19. "College Memories," Handwritten manuscript of a response to a toast at the Alumni Banquet, University of Alabama, June 20, 1899, in Alabama Collection.
20. *Laws of the University of the State of Alabama*, 1839, Chapter II, Sec. 3.
21. "Minutes of the Proceedings of the Faculty," 1841-1854, December 20, 1845, pp. 103-104.
22. *Laws of the University of the State of Alabama*, Chapter II, Sec. 4-8.
23. *Ibid.*
24. *Ibid.*, 1839 and 1850, Chapter IV.
25. *Ibid.*
26. Manuscript Papers, "University Library", Letters on Employment, 1845.
27. Old University Papers.
28. President Manly's "Diary", 1843-1847, January 29, 1847, pp. 118-121.
29. *Ibid.*, February 22, 1847, p. 130.
30. *Ibid.*, March 13, 1947, p. 131.
31. *Ibid.*, March 15, 1847, p. 130B.
32. *Ibid.*, March 15, 1847, pp. 130-131B.
33. Letter from F. W. Thomas to the Board of Trustees, March 20, 1847.
34. "Minutes of the Proceedings of the Faculty", 1841-1854, July 19, 1847, p. 138.
35. *Landon Cabell Garland, The Prince of Southern Educators*, Bulletin of Van-

derbilt University, Vol. XXXVIII, No. 2, January 15, 1938.
36. *Vanderbilt Observer,* Vol. XVII, No. 6, March 1895, p. 256.
37. Garland, *Prince of Southern Educators,* p. 22, Quoting from John Massey, *Reminiscences,* pp. 110, 139.
38. *Ibid.,* Quoting from letter to H. R. Fulton from B. M. Robinson, August 24, 1936.
39. *Ibid.,* p. 3.
40. Little, p. 13.
41. "Ordinances and Resolutions of the Board of Trustees," 1822-1841, December 16, 1841, p. 294.
42. Samuel Longfellow, *Life of Henry Wadsworth Longfellow,* Vol. I, p. 341, quoted in McCorvey, "Henry Tutwiler and the Influence of the University of Virginia, on Education in Alabama," *Transactions Of The Alabama Historical Society,* 1904, V, 87.
43. "Record of the Ordinances and Resolutions of the Trustees," 1842-1855, July 12, 1853, p. 53.
44. "Minutes of the Proceedings of the Faculty," 1841-1854, September 1, 1853, p. 286.
45. Little, p. 13.
46. Letter from F. A. P. Barnard to the Board of Trustees, December 16, 1846, quoted in Ray, pp. 12-13.
47. Ray, pp. 67-8.
48. "Record of the Ordinances and Resolutions of the Board of Trustees," 1842-1855, December 19, 1846, p. 30.
49. "Minutes of the Proceedings of the Faculty," 1841-1854, July 15, 1847, pp. 136-137.
50. Ray, p. 3.
51. "Minutes of the Proceedings of the Faculty," 1841-1854, December 16, 1848, p. 167.
52. *Catalogue of the Officers and Students of the University of Alabama,* 1855-1856, p. 5.
53. Ray, pp. 70-79. Letter from Elliott to Ray.
54. *Ibid.*
55. Incident related by Jennie C. M. Richardson, in Alabama Collection.
56. Letter from Crenshaw Hall to his mother, Tuscaloosa, Alabama, July 2, 1858.
57. "Minutes of the Proceedings of the Faculty," 1841-1854, July 17, 1852, p. 248.
58. *The Daily Post* (Montgomery), May 30, 1860.
59. Clark, p. 83.
60. *Ibid.,* pp. 133-134.
61. Sketch of Professor Brumby in LaBorde's *History of the South Carolina College,* quoted in Clark, p. 68.
62. Ray, p. 3.
63. Sir Charles Lyell, *Second Visit to the United States of America,* II, 64.
64. J. W. Mallet, "Redetermination of the Atomic Weight of Lithium," *The American Journal of Science and Arts,* November, 1856, Vol. XXII, pp. 349-356.
65. E. F. Smith, *Chemistry in America,* passim.
66. B. I. Wiley, *The Life of Johnny Reb.,* p. 303.
67. "Minutes of the Proceedings of the Faculty," 1841-1854, June 13, 1853, p. 281.
68. *Ibid.,* December 16, 1846, p. 122.
69. *Ibid.,* January 29, 1849, p. 169.
70. *Ibid.,* February 23, 1852, p. 232.
71. *Ibid.,* December 17, 1846, p. 122.
72. *Acts of the General Assembly,* 1821, pp. 3-8.
73. *Ibid.,* 1822, pp. 26-32.

THE OLD UNIVERSITY 591

74. "Ordinances and Resolutions of the Board of Trustees", 1822-1841, December 12, 1832, p. 157.
75. *Ibid.*, December 28, 1832, p. 164.
76. *Ibid.*, December 11, 1837, p. 245.
77. *Ibid.*, December 17, 1838, p. 258.
78. *Ibid.*, December 21, 1840, p. 284.
79. "Record of the Ordinances and Resolutions of the Board of Trustees," 1842-1855, December 18, 1844, p. 11.
80. *Ibid.*, December 27, 1844, p. 19.
81. *Ibid.*, August 13, 1847, p. 34.
82. *Ibid.*, December 18, 1844, p. 11.
83. *Ibid.*, July 13, 1848, p. 37.
84. *Ibid.*, July 15, 1853, p. 58.
85. *Ibid.*, 1822-1841, December 20, 1838, p. 262.
86. *Ibid.*, December 16, 1839, p. 274.
87. *Alabama Journal* (Montgomery), February 17, 1841.
88. "Ordinances and Resolutions of the Board of Trustees," 1822-1841, December 16, 1839, p. 274.
89. *Ibid.*, 1842-1855, September 28, 1854, p. 62.
90. *Ibid.*, 1822-1841, January 5, 1829, p. 71.
91. From the Annual Report to the General Assembly as written in the "Journal of the Proceedings of the Board of Trustees," 1822-1832, January 13, 1830.
92. "Journal of the Proceedings of the Board of Trustees," 1822-1832, January 7, 1830, p. 220.
93. "Ordinances and Resolutions of the Board of Trustees," 1822-1841, December 23, 1831; November 24, 1830, pp. 196, 138.
94. *Ibid.*, April 13, 1831, p. 109.
95. *Ibid.*, January 2, 1832, p. 142.
96. *Ibid.*, April 13, 1831, p. 110.
97. *Ibid.*, December 14, 1832, p. 159.
98. *Ibid.*, December 28, 1832, p. 165.
99. *Ibid.*, August 16, 1834, p. 204.
100. *Ibid.*, August 12, 1835, p. 208.
101. *Ibid.*, January 15, 1831 p. 106.
102. *Ibid.*, April 13, 1831, p. 110.
103. *Ibid.*, August 12, 1835; December 19, 1836, pp. 207 and 221-222.
104. *Ibid.*, December 21, 1836; December 14, 1837, pp. 223 and 249.
105. "Journal of the Proceedings of the Board of Trustees," 1822-1832, December 26, 1831, pp. 346 and 349.
106. "Ordinances and Resolutions of the Board of Trustees," 1822-1841, December 19, 1832, p. 160.
107. *Ibid.*, August 19, 1833, p. 180.
108. *Ibid.*, November 20, 1835, p. 165.
109. *Ibid.*, December 11, 1837, p. 245.
110. *Ibid.*, August 15, 1834, p. 197.
111. *Ibid.*, December 16, 1841, p. 294.
112. "Record of the Ordinances and Resolutions of the Board of Trustees," 1842-1855, December 17, 1842, p. 5.
113. *Ibid.*, p. 6.
114. "Minutes of the Proceedings of the Faculty," 1841-1854, October 18, 1843; November 17, 1843, pp. 47, 51-53.
115. "Record of the Ordinances and Resolutions of the Board of Trustees," 1842-1855, December 19, 1843, p. 12.
116. *Ibid.*, December 26, 1844, p. 18.

117. *Trustees of the University of Alabama v. Walden,* 15 *Ala.* 655, (1849) Quoted in Elliott and Chambers, *The College and the Courts,* p. 87.
118. "Record of the Ordinances and Resolutions of the Board of Trustees," 1842-1855, December 11, 1843, p. 8.
119. *Ibid.,* July 13, 1853, p. 53.
120. "Minutes of the Proceedings of the Faculty," 1841-1854, July 25, 1852, p. 249.
121. Clark, p. 75.
122. "Record of the Ordinances and Resolutions of the Board of Trustees." 1842-1855, July, 1855, p. 64.
123. "General Ledger," 1861-1865, pp. 15-21.

CHAPTER V

1. "Ordinances and Resolutions of the Board of Trustees," 1822-1841, March 24, 1828, p. 59.
2. *Ibid.,* p. 58.
3. *Ibid.,* January 13 and 18, 1830, pp. 79-80.
4. "Journal of the Proceedings of the Board of Trustees," 1822-1832, p. 258.
5. "Ordinances and Resolutions of the Board of Trustees," 1822-1841, January 3, 1831, p. 102.
6. Letter from D. Woodruff, of Smith and Woodruff, Tuscaloosa, Alabama, to President and Board of Trustees, University of Alabama, June 28, 1830, in Ms. papers, University Library, Lib.I, "Old Library," Alabama Collection.
7. "Journal of the Proceedings of the Board of Trustees," 1822-1832, December 7, 1830, p. 282.
8. "Ordinances and Resolutions of the Board of Trustees," 1822-1841, January 3, 1831, pp. 101-102.
9. "Journal of the Proceedings of the Board of Trustees," 1822-1832, December 27, 1831, p. 347.
10. "Ordinances and Resolutions of the Board of Trustees," 1822-1841, December 30, 1831, p. 141.
11. *Laws of the University of the State of Alabama,* 1839.
12. "Ordinances and Resolutions of the Board of Trustees," 1822-1841, December 8, 1837, p. 244.
13. "Faculty Minutes," 1831-1835, May 15, 1832; August, 1833.
14. *Ibid.,* May 15, 1832.
15. *Ibid.,* September 24, 1836, p. 51.
16. "Ordinances and Resolutions of the Board of Trustees," 1822-1841, December 15, 1838, p. 257.
17. "Minutes of the Proceedings, of the Faculty," 1841-1854, August 15, 1847, January 31, September 29, 1848, pp. 142-152, 161.
18. Manuscript Papers, University Library, Library I, "Old Library."
19. "Minutes of the Proceedings of the Faculty," 1841-1854, December 28, 1843, p. 57.
20. Roberts, p. 9.
21. "Minutes of the Proceedings of the Faculty," 1841-1854, December 28, 1843, p. 57.
22. Clark, p. 64.
23. Roberts, p. 19-20.
24. "Minutes of the Proceedings of the Faculty," 1841-1854, February 7, 1845, p. 86.
25. *Ibid.,* March 9, 1849, p. 170.
26. *Ibid.,* February 2, 1852, p. 228.
27. "Faculty Minutes," 1835-1837, March 23, 1837, p. 65.

THE OLD UNIVERSITY 593

28. "Minutes of the Proceedings of the Faculty," 1841-1854, February 9 and 16, 1844, pp. 66-67.
29. *Ibid.*, January 29, 1849, p. 169.
30. *Ibid.*, March 26, 1849, p. 171.
31. Roberts, p. 20.
32. "Journal of the Proceedings of the Board of Trustees," 1822-1832, January 8, 1831, p. 290.
33. *Ibid.*, January 13 and 17, 1832, pp. 361 and 364.
34. "Ordinances and Resolutions of the Board of Trustees," 1822-1841, January 13, 1832, p. 145.
35. "Ordinances and Resolutions of the Board of Trustees," 1822-1841, December 27, 1832, p. 164.
36. "Faculty Minutes," 1831-1835, November 6, 1832.
37. "Ordinances and Resolutions of the Board of Trustees," 1822-1841, December 21, 1832, p. 161.
38. "Journal of the Proceedings of the Board of Trustees," 1822-1832, December 20, 1832, p. 386.
39. "Ordinances and Resolutions of the Board of Trustees," 1822-1841, August 14, 1833, p. 177.
40. *Ibid.*, August 13, 1834, p. 192.
41. "Faculty Minutes," 1835-1837, August 3, 1835, p. 10.
42. *Ibid.*, February 1, 1836, p. 28.
43. "Ordinances and Resolutions of the Board of Trustees," 1822-1841, December 17, 1836, p. 221.
44. *Ibid.*, December 21, 1836, p. 226.
45. *Ibid.*, December 14, 1837, p. 248.
46. *Ibid.*, December 11, 1837, p. 246.
47. *Ibid.*, December 17, 1838, p. 263.
48. President Manly's "Diary", 1834-1846, 1839, p. 164.
49. *Ibid.*, December 16, 1841, p. 293.
50. "Minutes of the Proceedings of the Faculty," 1841-1854, January 6, 1842, p. 1.
51. *Ibid.*, December 22, 1843, p. 57.
52. *Ibid.*, December 28, 1843, p. 57.
53. *Ibid.*, December 28, 1843, p. 58-59.
54. *Ibid.*, January 12, 1844, pp. 62-63.
55. "Record of the Ordinances and Resolutions of the Board of Trustees," 1842-1855, December 25, 1844, p. 17.
56. *Ibid.*, July 14, 1848, p. 38.
57. "Minutes of the Proceedings of the Faculty," 1841-1854, September 30, 1848, p. 161.
58. *Ibid.*, November 5, 1849, p. 182.
59. *Ibid.*, February 4, 1850, p. 187.
60. *Ibid.*, October 4, 1851, p. 213.
62. *Ibid.*, July 17, 1852, p. 249.
63. *Ibid.*, October 2, 1852, p. 257.
64. "Ordinances and Resolutions of the Board of Trustees," 1822-1841, December 17, 1836, p. 221.
65. "Record of Ordinances and Resolutions of the Board of Trustees," 1842-1855, December 16, 1842, p. 4.
66. "Minutes of the Proceedings of the Faculty," 1841-1854, February 26, 1843, p. 30.
67. *Ibid.*, February 3, 17, March 3, 1843, pp. 29-30.
68. Letter from R. T. Brumby to the Board of Trustees, December 14, 1841.

69. "Record of the Ordinances and Resolutions of the Board of Trustees," 1842-1855, December 27, 1845, p. 23.
70. "Minutes of the Proceedings of the Faculty, " 1841-1854, February 18, 1846, p. 109.
71. "Ordinances and Resolutions of the Board of Trustees," 1822-1841, December 13, 1839, p. 273.
72. Letter from Brumby and Barnard to the Board of Trustees, 1846.
73. Old University Records, 1846.
74. "Minutes of the Proceedings of the Faculty," 1841-1854, January 28, 1844, p. 75.
75. *Ibid.*, June 17, 1842, p. 14.
76. *Ibid.*, July 21, 1843, p. 43.
77. *Ibid.*, May 24, 1847, p. 43.
78. Letter written at Lagrange, Alabama, November 11, 1840, from Henry Tutwiler to Dr. Manly, Manuscript Papers, University Library, Library I, "Old Library," Alabama Collection.
79. "Minutes of the Proceedings of the Faculty," 1841-1854, January 21, 1842, p. 3.
80. *Ibid.*, March 3, 1843, p. 30.
81. From Report on Library to the Legislative Committee, August 10, 1835, Filed in State Department of Archives and History, Montgomery, Alabama.
82. Manuscript Papers, Old University, Alabama Collection, February 3, 1854.
83. Manuscript Papers in Alabama Collection, January 24, 1854.
84. Manuscript Papers, February 17, 1844.
85. Manuscript Papers, November 11, 1856.
86. Manuscript Papers, no date.
87. "Minutes of the Proceedings of the Faculty," 1841-1854, October 11, 1847, p. 144.
88. "Faculty Minutes," 1835-1837, December 23, 1836, pp. 62-63.
89. President Manly's Diary," 1834-1846, 1839, p. 164.
90. "Minutes of the Proceedings of the Faculty, 1841-1854, February 7, 1845, p. 86.
91. *Ibid.*, November 28, 1845, p. 102.
92. *Ibid.*, April 29, 1842, pp. 11-12.
93. *Ibid.*, June 16, 1843, p. 39.
94. *Ibid.*, December 5, 1848, p. 166.
95. *Ibid.*, April 20, 1844, p. 71.
96. *Ibid.*, December 5, 1848, p. 166.
97. *Ibid.*, December 3, 1849, p. 183.
98. *Ibid.*, January 10, 1853, p. 266.
99. *Ibid.*, October 2, 1852, p. 257.
100. *Ibid.*, July 4, 1853, p. 284.
101. "Ordinances and Resolutions of the Board of Trustees," 1822-1841, July 17, 1837, p. 240.
102. *Ibid.*, December 15, 1838, p. 257.
103. "Minutes of the Proceedings of the Faculty," 1841-1854, August 15, 1847; January 31 and September 30, 1848, pp. 142, 152, 161.
104. Manuscript Papers, University Library, Library I, "Old Library."
105. Clark, p. 64.

CHAPTER VI

1. Message from Governor Collier to the Citizens of Alabama, *Advertiser and State Gazette*, (Montgomery), October 9, 1850.
2. Clark, p. 84.
3. "Ordinances and Resolutions of the Board of Trustees," 1822-1841, April 15, 1831, pp. 108-109.

4. *Ibid.*, April 16, 1831, p. 124.
5. *Ibid.*
6. Smith, p. 203.
7. "Reminiscences of the History of the University of Alabama," by Oran M. Roberts, (Typewritten pamphlet in Alabama Collection) pp. 1-2.
8. *Ibid.*
9. *Ibid.*
10. "Ordinances and Resolutions of the Board of Trustees," 1822-1841, April 16, 1831, pp. 132-133.
11. *Ibid.*, December 14, 1837, p. 249.
12. "Records of the Ordinances and Resolutions of the Board of Trustees," 1842-1855, December 15, 1842, pp. 1-2.
13. *Ibid.*, December 16, 1843, p. 9.
14. "Ordinances and Resolutions of the Board of Trustees," 1822-1841, July 14, 1837, p. 238.
15. "Record of the Ordinances and Resolutions of the Board of Trustees," 1842-1855, December 15, 1842, p. 1-2.
16. *Ibid.*, July 13, 1848, p. 36.
17. *Ibid., December* 16, 1843, p. 9.
18. *Ibid.*, August 12, 1847, p. 32.
19. *Ibid.*, December 27, 1845, p. 24.
20. "Ordinances and Resolutions of the Board of Trustees," 1822-1841, June 30, 1830, p. 88.
21. *Ibid.*, April 16, 1831, p. 133.
22. *Senate Journal*, 1833, pp. 6-22.
23. "Record of the Ordinances and Resolutions of the Board of Trustees," 1842-1855, December 15, 1842, p. 2.
24. *Ibid.*, p. 54.
25. Letter from Crenshaw Hall to his father, Tuscaloosa, Alabama, June 16, 1858.
26. *Laws of the University of Alabama*, 1839, Ch. XI, Sec. 7, p. 17.
27. *Laws of the University of Alabama*, 1850, Ch. XI, Sec. 7, p. 17.
28. "Faculty Minutes," 1831-1835, October 31, 1831.
29. *Ibid.*, February 5, 1833.
30. *Laws of the University of Alabama*, 1839-1850, Ch. XV, Sec. 1.
31. "Faculty Minutes," 1831-1835, October 21, 1833.
32. Letter from Bolling Hall to his mother, Tuscaloosa, Alabama.
33. "Faculty Minutes," 1831-1835, October 3, 4, 1831.
34. *Laws of the University of Alabama*, 1839, Ch. V, Sec. 5, pp. 9-10.
35. *Law of the University of Alabama*, 1850, Ch. V, Sec. 5, p. 10.
36. *Laws of the University of Alabama*, 1839, 1850, Ch. VIII, Sec. 1, p. 12.
37. "Minutes of the Proceedings of the Faculty," 1841-1854, October 19, 1842, p. 14.
38. "Ordinances and Resolutions of the Board of Trustees, 1822-1841, April 16, 1831, p. 125.
39. *Ibid.*, January 17, 1832, p. 145.
40. "Faculty Minutes," 1831-1835, February 3, 1832.
41. "Faculty Minutes," 1835-1837, March 1, 1836, p. 30.
42. *Laws of the University of Alabama*, 1839, Ch. IV, Sec. 4, p. 7.
43. "Minutes of the Proceedings of the Faculty, 1841-1854," April 29, 1842, p. 12.
44. *Ibid.*, October 10, 1845, p. 99.
45. *Ibid.*, October 1, 1853, p. 287.
46. "Ordinances and Resolutions of the Board of Trustees," 1822-1841, April 16, 1831, p. 129.
47. *Ibid.*, January 17, 1832, p. 149.
48. "Faculty Minutes," 1831-1835, August 10, 1833, and October 28, 1836, p. 56.

49. *Laws of the University of Alabama,* 1839, Ch. XI, Secs. 4, 5, 6.
50. *Laws of the University of Alabama,* 1850, Ch. XI, Sec. 5.
51. Letter from Bolling Hall to his father, Tuscaloosa, Alabama, January 6, 1857.
52. Letter from Bolling Hall to his father, Tuscaloosa, Alabama, October 6, 1857.
53. Little, p. 10.
54. "Ordinances and Resolutions of the Board of Trustees," 1822-1841, April 16, 1831, p. 129.
55. *Ibid.,* January 11, 1833, p. 168.
56. *Ibid.,* December 23, 1836, p. 211.
57. "Faculty Minutes," 1831-1835, February 1, 1834.
58. Roberts, p. 13.
59. *Laws of the University of Alabama,* 1839, Ch. XIV, Sec. 4.
60. "Records of the Ordinances and Resolutions of the Board of Trustees," 1842-1855-, August 13, 1847, p. 30.
61. Letter from Crenshaw Hall to his mother, Tuscaloosa, Alabama, October 20, 1857.
62. "Minutes of the Proceedings of the Faculty, 1841-1854," May 7, 1849, p. 172.
63. *Ibid.*
64. Little, p. 11.
65. "Ordinances and Resolutions of the Board of Trustees," 1822-1841, December 20, 1830, p. 199, August 14, 1834, p. 194, December 12, 1839, p. 271; 1842-1855, December 12, 1842, p. 1, December 19, 1843, p. 12.
66. *Ibid.,* December 20, 1830, p. 199.
67. *Ibid.,* April 6, 1831, p. 129.
68. *Ibid.,* August 14, 1834, p. 194.
69. Letter from Crenshaw Hall to his father, Tuscaloosa, Alabama, November 4, 1857.
70. "Faculty Minutes," 1835-1837, March 29, 1837, p. 66.
71. "Minutes of the Proceedings of the Faculty,," 1841-1854 May 7, 1849, p. 172.
72. *Ibid.,* November 14, 1853, p. 290.
73. *Ibid.,* May 16, 1853, p. 278.
74. *Ibid.,* January 24, 1848, p. 151.
75. "Faculty Minutes," 1831-1835, March 15, 1833.
76. *Ibid.,* January 23, 1833.
77. "Faculty Minutes," 1831-1835, March 15, 1833.
78. *Ibid.,* May 15, 1832.
79. "Minutes of the Proceedings of the Faculty," 1841-1854, November 29, 1852, p. 262.
80. "Faculty Minutes," 1831-1835, May 15, 1832.
81. Little, *Memoirs,* p. 16.
82. "Ordinances and Resolutions of the Board of Trustees," 1822-1841, April 16, 1831, p. 125.
83. "Record of Ordinances and Resolutions Passed by the Trustees, 1842-1855," December 17, 1846, p. 27.
84. "Faculty Minutes," 1831-1835, January 30, 1832.
85. *Ibid.,* June 8, 1832, p. . . . ., April 8, 1833.
86. *Laws of the University of Alabama, 1839.* Ch. VII, Sec. 4.
87. Letter from Bolling Hall to his mother, Tuscaloosa, Alabama, October 31, 1857.
88. *Laws of the University of Alabama, 1839-1850,* Ch. VII, Sec. 5.
89. *Ibid.,* Sec. 3.
90. Clark, p. 50.
91. "Ordinances and Resolutions of the Board of Trustees," 1822-1841, 1831, Ch. IX, Sec. 5, p. 134.

THE OLD UNIVERSITY

92. "Faculty Minutes," 1831-1835, January 24, 1833.
93. *Ibid.*, February 5, 1833.
94. *Laws of the University of Alabama*, 1839, Ch. VIII, Sec. 11.
95. "Minutes of the Proceedings of the Faculty," 1841-1854, January 7, 1842, p. 1.
96. *Ibid.*, July 15, 16, 1842, pp. 16-17.
97. *Ibid.*, July 15, 1842, p. 16.
98. *Ibid.*, May 26, 1843, p. 37.
99. "Record of the Ordinances and Resolutions of the Board of Trustees," 1842-1855, December 15, 1843, p. 8.
100. *Laws of the University of Alabama*, 1850, Ch. VIII, Sec. 11.
101. "Minutes of the Proceedings of the Faculty, 1841-1854," November 1, 1847, p. 145.
102. *Ibid.*, June 9, 1843, p. 38; see also June 3, 10, 1842, pp. 13-14.
103. Roberts, pp. 2-3.
104. Excerpts from the "Faculty Ledger," 1852.
105. *Ibid.*
106. *Ibid.*, May 29, 1848.
107. Little, p. 16.
108. Roberts, p. 2.
109. Little, pp. 14-15.
110. *Ibid.*, p. 18.
111. Letter from Crenshaw Hall to his father, November 18, 1857.
112. Letter from Crenshaw Hall to his Mother, May 15, 1858.
113. Letters from Crenshaw and Bolling Hall to his mother, April 13, and April 17, 1858.
114. "Faculty Minutes," 1831-1835, April 12, 1833.
115. "Faculty Minutes," 1835-1837, October 6, 1838, p. 55.
116. *Laws of the University of Alabama*, 1839-1850, Ch. VIII, Sec. 1.
117. Roberts, p. 7
118. Letters from Crenshaw Hall to his mother, July 2, 1858.
119. "Ordinances and Resolutions of the Board of Trustees," 1822-1841, January 17, 1832, p. 149.
120. Roberts, pp. 13-14.
121. "Minutes of the Proceedings of the Faculty," 1841-1854, November 12, 1846, p. 119.
122. *Ibid.*, June 7, 1847, p. 134.
123. *Ibid.*, April 30, 1849, p. 172.
124. *Ibid.*, July 17, 1846, p. 116.
125. *Ibid.*, May 15, 1854, pp. 303-304.
126. Little, p. 14.
127. President Basil Manly's "Diary" 1843-1848, July 3, 1847, p. 162.
128. "Ordinances and Resolutions of the Board of Trustees," 1822-1841, April 16, 1831, pp. 131-132.
129. "Faculty Minutes," 1831-1835, July 10, 1834.
130. "Ordinances and Resolutions of the Board of Trustees," 1822-1841, August 14, 1834, p. 195.
131. "Faculty Minutes," 1835-1837, November 6, 1835, p. 18.
132. "Ordinances and Resolutions of the Board of Trustees, 1822-1841, November 20, 1835, p. 217.
133. *Ibid.*, December 23, 1836, p. 231.
134. *Ibid.*, December 12, 1837, p. 247.
135. *Ibid.*, December 23, 1840, p. 288.
136. *Ibid.*, December 16, 1841, p. 292.

137. "Record of the Ordinances and Resolutions of the Board of Trustees," 1842-1855, December, 1846, p. 28.
138. *Ibid.*, August 13, 1847, p. 32.
139. Letter from Bolling Hall to his father, Tuscaloosa, Alabama, October 31, 1857.
140. Letter from Bolling Hall to his mother, December 1, 1857.
141. Letter from Crenshaw Hall to his mother, April 13, 1858.
142. "Minutes of the Proceedings of the Faculty," 1841-1854, March 20, 1848, p. 154.
143. *Ibid.*, March 17, 1851, p. 205.
144. Letter from Bolling Hall to his father, July 10, 1858.
145. "Faculty Minutes," 1831-1835, August 7, 1833.
146. Notes from the "Journals or Diary" of Sara Haynesworth Gayle, in private possession.
147. "Faculty Minutes," 1835-1837, June 5, 1835, pp. 2-3.
148. *Flag of the Union* (Tuscaloosa) June 30, 1841.
149. "Minutes of the Proceedings of the Faculty," 1841-1854, June 30, 1843, p. 40.
150. Letter from Crenshaw Hall, Tuscaloosa, Alabama, July 5, 1858.
151. "Minutes of the Proceedings of the Faculty, 1841-1854," July 9, 1849, p. 178.
152. *Ibid.*, July 5, 1844, p. 75.
153. *Ibid.*, December 5, 1845, p. 102.
154. Roberts, p. 7.
155. "Minutes of the Proceedings of the Faculty," 1841-1854, February 21, 1853, p. 271.
156. *Ibid.*, November 24, 1851, p. 219; November 22, 1852, p. 261.
157. *Ibid.*, February 18, 1842, p. 4.

CHAPTER VII

1. First Report of Dr. Manly to the Board of Trustees, Clark, pp. 49-50.
2. *Catalogues of the University of Alabama*, 1843 through 1845.
3. *Ibid.*, 1850-1851.
4. Letter from B. Manly to Capt. James A. Tait, January 23, 1850.
5. *Catalogues of the University of Alabama*, 1853-1854.
6. "Ordinances and Resoultions of the Board of Trustees," 1822-1841, April 16, 1831, Ch. 3, Sec. 3 p. 124; *Catalogue of Officers and Students of the University of Alabama*, 1837.
7. Message from Governor Collier to the Citizens of Alabama, *Advertiser and State Gazette*, (Montgomery) October 9, 1850.
8. "Faculty Minutes," 1835-1837, February 7, 1837, p. 64.
9. *Ibid.*, 1831-1835, January 24, 1833.
10. *Ibid.*, May 4, 1833.
11. "Ordinances and Resolutions of the Board of Trustees," 1822-1841, December 11, 1837, p. 247.
12. *Ibid.*, December 14, 1837, p. 250.
13. *Laws of the University of Alabama*, 1839, Ch. V, Sec. 2.
14. *Laws of the University of Alabama*, 1850, Ch. V, Sec. 2.
15. "Record of the Ordinances and Resolutions of the Board of Trustees," 1842-1855, December 18, 1843, p. 11.
16. "Minutes of the Proceedings of the Faculty," 1841-1854, December 30, 1842, p. 25; June 27, 1845, p. 96. Letter from Basil Manly, October 27, 1851, Alabama Collection.
17. Letter from Basil Manly, October 27, 1851, Alabama Collection.

THE OLD UNIVERSITY 599

18. Clark, pp. 69-70.
19. Clark, pp. 75-76.
20. J. Fulton, *Memoirs of Frederick A. P. Barnard,* pp. 169-171.
21. *Ibid.*
22. *Catalogue of the University of Alabama,* 1850-1851.
23. *Catalogue of the Officers and Students of the University of Alabama,* 1855-1856, p. 11.
24. *Ibid.,* 1857-1858, p. 10.
25. *Ibid.,* 1855-1856, p. 13.
26. Clark, pp. 75-76.
27. *Catalogue of the Officers and Students of the University* for 1859-60, p. 10.
28. Clark, pp. 84-85.
29. *Ibid.*
30. "Faculty Minutes," 1831-1835, December 18, 1834.
31. *Ibid.,* January 1835.
32. *Ibid.*
33. *Ibid.,* April 7, 1835.
34. *Ibid.,* August 17, 1835.
35. "Faculty Minutes," 1835-1837, February 6, 1837, p. 63.
36. *Ibid.,* February 6, 1837, p. 63.
37. *Ibid.,* July 29, 1837, pp. 78-79.
38. "Ordinances and Resolutions of the Board of Trustees," 1822-1841, December 21, 1836, p. 226.
39. *Ibid.,* December 7, 1837, p. 243.
40. "Message from Governor Collier to the Citizens of Alabama," *Advertiser and State Gazette* (Montgomery), October 9, 1850.
41. "Minutes of the Proceedings of the Faculty," 1841-1854, December 14, 1843, p. 56.
42. "Record of Ordinances and Resolutions of the Board of Trustees," 1842-1855, December 16, 1843, p. 10.
43. *Catalogue of the University of Alabama,* 1844.
44. Ms. Papers, "Old Library," Medicine Dept. University Library.
45. "Record of the Ordinances and Resolutions of the Board of Trustees, 1842-1855, December 27, 1845, pp. 23-25.
46. *Catalogue of the University of Alabama,* 1846.
47. "Minutes of the Proceedings of the Faculty," 1841-1854, February 3, 1851, p. 202.
48. *Acts Passed by the Third and Fourth Annual Session of the General Assembly,* 1821, p. 2-8; 1822, pp. 26-32.
49. "Message from Governor Collier to the Citizens of Alabama," *Advertiser and State Gazette,* October 9, 1850.
50. "Minutes of the Proceedings of the Faculty," 1841-1854, January 4, 1849, p. 168.
51. *Ibid.,* May 27, 1850, pp. 191-192.
52. Letter from Lucian Owen to his father, October 8, 1857.
53. *Flag of the Union* (Tuscaloosa), January 27, 1841.
54. Ray, pp. 36-7.
55. "Faculty Minutes," 1831-1835, February 5, 1833.
56. J. C. M. Richardson, "College Memories," Handwritten manuscript in Alabama Collection.
57. Roberts, "Reminiscences," pp. 4-5.
58. Letter from Crenshaw Hall to his mother, October 20, 1857.
59. Letter from Crenshaw Hall to his father, November 4, 1857.
60. Letter from Bolling Hall to his father, October 31, 1857.

61. *The Spirit of the Age* (Tuscaloosa), December 21, 1831.
62. "Faculty Minutes," 1831-1835, June 22, 1833.
63. *Ibid.*, July 16, 1833.
64. Roberts, p. 8.
65. *Catalogue of the University of Alabama,* 1855-1856, p. 12.
66. "Record of the Ordinances and Resolutions of the Board of Trustees, 1842-1855," December 18, 1843, p. 13.
67. "Minutes of the Proceedings of the Faculty," 1841-1854, June 28, 1844, p. 75.
68. "Record of the Ordinances and Resolutions of the Board of Trustees," 1842-1855," July 15, 1853, p. 58.
69. *Catalogue of the University of Alabama,* 1853-1854.
70. "Ordinances and Resolutions of the Board of Trustees," 1822-1841, April 16, 1831, Ch. 10, Sec. 2 p. 134.
71. *Ibid.*, April 16, 1831, Ch. 10, Sec. 4, 5, p. 135.
72. *Ibid.*, December 19, 1832, and "Journal of the Proceedings of the Board of Trustees," 1822-1832, December 19, 1832, p. 382.
73. "Faculty Minutes," 1835-1837, August 3, 1835, p. 9.
74. *Ibid.*, 1831-1835, May 16, 1833.
75. *Ibid.*
76. *Ibid.*
77. *Laws of the University of Alabama,* 1839 and 1850, Ch. X, Sec. 2 and 5.
78. "Minutes of the Proceedings of the Faculty," 1841-1854, October 9, 1848, p. 164.
79. *Ibid.*, October 24, 1848, p. 165.
80. *Ibid.*, June 30, 1849, p. 178.
81. *Ibid.*, May 13, 1851, p. 207.
82. *Catalogue of the University of Alabama,* 1855-1856, p. 14.
83. *Ibid.*, 1857-58, p. 14.
84. *Ibid.*, 1859-60, pp. 20-21.
85. President Basil Manly's "Diary," 1843-1848, December, 1846, p. 105.
86. "Message from Governor Collier to Citizens of Alabama," *Advertiser and State Gazette* (Montgomery), October 9, 1850.

CHAPTER VIII

1. "Journal of the Proceedings of the Board of Trustees," 1822-1832, December 22, 1831, p. 339.
2. *Ibid.*, December 14, 1832, p. 375.
3. "The Philomathic Society" written by William C. Davis, Jr., Material gathered by Roy L. Thomas. Typewritten booklet in Alabama Collection.
4. *Ibid.*
5. *The Spirit of the Age* (Tuscaloosa), May 30, 1832.
6. *Flag of the Union* (Tuscaloosa), November 13, 1839.
7. Jacksonville *Republican,* February 14, 1844.
8. *Acts of the General Assembly:* Act No. 94, 1843, p. 96; Act. No. 148, 1845, p. 97.
9. "Faculty Minutes," 1831-1835, February 23, 1833.
10. *Ibid.*, November 28, 1834.
11. Davis quoting from *Corolla* (yearbook) of 1893.
12. "Minutes of the Proceedings of the Faculty," 1841-1854, January 2, 1854, p. 292.
13. Letter from Bolling Hall to his father, October 17, 1857.
14. Roberts, p. 19.
15. Letter from Bolling Hall to his father, May 2, 1858.
16. Jacksonville *Republican,* November 16, 1837.

THE OLD UNIVERSITY 601

17. Letter written by Emma Augusta Jones in 1932, telling of her father's membership in the Erosophic Society in 1854.
18. *Catalougue of the University of Alabama*, 1857, as quoted in *The Monitor* (Tuscaloosa), May 6, 1858.
19. Davis.
20. "Minutes of the Proceedings of the Faculty," 1841-1854, March 13, 1846, p. 110.
21. *Ibid.*, May 22, 1846, p. 113.
22. *Ibid.*, May 30, 1845, p. 94.
23. *Ibid.*, July 26, 1847, p. 138.
24. *Ibid.*, December 5, 1848, p. 166.
25. *Ibid.*, March 19, 1849, p. 171.
26. *Ibid.*, May 13, 1850, p. 191.
27. Little, p. 15.
28. President Manly's "Diary," 1848-1855, November 3, 1851, p. 149.
29. "Minutes of the Proceedings of the Faculty, 1841-1854," July 9, 1852, p. 255.
30. President Manly's "Diary," 1845-1855, November 1852, pp. 202-204.
31. "Minutes of the Proceedings of the Faculty," 1841-1854, November 1, 1852, p. 260.
32. President Manly's "Diary," 1848-1855, April, 1854, p. 258.
33. "Record Book, Containing the Names of Students, time of Admission, Parents, Guardians, etc., 1831-1865," October 13, 1856.
34. "Minutes of the Proceedings of the Faculty," 1841-1854, July 6, 1849, p. 178.
35. *Ibid.*, November 11, 1850, p. 199.
36. *Ibid.*, March 17, 1851, p. 204.
37. *Ibid.*, July 9, 1852, p. 255.
38. *Ibid.*, July 13, 1852, p. 247.
39. *Ibid.*, July 15, 1852, p. 247-248.
40. *Ibid.*, October 17, 1845, p. 100.
41. *Ibid.*, May 22, 1846, p. 113.
42. *Ibid.*, June 12, 1846, p. 114.
43. *Ibid.*, October 16, 1848, p. 164.
44. *Ibid.*, December 16, 1848, p. 167.
45. *Ibid.*, September 29, 1849, p. 180-181.
46. *Ibid.*, March 4, 1850, p. 189.
47. "Faculty Minutes," 1831-1835, November 12, 1833.
48. "Faculty Minutes," 1835-1837, February 17, 1836, p. 29.
49. *Catalogue of the University of Alabama*, 1856-1857, p. 36.
50. *The Spirit of the Age* (Tuscaloosa), December 28, 1831.
51. "Faculty Minutes," 1831-1835, December 15, 1833.
52. *Ibid.*, July 10, 1834.
53. *Ibid.*, May 22, 1835.
54. Roberts, p. 23.
55. "Journal of the Proceedings of the Board of Trustees," 1822-1832, April 5, 1822, p. 2.
56. "Proceedings of the Faculty of the University of Alabama," 1871-1879, March 22, 1872, p. 71.
57. Letter from Professor Robert E. Jones, April 25, 1850.
58. A. W. Lawrence, *Classical Sculpture*, p. 203.
59. *An Oration Delivered Before the Society of Alumni at Its First Anniversary*, by A. B. Meek, December 17, 1836.
60. *Flag of the Union* (Tuscaloosa), November 13, 1839.
61. *The Advertiser and State Gazette* (Montgomery), July 31, 1850.
62. *The Independent* (Gainesville), August 1, 1857.

63. *The Monitor* (Tuscaloosa), July 15, 1858.
64. "Minutes of the Proceedings of the Faculty," 1841-1854, November 25, 1842, p 23.
65. *The Independent* (Gainesville), August 1, 1857.
66. *The Monitor* (Tuscaloosa), July 15, 1858.
67. "Ordinances and Resolutions of the Board of Trustees," 1822-1841, December 15, 1837, p. 252.
68. *Ibid.*, December 21, 1838, p. 262.
69. Clark, p. 51.
70. "Record of the Ordinances and Resolutions of the Board of Trustees," 1842-1855, December 27, 1844, p. 18.
71. *Ibid.*, December 19, 1846, p. 29.
72. *Alabama Baptist Advocate* (Marion), July 25, 1849.
73. *Ibid.*, January 14, and 21, 1850, p. 186.
74. *Advertiser and State Gazette* (Montgomery), August 7, 1850.
75. *Alabama Baptist Advocate* (Marion), July 31, 1850.
76. Jacksonville *Republican*, July 27, 1852.
77. "Minutes of the Proceedings of the Faculty," 1841-1854," May 11, 1852, p. 239.
78. *Advertiser and State Gazette* (Montgomery), July 30, 1851.
79. *The Independent* (Gainesville), July 26, 1856.
80. *Ibid.*, July 28, 1860.
81. Little, p. 18.

CHAPTER IX

1. See Chapter on First Faculty.
2. *Laws of the University of the State of Alabama, 1839,* pp. 11-12.
3. This is taken from the *Laws of 1839*. The wording of the *Laws of 1850* varies somewhat.
4. *Laws of the University of Alabama,* 1839, p. 25.
5. *Ibid.*
6. *Ibid.*, Ch. XVI, Sec. 4, pp. 23-24.
7. *Ordinances for the Government of the University of Alabama,* 1831, Ch. V, Sec. 1.
8. *Laws of the University of Alabama,* 1839, Ch. XVI, Sec. 1, p. 23.
9. *Ibid.*, Ch. XVI, Sec. 4, pp. 23-24.
10. Clark, p. 51-52.
11. *Ibid.*, p. 53-54.
12. *Ibid.*, pp. 59-60.
13. "Minutes of the Proceedings of the Faculty," 1841-1854, January 1, 3, 17, February 7, 14, 1848, pp. 148, 151-153.
14. "Faculty Minutes," 1831-1835, February 23, 1833.
15. *Ibid.*, May 8, 1835.
16. "Minutes of the Proceedings of the Faculty, 1841-1854," March 15, 16, 1842, pp. 6-7.
17. *Ibid.*, March 22, 31, 1842, pp. 9, 12.
18. *Ibid.*, May 5, 10, 1843, pp. 34-35.
19. *Ibid.*
20. *Ibid.*, February 25, March 4, 7, 10, 1842, pp. 4-6.
21. *Ibid.*, March 30, April 25, 1843, pp. 32-4.
22. *Ibid.*, March 20, 1848, p. 154.
23. *Ibid.*, March 30, May 10, 24, 1852, pp. 237, 239, 240-241.
24. *Ibid.*, December 10, 11, 1849, pp. 184-185.

THE OLD UNIVERSITY 603

25. See Chapter on First Faculty.
26. Ordinances and Resolutions of the Board of Trustees," 1822-1841, December 16, 1841, p. 293.
27. President Basil Manly's "Diary", 1834-1846, January 28, 1841, p. 221.
28. "Faculty Minutes," 1835-1837, March 15, 1836, p. 35.
29. "Minutes of the Proceedings of the Faculty," 1841-1854," December 18, 1851, p. 224.
30. Ibid., January 5, 1852, p. 224.
31. Ms. Papers, "Old University," Degrees and Awards, Ordinances of 1859, in Alabama Collection.
32. Little, pp. 12-13.
33. "Faculty Minutes," 1835-1837, October 30, 1835, p. 17.
34. Ibid., December 14, 1835, pp. 22; March 3, 1836, p. 30-31.
35. Laws of the University of Alabama, 1839, 1850, Ch. VII, Sec. 3, p. 11.
36. "Faculty Minutes," 1835-1837, October 28, 1836, p. 57.
37. Excerpts from "Faculty Ledger," 1843-1860.
38. "Minutes of the Proceedings of the Faculty," 1841-1854, February 3, 1843, p. 29.
39. Ibid., October 14, 1850, p. 198.
40. Ibid., April 17, 1852, p. 237.
41. "Faculty Minutes," 1835-1837, December 14, 1835, p. 23.
42. "Minutes of the Proceedings of the Faculty," 1841-1854, May 26, 1851, p. 208.
43. Ordinances for the Government of the University of Alabama, 1831, Ch. IV, Sec. 5.
44. Laws of the University of Alabama, 1839, Ch. VIII.
45. "Faculty Minutes," 1835-1837, April 14, 1837, p. 67.
46. "Minutes of the Proceedings of the Faculty," 1841-1854, October 25, and November 1, 1847, p. 145.
47. Ibid., March 13, 1848, p. 154. (The use of numerals to identify students of the same name was common.)
48. Ibid., May 12, 1843, p. 35.
49. Ibid., March 9, 1849, p. 171.
50. Ibid., November 3, and 9, 1843, pp. 49-50.
51. Ibid., February 16, 1852, p. 231.
52. Ibid., February 9, and 12, 1852, pp. 229-30.
53. Ibid., February 16, 1852, p. 231.
54. "Ordinances of 1831," Ch. IV, Sec. 10.
55. Laws of the University of Alabama, 1939, Ch. IX, Sec. 5, p. 14.
56. "Faculty Minutes," 1835-1837, December 14, 1835, p. 22.
57. Ibid., March 3, 1836, pp. 30-31.
58. Ibid., April 1, 1836, p. 36.
59. "Faculty Minutes," 1831-1835, February 23, 1833, January 31, 1834, February 24, 1834; "Minutes of the Proceedings of the Faculty," May 14, 1849, p. 173.
60. "Faculty Minutes," 1831-1835, March 6, 1834.
61. Ibid., 1831-1835, April 9, 1834.
62. Ibid., June 12, 1835, pp. 3-4.
63. Ibid., October 28, 1836, p. 56.
64. "Minutes of the Proceedings of the Faculty," 1842-1854, February 4, 1842, p. 3.
65. Ibid., February 3, 1843, p. 29.
66. Ibid., March 29 and April 3, 1844, p. 70.
67. Ibid., August 6, 1847, pp. 139-140.
68. Ibid., February 14, 1848, p. 152.
69. Ibid., March 5, and 19, 1849, pp. 170-171.
70. Ibid., January 19, 26; February 2, 9, 11, 1852, pp. 228-230.

71. *Ibid.*, February 9, 1852, p. 229.
72. See "Faculty Minutes," 1831-1835, March 27, 1832; *Ibid.*, 1835-1837, December 7, 1835, p. 32.
73. "Minutes of the Proceedings of the Faculty," 1841-1854, January 1, 1850, p. 185.
74. *Ibid.*, March 8 and 15, 1852, pp. 233-234.
75. *Ibid.*, July 27, 1843, pp. 43-44.
76. "Faculty Minutes," 1831-1835, July 24, August 10, 1833.
77. "Minutes of the Proceedings of the Faculty, 1841-1854," March 30 and 31, April 25, 1843, pp. 31-34.
78. *Ibid.*, November 22, 1847, p. 146.
79. *Ibid.*, September 31, October 2, 1848, pp. 162-164.
80. *Ibid.*, January 15, 1849, p. 169.
81. *Ibid.*, February 18, 1851, p. 203.
82. *Ibid.*, June 2, 1851, p. 208-9.
83. *Ibid.*, December 19, 1851, January 5, 1852, pp. 224 and 225.
84. *Ibid.*, December 12, 1853, p. 292.
85. Letter from Crenshaw Hall to his father, March 6, 1858.
86. Letter from Bolling Hall to his mother, March 4, 1858.
87. "Faculty Minutes," 1835-1837, May, 1836, p. 45.
88. Excerpts from "Faculty Ledger."
89. "Faculty Minutes," 1831-1835, November 12, 1833.
90. *Ibid.*, 1835-1837, April 10, 1836, p. 38.
91. "Minutes of the Proceedings of the Faculty," 1841-1854, June 10, 11, 1842, p. 14.
92. *Ibid.*, May 17, 1842, p. 13.
93. *Ibid.*, January 22, 1849, p. 169.
94. *Ibid.*, October 20, 1851, p. 216.
95. "Faculty Minutes," 1831-1835, March 6, 1834.
96. "Minutes of the Proceedings of the Faculty," 1841-1854, January 31, 1853, p. 267.
97. *Ibid.*, February 2, 1853, p. 268.
98. *Ibid.*
99. *Ibid.*, March 17, 1853, p. 272.
100. *Ibid.*, April 25, 1853, p. 275; May 23, 1853, p. 279.
101. *Ibid.*, March 29, 1852, p. 235.
102. Little, pp. 4-5.
103. Quoted from *Flag of the Union* (Tuscaloosa), February 8, 1843.
104. Thirty-three are listed as suspended in the faculty minutes of May 16, 1854. The Jacksonville *Republican,* June 6, 1854, gives the number as 35 and the Mobile *Daily Register,* of the same date, sets it at 34.
105. Little, p. 17.
106. Mobile *Daily Register,* June 6, 1854.
107. E. L. Green, *A History of the University of South Carolina,* p. 241.
108. *Ibid.*, p. 242.
109. P. A. Bruce, *History of the University of Virginia,* II, 298-299.
110. *Ibid.*, p. 294.
111. *Ibid.*, pp. 309-311.
112. E. W. Knight, "What Constitutes a Good History of a College," unpublished monograph.

CHAPTER X

1. "Report of Committee of Investigation, Appionted by the Board of Trustees, 1837", "Old University." See also, *Flag of the Union* (Tuscaloosa), August 9, 1837.
2. *Laws of the University of Alabama*, 1839, pp. 11-12.
3. Excerpts from the "Faculty Ledger."
4. "Faculty Minutes," 1835-1837, April 4, 1837, p. 67.
5. "Minutes of the Proceedings of the Faculty," 1841-1854, June 20, 1842, p. 15.
6. *Ibid.*, June 21, 1847, p. 135.
7. *Ibid.*, December 7, 1847, p. 147.
8. *Ibid.*, October 27 and 29, 1851, p. 217.
9. *Ibid.*, October 1, 1853, p. 287.
10. "Faculty Minutes," 1831-1835, n. d.
11. *Ibid.*, March 9, 1833.
12. Roberts, p. 2.
13. *Ibid.*, and "Faculty Minutes," 1831-1835, April 22, 1835.
14. "Faculty Minutes," 1831-1835, April 15, 1835.
15. *Ibid.*, April 22, 1835.
16. *Ibid.*, June 1, 1835.
17. "Faculty Minutes," 1835-1837, March 9-10, 1836, pp. 32-33.
18. *Ibid.*, June 2, 1837, p. 77.
19. "Minutes of the Proceedings of the Faculty," 1841-1854, November 17, 1843, p. 54.
20. *Ibid.*, June 11 and 13, 1844, pp. 73-74.
21. Letter from Bolling Hall to his mother, Tuscaloosa, Alabama, May 9, 1858.
22. Bruce, pp. 294-295.
23. E. M. Coulter, *College Life In The Old South*, p. 97.
24. "Faculty Minutes," 1835-1837, July 16, 1835, p. 6; March 14, 1836, p. 33.
25. *Ibid.*, September 20, 1836, p. 52.
26. *Ibid.*, April 26, 1836, p. 42.
27. "Faculty Minutes," 1831-1835, March 9, 1833.
28. *Ibid.*, March 8, 1834.
29. "Minutes of the Proceedings of the Faculty," 1841-1854, May 5, and 11, 1843, pp. 34-35.
30. "Faculty Minutes," 1835-1837, March 29, 1837, p. 66.
31. "Minutes of the Proceedings of the Faculty," 1841-1854, May 17, 1842, p. 13.
32. *Ibid.*, July 3, 1843, p. 40.
33. *Ibid.*, July 3, 1843, pp. 40-41.
34. *Ibid.*, July 5, 1843, p. 41.
35. *Ibid.*, July 7, 1843, p. 41.
36. *Ibid.*, October 2, 1843, p. 45.
37. *Ibid.*, January 22-24, 1844, p. 67.
38. *Ibid.*, March 24, 1845, p. 89.
39. *Ibid.*, April 26, 1845, p. 91.
40. *Ibid.*, February 16, and 20, 1846, p. 108-9.
41. *Ibid.*, February 27, 1846, p. 110.
42. *Ibid.*, December 12, 1851, to January 14, 1852, pp. 221-227.
43. *Ibid.*, June 1845, p. 94.
44. *Ibid.*, September 26, 1845, p. 98.
45. *President Manly's "Diary,"* 1848-1855, June 22, p. 85.

46. *Ibid.*, February 25, 1842, p. 4.
47. *Ibid.*, June 17 and 19, October 20, 1843, pp. 39 and 48.
48. *Ibid.*, November 3, 1843, p. 49.
49. *Ibid.*, October 20, 1843, p. 47.
50. *Ibid.*, May 24, 1847, p. 133.
51. *Ibid.*, September 30, 1848, p. 162.
52. *Ibid.*, October 13, 1851, p. 215.
53. *Ibid.*, October 20, 1843, p. 48.
54. *Ibid.*, October 3, 1845, p. 98.
55. *Ibid.*, March 13, 1846, p. 110.
56. *Ibid.*, January 29, 1849, p. 169.
57. *Ibid.*, November 30, 1846, p. 120.
58. *Ibid.*, November 27, 1848, p. 166.
59. *Ibid.*, March 13, 1851, p. 207.
60. *Ibid.*, January 31, 1853, pp. 267-268.
61. *Ibid.*, February 16, 1852, p. 231.
62. *Ibid.*, June 24, 1850, p. 169.
63. *Ibid.*, February 20, 1849, p. 169.
64. *Ibid.*, January 5, 1853, p. 265.
65. *Ibid.*, December 3, 1849, p. 183.
66. *Laws of 1831*, Ch. V, Sec. 2; *Laws of 1839*, Ch. XVII, Sec. 1.
67. "Faculty Minutes," 1831-1835, March 8, 1834.
68. "Faculty Minutes," 1835-1837, September 26, 1836, p. 53.
69. *Ibid.*, June 2, 1837, p. 77.
70. "Minutes of the Proceedings of the Faculty," 1841-1854, March 15, 1842, p. 6.
71. President Manly's "Diary," 1843-1848, January 19, 1848.
72. *Ibid.*, 1848-1855, January 18, 1851, p. 106.
73. *Ibid.*, October 31, 1851, p. 150.
74. Excerpts from the "Faculty Ledger," October, 1843 to July, 1860.
75. President Basil Manly's Diary," 1848-1855, January 21, 1851, pp. 106-107.
76. "Minutes of the Proceedings of the Faculty," 1841-1854, December 20-22, 1846, p. 123.
77. Excerpts from the "Faculty Ledger".
78. "Minutes of the Proceedings of the Faculty," 1841-1854, January 25, 1847, p. 127.
79. Excerpts from the "Faculty Ledger."
80. *Ibid.*
81. "Students' Ledger," 1838-1865.
82. President Manly's "Diary," 1843-1848, January 26, 1848, pp. 208, 211 and *Ibid.*, 1847-1857, January 26, 1848, p. 54.
83. *Ibid.*, 1846-1857, July 13, 1855, p. 378.
84. Bruce, p. 295.
85. *Ibid.*, p. 297.
86. Greene, pp. 244-246.
87. Morris Raymond Boucher, "Factors in the History of Tuscaloosa, Alabama, 1816-1846," Master's Thesis, University of Alabama, University, Alabama, 1847, pp. 21-23.
88. "Faculty Minutes," 1831-1835, October 3 and 4, 1831.
89. *Ibid.*, November 4, 1831.
90. *Ibid.*
91. *Ibid.*, April 12, 1833.
92. *Acts of the First Biennial Session of the General Assembly*, 1847, p. 63.

THE OLD UNIVERSITY

93. "Minutes and Records of the Circuit Court of Tuscaloosa County, 1848-1855," September, 1850, pp. 222-224.
94. *Ibid.*, March, 1854, pp. 522-523.
95. "Faculty Minutes," 1834-1835, January 14, 1833.
96. "Faculty Minutes," 1835-1837, March 14, 1836, pp. 33-34.
97. *Ibid.*, March 14, 1836, p. 34.
98. *Ibid.*, March 15, 1836, p. 34.
99. "Minutes of the Proceedings of the Faculty," 1841-1854, October 11, 1847, p. 144.
100. *Ibid.*, January 18, 1848, p. 150.
101. *Ibid.*, March 23, April 17, 1848, pp. 154 and 155.
102. *Ibid.*, January 1, 27, February 3, March 3, 1851, pp. 201-204.
103. *Ibid.*, November 3, 1851, p. 218.
104. *Ibid.*, December 1 and 8, 1851, p. 220.
105. *Ibid.*, January 6, 8, 12, 1852, pp. 226-227.
106. *Ibid.*, March 1, 8, 15, 1852, pp. 232-234.
107. *Ibid.*, December 13, 1852, p. 263.
108. *Ibid.*
109. "Report of the Grand Jury," *The Monitor* (Tuscaloosa), October 14, 1858.
110. *Flag of the Union* (Tuscaloosa), October 3, 1835.
111. "Faculty Minutes," 1831-1835.
112. Bruce, p. 97.
113. Coulter, p. 113.
114. Bruce, p. 279.
115. Coulter, p. 103.
116. *Independent Monitor* (Tuscaloosa), June 11, 1859.
117. Records of Tuscaloosa County, "Circuit Court Minutes, State and Civil Cases," Book II, 1856-1867, September term, 1859, October 5, p. 183.
118. "Faculty Minutes," 1835-1837, November 30, December 6, 1835, pp. 20-21.
119. *Ibid.*, November 20, and 27; "Minutes of the Proceedings of the Faculty," 1841-1854, December 16, 1848, pp. 166-167.
120. *Ibid.*, November 20, and 27, December 16, 1848, pp. 166-167.
121. *Ibid.*, February 9, 11, and 12, 1852, pp. 229-230.
122. *Ibid.*, June 23, 1851, p. 210.
123. This house, commonly called the Governor's Mansion, is now occupied by the University Club.
124. Reply to Circular Letter, printed in Mobile *Commercial Register*, June 6, 1835.
125. Circular Letter to the Parents and Trustees, "Faculty Minutes," 1831-1835, April 7, 1835.
126. Mobile *Commercial Register*, June 6, 1835.
127. Letter from Crenshaw Hall to his mother, March 20, 1858.
128. Letter from Crenshaw Hall to his father, July 2, 1858.
129. Letter from Bolling Hall to his father, June 8, 1858.
130. From the statement issued to the Patrons of the University in the *Tuscaloosa Monitor* and reprinted in *The Independent* (Gainesville), June 19, 1858. Other sources, of information on the Herring case include *The Monitor*, June 10, 24, July 1, 1858; *Daily Confederation* (Montgomery), June 11; *Advertiser and Gazette* (Montgomery), June 16, 23, 1858.
131. Reprinted in *The Monitor* (Tuscaloosa), February 26, 1859.
132. *Loc. cit.*, Another version of the party is given in the Chapter on Students.
133. *Loc. cit.*, March 19, 1859.

CHAPTER XI

1. C. Huse, "Personal Reminiscences and unpublished History".
2. *Weekly Advertiser* (Montgomery), February 6, 1861.
3. Quoted in *The West Alabamian* (Carrollton), March 6, 1861.
4. *Ibid.*
5. Letter from L. C. Garland to Governor J. G. Shorter, November 24, 1863.
6. Letter from L. C. Garland to Governor J. G. Shorter, September 5, 1863.
7. Letter from L. C. Garland to Governor J. G. Shorter, November 24, 1862.
8. Report of President L. C. Garland and Judge J. J. Ormond, 1860.
9. Huse.
10. Samuel Will John, "Alabama Corps of Cadets, 1860-65," *Confederate Veteran,* January, 1917.
11. *Ibid.*
12. Huse.
13. *Ibid.*
14. Letter from L. C. Garland to General Gideon J. Pillow, December 18, 1863.
15. J. A. Anderson, "Military History of the University of Alabama."
16. Letter from E. B. Thompson to his uncle, November 26, 1860.
17. Letter from L. C. Garland to Governor J. G. Shorter, November 24, 1862.
18. Anderson.
19. Letter to Governor A. B. Moore, June 14, 1861.
20. *The Beacon* (Greensboro), July 5, 1861.
21. Letter from L. C. Garland to Governor J. G. Shorter, September 5, 1863.
22. *The Beacon (Greensboro),* July 5, 1861.
23. Letter from L. C. Garland to Governor T. H. Watts, May 14, 1864.
24. The Virginia Military Institute, the Citadel Academy of South Carolina, and the Institute of Georgia limited their wartime curriculum to military studies.
25. "University of Alabama Record Book," 1838-1865.
26. Letter from L. C. Garland to Gen. Gideon J. Pillow, December 18, 1863.
27. John.
28. Report from L. C. Garland to Gov. J. G. Shorter, October 16, 1862.
29. Letter from L. C. Garland to Gov. J. G. Shorter, October 30, 1862.
30. Letter from L. C. Garland to Gov. T. H. Watts, March 10, 1864.
31. Letter from L. C. Garland to J. J. Thornton, Forkland, September 4, 1863.
32. Letter from L. C. Garland to Gov. J. G. Shorter, September 24, 1863.
33. Letter from L. C. Garland to Amos Jones, Camden, September 19, 1863.
34. Letter from L. C. Garland to R. Weaver, Eutaw, September 22, 1863.
35. Letter from L. C. Garland to Gov. J. G. Shorter, February 3, 1863.
36. Letter from L. C. Garland to B. E. Norris, Batesville, Miss., November 6, 1862.
37. Letters from L. C. Garland to Gov. T. H. Watts, January 25, April 13, 1864.
38. Letter from L. C. Garland to Confederate Sec. of War, April 30, 1864.
39. Letter from L. C. Garland to Gen. G. J. Pillow, December 18, 1863.
40. Letter from L. C. Garland to Gov. J. G. Shorter, February 3, 1863.
41. Letter from L. C. Garland to Gov. J. G. Shorter, October 16, 1862.
42. Letter from L. C. Garland to Gov. J. G. Shorter, February 3, 1863.
43. Letter from L. C. Garland to Col. Spann, Commander, Post at Tuscaloosa, September 22, 1863.
44. Letters from L. C. Garland to Gov. T. H. Watts, December 7, 1863.
45. Letter from L. C. Garland to Gov. T. H. Watts, March 29, 1854.
46. Letter from Prof. Jno. W. Pratt, to Dr. G. G. Griffin, Demopolis, October 1, 1862.
47. Letter from L. C. Garland to Gov. J. G. Shorter, February 17, 1863.

THE OLD UNIVERSITY 609

48. Letter from L. C. Garland to Gov. T. H. Watts, May 14, 1864.
49. Letter from L. C. Garland to Gov. J. G. Shorter, September 27, 1862.
50. Letter from L. C. Garland to Gov. T. H. Watts, March 29, 1864.
51. Letter from L. C. Garland to President of the Board of Trustees, May 14, 1864.
52. *Ibid.*
53. Letter from L. C. Garland to R. Weaver, Eutaw, November 19, 1863.
54. "Governors' Answers to Letters," December 6, 1861-May 13, 1863. Letter from Gov. J. G. Shorter to L. C. Garland, February 16, 1863, p. 324.
55. Letter from L. C. Garland to Hon. J. M. Calhoun, Richmond, Alabama, May 23, 1864.
56. Letter from L. C. Garland to Gov. J. G. Shorter, February 3, 1863.
57. "Old University Records."
58. Letter from L. C. Garland to Gov. T. H. Watts, January 25, 1864.
59. Letter from Gov. T. H. Watts to Sec. of War, February 1, 1864.
60. Letter from L. C. Garland to Capt. Slaughter, enrolling officer at Tuscaloosa, June 15, 1864.
61. Letter from L. C. Garland to Gov. T. H. Watts, March 17, 1864.
62. Letter from L. C. Garland to Gov. T. H. Watts, April, 1864.
63. *Ibid.*
64. Letter from L. C. Garland to Lt. Gen. Polk, March 1864.
65. Letter from L. C. Garland to Brigadier-Gen. W. H. Jackson, March 30, 1865.
66. Letter from L. C. Garland to Gov. J. G. Shorter, October 31, 1862.
67. Letter from L. C. Garland to Gov. J. G. Shorter, May 4, 1863.
68. Letter from L. C. Garland to Gov. J. G. Shorter, May 7, 1863.
69. *Ibid.*
70. *Ibid.*
71. Letters from L. C. Garland to Gov. J. G. Shorter, May 4 and 7, 1863.
72. Letter from L. C. Garland to Gov. T. H. Watts, January 22, 1864.
73. Petition to the Governor of Alabama, December 28, 1863.
74. John.
75. *Ibid.*
76. *Ibid.*

CHAPTER XII

1. Report of Gen. J. T. Croxton, *Records of the War of the Rebellion*, Series 1, Vol. 49, Part 1, p. 418.
2. *Ibid.*
3. *Ibid.*, See also T. P. Clinton, "The Military Operations of Gen. John T. Croxton In West Alabama," *Transactions Of The Alabama Historical Society*, 1899-1903, IV, 449-463.
4. Report of Gen. J. T. Croxton.
5. Clinton.
6. Report of Capt. A. B. Hardcastle, *Records of the War of the Rebellion*, Series 1, Vol. 49, Part 1, p. 505.
7. Clinton.
8. *Ibid.*
9. Report of Gen. J. T. Croxton.
10. Clinton.
11. Anderson.
12. Clinton.
13. John.

14. Clinton.
15. Tuscaloosa *News,* The Tuscaloosa Story Edition, July 31, 1949.
16. Report of Capt. A. B. Hardcastle.
17. Clinton.
18. John.
19. Clinton.
20. Anderson.
21. *Ibid.*
22. *Ibid.*
23. Report of Gen. J. T. Croxton.
24. Clinton.
25. John.
26. *Ibid.*
27. *Campaigns of Forrest* (1868).
28. Taken from bronze tablet in Morgan Hall.
29. T. W. Palmer, *A Register of the Officers and Students of the University of Alabama,* 1831-1901, *passim.*

In 1907 a legislative act provided that all students enrolled from 1861 to 1865 be classed as graduates of the University, regardless of the length of time they attended. Diplomas in blank form were prepared and sent to those present at next commencement or the next of kin. This honor roll listed 624 names.

CHAPTER XIII

1. "Minutes of the Board of Trustee," 1865-1868, December 7, 1865, pp. 5-7.
2. *Ibid.,* p. 7.
3. *Ibid.,* pp. 9-11.
4. *Ibid.,* p. 13.
5. *Ibid.*
6. *Ibid.,* p. 17.
7. *Acts of the General Assembly,* Approved, February 20, 1866.
8. "Minutes of the Board of Trustees," 1865-1868, February 27, 1866, p. 21.
9. *Ibid.,* p. 21.
10. *Ibid.,* May 12, 1866, pp. 28-31.
11. *Ibid.,* p. 39.
12. *Ibid.,* p. 33.
13. *Ibid.,* pp. 39-41.
14. *Ibid.,* June 4, 1866, p. 43.
15. *Ibid.,* July 19, 1866, pp. 47-53.
16. *Ibid.,* November 20, 1866, pp. 70-71.
17. *Ibid.,* November 20, 1866, p. 68.
18. *Ibid.,* November 21, 1866, p. 73.
19. *Ibid.,* November 22, 1866, pp. 77-79.
20. *Ibid.,* November 22, 1866, p. 80.
21. *Ibid.,* November 20, 1866, p. 68.
22. *Ibid.,* December 8, 1866, pp. 85-87.
23. *Ibid.,* March 12, 1867, p. 97.
24. *Ibid.,* June 25, 1867, p. 100.
25. *Ibid.,* July 15, 1867, pp. 109-110.
26. *Ibid.,* March 13, 1868, p. 126.
27. *Ibid.,* April 28, 1868, pp. 133-134.
28. *Ibid.,* April 29, 1868, p. 138.

REBUILDING THE UNIVERSITY

29. J. T. Murfee, "Book of Letters," 1867-1887.
30. "Minutes of the Board of Trustees," 1865-1868, April 29, 1868, p. 137.
31. *Ibid.*, April 28, 1868, pp. 135-150.
32. *Ibid.*, June 12, 1868, pp. 155-156.
33. *Alabama Constitution of 1867*, Article XI, Sections 4 & 6.
34. Tuscaloosa *Times*, April 1, 1874.
35. Montgomery *Mail*, Quoted in the *Independent Monitor*, August 18, 1868.
36. "Minutes of the Board of Regents," 1868-1869, August 5, 1868, p. 162.
37. *Ibid.*, August 5, 1868, p. 163.
38. *Ibid.*, August 5, 1868, p. 165.
39. *Independent Monitor* (Tuscaloosa), August 18, 1868.
40. "Minutes of the Board of Regents," 1868-1869, August 5, 1868, p. 163; and *Independent Monitor*, August 18, 1868.
41. "Minutes of the Board of Regents," 1868-1869, August 6, 1868, pp. 164-165.
42. *Independent Monitor* (Tuscaloosa), September 15, 1868.
43. S. Horn, *Invisible Empire*, p. 117.
44. *Independent Monitor*, August 11, 1868.
45. Horn, p. 129.
46. "Minutes of the Board of Regents," 1868-1869, December 15, 1868, p. 168.
47. Horn, p. 129.
48. *Independent Monitor*, January 5, 1869.
49. "Minutes of the Board of Regents," December 16, 1868, pp. 171-172.
50. *Ibid.*, December 23, 1868, p. 191.
51. Tuscaloosa *Observer*, January 2, 1869.
52. Independent *Monitor*, February 9, 1869.
53. *Ibid.*, March 23, 1869.
54. *Ibid.*, April 13, 1869.
55. Montgomery *Advertiser*, June 12, 1869.
56. *Independent Monitor*, July 27, 1869.
57. *Weekly State Journal* (Montgomery), August 14, 1869.
58. "Minutes of the Board of Regents," 1868-1869, August 21, 1869, pp. 230-231.
59. *Independent Monitor*, August 28, 1869.
60. *Ibid.*, September 25, 1869.
61. "Minutes of the Board of Regents," 1868-1869, August 21, 1869, p. 236.
62. *Weekly State Journal* (Montgomery), August 28, 1869.
63. Tuscaloosa *Observer*, August 21, 1869.
64. *Independent Monitor*, August 24, 1869.
65. *Ibid.*, April 5, April 26, and May 3; and *Alabama State Journal* (Montgomery), April 8, 1869.
66. Montgomery *Advertiser*, quoted in *Independent Monitor*, July 12, 1870.
67. *Independent Monitor*, September 13, 1870.
68. *Ibid.*, June 28, 1870.
69. "Address from the Board of Education to the Alumni of the University of Alabama," reprinted in *Independent Monitor*, March 21, 1871.
70. *Daily State Journal* (Montgomery), April 1, 1871.
71. Montgomery *Advance*, July 18, 1871.
72. *Southern Argus*, quoted in *Independent Monitor*, July 5, 1871.
73. *Independent Monitor*, September 27, 1871 "Faculty Minutes," 1871-1878, July 17, 1871, p. 1.
74. "Faculty Minutes," 1871-1878, September 21, October 2, 1871, pp. 2-3.
75. *Independent Monitor*, November 8, 1871.
76. *Corolla*, 1893, pp. 94-95.

CHAPTER XIV

1. *Corolla*, 1895, p. 78.
2. "Faculty Minutes," 1871-1878, November 17 to December 1, 1871, pp. 29-31, 37 and 47.
3. *House Journal*, 1866-1867, pp. 97-98.
4. *State Documents*, 1871-1872, October 25, 1871, pp. 28-31.
5. *Daily State Journal* (Montgomery), February 16, 1872.
6. *The Spectator* (Northport), February 24, 1874.
7. "Faculty Minutes," 1871-1878, December 18, 1872, pp. 116-117.
8. *Ibid.*, May 24, 1873, pp. 128-129.
9. *Ibid.*, June 26, 1873, p. 133.
10. *Ibid.*, July 4, 1874, p. 154.
11. "Regents Minutes," 1873-1874, June 29, 1874, pp. 64-65, 67.
12. *Ibid.*, June 30 and July 2, 1874, pp. 72-74, 82-84.
13. *Corolla*, 1895, pp. 79-80.
14. Huntsville *Democrat*, reprinted in Tuscaloosa *Times*, October 7, 1874.
15. "Regents Minutes," 1874-1875, November 21, 1874, p. 2.
16. *Ibid.*, November 28, 1874; July 6 and 8, 1875, pp. 27-28, 56, 59.
17. *Acts of the General Assembly of Alabama*, Session of 1875-76, pp. 268-272.
18. "Trustees Minutes," 1876-1888, July 1878, pp. 99-103.
19. Quote from Selma *Times*, as reprinted in Tuscaloosa *Gazette*, July 18, 1878.
20. Tuscaloosa *Gazette*, July 18, 1878.
21. Selma *Argus*, reprinted in Tuscaloosa *Gazette*, August 8, 1878.
22. "Trustees Minutes," 1876-1888, July 1878, pp. 99-103.
23. *Corolla*, 1895, pp. 79-80.
24. Tuscaloosa *Gazette*, August 1, 1878.
25. From the Montgomery *Advertiser*, reprinted in the Tuscaloosa *Gazette*, February 27, 1879.
26. "Annual Report of W. S. Wyman, President *pro tem* to the Board of Trustees," July 1879, p. 77.
27. "Trustees Minutes," 1876-1888, July, 1879, pp. 148-151.
28. *Ibid.*, September, 1879, pp. 166-167.
29. *Ibid.*, September 30, 1879, printed in Tuscaloosa *Gazette*, October 9, 1879.
30. *Ibid.*, June, 1883, p. 267.
31. *Ibid.*, June 1883, pp. 284, 287.
32. *Ibid.*, September, 1879, p. 160.
33. *Ibid.*, September 1879, pp. 165-166.
34. Mobile *Register*, reprinted in Tuscaloosa *Gazette*, July 24, 1879.
35. *Corolla*, 1895, pp. 83-84.
36. Eufaula *Times and News*, reprinted in Tuscaloosa *Gazette*, October 9, 1879.
37. Tuscaloosa *Gazette*, October 2, 1879.
38. "Trustees Minutes," 1876-1888, November, 1885, pp. 402-406.
39. Tuscaloosa *Times*, May 19, 1886.
40. *Ibid.*, June, 1886, p. 410.
41. "Trustees Minutes," 1876-1888, June, 1886, p. 421.
42. "Faculty Minutes," September 21, 1886-June 5, 1893, October 21, 1889, p. 144.
43. Tuscaloosa *Gazette*, June, 1886, p. 419.
44. *Ibid.*, September 23, 1886.
45. "Trustees Minutes," 1876-1888, June, 1888, p. 540.
46. *Ibid.*, 1888-1889, June 20, 1890, pp. 173-174.
47. *Ibid.*, 1876-1888, June, 1888, p. 516.
48. "Trustees Minutes," 1876-1888, 1877, p. 61.

REBUILDING THE UNIVERSITY

49. "Trustees Minutes," 1876-1888, June, 1888, p. 527.
50. "Trustees Minutes," 1888-1895, June 21, 1889, p. 50.
51. *Ibid.,* June, 1889, p. 99.
52. "Trustees Minutes," 1876-1888, June, 1888, p. 533.
53. "Trustees Minutes," 1888-1895, November 14, 1889, pp. 12, 114.
54. Tuscaloosa *Gazette,* October 24, 1889.
55. *Ibid.,* June 19, 1890.
56. "Trustees Minutes," 1888-1895, June 18, 1890, pp. 163-164.
57. *Ibid.,* June 19, 1890, p. 176.
58. Tuscaloosa *Gazette,* June 26, 1890.
59. "Trustees Minutes," 1896-1901, June 17, 18, 1896, pp. 15, 18, 19.
60. Mobile *Register,* reprinted in Tuscaloosa *Gazette,* August 27, 1896.
61. Tuscaloosa *Gazette,* September 10, 1896.
62. *Ibid.,* August 27, 1896.
63. Tuscaloosa *Times,* February 3, 1897.
64. *Ibid.,* March 24, 1897.
65. "Trustees Minutes," 1896-1901, January 10, 1901, p. 505.
66. Tuscaloosa *Gazette,* October 8, 1879.
67. "Faculty Minutes," 1871-1878, March 8, 1872, p. 67.
68. Tuscaloosa *Times,* January 13, 1899.
69. "Trustees Minutes," 1908-1916, May 28, 1908, p. 61.

CHAPTER XV

1. "Minutes of the Board of Trustees," 1876-1888, July 3, 1877, p. 48.
2. *Trustees of University V. Moody,* 62 *Alabama,* 389.
3. "Minutes of the Board of Trustees," 1876-1888, July 5, 1881, pp. 200-201.
4. *Ibid.,* July 5, 1881, pp. 200-201.
5. Hayneville *Examiner,* September 5, 1883.
6. Greenville *Advocate,* February 28, 1883.
7. "Minutes of the Trustees," 1876-1888, June 20, 1883, pp. 272-335.
8. *Ibid.,* May 5, 1884, pp. 300, 302.
9. *Ibid.,* June 18, 1885, pp. 379-386.
10. *Ibid.,* April 14, 1885, pp. 335-337.
11. *Alabama Acts,* 1884-1885, p. 109.
12. "Minutes of the Board of Trustees," 1876-1888, June 16, 1885, pp. 352-355.
13. *Ibid.,* June 18, 1885, pp. 372-376.
14. *Ibid.,* June 14, 1885, p. 369.
15. *Ibid.,* June 24, 1886, pp. 445-451.
16. *Ibid.,* June 20, 1887, pp. 466, 491, 494.
17. *Ibid.,* June 22, 1888, pp. 561-564.
18. *Ibid.,* June 19, 1888, p. 518.
19. *Ibid.,* June 18, 1888, pp. 518-519; also July 6, 1881, p. 216.
20. *Ibid.,* 1888-1895, June 15, 1889, pp. 106-109.
21. *Ibid.,* February 12, 1890, pp. 135-136.
22. *Ibid.,* June 18, 1890, p. 159.
23. *Ibid.,* June 18, 1890, pp. 206-209.
24. *Ibid.,* 1896-1901; December 20, 1899, p. 365.
25. *Ibid.,* 1888-1895, June 15, and 20, 1891, pp. 300-303, 304.
26. *Ibid.,* February 9, 1892, pp. 312-313.
27. *Ibid.,* June 20, 1892, pp. 384-389.
28. *Ibid.,* June 18, 1892, pp. 418-423.
29. *Ibid.,* June 20, 1892, pp. 384-389.

30. *Ibid.*, February 9, 1892, pp. 309-312.
31. *Ibid.*, June 20, 1893, pp. 495-463.
32. *Ibid.*, June 20, 1894, pp. 565-568.
33. *Ibid.*, June 15, 1895, Appendix, p. 14.
34. *Ibid.*, 1896-1901, June 20, 1897, pp. 171-177.
35. *Ibid.*, June 20, 1898, pp. 255-256.
36. *Ibid.*, June 20, 1897, pp. 171-177.
37. *Ibid.*, 1901-1907, January 23, 1902, p. 142.
38. *Ibid.*, 1896-1901, June 19, 1896, pp. 33-35; June 20, 1897, p. 175; February 25, 1898, p. 206.
39. *Ibid.*, 1896-1901, June 20, 1898, p. 225.
40. *Ibid.*, June 21, 1899, pp. 332-338.
41. *Ibid.*, June 20, 1898, pp. 255-256.
42. Birmingham *Ledger,* quoted in Tuscaloosa *Gazette,* January 30, 1902.
43. "Minutes of the Trustees," 1896-1901, June 14, 1900, pp. 466-470.
44. *Ibid.*, 1901-1907, May 30, 1905, pp. 387-388, 409-470.
45. *Ibid.*, 1896-1901, September 22, 1899, pp. 344-350.
46. *Ibid.*, December 20, 1899, p. 361.
47. *Ibid.*, December 20, 1899, pp. 363; 366; 370.
48. *Ibid.*, June 14, 1900, pp. 466-470.
49. *Sloss-Sheffield Steel & Iron Company v. the Board of Trustees of The University of Alabama,* 130 *Alabama,* 403.
50. "Minutes of the Trustees," 1901-1907, June 3, 1901, pp. 69-76.
51. *Ibid.*, May 30, 1905, p. 387.
52. *Ibid.*, June 1, 1903, pp. 265-267.
53. *Ibid.*, 1876-1888, June 20, 1883, pp. 260-261.
54. *Ibid.*, November 6, 1883, pp. 292-294.
55. *Ibid.*, November 5, 1883, pp. 289-290.
56. *Ibid.*, June 17, 1884, p. 311.
57. *Ibid.*, June 17, 1884, pp. 313-317; Alabama University *Monthly,* XI June, 1884.
58. Alabama University *Monthly,* XI, May, 1884; "Trustees Minutes," 1876-1888.
59. *Ibid.*, June 18, 1885, pp. 396-398.
60. *Ibid.*, June 23, 1886, p. 443.
61. *Ibid.*, June 24, 1886, p. 420.
62. *Ibid.*, 1888-1895, June 16, 1888, p. 2.
63. *Ibid.*, June 19, 1889, p. 35.
64. *Ibid.*, June 16, 1888, pp. 9-10.
65. *Ibid.*, June 15, 1889, p. 79.
66. *Ibid.*, June, 1885, pp. 351-352.
67. *Ibid.*, June, 1888, p. 490.
68. *Ibid.*, October, 1876, p. 31; July, 1877, p. 58.
69. *Ibid.*, June, 1865, pp. 351-352.
70. *Ibid.*, July 3, 1878, p. 79.
71. *Ibid.*, July 3, 1879, p. 135.
72. *Ibid.*, July 1879, p. 138.
73. *Ibid.*, June, 1882, p. 250.
74. *Ibid.*, June, 1887, p. 473.
75. *Ibid.*, June, 1888, pp. 547-548.
76. *Ibid.*, June, 1888, pp. 539, 555.
77. *Ibid.*, June, 1888, p. 539.
78. *Ibid.*, June, 1888, p. 525.
79. *Ibid.*, June 21, 1888, p. 530.
80. *Ibid.*, June, 1884, p. 307-327.
81. *Ibid.*, June, 1887, p. 502.

… REBUILDING THE UNIVERSITY

82. *Ibid.*, June 23, 1887, p. 489-490.
83. *Ibid.*, 1888-1895, February 12, 1890, p. 134.
84. *Ibid.*, 1896-1901, June 21, 1899, p. 332-338.
85. *Ibid.*, 1876-1888, June, 1887, p. 500.
86. *Ibid.*, November, 1883, pp. 291-292, 296.
87. *Ibid.*, September, 1879, pp. 163-165.
88. *Ibid.*, September, 1879, pp. 166, 189-194.
89. *Ibid.*, June 1888, p. 543.
90. *Ibid.*, June, 1883, p. 271.
91. *Ibid.*, June, 1884, p. 326.
92. *Ibid.*, June, 1887, pp. 458, 490.
93. *Ibid.*, January 14, 1879, p. 116.
94. *Ibid.*, June, 1889, pp. 498-499.
95. *Ibid.*, 1896-1901, June 18, 1896, p. 16.
96. J. H. Fitts, *An Appeal from the Alumni of the University of Alabama*, Tuscaloosa, October, 1896.
97. *Senate Journal*, 1898, December 13, p. 35.
98. *Ibid.*, 1898, December 13, pp. 1031-1049.
99. *Ibid.*, p. 351.
100. *Ibid.*, 1898, December 13, pp. 1052-1066.
101. *Alabama Acts*, 1896-7, p. 901; An act of 1899 provided for the same appropriation for the years 1900-1901.
102. *Alabama Constitution*, 1901, Article 14, Selection 265.
103. *Reports of the Auditor of the State of Alabama*, for years 1869-1901.

CHAPTER XVI

1. *Catalogue*, 1872-1873, p. 18; see also *Catalogue*, 1873-1874.
2. "Trustees Minutes," 1896-1901, June 21, 1899, pp. 305-306.
3. *Ibid.*, June 19, 1899, p. 270.
4. *Catalogue*, 1894-1895, pp. 52-53.
5. "Trustees Minutes," 1876-1888, June, 1883, pp. 268-269.
6. *Ibid.*, 1896-1901, p. 108.
7. "Trustees Minutes," 1896-1901, June 21, 1897, pp. 118-120.
8. *Catalogue*, 1871-1872, p. 25.
9. The *Catalogue* says that Bachelor of Letters was similar to the Bachelor of Philosophy with the omission of mathematics. But mathematics was not required for the Bachelor of Philosophy. There is an obvious error here. Study of the currimulum indicates that the Bachelor of Arts course was meant.
10. *Catalogue*, 1874-1875, pp. 15-16.
11. *Ibid.*
12. *Catalogue*, 1890-1891, p. 35.
13. *Catalogue*, 1893-1894, pp. 30-31.
14. *Catalogue*, 1889-1890, p. 29.
15. "Trustees Minutes," 1876-1888, July, 1879, p. 142.
16. "Faculty Minutes," 1878-1886, October 8, 1880, pp. 46-47.
17. *Ibid.*, September 21, 1881.
18. "Faculty Minutes," 1893, 1899, October 18, 1897, p. 231-233.
19. Material on the contents of courses is taken from the *Catalogues* for 1878-1879; and 1898-1899.
20. "Faculty Minutes," 1878-1886, October 27, 1871, p. 8.
21. *Catalogue*, 1871-1872, p. 24.
22. *Ibid.*
23. *Catalogue*, 1872-1873, pp. 32-33.

24. *Ibid.*
25. *Ibid.*, 1878-1879, p. 30.
26. *Ibid.*, 1872-1873, pp. 32-33.
27. "Trustees Minutes," 1876-1888, June, 1886, pp. 432-433.
28. *Ibid.*, 1896-1901, March 11, 1897, pp. 107-108.
29. *Ibid.*, July 8, 1897, p. 196.
30. *Catalogue*, 1875-1876, pp. 25-27.
31. *Ibid.*, 1879-1880, pp. 26-27.
32. "Trustees Minutes," 1888-1895, June, 1899, p. 548.
33. *Catalogue*, 1897-1898, pp. 75-76.
34. *Catalogue*, 1875-1876, p. 27.
35. *Ibid.*, 1897-1898, pp. 70-72.
36. *Acts of the Seventh Biennial Session of the General Assembly of Alabama . . .* 1859, pp. 350-351.
37. "Trustees Minutes," 1888-1895, June 20, 21, 1889, pp. 40-41, 53.
38. *Ibid.*, 1896-1901, March 11, 1897, pp. 99-100.
39. "Faculty Minutes," 1893-1899, January 11, 1897, pp. 179-180.
40. "Faculty Minutes," 1893-1899, March 8, 1897, pp. 183-185.
41. "Trustees Minutes," 1896-1901, March 11, 1897, pp. 95, 104.
42. Summary of points in "Faculty Minutes," April 5, 1897, pp. 188-191.
43. "Trustees Minutes," 1896-1901, June 21, 1897, p. 114.
44. *General Laws of the Legislature of Alabama . . . 1907,* Approved, March 6, 1907.
45. *Corolla,* 1897, pp. 98-102.
46. *Ibid.*
47. *Ibid.*
48. *Catalogue,* 1896-1897, pp. 59-62.
49. *Catalogue,* 1877-1878, p. 23.
50. "Faculty Minutes," 1886-1893, November 24, December 1, 1890, p. 195.
51. *Catalogue,* 1898-1899, pp. 44-45.
52. This includes the seven presidents who taught regular classes.
53. "Faculty Minutes," 1893-1899, October 1, 4, 1898, pp. 283-285.
54. *Ibid.*, 1871-1878, January 27, 1872, p. 57.
55. "Report of Carlos G. Smith to the Board of Trustees," 1878, p. 51.
56. "Faculty Minutes," 1878-1886, December 24, 1880.
57. *Ibid.*, 1878-1886, September 30, 1881.
58. *Catalogue,* 1898-1899, p. 58.
59. *Ibid.*, 1899-1900, p. 61.
60. "Trustees Minutes," 1895-1901, June 14, 1900, p. 499.
61. *Catalogue,* 1898-1899, p. 72.
62. "Faculty Minutes," 1893-1899, April 3, 1899, pp. 347-350.
63. *Ibid.*, April 10, 1899, pp. 352-353.
64. "Trustees Minutes," 1896-1901, June 14, 1900, p. 446.

CHAPTER XVII

1. "Trustees Minutes," 1866-1868, November 22, 1866, pp. 77-79.
2. *Independent Monitor,* March 7, 1871, referring to report made by Smith January 25, 1871.
3. Clark, *History of Education in Alabama,* 1702-1889, p. 101.
4. "Regents Minutes," 1868-1869, p. 200.
5. "Faculty Minutes," 1871-1878, October 3, 20, 1871, pp. 4, 7.
6. "Trustees Minutes," 1876-1888, September, 1879, pp. 160-161, 166.

7. *Ibid.*, June, 1882, pp. 230-231.
8. *Ibid.*, 1895-1901, March 11, 1897, pp. 109-110.
9. *Ibid.*, June 18, 1896, pp. 23-24.
10. "Faculty Minutes," 1871-1878, September 29, 1873, p. 134.
11. *Ibid.*, October 5, 1874, p. 156.
12. *Ibid.*, March 5, 1875, p. 166.
13. Tuscaloosa *Gazette,* May 17, 1888.
14. "Trustees Minutes," 1888-1895, June, 1888, p. 17.
15. "Regents Minutes," 1873-1874, November 26, 1873, p. 20.
16. "Faculty Minutes," 1871-1878, October 5, 1874, p. 156.
17. "Trustees Minutes," 1876-1888, July & October, 1876, pp. 17-19, 31.
18. *Ibid.*, January, 1879, p. 118.
19. *Ibid.*, June, 1883, p. 266.
20. *Ibid.*, June, 1884, p. 310.
21. *Ibid.*, June, 1887, p. 467.
22. *Ibid.*, p. 475.
23. "Faculty Minutes," 1871-1878, January 2, 1874, p. 143.
24. "Regents Minutes," 1873-1874, June 29, 1874, p. 59.
25. "Trustees Minutes," 1876-1883, July 1877, pp. 53-54.
26. "Faculty Minutes," 1871-1878, May 18, 1877, p. 208.
27. *Catalogue,* 1878-1879, p. 34.
28. "Faculty Minutes," 1878-1886, March 5, 1880, pp. 35-37.
29. "Trustees Minutes," 1901-1907, January 10, 1901, pp. 512-513.
30. "Faculty Minutes," 1871-1878, September 29, 1873, p. 134.
31. "Trustees Minutes," 1876-1888, June, 1887, p. 476.
32. *Ibid.*, 1888-1895, June, 1891, pp. 285-286.
33. *Ibid.*, February, 1890, p. 137.
34. *Catalogue,* 1899-1900, pp. 61-63.
35. "Faculty Minutes," 1893-1899, October 16, 1897, pp. 228-229.
36. "Trustees Minutes," 1876-1888, July, 1877, pp. 53-54.
37. "Faculty Minutes," 1893-1899, June 22, 1895, p. 127.
38. *Ibid.*, June 13, December 5, 1879, p. 18, 28.
39. Summarized from "Faculty Minutes," 1871-1878, November 7, 1871, pp. 21-27.
40. *Ibid.*, 1878-1886, October 10, 1879, p. 25.
41. *Ibid.*, October 31, 1879, p. 26.
42. "Faculty Minutes," 1878-1886, April 29, 1881, pp. 63-65.
43. "Trustees Minutes," 1876-1888, July 1881, p. 211.
44. *Catalogue.*
45. Quoted in Clara L. Verner, *Amelia Gayle Gorgas,* printed pamphlet in Alabama Collection.
46. *Corolla,* 1894, p. 182.
47. *Corolla,* 1896, p. 3.
48. *Corolla,* 1896, p. 6.

CHAPTER XVIII

1. *Catalogue,* 1878-1879, pp. 20-21.
2. "Faculty Minutes," 1871-1878, April 12, 1872, p. 77.
3. "Faculty Minutes," 1871-1878, October 2, 5, 1871, p. 5.
4. "President's Report to the Board of Trustees," July 1879, pp. 79-80, (Professor Wyman).
5. "Faculty Minutes," 1871-1878, January 10, 1873, p. 117.
6. *Catalogue,* 1880-1881, p. 15.

7. "Faculty Minutes," 1871-1878, September 25, 1874, p. 155.
8. *Ibid.*, January 8, 1875, p. 163.
9. *Ibid.*, February 15, 1875, p. 165.
10. *Ibid.*, May 2, 1873, p. 127.
11. "Trustees Minutes," 1876-1888, January 1879, p. 212.
12. "Faculty Minutes," 1878-1888, May 8, 1879, p. 16.
13. *Catalogue*, 1879-1880, p. 16.
14. "President's Report to the Board of Trustees," July 1879, p. 83, (Professor Wyman).
15. *Ibid.*, 1880, pp. 98-99.
16. *Ibid.*
17. *Catalogue*, 1882-1883, p. 14.
18. *Catalogue*, 1886-1887, p. 15.
19. *Ibid.*, p. 14.
20. "Faculty Minutes," 1876-1886, October 4, 5, 1880, pp. 43-44.
21. *Ibid.*, 1886-1893, p. 65.
22. Tuscaloosa *Gazette*, February 14, 1884.
23. "Report of President Lewis to the Board of Trustees," 1881, p. 109.
24. "Faculty Minutes," 1886-1893, May 30, June 23, 1887, p. 109.
25. *Ibid.*, June 6, 14, 1889, pp. 127-129.
26. *Ibid.*, September 19, 1889, p. 132.
27. *Ibid.*, June 9, 1890, pp. 173-174.
28. "Trustees Minutes," 1888-1895, June, 1890, pp. 207-209.
29. "Faculty Minutes," 1886-1893, May 23, 1892, pp. 247-248.
30. *Ibid.*, July 4, 1892, pp. 254-255.
31. *Ibid.*, 1893-1899, October 4, 1898, p. 295.
32. *Catalogue*, 1899-1900, pp. 17-19.
33. "Faculty Minutes," 1893-1899, October 6, 1897, pp. 216-217.
34. *Catalogue* 1899-1900, pp. 131-134.
35. "Faculty Minutes," 1871-1878, November 3, 1871, pp. 11-13.
36. *Ibid.*, January 5, 1872, p. 51.
37. *Ibid.*, July 13, 1875, p. 175.
38. *Ibid.*, 1886-1893, November 8, 1887, pp. 14-15.
39. *Ibid.*, 1878-1886, June 20, 1879, p. 19.
40. *Ibid.*, 1886-1893, November 8, 1887, pp. 14-15.
41. *Catalogue*, 1897-1898, p. 50.
42. "Faculty Minutes," 1886-1893, November 8, 1887, pp. 14-15.
43. *Ibid.*, November 11, 1889, p. 144.
44. *Ibid.*
45. *Ibid.*, 1893-1899, June 23, 1894, pp. 83-84.
46. "Trustees Minutes," 1876-1888, June, 1887, p. 477.
47. "Faculty Minutes," 1886-1893, June 30, 1888, p. 100.
48. *Ibid.*, 1871-1878, January 12, 1872, p. 55.
49. *Ibid.*, 1878-1886, June 13, 1879.
50. "Faculty Minutes," 1886-1893, p. 59.
51. *Ibid.*, February 13, 1888, p. 82.
52. *Catalogue*.
53. "Faculty Minutes," 1871-1878, May 24, 1872, p. 87.
54. "Trustees Minutes," 1888-1895, June 18, 1889, p. 29.
55. *Catalogue*, 1899-1900, p. 51.
56. *Catalogue*, 1875-1876, p. 18.
57. *Ibid.*, 1885-1886, p. 33.
58. *Ibid.*, 1886-1887, p. 35.

59. *Ibid.,* 1887-1888, p. 56.
60. *Ibid.,* 1890-1891, p. 64.
61. *Ibid.,* 1898-1899, pp. 67-68.

CHAPTER XIX

1. "Faculty Minutes," 1871-1878, November 7, 1871, pp. 17-21.
2. *Ibid.,* September 23, 1881, p. 74.
3. *Ibid.,* September 22, 1881, pp. 73-74.
4. *Ibid.,* September 30, 1881, pp. 74-75.
5. *Ibid.,* 1886-1893, November 7, 1886, p. 13.
6. *Ibid.,* 1893-1899, June 22, 1896, p. 164.
7. *Ibid.,* 1886-1893, June 22, 1889, p. 130.
8. *Ibid.,* November 16, 1890, pp. 224-225.
9. *Ibid.,* 1893-1899, May 13, 1895.
10. *Ibid.,* October 14, 1895, p. 134.
11. *Ibid.,* January 14, 1896, p. 144.
12. *Ibid.,* October 25, 1897, pp. 235-236.
13. *Ibid.,* October 27, November 15, 1897, pp. 237, 239-240.
14. "Regents Minutes," 1874-1875, November 21, 1874, pp. 9-16.
15. "Faculty Minutes," 1886-1893, June 30, 1888, p. 99.
16. *Catalogue,* 1887-1888, p. 15.
17. "Faculty Minutes," 1886-1893, October 8, 1886, p. 9.
18. *Ibid.,* November 29, 1886, p. 22.
19. *Ibid.,* February 21, 1887, p. 35.
20. *Ibid.,* May 30, 1887, p. 49.
21. "Trustees Minutes," 1876-1888, July 4, 1879, p. 152.
22. "Trustees Minutes," 1888-1895, June 30, 1892, p. 371.
23. *Ibid.*
24. *Ibid.,* 1876-1888, July, 1879, p. 143.
25. *Catalogue,* 1897-1898, pp. 42-43.
26. *Ibid.,* 1881-1882, p. 25.
27. "Faculty Minutes," 1878-1886, December 1, 1882, p. 102.
28. *Ibid.,* 1871-1878, March 28, 1873, p. 124.
29. *Ibid.,* 1886-1893, April 29, 1889, p. 122.
30. *Ibid.,* May 11, 1891, p. 210.
31. "Trustees Minutes," 1888-1895, June 25, 1891, p. 285.
32. *Independent Monitor* (Tuscaloosa), July 5, 1871.
33. "Regents Minutes," 1869-1873, missing.
34. "Regents Minutes," 1873-1874, December 1, 1873, p. 33.
35. *Ibid.,* November 21, 25, 1874, pp. 8, 19.
36. *Ibid.,* July 2, 1874, pp. 91-92.
37. *Ibid.,* July 8, 1875, p. 53.
38. "Trustees Minutes," 1876-1888, July, 1876, pp. 10-11.
39. *Ibid.,* July, 1877, p. 54 .
40. *Ibid.,* July, 1878, p. 85.
41. "Trustees Minutes," 1876-1888, June 22, 1888, p. 549.
42. "Trustees Minutes," 1889-1895.
43. *Ibid.,* 1895-1901, June, 1896, pp. 13-14.
44. *Ibid.,* June 1897, p. 142.
45. *Ibid.,* June, 1897, p. 145.
46. *Ibid.,* June, 1899, p. 315.
47. *Ibid.,* 1876-1888, June, 1884, p. 329.

48. *Ibid.*, June 1885, pp. 359-360, 368.
49. "Faculty Minutes," 1886-1893, September 21, 1887, p. 65.
50. *Ibid.*, September 21, 1887, p. 1.
51. "Trustees Minutes," 1876-1888, June, 1888, pp. 530, 540, 547.
52. "Faculty Minutes," 1886-1893, October 14, 1887, p. 71.
53. "Trustees Minutes," 1888-1895, February and June, 1890, pp. 136, 211.
54. *Ibid.*, June 15, 1889, p. 102.
55. *Ibid.*, June 21, 1889, p. 49.
56. *Ibid.*, June 1890, p. 211.
57. "Trustees Minutes," 1895-1901.
58. *Ibid.*, July, 1879, pp. 144-145; September, 1879, p. 169.
59. *Ibid.*
60. *Ibid.*, 1888-1895, November 14, 1889, pp. 123-124.
61. *Ibid.*, June 14, 1900, pp. 448-449.
62. "Annual Report of President B. B. Lewis to Board of Trustees," 1881, pp. 116-117.
63. *Ibid.*, p. 130. Charles R. McCall served as an assistant in the Latin department from 1878 to 1881. There is no McCalley listed on the faculty at that time.
64. "Trustees Minutes," 1876-1888, June, 1883, p. 278.
65. *Ibid.*, June. 1888, p. 530.
66. "Report of President Lupton to the Board of Regents," November 26, 1873, pp. 1-2 (in Regents Minutes).
67. *Report of the Committee on the University to the Board of Regents*, no date, p. 17 (Probably 1870 to 1871).
68. *Ibid.*
69. "Report of President Lupton to the Board of Regents," November 26, 1873, pp. 1-2.
70. "Regents Minutes," 1873-1874, December 1, 1873, pp. 29-31.
71. *Ibid.*, December 4, 1873, p. 45.
72. "Trustees Minutes," 1876-1888, July 1, p. 9.
73. *Ibid.*, July 4, 1877, p. 65.
74. *Ibid.*, July 1879, p. 147.
75. *Ibid.*, June, 1885, pp. 366-367.
76. *Ibid.*, June, 1888, p. 511, 528.
77. *Ibid.*, 1895-1901, June 22, 1897, p. 130.

CHAPTER XX

1. *Corolla*, 1893, p. 75.
2. "Faculty Minutes," 1893-1899, March 12, 1894, p. 65.
3. Tuscaloosa *Times*, January 13, 1875.
4. "Faculty Minutes," 1871-1878, October 16, 1874, p. 157.
5. *Ibid.*, October 1, 1873, p. 135.
6. *Ibid.*, October 7, 1873, p. 144.
7. "Trustees Minutes," 1876-1888, July 5, 1876, pp. 18-20.
8. *Ibid.*, January, 1879, p. 115.
9. Alabama University *Monthly*, Vol. X, June, 1884.
10. *Catalogue*, 1884-1885.
11. The *Journal*, Vol. II, November, 1891, June, 1892.
12. *Catalogue*, 1894-1895.
13. *Ibid.*, 1897-1898.
14. "Trustees Minutes," 1876-1888, July 5, 1876, p. 20.
15. *Ibid.*, July 1, 1878, p. 27.
16. "Reports of the Presidents to the Board of Trustees," 1878-1882, pp. 27-28.

REBUILDING THE UNIVERSITY

17. Alabama University *Monthly*, Vol. VI, February, 1879.
18. "Reports of the Presidents to the Board of Trustees," 1878-1882, pp. 77-79.
19. "Trustees Minutes," 1876-1888, June, 1887, p. 475.
20. *Ibid.*, June 1886, p. 418.
21. *Ibid.*, June, 1888, p. 556.
22. Sam Friedman, Letter to author, June, 1950.
23. "Trustees Minutes," 1888-1895, June, 1888, p. 16.
24. *Ibid.*, June, 1887, p. 477.
25. *Ibid.*, June, 1888, p. 14.
26. *Ibid.*, June, 1888, p. 14.
27. "Reports of the Presidents to the Board of Trustees," 1876-1882, p. 110.
28. "Faculty Minutes," 1876-1886, December 16, 1881.
29. Alabama University *Monthly*, 1886-1887, Vol. XIV, October, 1886, p. 23.
30. *Corolla*, 1894, pp. 178-183.
31. "Trustees Minutes," 1888-1895, June 27, 1889, p. 44. *Rules and Regulations of the University*, 1873, pp. 6-16.
32. Friedman, *loc. cit.*
33. Alabama University *Monthly*, Vol. XIV, January, 1887.
34. "Trustees Minutes," 1876-1888, June, 1887, p. 477.
35. *Tuscaloosa Gazette*, July 7, 1881.
36. *Corolla*, 1896, p. 92; Alabama University *Monthly*, Vol. XIV, January, 1887.
37. *Corolla*, 1898, pp. 58-59.
38. *Ibid.*, 1898, p. 59.
39. *Ibid.*
40. "Trustees Minutes," 1876-1888, January 14, 1879, p. 113.
41. *Ibid.*, January 14, 1879, p. 114.
42. *Ibid.*, September, 1879, p. 169.
43. "Reports of the Presidents to the Board of Trustees," 1878-1882, p. 43.
44. *Ibid.*, p. 118.
45. "Trustees Minutes," 1888-1895, June, 1888, p. 16.
46. *Ibid.*, June 21, 1882, p. 246.
47. "Reports of the Presidents to the Board of Trustees," 1878-1882, pp. 127-128.
48. "Trustees Minutes," 1876-1888, June 21, 1882, p. 240.
49. Alabama University *Monthly*, 1874-1875, Vol. II, December, 1874.
50. Tuscaloosa *Times*, May 22, 1889.
51. "Trustees Minutes," 1888-1895, February 12, 1890, pp. 137-138; Tuscaloosa *Gazette*, April 2, 1891.
52. "Faculty Minutes," 1878-1886, September 19, 1881.
53. *Ibid.*, 1899-1906, May 5, 1890, p. 165.
54. *Ibid.*, 1886-1893, January 31, 1887, p. 31.
55. "Trutees Minutes," 1888-1895, June 25, 1891, p. 285.
56. *Ibid.*, 1895-1901, June June 23, 1897, p. 135.
57. "Faculty Minutes," 1893-1899, October 3, 1897, p. 216.
58. Friedman, *loc. cit.*
59. *Ibid.*
60. *Ibid.*
61. *Ibid.*
62. Hill Ferguson, "The University During the Gay Nineties," University of Alabama *Alumni News*, March, 1948, pp. 90-91.
63. *Ibid.*
64. *Ibid.*
65. *Ibid.*
66. Alabama University *Monthly*, Vol. IX, April, 1882, p. 229.
67. "Faculty Minutes," 1878-1886, October 16.

68. *Corolla*, 1901, p. 218.
69. Tuscaloosa *Times*, February 25, 1891.
70. "Faculty Minutes," 1871-1901. *Passim*.
71. *Ibid.*, 1893-1899, October 4, 1898, pp. 263-264.
72. *Ibid.*, May 9, 1898, pp. 263-264.
73. *Ibid.*, March 26, 1894, pp. 67-68.
74. *Ibid.*, 1871-1878, January 30, 1872, p. 61.
75. *Ibid.*, 1878-1886, May 8, 1884.
76. *Independent Monitor* (Tuscaloosa), December 13, 1871.
77. "Faculty Minutes," 1871-1878, January 17, 1879, pp. 242-243.
78. Friedman, *loc. cit.*
79. "Faculty Minutes," 1878-1886, March 25, 1881, p. 61.
80. *Ibid.*, 1886-1893, November 21, 1887, p. 75.
81. "Trustees Minutes," 1888-1895, June 15, 1889, pp. 92-95.
82. *Ibid.*, June 18, 1890, p. 153.
83. *Ibid.*, June 23, 1891, pp. 264-265.
84. Tuscaloosa Times, July 5, 1893; "Faculty Minutes," 1893-1899, May 11, 1896, p. 155.
85. "Faculty Minutes," 1893-1899, December 11, 1893, p. 58.
86. *Corolla*, 1899, p. 117.
87. "Faculty Minutes," 1893-1899, November 9, 1896, p. 174.
88. Ferguson.
89. Tuscaloosa *Times*, July 5, 1893.
90. Ferguson.
91. *Acts Passed at the Third Annual Session of the General Assembly of the State of Alabama*, 1821, pp. 3-8; *An Act Supplementary to an Act to Establish a State University*, Sec. 22.
92. Israel Pickens, Governor of Alabama, November 13, 1821, *Senate Journal*, (1821), pp. 8-17.
93. Israel Pickens, Governor of Alabama, November 19, 1823, *Senate Journal*, 1823, pp. 8-17.
94. *Report of the Committee on the University to the Board of Regents*, pp. 15-16. No date on pamphlet. In Alabama Collection.
95. "Report of President Carlos G. Smith to the Board of Trustees," July 2, 1878, pp. 70-73.
96. Alabama University *Monthly*, Vol. XI, No. 8, May, 1884, pp. 308-309.
97. *Alabama Christian Advocate* (Birmingham), October 30, 1890.
98. *Corolla*, 1899, pp. 55-56.
99. "Trustees Minutes," 1888-1895, June 29, pp. 352-353.
100. *Corolla*.
101. "Faculty Minutes," 1893-1899, January 16, 1893, p. 271.
102. *Ibid.*, February 6, 1893, pp. 273-274.
103. "Trustees Minutes," 1888-1895, June 28, 1893, p. 439.
104. "Faculty Minutes," 1893-1899, July 1, 1893; July 11, 1893, pp. 35-37.
105. It was to honor these two young ladies as the first women students that the Adams-Parker dormitory on Denny Field was named.
106. *Corolla*, 1894, p. 71.
107. *Ibid.*, pp. 121-123.
108. "Faculty Minutes," 1893-1899, April 9, 1894, p. 69.
109. *Corolla*, 1895, pp. 23-29.
110. *Ibid.*, pp. 141, 142, 143.
111. *Catalogue*, 1896-1897, pp. 92-93, 96.
112. *Corolla*, 1896, p. 26.

REBUILDING THE UNIVERSITY

113. Special students were those who did not take the full number of studies, while eclectic students took full time work but did not follow any regular course.
114. *Corolla,* 1897, pp. 65-69; 88-89.
115. *Ibid.,* p. 35.
116. "Trustees Minutes," 1896-1901, March 11, 1897, pp. 101-102.
117. *Ibid.,* July 8, 1897, pp. 191-192.
118. *Corolla,* 1898, p. 43.
119. *Ibid.,* pp. 60-64.
120. "Trustees Minutes," 1896-1901, February 19, 1898, pp. 203-205.
121. Conversation with Mrs. Annie Sercy Snow in 1949.
122. "Trustees Minutes," 1896-1901, June 21, 1898, p. 224.
123. *Corolla,* 1899, pp. 55-56.
124. "Trustees Minutes," 1896-1901, June 21, 1899, pp. 298-299.
125. *Corolla,* 1899, pp. 57-58.
126. *Ibid.,* p. 161.
127. *Ibid.,* p. 142.
128. *Ibid.,* p. 44.
129. *Ibid.,* p. 163.
130. Tuscaloosa *Times,* October 15, 1898.
131. *Ibid.,* May 26, 1899.
132. *Catalogue,* 1899-1900, pp. 123-126.
133. *Ibid.,* 1900-1901, pp. 189-190.
134. The honorary degree of Mistress of Science was awarded in 1901 to Miss Bessie Parker, who was teaching at that time at Converse College, Spartansburg, South Carolina.

CHAPTER XXI

1. *Independent Monitor* (Tuscaloosa), November 29, 1871.
2. "Trustees Minutes," 1876-1888, July, 1876, p. 13.
3. *Ibid.,* July 1876, p. 13.
4. Ferguson, *loc. cit.*
5. Tuscaloosa *Times,* September 24, 1884.
6. "Trustees Minutes," 1888-1895, June 30, 1892, pp. 267-268.
7. *Ibid.,* 1896-1901, p. 445.
8. *Ibid.,* 1888-1895, June 25, 1891, pp. 281, 282.
9. Tuscaloosa *Times,* June 24, 1891.
10. Alabama University *Monthly,* Vol. XII, June, 1885, p. 357; "Trustees Minutes," 1876-1888, June, 1885, pp. 364-365.
11. *Corolla,* 1893, p. 96.
12. Alabama University *Monthly,* Vol. I, December, 1873, p. 12.
13. "Trustees Minutes," 1888-1893, June, 1887, p. 468.
14. "Faculty Minutes," 1871-1878, May 23, 24, 1873, p. 128.
15. "Regents Minutes," 1873-1874, December 2, 3, 1873, pp. 40-42.
16. *Ibid.,* December 2, 1873, pp. 36-39.
17. "Faculty Minutes," 1871-1878, October 3, 1873, pp. 80-81.
18. *Ibid.,* July 4, 1874, p. 100.
19. "Trustees Minutes," 1876-1888, July 1879, p. 145.
20. *Ibid.,* 1888-1895, June 17, 1889, pp. 23-24.
21. *Ibid.,* June 23, 1891, pp. 257-258.
22. *Corolla,* 1893, p. 96.
23. "Faculty Minutes," 1878-1886, October 4, 1880, pp. 43-44.
24. "Trustees Minutes," 1888-1895, June 30, 1892, pp. 367-368.

25. *Ibid.*, 1896-1901, June 19, 1896, p. 33.
26. "Faculty Minutes," 1886-1893, September 20, 1887, p. 64.
27. "Reports of the Presidents to the Board of Trustees," 1878-1882, pp. 135-136; 64-65.
28. "Trustees Minutes," 1876-1888, June, 1882, p. 241.
29. *Ibid.*, June, 1885, p. 393.
30. "Faculty Minutes," 1878-1886, February 27, 1880, p. 34.
31. *Ibid.*, February 15, 1882, p. 85.
32. *Ibid.*, February 17, 1882, p. 85.
33. *Ibid.*, 1886-1893, May 18, 1887, pp. 46-47.
34. *Ibid.*, 1871-1879, July 8, 1878, p. 229.
35. *Ibid.*, 1886-1893, June 25, 1887, pp. 58-59.
36. *Ibid.*, 1871-1878, November 30, 1871, p. 43.
37. *Ibid.*, 1893-1899, December 5, 1898, pp. 312-313; December 12, 1898, pp. 312-316.
38. *Ibid.*, December 12, 1898, p. 316.
39. *Ibid.*, December 19, 1898, pp. 317-318.
40. *Corolla*, 1899, p. 7.
41. "Faculty Minutes," 1899-1906, September 23, 1901, pp. 149-156.
42. Alabama University *Monthly*, 1872-1874, Vol. I, April 1874, p. 101.
43. *Crimson-White*, March 11, 1902.
44. "Trustees Minutes," 1888-1895, June 15, 1889, pp. 20-25.
45. "Faculty Minutes," 1886-1893, December 6, 1888, p. 110.
46. *Corolla*, 1896, p. 113.
47. "Faculty Minutes," 1899-1906, December 12, 1900, p. 119.
48. *Ibid.*, 1886-1893, May 20, 1889, p. 125.
49. *Ibid.*, May 20, 1889, p. 125.
50. *Ibid.*, 1878-1886, July 5, 1880.
51. *Ibid.*, June 23, 1882.
52. "Trustees Minutes," 1876-1888, June, 1888, pp. 534-555; "Reports of the Presidents to the Board of Trustees," 1878-1882, pp. 81-82.
53. "Reports of the Presidents to the Board of Trustees," 1878-1882, p. 113; Faculty Minutes," 1878-1886, July 5, 1880, p. 43.
54. "Trustees Minutes," 1876-1888, June 1882 p, 239.
55. *Ibid.*, 1896-1901, June 16, 1896, pp. 10-11.
56. "Faculty Minutes," 1899-1906, December 4, 1899, p. 16.
57. *Ibid.*, 1871-1879, February 24, 1879, p. 246.
58. "Reports of the Presidents to the Board of Trustees," 1878-1882, pp. 85-86.
59. "Faculty Minutes," 1871-1879, March 24, 1879, p. 250.
60. *Ibid.*, 1878-1886, October 4, 1880.
61. "Reports of the Presidents to the Board of Trustees," 1878-1882, pp. 125-126.
62. "Faculty Minutes," 1878-1886, December, 21-1883, p. 131.
63. "Trustees Minutes," 1876-1888, July 1879, p. 152.
64. *Ibid.*, 1888-1895, June 29, 1892, p. 351.
65. Tuscaloosa *Times,* April 9, 1890.
66. *Ibid.*, January 9, 1889.
67. Ferguson, *loc. cit.*
68. Tuscaloosa *Times*, February 27, 1878.
69. *State vs. Harrison*, Circuit Court Minutes of Tuscaloosa County, Vol. I, 1874-1880, Spring Term, 1879, p. 469.
70. "Reports of the Presidents to the Board of Trustees," 1878-1882, pp. 46-47.
71. "Trustees Minutes," 1876-1888, June 29, 1878, p. 69.
72. *Ibid.*, July 4, 1878, p. 94.
73. *Ibid.*, July 1878, pp. 95-96.

REBUILDING THE UNIVERSITY

74. "Reports of the Presidents to the Board of Trustees," 1878-1882, pp. **84-85**.
75. "Faculty Minutes," 1878-1886, November 15, 1880, p. 51.
76. *Ibid.*, April 6, 1881, p. 61.
77. "Trustees Minutes," 1896-1901, February 19, 1898, pp. 203-205.
78. *Corolla*, 1895, pp. 155-158.
79. *Independent Monitor* (Tuscaloosa), November 29, 1871.
80. "Regents Minutes," 1873-1874, December 2, 1873, pp. 36-39; July 2, 1874, p. 85.
81. *Ibid.*, November 21, 1874, p. 5.
82. "Faculty Minutes," 1871-1879, November 21, 1873, p. 142.
83. *Ibid.*, October 9, 1874, p. 156.
84. *Ibid.*, January 8, 1875, p. 163.
85. *Ibid.*, January 29, 1875, p. 164.
86. Tuscaloosa *Times*, January 13, 1875.
87. "Reports of the Presidents to the Board of Trustees," 1878-1882, 1878, pp. 66-67.
88. "Faculty Minutes," 1886-1893, February 9, 1891, pp. 203-204.
89. Montgomery *Advertiser*, June 26, 1891.
90. The *Senior Battery*, University of Alabama, June 1891, pp. 9, 12.
91. *Ibid.*
92. "Faculty Minutes," 1886-1893, February 6, 1893, p. 274.
93. "Trustees Minutes," 1888-1895, June 19, 1894, p. 505.
94. *Ibid.*, June 21, 1894, pp. 526-527.
95. *Ibid.*, June 19, 1895, p. 567.
96. *Ibid.*, 1896-1901, June 17, 1896, p. 8.
97. *Ibid.*, June 21, 1899, pp. 299-300.
98. *Ibid.*, June 14, 1900, pp. 438-452.
99. McQueen, John D., Statement on the 1900 Student Rebellion at the University of Alabama, Tuscaloosa, July 11, 1847.
100. *Ibid.*
101. *Ibid.*
102. "Faculty Minutes," 1899-1906, December 8, 1900, pp. 82-83.
103. *Ibid.*, December 8, 1900, pp. 81-82.
104. *Ibid.*, December 10, 1900, pp. 84-85.
105. *Ibid.*
106. *Ibid.*, December 12, 1900, pp. 111-114.
107. McQueen, *loc. cit.*
108. "Faculty Minutes," 1899-1906, December 12, 1900, pp. 111-114.
109. *Ibid.*, pp. 115-126.
110. "Trustees Minutes," 1896-1901, December 14, 1900, pp. 478-493.
111. *Ibid.*
112. McQueen, *loc. cit.*

CHAPTER XXII

1. "Faculty Minutes," 1871-1878, October 20, 1871, p. 7.
2. Alabama University *Monthly*, Vol. III, December, 1875.
3. *Ibid.* Vol. II, March, 1874.
4. *Ibid.*, Vol. II, December, 1874.
5. *Ibid.*, Vol. III, December, 1875.
6. Tuscaloosa *Gazette*, April 24, 1879.
7. *Ibid.*, May 23, 1878.
8. "Faculty Minutes," 1878-1886, May 2, 1886.
9. Tuscaloosa *Gazette*, July 7, 1881.
10. *Corolla*, 1897, p. 28.

11. Alabama University *Monthly*, Vol. XII, November, 1884.
12. *Corolla*, 1893, p. 113.
13. *The Journal*, Vol. II, November, 1891.
14. *Ibid.*, April, 1892, pp. 246-247.
15. "Trustees Minutes," 1888-1895, June, 1888, pp. 556-557.
16. *Ibid.*, June 20, 1889, p. 37.
17. *Corolla*, 1898, p. 56.
18. "Faculty Minutes," 1871-1878, January 23, 1874, p. 144.
19. "Faculty Minutes," 1878-1886, July 8, 1879.
20. "Faculty Minutes," 1878-1886, July, 1879.
21. *Ibid.*, January 28, 1881.
22. "Trustees Minutes," 1876-1888, April, 1885, p. 334.
23. *Ibid.*, June, 1885, pp. 362-364.
24. *Ibid.*, June, 1885, pp. 362-364.
25. "Faculty Minutes," 1878-1886, October 23, 1885.
26. "Trustees Minutes," 1876-1888, November, 1885, p. 405.
27. *Ibid.*, 1888-1895, June, 1888, p. 524.
28. *Corolla*, 1893, pp. 47-48; 50-52.
29. *Ibid.*, pp. 53-55; 61-63; 64-66.
30. *Ibid.*, pp. 56-59.
31. *Ibid.*, 1899.
32. *Ibid.*, 1902.
33. *Ibid.*, 1902, p. 109.
34. *Ibid.*, 1893, p. 142.
35. *Ibid.*, 1895, p. 119.
36. *Ibid.*, 1893, p. 145.
37. *Ibid.*, 1893, p. 145.
38. *Ibid.*, 1893, p. 142.
39. *Ibid.*, 1901, pp. 175-176.
40. *Ibid.*, 1899; *(Crimson-White*, November 1, 1898).
41. "Faculty Minutes," 1871-1878, October 24, 1873, p. 239.
42. Alabama University *Monthly*, Vol. XI, April, 1884, p. 265.
43. "Faculty Minutes," 1871-1878, June 1, 1877, p. 210.
44. *Ibid.*, October 26, 1877, pp. 213-214.
45. *Ibid.*, 1878-1886, October 22, 1880.
46. *Ibid.*, June 23, 1882.
47. Alabama University *Monthly*, Vol. XIV, February, 1887, p. 187.
48. "Faculty Minutes," 1878-1886, June 25, 1886.
49. *Ibid.*, 1886-1893, June 24, 1887, p. 60.
50. *Ibid.*, November 3, 1890, pp. 191-192.
51. *Corolla*, 1894, p. 121.
52. *Ibid.*, p. 121.
53. "Faculty Minutes," 1893-1899, February 12, 1894, p. 62.
54. *Ibid.*, October 9, 1894, p. 91.
55. *Ibid.*, June 17, 1895, p. 123.
56. *Ibid.*, February 17, 1896, p. 147.
57. *Ibid.*, October 19, 1896, p. 171.
58. *Catalogue*, 1894-1895.
59. "Faculty Minutes," 1886-1893, November 28, 1892, p. 267.
60. *Corolla*, 1893, p. 8.
61. Alabama University *Monthly*, 1874-1875, Vol. II, December, 1874.
62. "Faculty Minutes," 1871-1878, March 12, 1875.
63. Tuscaloosa *Gazette*, June 29, 1882.
64. "Faculty Minutes," 1886-1893, March 14, 1892, p. 236.

65. *Corolla*, 1893, p. 148.
66. *Ibid.*, 1894, p. 95.
67. *Crimson-White*, Centennial Issue, May, 1931, p. 61.
68. *Ibid.*, p. 61.
69. *Ibid.*, p. 60.
70. "Faculty Minutes," 1886-1893, November 7, 1892, pp. 266-267.
71. *Crimson-White*, Centennial Issue, May, 1931, p. 19.
72. *Ibid.*, p. 60.
73. *The Journal*, January, 1892, Vol. III, p. 77.
74. *Corolla*, 1893, p. 126.
75. "Trustees Minutes," 1888-1895, February, 1892, pp. 310-311.
76. "Faculty Minutes," 1886-1893, February 8, 1892, pp. 233-234.
77. *Corolla*, 1902, pp. 202-203.
78. *Ibid.*, 1895, p. 116.
79. "Faculty Minutes," 1886-1893, May 1, 1893, p. 284.
80. Tuscaloosa *Times*, November 29, 1893.
81. Letter from Hill Ferguson to James B. Sellers, September 25, 1950, and Birmingham *News*, December 1, 1950.
82. *The Journal*, November, 1892, Vol. III, p. 25.
83. *Ibid.*, March, 1893, Vol. IV, p. 135.
84. *Tuscaloosa* Times, July 5, 1893.
85. "Faculty Minutes," 1893-1899, October 19, 1896, p. 170.
86. *Ibid.*, 1886-1893, November 10, 1890, p. 193.
87. *Crimson-White*, December 1, 1896.
88. "Faculty Minutes," 1886-1893, May 1, 1893, p. 284.
89. Corolla, 1894, pp. 93-94.
90. *Ibid.*, 1893.
91. *Ibid.*, p. 102.
92. *Corollas*, 1893-1902, *passim*.
93. *Corolla*, 1895, pp. 93-99.
94. "Faculty Minutes," 1893-1899, June 3, 1895, pp. 19-20.
95. *Ibid.*, June 1, 1896, p. 157.
96. *Ibid.*, October 19, 1895, p. 170.
97. *Ibid.*, October 19, 1896, p. 170.
98. *Corolla*, 1896, pp. 76-77.
99. *Ibid.*, 1897, p. 8.
100. *Corolla*, 1898, p. 141.
101. *Tuscaloosa Sunday Times,* June 13, 1897.
102. *Corolla*, 1898, pp. 105-106.
103. "Trustees Minutes," 1896-1901, June 21, 1899, pp. 304-305.
104. "Faculty Minutes," 1899-1906, June 11, 1900, p. 47.
105. *Corolla*, 1900, p. 123.
106. *Ibid.* p. 8.
107. "Faculty Minutes," 1899-1906, October 18, 1901. p. 164.
108. Tuscaloosa *Weekly Times*, November 1, 1901.
109. *Crimson -White*, Centennial Issue, May, 1931, p. 19.
110. *Corolla*, 1901, p. 164.
111. "Trustees Minutes," 1896-1901, June 14, 1900, pp. 439-440.

CHAPTER XXIII

1. "Faculty Minutes," 1871-1878, May 24, 1872, p. 85.
2. *Ibid.*, April 6, 1872, p. 75.
3. *Ibid.*, March 29, 1872, p. 73.

4. *Ibid.,* June 11, 1872, p. 91.
5. *Ibid.,* June 21, 1872, p. 93.
6. *Ibid.,* June 5, 1874, p. 151; March 21, 1873, p. 123.
7. *Ibid.,* April 15, 1873, p. 125.
8. *Ibid.,* May 16, 1873, p. 127.
9. *Ibid.,* May 30, 1873, p. 130.
10. *Ibid.,* June 6, 1873, p. 130.
11. *Ibid.,* February 19, 1875, p. 165.
12. *Ibid.,* March 19, 1875, p. 165; April 2, 1875, p. 169.
13. *Ibid.,* April 16, 1875, p. 170.
14. *Ibid.,* May 21, 1875, p. 172.
15. *Catalogue,* 1872-1875, p. 25.
16. "Faculty Minutes," 1878-1886, February 9, 1883, p. 107.
17. *Ibid.,* March 16, 1883, p. 110.
18. "Trustees Minutes," 1876-1888, July, 1876, p. 24.
19. *Ibid.,* July, 1877, p. 55.
20. *Ibid.,* July, 1878, p. 72.
21. *Ibid.,* July 1879, pp. 123, 130.
22. *Ibid.,* June, 1880, p. 177.
23. *Ibid.,* July 1881, p. 204.
24. "Faculty Minutes," 1871-1878, May 8, 1875, pp. 221-222.
25. *Ibid.,* April 7, 1876, p. 189.
26. *Ibid.,* December 8, 1876, p. 201.
27. "Faculty Minutes," 1878-1886, September 19, 1881, pp. 70-71.
28. *Ibid.,* June 21, 1883.
29. "Report of the President to the Trustees," 1878-1882, p. 114.
30. *Corolla,* 1893, p. 164.
31. "Trustees Minutes," 1876-1888, September, 1879, pp. 168-169.
32. *Ibid.,* July, 1879, p. 145.
33. *Corolla,* 1894, p. 137.
34. "Trustees Minutes," 1888-1895, June 22, 1891, p. 254. Unless otherwise specified, all the material on honors was taken from Catalogues for the Years from 1871 to 1900.
35. "Faculty Minutes," 1893-1899, June 29, 1893, pp. 33-35.
36. John D. Yerby, A. M., 1896.
37. "Faculty Minutes," 1893-1899, June 17, 1895, pp. 33-35.
38. "Trustees Minutes," 1888-1895, June 30, 1892, p. 273.
39. *Catalogue,* 1894, 1895, p. 48.
40. "Faculty Minutes," 1899-1906, June 16, 1899, p. 369.
41. "Report of Carlos G. Smith to the Board of Trustees," 1877-1878, "Annual Reports of the Presidents," p. 63.
42. "Trustees Minutes," 1876-1888, July 2, 1878, p. 75.
43. "Faculty Minutes," 1878-1886, June 27, 1879, pp. 19-20.
44. *Ibid.,* 1893-1899, June 12, 1896, p. 159.
45. "Trustees Minutes," 1876-1888, July 3, 1879, p. 136. At that time, the Master's degree was sometimes given rather automatically, upon application, to those graduates with Bachelor's degree of three years' standing who had followed a learned field of endeavor after graduating from the University.
46. *Ibid.,* June 19, 1882, p. 225.
47. *Ibid.,* 1888-1895, June 18, 1889, p. 29.
48. *Ibid.,* June 19, 1889, p. 33.
49. *Ibid.,* June 18, 1889, pp. 29-30.
50. "Faculty Minutes," 1886-1893, June 6, 1887, p. 50.

REBUILDING THE UNIVERSITY 629

51. *Ibid.*, 1893, 1899, June 26, 1893, pp. 32-33.
52. "Trustees Minutes," 1888-1895, February 12, 1890, pp. 138-139.
53. "Faculty Minutes," 1871-1878, June 23, 1876, p. 193.
54. "Trustees Minutes," 1876-1888, 1878, pp. 73 and 83.
55. "Faculty Minutes," 1878-1886, March 13, 1885, p. 157.
56. *Ibid.*, 1893-1899, June 16, 1899, p. 369.
57. Diploma presented to Anna Byrne Adams, 1895, framed in Alabama Collection, University of Alabama. Words underscored were written in by hand.
58. "Trustees Minutes," 1876-1888, July, 1879, pp. 133-134.
59. *Ibid.*, October, 1879, p. 172.
60. *Ibid.*, June, 1880, pp. 175-176.
61. *Ibid.*, 1876-1888, June, 1883, pp. 259-260.
62. *Ibid.*, June, 1887, p. 457.
63. *Ibid.*, 1888-1895, June 19, 1889, pp. 35-36.
64. The Tuscaloosa *Gazette*, July 13, 1876.
65. The Tuscaloosa *Times*, June 27, 1883.

CHAPTER XXIV

1. J. J. Garrett, "Alumni Address," 1873.
2. Tuscaloosa *Times*, March 25, 1874.
3. *Ibid.*, April 1, 1874.
4. *Ibid.*
5. *Ibid.*, April 8, 1874.
6. Hayneville *Examiner*, August 22, 1883.
7. *Ibid.*, August 15, 1883.
8. Tuscaloosa *Gazette*, quoted in Hayneville *Examiner*, August 22, 1883.
9. Hayneville *Examiner*, August 22, 1883.
10. Eufaula *Times*, quoted in Hayneville *Examiner*, August 8, 1883.
11. Fort Payne *Journal*, quoted in Hayneville *Examiner*, November 7, 1883.
12. Montgomery *Advertiser*, quoted in Hayneville *Examiner*, July 18, 1883.
13. Ashville *Aegis*, quoted in Hayneville *Examiner*, August 15, 1883.
14. Greenville *Advocate*, quoted in Tuscaloosa *Times*, February 28, 1883.
15. Mobile *Register*, quoted in Tusacloosa *Times*, September 13, 1883.
16. Tuscaloosa *Gazette*, October 11, 1883.
17. *Sunday Morning Chronicle* (Birmingham), February 10, 1884.
18. Tuscaloosa *Gazette*, February 14, 1884.
19. Birmingham *News*, quoted in Tuscaloosa *Gazette*, May 24, 1888.
20. Montgomery *Dispatch*, quoted in Tuscaloosa *Gazette*, May 24, 1888.
21. Birmingham *Age*, quoted in Tuscaloosa *Gazette*, May 24, 1888.
22. Birmingham *News*, September 3, 1896.
23. Mobile *Daily Register*, January 28, 1897.
24. *Methodist Quarterly Review* (Nashville), Vol. 62, 1880, p. 306; 310-312; Vol. 6, 1884, p. 681.
25. *Alabama Baptist* (Birmingham), April 6, 1885.
26. *North American Review*, quoted in *Alabama Baptist*, June 11, 1885.
27. *Alabama Baptist* (Birmingham), June 11, 1885.
28. *Wesleyan Christian Advocate*, quoted in *Alabama Baptist*, April 30, 1885.
29. *Alabama Baptist* (Birmingham) June 11, 1885.
30. *Ibid.*, March 11, 1886.
31. *Alabama Christian Advocate* (Birmingham), March 1, 1888.
32. *Baptist Quarterly Review*, quoted in Alabama Baptist, August 19, 1886.
33. *Alabama Baptist* (Birmingham), April 16, 1885.

34. *The Alabama Beacon* (Greensboro), April 14, 1885.
35. *Ibid.*
36. Tuscaloosa *Gazette,* April 23, 1885.
37. *Ibid.,* April 23, 1885.
38. *Alabama Beacon* (Greensboro), May 5, 1885.
39. Tuscaloosa *Gazette,* April 2, 1885.
40. *Ibid.,* April 30, 1885.
41. *Alabama Beacon* (Greensboro), May 12, 1885.
42. Tuscaloosa *Times,* November 29, 1893.
43. *Alabama Christian Advocate* (Birmingham), July 5, 1894.
44. *Daily Register* (Mobile), January 28, 1897.
45. Tuscaloosa *Times,* February 3, 1897.

Index

Abbott, Eli, 400, 524, 528, 529, 530
Acklin, William, 18, 51
Acker, P. J., 398
Adams, Anna Byrne, 478, 479, 548
Adams, Benjamin C., 240
Adams, ... 242, 243
Adams, Dan, 288
Adams, J. T., 424
Addison, Joseph, 187
Admission of Women to University, 475-485
Advertiser, 303, 325, 326
Advertiser and State Gazette, 194
Advocate, 33, 34, 345
Agassiz, Louis, 154, 172
Agricultural and Mechanical College at Auburn, 382
Agricultural and Mechanical College of Mississippi, 400
Agricultural Chemistry, 149, 155
Agricultural College, 553
Alabama Athenaeum, 202
Alabama Baptist, 560, 561, 562, 563
Alabama Christian Advocate, 476, 477, 560, 563, 568
Alabama Central Female College of Tuskegee, 544
Alabama Constitutional Convention, 390
Alabama Education Association, 340
Alabama Geological Survey, 83, 86
Alabama Great Southern Railroad, 16
Alabama Historical Society, 192, 409, 549
Alabama Journal, 91
Alabama Normal College for Girls, Livingston, 424
Alabama Polytechnic Institute, 315
Alabama Regiment Band, 548
Alabama Supreme Court, 9, 95, 143, 390, 406, 413

Alabama State Hospital, 544
Alabama and Tennessee Rivers Railroad, 279
Alabama Territory, 7
Aldrich Coal Mining Company, 353
Algebra, 167
Allen, Leroy P., 116
Alpha Delta Phi, 181
Alpha Tau Omega, 519
Alston, William W., 499, 500, 501, 516
Altman, W. H., 424
Alumni Society, 190, 344, 358, 364, 365, 551
American Journal of Education, 71
American Journal of Science, 87
American Protestant Association, 110
Amherst College, 83
Ancient History, 149
Anderson, Edward B., 543
Anderson, James A., 520
Anderson, John J., 420
Anderson, John M., 488
Anderson, Dr. W. H., 396
Andover Theological Seminary, 49
Andrews, A. S., 538, 551
Andrews, William F., 540
Anglo-Saxon, 382, 384
Annex, Julia S. Tutwiler, 482
Arcite, 425
Argus, 323
Armstrong, H. C., 358
Arnold, Thomas, 112
Arnold, Thomas K., 154, 155
Arrington, J. N., 182
Arthur, a slave, 39
Ashe, Paoli Pascal, 36, 47, 318
Ashe, William C., 116
Ashford, John B., 218
Association of College and Preparatory Schools of the Southern States, 425

Astronomy and Its Applications, 149
Asylum, 362, 363
Athletic Association, 525, 532
Athletic Field Day, 523
Atkinson, T. P., 219
Atlantic, 410
Attica, 189
Auburn, 328, 488, 511, 528, 529, 530, 531, 535, 556
Augustus, William B., 181
Auxiliary Schools, 423-425
Avery, Sallie J., 482

Bachelor of Engineering, 381
Bachelor of Letters, 382
Bachelor of Mining Engineering, 381
Babcock, 361
Bailey, James F., 53, 157, 158, 187
Baine, Thomas, 556, 558, 559
Baird, Alex, 40, 129
Baird, Mrs. Alex, 253
Baker, Jacob H., 117
Baker, J. R., 425
Baker place, 129
Baldwin, Marion, 103, 107, 188
Bank of the State of Alabama, 22
Bankhead, Henry M., 529
Bankhead, W. B., 524
Banks, James S., 139
Banks, Mrs. James S., 37
Banks, Marion, 116, 118, 170, 187, 319
Baptist Church, 560
Baptist denomination, 129, 537, 561
Baptist, Edward, 151, 194
Baptist, Edward G., 241, 242
Baptist Quarterly Review, 563
Baptist Theological Seminary, 67
Barker, Thomas of Rugby, 385
Barnard College, 73
Barnard, Frederick Augustus Porter, 35, 68, 69, 70, 71, 72, 73, 74, 78, 81, 82, 84, 85, 86, 87, 90, 97, 106, 108, 109, 110, 149, 151, 152, 177, 183, 215, 359
Barnard Hall, 354, 359, 464
Barnes, William K., 232
Barnwell, Charles H., 374, 497
Barr, John Gorman, 108, 191
Baseball, 524, 532
Baskins, Thomas L., 19
Battle, Archibald John, 84, 109, 327
Baylies, James, 481, 491
Beale, William L., 229
Beauchini, 53

Beaumont, Eugene B., 524, 528
Beeson, Jasper L., 448
Bell, 242
Ben, a slave, 38, 39
Benagh, George, 38, 84, 85, 88, 143, 151, 152, 166, 213, 221, 265
Benson, N. E., 30, 47
Benton County, 193
Berry, Obediah, 284
Bessemer High School, 425
Bestor, D. P., 174
Bestor, George T., 529
Betts, Edward C., 320
Bibb, Thomas, 13
Bibb, William W., 8
Bible, 65, 201, 202, 238, 463, 561
Bibliography, 573-580
Billingslea, Clement C., 10
Biology, 377-378
Birmingham *Age*, 556, 559
Birmingham Athletic Club, 528, 529, 530, 532
Birmingham High School, 424, 530
Birmingham High School Stars, 528
Birmingham *News*, 556, 559
Birmingham *Sunday Morning Chronicle*, 558
Birney, James G., 48, 179
Bishop, Alma, 482
Bishop, John W., 109, 334
Black, 83
Blackstone, 112
Blanchard, M. C., 194
Blanche, a horse, 223
Boggs, W. L., 265
Boise, James R., 384
Bonaparte, 188
Bondurant, E. D., 397
Bonfils, Francois, 53, 55, 62, 80, 89, 93, 119, 127, 131, 149, 157, 158, 168, 204, 251
Book Buyer, 410
Booker, William E., 488
Booth, S. S., 438
Boothe, William J., 488
Boston Quarterly Review, 110
Bottle Corps, 330
Bouchelle, Ezra F., 213
Bouchelle, Frank, 118
Bourbon, 154
Bowden, F. W., 178, 188, 229
Bowie, Alexander, 192, 193
Boyce, J. P., 67

INDEX

Boyd, B. H., 424
Boyd High School, 424
Boykin, Burwell, 116, 117, 142, 187, 191, 488
Boyle, John P., 266
Boyle, R. E., 524
Boysey, a slave, 91
Boy's High School, 424
Bracy, John D., 117
Bradfield, George Hamilton, 536
Bragg, B. B., 277
Brandon, F. T. J., 538
Brettieru, 424
Bridges, Charles E., 192
British, 87, 542
British Government, 112
Brooks, Franklin H., 110
Brooks, Henry, 96
Brooks, Miss Maria, 69
Brothers, William P., 540
Brougham, Henry, 187
Brown, Beaufort W., 230
Brown, Cy, 534
Brown, Judge, 128, 158
Brown, N. H., 254, 334, 335
Brown, Sidney, 230, 232
Brown, Thomas P., 488
Brown University, 49, 65
Browning, Robert, 542
Brumby, Arnoldus V., 84, 85, 107
Brumby, Richard T., 37, 53, 62, 64, 65, 68, 72, 78, 82, 84, 85, 86, 89, 93, 107, 108, 109, 110, 149, 163, 172, 174, 203, 204
Brundidge High School, 423
Bryce, Dr. Peter, 283, 544
Bryce, Mrs. Peter, 469, 476
Buchanan, George, 11
Buchannan, Mrs. J. C., 39
Bugbee, Francis, 10, 182, 183, 194, 236
Bullock, E. C., 191
Bullock, Mamie, 482
Bunsen, C. C. J., 315
Burford, Charles M., 191, 192
Burgett, James R. Jr., 543
Burke, Malcolm, 220
Burkett, Dr., 72
Burns, Robert, 425
Bush, F. T., 528
Business Directory of the Western Valley, 112
Business Management, 28-42; 343-371
Butler County, 30, 541
Butler High School, 423

Butler, Pierce M., 242, 243
Byrd, William, 306, 307, 308
Byson, J. H., 334

C. E. degree, 379
Caesar, 147, 417, 419, 427
Cahaba coal fields, 347
Cahaba Southern Mining Company, 353
Cairnes, John E., 443
Calculus, 154
Caldwell, Charles W., 117
Caldwell, John W., 117
Calhoun, John C., 319, 335, 373, 410, 438, 466
Callans, Jasper, 300, 302
Cambridge University, 49
Cammer, 106
Campbell, William W., 488
Cannon, William, 47
Capers, Richard Legrand, 207
Carlisle, Horace, 423
Carlisle, James, 107
Carlyle, Thomas, 425
Carnshaw, Wallace, 542, 543
Carpenter, James, 283
Carpenter, John D., 231
Carrill, Cog, 99
Carrolton Academy, 424
Carson, Thomas L., 117
Carter, J. C., 401
Carter, Robert W., 10, 12
Caruthers, 205
Cassandra, 427
Castle Hill Land and Manufacturing Company, 363
Catiline, 147, 427
Catalogue, 62, 64, 123, 131, 159, 160, 161, 168, 169, 170, 372, 381, 388, 397, 401, 402, 420, 432, 433, 434, 441, 443, 479, 538, 542
Centenary Institute, 85
Central Female College, 550
Central University, 535
Centre College, 80
Century, 409
Chamberlin, Jeremiah, 225
Chambliss, N. R., 303, 304
Chapel Hill, 454
Chapin, W. R., 507
Chapman, 236
Charles V, 172
Chaucer, 384
Chaucerian, 542

Chemistry, 65, 149
Childress, James L., 117
Childress' place, 30
Chilton, C. L., 567, 568
Chinese, 514
Chisholm, 359
Chisholm's Orchestra, 330
Christ Church, 71, 542
Christian, 121, 322, 329, 335, 538, 561, 562, 563, 564, 565, 566, 569
Christianity, 55, 188, 190
Christmas, 42, 139, 140, 141, 246, 469, 470, 472, 527
Cicero, 44, 147, 154, 383, 417, 419, 427
Citadel, 260
Citations, 583-630
Citronelle College, 425
Citronell and Fruitdale School Co., 424
City Hall, 472
Civil Engineering, 65, 74, 149, 155, 310, 378, 379, 380
Clark Hall, 357, 359, 361, 406, 461, 483
Clark, Louis V., 488
Clark, Thomas W., 405
Clark, W. G., 57, 69, 151, 155, 286, 319, 338, 344, 357, 358, 394, 395, 405, 548, 549
Clarke, T. C., 408
Clausell School, 318
Clay, Clement, 59, 60, 187
Clay, Hugh L., 230
Clayton, H. D., 314, 330, 331, 332, 335, 336 341, 390, 394, 406
Clayton, Mrs. H. D., 333
Clayton, J. P., 422
Cleary, Augusta, 482, 484
Clements, Julius M., 488
Clements, Luther M., 158
Clements, Newton N. Jr., 488
Clemson, 530, 535
Cleveland, Grover, 222
Cleveland, J., 36
Cloud, N. B., 301
Coachman, W., 438
Cobb, R. W., 328
Cobbs, R. H., 537, 538
Cochran, William A., 117, 182, 188
Cochrane, John, 230
Cockerel, N. E., 195
Code of Alabama, 392
Coleman, Phares, 540
Coleman, W. L., 165

Colgin, John, 116
College of Physicians and Surgeons, 50
Collier, H. W., 63, 112, 115, 147, 151, 158, 161, 162, 174
Collins, Robert B., 162
Columbia University, 40, 50, 73
Comegys, William C., 219
Comigys, 249
Commandants: Huse; Murfee; Harrison; Goodfellow; McConnell; Johnston; McCorvey; Hixson; Moore, T. W.; Taylor; Elliott; Bailies; Pettus; Moore, P. H.; West; Forman; Parker; Elmore; Sprott; Lee. See also entries under individual names.
Commencement exercises, 536-551
Commencement Hop, 470, 471, 472, 548, 550, 567
Commentaries on American Law, 172
Commerce, 538, 539, 542
Commercial Review, 110
Company C Wins Prize, 488
Compromise of 1850, 225
Compton, W. N., 438
Comstock, J. L., 162
Conchology, 149
Congress, 8, 16, 272, 293, 310, 311, 315, 316, 328, 329, 343, 345, 346, 347, 348, 358, 407
Congressional, 3
Conniff, W. J., 507
Conner, Ephraim D., 230
Connor, William D., 230
Convention of the Territory of Alabama, 7
Cook, Thomas A., 474
Cook, Walter, 192
Cooper, Peter, 541
Cooper, Dr. Thomas, 223
Cope, R. E. L., 524
Cork, 81
Corneille's *Cid*, 385
Corolla, 315, 396, 397, 408, 414, 478, 479, 480, 481, 482, 483, 522, 532, 533, 543
Cosmopolitan, 410
Cottingham, Elisha B., 488
Crabb, John Thomas, 117
Crawford, William, 47, 91, 143, 174
Creek Indian, 418
Crenshaw, Walter H., 188, 190
Crimson-White, 479, 480, 495, 521, 522, 534
Crimson and White Colors, 525-527
Crook, James, 319, 334

INDEX

Crook, J. Flournoy, 448, 477
Croom, Richard, 204
Croxton, John T., 6, 281, 282, 283, 285, 287, 293, 404
Cuba Institute, 424
Cumberland, 531, 535
Cunningham, J. B., 49, 424
Curriculum, 74, 145-174; 372-403
Curry, Thomas W., 217

Daguerron, 70
Daily Gazette, 409
Daily State Journal, 309
Dana, James D., *Zo-ophytes of the Exploring Expedition,* 112
Dana, James D., 155
Dances: Grand March, Waltz, Polka, Mazourka, Lancers, 473
Daniel, John, 543
Darwin, Charles, 541
Daugette, C. W., 424
Davenport, John G., 107, 116, 118, 170, 171, 187
Davidson College, 454
Davis, Adrian Marie, 417
Davis, Hubert, 547
Davis, John A. G., 224
Davis, Nicholas, 10
Davis, William C., Jr., 175, 176
Davis, Zebulon P., 230
Davy, Sir Humphrey, 83
Dawson, Henry R., 488
Dawson, N. H. R., 319, 334, 358, 359, 490
Day, Henry N., 154
Dearing, James H., 62, 63, 250, 252
DeBardeleben, Mary Christine, 482, 484
DeBow's *Commercial Review,* 110
Decatur City Schools, 425
Declaration of Independence, 143
Defoe, Daniel, 420
Degree of Civil Engineer, 379
DeLoffre, André, 81, 109, 265, 285
DeLow's Band, 472
Delta Kappa Epsilon, 180, 181, 183, 519
Democrat, 318
Demosthenes, 105, 130, 154
Dennis, John, 81
Dent, Dennis, 47
Dent, W. E., 495
DeSoto, 193
Destruction of the University, 281-288
DeVotie, N. L., 195

Dew, Duncan, 217
Dew, John G., 212
Dewberry, J. R., 528
Dickens, Charles, 401
Dickinson College, 314
Dickson, T. A., 438
Dill, J. M., 359, 423
Discipline, 197-257; 486-513
Distinguished Students, 433, 434
Dixon, E. R., 266
Doby, James M., 221, 222
Doby Rebellion, 125, 224, 249
Dockery, Professor James C., 38, 72, 78, 80, 85, 90, 108, 109, 206, 207
Donne, John, 112
Donoho, 362
Drennen, W. Earl, 507, 529, 530
Drumondra House, 82
Drysdale, Mary A., 92
Duke of Wellington, 541
Duncan, 425

Earle, Joseph B., 540
Earle, S. L., 438
Early English Text Society, 542
East Alabama Male College, 316
Eddins, Lollie, 484
Edgar, George M., 336, 375, 394, 428, 438, 478
Edinburgh, 113
Edinburgh University, 49
Education Society, 110
Edward, a slave, 39
Electricity and Magnetism, 154
Eliot, George, 401
Elliot, Bishop of Georgia, 194
Elliot, John, 46
Elliott, William G., 491
Ellis, Francis, 231
Elmore, Henry M., 234
Elmore, Physic Rush, 212, 233
Elmore, V. M., Jr., 491
Emory and Henry College, 330
Endowment Fund, 343
Engineering, 392-393
English, 53, 55, 59, 65, 68, 74, 75, 76, 80, 82, 93, 116, 147, 155, 158, 164, 165, 167, 168, 191, 195, 310, 339, 373, 379, 380, 381, 383, 388, 391, 399, 418, 420, 425, 432, 438, 447, 466, 467, 478, 479, 480, 514, 536, 540, 547, 548
English Language and Literature, 373
Enrollment of students, 1831-1902, 581

Entrance Examinations, 425-427
Entrance Requirements, 418-427
Episcopal Church, 3, 71
Episcopalians, 537
Erosophic Hall, 190
Erosophic Society, 35, 143, 167, 175, 176, 177, 178, 179, 180, 182, 190, 193, 194, 210, 514, 515, 520
Erskine College, 454
Eschenburg, John J., 154
Euclid, 557
Eufaula City Schools, 424
Eufaula *Times*, 555, 556, 557
Euripedes, 167, 384
European, 224
Eutrapelian, 180
Evening Post, 364
Evidences of Christianity, 149
Examiner, 345
Extension Work, 161, 401
Extra Curricular Activities, 175-196; 514-535

Faculty, 1831-37, 43; 1837-60, 67; 1871-1901, 372; Problems, 435
Faraday, Michael, 86
Farewell Address, 144
Fashion, 111
Fasquelle, Louis, 154
Fawcet, Henry, 387, 443
Feagin, George W., 488
Fearn, Mary, 526
Fearn, Thomas, 10, 46
Fearn, Walter, 526
Female Education, 161-162
Ferguson, Burr, 524
Ferguson, Hill, 468, 472, 486, 487, 498, 499, 525
Ferguson, James, 113
Field, Hume R., 10, 30, 47
Figh, G. M., & Company, 296, 297
Finley, Peyton, Negro trustee, 310, 311
Fisher, Lorenzo C., 219
Fitts, Alston, 488
Fitts, James H., 192, 293, 344, 364, 365
Fitts, J. H. & Co., 296, 297, 358
Fitts, P. A., 537
Fitts, Waverly, 500
Fitts, William C., 356
Fitzpatrick, Benjamin, 24, 541
Fitzpatrick, Byre, 234
Fitzpatrick, James M., 213
Fitzpatrick, Phillip, 192

Flag of the Union, 163
Fleming, John, 241
Florence State College, 340
Football; first team, 524; coaches, 528-530; comes to the campus, 524-526; declines, 532-533; games played 1892-1901, 528-530; captains and managers, 528-530; lean years, 532-533; schedules 1892-1901, 528-530
Forman, J. R., 491, 507
Forney, George H., 488
Forney, Jacob, 400, 543
Forney, John H., 298, 299, 300
Forney, William H., 151, 194, 317, 358
Forrest, N. B., 274
Fort Payne Journal, 555, 556
Fortson, John T., 117
Forum, 409
Foster, Glenn, 488
Foster, James M., 231, 234, 235
Foster, Jesse G., 182
Foster, John A., 177, 319, 334, 358
Foster, John Manly, 541
Foster, Joshua H., 193, 205, 316, 375, 410, 215, 335, 440, 441, 467
Foster, N., 150
Foster, Stephen, 469
Foster, W., 195
Fourcroy, A. F., 83
Fourth of July, 142, 143, 249
Fowler, 127, 129
Fowler House, 360
Francis, John M., 448, 543
Franklin, Benjamin, 187
Franklin College, 223
Franklin, D., 113
Franklin Hall, 34, 35, 40, 116, 122, 123, 135, 210, 219, 227, 238, 358
Fraternities, 181, 516; see also individual listings
Frazer, T. H., 397
Frazer, T. Sidney, 524
Freedmen's Bureau, 299
French, 55, 74, 83, 94, 109, 112, 154, 196, 210, 379, 381, 385, 407, 432, 440, 467, 476, 484
French Republic, 426
French, S. G., 278
Freret, W. A., 357, 438
Friedman & Loveman, 525
Friedman, Sam, 457, 466, 467, 468, 471
Fry, C. P., 438
Fry, E. M., 438

INDEX

Fulton, W. B., 248
Furman Academy, 424
Furman, Richard, 93, 107, 113, 130
Furnivall, F. J., 542
Furman University, 67, 535

Gage's Place, 28
Gaines, George W., 117, 188
Gamble, W. C., 196
Garber, Alexander M., 488
Garland, Jennie, 78, 374
Garland, Landon Cabell, 38, 78, 79, 80, 84, 85, 87, 90, 96, 97, 136, 156, 166, 172, 194, 240, 252, 254, 256, 257, 258, 259, 260, 261, 262, 263, 264, 265, 266, 267, 268, 269, 283, 284, 285, 287, 291, 292, 293, 294, 295, 296, 297, 298, 341, 359, 404, 408, 489, 552
Garland, Mrs. L. C., 286, 291
Garland Hall, 354, 357, 359, 457, 458, 480
Garland, Landonia, 78
Garland, Louise, 78
Garland, Lucinda Rose, 78, 136
Garland, Maurice Hamner, 78
Garner, Tom, 414
Garnett, A. S., 310, 311, 313, 374, 405
Garrett, J. J., 195, 552, 553, 567, 568
Garth, Jesse, 51
Gary, Thomas F., 488
Gasset, Henry, 112
Gay, John L., 53, 65
Gay, William D., 488
Gayle, Amelia, 325
Gayle, Gov. John, 121, 176, 325, 413
Gayle, Sara Haynesworth, 59, 142
Gaylesville High School, 424
Gazette, 314, 321, 322, 323, 324, 329, 331, 333, 335, 337, 340, 549
Geary, J. B., 300, 302
General Assembly, 7, 8, 10, 11, 13, 15, 16, 17, 21, 22, 23, 24, 25, 28, 29, 46, 88, 121, 244, 256, 258, 260, 293, 298, 335, 341, 343, 344, 356, 358, 365, 366, 367, 368, 390, 396, 553, 554, 570
Geographical Society of England, 86
Geometry, 154, 167
George, David R., 213
Georgia Tech, 535
German, 83, 379, 381, 385, 407, 432, 438, 440, 442, 467, 472, 479, 523, 548, 567
Gibbs, John F., 266
Gibson, Charlie B., 543
Gilbert, John W., 447

Gilbert and Sullivan, 469
Gilkey, Walter M., 253
Gilmore, W. J., 206
Gindrat, John H., 117
Givhan, W. P., 233
Glasgow University, 49
Glassell, 236
Goethe, 385
Goldsby, Guy S., 212
Goldsby, Mrs., 410
Goldsmith, 384, 420
Goldthwaite, Judge, 143
Goode, Rhett, 397
Goodfellow, T. M., 300, 302
Goodwin, Park, 384
Gordon and Curry, 112
Gordon, F. E., 396
Gordon, Thomas Jefferson, 210
Gorgas, Mrs. Amelia G., 326, 335, 405, 409, 413, 414, 415, 450, 463
Gorgas Home, 31, 33, 91, 127, 386, 326, 463
Gorgas, Josiah, 83, 87, 314, 321, 324, 325, 326, 327, 341, 378, 405, 412, 414, 419, 463
Gorgas, Mary, 176
Gossage, William H., 266
Göttingen, University, 83
Gould, R. S., 106, 108, 154, 172, 212, 241
Grace, John T., 213, 219
Grading System, 427, 428, 429
Graduates 1831-1902, 581
Graduate work, 172, 173, 398, 399
Graham, John Y., 377, 378, 439
Grant, President U. S., 308
Graves, Bibb, 524, 542
Graves, John Temple, 468
Gray, Oscar L., 488, 526
Gray, Thomas, 139
Grayson, D. A., 524, 542
Greek, 34, 45, 46, 74, 84, 109, 112, 116, 119, 147, 149, 154, 155, 156, 157, 167, 181, 183, 291, 319, 321, 335, 340, 373, 379, 380, 381, 382, 384, 387, 399, 417, 419, 420, 424, 432, 437
Greene Academy, 318
Greene, John H., 230, 231
Greenbank House, 112
Greensboro *Beacon*, 567
Greensborough Avenue, 287
Greensborough Southern, 556
Greenville *Advocate*, 556, 558
Greenville Public School, 423

Griffin, Malcomb, 529
Griffin, W. E., 269
Griggs, W. C., 425
Griswold, J. G., 310, 311, 313, 537
Gwin, D. W., 536
Guild, James, 35
Guild, Joseph C., 234
Gulf States Inter-Collegiate Oratorical Association, 519
Gunn, Silas L., 116

Hale, Nathan, 192
Hall, Bolling, 11, 123, 127, 132, 136, 141, 166, 178, 179, 217, 231, 232, 253
Hall, Crenshaw, 83, 121, 127, 129, 136, 137, 141, 165, 217, 252, 254
Hall, Robert, 187
Hallam, Henry, 172
Hamilton, Peter, 161, 550
Hampden-Sidney College, 78
Hardaway, B. H., 438, 444, 541, 543
Hardaway, Robert, 335
Harding, Horace, 319, 378, 543
Hargrove, A. C., 195, 336, 342, 346, 349, 350, 351, 354, 390, 570
Hargrove, Robert K., 85, 194, 447
Harkness, Albert, 154
Harper, R. D., 229, 301, 302, 304
Harper's Weekly, 301, 410
Harrington, Dr., 70
Harris House, 482
Harris, John J., 220, 336
Harris, Nathaniel, 47, 49
Harris, R. R., 425
Harris, Samuel S., 538
Harris, Stephen W., 117
Harrison, Gessner, 63, 224, 310
Harrison, James F., 398
Harrison, Kibble J., 499, 500
Harrison, W. P., 538
Hart, 417
Harvard, 49, 56, 57, 80, 87, 198, 210, 340, 374
Harvey, M. H., 530
Haven, Joseph, 387
Hawthorne, Nathaniel, 401
Hayden, Bessie Leach, 468
Hayes, Andrew W., 541
Hayes, Marcellus T., 332, 400, 527
Hayneville Examiner, 555, 556
Hays Bill, 343
Hays, Charles, 316
Helvetians, 427

Henderson, Ebenezer, 112, 113
Henderson, S. W., 524
Henley, John C., 407, 408
Henley, Thomas M., 407
Henry, Charles F., 80, 109, 211
Henry, William, 83
Henry, William C., 117
Herald, 409
Herbert, Hilary Abner, 222, 319
Herbert, P. T., 231
Herndon, Robert E., 204
Herndon, Tom, 139
Herodotus, 154, 384
Herring, David A., 253
Hester, Manly L., 192
Heustis, J. H., 396
Hiawathas, 523
Hibbard, B. L., 408
Hibbard, John Leslie, 408
Hill, A., 476
Hill, D. H., 327
Hill, John J., 117
Hill, Mary Carter, 479
Hilliard, Henry W., 53, 54, 55, 59, 76, 85, 89, 93, 119, 125, 153, 168, 174, 177
History of Education in Alabama, 150
Historical Society, 540
Hitchcock, Henry, 10, 11, 65
Hixson, James Courtney, 332, 490, 543
Hobdy, Oliver A., 488
Hodgson, Joseph, 474
Hodgson, Telfair, 310, 313, 316, 375, 408
Hogan, Abby, 484
Hogan and Foster, 111
Hogan, John B., 59
Hogan, Richard I., 216
Holtzclaw, James Thaddeus, 542
Homer, 384
Honorary degrees, 174, 543-547
Hooper, William, 47
Hopkins, Arthur F., 11
Hopkins, Benjamin B., 47
Hopkins, Charles, 541
Horace, 44, 154, 167, 220, 383, 557
Horn, John L., 488
Horn, Kate, 482
Houston, George S., 549
Houston, John C., 216
Howard College, 66, 511, 556, 562
Howerton, B. T., 424
Hubbard, David, 47, 59, 60
Hubert, Numa, 117

INDEX

Hudson, William W., 53, 59, 60, 61, 93, 119, 133, 157, 168, 251
Huguenot, 81
Hullum, Dr., 112
Hume Academy, 318
Humphries, David, 299, 302
Hunley, Peter F., 192
Hunter, Anna Trott, 484
Hunter, John, 14
Huntsville Advocate, 5, 56
Huntsville Male Academy, 424
Huntsville Road, 5, 37, 243, 250, 280, 291, 301, 307
Huntsville Southern Advocate, 4
Hurricane Creek, 287
Huse, Caleb, 84, 258, 261, 265
Hygiene, 377

Independent, 190
Independent Monitor, 66, 300, 308
Indian, 16, 57, 193
Indian Territory, 438
Inge, John, 205
Inge, Richard F., 212
Inge, Samuel W., 117, 228
Inge, William B., 117, 188, 228, 229
Ingersoll, Fannie, 482
Ingersoll, Thomas, 329, 564, 565
Innerarity, John F., 408
Insane Hospital, 293
Institution for the Deaf and Dumb at Hartford, 69
Ionic, 32, 34
Isac, a slave 40
Isocrates, 154
Italian, 74
Ivanhoe, 421

Jack, a slave, 91
Jackson, Gen. Andrew, 426
Jackson, Edward, 154
Jackson, W. H., 274, 281, 287
Jacksonville Republican, 193
Jacksonville State Normal College, 400
James, a slave, 39
James, Samuel, 91
Jacob, Frederick, 417
Jefferson, Thomas, 178
Jefferson Hall, 5, 31, 32, 33, 116, 121, 125, 218, 220, 238, 242
Jefferson, Thomas, 151, 223, 333
Jemison, R. Jr., 293, 296

Jemison, W. C., 520
Jenkins, Andrew J., 192
Jenkins, Joseph Dunnam, 64, 107
Jennie Rogers, 302
John, Samuel Will, 279
Johns Hopkins University, 373, 525, 547
Johnson, D. B., 524
Johnson, James A., 116
Johnson, Mrs. Nancy, 248
Johnson, Richard S., 230
Johnson, Richard T., 188
Johnson, Samuel, 165
Johnston, David, 129
Johnston, George D., 316, 489
Johnston, Joseph F., 355, 366
Johnston's surrender, 287
Jones, Aaron, 230, 437
Jones and Boise, 384
Jones, Calvin, 53, 54, 55, 59
Jones, Edward L., 192
Jones, Edward N., 546
Jones, John A., 125, 168, 190
Jones Literary Society, 515
Jones, Richard C., 314, 334, 335, 336, 339, 340, 390, 428, 478, 548
Jones, Robert E., 189
Journal, 521, 525, 526
Judson, 556

Kappa Alpha, 519
Kappa Sigma, 519
Keane, Bishop John J., 561
Kellerman, Charles, R., 378
Kelly, D. C., 538
Kelly, Isham H., 187
Kent Club, 520
Kent, James, 172
Kentucky State, 535
Ketchum, George A., 396, 397
Key, Thomas H., 224
Killough, James T., 241, 242, 245
Kimball, Joseph, 300
Kincaid, William A., 224
King, Frank, 232
King, E. D., 193, 351
King, H. S., 139
King, John Warren, 536
King, Judge P., 293
King, Peyton, 230, 231
King, William A., 48
King, William T., 268
King, William W., 116, 118, 170, 171, 187
Kinney, 111

640 INDEX

Knight, John, 424
Knott High School, 425
Koran, 285, 405
Kuklos, Adelphon, 181, 300, 301, 302, 307, 308
Kyser, G. H., 524, 428

L. F. T. Hall, 472
Lafayette, General Gilbert-Mottier, 143, 188, 409
Lagrange College, 66
Lakin, Rev. A. S., 299, 300, 301, 302
Lalande, Alexander D., 233
Langdon, Daniel Webster, 447, 449
Lanneau, J. F., 550
Lapsley, James W., 365
Lapsley, Samuel, 543
Larrabee, B. F., 538
Latin, 45, 46, 55, 74, 109, 116, 119, 147, 149, 155, 156, 157, 167, 178, 180, 188, 192, 195, 196, 209, 217, 291, 310, 331, 334, 335, 340, 342, 373, 379, 380, 381, 382, 383, 391, 399, 408, 417, 419, 420, 424, 427, 432, 437, 478, 536, 542, 547
Lavosier, A. L., 83
Lawhon, Rosa, 484
Lawler, Joab, 59
Laws of Nations, 172
Leach, S. J., 283
Leach, Mrs. S. J., 283
Leach, Emily, 283
Leatherwood, 362
LeConte, Joseph, 223, 386
Lectures on History, 172
Lectures on Modern History, 112
Lee, Alto V., Jr., 491, 547
Lee, John H., 192
Lee, P. C., 195
Lee, Stephen D., 317, 327
Lee's surrender, 287
Legendre, Adrian, 154
Ledger, 355
Legislature, 365, 366
Leiber, Francis, 223
Leland, John D., 546
Lenoir, William T., 488
Letters of John Quincy Adams on Free Masonry, 112
Lewis, Burwell Boykin, 314, 326, 327, 328, 329, 330, 341, 344, 345, 374, 390, 421, 449, 450, 463, 492, 496, 498, 540, 551, 564, 565, 566
Lewis, Mrs. B. B., 330, 476

Lewis, Dixon H., 46
Lewis, John W., 117
Library, 98-114; 404-415
Library, Amelia Gayle Gorgas, 415
Liddell, Charles P., 541
Life, 410
Life of Washington, 111
Lincoln, President Abraham, 263, 274, 275
Lindsley, Dr. Philip, 47, 48, 49
Lipscomb, Abner S., 174
Lister, George, 209
"Little Doc," 466
Little, George, 69, 81, 129, 135, 136, 138, 181, 195, 210, 220, 327
Little, James, 546
Little, John B., 447, 541, 543
Littell's Living Age, 410
Little, W. G., 524, 528
Livingston *Messenger*, 254
Livingston Military Academy, 423
Lockhart's Battallion, 279
Locket, Samuel H., 327
Logic, 154
Logic and Moral Philosophy, 167
Lomax, Tenant, 512
Lomis, Professor John C., 154, 302
Long, George, 224
Longfellow, Henry Wadsworth, 80
Lord, W. W., 196
Louisiana State University, 519, 529
Louisville and Nashville Railroad, 444
Loughridge, James Allen, 541
Lovejoy, G. M., 425
Loveless, E. L., 538
Lowar and Hogan, 99
Lowry, A. P., 424
Lyceum, 5, 31, 32, 204, 238
Lyell, Sir Charles, 86
Lumsden, Charles L., 261
Luna, a slave, 236
Lupton, N. T., 308, 309, 310, 311, 312, 313, 315, 316, 317, 341, 375, 376, 435, 451, 452, 489, 536

McCall, Charles R., 408, 417
McCalla, Richard C. Jr., 541
McCalley, Henry, 450, 543, 546
McCants, A. G., 524, 529
McConnell, Roscoe, 541
McCook, F. M., 281
McCord, Charles E., 488
McCord, D. J., 234

INDEX

McCorvey, Thomas C., 312, 317, 332, 335, 375, 428, 441, 443, 465, 478, 489, 490, 543, 548, 550
McCoy, A. S. J., 488
McCoy, W. C., 329, 564, 565, 566
McDonough, William S., 284
McDow, Alexander, 231
McEachin, A. B., 355
McGehee, Laura Scott, 484
McHelm, 150
McIver, W. C., 319
McKenzie, Daniel B., 448
McKinley, John, 10, 11
McKinnon, H. A., 424
McLaughlin, John, 143
McLeod, W. A., 423
McLester Hotel, 495
McLester, R. & J., 294
McMahon, Leila, 482
McMillan, William, 52, 93, 107, 163
McMorries, E. Y., 424
McMullen, Robert B., 116, 118, 170, 187, 190
McPherson, C. G., 174
McQueen, James W., 117
McQueen, John D., 507, 508, 509, 512, 530
McTyeire, Bishop H. N., 562, 563
M. & O. Railroad, 470
Maapen, 360
Macbeth, 425
Madison Hall, 34, 35, 116
Madison, James, 35
Magill, B. F., 242
Mahaffy, 384
Mail, 299
Mallet, John William, 82, 83, 84, 85, 86, 149, 162, 210, 240, 265, 291, 292, 327
Malone, John N., 151
Manly, Basil, 37, 66, 67, 68, 69, 72, 73, 74, 76, 78, 81, 85, 89, 90, 91, 103, 105, 108, 111, 135, 145, 147, 149, 150, 151, 156, 158, 181, 191, 195, 196, 207, 209, 236, 240, 242, 317, 408, 538
Manly, Basil, Jr., 549
Manly, Charlie, 81, 196
Manly Hall, 357, 359, 483, 506
Mardis, S. W., 18
Marengo Military Academy, 423
Marks, Robert M., 541
Marlowe, Nicholas, 220
Marr, Daniel P., 117
Marr, John H., 233
Marr's Field, 30, 46, 89

Marshall, John, 68
Martin, Alburto, 192
Martin, H. L., 248, 249
Martin, Governor J. L., 24, 25, 319, 390, 334
Martin, Lucian F. L., 192, 241, 242
Martin, Lucy Grace Archer, 479, 480
Martin, W. A., 529
Martin, Wolsey R., 541
Mason, Leila St. Clair, 484
Mason, Sadie, 482, 484
Masonry, 112
Massey, J. W., 295
Massey, James, 544
Massey, John, 327
Mastin, James H., 187
Mathews, Thomas M., 204
Mathematics, 46, 374
Matthews, Thomas E., 233
Maull, John C., 117
Maury, Matthew F., 87, 310, 311, 312, 444, 445
Maxwell, Thomas Harris, 542, 549
Mayfield, Surry F., 448
Mayfield, Susie Fitts Martin, 484
M. W. L. Arkansas Female College, 484
Mechanical Drawing, 380
Medical College of Alabama, 393-398
Medical College of Atlanta, Georgia, 546
Medical School, 33
Meek, Alexander B., 116, 118, 190, 135, 142, 170, 171, 187, 215, 312
Meek, Professor B. F., 310, 311, 317, 327, 335, 373, 408, 410, 417, 422, 438, 440, 466, 467, 478, 548, 549, 550
Meek, F. M., 546
Meek, Samuel M., 192, 536
Memorial Day, 469
Memorial Stone, 288
Mercer, 454, 535
Meriwether, James, 117
Merrill, A. H., 401
Merriwether, George, 188
Messenger, 254
Meteorology, 149
Methodist, 561, 562, 564, 566
Methodist Church, 85
Methodists, 537, 565
Methodist Episcopal Church, 560
Methodist Quarterly Review, 561
Middle Ages, 172
Mill, J. Stuart, 443
Milar, W. J. L., 150

Military, Company E Wins Honors, 488
Military organization, 258-280; 486-513
Military Rebellion, 507-513
Miller, A. A., 3
Miller, R. H., 541
Miller, Washington D., 93, 188
Mills, Capt., 307
Millwood School, 423, 424
Milton, John, 425
Mineralogy and Geology, 149
Mines and Metallurgy, 376
Minerva, 189
Minor, Henry, 10, 11
Mississippi A. & M. College, 529, 530, 535
Mitchell, Dr. Elisha, 47
Mitchell, John J., 365
Mobile and Ohio Railroad, 353
Mobile *Commercial Register*, 18, 23
Mobile *Daily Register*, 556, 558, 559, 560
Mobile *Tribune*, 41
Mobley, Tom, 232
Modern History, 149
Mohr, Charles A., 397, 398
Mohr, H. B., 398
Moliere, J. B. P., 385
Monitor, 190, 193, 194, 254, 301, 302, 303, 304, 305, 444
Monk, A., 476, 546, 547
Montgomery *Advertiser*, 555, 557
Montgomery Athletic Club, 529
Montgomery *Dispatch*, 559
Monthly, 494
Moody, Dr. H. A., 394, 395, 397, 401
Moody, Mary Washington, 484
Moody, Washington, 193, 343, 344
Moore, Governor A. B., 26, 263
Moore, David, 12
Moore, J. Burns, 346
Moore, John, 188, 192
Moore, Nathaniel, 117
Moore, Peyton Herndon, 491
Moore, Samuel B., 3
Moore, Sydenham, 248, 249
Moore, Tredwell W., 490, 491
Moral and Intellectual Philosophy, 149
Morgan Bill, 349, 350, 358
Morgan, Enoch, 319, 408
Morgan Land Bill, 346
Morris, D., 53
Morrisett, E. P., 195
Morrissette, Edward H., 549
Morrison, James H., 261
Morrison, William, 36

Morrow, Hugh, 542
Morton, Quin, 14, 30, 51
Mosley, Benjamin A., 117
Moses, a slave, 38, 39, 40, 41, 235, 236
Moss, 196
Mountain Home Academy, 318
Mt. Willing High School, 424
Mudd, W. S., 293
Muller, Albert A., 174
Mundy, Reuben, 188
Munsel, Joel, 408
Murfee, H. H., 266
Murfee, J. T., 97, 265, 266, 284, 285, 296, 298, 327
Murphy, John, 10, 29, 424
Murphy, Samuel S., 215
Mustrat, 49
Mythology, 154

Nabers, Edward L., 249, 253, 254
Nashville University, 260
National Education Association, 331
Natural Philosophy, 149
Ned, a slave, 40
Neely, P. P., 195
Negro, 38, 78, 111, 120, 234, 235, 240, 260, 283, 284, 285, 286, 299, 300, 306, 310, 499, 136, 139, 282
Nelson, William P., 488
Nevius, Rev. R. D., 194
Newell Bill, 347
Newman, Zipp, 525
New Shakespeare Society of Great Britain, 542
Nesmith, C. C., 524
Newton Theological Institution, 65
New Year, 498
New Year's Day, 469
New York Institution for the Deaf and Dumb, 69
Nicaraugua Canal, 542
Nicoloson, A. S., 193
Nichols, William, 30, 34
Noel and Chapsal, 385
Nooe, John A., 118, 171, 187
Normal Department, 159-160, 387-388
North American, 409
North American Review, 414
Northington, W. T., 477
North-East and South-West Railroad, 80
Northrop, Cyrus, 304
Nott, Edward F., 213
Nott, J. C., 396, 408

INDEX
643

Nuttall, Thomas, 100

Oakland College, Mississippi, 225
Oberlin College, Ohio, 474
Observatory, 34, 239, 286, 443
Observer, 190, 258, 305
Odd Fellows, 185
Olin, Stephen, 76, 78, 174
Oliver, Samuel W., 12, 30, 47
Oliver, Isaac, 541
Oliver, William B., 488
Olmsted, Denison, 70
O'Neal, E. A., 346, 488, 551
O'Neal, Mrs. Mary C., 358
Oppett, Benjamin, 19
Opposition to University, 552-571
Optics, 149, 154
Ordinance Laboratories, 87
Organic Chemistry, 154
Ormand, John J., 102
Ormond, W. B., 184, 194, 220
Osborne, 307
Othomisian Debating Society, 180
Otis, Lelius McC., 438
Otto, Dr. Emil, 385
Owen, Dr., 398
Owen, George W., 10, 11
Owen, John M., 192
Owen, Joseph R. N., 117
Owen, Laura, 196
Owen, Lucien, 162
Owen, Thomas, 14, 51
Oxford University, 49, 73

Palamon, 425
Palmer, Thomas W., 334, 335, 375, 430, 438, 439, 463, 478, 509, 515
Pape, W. B., 397
Parham, William, 187, 188
Parker, Bessie, 478, 479
Parker, John, 421
Parker, Osborne, 196
Parker, Thornton, 502
Parker, William A., 196, 310, 313, 317, 327, 335, 342, 373, 407, 417, 428, 438, 439, 440, 442, 467, 478, 544, 548
Parker, Mrs. William A., 467
Parkes, William J., 491
Parsons, Governor L. E., 292
Parsons, Augustus, 376
Parthenon, 189
Pate, Franklin S., 214
Patterson, Dr. R. M., 47

Patton, M. K., 438
Patton, R. M., 294, 316
Paul, a slave, 40
Paul, James, 30
Payne, Martyn, 112
Peabody, A. P., 387
Peck, David L., 236, 310, 311, 312, 313, 317, 375, 417
Peck, Samuel Mintern, 242, 358
Pegues, Sheriff, 307
Peithonian Literary Society, 515, 516, 521
Pelham, Samuel C., 424
Pennsylvania Mobile Coal Company, 349
Perkins, Constantine, 31
Perkins, Mrs. Eliza, 240
Perrin, Robert, 182
Perry, Thaddeus, H., 241
Peters, a squatter, 294
Peters, Thomas M., 107, 197, 188, 408
Petrarch, 71
Pettus, Erle, 491
Pettus, R. Emmett, 405
Pettway, 495
Pharr, E. A., 236
Phi Beta Kappa, 183, 184, 194
Phi Delta Theta, 519
Phi Gamma Delta, 181, 519
Phillips-Andover, 524
Phillips Academy, 49
Phillips, George, 10, 30, 47, 59
Phillips, J. H., 424
Phillips, William B., 335, 336, 374, 376, 398
Philomathic Hall, 509
Philomathic Society, 35, 143, 175, 176, 177, 178, 179, 180, 182, 190, 193, 194, 476, 514, 515, 520
Physical culture, 376-377
Pickel, James M., 336, 376
Pickens, A. L., 188
Pickens, Israel, 10, 13, 474
Pickens Stage, 142
Pierce, C. W., 405
Pierce, George, 538
Pierce, Henry Niles, 537
Pierce, James T., 266
Pierson, W. P., 424
Pilgrims, 188
Pillow, Gideon, 265, 268
Pinkston, Algernon S., 117
Plato, 384
Poe, Edgar Allen, 542
Political Economy, 46, 149, 155, **374**

Polk, Leonidas, 273
Pollard, 279
Pollock-Stephens Institute, 424
Pope, Alexis D., 117
Popular Science Monthly, 410
Porter, Benjamin F., 21, 63, 85, 160
Powe, William E., 188
Powers, James K., 314, 334, 339, 340, 402, 481, 508, 510, 511, 512, 522, 532
Powers, Lula Knox, 484
Poyner, D., 266
Pratt, Daniel, 174
Pratt House, 463
Pratt, H. S., 39, 68, 76, 89, 90, 91, 92, 132, 149, 151, 152, 165, 166, 206, 209, 212, 213, 217, 269, 291, 292, 524
Pratt, Mrs. H. S., 91
Pratt, Mrs. Isabella Drysdale, 92
Pratt, Jane Horatio, 92
Pratt, John Wood, 80, 265
Pratt, L. C., 382
Prattville Academy, 424
Preparatory school, 157
Presbyterian, 377, 378
Presbyterians, 69, 537
Presbyterian Church, 91
Presbyterian Female Institute, 69
Presidents: Woods, Manly, Garland, Lakin, Harper, Richards, Chambliss, W. R. Smith, Northrop, Maury, Lupton, C. G. Smith, Lewis, Clayton, Jones, Powers, Wyman; See references under individual names
President's Mansion, 34, 37, 90, 91, 286, 291, 303, 317, 324
Price, George W. F., 538
Price, W. H. C., 194
Prince and Garrett, 111
Prince, a slave, 120
Prince, Edmund, 16, 17
Prince, Oliver T., 206
Prince, S. R., 529
Princeton, 50, 377, 378
Principles of Zoology, 172
Professional Education, department of, 372, 378
Public examinations, 431-432
Puck, 410
Pugh, John C., 488
Puritan, 262
Puritans, 55
Puryear, Frank, 424
Pyncheon, Alice, 425

Quarles, W. W., 438, 488
Quarterly Review, 110
Queen City Avenue, 16, 243
Quentin Durward, 421
Quinn, 362

Randolph place, 141
Randolph, J. B., 195
Randolph, Ryland, 300, 302, 306, 307, 308
Randolph-Macon College, 78, 84, 304, 314, 400, 454
Read, John B., 187, 188, 266, 279
Ready Writer Prize, 542
Redwood, George E., 279
Reese, Henry F., 541
Reese, Joseph S., 117
Register, 19, 327, 337
Registrar employed, 430
Reminiscences, William R. Smith, 43, 44
Renfro, J. L., 495
Rensselaer Institute, 81
Report, 83
Review of Reviews, 410
Rhetoric, 149, 154
Rhett, R. B., 334, 335
Rhodes, Editor, 559
Rhodes, Henry W., 47
Rhodes, Josias Duckett, 109, 195
Rich, O., 109
Richards, J. DeForest, 302
Richardson, A. W., 103, 108
Richardson, Warfield, 6, 73, 194, 373, 374
Richardson, William, 164, 165, 391, 481
Richardson, Wilson G., 72, 106, 108, 113, 401
River and Harbor Bill, 352
Rives, Samuel H., 107
Rives, Whitmill W., 117
Roach, a student in South Carolina, 242, 243
Robert Donell High School, 425
Roberts, H. W., 519
Roberts, Oran, 63, 103, 104, 106, 107, 119, 120, 128, 134, 135,, 137, 138, 164, 165, 168, 178, 188, 229, 544
Robertson, William D., 172
Robinson, A. P., 235
Robinson Crusoe, 420
Robinson, Francis M., 205
Robinson, William, 76
Robinson, William, Jr., 77
Roger, Sir, 425

INDEX

Roman Catholic Church, 561
Roseneau, Monroe, 422
Ross, F. A., 396
Ross, S. H., 139
Rosser, L. V., 424
Rotunda, 5, 31, 33, 35, 36, 103, 104, 105, 130, 131, 132, 136, 138, 190, 191, 195, 201, 204, 237, 238, 240, 270, 285, 404
Round House, 262, 286, 463, 504
Rousseau, 279
Royall, Julia Trent, 481, 483
Royal Society, 82
Russell, E. L., 401
Russian Zoological Laboratory in France, 377

Saffold, Adison J., 117
Saffold, Benjamin J., 235
Saffold, Milton J., 236
Saffold, William B., 204, 373, 439, 543
Salary schedule, 92-97, 446-450
Saltonstall, Gurdon, 7, 43, 44, 47, 48, 50, 51, 53, 55, 58, 59, 65, 89, 93, 116, 117, 118, 125, 145
Sam, a slave, 39, 41, 70, 236
Sample, A. H., 174
Sanders, Jeremiah E., 205, 233
Sanders, W. H., 397
Sanford, John W. A., 327
Saratoga Academy, 69
Saunders, William, 215, 234
Savage, F. M., 524
Sayre, Herbert A., 375, 547
Scherb, E. V., 40, 80, 81, 96, 210, 219, 220
Schiller, 385
Scientific American, 410
School of Biology, 387
School of Chemistry and Metallurgy, 385
School of Engineering, 392-393
School of the English Language and Literature, 384
School of Geology and Mineralogy, 386
School of Geology and Natural History, 386
School of Greek, 384
School of History and Philosophy, 374, 387
School of Latin, 383
School of Latin and Greek, 373
School of Law, 160-161, 388-392
School of Mathematics, 386

School of Medicine, 160, 387
School of Mental and Moral Philosophy, 387
School of Mining and Metallurgy, 376
School of Modern Languages, 373, 385
School of Natural Philosophy and Astronomy, 386
School of Pedagogy and Psychology, 388
School of Pharmacy, 387
School of Physics and Astronomy, 374, 386
Scott, Sir Walter, 384, 401, 421
Searcy, Abbie, 481, 483
Searcy, Dr. Reuben, 40, 543
Searles, T. S., 397
Seay, Thomas, 334
Seed, Walter D., 541
Selma Printing Company, 565
Seminary of Learning, 7, 8, 556
Seminole Indians, 84
Semmes, Joseph E., 224
Semmes, Raphael, 303
Seniors become "ex-military," 506
Sentinel, 409
Sewanee, 525, 527, 528, 529, 531, 535
Shackelford, Jack, 10, 30
Shakespeare, 407, 542
Shakespeare Society, 520
Sherman, Sterling, 107
Shelby *Sentinel*, 409
Shockley, Bascom T., 288
Shorter, J. G., 259, 264, 265, 268, 271, 274, 276, 278
Shortridge, George D., 117, 118, 170, 184, 187
Shortridge, Judge, 167
Sibert, Martin D., 448, 543
Sigma Alpha Epsilon, 181, 519
Sigma Nu, 519
Signet Library, 113
Simms of London, 35
Sims, Professor Edward D., 76, 90, 108, 109, 111
Simone, T., 155
Slade, Thomas B., 192
Slaves, 38-40
Slone, S. B., 528
Sloss-Sheffield Company, 355, 356
Smith, Adam, 443
Smith, Boling, 228
Smith, Carlos G., 314, 317, 318, 319, 321, 322, 323, 324, 375, 400, 401, 418, 440, 445, 453, 475, 476, 492, 501, 504, 545

Smith, Daniel Holt, 439, 524, 542
Smith, Eugene A., 266, 279, 310, 311, 313, 316, 317, 327, 335, 346, 355, 356, 365, 374, 376, 394, 395, 406, 408, 466, 489, 570
Smith, G. A., 306
Smith, John L., 234, 235
Smith, John M., 52, 53, 65, 158, 187, 188
Smith, Kirby, 327
Smith, M. M., 424
Smith, Paoli, 418
Smith, T. H., 401
Smith, William A., 306, 307, 308
Smith, W. H., 307
Smith, William R., 43, 45, 50, 51, 63, 70, 71, 117, 175, 187, 308, 309, 314, 405, 440
Smythe, William 172
"Smoky Row," 499
Snow, Henry A., 22
Snowden, 423, 424
Snowden Academy, 423, 424
Society of the Alumni, 550
Somerville, an author, 172
Somerville, Henderson M., 195, 266, 319, 390, 544
Somerville, James, 108, 447
Somerville, Ormond, 336, 390, 448, 543
Somerville, Percy R., 541
Somerville, William O., 377
Sons of Temperance, 186, 240, 245
Sophocles, 384
Sorsby, Thomas, 117
Sousa, John Phillip, 469
South Carolina College, 67, 68, 69, 82, 223, 374,
South Highland Academy, 423
Southern Advocate, 17, 18, 19, 32
Southern Argus, 311
Southern Association of Schools and Colleges, 439
Southern Athletic Club, 529
Southern College Association, 525, 535
Southern Educational Journal, 110
Southern Medical College Association, 397
Southern University, 564, 566
Southron, 71
Southwestern Presbyterian University, 535
Spanish, 55, 74, 109, 149, 155, 193, 196, 381, 438
Spaulding, 154
Spartan, 123, 303, 456
Speed, Joseph H., 474
Spencer, Senator, 405

Spessard, A. M., 424
Spherical Trigonometry, 155
Spraggins, a student, 499, 500
Spring Lake College, 425
Sprott, Samuel H., 491
St. John's, 525
St. Joseph, 556
St. Michael's Day, 81
Stafford School, 69
Stafford, Samuel M., 68, 69, 72, 84, 89, 108, 110, 111, 149, 219, 407
Stafford, Mrs. Samuel M., 83, 84, 162, 240, 408
Starr, George, 51, 59
Starke, J. M., 423
State Bank, 365
State Herald, 559
State Normal College at Florence, 339, 340, 423, 424
State Normal School at Jacksonville, 424
Stephens, Alexander Hamilton, 541
Stevens, Thomas M., 488
Stevenson, Robert Louis, 401
Steward's Hall, 5, 42, 62, 90, 107, 127, 128, 138, 159, 205, 230, 233
Stickney, Fred G., 507
Stickney, J. W., 529
Stone, Sardine G., 117
Stone, William D., 37
Storrs, Charles P., 288, 328
Summer School, 402
Sun, 409
Sunday Times, 409
Supreme Court, state, 10, 21, 96, 235, 344, 356
Swartout, Samuel, 50
System of grading, 428

Taber's place, 30
Tacitus, 167
Tait, Charles, 58, 188
Tait, Felix, 194
Tait, James, 146
Tait, Robert, 205, 206, 215
Taliaferro, Mrs. E. T., 424
Taylor, Governor of Tennessee, 516
Taylor, J. W., 536
Taylor, John, 223
Taylor School of Birmingham, 529
Taylor, Steward, 233
Taylor's Surrender, 287
Taylor, Walter L., 491
Teachers, 43-97, 399-401

INDEX 647

Teachers' Salaries, 92-97, 310, 444-453
Teaching Load, 440-441
Tennessee Female College, 85
Tennessee Valley, 277
Tennyson, Alfred Lord, 384
Texas, 116, 137, 174, 179, 224, 535, 544, 546
Thackery, William M., 401
Thanksgiving Day, 143, 469, 527
Thomas, Frederick W., 76, 77, 78
Thompson, 83
Thompson, Henry, 174
Thorington, William Sewell, 391, 394
Thornton, A. Q., 298
Thucydides, 384, 557
Times, 298, 321, 339
Times and News, 328
Tindall, John L., Jr., 116, 135
Todd, James Berwick, 438
Tom, a slave, 40
Townes, Eggleton D., 188
Transylvania College, 49, 51, 57, 100, 118
Trigonometry, 154
Troy *Standard*, 409
Trustee Prize, 543
Trustees of the University of Alabama v. Winston, 21
Tryon, Battle of, 281
Tucker, Rev., 538
Tulane University, 519, 523, 528, 529, 530, 531, 535
Tunstall, Alfred M., 541
Tuomey Hall, 354, 359
Tuomey, Michael, 81, 82, 83, 85, 86, 87, 90, 96, 97, 105, 109, 111, 136, 149, 163, 193, 211, 238, 240, 241, 359
Turk, Annie, 482, 483
Tuscaloosa District High School, 424
Tuscaloosa Female Institute, 73
Tuscaloosa *Gazette*, 462, 556, 558, 566
Tuscaloosa *Inquirer*, 18
Tuscaloosa Insurance Company, 343
Tuscaloosa Northern Railroad, 444
Tuscaloosa *Times*, 473, 484, 500, 504, 527, 532, 540, 551, 552, 554, 555, 567, 569, 570
Tutwiler, Henry, 7, 43, 45, 49, 50, 51, 55, 60, 61, 63, 64, 66, 69, 85, 92, 111, 116, 117, 119, 125, 133, 168, 174, 252, 297, 298, 317, 318, 321, 322, 323
Tutwiler Hall, 483
Tutwiler, Julia, 424, 477, 478, 482
Tutwiler, Netta, 375

Union College, 47, 50
Union Springs Institute, 424
Uniontown High School, 424
University Auxiliary Schools, 422
University Dramatic Club, 520
United Daughters of the Confederacy, 288
University of Dublin, 82
University of Georgia, 519
University of Göttingen, 82, 85
University of Heidelberg, 315
University Mandolin, Glee, and Guitar Club, 520
University Military School, 423, 424
University of Mississippi, 73, 80, 152, 519
University *Monthly*, 358, 464, 520, 521
University of Munich, 377
University of Nashville, 318
University of North Carolina, 76
University of Pennsylvania, 318, 528, 529
University of Pisa, 53
University School, 423
University of Tennessee, 505
University of Texas, 137
University of Transylvania, 56
University of Virginia, 30, 47, 50, 115, 150, 152, 224, 248, 454, 529

Van de Graaf, Adrian, 336, 390, 446
Vanderbilt University, 79, 80, 315, 401, 439, 525, 531, 535
Vanhoose, 242
Vattel, Emmerich de, 172
Vaughan, Vernon H., 302, 306, 307, 311
Vaughn, William J., 266, 310, 312, 313, 317, 375, 378
Vauquelin, 83
Vergil, 44, 146, 147, 167, 417, 419, 476
Veritates, Amicus, 56, 58
Verner, C. B., 354
Verner Military Academy, 423
Verner, W. H., 423
Vicar of Wakefield, 420
Vidmer, John R., 488, 526
Virginia Military Institute, 260, 261, 268, 454, 491
Volunteer Military Company of Tuscaloosa, 185

Waddel, M., 248
Wagenhurst, Otto, 529
Wake Forest, 525
Walden, George S., 96, 205

INDEX

Walke, a student at the University of Virginia, 242
Walker, H. L., 425
Walker Home, 141
Walker, Amasa, 443
Walker, M. P., 524
Walker, Percy, 408
Walker, Thomas A., 187
Walker, William M., 524
Wallace, Elijah, 188
Wallace, John P., 234
Wallis, Ann Eliza, 45, 46
Wallis, John F., 36, 43, 44, 47, 48, 50, 51, 53, 55, 60, 61, 62, 63, 65, 68, 84, 92, 93, 98, 100, 107, 119, 125, 162, 168
Walthall, R. B., 209, 210, 212, 217
Warner, Willard, 307, 308, 405
Warren, Bessie, 468
Warrior Coal Fields, 347
Washington's Birthday, 143
Washington College, 78
Washington, George, 144, 187
Washington Hall, 5, 31, 32, 33, 116, 119, 121, 125, 186, 196, 203, 472
Washington and Lee, 454
Washington Monument, 413
Watchman, 324
Watermelon Road, 282
Watkins, J. M., 423
Watts, Thomas H., 273, 277, 278, 292, 520
Wayland, F., 155
Webb, James D., 117, 192
Webb, James E., 334, 335, 338, 391, 477
Webb, J. S., 528
Weeden, John David, 390, 547
Weekly State Journal, 304, 305
Weissinger, Alexander J., 233
Wellborn, A. H., 529
Wert, T. W., 529, 534
Wesleyan Christian Advocate, 562
Wesleyan Universtiy, 174
West Alabama Breeze, 409
West Alabama Agricultural School, 424
West, James W., 340, 491, 507, 508, 510, 511, 512
West Point Military Academy, 260, 261, 268, 314, 325, 487, 486, 511
Whately, Richard, 154
Wheelock, Charles F. Jr., 545
Whelan, Benjamin L., 215
White, F. S., 481
White, John W., 384
White, Frank, 502, 529, 534
White, James, 423, 479, 543
White, P. W., 421
Whitfield, Benjamin, 39, 129
Whitfield, H. S., 299, 300, 316, 375, 440, 441, 444
Whitfield, Luke James, 184
Whiting, William J., 201, 202
Whitney, W. D., 385
Wiatt, John E., 424
Wilcox, Cadmus M., 334
Wildman, Alyce, 479, 480
Wiley, John, 162
Wiley and Putnam, 110
Wilkins, George S., 378
William, a slave, 39, 40
Williams, Charles L., 117
Williams, Henry P., 488
Williams, James M., 117
Wilmer, Bishop, 537
Wilson, H. F., 438, 488
Wilson's Hill, 28
Wilson, J. H., 281
Wilson, John, 166
Wilson, Joseph R., 327, 538
Wilson, Lucy, 481
Wilson's Raid, 481
Wilson's Raiders, 287
Wilson, Woodrow, 382
Winston, John A., 151
Winston, John J., 21
Wofford College, 454
Wood, Bernard A., 488
Wood, Green M., 117
Wood, Leila, 484
Wood, Sterling, A. M., 390
Woodruff, David, 98, 99
Woodruff, Milford F., 172, 220
Woods, Alva, 4, 5, 43, 45, 49, 50, 51, 52, 54, 55, 56, 57, 58, 59, 60, 62, 63, 64, 65, 85, 90, 92, 100, 102, 111, 112, 118, 119, 132, 157, 158, 164, 168, 198, 200, 207, 251, 252
Woods, Mrs. Alva, 46
Woods Hall, 31, 296, 357, 359, 362, 363, 406, 456, 458, 478, 480, 500, 507
Woodward-Warren Company, 468
Woolsey, 49
Wooten, Richard Council, 542
Wright, Julius T., 423
Wright, Ruffin A., 398
Wyche, John I., 48
Wyman, Alice Searcy, 479

INDEX

Wyman, William Stokes, 84, 109, 111, 177, 241, 265, 286, 291, 292, 297, 299, 300, 310, 311, 312, 313, 314, 315, 317, 326, 327, 330, 332, 333, 334, 335, 340, 342, 351, 358, 373, 374, 394, 405, 406, 407, 409, 410, 419, 420, 428, 430, 432, 434, 438, 454, 478, 502, 534
Wynne, W. A., a student, 236

Xenophon, 147, 154, 167, 384, 419

Y. M. C. A., 462
Yale College, 53, 69, 70, 183, 185, 304
Yancey, R. C., 195
Yancey, William L., 194
York Academy, 424
Young, C. H., 507
Young, J. W., 195

Ziegler, Annie F., 479
Zoölogy, 149